FROMMER'S

COMPREHENSIVE TRAVEL GUIDE

YUCATÁN '95-'96

INCLUDES CANCÚN & COZUMEL

by Marita Adair
Assisted by Maribeth Mellin

MACMILLAN • USA

Macmillan Travel
A Prentice Hall Macmillan Company
15 Columbus Circle
New York, NY 10023

ISBN 0-671-88384-4
ISSN 1064-1416

Design by Robert Bull Design
Maps by Geographix, Inc.

SPECIAL SALES

Bulk purchases (10+ copies) of Frommer's Travel Guides are available to corporations at
special discounts. The Special Sales Department can produce custom editions to be used as
premiums and/or for sales promotion to suit individual needs. Existing editions can be
produced with custom cover imprints such as corporate logos. For more information write
to: Special Sales, Prentice Hall, 15 Columbus Circle, New York, NY 10023.

Manufactured in the United States of America

CONTENTS

LIST OF MAPS

INVITATION TO THE READERS

In researching this book, I have come across many wonderful establishments, the best of which I have included here. I am sure that many of you will also come across appealing hotels, inns, restaurants, guesthouses, shops, and attractions. Please don't keep them to yourself. Share your experiences, especially if you want to comment on places that have been included in this edition that have changed for the worse. You can address your letters to:

Marita Adair
Frommer's Yucatán
c/o Macmillan Travel
15 Columbus Circle
New York, NY 10023

A DISCLAIMER

Readers are advised that prices fluctuate in the course of time, and travel information changes under the impact of the varied and volatile factors that affect the travel industry. Neither the author nor the publisher can be held responsible for the experiences of readers while traveling. Readers are invited to write to the publisher with ideas, comments, and suggestions for future editions.

A WORD ABOUT PRICES

Mexico has a value-added tax of 10% (*Impuesto de Valor Agregado,* or "IVA," pronounced "*ee*-bah") on almost everything, including hotel rooms, restaurant meals, bus tickets, tours, and souvenirs. Due to a change in the law, this tax will not necessarily be included in prices quoted to you. In addition, prices charged by hotels and restaurants have been deregulated. Mexico's new pricing freedom may cause some price variations from those quoted in this book; always ask to see a printed price sheet and ask if the tax is included. All prices given in this book already include the tax.

In this book, I've listed only dollar prices, which are a more reliable guide than peso prices. In this age of inflation, prices may change by the time you reach Mexico. Mexico's officially reported inflation rate is around 8%, but hotel and restaurant prices have been going up 15% to 40% annually for the last several years.

Important note: In 1993 Mexico introduced the New Peso, which knocks three zeros off the old currency. The value remains the same—just over 3 New Pesos to each U.S. dollar. Old peso notes will be accepted until 1996; there's no announced time limit yet on coins.

SAFETY ADVISORY

Whenever you're traveling in an unfamiliar city or country, stay alert. Be aware of your immediate surroundings. Wear a moneybelt and keep a close eye on your possessions. Be particularly careful with cameras, purses, and wallets, all favorite targets of thieves and pickpockets.

CHAPTER 1

GETTING TO KNOW MEXICO & THE YUCATÁN

When you travel in the Yucatán, you'll be especially struck by Mexico's contrasting layers: Glitzy resorts, economical beachside hostelries, and lagoons with world-class snorkeling lie along the coasts, as do miles of jungle and a few archeological sites. Inland there is more jungle, and other ancient sites reached by passing neat, rock-fenced villages comprised of white stucco or stick- and mud-walled cottages, usually decorated with potted plants and surrounded by fruit trees. Maya village women wear cool cotton embroidered shifts and go about village life oblivious to the peninsula's fame as a premier resort destination. Their day-to-day cultural and belief system holds many elements that can be traced to pre-Hispanic times. Though shy, the Maya are immensely courteous and helpful, and eagerly chat with strangers even when neither can speak the other's language. More than 350,000 Maya living in the Yucatán's three states speak Maya and most, especially men, speak Spanish too. Many, especially those serving tourists, slip easily between Maya, Spanish, and English. You'll get along even if English is your only language.

Crumbling henequén haciendas surrounded by fields of maguey dot the peninsula. Henequén, a yuccalike plant from which hemp is made, was the king crop in the Yucatán in the 19th century, and the industry is still going strong, with rope, packing material, shoes, and purses manufactured from the spiny plant. Besides henequén, other crops in the mostly agricultural peninsula are corn, coconuts, oranges, mangoes, and bananas.

Three states are included in the peninsula (although for touring purposes I have also covered the states of Tabasco and Chiapas). The Caribbean state of **Quintana Roo** in the east has the best beaches and is also blessed with the resort islands of Cancún, Cozumel, and Isla Mujeres; the ruins of Tulum and Cobá; and the 1.3 million-acre Sian Ka'an Biosphere Reserve south of Cancún. Sultry, rough-edged, and unfriendly, Quintana Roo's capital, Chetumal, seems far removed, sitting at the southernmost edge of the state, almost an inappropriate capital for an area with such natural and touristic riches.

Wedge-shaped **Yucatán** state, in the middle of the region, with delightful Mérida as its capital, has among its crowning attractions the ruins of Uxmal and Chichén-Itzá. The state's nature reserves include those for flamingos at Celestún and Río

WHAT'S SPECIAL ABOUT THE YUCATÁN

Archeology
Uxmal, most beautiful of the Yucatán's pre-Hispanic Maya cities. Chichén-Itzá, grand Maya/Toltec site famed for its architecture.

Beaches
The Yucatán's fine white-sand beaches, unequaled in Mexico, are best on Quintana Roo's Caribbean coast.

Crafts
Beautiful multicolored baskets from Halacho, Panama hats woven in Becal, and hammocks, plus silver and gold filigree work.

Cuisine
Fresh lobster and shrimp, the Yucatán's most tempting seafoods. Regional Yucatecan cuisine, some of the most flavorful in Mexico, especially pit-baked cochinita or pollo pibil and achiote-grilled fish.

Nature
Sian Ka'an Reserve, a 1.3 million-acre coastal area south of Cancún. El Palmar Reserve, a 1.2 million-acre area on Yucatán's upper coast. Celestún, winter home to flamingos, and Río Lagartos, flamingo nesting grounds. Isla Contoy, a national wildlife refuge island habitat for more than 70 bird species near Isla Mujeres. Coastal Quintana Roo, nesting grounds of sea turtles. The Yucatán peninsula itself, with over 400 species of birds, and 200 reptiles and mammals, including the endangered manatee.

People and Customs
The Maya people, many of whom live in pre-Hispanic–style homes and respect regional customs, are well known for courtesy.

Resorts
Cancún, an island with some of the most sophisticated resorts in the country, and mainland Cancún City, with economical hotels. Akumal, Pamul, Playa del Carmen, and the Punta Allen peninsula south of Cancún, for economical hotels and good diving, snorkeling, fishing, and bird-watching. Isla Mujeres, the poor man's Cancún, with good beaches, reasonably priced lodgings, good restaurants, and a relaxing pace. Cozumel, less expensive and more laid-back than Cancún.

Special Cities and Villages
Mérida, with colonial architecture, free nightly cultural events, and the beautiful Museum of Anthropology. Whitewashed, rock-walled, thatched-roofed villages, including Tinum, where visitors stay with locals, and Ticul, village of tricycle taxis. Campeche, a unique walled city, uses baluartes for museums.

Water Sports
Reef diving off Cozumel and along the Caribbean coast to see geologic formations and an abundance and diversity of marine life unequaled in Mexico. Snorkeling in clear Caribbean waters off Yucatán, especially Xcaret and Xel-Ha lagoons, south of Cancún, and Chancanab Park on Cozumel Island.

Lagartos and a new one, El Palmar, a 1.2 million-acre reserve established in 1990 on the upper Yucatán coast.

Campeche, on the peninsula's west coast, faces the Gulf of Mexico and has as its capital the beautiful walled city of Campeche. The region is off the beaten path for most tourists, who are drawn to the middle and eastern parts of the peninsula. Among its attractions are the hat- and basket-weaving towns of Becal and Halacho, and the ruins of Edzná. The Gulf coast beaches are coarser than those on the Caribbean, and the water tends to be rough and choppy.

The countries of Belize and Guatemala border the Yucatán on the east and south.

1. GEOGRAPHY, ECOLOGY, HISTORY & POLITICS

GEOGRAPHY & ECOLOGY

Many people think that the Yucatán is somewhere in the extreme southeast of Mexico. A look at the map shows that the land of the Maya is actually the far east-central part of the republic. Mérida is north of the major population centers of Mexico City, Guadalajara, Puebla, and Veracruz. Mérida is also surprisingly close to the tip of Florida: From Mexico City to Mérida it's about 600 miles as the crow flies, and from Mérida to Miami it's a mere 675 miles.

Edged by the rough and deep-blue aquamarine Gulf of Mexico on the west and north, and the clear cerulean blue Caribbean Sea on the east, the peninsula covers almost 84,000 square miles, with nearly 1,000 miles of shoreline. Covered with dense jungle, the porous limestone peninsula is mostly flat, with thin soil supporting a low, scrubby jungle, with almost no surface rivers. Rainwater is filtered by the limestone into underground rivers. Cenotes, or collapsed caves, are natural wells dotting the region. The only sense of height comes from the curvaceous terrain rising from the western shores of Campeche inland to the border with Yucatán state. This rise, called the Puuc hills, is the Maya "Alps," a staggering 980 feet high. Locally the hills are known as the Sierra de Ticul or Sierra Alta. The highways undulate a little as you go inland, and south of Ticul there's a rise in the highway that provides a marvelous view of the "valley" and misty Puuc hills lining the horizon. Maya towns near the Puuc hills favored a decorative style that incorporated geometric patterns and masks of Chaac, thus giving the style its name—Puuc.

Enormous strides in protecting the Yucatán's abundant natural life have been made in the last decade. The nature reserves have not been significantly opened to tourism, and may never be since the idea is to protect them, and money is lacking

IMPRESSIONS

Even a short stay in Mexico will telescope you through many centuries and, in imagination at least, will transport you to far away countries. Only Egypt has pyramids and prehistoric ruins as monumental as those of Teotihuacán and Chichén-Itzá. Taxco's and Mexico City's cathedrals rival those of Spain and Italy. Even Switzerland can hardly claim grander mountain scenery than Mexico's.
—BYRON STEEL, *LET'S VISIT MEXICO,* 1946

to staff and patrol opened areas. But wildlife, especially birds, are easy to see in or out of a reserve, once you get away from commercialized and developed areas.

Yucatán state's nature reserves include the 118,000-acre Río Lagartos Wildlife Refuge north of Mérida, where North America's largest flock of flamingos nests; the Celestún Wildlife Refuge, covering more than 14,000 acres, for the protection of flamingos and other tropical birds and plant life; and, adjacent to it, the 123,398-acre El Palmar Wildlife Refuge, important for its springs, cenotes, and black mangroves, established in 1990 on the upper Yucatán coast. Besides these, the state has incorporated nature trails into the archeological site of Dzibilchaltún, north of Mérida.

In 1989 Campeche state set aside 178,699 acres in the Calakmul Biosphere Reserve that it shares with the country of Guatemala. The area includes the state's ruins of Calakmul, as well as significant plants, animals, and birdlife.

Quintana Roo's protected areas are some of the region's most beautiful, wild, and important. In 1986 the state ambitiously set aside the 1.3 million-acre Sian Ka'an Biosphere Reserve, protecting a significant part of the coast from development south of Tulum. Isla Contoy, also in Quintana Roo, off the coast from both Isla Mujeres and Cancún, is a beautiful island refuge for hundreds of bird species, turtles, and other plant and wildlife. And in 1990 the 150-acre Jardín Botánica, south of Puerto Morelos, was opened to the public; along with the Botanical Garden at Cozumel's Chancanab Lagoon, it gives visitors an excellent idea of the Yucatán's forest life. Some effort has been made to protect turtle nesting areas on the state's lengthy shoreline, since four of the world's nine marine turtles nest on Quintana Roo's shores—loggerhead, green, hawksbill, and leatherback. More than 600 species of birds, reptiles, and mammals have been counted.

El Triunfo Biosphere Reserve, near the Lagunas de Montebello in Chiapas, preserves 25,000 acres of the rain forest habitat of the rare and endangered quetzal bird.

HISTORY

DATELINE

- **10,000–2300 B.C.** Prehistoric Period: Chiles, corn, beans, avocado, amaranth, and pumpkin are cultivated. Stone bowls and jars, obsidian knives, and open-weave basketry developed.
- **1500–300 B.C.** Preclassic Period: Olmec culture spreads and develops over gulf coast, southern Mexico, Central America, and lower Mexican Pacific coast.

(continues)

The earliest "Mexicans" were Stone Age men and women, descendants of the race that had crossed the Bering Strait and reached North America before 10,000 B.C. These were *Homo sapiens* who hunted mastodons and bison, and gathered other food as they could. Later (Archaic Period, 5200–1500 B.C.), signs of agriculture and domestication appeared: baskets were woven; corn, beans, squash, and tomatoes were grown; turkeys and dogs were kept for food. By 2400 B.C. the art of pot making had been discovered (the use of pottery was a significant advance). Life in these times was still very primitive, of course, but there were "artists" who made clay figurines for use as votive offerings or household "gods." Actually, "goddesses" is a better term, for all the figurines found so far have been female, and are supposed to symbolize Mother Earth or Fertility. (Use of these figurines predates any belief in well-defined gods.)

The Yucatán's history, in particular, has fascinated the rest of the world since Lord Kingsborough published a study of its ruins in 1831. Just a few years later, New York lawyer John L. Stephens and artist Frederick Catherwood made several trips through the Yucatán and Central America. Stephens recorded his adventures in a fascinating series of travel books, illustrated by Catherwood's superb drawings, which achieved immediate and lasting popularity. The books are still wonderful reading, and are available through bookstores in North America and Mexico.

Ever since Stephens's adventures, foreigners have been touring the Yucatán to view its vast crumbling cities and ponder the fall of the great Maya civilization, which developed mathematical theories far in advance of European thought, and perfected an extremely accurate calendar.

THE PRECLASSIC PERIOD   It was in the Preclassic Period (1500 B.C.–A.D. 300) that the area known by archeologists as Mesoamerica (from the northern Mexico Valley to Costa Rica) began to show signs of a farming culture. They farmed either by the "slash-and-burn" method of cutting grass and trees, then setting fire to the area to clear it for planting; or by constructing terraces and irrigation ducts, a method used principally in the highlands around Mexico City, where the first large towns developed. At some time during this period, religion became an institution as certain men took the role of shaman, or guardian of magical and religious secrets. These were the predecessors of the folk healers and nature priests still found in modern Mexico.

The most highly developed culture of this Preclassic Period was that of the Olmecs, which flourished from 1500 to 100 B.C. Their influence is substantial in the Yucatán peninsula, but their primary stronghold was in what are today the states of Veracruz and Tabasco. They used river rafts to transport colossal multiton blocks of basalt, which were used to carve roundish heads. These sculptures still present problems to archeologists: What do they signify? The heads seem infantile in their roundness, but all have the peculiar "jaguar mouth" with a high-arched upper lip that is the identifying mark of the Olmecs, and that was borrowed and adapted by many later cultures. The artists seemed obsessed with deformity, and many smaller carved or clay figures are of monstrosities or misshapen forms. Those with open eyes are slightly cross-eyed. Besides their achievements in sculpture, the Olmecs were the first in Mexico to use a calendar and to develop writing, both of which were later perfected by the Maya.

Historians speculate that the Maya were descended from the mysterious Olmecs, but a definitive link between the cultures is missing, except for a few archeological finds like Izapa, a huge site found almost intact on the Pacific coast of Chiapas. Izapa, considered the home of a transition culture between the Olmec and the Maya, rose between 400 B.C. and A.D. 400. El Pital, a large site being excavated in Veracruz state, may provide additional links between the Olmecs and other cultures.

Other than conclusions drawn from the stone carvings and historic interpretations of Izapa, the Mayas' developmental

DATELINE

• **1000–900 B.C.**   Olmecs' San Lorenzo center is destroyed; they begin anew at La Venta.

• **600 B.C.**   La Venta Olmec cultural zenith; Cholula begins 2,000-year history as huge ceremonial/civic center.

• **500–100 B.C.**   Zapotecs flourish; Olmec culture disintegrates. Teotihuacán settlement is started, and first pyramid at El Tajín is started.

• **A.D. 100**   Building begins on Sun and Moon pyramids at Teotihuacán; Palenque dynasty emerges in Yucatán.

• **300–900**   Classic Period: Xochicalco established; Maya civilization develops in Yucatán and Chiapas.

• **683**   Maya Lord Pacal is buried in Mexico's only pyramid built as a tomb—the Palace of the Inscriptions at Palenque.

• **650–800**   El Tajín reaches

(continues)

years remain a mystery. Somewhere along the way they perfected the Olmec calendar, refined and developed their ornate system of hieroglyphic writing and their early architecture. The Maya religion, with its 166 deities, was also being shaped in these early centuries, which were contemporaneous with the Roman Empire. The Maya guided their lives by using a number of interwoven and complex calendars (see the section on Chichén-Itzá in Chapter 5).

THE CLASSIC PERIOD Most artistic and cultural achievement came about during Mexico's Classic Period (A.D. 300–900), when life began to center in cities. Class distinctions arose as the military and religious aristocracy took control; a class of merchants and artisans grew, with the independent farmer falling under a landlord's control. The cultural centers of the Classic Period were Yucatán and Guatemala (also home of the Maya), the Mexican Highlands at Teotihuacán, the Zapotec cities of Monte Alban and Mitla (near Oaxaca), and the cities of El Tajín and Zempoala on the gulf coast.

The Maya are at the apex of pre-Columbian cultures. Besides their superior artistic achievements, the Maya made significant discoveries in science, including the use of the zero in mathematics and a complex calendar with which the priests could predict eclipses and the movements of the stars for centuries to come.

The Maya were warlike, raiding their neighbors to gain land and subjects as well as to take captives for their many blood-centered rituals. Recent studies, notably *Blood of Kings* (Braziller, 1986) by Linda Schele and Mary Ellen Miller, debunked the long-held theory that the Maya were a peaceful people. Scholars continue to decipher the Maya hieroglyphs, murals, and relief carvings to reveal a Maya world tied to a belief that blood sacrifice was necessary to communicate with celestial gods and ancestors and to revere the dynasties of earthly blood kin. Thus, through bloodletting and sacrifice they nourished their gods and ancestors, and honored royal births, deaths, marriages, and accessions during a calendar full of special occasions. Numerous carvings and murals show that members of the ruling class, too, ritualistically mutilated themselves to draw sacrificial blood.

The Classic Period ended with a century of degradation and collapse, roughly corresponding to the A.D. 800s. By the early 900s, the great ceremonial centers were abandoned and the jungle took them over, but why classic Maya culture collapsed so quickly is still something of a mystery.

Who exactly inhabited Teotihuacán (100 B.C. to 700 A.D.—near present-day Mexico City) isn't known, but it is thought to have been a city of 200,000 or more inhabitants covering nine square miles. At its height, Teotihuacán was the greatest cultural center in Mexico, with influence as far southeast as Guatemala and including the Yucatán peninsula.

Its layout has religious significance; on the tops of its pyramids consecrated to the sun and moon, high priest's rituals were attended, but not observed, by the masses of the people at the foot of the pyramid. Some of the magnificent reliefs and frescoes that decorated the religious monuments can be seen in Mexico City's museums.

THE POSTCLASSIC PERIOD In the Postclassic Period (A.D. 900–1500), warlike cultures developed impressive societies of their own, although they never surpassed the Classic peoples. All paintings and hieroglyphs of this period show war, migration, and disruption. Somehow the glue of society became unstuck, people wandered from their homes, and the religious hierarchy lost influence.

After the Classic Period, the Maya migrated from their historic home in Guatemala and Chiapas into the northern lowlands of the Yucatán (roughly the modern states of Yucatán and Campeche), where they spent six centuries, from A.D. 900 to 1500, trying to recover their former greatness.

During this period, the cities near the Yucatán's low western hills were built. The architecture of the region, called **Puuc style**, is generally characterized by elaborate exterior stonework appearing above door frames and extending to the roofline. Examples of this architecture can be seen in Kabah, Sayil, Labná, and Xlapak. Even though Maya architecture never regained the heights achieved at Palenque or Tikal, the Puuc buildings, such as the Codz Poop at Kabah and the palaces at Sayil and Labná, are quite beautiful and impressive.

Finally, in the 1300s, the warlike Aztecs settled west of the Yucatán, in the Mexico Valley on Lake Texcoco (site of Mexico City), with the island city of Tenochtitlán as their capital. Legend has it that as the wandering Aztecs were passing the lake they saw a sign predicted by their prophets: an eagle perched on a cactus plant with a snake in its mouth. They built their city there and it became a huge (pop. 300,000) and impressive capital. The Aztec empire was a more or less loosely united territory of great size. The high lords of the capital became fabulously rich in gold, stores of food, cotton, and perfumes; skilled artisans were prosperous; events of state were elaborately ceremonial. Victorious Aztecs returning from battle sacrificed thousands of captives on the altars atop the pyramids, cutting their chests open with stone knives and ripping out their still-beating hearts to offer to the gods.

QUETZALCOATL The legend of Quetzalcoatl, a holy man who appeared during the time of troubles at the end of the Classic Period, is one of the most important tales in Mexican history and folklore, and contributed to the overthrow of the Aztec empire by the Spaniards. Quetzalcoatl means "feathered serpent." Learned beyond his years, he became

DATELINE

today Campeche. Juan de Grijalva lands on the island of Cozumel and names it Santa Cruz.

• **1519** Conquest of Mexico begins: Hernán Cortés and troops arrive near present-day Veracruz.

• **1521** Conquest is complete after Aztec defeat at Tlaltelolco in 1521.

• **1521–24** Cortés organizes Spanish empire in Mexico and begins building Mexico City on the ruins of Tenochtitlán.

• **1524** First Franciscan friars arrive from Spain.

• **1524–35** Cortés removed from leadership.

• Spanish king sends officials, judges, and finally an audiencia to govern.

• **1526** Francisco Montejo permitted to colonize the Yucatán.

• **1535–1821** Viceregal Period: Mexico governed by 61 viceroys appointed by king of Spain; landed aristocracy emerges with ownership of huge portions of land (haciendas).

• **1537** Mexico's

(continues)

DATELINE

first printing press is installed in Mexico City.
1540 Campeche, Mérida, and Valladolid are founded.
1559 French and Spanish pirates attack Campeche.
1562 Friar Diego de Landa destroys 5,000 Mayan religious stone figures and burns 27 hieroglyphic painted manuscripts at Maní, Yucatán.
1571 The Inquisition is established in Mexico.
1704 Campeche's fortified walls are finished, surrounding the city.
1767 Jesuits expelled from New Spain.
1810–21 War of Independence: Fr. Miguel Hidalgo starts movement for Mexico's independence from Spain, but is executed within a year. Compromise between monarchy and a republic is outlined by Agustín de Iturbide.
1821 Independence from Spain is achieved.
1822 First Empire: Agustín de Iturbide, independence leader, ascends throne as

(continues)

the high priest and leader of the Toltecs at Tula, and put an end to human sacrifice. His influence completely changed the Toltecs from a group of warriors to peaceful and productive farmers, artisans, and craftsmen. But his successes upset the old priests, and they called upon their ancient god of darkness, Texcatlipoca, to degrade Quetzalcoatl in the eyes of the people. One night the priests conspired to dress Quetzalcoatl in ridiculous garb, get him drunk, and tempt him to break his vow of chastity. The next morning the shame of this night of debauchery drove him out of his own land and into the wilderness, where he lived for 20 years. He emerged in Coatzacoalcos, in the Isthmus of Tehuantepec, bade his few followers farewell, and sailed away, having promised to return in a future age. Toltec artistic influences noted at Chichén-Itzá in the Yucatán seemed to suggest that in fact he landed there and, among the Maya, began his "ministry" again, this time called Kukulkán. He supposedly died there, but the legend of his impending return remained. (In "Spanish Conquistadores," below, we'll see how this legend brought down the Aztec empire.)

Kukulkán leading the invasion of Chichén-Itzá was a long-held scholarly theory, but now the scholarly school is out again. That Kukulkán existed isn't in doubt, but precisely how he fit in is being reexamined. Research revealed in *A Forest of Kings* by Linda Schele and David Freidel (William Morrow and Co., Inc., 1990) shows that the bas-relief history at Chichén-Itzá does not support a Toltec invasion theory. They believe Chichén-Itzá's adoption of Toltec architecture demonstrates it was a cosmopolitan city that absorbed elements brought by the Itzáes from another region, but that the continuity of buildings and bas-relief figures show it was a continuous Maya site (sans Toltecs).

The Yucatán was profoundly affected by a strong influence from central Mexico. Some theories claim that a distantly related branch of the Maya people, called the **Putún Maya,** came from the borders of the Yucatán peninsula and controlled the trade routes along the coast and rivers between mainland Mexico and the classic Maya lands in Petén and Chiapas. They spoke the Maya language poorly and used many Nahuatl (Aztec) words.

When the Putún Maya left their ships and moved inland, they became known as the **Itzáes** because, after unsuccessfully trying to conquer Yaxuná, they settled 12 miles north in what eventually became known as Chichén-Itzá (well of the Itzá), a perfect place because of its access to water and its proximity to centers ripe for conquering. They brought with them years of experience in trading far and wide (thus the influence of the Toltecs that shows up so strongly at Chichén-Itzá). Eventually they were successful in conquering other peninsular kingdoms and creating the vast city of Chichén-Itzá.

According to some authorities, Uxmal was inhabited during this same period (around A.D. 1000), by the tribe known as the **Tutul Xiú** who came from the region of Oaxaca and Tabasco. Some scholars think that the Xiú took the city from earlier builders because evidence shows that the region around Uxmal was inhabited as early as 800 B.C.

The three great centers of Chichén-Itzá, Mayapán, and Uxmal lived in peace under a confederation: The Itzá ruled in Chichén-Itzá, the Cocom tribe in Mayapán, and the Xiú in Uxmal. Authorities don't agree on the exact year, but sometime during the 12th century A.D. the people of Mayapán overthrew the confederation, sacked Chichén-Itzá, conquered Uxmal, and captured the leaders of the Itzá and the Xiú. Held in Mayapán, the Itzá and the Xiú princes reigned over, but did not rule, their former cities. Mayapán remained the seat of the confederation for over 200 years.

The Xiú took their revenge in 1441 when they marched from Uxmal on Mayapán, capturing and destroying the city, and killing the Cocom rulers. They founded a new city at Maní. Battles and skirmishes continued to plague the Maya territory until it was conquered by the Spanish conquistadores.

SPANISH CONQUISTADORES In 1517, the first Spaniards to arrive in what is today known as Mexico skirmished with Maya Indians off the coast of the Yucatán peninsula. One of these fledgling expeditions ended in shipwreck, leaving several Spaniards stranded as prisoners of the Maya. When word of this new land of riches spread in Cuba, where Hernán Cortés resided, another expedition became reality under his leadership. When he showed up on the same route as the previous expeditions and landed on the island of Cozumel in February 1519, it changed the course of Mexican history. There he heard of the stranded Spaniards on the mainland and later made contact with them. Soon after, he met the Indian slave Malinche, who spoke both Maya and Nahuatl (the Aztec language), and who, together with one of the shipwrecked Spaniards, provided the language link between the conquerors and the Aztecs. This liaison facilitated the Spanish conquest of Mexico. When Cortés arrived, the Aztecs didn't rule the Yucatán Maya, but conquering the Aztecs led to total Spanish domination of not only the Yucatán, but of all Mexico. Following the hint of gold, the Spaniards continued on around the Yucatán peninsula to Campeche and Tabasco, eventually landing on the east coast at what today is Veracruz. From there the conquest was eventually launched. While in Tabasco, Cortés first heard of the Aztecs when he asked the source of the gold the Maya possessed.

When Cortés and his men landed, the Aztec empire was ruled by Moctezuma (often misspelled Montezuma) in great

DATELINE

emperor of Mexico.

• **1824** Iturbide is expelled, returns, and is executed by firing squad.

• **1824–55** Federal Republic Period: Guadalupe Victoria is elected first president of Mexico in 1824, and is followed by 26 presidents and interim presidents, among them Santa Anna.

• **1828** Slavery abolished.

• **1835** Texas declares independence from Mexico.

• **1836** Santa Anna defeats Texans at Battle of the Alamo, at San Antonio, Texas, but is later defeated and captured at the Battle of San Jacinto outside Houston, Texas.

• **1838** France invades Mexico at Veracruz.

• **1845** United States annexes Texas.

• **1846–48** War with the United States: For $15 million Mexico relinquishes half of its national territory to the U.S. in Treaty of Guadalupe Hidalgo.

• **1847–66** War of the Castes: Segregationist

(continues)

DATELINE

policies by Yucatán
leaders against the
Maya cause revolt,
upheaval, and
decimation of half
the Maya
population. Strife
continues until well
into 20th century.

1855–72 Reform
Years: A three-year
war pits cities
against villages and
rich against poor, in
a search for
ideology, stability,
and political
leadership. Benito
Juárez is president
in fact and in exile
off and on between
Reform Wars and
leadership by
Emperor Maximilian.
Juárez nationalizes
church property and
declares separation
of church and state.

1858 Campeche
and Yucatán
become territories.

1862 England,
Spain, and France
send troops to
demand debt
payment and all
except France
withdraw.

1863 Campeche
gains statehood.

1864–67 Sec-
ond Empire: French
Emperor Napoléon
III sends Maximilian
of Hapsburg to be
emperor of Mexico.

1867 Juárez
orders execution of
Maximilian at
Querétaro and

(continues)

splendor. The emperor was not certain what course to pursue: If the strangers were Quetzalcoatl and his followers returning at last, no resistance must be offered; on the other hand, if the strangers were not Quetzalcoatl, they might be a threat to his empire. Moctezuma tried to bribe them with gold to go away, but this only whetted their appetites. Despite the fact that Moctezuma and his ministers received the conquistadores with full pomp and glory when they reached Mexico City, Cortés eventually took Moctezuma captive.

Though the Spaniards were no match for the hundreds of thousands of Aztecs, they skillfully kept things under their control until a revolt threatened Cortés's entire enterprise. He retreated to the countryside, made alliances with non-Aztec tribes, and finally marched on the empire when it was governed by the last Aztec emperor, Cuauhtémoc. Cuauhtémoc defended himself and his people valiantly for almost three months, but was finally captured, tortured, and executed.

The Spanish conquest had started out as an adventure by Cortés and his men, unauthorized by the Spanish crown or its governor in Cuba. Soon Christianity was being spread through "New Spain." Guatemala and Honduras were explored and conquered, and by 1540 the territory of New Spain included Spanish possessions from Vancouver to Panama. In the two centuries that followed, Franciscan and Augustinian friars converted great numbers of Indians to Christianity, and the Spanish lords built up huge feudal estates on which the Indian farmers were little more than serfs. The silver and gold that Cortés had sought made Spain the richest country in Europe.

The **conquest of Yucatán** took 20 years and was achieved by three men all with the same name: Francisco de Montejo the Elder (also called El Adelantado, the pioneer), who started the process; his son, Francisco Montejo the Younger (known as El Mozo, the lad); and a cousin. Montejo the Elder sailed from Spain in 1527 with 400 soldiers and landed at Cozumel, but was forced to relaunch his campaign from the western coast, where he could more easily receive supplies from New Spain (Mexico).

From Mexico, he conquered what is now the state of Tabasco (1530), pushing onward to the Yucatán. But after four difficult years (1531–35) he was forced to return to Mexico penniless and exhausted. In 1540, Montejo the Younger and his cousin (another Francisco de Montejo) took over the cause, successfully establishing a town at Campeche, and another at Mérida (1542); by 1546 virtually all of the peninsula was under his control.

A few weeks after the founding of Mérida, the greatest of the several Maya leaders, Ah Kukum Xiú, head of the Xiú people, offered himself as Montejo's vassal and was baptized, giving himself the name Francisco de Montejo

Xiú. With the help of Montejo's troops Montejo the Younger and his cousin then accomplished their objective, the defeat of the Cocoms. By allying his people with the Spaniards, Xiú triumphed over the Cocoms, but surrendered the freedom of the Yucatecan Maya. In later centuries warfare, disease, slavery, and emigration all led to the decline of the peninsula's population. Fray Diego de Landa, second bishop of the Yucatán, destroyed much of the history of the Maya culture when he ordered the mass destruction of the priceless Maya codices, or "painted books," at Maní in 1562; only three survived.

INDEPENDENCE Spain ruled Mexico until 1821, when Mexico finally gained its independence after a decade of upheaval. The independence movement had begun in 1810 when a priest, Fr. Miguel Hidalgo, gave the cry for independence from his pulpit in the town of Dolores, Guanajuato. The revolt soon became a revolution, and Hidalgo, Ignacio Allende, and another priest, José María Morelos, gathered an "army" of citizens and threatened Mexico City. Ultimately Hidalgo was executed, but he is honored as "the Father of Mexican Independence." Morelos kept the revolt alive until 1815, when he, too, was executed.

When independence finally came, Agustín de Iturbide was ready to take over. In 1822 Iturbide founded a short-lived "empire" with himself as emperor. The next year it fell and was followed by the proclamation of a republic, with Gen. Guadalupe Victoria as the first president.

In 1821 the Spanish governor of Yucatán resigned and Yucatán, too, became an independent country. Though it decided to join in a union with Mexico two years later, this period of sovereignty is testimony to the Yucatecan spirit of independence. That same spirit arose again in 1846 when Yucatán seceded from Mexico.

After the war, sugarcane and henequén cultivation were introduced on a large scale, organized around vast landed estates, called haciendas, each employing hundreds of Maya virtually as slaves. During the war for secession, weapons were issued to the Maya to defend independent Yucatán against attack from Mexico or the United States. The Maya turned these same weapons on their local oppressors, setting off the War of the Castes in 1847.

WAR OF THE CASTES The Maya ruthlessly attacked and sacked Valladolid, and strengthened their forces with guns and ammunition bought from British merchants in Belize (British Honduras). By June 1848 they held virtually all of the Yucatán except Mérida and Campeche—and Mérida's governor had already decided to abandon the city.

Then followed one of the strangest occurrences in Yucatán history. It was time to plant the corn, and the Maya fighters went off to tend the fields. Meanwhile,

DATELINE

resumes presidency in Mexico City until his death in 1872.

• **1872–84** Post-Reform Period: Only four presidents hold office but country is nearly bankrupt.

• **1876–1911** Porfiriato: Porfirio Díaz is president/dictator of Mexico for 35 years, leading country to modernization at the expense of human rights.

• **1902** Quintana Roo becomes Mexican territory.

• **1911–17** Mexican Revolution: Francisco Madero drafts revolutionary plan. Díaz resigns. Leaders jockey for power during period of great violence, national upheaval, and tremendous loss of life.

• **1913** President Madero assassinated.

• **1914–16** Two U.S. invasions of Mexico.

• **1915** Payo Obispo becomes capital of territory of Quintana Roo.

• **1917–40** Reconstruction: Present constitution of Mexico is signed. Land and education reforms are initiated and labor

(continues)

DATELINE

unions strengthened. Mexico expels U.S. oil companies and nationalizes all natural resources and railroads. Presidents Obregón and Carranza, Pancho Villa, and Zapata are assassinated.

- **1926–29** President Calles limits the Catholic church, leading to the Cristero Rebellion; in protest, the clergy strikes and incites violence between church and government.
- **1931** Quintana Roo territory is divided between the states of Yucatán and Campeche, causing popular protest.
- **1935** Quintana Roo is restored to territorial status.
- **1936** Payo Obispo becomes Chetumal.
- **1940** Mexico enters period of political stability and makes tremendous economic progress and improvement in the quality of life.
- **1950** The first train links Campeche with Coatzacoalcos.
- **1955** Women are given full voting rights.
- **1974** Quintana Roo achieves statehood and

(continues)

Mexico sent reinforcements in exchange for Yucatán's resubmission to Mexican authority. Government troops took the offensive, driving many of the Maya to the wilds of Quintana Roo, in the southeastern reaches of the peninsula.

Massed in southern Quintana Roo, the Maya, seeking inspiration in their war effort, followed the cult of the **Talking Crosses,** which was started in 1850 by a Maya ventriloquist and a mestizo "priest," who carried on a tradition of "talking idols" that had flourished for centuries in several places, including Cozumel. The "talking cross" first appeared at Chan Santa Cruz, and soon several crosses were talking and inspiring the Maya.

The Yucatecan authorities seemed content to let the rebels and their talking crosses rule the southern Caribbean coast, which they did with only minor skirmishes until the late 1800s. The rebel government received arms from the British in Belize, and in return allowed the British to cut lumber in rebel territory.

But at the turn of the century, Mexican troops with modern weapons penetrated the rebel territory, soon putting an end to this bizarre, if romantic, episode of Yucatecan history. The town of Chan Santa Cruz was renamed in honor of a Yucatecan governor, Felipe Carrillo Puerto, and the Yucatán was finally a full and integral part of Mexico.

At the national level, a succession of presidents and military dictators followed Guadalupe Victoria until the French intervention, one of the most bizarre and extraordinary episodes in modern times. In the 1860s, Mexican factions offered Archduke Ferdinand Maximilian Joseph of Hapsburg the crown of Mexico, and with the support of the ambitious French emperor, Napoléon III, the young Austrian actually came to Mexico and "ruled" for three years (1864–67), while the country was in a state of civil war. This European interference in New World affairs was not welcomed by the United States, and the French emperor finally withdrew his troops, leaving the misguided Maximilian to be captured and executed by a firing squad in Querétaro. His adversary and successor (as president of Mexico) was Benito Juárez, a Zapotec Indian lawyer and one of the most heroic figures in Mexican history. After victory over Maximilian, Juárez did his best to unify and strengthen his country before dying of a heart attack in 1872. His effect on Mexico's future was profound, however, and his plans and visions bore fruit for decades.

THE PORFIRIATO & THE REVOLUTION From 1877 to 1911, a period now called the "Porfiriato," the prime role in Mexico was played by Porfirio Díaz, a general under Juárez. Recognized as a modernizer, he was a terror to his enemies and to challengers of his absolute power. During the Díaz years, many who fell into disfavor wound up enslaved in the Yucatán, including the Yaqui Indians of northwestern Mexico. These shockingly brutal years are recorded in *Barbarous Mexico* by John Kenneth Turner (University of Texas Press, 1969). He was forced to abdicate in 1911 by Francisco Madero and public opinion.

After the fall of the Porfirist dictatorship, several factions split the country, including those led by "Pancho Villa" (whose real name was Doroteo Arango), Alvaro Obregón, Venustiano Carranza, and Emiliano Zapata. The decade that followed is referred to as the Mexican Revolution. Drastic reforms occurred in this period, and the surge of vitality and progress from this exciting if turbulent time has inspired Mexicans to the present. Succeeding presidents have invoked the spirit of the Revolution, which is still studied and discussed.

THE 20TH CENTURY After the turmoil of the Revolution, Mexico sought stability in the form of the Partido Revolucionario Institucional (el PRI), the country's dominant political party. With the aim of "institutionalizing the revolution," el PRI (pronounced "ell-*pree*") literally engulfed Mexican society, leaving little room for vigorous, independent opposition. For over half a century the monolithic party has had control of the government, labor unions, trade organizations, and other centers of power in Mexican society.

The most outstanding Mexican president of the century was Gen. Lázaro Cárdenas (1934–40). An effective leader, Cárdenas broke up vast tracts of agricultural land and distributed parcels to small cooperative farms called *ejidos*, reorganized the labor unions along democratic lines, and provided funding for village schools. His most famous action was the expropriation of Mexico's oil industry from U.S. and European interests, which became Petroleros Mexicanos (Pemex), the government petroleum monopoly.

Since the days of Cárdenas, the president of Mexico has selected his successor, which to date has always been a PRI-party member. Vocal opposition candidates in recent elections have challenged this entrenched system. However, the national election has, in effect, been a confirmation of his choice for president. Among the selected presidents have been Ávila Camacho, who continued many of Cárdenas's policies; Miguel Aleman, who expanded national industrial and infrastructure development; Adolfo López Mateos, who expanded the highway system and increased hydroelectric power sources; and Gustavo Díaz Ordaz, who provided credit and technical help to the agricultural sector.

In 1970 Luis Echeverría came to power, followed in 1976 by José López Portillo. During their presidencies there emerged a studied coolness in relations with the United States and an activist role in international affairs. This period also saw an increase in charges of large-scale corruption in the upper echelons of Mexican society. The corruption, though endemic to

DATELINE

Cancún opens to tourism.

• **1982** Banks are nationalized.

• **1988** Mexico enters the General Agreement on Tariffs and Trade (GATT).

• **1991** Mexico, Canada, and the United States begin Free Trade Agreement negotiations.

• **1992** Sale of ejido land (peasant communal property) to private citizens is allowed; Mexico and the Vatican establish diplomatic relations after an interruption of 100 years.

• **1993** Mexico deregulates hotel and restaurant prices; New Peso currency begins circulation. The North American Free Trade agreement is approved by all three countries.

• **1994** A January Indian uprising in Chiapas sparks protests countrywide over land distribution, bank loans, health care, education, voting, and human rights. In an evidently unrelated incident, PRI candidate Luís

(continues)

the system, was encouraged by the river of money from the rise in oil prices. When oil income skyrocketed, Mexican borrowing and spending did likewise. The reduction of oil prices in the 1980s left Mexico with an enormous foreign bank debt and serious infrastructure deficiencies.

MEXICO TODAY Without King Oil, Mexico must rebuild agriculture and industry, cut expenditures, tame corruption, and keep its creditors at bay. Pres. Miguel de la Madrid Hurtado, who assumed the presidency in 1982, struggled with these problems and made important progress. The current president, Carlos Salinas de Gortari, has managed to slow inflation from 200% annually to between 8% and 15%. In January 1994, Mexico joined with the U.S. and Canada in the North American Free Trade Agreement, which will be phased in over a 15-year period and which will eliminate many trade barriers between the three countries. But the economy, and society, are still under tremendous economic pressure, and charges of government corruption, although fewer than in the past, still exist. The next president of Mexico will be elected in August 1994.

Peasant revolts began in Chiapas in January 1994 and spread to other areas of the country. The protestors' grievances over land, voting, human rights, and access to loans mimics the same unresolved ills that led to Mexico's revolution early this century. Careful handling by governmental leaders could defuse this powder keg, but it remains to be seen how this and successive governments will handle the issues.

Economically, Mexico is not by any means a poor country. Only about a sixth of the economy is in agriculture. Mining is still fairly important. Gold, silver, and many other important minerals are still mined, but the big industry today is oil. Mexico is also well industrialized, manufacturing textiles, food products, and everything from cassette tapes to automobiles.

POLITICS

The Republic of Mexico today is headed by an elected president and a bicameral legislature. It is divided into 31 states, plus the Federal District (Mexico City).

Mexico's current economic difficulties have led to a newly vigorous and open political life, with opposition parties gaining strength. The traditionally victorious PRI party won the hotly contested presidential election in 1988, but its candidate, Carlos Salinas de Gortari, only managed to claim a historically low 50.36% of the vote amid claims of fraud by his chief rival, Cuauhtémoc Cárdenas of the newly formed National Democratic Front (FDN). Ironically, Cárdenas is the son of Mexico's beloved president, who founded the PRI. However, opposition parties managed to win a few Senate seats for the first time since the PRI came to power, and recent local elections produced strong opposition candidates. Mexico's new president was to be elected as this book went to press. The campaign was doubly troubled by the assassination of PRI candidate Luís Donaldo Colosio and the replacement candidacy of

IMPRESSIONS

It becomes a virtue, almost a necessity, to do some loafing. The art of leisure is therefore one of Mexico's most stubbornly defended practises [sic] and one of her subtle appeals: a lesson in civilization which we of the hectic north need very badly to learn.
—ANITA BRENNER, *YOUR MEXICAN HOLIDAY,* 1932

DID YOU KNOW ...?

- The Celestún estuary, on the Yucatán Gulf coast, is home to the largest flock of flamingos in North America.
- Cacao beans, grown in Tabasco and Chiapas, were Aztec currency.
- Cancún opened to tourism in 1974 with one hotel.
- In 1841 Yucatán hired the Texas Navy to protect the peninsula from invasion by Mexico.
- The Maya predicted the earth's destruction by earthquakes in the year A.D. 2012.
- During the 300 years that Mexico belonged to Spain, no Spanish king ever visited the country.
- Mexico's Indian population was approximately 30 million in 1519. By 1550, it was down to only three million, largely because of the spread of smallpox, measles, and other diseases brought by the Spaniards.
- Half the population of Mexico is under the age of 16.
- Cortés prevented his troops from returning to Spain by sinking all of his ships.

Ernesto Zedillo Ponce de León, his campaign manager, just five months before the election. The main opposition candidate, from the PAN party, was Diego Fernandez de Cevallos. Whether promised reforms for greater democracy will be lasting is debatable, but Mexico has been one of the most stable countries in Latin America.

In short, Mexico is well into the 20th century, with all the benefits and problems of contemporary life, and although vast sums are spent on education and public welfare, a high birthrate, high unemployment, and unequal distribution of wealth show that much remains to be done.

2. FAMOUS MEXICANS

Porfirio Díaz (1830–1915) Born in Oaxaca and schooled in law, Díaz distinguished himself at the famous Puebla battle and within 14 years became president of Mexico. He remained as dictator for the next 34 years, with one four-year interruption. His contributions were enormous: He moved the country from turmoil and bankruptcy into peace and stability through improvements in communication, railroads, agriculture, industry, and foreign investment. He built lavish public buildings, and sent promising art students to Europe on full scholarships. Yet these successes were achieved by disregarding the law and at the expense of the poor, Indians, and intellectuals who opposed his methods.

Since the Yucatán peninsula was distant from the power brokers of the capital, those considered obstacles to Díaz's plans often ended up enslaved in the Yucatán, which was dubbed "Mexico's Siberia." Those exiled at his request included Yaqui Indians from northwestern Mexico and out-of-favor soldiers and politicians. This cruel and lawless enslavement constitutes one of the blackest episodes in Mexico's history and one of the many reasons Díaz is so disdained today. His excesses brought about his downfall in 1911 and the Mexican Revolution, which lasted until 1917. Díaz died in exile in Paris.

Miguel Hidalgo y Costilla (1753–1811) A small-town priest in the town of Dolores, Guanajuato, Hidalgo won fame as the Father of Mexican Independence. He was among several in his area who secretly conspired to free Mexico from Spanish domination. On the morning of September 16, 1810, a messenger from Josefa Ortiz de Dominguez brought Hidalgo word that the conspiracy was uncovered. He quickly decided to publicly call for independence (an act known today as the *grito* or "cry") from his parish church, after which he galloped from village to village spreading the news and gathering troops.

Benito Juárez (1806–1872) A full-blooded Zapotec Indian, Juárez became governor of Oaxaca in 1847, after which he was exiled to New Orleans by grudge-holding President Santa Anna because Juárez had refused to grant him asylum in Oaxaca years before. He first became president of Mexico in 1858, though his terms were interrupted once during the Reform Wars and again during the French intervention. Juárez cast the deciding vote in favor of executing Maximilian. He died from a heart attack before completing his fourth term. Devoid of personal excesses, Juárez had a clear vision for Mexico that included honest leadership, separation of church and state, imposition of civilian rule, reduction of the military, and education reform.

Doña Marina (La Malinche) (early 1500s) Born to Nahuatl-speaking parents in Veracruz, but sold into slavery in the Maya-speaking Yucatán when her mother remarried, this young Indian girl knew two languages when she met Cortés in 1519. With Jerónimo de Aguilar, a Spaniard who had been shipwrecked off the coast of the Yucatán and knew Maya, she translated conversations for Cortés to Nahuatl speakers of central Mexico while also becoming Cortés's mistress and bearing him a son, Martín. Later she married a Spaniard, Juan Jaramillo. To Mexicans her name, Malinche (*malinchismo*), means traitor or harboring a preference for foreign people and their customs. Her burial place is unknown.

Moctezuma II (1468–1520) At age 52, after consolidating an empire that included all the territory surrounding his magnificent capital, Tenochtitlán, plus today's Veracruz, Chiapas, and Oaxaca, Moctezuma (misspelled Montezuma) fell victim to a superstitious belief about the return of the white-skinned god Quetzalcoatl, a belief that cost him his life and his empire. Though so exalted that no one was allowed to look at him or sit in his presence, Moctezuma went out to meet Cortés when he arrived in Tenochtitlán, hosted him lavishly, and even toured the city with him. Eventually the Spaniards made Moctezuma a prisoner. During one confusing night, the Aztecs rebelled with every weapon in their arsenal, including stones. Moctezuma was sent to the rooftop to quell the rebellion, and was accidentally hit by a stone. He died three days later.

António López de Santa Anna (1794–1876) One of the most scorned characters in Mexican history, he was president of Mexico 11 times between 1833 and 1855. His outrageous exploits disgust and infuriate Mexicans even today, but none more than his role in losing half the territory of Mexico to the United States. Defeated and captured at the Battle of San Jacinto outside Houston, Texas, in 1836, he agreed to allow Texas to be a separate republic and to mark the boundary at the Rio Grande. When the U.S. voted to annex Texas, it sparked the Mexican-American War, which the U.S. won in 1848. In the Treaty of Guadalupe that followed, the U.S. paid Mexico $15 million for Texas, New Mexico, California, Arizona, Nevada, Utah, and part of Colorado. Eventually Santa Anna was exiled, but he returned to Mexico two years before he died—poor, alone, and forgotten.

3. ART, ARCHITECTURE & LITERATURE

ART & ARCHITECTURE Mexico's artistic and architectural legacy began more than 3,000 years ago. Until the fall of the Aztec Empire in A.D. 1521, art, architecture, politics, and religion in Mexico were inextricably intertwined and remained so in different ways through the colonial period.

World-famous archeological sites in Mexico—more than 15,000 of them—are individually unique even if built by the same groups of people. Each year scholars decipher more information about the ancient indigenous groups who built these cities, using information they left in bas-relief carvings, sculptures, murals, and hieroglyphics.

Mexico's pyramids are truncated platforms, not true pyramids, and come in many different shapes. At Tzintzuntzán, near Lake Pátzcuaro, the buildings, called *yacatas*, are distinguished by semicircular buildings attached to rectangular ones. Many sites have circular buildings, usually called the observatory and dedicated to Ehécatl, god of the wind. At El Tajín, the

○ **Amazing stone murals or mosaics using thousands of pieces of fitted stone to form figures of warriors, snakes, or geometric designs decorate the pyramid facades at Uxmal and Chichén-Itzá.**

Pyramid of the Niches has 365 niches, one for every day of the year, while El Castillo at Chichén-Itzá has 365 steps. The Temple of the Magicians at Uxmal has beautifully rounded and sloping sides. The Huastecas of northern Veracruz and Tamaulipas states were known for their many circular ceremonial platforms. Evidence of building one pyramidal structure on top of another, a widely accepted practice, has been found throughout Mesoamerica.

The largest pyramid by volume is the Tepanapa pyramid at Cholula. The Temple of the Inscriptions at Palenque is the only pyramid built specifically as a tomb, although tombs have been found in many other pyramids. Cobá has the longest road (*sacbe*), stretching 62 miles. Numerous sites in Mesoamerica had ballcourts. In Mexico the longest is at Chichén-Itzá—nearly the length of a football field. El Tajín, with 17 ballcourts, has the most.

Architects of many Toltec, Aztec, and Teotihuacán edifices used a sloping panel (*tablud*) alternating with a vertical panel (*tablero*). Elements of this style occasionally show up in the Yucatán. Dzinbanché, a newly excavated site near Lago Bacalar in southern Quintana Roo state, has at least one temple with this characteristic.

The true arch was unknown in Mesoamerica, so the Maya made multiple use of the corbeled arch in which a keystone juts out over the others and is used to build a modified inverted V-shaped arch.

The Olmecs, considered the parent culture in Mexico, built pyramids of earth, so little remains to tell us what their buildings looked like. The Olmecs, however, left an enormous sculptural legacy from small, intricately carved pieces of jade to 40-ton carved basalt rock heads that were, amazingly, shipped to their homesites by river raft.

Throughout Mexico, the pyramids were embellished with carved stone or mural art, not for the purpose of pure adornment, but for religious and historic reasons. Hieroglyphs, picture symbols etched on stone or painted on walls or pottery, functioned as the written language of the ancient peoples, particularly the Maya. By deciphering the glyphs, scholars allow the ancients to speak again, giving us specific names to attach to rulers and their families, demystifying the great dynastic histories of the Maya. For more on this, be sure to read *A Forest of Kings* (1990) by Linda Schele and David Freidel. Good hieroglyphic examples can be seen in the site museum at Palenque.

Carving important historic figures on free-standing stone slabs, or *stelae*, was a common Maya commemorative device. Several are in place at Cobá, and good examples are in the Museum of Anthropology in Mexico City and the Carlos Pellicer Museum in Villahermosa.

Pottery played an important role, and different indigenous groups are distinguished by their use of color and style in pottery. The Cholulans had distinctive red-clay pottery decorated in cream, red, and black; Teotihuacán was noted for its three-legged painted orangeware; Tenochtitlán for its use of brilliant blue and red; Casas Grandes for anthropomorphic and zoomorphic images on clay vessels; and the Maya for pottery painted with scenes from daily and historic life. Besides regional museums, the best collection of all this work is in the Museum of Anthropology in Mexico City.

Pre-Hispanic cultures left a number of fantastic painted murals, some of which are remarkably preserved, such as those at Bonampak and Cacaxtla, and others of which are fragmentary, such as those at Teotihuacán, Cholula, and El Tajín. Amazing stone murals or mosaics using thousands of pieces of fitted stone to form figures of warriors, snakes, or geometric designs decorate the pyramid facades at Uxmal and Chichén-Itzá.

With the arrival of the Spaniards a new form of architecture came to Mexico (the next 300 years are known as the Viceregal Period, when Spain's appointed viceroys ruled Mexico). Many sites that were occupied by indigenous groups at the time of the conquest were razed, and in their place appeared Catholic churches, public buildings, and palaces for conquerors and the king's bureaucrats. In the Yucatán existing churches at Izamal, Calkani, Santa Elena, and Muná rest atop former pyramidal structures. Indian artisans, who formerly worked on pyramidal structures, were recruited to give life to the new buildings, often guided by drawings of European buildings the Spanish architects tried to emulate. Frequently left on their own, the indigenous artisans sometimes implanted traditional symbolism in the new buildings: a plaster angel swaddled in feathers, reminiscent of the god Quetzalcoatl; or the face of an ancient god surrounded by corn leaves. They used pre-Hispanic calendar counts, the 13 steps to heaven, or the nine levels of the underworld to determine how many flowerettes to carve around the church doorway.

To convert the native populations, New World Spanish priests and architects altered their normal ways of building and teaching. Often before the church was built, an open-air atrium was first constructed so that large numbers of parishioners could be accommodated for service. *Posas* (shelters) at the four corners of churchyards were another architectural technique unique to Mexico, again for the purpose of accommodating crowds during holy sacraments. Because of the language barrier between the Spanish and the natives, church adornment became more graphic. Biblical tales came to life in frescoes splashed across church walls; Christian symbolism in stone supplanted that of pre-Hispanic times. Out went the eagle (sun symbol), feathered serpent (symbol of fertility, rain, earth, and sky), and jaguar (power symbol), and in came Christ on a cross, saintly statues, and Franciscan, Dominican, and Augustinian symbolism. It must have been a confusing time for the indigenous peoples, which accounts for the continued intermingling of Christian and pre-Hispanic ideas as they tried to make sense of it all. The convenient apparition of the Virgin Mary on former pre-Hispanic religious turf made it "legal" to return there to worship and build a "Christian" shrine. Baroque became even more baroque in Mexico and was dubbed *churrigueresque*.

Almost every village in the Yucatán peninsula has the hulking remains of enormous fortresslike missions, monasteries, convents, and parish churches. Many were built in the 16th century following the early arrival of Franciscan friars (the Franciscans were the only sect allowed in the Yucatán to Christianize the natives). Highlights include the Mission of San Bernardino de Sisal in Valladolid; the fine altarpiece at Teabo; the folk art retablo at Calkani; the large church and convent at

Maní with its unique retablos and limestone crucifix; the facade, altar, and central retablo of the church at Oxkutzcab; the 16-bell espadaña at Ytholin; the baroque facade and altarpiece at Maxcanu; the cathedral at Mérida; the vast atrium and church at Izamal; and the baroque retablo and murals at Tabi.

In the Yucatán the term *plateresque* was given to facade decorations resembling silver design, which seem to be planted on a structure rather than a part of it.

Concurrently with the building of religious structures, public buildings took shape, modeled after those in European capitals. Colorful locally made tile, made in a fusion of local art and Talavera style from Spain, decorated public walls and church domes. The hacienda architecture sprang up in the countryside, resulting in massive, thick-walled, fortresslike structures built around a central patio. Remains of haciendas, some of them still operating, can be seen in almost all parts of Mexico. The San Carlos Academy of Art was founded in Mexico City in 1785, taking after the renowned academies of Europe. Though the emphasis was on a Europeanized Mexico, by the end of the 19th century the subject matter of easel artists was becoming Mexican: Still lifes with Mexican fruit and pottery, and Mexican landscapes with cactus and volcanoes appeared, as did portraits whose subjects wore Mexican regional clothing. José María Velasco (1840–1912), the father of Mexican landscape painting, emerged during this time. His work and that of others of this period are at the National Museum of Art in Mexico City.

With the late 19th century entry of Porfirio Díaz into the presidency came another infusion of Europe. Díaz idolized Europe, and during this time he lavished on the country a number of striking European-style public buildings, among them opera houses still used today. He provided European scholarships to promising young artists who later returned to Mexico to produce clearly Mexican subject paintings using techniques learned abroad. Partly because of the vast henequén hacienda wealth and partly because the Yucatán peninsula was so far from the heart of Mexico, it too developed more of an affinity with European and Cuban cultures than it did with Mexico.

While the Mexican Revolution, following the resignation and exile of Díaz, ripped the country apart between 1911 and 1917, the result was the birth of Mexico, a claiming and appreciation of it by Mexicans. In 1923 Minister of Education José Vasconcelos was charged with educating the illiterate masses. As one means of reaching many people, he started the muralist movement when he invited Diego Rivera and several other budding artists to paint Mexican history on the walls of the Ministry of Education building and the National Preparatory School in Mexico City. From then on, the "big three" muralists—David Siquieros, José Clemente Orozco, and Rivera—were joined by others in bringing Mexico's history in art to the walls of public buildings throughout the country for all to see and interpret. The years that followed eventually brought about a return to easel art, an exploration of Mexico's culture, and a new generation of artists and architects who were free to invent and draw upon subjects and styles from around the world. Among the 20th-century greats are the "big three" muralists, as well as Rufino Tamayo, Gerardo Murillo, José Guadalupe Posada, Saturnino Herrán, Francisco Goitia, Frida Kahlo, José María Velasco, Pedro and Rafael Coronel, Miguel Covarrubias, Olga Costa, and José Chávez Morado. Among important architects during this period, Luis Barragán incorporated design elements from haciendas, and from Mexican textiles, pottery, and furniture, into sleek, marble-floored structures splashed with the vivid colors of Mexico. His ideas are used by Mexican architects all over Mexico today.

LITERATURE   By the time Cortés arrived in Mexico, the indigenous people were already masters of literature, recording their poems and histories by painting in fanfold books (codices) made of deerskin and bark paper or carving on stone. To record history, gifted students were taught the art of bookmaking, drawing, painting, reading, and writing, abilities the general public didn't have. The ancient Maya produced two important epic works, the *Book of Popol Vuh* and the *Chilam Balam*. Unfortunately, other than these two works, very little survives, for after the conquest the Spaniards deliberately destroyed native books. However, several Catholic priests, among them Bernardo de Sahugun and Diego de Landa (who was one of the book destroyers), encouraged the Indians to record their customs and history. These records are among the best we have to document life before the conquest.

During the conquest, Cortés wrote his now-famous five letters to Charles V, which give us the first printed conquest literature, but the most important record is that of Díaz de Castillo. Enraged by an inaccurate account of the conquest written by a flattering friend of Cortés, 40 years after the conquest Bernal Díaz de Castillo, one of the conquerors, wrote his lively and very readable version of the event, *True History of the Conquest of Mexico*; it's regarded as the most accurate.

In an attempt to defend himself for burning 27 Maya hieroglyphic rolls in 1562, Friar Diego de Landa collected contemporary Maya customs, beliefs, and history and wrote *Relación de las Cosas de Yucatán* (today entitled *Yucatán Before and After the Conquest*, Dover Press, 1978). It was published in 1566 and remains the most significant record of its kind.

The first printing press appeared in Mexico in 1537 and was followed by a proliferation of printing, mostly on subjects about science, nature, and getting along in Mexico. The most important literary figure during the 16th century was Sor Juana Inés de la Cruz, child prodigy and later poet-nun whose works are still treasured. The first Spanish novel written in Mexico was *The Itching Parrot* by José Joaquín Fernández de Lizardi, about 19th-century Mexican life. The first daily newspaper appeared in 1805. Nineteenth-century writers produced a plethora of political fiction and nonfiction. Among the more explosive was *The Presidential Succession of 1910* by Francisco Madero (who later became president), which contributed to the downfall of Porfirio Díaz, and *Regeneración*, a weekly anti-Díaz magazine published by the Flores Mignon brothers.

Among 20th-century writers of note are Octavio Paz, author of *The Labyrinth of Solitude* and winner of the 1991 Nobel Prize for literature, and Carlos Fuentes, who wrote *Where the Air Is Clear*.

Books in Mexico are expensive, and editions are not produced in great quantity. Newspapers and magazines proliferate, but the majority of those who read devour comic-book novels, the most visible form of literature.

4. RELIGION, MYTH & FOLKLORE

Mexico is a predominantly Roman Catholic country, a religion introduced by the Spaniards during the Conquest of Mexico. Despite its preponderance, the Catholic faith, in many places (Chiapas and Oaxaca, for example), has pre-Hispanic overtones. One need only visit the *curandero* section of a Mexican market, or attend a village festivity featuring pre-Hispanic dancers, to understand that supernatural beliefs often run parallel to Christian ones.

IMPRESSIONS
We both learned that the Maya are not just a people of the past. Today, they live in their millions in Mexico, Guatemala, Belize and western Honduras, still speaking one of the thirty-five Mayan languages as their native tongue. They continue to cultivate their fields and commune with their living world in spite of the fact that they are encapsulated within a larger modern civilization whose vision of reality is often alien to their own.
—LINDA SCHELE AND DAVID FREIDEL, *A FOREST OF KINGS*, 1990

Mexico's complicated mythological heritage from pre-Hispanic literature is jammed with images derived from nature—the wind, jaguars, eagles, snakes, flowers, and more—all intertwined with elaborate mythological stories to explain the universe, climate, seasons, and geography. So strong were the ancient beliefs that Mexico's indigenous peoples built their cities according to the four cardinal points of the compass, with each compass point assigned a particular color (the colors might vary from group to group). The sun, moon, and stars took on godlike meaning and the religious, ceremonial, and secular calendars were arranged to show tribute to these omnipotent gods.

Most groups believed in an underworld (not a hell), usually of 9 levels, and a heaven of 13 levels, so the numbers 9 and 13 become mythologically significant. The solar calendar count of 365 days and the ceremonial calendar of 260 days are numerically significant. How one died determined where one wound up after death: in the underworld, in heaven, or at one of the four cardinal points. Everyone had first to make the journey through the underworld.

One of the richest sources of mythological tales is the *Book of Popol Vuh*, a Maya bible of sorts, which was recorded after the conquest. The *Chilam Balam*, another such book, existed in hieroglyphic form at the conquest and was recorded, using the Spanish alphabet to transliterate Maya words that could be understood by the Spaniards. The *Chilam Balam* differed from the *Popol Vuh* in that it is the collected histories of many Maya communities.

Each of the ancient cultures had its set of gods and goddesses, and while the names might not cross cultures, their characteristics or purpose often did. Chaac, the hook-nosed rain god of the Maya, was Tlaloc, the mighty-figured rain god of the Aztecs; Queztalcoatl, the plumed-serpent god/man of the Toltecs, became Kukulkán of the Maya. The tales of the powers and creation of these deities make up Mexico's rich mythology. Sorting out the pre-Hispanic pantheon and mythological beliefs in ancient Mexico can become an all-consuming study (the Maya alone had 166 deities), so below is a list of some of the most important gods:

Chaac	Maya rain god
Cocijo	Zapotec rain god
Ehécatl	Wind god, whose temple is usually round; another aspect of Quetzalcoatl
Itzamná	Maya god above all, who invented corn, cacao, and writing and reading
Ixchel	Maya goddess of water, weaving, and childbirth
Kinich Ahau	Maya sun god
Kukulkán	Quetzalcoatl's name in the Yucatán
Mayahuel	Goddess of pulque
Ometeotl	God/goddess all-powerful creator of the universe, ruler of heaven, earth, and the underworld

Quetzalcoatl	A mortal who took on legendary characteristics as a god (or vice versa). When he left Tula in shame after a night of succumbing to temptations, he promised to return. He reappeared in the Yucatán. He is also symbolized as Venus, the morning star, and Ehécatl, the wind god. Quetzalcoatl is credited with giving the Maya cacao (chocolate), and teaching them how to grow it, harvest it, roast it, and turn it into a drink with ceremonial and magical properties.
Tláloc	Aztec rain god

5. CULTURAL & SOCIAL LIFE

The population of Mexico is 85 million, 15% of which is white (most of Spanish descent), 60% mestizo (mixed Spanish and Indian), and 25% pure Indian (descendants of the Maya, Aztecs, Huastecs, Otomies, Totonacs, and other peoples). Added to this ethnic mix are Africans brought as slaves, European merchants and soldiers of fortune, and the lingering French influence from the time of Maximilian's abortive empire in the New World.

Although Spanish is the official language, about 50 Indian languages are still spoken, mostly in the Yucatán peninsula, Oaxaca, Chiapas, Chihuahua, Nayarit, Puebla, Sonora and Veracruz, Michoacán, and Guerrero.

Modern Mexico clings to its identity while embracing outside cultures, so Mexicans enjoy the Bolshoi Ballet as easily as a family picnic or village festival. Mexicans have a knack for knowing how to enjoy life, and families, weekends, holidays, and festivities are given priority. They also enjoy stretching a weekend holiday into four days called a *puente* (bridge) and, with the whole family in town, flee the cities en masse to visit relatives in the country, picnic, or relax at resorts.

The Mexican work day is a long one: laborers begin around 7am and get off at dusk; office workers go in around 9am and, with a two- or three-hour lunch, get off at 7 or 8pm. Once a working career is started, there is little time for additional study. School is supposedly mandatory and free through the sixth grade, but many youngsters quit long before that, or never go at all.

Sociologists and others have written volumes trying to explain the Mexicans' special relationship with death. It is at once mocked and mourned. The Days of the Dead, November 1 and 2, a cross between Halloween and All Saints' Day, is a good opportunity to observe Mexico's relationship with the concept of death.

MUSIC & DANCE One has only to walk down almost any street or attend any festival to understand that Mexico's vast musical tradition is inborn; it pre-dates the conquest. Musical instruments were made from almost anything that could be made to rattle or produce a rhythm or a sound—conch-shell trumpets, high-pitched antler horns, rattlers from sea shells and rattlesnake rattlers, drums of turtle shell as well as upright leather-covered wood (*tlalpanhuéhuetl*), and horizontal hollowed logs (*teponaztli*), bells of gold and copper, wind instruments of hollow reeds or fired clay, and soundmakers from leather-topped armadillo shells and gourds. Many were elaborately carved or decorated, befitting the important ceremonies they accompanied. So important was music that one of Moctezuma's palaces, the Mixcoacalli, was devoted to the care and housing of musical instruments, which were guarded around the clock. Music, dance, and religion were tied together with literature. Music was usually intended to accompany the poems that were written for religious ceremonies. Children with talent were separated and trained to adulthood especially as musicians and poets, two exacting professions in which mistakes carried extreme consequences. The dead were buried with musical instruments for their journey into the afterlife.

Music and dance in Mexico today are divided into three kinds: pre- and post-Hispanic and secular. Post-Hispanic music and dance evolved first in order to teach the native inhabitants about Christianity with such dances as "Los Santiagos," with St. James battling heathens, and "Los Moros," with Moors battling Christians. Others, like "Los Jardineros," were spoofs on pretentious Spanish life. Secular dances are variations of Spanish dances performed by both men and women characterized by lots of foot-tapping, skirt-swishing, and innocent flirtation. No "Mexican fiesta night" would be complete without the "Jarabe Tapatío," the national folk dance of Mexico. "Jaranas" are folk dances of the Yucatán, danced to the lively beat of a ukulelelike instrument and drums.

Besides the native music and dances, there are regional, state, and national orchestras. On weekends state bands often perform free in central plazas. In Mérida, almost any night and all day Sunday the city hosts free public concerts and regional dancing. Performing arts groups from all over the world frequently tour Mexico. Mexicans have a sophisticated understanding and enjoyment of visual and performing arts and any special show will be a sell-out.

6. SPORTS & RECREATION

The precise rules of the ball game played by pre-Hispanic Mexicans isn't known, but it is fairly well established that some of the players were put to death when the game was over—whether it was the victors or the losers is unknown. Stone carvings of the game left on the walls of ballcourts throughout Mesoamerica depict heavily padded players elaborately decked out. With that interesting beginning, team sports are popular in Mexico. Probably the most popular team sport today is soccer; turn on the TV almost anytime to catch a game.

Bullfighting, introduced by the Spaniards, is performed countrywide today. By the 18th century the Mexican gentleman-cowboy, the *charro*, displayed skillful horsemanship during the *charreada*, a Mexican-style rodeo; today charro associations countrywide compete all year, usually on Sunday mornings. Although supposedly illegal, in many places cockfights are held in specially built arenas.

Mexico has numerous golf courses, especially in the resort areas. It is sometimes easier to rent a horse in Mexico than a car, since horseback riding is a pastime enjoyed by many people at beach resorts as well as in the country. Sport bicycling has grown in popularity, so it isn't unusual to see young men along public highways during cycling club marathons.

Tennis, racquetball, squash, waterskiing, surfing, and scuba diving are all sports visitors can enjoy in Mexico. While it's possible to scuba dive in the Pacific, the best

IMPRESSIONS

The Yucatecans are very generous and hospitable; no one enters their houses without being offered food and drink, what drink they may have during the day, or food in the evening. If they have none, they seek it from a neighbor; if they unite together on the roads, all join in sharing even if they have little for their own need.
—FRIAR DIEGO DE LANDA, *YUCATÁN BEFORE AND AFTER THE CONQUEST*, 1566

place for that sport is Mexico's Yucatán Caribbean coast. Mountain climbing and hiking volcanoes is a rugged sport where you'll meet like-minded folks from around the world.

7. FOOD & DRINK

Mexican food served in the United States isn't really Mexican food, it's a transported variation that gets less Mexican the farther you get from the border. True Mexican food usually isn't fiery hot; hot spices are added from sauces and garnishes at the table. While there are certain staples like tortillas and beans that appear almost universally, Mexican food and drink varies considerably from region to region; even the beans and tortillas sidestep the usual in some areas just to keep you on your toes.

DINING CUSTOMS Who you are and what you do makes a difference when it comes to when you eat. If you're a businessperson, you may grab a cup of coffee or *atole* and a piece of sweet bread just before heading for work around 8am. Around 10 or 11am it's time for a real breakfast, and that's when restaurants fill with men (usually) eating hearty breakfasts that may look more like lunch with steak, eggs, beans, and tortillas. Between 1 and 5pm patrons again converge for lunch, the main meal of the day, which begins with soup, then rice, then the main course with beans and tortillas and maybe a meager helping of a vegetable, followed by dessert and coffee. Workers return to their jobs until 7 or 8 pm. Dinner is late, usually around 9 or 10pm. Although you may see many Mexicans eating in restaurants at night, big evening meals aren't traditional; a typical meal at home would be a light one with leftovers from breakfast or lunch, perhaps soup, or tortillas and jam, or a little meat and rice.

Foreigners searching for an early breakfast will often find that nothing gets going in restaurants until around 9am; that's a hint to bring your own portable coffee pot and coffee, buy bakery goodies the night before, and make breakfast yourself. Markets, however, are bustling by 7am and that's the best place to get an early breakfast. Though Mexico grows flavorful coffee in Chiapas, Veracruz, and Oaxaca, a jar of instant coffee is often all that's offered, especially in budget restaurants.

Some of the foreigner's greatest frustrations in Mexico have to do with getting and retaining the waiter and receiving the final bill. If the waiter arrives to take your order before you are ready, you may have trouble getting him again when you *are* ready. Once your meal is before you, and you're close to savoring your last morsel, amazingly an eager waiter often appears to whisk away your plate before you're finished! "¿Puedo retirar?" ("Can I take your plate away?") he asks, nearly clicking his heels with efficiency. At this point guard your plate, for at any moment it could disappear midfork. Finding your waiter to get the check, however, is another matter. It's considered rude for the waiter to bring it before it's requested, so you have to ask for it (sometimes more than once, when at last you've found the waiter). To summon the waiter, wave or raise your hand, but don't motion with your index finger, a demeaning gesture that may even cause the waiter to ignore you. Or if it's the check you want, a smile and a scribbling motion into the palm of your hand can send the message across the room. In many budget restaurants, waiters don't clear the table of finished plates or soft-drink bottles because they use them to figure the tab. Always double-check the addition.

REGIONAL CUISINE   Mexico's regional foods are a mixture of pre-Hispanic, Spanish, and French cuisines, and at their best are among the most delicious in the world. Recipes developed by nuns during colonial times to please priests and visiting dignitaries have become part of the national patrimony, but much of Mexico's cuisine is derived from pre-Hispanic times. For the visitor, finding hearty, filling meals is fairly easy on a budget, but finding truly delicious food is not as easy. However, some of the best food is found in small, inexpensive restaurants where regional specialities are made to please discerning locals.

Tamales are one of Mexico's traditional foods, but regional differences make trying them a treat as you travel. Chiapas has many tamal types, but all are plump and usually come with a sizable hunk of meat and sauce inside.

Tortillas, another Mexican basic, are not made or used universally. In northern Mexico flour tortillas are served more often than corn tortillas. Blue-corn tortillas, once a market food, have found their way to gourmet tables throughout the country. Tortillas are fried and used as garnish in tortilla and Tarascan soup. Soft tortillas become *tacos* when filled with any number of meats; however, in some places in Mexico what's called a taco on the menu may be more like a flauta elsewhere. A tortilla stuffed, rolled, or covered in a sauce and garnished results in an *enchilada*. A tortilla filled with cheese and lightly fried is a *quesadilla*. Rolled into a narrow tube, stuffed with chicken, then deep-fried, it's known as a *flauta*. Leftover tortillas cut in wedges and crispy fried are called *totopos* and used to scoop up beans and guacamole salad. Yesterday's tortillas mixed with eggs, chicken, peppers, and other spices are called *chilaquiles*. Small fried-corn tortillas are delicious with ceviche, or when topped with fresh lettuce, tomatoes and sauce, onions, and chicken they become *tostadas*. Each region has a variation of these tortilla-based dishes.

The Yucatán peninsula has some of the most varied regional food, including papadzul, huevos motuleños, poc-chuc, cochinita and pollo pibil, escabeche, and lime soup.

Regional drinks are almost as varied as the food in Mexico. Tequila comes from the blue agave grown near Guadalajara. Hot *ponche* (punch) is often found at festivals and is usually made with fresh fruit and spiked with tequila or rum. Baja California and the region around Querétaro are prime grape-growing land for Mexico's wine production. The best *pulque* supposedly comes from Hidalgo state. Beer is produced in Monterrey, the Yucatán, and Veracruz. Delicious fruit-flavored waters appear on tables countrywide made from hibiscus flowers, ground rice and melon seeds, watermelon, and other fresh fruits. Sangría is a spicy tomato/orange-juice and pepper-based chaser for tequila shots.

8. RECOMMENDED BOOKS, FILMS & RECORDINGS

BOOKS

There is an endless supply of books written on the history, culture, and archeology of Mexico and Central America. I have listed those that I especially enjoyed.

HISTORY   Dennis Tedlock produced an elegant translation of the *Popul Vuh* a collection of ancient Maya mythological tales (Simon & Schuster, 1985). *A Short History of Mexico* (Doubleday, 1962), by J. Patrick McHenry, is a concise historical account. A remarkably readable and thorough college textbook is The *Course of Mexican History* (Oxford University Press, 1987), by Michael C. Meyer and William L. Sherman. *The Conquest of New Spain* (Shoe String, 1988), by Bernal Díaz, is the famous story of the Mexican conquest written by Cortés's lieutenant.

Sons of the Shaking Earth (University of Chicago Press), by Eric Wolf, is the best single-volume introduction to Mexican history and culture that I know of. *Ancient Mexico: An Overview* (University of New Mexico Press, 1985), by Jaime Litvak, is a short, very readable history of pre-Hispanic Mexico.

The Wind That Swept Mexico (University of Texas Press, 1971), by Anita Brenner, is a classic illustrated account of the Mexican Revolution.

Barbarous Mexico, by John Kenneth Turner (University of Texas Press, 1984), was written in the early 1900s as a shocking exposé of the atrocities of the Porfirio Díaz presidency, which included enslaving Yaqui Indians from Sonora in camps in the Yucatán and Oaxaca. *The Lost World of Quintana Roo*, by Michel Peissel (E.P. Dutton, 1963), is the thrilling account of a young man's journey on foot in search of undiscovered ruins along the Yucatán's almost uninhabited Caribbean coast in the late 1950s.

CULTURE *Mexican and Central American Mythology* (Peter Bedrick Books, 1983), by Irene Nicholson, is a concise illustrated book that simplifies the subject.

A good, but controversial, all-around introduction to contemporary Mexico and its people is *Distant Neighbors: A Portrait of the Mexicans* (Random House, 1984), by Alan Riding. In a more personal vein is Patrick Oster's *The Mexicans: A Personal Portrait of the Mexican People* (Harper & Row, 1989), a reporter's insightful account of ordinary Mexican people. A novel with valuable insights into the Mexican character is *The Labyrinth of Solitude* (Grove Press, 1985), by Octavio Paz.

Anyone going to San Cristóbal de las Casas, Chiapas, should first read *Living Maya* (Harry N. Abrams, 1987), by Walter F. Morris, with excellent photographs by Jeffrey J. Foxx, all about the Maya living today in the state of Chiapas.

The best single source of information on Mexican music, dance, and mythology is Frances Toor's *A Treasury of Mexican Folkways* (Crown, 1967).

Passionate Pilgrim, by Antoinette May (Paragon House, 1993), is the fascinating biography of Alma Reed, an American journalist and amateur archeologist whose life spanned the exciting 1920s to 1960s. Her journalistic assignments included early archeological digs at Chichén-Itzá, Uxmal, and Palenque; breaking the story to *The New York Times* of archeologist Edward Thompson's role in removing the contents of the sacred cenote at Chichén-Itzá to the Peabody Museum at Harvard; and serving as a columnist for the *Mexico City News*. She also had a love affair with Felipe Carrillo Puerto, the governor of Yucatán, who commissioned the famous Mexican song "La Peregrina" in her honor; and she championed the career of Mexican muralist José Clemente Orozco at her art gallery in New York.

Mexico Insight published by Excelsior in Mexico City, Bucarelli No. 1, 5 Piso, Mexico, D.F. Mexico 06600, is a twice-monthly hard-hitting newsmagazine in English. It's the best way to keep on top of what's happening from economics, to politics, to day-to-day issues such as police, Mexico City's earthquake-warning system, border agents, developers, business, free trade, the Chiapas uprising—well, you name it. Subscriptions cost $46 for 24 issues.

ART, ARCHEOLOGY & ARCHITECTURE Anyone heading for the Yucatán should first read the wonderfully entertaining accounts of travel in that region by the 19th-century traveler, New York lawyer, and amateur archeologist John L. Stephens. His books, *Incidents of Travel in Central America, Chiapas and Yucatán*, and also the account of his second trip, *Incidents of Travel in Yucatán*, have been reprinted by Dover Publications. The series also includes Friar Diego de Landa's *Yucatán Before and After the Conquest* (Dover, 1978) written in the 1560s. Friar Diego's account is a detailed description of Maya daily life, much of which has remained the same from his time until today. Another must is *The Maya* (Thames and Hudson, 1987), by Michael Coe, which is helpful in relating to the different Maya periods. *A Forest of Kings: The Untold Story of the Ancient Maya* (William Morrow, 1990), by Linda Schele and David Freidel, uses the written history of Maya hieroglyphs to tell the dynastic history of selected Maya sites. *The Blood of Kings: Dynasty and Ritual in Maya Art* (George Braziller, Inc., 1986), by Linda Schele and Mary Ellen Miller, a pioneer work, unlocks the bloody history of the Maya.

Try a used bookstore for *Digging in Mexico*, by Ann Axtell Morris, (Doubleday, Doran, 1931). The book is as interesting for its photographs of Chichén-Itzá before and during the excavations as it is for the author's lively and revealing anecdotes. Morris was the young writer and artist wife of Earl Morris, director of excavations at Chichén-Itzá during the Carnegie Institution's work there in the 1920s.

Maya History, by Tatiana Proskouriakoff (University of Texas Press, 1993), is the last work of one of the most revered Maya scholars. Linda Schele, a contemporary Maya scholar, calls Proskouriakoff "the person who was to our field as Darwin was to biology." Her contributions included numerous drawings of now-ruined Maya temples and glyphs, of which there are over 300 in this book.

Maya Missions, by Richard and Rosalind Perry (Espadaña Press, 1988), will enhance any extensive Yucatán trip. The authors reveal the mysteries of the Yucatán peninsula's many centuries-old colonial-era missions with inviting detail. It's a must-have book. Another must is the most comprehensive guide to Maya ruins, *An Archeological Guide to Mexico's Yucatán Peninsula* by Joyce Kelly (University of Oklahoma, 1993). These two books will enrich your visit a thousandfold.

A book that tells the story of the Indians' "painted books" is *The Mexican Codices and Their Extraordinary History* (Ediciones Lara, 1985), by María Sten. *Mexico: Splendors of Thirty Centuries* (Metropolitan Museum of Art, 1990), the catalog of the 1991 traveling exhibition, is a wonderful resource on Mexico's art from 1500 B.C. through the 1950s. Another superb catalog, *Images of Mexico: The Contribution of Mexico to 20th Century Art* (Dallas Museum of Art, 1987) is a fabulously illustrated and detailed account of Mexican art gathered from collections around the world. *Art and Time in Mexico: From the Conquest to the Revolution* (Harper & Row, 1985), by Elizabeth Wilder Weismann, illustrated with 351 photographs, covers Mexican religious, public, and private architecture with excellent photos and text. *Casa Mexicana* (Stewart, Tabori & Chang, 1989), by Tim Street-Porter, takes readers through the interiors of some of Mexico's finest homes-turned-museums or public buildings and private homes using color photographs. *Mexican Interiors* (Architectural Book Publishing Co., 1962), by Verna Cook Shipway and Warren Shipway, uses black-and-white photographs to highlight architectural details from homes all over Mexico.

FOLK ART Chloë Sayer's *Costumes of Mexico* (University of Texas Press, 1985) is a beautifully illustrated and written work. *Mexican Masks* (University of Texas Press, 1980), by Donald Cordry, based on the author's collection and travels, remains the definitive work on Mexican masks. Cordry's *Mexican Indian Costumes* (University of Texas Press, 1968) is another classic on the subject. Carlos Espejel wrote both *Mexican Folk Ceramics* and *Mexican Folk Crafts* (Editorial Blume, 1975 and 1978), two comprehensive books that explore crafts state by state. *Folk Treasures of Mexico* (Harry N. Abrams, 1990), by Marion Oettinger, curator of folk art and Latin American art at the San Antonio Museum of Art, is the fascinating illustrated story behind the 3,000-piece Mexican folk-art collection amassed by Nelson Rockefeller over a 50-year period, as well as much information about individual folk artists.

NATURE *Peterson Field Guides: Mexican Birds* (Houghton Mifflin), by Roger Tory Peterson and Edward L. Chalif, is an excellent guide to the country's birds. *Birds of the Yucatán* (Amigos de Sian Ka'an) has color illustrations and descriptions of 100 birds found primarily in the Yucatán peninsula. *A Guide to Mexican Mammals & Reptiles* (Minutiae Mexicana), by Normal Pelham Wright and Dr. Bernardo Villa Ramírez, is a small but useful guide to some of the country's wildlife.

FILMS

Mexico's first movie theater opened in 1897 in Mexico City. Almost immediately men with movie cameras began capturing everyday life in Mexico as well as both sides of the Mexican Revolution. All these early films are safe in Mexican archives. The movie industry had its Mexican start with the 1918 film *La Banda del Automóvil Gris* (The Gray Automobile Gang) by Enrique Rosas Priego, based on an actual cops-and-robbers event in Mexico, but the industry's heyday really began in the 1930s and lasted only until the 1950s. Themes revolved around the Mexican Revolution, handsome but luckless singing cowboys, and helpless, poor-but-beautiful maidens, all set against a classic Mexican backdrop, at first a rural or village (*rancho*) setting and later city neighborhood scenes.

Classic films from that era are *Allá en el Rancho Grande* and *Vámonos Con Pancho Villa,* both by Fernándo de Fuentes; *Campeón sin Corona* (Champion without a Crown), a true-life boxing drama, by Alejandro Galindo; *La Perla* (The Pearl), by Emilio Fernández, based on John Steinbeck's novel; *Yanco,* by Servando González, about a poor, young boy of Xochimilco who learned to play a violin; and the sad tale of *María Candelaria,* also set in Xochimilco, another Fernández film starring Dolores del Rio. Comedian Cantinflas starred in many Mexican films, and became known in the U.S. for his role in *Around the World in Eighty Days.*

The most recent well-known film produced in Mexico is *Like Water for Chocolate,* a wonderful movie based on the novel by Laura Esquivel (Doubleday, 1992). Lusty and intimate, the story intertwines the secrets of traditional Mexican food preparation with a magical and surrealistic yet believable account of Mexican hacienda family life along the Río Grande/Río Bravo at the turn of the century.

Mexico as subject matter and location has had a long life. The Durango mountains have become the film backdrop capital of Mexico. *The Night of the Iguana* was filmed in Puerto Vallarta, putting that seaside village on the map. *The Old Gringo* was filmed in Zacatecas and *Viva Zapata* and *Under the Volcano* were both set in Cuernavaca.

RECORDINGS

Mexicans take their music very seriously—notice the tapes for sale almost everywhere, ceaseless music in the streets, and the bus drivers with collections of tapes to entertain passengers. For the collector there are choices from contemporary rock to revolutionary ballads, ranchero, salsa, and romantic trios.

For trio music, some of the best is by Los Tres Diamantes, Los Tres Reyes, and Trio Los Soberanos. If you're requesting songs of a trio, good ones to ask for are "La Peregrina," "Sin Ti," "Usted," "Adios Mi Chaparita," "Amor de la Calle," and "Cielito Lindo." Traditional ranchero music to request, which can be sung by soloists or trios, are "Tú Solo Tú," "No Volveré," and "Adios Mi Chaparita."

Music from the Yucatán would include the recordings by the Trio Los Soberanos and Dueto Yucalpetén. Typical Yucatecan songs are "Las Golondrinas Yucatecas," "Peregrina," "Ella," "El Pájaro Azul," and "Ojos Tristes." Heartthrob soloists from years past include Pedro Vargas, Pedro Enfante, Hector Cabrera, Lucho Gatica, Pepe Jara, and Alberto Vazquez.

Peña Ríos makes excellent marimba recordings. Though marimba musicians seldom ask for requests, some typical renditions would include "Huapango de Moncayo" and "El Bolero de Ravel."

Mariachi music is played and sold all over Mexico. Among the top recording artists is Mariachi Vargas. No mariachi performance is complete without "Guadalajara," "Las Mañanitas," and "Jarabe Tapatío."

One of the best recordings of recent times is the Royal Philharmonic Orchestra's rendition of classic Mexican music titled *Mexicano*; it's one purchase you must make.

PLANNING A TRIP TO MEXICO & THE YUCATÁN

In this chapter, the where, when, and how of your trip is discussed—the advance planning that gets your trip together and takes it on the road.

After they decide where to go, most people have two fundamental questions: What will it cost? and How do I get there? This chapter not only answers those questions, but addresses such important issues as when to go, whether or not to take a tour, what pretrip health precautions should be taken, what insurance coverage to investigate, where to obtain additional information, and more.

1. INFORMATION, ENTRY REQUIREMENTS & MONEY

SOURCES OF INFORMATION

TOURIST OFFICES Mexico has tourist offices throughout the world, including the following:

United States: 70 E. Lake St., Suite 1413, Chicago, IL 60601 (tel. 312/565-2778); 2702 N. Loop W., Suite 450, Houston, TX 77008 (tel. 713/880-5153); 10100 Santa Monica Blvd., Suite 224, Los Angeles, CA 90067 (tel. 310/203-8191); 233 Ponce de Leon Blvd., Suite 710, Coral Gables, FL 33134 (tel. 305/443-9160); 405 Park Ave., Suite 1401, New York, NY 10022 (tel. 212/755-7261); and 1911 Pennsylvania Ave. NW, Washington, D.C. 20006 (tel. 202/728-1750).

Canada: One Place Ville-Marie, Suite 1526, Montréal, PQ H3B 2B5 (tel. 514/871-1052); and 2 Bloor St. W., Suite 1801, Toronto, ON M4W 3E2 (tel. 416/925-0704).

United Kingdom: 60-61 Trafalgar Sq., London WC2N 5DS (tel. 44-071/839-3177).

Europe: Weisenhüttenplatz 26, 6000 Frankfurt-am-Main 1, Germany (tel. 4969/25-3413); Calle de Valázquez 126, Madrid 28006, Spain (tel. 341/261-1827); 4 rue

Notre-Dame-des-Victoires, 75002 Paris, France (tel. 331/40-20-07-34); and via Barberini 3, 00187 Roma, Italy (tel. 396/482-7160).

Asia: 2.15.1 Nagata-Cho, Chiyoda-Ku, Tokyo 100, Japan (tel. 813/580-2962).

OTHER SOURCES The following newsletters may be of interest to readers:

Mexico Meanderings, P.O. Box 33057, Austin, TX 78764, is a six- to eight-page newsletter with photographs featuring off-the-beaten-track destinations in Mexico. It's aimed at readers who travel by car, bus, or train, and is published six times annually. A subscription costs $18.

Travel Mexico, Apdo. Postal 6-1007, México, DF 06600, is issued six times a year by the publishers of *Traveler's Guide to Mexico*, the book frequently found in hotel rooms in Mexico. The newsletter covers a variety of topics from news about archeology to hotel packages, new resorts and hotels, and the economy. A subscription costs $15.

ENTRY REQUIREMENTS

DOCUMENTS All travelers are required to:

1. Present proof of citizenship, such as an original birth certificate with a raised seal, a valid passport, or naturalization papers. This proof of citizenship may also be requested to reenter both the United States and Mexico. Note that photocopies are not acceptable.
2. Carry a Mexican Tourist Permit, which is issued free of charge by Mexican border officials after proof of citizenship is accepted. The tourist permit is more important than a passport in Mexico, so guard it carefully—if you lose it, you may not be permitted to leave the country until you can replace it; that bureaucratic hassle takes several days or a week at least.

   A Tourist Permit can be issued for up to 180 days, and although your stay south of the border may be less than that, you should get the card for the maximum time, just in case. Sometimes the officials don't ask, they just stamp a time limit, so be sure and say "180 days," or at least twice as long as you think you'll stay. You may decide to stay, and you'll eliminate hassle by not needing to renew your papers. This hint is especially important for people who take cars into Mexico.

Other Requirements:

1. Children under age 18 traveling without parents or with only one parent must have a notarized letter from the absent parent or parents authorizing the travel.
2. Additional documentation is required for driving a personal vehicle to Mexico. (See Section 7, "Getting There.")

Lost Documents To replace a lost passport, contact your embassy or nearest consular agent, listed in "Fast Facts: Mexico," below. You must establish a record of your citizenship, and also fill out a form requesting another Mexican Tourist Permit. Without the tourist permit you can't leave the country, and without an affidavit affirming your passport request and citizenship, you may have hassles at Customs when you get home. So it's important to clear everything up *before* trying to leave.

CUSTOMS When you enter Mexico, Customs officials will be tolerant as long as you have no illegal drugs or firearms. You're allowed to bring in two cartons of cigarettes, or 50 cigars, plus a kilogram (2.2 lb.) of smoking tobacco; the liquor allowance is two bottles of anything, wine or hard liquor.

When you're reentering the United States, federal law allows, duty free, up to $400 in purchases every 30 days. The first $1,000 over the $400 allowance is taxed at 10%. You may bring in a carton (200) of cigarettes, or 50 cigars, or 2 kilograms (total, 4.4 lb.) of smoking tobacco, plus 1 liter of alcoholic beverage (wine, beer, or spirits).

Canadian citizens are allowed $20 in purchases after a 24-hour absence from the country or $100 after a stay of 48 hours or more.

MONEY

CASH/CURRENCY In 1993 the Mexican government dropped three zeroes from its currency. The new currency is called the Nuevo Peso or New Peso. The change doesn't devalue the peso; it simplifies accounting—all those zeroes were becoming too difficult to manage. Old Peso notes will be valid until 1996; no date for last use of old coins has been announced. Paper currency comes in denominations of 2, 5, 10, 20, 50, and 100 New Pesos. Coins come in denominations of 1, 2, 5, and 10 pesos and 20 and 50 centavos (100 centavos equal 1 New Peso). The coins are somewhat confusing because different denominations have a similar appearance. New Peso prices appear written with an N or NP beside them; and for a while the Old Peso prices will appear as well. Currently the U.S. dollar equals just over NP$3; an item costing NP$5, for example, would be equivalent to U.S. $1.66.

These changes are likely to cause confusion among U.S. and Canadian travelers to Mexico in several ways. First, Nuevo Peso prices are close enough to those in the U.S. and Canada to ensure some confusion; some people will take advantage of the similarity. Then, for the first time in years, everyone must become accustomed to making small change and seeing it on restaurant bills and credit cards. On restaurant bills that you pay in cash, for example, the change will be rounded up or down to the nearest five-centavo multiple. But credit-card bills will show the exact amount and will have N written before the amount to denote that the bill is in New Pesos. Be sure to double-check any credit-card vouchers to be sure the N or NP appears on the total line.

Getting change continues to be a problem in Mexico. Small denomination bills and coins are hard to come by, so start collecting them as soon as you cross the border and continue as you travel. Shopkeepers everywhere seem always to be out of change and small bills; that's doubly true in a market.

Take stock of your cash needs before a weekend, when banks are closed. Once away from a major touristic center, such as Cancún or Mérida, banks are hard to come by, and credit cards and even traveler's checks can be virtually useless. See also "Wire Funds" in "Fast Facts: Mexico," below.

The dollar sign ($) is used to indicate pesos in Mexico. To avoid confusion, from now on I will use the dollar sign in this book *only* to denote U.S. currency.

Many establishments dealing with tourists also quote prices in dollars. To avoid confusion, they use the abbreviations "Dlls." for dollars, and "m.n." (*moneda nacional*—national currency) for pesos.

EXCHANGING MONEY Cash can sometimes be difficult to exchange because counterfeit U.S. dollars have been circulating recently in Mexico; merchants and banks are wary, and many, especially in small towns, refuse to accept dollars in cash.

Banks in Mexico often give a rate of exchange below the official daily rate, and hotels usually exchange below the bank's daily rate. Personal checks may be cashed, but will delay you for weeks since a bank will wait for your check to clear before giving you your money. Canadian dollars seem to be most easily exchanged for pesos at branches of Banamex and Bancomer.

Banks are open Monday through Friday from 9am to 1:30pm; a few banks in large cities offer extended afternoon hours. You'll save time at the bank or currency-exchange booths by arriving no earlier than 10am, about the time the official daily rate is received. Usually they won't exchange money until they have the official rate. Large airports have currency-exchange counters that sometimes stay open as long as flights are arriving or departing.

TRAVELER'S CHECKS For the fastest and least complicated service, you should carry traveler's checks, which are readily accepted nearly everywhere. Mexican banks pay more for traveler's checks than for dollars in cash—but Casas de Cambio (exchange houses) pay more for cash than for traveler's checks. Some banks, but not all, charge a service fee, as high as 5%, to exchange either traveler's checks or dollars. Sometimes banks post the service charge amount so you can see it, but they might not, so it pays to ask first and shop around for a bank without a fee.

CREDIT CARDS You'll be able to charge some hotel and restaurant bills, almost all airline tickets, and many store purchases on your credit cards. You can get cash advances of several hundred dollars on your card, but there may be a wait of 20 minutes to two hours. However, you can't charge gasoline purchases in Mexico.

VISA ("Bancomer" in Mexico), MasterCard ("Carnet" in Mexico), and, less widely, American Express are the most accepted cards. The Bancomer bank, with branches throughout the country, has inaugurated a system of automatic teller machines linked to VISA International's network. If you are a VISA customer, you may be able to get peso cash from one of the Bancomer ATMs.

But I must warn you not to depend too heavily on your credit cards if you plan to venture beyond Cancún or Mérida. Pesos are a must. In addition, for some unknown reason, some places don't accept credit cards on Sunday.

BRIBES Called a *propina* (tip), *mordida* (bite), or worse, the custom is probably almost as old as mankind. Bribes exist in every country, but in developing countries the amounts tend to be smaller and collected more often. You will meet with bribery, so you should know how to deal with it.

Border officials have become more courteous, less bureaucratic, and less inclined to ask/hint for a bribe. I'm still wary, however; just so you're prepared, here are a few hints based on the past.

Some border officials will do what they're supposed to do (stamp your passport or birth certificate and inspect your luggage) and then wave you on through. If you don't offer a tip of a few dollars to the man who inspects your car (if you're driving), he may ask for it, as in "Give me a tip (*propina*)." If you're charged for the stamping or inspection, ask for a receipt. If you get no receipt, you've paid a bribe.

Officials don't ask for bribes from everybody. Travelers dressed in a formal suit and tie, with pitch-black sunglasses and a scowl on the face, are rarely asked to pay a bribe. Those who are dressed for vacation fun or seem good-natured and accommodating are charged every time. You should at least act formal, rather cold, dignified, and businesslike, perhaps preoccupied with "important affairs" on your mind. Wear those dark sunglasses. Scowl. Ignore the request. Pretend not to understand. Don't speak Spanish. But whatever you do, avoid impoliteness, and absolutely *never* insult a Latin American official! When an official's sense of machismo is roused, he can and will throw the book at you, and you may be in trouble. Stand your ground—politely.

SCAMS As you travel in Mexico, you may encounter several types of scams. The **shoeshine scam** is an old trick. Here's how it works. A tourist agrees to a shine for, say, 3 pesos. When the work is complete the vendor says "that'll be 30 pesos" and insists that the shocked tourist misunderstood. A big brouhaha ensues involving bystanders who side with the shoeshine vendor. The object is to get the bewildered tourist to succumb to the howling crowd and embarrassing scene and fork over the money. A variation of the scam has the vendor saying the price quoted is per shoe. To avoid this scam, ask around about the price of a shine, and when the vendor quotes his price, write it down and show it to him *before* the shine.

Tourists are suckered daily into the **iguana scam.** Someone, often a child, strolls by carrying a huge iguana and says "Wanna take my peekchur." Photo-happy tourists seize the opportunity. Just as the camera is angled properly, the holder of the iguana says (more like mumbles), "One dollar." That means a dollar per shot. Sometimes they wait until the shutter clicks to mention money.

Because hotel desk clerks are usually so helpful, I hesitate to mention the **lost objects scam** for fear of tainting them all. But here's how it works. You "lose" your wallet after cashing money at the desk, or you leave something valuable such as a purse or camera in the lobby. You report it. The clerk has it, but instead of telling you that he does, he says he will see what he can do; meanwhile, he suggests that you offer a high reward. This one has all kinds of variations. In one story a reader wrote about, a desk clerk in Los Mochis was in cahoots with a bystander in the lobby who lifted her wallet in the elevator.

Another scam readers have mentioned might be called the **infraction scam.** Officials, or men presenting themselves as officials, demand money for some supposed infraction. Never get into a car with them. I avoided one begun by a bona fide policeman-on-the-take in Chetumal when my traveling companion feigned illness and began writhing, moaning, and pretending to have the dry heaves. It was more than the policeman could handle.

Legal and necessary car searches by military personnel looking for drugs are mentioned elsewhere. But every now and then there are police-controlled illegal roadblocks where motorists are forced to pay before continuing.

Along these lines, if you are stopped by the police, I also suggest that you avoid handing your driver's license to a policeman. Hold it so that it can be read, but don't give it up.

Although you should be aware of such hazards and how to deal with them, I log thousands of miles and many months in Mexico each year without serious incident, and I feel safer there than at home (see also "Emergencies" and "Safety" in "Fast Facts: Mexico," below).

2. WHEN TO GO—CLIMATE, HOLIDAYS & EVENTS

CLIMATE

Most of Mexico offers one of the world's most perfect winter climates—dry, balmy, with temperatures ranging from the 80s by day to the 60s at night.

The winter climate on the Gulf coast has a big effect on Yucatán weather. Freezing blasts out of Canada via the Texas Panhandle swoop across the Gulf of Mexico to the Yucatán peninsula. The most disconcerting thing about *nortes* (the name given to these freezing blasts) is that they strike so suddenly. You can be luxuriating on a Cancún beach, enjoying flawless weather, when all of a sudden you'll notice a slight haze obscuring the sun. Within an hour it's like March in New York—gray skies, a boisterous wind, and chilly rain whipping your cheeks. In that brief hour the temperature will have dropped as much as 40°. But here's an interesting twist. While nortes hit Veracruz (latitude 19) with vicious intensity, their sting is far less severe in the most northerly Yucatán peninsula. Gales hit Veracruz over land and Mérida over water; the Gulf has a warming effect.

In summer the difference between west coast and Gulf coast temperatures is much less. Both areas become warm and rainy. Of the two regions, the Gulf is far rainier, particularly in the states of Tabasco and Campeche.

HOLIDAYS

On national holidays, banks, stores, and businesses are closed, hotels fill up quickly, and transportation is crowded. Mexico celebrates the following national holidays:

January 1	New Year's Day
February 5	Constitution Day
March 21	Birthday of Benito Juárez
March–April (movable)	Holy Week (Good Friday through Easter Sunday)
May 1	Labor Day
May 5	Battle of Puebla, 1862 (Cinco de Mayo)
September 1	President's Message to Congress
September 16	Independence Day
October 12	Day of the Race (Columbus Day in the U.S.)
November 1–2	All Saints' and All Souls' days (Days of the Dead)
November 20	Anniversary of the Mexican Revolution
December 11–12	Feast Day of the Virgin of Guadalupe (Mexico's patron saint)
December 24–25	Christmas Eve and Christmas Day

MEXICO CALENDAR OF EVENTS

JANUARY

Three Kings Day (Día de los Santos Reyes). Commemorates the Three Kings' bringing of gifts to the Christ Child. On this day the Three Kings "bring" gifts to children. January 6. In Tizimín, Yucatán, January 6 begins the region's biggest festival, which lasts three days and honors the patron saints of the local church—Santos Reyes.

FEBRUARY

Candlemas. On January 6, Rosca de Reyes, a round cake with a hole in the middle is baked with a tiny doll inside representing the Christ Child. Whoever gets the slice with the doll must give a party on February 2. Tecoh and Kantunil both have candlelit processions climaxing at the central church where parishioners almost cover the floors with lighted candles.

⊙ *CARNAVAL Resembles New Orleans's Mardi Gras, a festival atmosphere with parades. In Chamula, however, the event hearkens back to pre-Hispanic times with ritualistic running on flaming branches.*
    ***Where:** Especially celebrated in Mérida and Hocaba, Yuc.; Chamula, Chi.; and Cozumel, Q. Roo. **When:** Date variable, but always the three days preceding Ash Wednesday and the beginning of Lent. **How:** Transportation and hotels may be clogged, so it's best to make reservations six months in advance and arrive a couple of days ahead of the beginning of celebrations.*

Ash Wednesday. The start of Lent and a time of abstinence. It's a day of reverence nationwide, but some towns honor it with folk dancing and fairs. Movable date.

MARCH

Benito Juárez's Birthday. Small hometown celebrations countrywide, but especially in Juárez's birthplace, Gelatao, Oaxaca.

⊙ *HOLY WEEK Celebrates the last week in the life of Christ from Good Friday through Easter Sunday with almost nightly somber religious processions, spoofing of Judas, and reenactments of specific biblical events, plus food and craft fairs. Businesses close and Mexicans travel far and wide during this week.*
    ***Where:** Ticul, Yuc., celebrates Easter and a tobacco fair at the same time. **When:** March or April. **How:** Reserve early with a deposit. Airlines into and out of the country will be reserved months in advance. Buses almost anywhere in Mexico will be full, so try arriving on the Wednesday or Thursday before Good Friday. Easter Sunday is quiet.*

MAY

Labor Day. Workers' parades countrywide and everything closes. May 1.
Holy Cross Day (Día de la Santa Cruz). Workers place a cross on top of unfinished buildings and celebrate with food, bands, folk dancing, and fireworks around the worksite. Celebrations are particularly colorful in Izamal, Yuc.
Cinco de Mayo. A national holiday that celebrates the defeat of the French at the Battle of Puebla. May 5.
Feast of San Isidro. The patron saint of farmers is honored with a blessing of seeds and work animals. May 15.

JUNE

Navy Day. Celebrated by all port cities. June 1.

⊙ *CORPUS CHRISTI Honors the Body of Christ—the Eucharist—with religious processions, mass, food. Celebrated nationwide. Festivities include numerous demonstrations of the voladores (flying pole dancers) beside the church and at the ruins of El Tajín.*
    ***Where:** Particularly special in Papantla, Ver. **When:** Variable date 66 days after Easter. **How:** By bus from Tampico, Tuxpan, or Poza Rica. Make reservations well in advance.*

Saint Peter's Day (Día de San Pedro). Celebrated wherever St. Peter is the patron saint and honors anyone named Pedro or Peter.

JULY

Virgin of Carmen. A nationally celebrated religious festival centered at churches nationwide. Motul, Yuc., celebrates with a lively festival. July 16.

Saint James Day (Día de Santiago). Observed countrywide wherever St. James is the patron saint, and for anyone named Jaime or James, or any village with Santiago in the name. Often celebrated with rodeos, fireworks, dancing, and food. July 25.

AUGUST

✪ *ASSUMPTION OF THE VIRGIN MARY* *Celebrated throughout the country with special masses and, in some places, processions. Streets are carpeted with flower petals and colored sawdust. At midnight on the 15th a statue of the Virgin is carried through the streets; the 16th is a running of the bulls.*
Where: Special in Oxkutzcab, Yuc. When: August 10–17.

SEPTEMBER

Independence Day. Celebrates Mexico's independence from Spain. A day of parades, picnics, and family reunions throughout the country. At 11pm on September 15 the president of Mexico gives the famous independence *grito* (shout) from the National Palace in Mexico City. September 16 (parade day).

OCTOBER

Cervantino Festival. Begun in the 1970s as a cultural event bringing performing artists from all over the world to the Guanajuato, a picturesque village northeast of Mexico City. Now the artists travel all over the republic after appearing in Guanajuato. Check local calendars for appearances. Mid-October through November.

Feast of San Francisco de Asis. Anyone named Frances or Francis or Francisco, and towns whose patron saint is Francis of Assisi, will be celebrating with barbecue parties, regional dancing, and religious observances. October 4.

Día de la Raza. Day of the Race, or Columbus Day (the day Columbus discovered America), commemorates the fusion of two races—Spanish and Mexican. October 12.

NOVEMBER

✪ *DAY OF THE DEAD* *What's commonly called the Day of the Dead is actually two days: All Saints' Day, honoring saints and deceased children, and All Souls' Day, honoring deceased adults. Relatives gather at cemeteries countrywide, carrying candles and food, often spending the night beside graves of loved ones. Weeks before, bakers begin producing bread formed in the shape of mummies or round loaves decorated with bread bones. Decorated sugar skulls emblazoned with glittery names are sold everywhere. Many days ahead, homes and churches erect special altars laden with Day of the Dead bread, fruit, flowers, candles, and favorite foods and photographs of saints and of the deceased. On the two nights of the Day of the Dead children dress in costumes and masks, often carrying mock coffins through the streets and pumpkin lanterns into which they expect money will be dropped.*

Where: San Cristóbal de las Casas, Chi., and surrounding villages are worth visiting. Mérida is rich in graveside ritual as well. **When:** *November 1–2.*

Revolution Day. Commemorates the start of the Mexican Revolution in 1910, with parades, speeches, rodeos, and patriotic events. November 20.

DECEMBER

Feast of the Virgin of Guadalupe. Throughout the country the Patroness of Mexico is honored with religious processions, street fairs, dancing, fireworks, and masses. The Virgin of Guadalupe appeared to a small boy, Juan Diego, in December 1531 on a hill near Mexico City. He convinced the bishop that the apparition had appeared by revealing his cloak, upon which the Virgin was emblazoned. It's customary for children to dress up as Juan Diego, wearing mustaches and red bandannas. The most famous and elaborate celebration takes place at the Basilica of Guadalupe, north of Mexico City, where the Virgin appeared. But almost every village celebrates this day, often with processions of children carrying banners of the Virgin, and with *charreadas*, bicycle races, dancing, and fireworks. December 12.

Christmas Posadas. Each of the 12 nights before Christmas it's customary to reenact the Holy Family's search for an inn, with door-to-door candlelit processions in cities and villages nationwide.

Christmas. Mexicans extend this celebration and leave their jobs, often beginning two weeks before Christmas, all the way through New Year's. Many businesses close and resorts and hotels fill up. December 23 there are significant celebrations.

New Year's Eve. As in the U.S., New Year's Eve is the time to gather for private parties of celebration and to explode fireworks and sound noisemakers.

3. HEALTH & INSURANCE

HEALTH PREPARATIONS

Of course, the very best way to avoid illness or to mitigate its effects are to make sure that you're in top health when you travel and that you don't overdo it. Travel tends to take more of your energy than a normal working day, and missed meals mean that you get less nutrition than you need. Make sure that you have three good, wholesome meals a day, get more rest than you normally do, and don't push yourself if you're not feeling in top form.

COMMON AILMENTS

TURISTA *Turista* is the name given to the pervasive diarrhea, often accompanied by fever, nausea, and vomiting, that attacks so many travelers to Mexico on their first trip. Doctors, who call it travelers' diarrhea, say it's not just caused by one "bug," or factor, but by a combination of different food and water, upset schedules, overtiring, and the stresses that accompany travel. Being tired and careless about food and drink is a sure ticket to turista. A good high-potency (or "therapeutic") vitamin supplement, and even extra vitamin C, is a help; yogurt is good for healthy digestion, but is not available everywhere in Mexico.

Preventing Turista The U.S. Public Health Service recommends the following measures for prevention of travelers' diarrhea:

- Drink only purified water. This means tea, coffee, and other beverages made with boiled water; canned or bottled carbonated beverages and water; beer and wine; or water that you yourself have brought to a rolling boil or otherwise purified. Avoid ice, which is usually made with untreated water.
- Choose food carefully. In general, avoid salads, uncooked vegetables, and unpasteurized milk or milk products (including cheese). Choose food that is freshly cooked and still hot. Peel fruit yourself. Don't eat undercooked meat, fish, or shellfish.

The Public Health Service does not recommend that you take any medicines as preventatives. All the applicable medicines can have nasty side effects if taken for several weeks.

How to Get Well If you get sick, there are lots of medicines available in Mexico that can harm more than help. You should ask your doctor before you leave home what medicine he or she recommends for travelers' diarrhea, and follow that advice.

Public Health Service guidelines are these: If there are three or more loose stools in an eight-hour period, especially with other symptoms such as nausea, vomiting, abdominal cramps, and fever, it's time to go to a doctor.

The first thing to do is go to bed and don't move until the condition runs its course. Traveling makes it last longer. Drink lots of liquids: Tea without milk or sugar, or the Mexican *té de manzanilla* (chamomile tea), is best. Eat only *pan tostada* (dry toast). Keep to this diet for at least 24 hours and you'll be well over the worst of it. If you fool yourself into thinking that a plate of enchiladas can't hurt, or that beer or liquor will kill the germs, you'll have a total relapse.

The Public Health Service advises that you be especially careful to replace fluids and electrolytes (potassium, sodium, etc.) during a bout of diarrhea. Do this by drinking glasses of fruit juice (high in potassium) with honey and a pinch of salt added; and also a glass of boiled pure water with a quarter teaspoon of sodium bicarbonate (baking soda) added.

ALTITUDE SICKNESS At high altitudes it takes about 10 days to acquire the extra red blood corpuscles you need to adjust to the scarcity of oxygen. At very high-altitude places such as San Cristóbal de las Casas, your car won't run very well, you may have trouble starting it, and you may not even sleep well at night.

This ailment results from the relative lack of oxygen and decrease in barometric pressure that come from being at high altitudes (5,000 ft./1,500m, or more). Mexico City is at an altitude of more than 7,000 feet, as are a number of other central Mexican cities, so discomfort is possible. Symptoms include shortness of breath, fatigue, headache, and even nausea.

Avoid altitude sickness by taking it easy for the first few days after you arrive at high altitude. Drink extra fluids, but avoid alcoholic beverages, which not only tend to dehydrate you, but also are more potent in a low-oxygen environment. If you have heart or lung problems, talk to your doctor before going above 8,000 feet.

BUGS & BITES Mosquitoes and gnats are prevalent along the coast and in the Yucatán lowlands. Insect repellent (*repelente contra insectos*) is a must, and it's not always available in Mexico. If you're sensitive to bites, pick up some antihistamine cream from a drugstore at home (Di-Delamine is available without a prescription). Rubbed on a fresh mosquito bite, the cream keeps down the swelling and reduces the itch. In Mexico, ask for Camfo-Fenicol (Campho-phenique), the second-best remedy.

Most readers won't ever see a scorpion, but if you're stung go to a doctor.

SUNBURN In the Yucatán, especially while visiting ruins or lying on the beach, be aware that the sun is more intense at this latitude and therefore more likely to cause sunburn in a short time. Use sunscreen lavishly at the beach and archeological sites. At the ruins wear a hat and carry water, or stop for nonalcoholic refreshment often.

MORE SERIOUS DISEASES

You don't have to worry about tropical diseases if you stay on the normal tourist routes. You can protect yourself by taking some simple precautions. Besides being careful about what you eat and drink, don't go swimming in polluted waters. This includes any stagnant water such as ponds, slow-moving rivers, and Yucatecan cenotes. Mosquitoes can carry malaria, dengue fever, and other serious illnesses. Cover up, avoid going out when mosquitoes are active, use repellent, sleep under mosquito netting, and stay away from places that seem to have a lot of mosquitoes. The most dangerous areas seem to be on Mexico's west coast away from the big resorts (which are relatively safe).

To prevent malaria if you go to a malarial area, you must get a prescription for antimalarial drugs and begin taking them before you enter the area. You must also continue to take them for a certain amount of time after you leave the malarial area. Talk to your doctor about this. It's a good idea to be inoculated against tetanus, typhoid, and diphtheria, but this isn't a guarantee against contracting the disease.

The following list of diseases should not alarm you, as their incidence is rare among tourists. But if you become ill with something more virulent than travelers' diarrhea, I want you to have this information ready at hand:

CHOLERA Cholera comes from sewage-contaminated water and is transmitted by using the contaminated water to drink, cook, or to wash food. Thus raw fish and raw or lightly cooked vegetables are good candidates for transmitting the disease. Outbreaks of cholera in Mexico have been isolated and contained immediately and have not occurred in any major tourist area. Symptoms are extreme diarrhea, vomiting, abdominal pain, and rapid incapacitation. Get to a hospital immediately. Dehydration can be immediate and deadly so drink plenty of nonalcoholic liquids.

DENGUE FEVER Transmitted by mosquitoes, it comes on fast with high fever, severe headache, and joint and muscle pain. About three or four days after the onset of the disease, there's a skin rash. Highest risk is during July, August, and September.

DYSENTERY Caused by contaminated food or water, either amoebic or bacillary in form, it is somewhat like travelers' diarrhea, but more severe. Risk for tourists is low.

HEPATITIS, VIRAL This virus is spread through contaminated food and water (often in rural areas), and through intimate contact with infected persons. Risk for tourists is normally low.

MALARIA Spread by mosquito bites, malaria can be effectively treated if caught soon after the disease is contracted. Malaria symptoms are headache, malaise, fever, chills, sweats, anemia, and jaundice.

RABIES This virus is almost always passed by bites from infected animals or bats, rarely through broken skin or the mucous membranes (as from breathing rabid bat-contaminated air in a cave). If you are bitten, wash the wound at once with large amounts of soap and water—this is important! Retain the animal, alive if possible, for rabies quarantine. Contact local health authorities to get rabies immunization. This is essential, as rabies is a fatal disease that may be prevented by prompt treatment.

SCHISTOSOMIASIS This is a parasitic worm, passed by a freshwater snail larva that can penetrate unbroken human skin. You get it by wading or swimming in fresh water where the snails are, such as in stagnant pools, streams, or cenotes. About two or three weeks after exposure, there's fever, lack of appetite, weight loss, abdominal pain, weakness, headaches, joint and muscle pain, diarrhea, nausea, and coughing. Some six to eight weeks after infection, the microscopic snail eggs can be found in the stools. Once diagnosed (after a very unpleasant month or two), treatment is fast, safe, effective, and cheap. If you think you've accidentally been exposed to schistosomiasis-infected water, rub yourself vigorously with a towel and/or spread rubbing alcohol on the exposed skin.

TYPHOID FEVER Protect yourself by having a typhoid vaccination (or booster, as needed). Protection is not total—you can still get this very serious disease from contaminated food and water. Symptoms are similar to those for travelers' diarrhea, but much worse. If you get typhoid fever, you'll need close attention by a doctor, perhaps hospitalization for a short period.

TYPHUS FEVER You should see a doctor for treatment of this disease, which is spread by lice. Risk is very low.

EMERGENCY EVACUATION

For extreme medical emergencies there's a service from the United States that will fly people to American hospitals: **Air-Evac**, 24-hour air ambulance (tel. collect, 713/880-9767 in Houston, 619/278-3822 in San Diego, or 305/772-0003 in Miami, 24 hours daily).

INSURANCE

HEALTH/ACCIDENT/LOSS It can happen anywhere in the world—you discover you've lost your wallet, your passport, your airline ticket, and your tourist permit. Always keep a photocopy of these documents in your luggage—it makes replacing them easier. To be reimbursed for insured items once you return, you'll need to report the loss to the Mexican police and get a written report. If you don't speak Spanish, take along someone who does. If you lose official documents, you'll need to contact both Mexican and U.S. officials in Mexico before you leave the country.

Health Care Abroad, 107 W. Federal St., P.O. Box 480, Middleburg, VA 22117 (tel. 703/687-3166, or toll free 800/237-6615), and **Access America,** 6600 W. Broad St., Richmond, VA 23230 (tel. 804/285-3300, or toll free 800/628-4908), offer medical and accident insurance as well as coverage for luggage loss and trip cancellation. But always read the fine print to be sure that you're getting the coverage that you want.

For British Travelers Most big travel agents offer their own insurance, and will probably try to sell you their package when you book a holiday. Think before you sign. Britain's Consumers' Association recommends that you insist on seeing the policy and reading the fine print before buying travel insurance.

You should also shop around for better deals. Try **Columbus Travel Insurance Ltd.** (tel. 071/375-0011) or, for students, **Campus Travel** (tel. 071/730-3402). If you're unsure about who can give you the best deal, contact the **Association of British Insurers,** 51 Gresham St., London EC2V 7HQ (tel. 071/600-333).

4. WHAT TO PACK

CLOTHING High-elevation cities such as San Cristóbal de las Casas require a coat, gloves, and warm socks in winter and preferably a couple of sweaters. In summer it gets warm during the day and cool, but not cold, at night. Generally speaking, throughout Mexico it rains almost every afternoon or evening between May and October—so take rain gear. Mexico tends to be a bit conservative in dress, so shorts and halter tops are generally frowned upon except at seaside resorts. Lightweight cotton clothes are preferable for the lowlands (the Yucatán and coastal areas).

GADGETS Bring your own washcloth, or better yet a sponge (which dries quickly)—you'll rarely find washcloths in a budget-category hotel room and perhaps not even in first-class accommodations. A bathtub plug (one of those big round ones for all sizes) is a help since fitted plugs are frequently missing, or don't work. Inflatable hangers and a stretch clothesline are handy. I never leave home without a luggage cart, which saves much effort and money, and is especially useful in small towns where there are no porters at bus stations. Buy a sturdy one with at least four-inch wheels that can take the beating of cobblestone streets, stairs, and curbs. A heat-immersion coil, plastic cup, and spoon are handy for preparing coffee, tea, and instant soup. For power failures, and if you plan to visit archeological sites with dark interiors, a small flashlight is a help. A combo pocketknife (for peeling fruit) with a screwdriver (for fixing cameras and eyeglasses), bottle opener, and corkscrew is a must.

5. TIPS FOR THE DISABLED, SENIORS, SINGLES, FAMILIES & STUDENTS

FOR THE DISABLED Travelers unable to walk, or who are in wheelchairs or on crutches, discover quickly that Mexico is one giant obstacle course. Beginning at the airport on arrival you may encounter steep stairs before finding a well-hidden elevator or escalator—if one exists. Airlines will often arrange wheelchair assistance for passengers to the baggage area. Porters are generally available to help with luggage at airports and large bus stations, once you've cleared baggage claim. Escalators (and there aren't many in the country) are often not operating. Few handicapped-equipped restrooms exist, or when one is available, access to it may be via a narrow passage that won't accommodate a wheelchair or someone on crutches. Many deluxe hotels (the most expensive) now have rooms with bathrooms for the handicapped and handicapped access to the hotel. For those traveling on a budget, stick with one-story hotels or those with elevators. Even so, there will probably still be obstacles somewhere. Stairs without handrails abound in Mexico. Intracity bus drivers generally don't bother with the courtesy step upon boarding or disembarking. On city buses the height between the street and the bus step can require considerable force to board. But generally speaking, no matter where you are, someone will lend a hand, although you may have to ask for it.

FOR SENIORS Handrails are often missing. Unmarked or unguarded holes in sidewalks countrywide present problems for all visitors.

Retiring Mexico is a popular country for retirees, although income doesn't go nearly as far as it once did. Do several things before venturing south permanently: Stay for several weeks in any place under consideration; rent before buying; and check on the availability and quality of health care, banking, transportation, and rental costs. How much it costs to live depends on your lifestyle and where you choose to live. Car upkeep and insurance, and clothing and health costs are important variables to consider.

The Mexican government requires foreign residents to prove a specific amount of income before permanent residence is granted, but you can visit for six months on a tourist visa and renew it every six months without committing to a "legal" status. Mexican health care is surprisingly inexpensive. You can save money by living on the local economy: Buy food at the local market, not imported items from specialty stores; use local transportation and save the car for long-distance trips.

The following newsletters are written for prospective retirees: **AIM,** Apdo. Postal 31-70, Guadalajara, Jal. 45050, México, is a well-written, plain-talk and very informative newsletter on retirement in Mexico. Recent issues reported on retirement background and considerations for Lake Chapala, Aguascalientes, Alamos, Zacatecas, West Coast beaches, Acapulco, and San Miguel de Allende. It costs $16 for a subscription in the U.S. and $19 in Canada. Back issues are three for $5.

Retiring in Mexico, Apdo. Postal 50409, Guadalajara, Jal. (tel. 36/21-2348 or 47-9924), comes in three editions—a large January issue and smaller spring and fall supplements—all for $12. Each newsletter is packed with information about retiring in Guadalajara. It's written by Fran and Judy Furton, who also sell other packets of information as well as host an open house in their home every Tuesday for $12.

Finally, **Sanborn Tours,** 1007 Main St., Bastrop, TX 78602 (tel. toll free 800/ 531-5440), offers a "Retire in Mexico" Guadalajara orientation tour.

FOR SINGLE TRAVELERS Mexico may be the land for romantic honeymoons, but it's also a great place to travel on your own without really being or feeling alone. Although combined single and double rates is a slow-growing trend in Mexico, most of the hotels mentioned in this book still offer singles at lower rates. There's so much to see and do that being bored needn't be a problem. Mexicans are very friendly and it's easy to meet other foreigners. Singles can feel quite comfortable anywhere in the Yucatán peninsula. There's a good combination of beachlife, nightlife, and tranquillity, whichever is your pleasure.

If you don't like the idea of traveling alone, you might try **Travel Companion Exchange,** P.O. Box 833, Amityville, NY 11701 (tel. 516/454-0880; fax 516/454-0170), which brings prospective travelers together. Members complete a profile, then place an anonymous listing of their travel interests in the newsletter. Prospective traveling companions then make contact through the exchange. Membership costs $36 to $66 for six months.

For Women   As a frequent female visitor to Mexico, mostly traveling alone, I can tell you firsthand that I feel safer traveling in Mexico than in the United States. Mexicans are a very warm and welcoming people, and I'm not afraid to be friendly wherever I go. But I use the same common-sense precautions I use traveling anywhere else in the world: I'm alert to what's going on around me.

Mexicans in general, and men in particular, are nosy about single travelers, especially women. They want to know with whom you're traveling, whether you're married or have a boyfriend, and how many children you have. My advice to anyone asked these details by taxi drivers, or other people with whom you don't want to become friendly, is to make up a set of answers (regardless of the truth): I'm married, traveling with friends, and I have three children. Divorce may send out a wrong message about availability.

Drunks are a particular nuisance to the lone female traveler. Don't try to be polite—just leave or duck into a public place.

Generally women alone will feel comfortable going to a hotel lobby bar, but are asking for trouble by going into a pulquería or cantina. In restaurants, as a general rule, single women are offered the worst table and service. You'll have to be vocal about your preference and insist on service. Tip well if you plan to return. Don't tip at all if service is bad.

And finally, remember that Mexican men learn charm early. The chase is as important as the conquest (maybe more so). Despite whatever charms *you* may possess, think twice before taking personally or seriously all the adoring, admiring words you'll hear.

For Men   I'm not sure why, but non-Spanish-speaking foreign men seem to be special targets for scams and pickpockets. So if you fit this description, whether traveling alone or in a party, exercise special vigilance.

FOR FAMILIES   Mexicans travel extensively with their families, so your child will feel very welcome. Hotels will often arrange for a babysitter. Several hotels in the mid to upper range have small playgrounds and pools for children and hire caretakers on weekends to oversee them. Few budget hotels offer these amenities.

Before leaving, you should check with your doctor to get advice on medications to take along. Bring a supply, just to be sure. Disposable diapers are made and sold in Mexico (one popular brand is Kleen Bebé). The price is about the same as at home, but the quality is poorer. Gerber's baby foods are sold in many stores. Dry cereals, powdered formulas, baby bottles, and purified water are all easily available in mid-size to large cities.

Cribs, however, may present a problem. Except for the largest and most luxurious hotels, few Mexican hotels provide cribs.

Many of the hotels I mention, even in noncoastal regions, have swimming pools, which can be dessert at the end of a day of traveling with a child who has had it with sightseeing.

Take along a "security blanket" for your child. This might be a favorite toy or book to make the child feel at home in different surroundings. And draw up rules for your family to follow—guidelines on bedtime, eating, and spending can help make everyone's vacation more enjoyable.

FOR STUDENTS   Students traveling on a budget may want to contact the student headquarters in the various cities that can supply information on student hostels. Maps and local tourist information are also available. For more information see "Youth Hostels," in Section 9 later in this chapter.

6. EDUCATIONAL/ADVENTURE TRAVEL

EDUCATIONAL/STUDY TRAVEL

SPANISH LESSONS Of the towns listed in this book, San Cristóbal de las Casas is the only one with a Spanish-language school catering to foreign students; several readers have written to recommend it. A dozen other towns south of the border are famous for their Spanish-language programs. Most of these are covered in *Frommer's Mexico on $45 a Day*. Enrolling is simple: Write to those in towns that interest you and ask for their course outline, prices, and recommended housing list. Some schools can arrange your stay with a host family. Go any time of year since there's no need to wait for a "semester" or course year to start. The Mexican Government Tourism Office nearest you may also have information about schools.

Don't expect the best and latest in terms of language texts and materials—many are well out-of-date. Teachers tend to be underpaid and perhaps undertrained, but very friendly and extremely patient.

The **National Registration Center for Studies Abroad (NRCSA),** 823 N. 2nd St., Milwaukee, WI 53203 (tel. 414/278-0631), has a catalog ($5) of schools in Mexico. They will register you at the school of your choice, arrange for room and board with a Mexican family, and make your airline reservations. Charges for their service are reflected in a fee that's included in the price quoted to you for the course you select.

Folk-art collectors may be interested in trips organized by the San Antonio Museum of Art. The **Friends of Folk Art** of the San Antonio Museum Association, P.O. Box 2601, San Antonio, TX 78299-2601 (tel. 210/978-8100), organizes small groups for once-a-year trips led by the museum's folk-art curator, usually concentrating on a single region in Mexico.

HOMESTAYS Living with a Mexican family is another way to learn Spanish. Family stays are not particularly cheap, so you should get your money's worth in terms of interaction and language practice.

Spanish-language schools frequently provide lists of families who offer rooms to students. Often the experience is just like being one of the family.

World Learning Inc., The U.S. Experiment in International Living, Kipling Road, P.O. Box 676, Brattleboro, VT 05302-0676 (tel. 802/257-7751; fax 802/258-3248), offers a wide range of options for international experiences ranging from accredited programs to homestays and Elderhostel affiliation.

ADVENTURE/WILDERNESS TRAVEL

Mexico is behind the times in awareness of tourist interest in ecology-oriented adventure and wilderness travel. As a result, most of the national parks and nature reserves are understaffed and/or not staffed by knowledgeable people. Most companies offering this kind of travel are U.S. operated and trips are led by specialists. The following companies offer a variety of off-the-beaten-path travel experiences:

Victor Emanuel Tours, P.O. Box 33008, Austin, TX 78764 (tel. 512/328-5221, or toll free 800/328-8368), is an established leader in birding and natural-history tours.

Far Flung Adventures, P.O. Box 377, Terlingua, TX 79852 (tel. 915/371-2489, or toll free 800/359-4138), takes clients on specialist-led Mexico river trips, in

Veracruz and Río Usumacinta, for example, that combine rafting and camping at Yucatán's archeological sites.

The **Foundation for Field Research,** P.O. Box 2010, Alpine, CA 91903 (tel. 619/445-9264), accepts volunteers who contribute a tax-deductible share to project costs during scientific work at Bahía de los Angeles and Isla de Cedros in Baja California, Mexiquillo Beach in Michoacán state, Alamos in the state of Sonora, and in the state of Chiapas.

ATC Tours & Travel, Calle 5 de Febrero no. 15, San Cristóbal de las Casas, Chi. 29200 (tel. 967/8-2550; fax 967/8-3145), offers a wide assortment of natural-history and other adventure tours in Yucatán, Chiapas, and Guatemala.

Wings, Inc., P.O. Box 31930, Tucson, AZ 85751 (tel. 602/749-1967), has a wide assortment of trips, including birding in Oaxaca, Chiapas, Colima, and Jalisco.

The **Texas Camel Corps,** affiliated with the Witte Museum, 3801 Broadway, San Antonio, TX 78209 (tel. 210/820-2167 or 210/820-2168; fax 210/820-2109), offers several trips annually with nature, history, or archeology themes. One goes to San Cristóbal de las Casas for the Day of the Dead, and another explores the fascinating but little-known Río Bec route near Lago Bacalar in the southern part of the Yucatán peninsula.

Remarkable Journeys, P.O. Box 31855, Houston, TX 77231-1855 (tel. 713/721-2517, or toll free 800/856-1993 in the U.S.; fax 713/728-8334), offers unusual trips in Mexico including Carnaval and the Day of the Dead in Mérida.

Zapotec Tours, 500 N. Michigan Ave., Chicago, IL 60611 (tel. 312/973-2444, or outside IL, toll free 800/326-7251 in the U.S.; fax 312/248-5245), offers an intriguing variety of specialist-led, eight-day trips, primarily to Oaxaca. But at least one trip includes the chocolate route near Villahermosa, Tabasco. Highlights include numerous introductions to local specialists whose knowledge of architecture, archeology, art, and food provide cultural experiences unavailable to the casual tourist.

7. GETTING THERE

BY PLANE

The airline situation is changing rapidly, with many new regional carriers offering scheduled service to areas previously not served. Besides regularly scheduled service, charter service direct from U.S. cities to resorts is making Mexico more accessible. The Yucatán is served by major airline routes to Cancún, Mérida, and Cozumel, and marginally to Campeche and Chetumal. Regional airlines cover shorter and lesser routes to Cozumel, Chetumal, Chichén-Itzá, and Palenque.

THE MAJOR INTERNATIONAL AIRLINES The main airlines operating direct or nonstop flights from the United States to points in Mexico include **Aero California** (tel. toll free 800/237-6225), **Aeroméxico** (tel. toll free 800/237-6639), **Air France** (tel. toll free 800/237-2747), **Alaska Airlines** (tel. toll free 800/426-0333), **American** (tel. toll free 800/433-7300), **Continental** (tel. toll free 800/231-0856), **Delta** (tel. toll free 800/221-1212), **Lacsa** (tel. toll free 800/225-2272), **Lufthansa** (tel. toll free 800/645-3880), **Mexicana** (tel. toll free 800/531-7921), **Northwest** (tel. toll free 800/225-2525), and **United** (tel. toll free 800/241-6522). **Southwest Airlines** (tel. toll free 800/435-9792) serves the U.S. border. International airline main departure points are Chicago, Dallas/Fort Worth, Denver, Houston, Los Angeles, Miami, New Orleans,

New York, Orlando, Philadelphia, Raleigh/Durham, San Antonio, San Francisco, Seattle, Toronto, Tucson, and Washington, D.C.

Bargain hunters, rejoice! Excursion and package plans proliferate, especially in the off-season. A good travel agent will be able to give you all the latest schedules, details, and prices, but you may have to sleuth regional airlines for yourself (see "By Plane" in Section 8, "Getting Around," below). The lowest airline prices are mid week all year, and in the off-season (after Easter to December 15).

CHARTERS   Charter service is growing and usually is sold as a package combination of air and hotel. Charter airlines, however, may sell air only, without hotel. Charter airlines include **Latur,** which offers charters from New York, Chicago, and Boston. **Taesa Airlines** also has service from several U.S. cities.

Tour companies operating charters include: Club America Vacations, Apple Vacations, Friendly Holidays, and Gogo Tours.

FLIGHTS FROM THE U.K.

British travelers should comparison shop carefully to find the best airfare bargains. **British Airways** (tel. 081/897-4000 in London) offers nonstop service three times a week from London to Mexico City, where there are frequent daily flights to points within the Yucatán peninsula. Another option is to fly to a major hub in the United States, from which you will be able to connect with a flight to your Yucatán destination.

Your best bet is to have a reputable travel agent, such as Thomas Cook, sort out the many possibilities and look for the best price available on your travel dates.

BY TRAIN

For getting to the border by train, call **Amtrak** (tel. toll free 800/872-7245) for fares, information, and reservations. Trains connect the upper interior of Yucatán from Mérida to Valladolid with the gulf coast from Villahermosa, Palenque, and Campeche. Although I wouldn't recommend it because of long delays, you could even board a train in Mexico City and arrive in the Yucatán. Generally speaking, these trains, especially the longer runs, are slow and prone to thievery. Shorter hauls, say between Mérida and Tinum or Valladolid, can be quite pleasant.

BY BUS

Greyhound-Trailways, or its affiliates, offers service from around the U.S. to the border, where passengers disembark, cross the border, and buy a ticket for travel into the interior of Mexico. At many border crossings there are scheduled buses from the U.S. bus station to the Mexican bus station.

BY CAR

Driving is certainly not the cheapest way to get to Mexico, but it's the best way to see the country.

Unleaded gas (Magna Sin) costs around $1.60 a gallon, and regular gas (Nova) only slightly less.

Insurance costs are high (see below). Parking is a problem in the cities. Unless you have a full carload, the bus comes out cheaper per person.

If you want to drive to the Mexican border but not into Mexico, border area chambers of commerce or convention and visitor's bureaus can supply names of secured parking lots. You can leave your car there while you see the country by rail, bus, or plane.

CAR DOCUMENTS   To drive a car into Mexico, you'll need a Temporary Car Importation Permit, granted upon satisfaction of a long and strictly required list of documents. The permit can be obtained through Mexican border officials at the time you cross the border *or,* before you travel, through American Automobile Association (AAA) offices. AAA offices may charge a fee for this service, but it may be worth it if it improves the uncertain prospects of traveling all the way to the border without proper car documents for crossing.

You'll need:

1. A valid driver's license.
2. The car's current registration. (It wouldn't hurt to carry a photocopy of the car title as well.) If the registration is in more than one name, and one person on the registration is not traveling, then a notarized letter from the absent person(s) authorizing the use of the vehicle for the trip will be required.
3. A letter from the lien holder, if your registration shows a lien, giving you permission to take the vehicle into Mexico.
4. A valid international credit card. Using only your credit card (no cash or checks) you are required to pay a $10 car-importation fee.
5. Those without credit cards to pay the $10 importation fee will be required to post a cash bond equal to the value of the car which will be determined by the Mexican border official; generally the bond is about 2% of the car's value. If you post a bond you must also leave your **original car title** with the bond, both of which are returned to you when you return with your car. This also requires coming and going through the same border entry.
6. You must sign a declaration promising to return to your country of origin with the vehicle.

RETURNING YOUR CAR DOCUMENTS   The Temporary Car Permit papers you obtained when you entered Mexico must be returned when you cross back with your car. If they aren't returned, heavy fines are imposed and your car may be confiscated if you ever cross the border in the same car again. At the 16-mile checkpoint on the Mexican side, just before Laredo, Mexican officials will usually accept your papers there and remove the decal from your window. At other crossings you *may* be able to return them at a similar checkpoint. If you have to wait until reaching the border crossing, sometimes there's an authorized Hacienda official (that's the only one you can deal with) on duty to receive your papers, and sometimes there isn't. When there isn't, you must hunt him down wherever he is in town. Whatever you do, don't cross back without turning in your papers. Late nights, weekends, and Mexican holidays may pose special problems for this.

OTHER RULES   You must carry your vehicle permit, tourist permit, and proof of insurance in the car at all times. Remember too that the driver of the car will not be allowed to leave the country without the car (even if it's wrecked or stolen) unless he or she satisfies Customs that the import duty will be paid. In an emergency, if the driver of the car must leave the country without the car, the car must be put under Customs seal at the airport and the driver's tourist permit must be stamped to that effect. There may be storage fees.

The car-permit papers will be issued for the same length of time as your tourist permit was issued for. It's a good idea to greatly overestimate the time you'll spend in Mexico when applying for your permit, so that if something unforeseen happens and you have to (or want to) stay longer, you don't have to go through the long hassle of getting your papers renewed. The maximum term for tourist permit and temporary vehicle-importation permit is six months.

Other documentation is required for permission to enter the country (see "Entry Requirements," above).

MEXICAN AUTO INSURANCE Although auto insurance is not legally required in Mexico, anyone who drives without it is foolish. U.S. and Canadian insurance is invalid in Mexico. To be insured there, you must purchase Mexican insurance. Any party involved in an accident who has no insurance is automatically sent to jail and the car is impounded until fault is determined and all claims are settled. This is true even if you just drive across the border to spend the day—and it may be true even if you're injured.

The insurance agency will show you a full table of current rates and will recommend the coverage it thinks adequate. The policies are written along lines similar to those north of the border. Again, it's best to overestimate the period of coverage you'll need, because it's a real runaround to get your policy term lengthened in Mexico. Any part of the term unused will be prorated and that part of your premium refunded to you in cash at the office on the American side on your return, or by mail to your home. Be sure the policy you buy will pay for repairs in either the U.S. or Mexico, and that it will pay out in dollars, not pesos.

One of the best insurance companies for south-of-the-border travel is **Sanborn's Mexico Insurance,** with offices at all border crossings. I never drive across the border without Sanborn's insurance. It costs the same as the competition, and you get a Travelog that's a mile-by-mile guide along your proposed route. Information occasionally gets a bit dated, but for the most part it's like having a knowledgeable friend in the car telling you how to get in and out of town, where to buy gas (and which stations to avoid), highway conditions, and scams. It's especially helpful in remote places. Most of Sanborn's border offices are open Monday through Friday, and a few are staffed on Saturday and Sunday as well. You can purchase your auto liability and collision coverage by phone in advance and have it waiting at a 24-hour location if you are crossing when their office is closed. As for costs, a car with a value of $10,000 costs $133.45 to insure for two weeks, or $72 for one week. An annual policy for a car valued between $10,000 and $15,000 would be $397. For information, contact Sanborn's Mexico Insurance, P.O. Box 310, Dept. FR, 2009 S. 10th, McAllen, TX 78502 (tel. 512/686-0711; fax 512/686-0732).

AAA auto club also sells insurance.

PREPARING YOUR CAR Check the condition of your car thoroughly before you cross the border. Parts made in Mexico may be inferior, but service generally is quite good and relatively inexpensive.

Carry a spare radiator hose and spare belts for the engine fan and air conditioner. Can your tires last a few thousand miles on Mexican roads?

Take simple tools along if you're handy with them, also a flashlight or spotlight, a cloth to wipe the windshield, toilet paper, and a tire gauge—Mexican filling stations generally have air to fill tires, but no gauge to check the pressure. When driving, I always bring along a combination gauge/air compressor sold at U.S. automotive stores; it plugs into the car cigarette lighter, making it a simple procedure to check the tires every morning and pump them up at the same time.

Not that many Mexican cars comply, but Mexican law requires that every car have **seat belts** and a **fire extinguisher.** Be prepared!

CROSSING THE BORDER WITH YOUR CAR After you cross the border into Mexico from the U.S., you'll stop to get your tourist/car permit (now all in one),

N

0   50 mi
      80 km

Gulf of Mexico

Progreso
Yucalpetén
Sisal
Celestún
Nature
Reserve
25
Dzibilchal
Mérida
Celestún
281
Oxkintoc
M
Halacho
Becal
Calkini
Uxmal
I. Jaina
La
Sàyil
Xla
Campeche
Hopelchen
180
Edzná
Champotón
Sabancuy
CAMPECHE
180
261
Ciudad del
Carmen
Francisco
Escárcega
Chica
186
TABASCO
Calakmul
Calakmu
Biospher
Reserve
GUATEMALA

5853

YUCATÁN

Gulf of Mexico

Isla Holbox

Isla Contoy
Bird Sanctuary

Río Lagartos   El Cuyo
                Holbox
Telchac   Río Lagartos Nature Reserve
Puerto   San Felipe Nature Reserve

295

Punta Sam   Isla Mujeres
Puerto Juárez

172

Cancún

Motul   Tizimín   180
                                                    D
anacin Izamal Itzamná   Ekbalám   Puerto
                          Nuevo Xcan   307   Morelos
ancéh   180
        Balancanché   Punta Bete
Telchquillo Caves Valladolid   Chemax   Playa del Carmen
        Pisté   Xcaret
        Chichén-Itzá   Dzitnup   Pamul
yapán   YUCATÁN   Xpuha   Isla de Cozumel
            Yaxuná   Cobá   Puerto Aventuras
cul   Akumal
tún Cave   Xelha Lagoon   Chemuyil
    Oxkutzcab   National Park
184   Tulúm
    Tekax   San José
hacmultún
        Melchor Ocampo Chunyaxche
            Chumpón   Muyil
        295   Boca Paila

                                     Punta Allen

            Vigía Chico
                            Bahía de
                            la Ascensión
        184 Felipe
             Carrillo
    QUINTANA   Puerto   Sian Ka'an
                        Biosphere Reserve
    ROO   Bahía del
                                 Espíritu Santo
        Valle Hermoso

alakmul
iosphere
Reserve   Lázaro Cárdenas   Los Limones

            Bacalar   Majahual
án Ruins Dzinbanché Ruins   Banco Chinchorro
ujil   Chetumal
        186
        Kohunlich
                            Xcalak

                            Caribbean   Sea

    BELIZE

and a tourist decal will be affixed to the front window. Somewhere between 12 and 16 miles down the road you'll come to a Mexican Customs post. In the past all motorists had to stop and present travel documents and possibly have their cars inspected. Now, there is a new system that chooses some motorists at random for inspection. If the light is green, no inspection; if it's red, stop for inspection. All car papers are examined, however, so you must stop. In the Baja Peninsula the procedures may differ slightly—first you get your tourist permit, then on down the road you may not be stopped for the car permit. Theoretically, you should not be charged for your tourist permit and inspection, but the uniformed officer may try to extract a bribe (see "Bribes" in Section 1, above).

Incidentally, when you cross back into the U.S. after an extended trip in Mexico, the American Customs officials may inspect every nook and cranny of your car, your bags, even your person. They're looking for drugs, which include illegal diet pills.

BY SHIP

Numerous cruise lines serve Mexico. Possible trips might cruise from California down to the Baja Peninsula (including specialized whale-watching trips) and ports of call on the Pacific coast, or from Miami to the Caribbean (which often includes stops in Cancún, Playa del Carmen, and Cozumel).

Among the companies offering trips to ports of call in the Yucatán are Carnival Cruise Lines (tel. toll free 800/327-9501), Commodore Cruise Line (tel. toll free 800/237-5361), Costa Cruises (tel. toll free 800/462-6782), Cunard Crown Cruises (tel. toll free 800/528-6273), Norwegian Cruise Line (tel. toll free 800/327-7030), Premier Cruise Lines (tel. toll free 800/473-3262), Princess Cruise Lines (tel. toll free 800/LOVE-BOAT), and Regal Cruises (tel. toll free 800/270-SAIL).

From a budget point of view, these are expensive if you pay full price. However, if you don't mind taking off at the last minute, several cruise tour specialists arrange substantial discounts on unsold cabins. One such company is **The Cruise Line, Inc.,** 4770 Biscayne Blvd., Penthouse 1–3, Miami, FL 33137 (tel. 305/576-0036 or toll free 800/327-3021 or 800/777-0707).

PACKAGE TOURS

Package tours, which include airfare and accommodations for one price, perhaps with other items included, such as meals, transfers, or sightseeing tours, offer some of the best values to the coastal resorts, especially during high season from December until after Easter. Off-season packages can be real bargains. But to know for sure if the package is a cost saver, you must price the package yourself by calling the airline for round-trip flight costs and the hotel for rates. Add in the cost of transfers to and from the airport (which packages usually include) and see if it's a deal. Packages are usually per person, and single travelers pay a supplement. In the high season a package may be the only way of getting there because wholesalers have all the airline seats. The cheapest package rates will be those in hotels in the lower range, always without as many amenities. But you can use the public areas and beaches of more costly hotels without being a guest.

Travel agents have information on specific packages.

TOUR OPERATORS IN GREAT BRITAIN BA Holidays, Airtours, and Sunset Travel are three of the largest such companies offering package tours to Mexico. I recommend you pay a visit to the Mexican Government Tourist Office in London, 60–61 Trafalgar Sq., London WC2 N5DS, U.K. (tel. 441/734-1058).

8. GETTING AROUND

BY PLANE

To fly from point to point within the country you'll rely on Mexican airlines. Mexico has two privately owned, large national carriers, **Mexicana** (tel. toll free 800/531-7921 in the U.S.) and **Aeroméxico** (tel. toll free 800/237-6639 in the U.S.), and several up-and-coming regional carriers. Mexicana is Latin America's largest air carrier, and offers extensive connections to the U.S. as well as within Mexico. Aeroméxico also has U.S. connections.

Several of the new regional carriers are operated by, or can be booked through, Mexicana or Aeroméxico. Regional carriers are: **Aero Cancún** (see Mexicana), **Aero Caribe** (see Mexicana), **Aero Leo López** (tel. 914/778-1022 in El Paso; fax 915/779-3534), **Aerolitoral** (see Aeroméxico), **AeroMar** (tel. toll free 800/950-0747 in the U.S. or see Mexicana), **Aero Monterrey** (see Mexicana), **Aero Morelos** (tel. 73/17-5588 in Cuernavaca; fax 73/17-2320), and **Aerovias Oaxaqueñas** (tel. 951/ 6-3824 in Oaxaca). The regional carriers are expensive, but they go to places that are difficult to reach. In each section of this book, I've mentioned regional carriers with all pertinent telephone numbers.

Because major airlines can book some regional carriers, read your ticket carefully to see if your connecting flight is on one of these smaller carriers—they may leave from a different airport or check in at a different counter.

AIRPORT TAXES Mexico charges an airport tax on all departures. Passengers leaving the country on an international departure pay $12 in cash—dollars or the peso equivalent—to get out of the country. Each domestic departure you make within Mexico costs around $6 unless you're on a connecting flight and have already paid at the start of the flight—you won't be charged again if you have to change planes for a connecting flight.

RECONFIRMING FLIGHTS Although airlines in Mexico say that it's not necessary to reconfirm a flight, I always do. On several occasions I have arrived to check in with a valid ticket only to discover that my reservation had been canceled. Now I leave nothing to chance. Also, be aware that airlines routinely overbook. To avoid getting bumped, check in for an international flight the required hour and a half in advance of travel. That will put you near the head of the line.

BY TRAIN

No truly first-class trains operate in the area covered by this book. However, wherever train travel is possible, I've listed it under the pertinent city or town. I don't recommend train travel east of the Isthmus of Tehuantepec (that is, into the Yucatán or Chiapas), although in the Yucatán interior there are a few short routes that are acceptable around Valladolid. Trains from Mexico City to the Yucatán are notorious for running as much as 24 hours behind schedule.

Purchase your ticket as far in advance as possible, as soon as your travel plans are firm.

SERVICE CLASSES Traveling **segunda** (second class) is usually hot, overcrowded, dingy, and unpleasant. **Primera** (first class) can be the same way unless you are sure to ask for **primera especial** (first-class reserved seat) a day or so in advance, if possible.

Service and cleanliness may vary dramatically. This qualified statement means that the cars will be clean at the start of the journey, but little may be done en route to keep them that way. Trash may accumulate, toilet paper vanishes, the water cooler runs dry or has no paper cups, and the temperature may vary between freezing and sweltering. Conductors range from solicitous to totally indifferent.

BY BUS

The most economical way to see the Yucatán is by bus. Although service is still best between the Yucatán's major cities, since 1992 it has improved considerably to other parts of the peninsula as well. In most places travelers can choose to use "deluxe" service buses with refreshments and movie entertainment aboard. Frequency of service between towns has improved as has commuter-type service (lots of departures) between established cities such as Cancún and emerging meccas such as Playa del Carmen. Many places that once depended only on vacancies on buses passing through (*de paso*) now originate buses, and you can purchase tickets in advance—often selecting your seat on a computer screen.

Though service has improved, if you plan to use buses as the primary means of transportation, plan also to add more days to your trip—bus travel takes longer. On highways you can still flag buses down that are going your way and hop aboard. You'll spend a lot of time waiting at highway intersections, particularly near Uxmal and Kabah, and along the Caribbean coast. If you're waiting on a busy route, say between Cancún and Tulum, many buses will pass you up because they are full. You could easily spend several weeks trying to get to all the major ruins, cities, and beaches in the Yucatán by bus. For example, a bus trip using the new highway from Mérida to Cancún takes 3¹/₂ hours; bus travel between Mérida and Palenque takes 9 hours. To find the fastest bus, get in the habit of asking if a bus goes *sin escalas*, or *directo* (non-stop or direct), which may mean no stops or only a couple of stops as opposed to many stops on a regular bus.

Keep in mind that routes, times, and prices may change, and as there is no central directory of schedules for the whole country, current information must be obtained from local bus stations or travel offices.

For long trips, carry some food, water, toilet paper, and a sweater (in case the air conditioning is too strong).

See the Appendix for a list of helpful bus terms in Spanish.

BY CAR

The best way to see the Yucatán is by car. It's one of the most pleasant parts of the country for a driving vacation. The jungle- and beach-lined roads, while narrow and without shoulders, are in generally good condition. And they are straight, except in the southern part of Yucatán state and west to Campeche where they undulate through the Yucatán "Alps."

The four-lane toll road between Cancún and Mérida is complete but actually ends short of either city. It costs around $53 one-way to use, and cuts the trip from five hours to around four hours. The old two-lane free road is still in fine enough shape and passes through numerous villages with many speed-control bumps (*topes*), and is much more interesting. New directional signs seem to lead motorists to the toll road (*cuota*) and don't mention the free road (*libre*), so if you want to use it, ask locals for directions.

A new four-lane stretch of road is finished from Cancún almost to Puerto Morelos. Originally it was to extend to Chetumal, but the local rumor is that instead, a new toll road will parallel the existing two-lane road and connect Cancún and Chetumal. Construction hasn't begun. Meanwhile, traffic on the remaining two-lane road has increased a thousandfold and the route is becoming hazardous to drive due to the lack of shoulders, among other things. See important information in Chapter 4, "Isla Mujeres, Cozumel & the Caribbean Coast," on how to use local driving customs to drive this stretch safely.

Be aware of the long distances in the Yucatán. Mérida, for instance, is 400 miles from Villahermosa, 125 miles from Campeche, and 200 miles from Cancún. Leaded gas (Nova) is readily available in the Yucatán; unleaded gas (Magna Sin) is available at most stations. Stations close early in the evening.

Most Mexican roads are not up to northern standards of smoothness, hardness, width of curve, grade of hill, or safety marking. *Cardinal rule*: Never drive at night if you can avoid it—in the Yucatán there are no shoulders; the roads aren't good enough; the trucks, carts, pedestrians, and bicycles usually have no lights; you can hit potholes, animals, rocks, dead ends, or bridges out with no warning. Enough said!

You will also have to get used to the spirited Latin driving styles, which tend to depend more on flair and good reflexes than on system and prudence. Be prepared for new procedures, as when a truck driver flips on his left-turn signal when there's not a crossroad for miles. He's probably telling you that the road's clear ahead for you to pass—after all, he's in a better position to see than you are. It's difficult to know, however, whether he really means that he intends to pull over on the left-hand shoulder.

You may have to follow trucks without mufflers and pollution-control devices for miles. Under these conditions, drop back and be patient, take a side road, or stop for a break when you feel tense or tired.

Take extra care not to endanger pedestrians. People in the countryside are not good at judging the speed of an approaching car, and often panic in the middle of the road even though they could easily have reached the shoulder.

CAR RENTALS With some trepidation I wander into the subject of car-rental rules, which change often in Mexico. The best prices are obtained by reserving your car a week in advance in the U.S.

Most large Yucatán cities have rental offices representing the various big firms and some smaller ones. You'll find rental desks at airports, at all major hotels, and at many travel agencies. The large firms like Avis, Hertz, National, and Budget have rental offices on main streets as well.

Cars are easy to rent if you have a credit card (American Express, VISA, MasterCard, etc.), are 25 or over, and have a valid driver's license and passport with you. Without a credit card you must leave a cash deposit, usually a big one. Rent-here, leave-there arrangements are usually simple to make, but are very costly.

Costs Don't underestimate the cost of renting a car. For a short one-day trip to Villahermosa, Cancún, or Mérida, you'll pay $68 to rent a VW Beetle through Avis Rental Cars with unlimited mileage, including 10% tax and $15.50 daily insurance. Renting by the week gives a cheaper daily rate: Through Avis, the seven-day rate, including mileage, insurance, and tax, is $349, in Cancún or Mérida. It makes a difference where you rent and for how long. When you rent makes a difference as well, with high-season rates in some places being almost double the low-season rates for the same car and length of rental. Mileage-added rates, at more than 25¢ a kilometer, can run the bill up considerably, so I recommend renting with mileage included rather than with mileage added.

A VW Beetle, rented for one day through Avis in Cancún (which from the U.S. only rents with unlimited mileage) would be:

Basic daily rental	$46.00
Insurance	$15.50
IVA Tax 10%	$6.15
Subtotal	$67.65
Gas $1.60/gallon (5 gallons)	$9.60
Total	$77.25

The Avis weekly rate of a VW Beetle in Cancún is:

7-day rental	$199.00
$15.50 daily insurance	$108.50
IVA Tax 10%	$30.75
Subtotal	$338.25
5 tanks of gas	$104.00
Total	$442.25

Rental Confirmation   Make your reservation directly with the car-rental company using their toll-free 800 number. Write down your **confirmation number** and request a copy of the confirmation be mailed to you; rent at least a week in advance so the confirmation has time to reach you. Present that confirmation slip when you appear for your car. If you're dealing with a U.S. company, the confirmation must be honored, even if they must upgrade you to another class of car. Don't allow them to send you to another agency. The rental confirmation also has the agreed-on price which prevents you from being charged more in case there is a price change before you arrive. Insist on the rate printed on the confirmation slip.

Deductibles   Be careful—deductibles vary greatly. Some are as high as $2,500, which comes out of your pocket immediately in case of car damage, so don't fail to get that information.

Insurance   Many credit-card companies offer their card holders free rental-car insurance as a perk for having the card. Don't use it in Mexico, for several reasons. Even though rental-car insurance is supposedly optional in Mexico, there are major consequences if you don't take it. First, even if your credit card eventually pays you back, if you have an accident or the car is vandalized, or stolen, you'll have to pay for everything before you can leave the rental-car office (or jail as the case may be). This includes full value of the car if it is unreparable—a determination made only by the rental-car company. Second, if you buy insurance, you pay only the deductible, which limits your liability. Third, if an accident occurs everyone may wind up in jail until guilt is determined; if you are determined guilty you may not be released from jail until all restitution is paid to the rental-car owners and to injured persons—made doubly difficult if you have no insurance. Insurance is offered in two parts: Collision and damage covers your car and others if the accident is your fault, and personal accident covers you and anyone in your car. I always take both. If you don't purchase the insurance, you may be required to pay a huge cash deposit.

Damage   Always inspect your car carefully using this checklist:

1. Hubcaps
2. Windshield for nicks and cracks
3. Tire tread
4. Body dents, nicks, etc.

5. Fenders—dents
6. Muffler—is it smashed?
7. Trim—loose or damaged
8. Head- and taillights
9. Fire extinguisher—under driver's seat, required by law
10. Spare tire and tools—in trunk
11. Seat belts—required by law
12. Gas cap
13. Outside mirror
14. Floor mats

Note every damaged or missing area, no matter how minute, on your rental agreement or you will be charged for all missing or damaged parts, including missing car tags, should the police confiscate your tags for a parking infraction (very costly). I can't stress enough how important it is to check your car carefully. Car companies have attempted to rent me cars with bald tires and tires with bulges, a car with a new car license that would expire before I returned the car, windshield dings that become cracks, as well as cars with missing trim, floor mats, fire extinguisher, etc.

Fine Print   Read the fine print on the back of your rental agreement and note that insurance is invalid if you have an accident while driving on an unpaved road.

Trouble Number   One last recommendation. Before starting out with a rental car, be sure you know their trouble number. Get the direct number to the agency where you rented the car and write down their office hours. The large firms have toll-free numbers, which may not be well staffed on weekends.

Problems, Perils, Deals   Presently, I find the best prices are through Avis, and that is the company I use; generally I am a satisfied customer, even though I sometimes have to dig in my heels and insist on proper service. These are the kinds of situations I have encountered within the past three years, which could occur with any company: Attempting to push me off to a no-name company rather than upgrade me to a more expensive car when a VW Beetle wasn't available; poorly staffed offices with no extra cars, parts, or mechanics in case of a breakdown; bald and bulging tires; and insisting that I sign an open credit-card voucher for 75% of the value of the car in case of accident, even though I had purchased insurance (I refused and still rented the car). Since the potential problems are varied I'd rather deal with a company based in the States so that I have recourse if I am not satisfied.

Signing the Rental Agreement   Once you've agreed on everything, the rental clerk will tally most of the bill before you leave and you will sign an open credit-card voucher, which will be filled in when you return the car. Read the agreement and double-check all of the addition. The time to catch mistakes is before you leave, not when you return.

Picking Up/Returning the Car   When you rent the car you agree to pick it up at a certain time and return it at a certain time. If you are late in picking it up or cancel the reservation, there are usually penalties—ask what they are when you make the reservation. If you return it more than an hour late, an expensive hourly rate kicks in. Also, you must return the car with the same amount of gas as it had when you drove out. If you don't, their charge for the difference is much more than gas bought at a public station and it will be added to your bill.

GASOLINE There's one government-owned brand of gas and one gasoline station name throughout the country—Pemex (Petroleras Mexicanas). Each station has a franchise owner who buys everything from Pemex. There are two types of gas in Mexico: Nova, an 82-octane leaded gas, and Magna Sin, 87-octane unleaded gas. Magna Sin is sold from brilliantly colored pumps and costs around $1.60 a gallon; Nova costs slightly less. In Mexico, fuel and oil are sold by the liter, which is slightly more than a quart (40 liters equals about $10^{1}/_{2}$ gallons). Nova is readily available. Magna Sin is now available in most areas of Mexico, along major highways, and in the larger cities. Even in areas where it should be available, you may have to hunt around. The usual station may be out of Magna Sin for a couple of days—on weekends especially. Or you may be told that none is available in the area, just to get your business. Plan ahead: Fill up every chance you get; keep your tank topped off. Pemex publishes a helpful *Atlas de Carreteras* (road atlas), which includes a list of filling stations with Magna Sin gas, although there are some inaccuracies in the list. *No credit cards are accepted for gas purchases.*

Here's what to do when you have to fuel up: Drive up to the pump, close enough so that you will be able to watch the pump run as your tank is being filled. Check that the pump is turned back to zero, go to your fuel filler cap and unlock it yourself, and watch the pump and the attendant as the gas goes in. Though many service-station attendants are honest, many are not. It's good to ask for a specific peso amount rather than saying "full." This is because the attendants tend to overfill, splashing gas on the car and anything within range.

As there are always lines at the gas pumps, attendants often finish fueling one vehicle, turn the pump back quickly (or don't turn it back at all), and start on another vehicle. You've got to be looking at the pump when the fueling is finished, because it may show the amount you owe for only a few seconds. This "quick draw" from car to car is another good reason to ask for a certain peso amount of gas. If you've asked for a certain amount, the attendant can't charge you more.

Once the fueling is complete, let the attendant check the oil, or radiator, or put air in the tires. Do only one thing at a time, be with him as he does it, and don't let him rush you. Get into these habits or it'll cost you.

If you get oil, make sure that the can that is tipped into your engine is a full one. If in doubt, have the attendant check the dipstick again after the oil has supposedly been put in. Check your change, and again, don't let them rush you. Check that your locking gas cap is back in place.

DRIVING RULES If you park illegally, or commit some other infraction, and you are not around to discuss it, police are authorized to remove your license plates (*placas*). You must then trundle over to the police station and pay a fine to get them back. Mexican car-rental agencies have begun to weld the license tag to the tag frame; you may want to devise a method of your own to make the tags difficult to remove on your personal car. Theoretically, this will make the policeman move on to another set of tags easier to confiscate. On the other hand, he could get his hackles up and decide to have your car towed. To weld or not to weld is up to you.

Be attentive to road signs. A drawing of a row of little bumps means that there are speed bumps (*topes*) across the road to warn you to reduce speed while driving through towns or villages. Slow down when coming to a village whether you see the sign or not—sometimes they install the bumps but not the sign! See also "Traveler's Advisory," for specific driving suggestions for the Yucatán area.

Kilometer stones on main highways register the distance from local population centers. There is always a shortage of directional signs, so check quite frequently that you are on the right road. Some of the most common road signs include the ones listed below (their English translations are on the right):

Camino en Reparación	Road Repairs
Conserva Su Derecha	Keep Right
Cuidado con el Ganado	Watch Out for Cattle
Cuidado con el Tren	Watch Out for Trains
Curva Peligrosa	Dangerous Curve
Derrumbes	Earthquake Zone
Deslave	Caved-in Roadbed
Despacio	Slow
Desviación	Detour
Disminuya Su Velocidad	Slow Down
Entronque	Highway Junction
Escuela	School (Zone)
Grava Suelta	Loose Gravel
Hombres Trabajando	Men Working
No Hay Paso	Road Closed
Peligro	Danger
Puente Angosto	Narrow Bridge
Raya Continua	Continuous (Solid) White Line
Tramo en Reparación	Road Under Construction
Un Solo Carril a 100 m.	One-Lane Road 100 Meters Ahead
Zona Escolar	School Zone

MAPS Guía Roji and AAA have good maps to Mexico. AAA maps are available free to members at any AAA office in the U.S. In Mexico, maps are sold at large drugstores like Sanborn's, at bookstores, and in hotel gift shops.

BREAKDOWNS Your best guide to repair shops is the yellow pages. For specific makes and shops that repair them, look under "Automoviles y Camiones: Talleres de Reparación y Servicio"; auto-parts stores are listed under "Refacciones y Accesorios para Automoviles." On the road, often the sign of a mechanic simply says TALLER MECÁNICO.

I've found that the Ford and Volkswagen dealerships in Mexico give prompt, courteous attention to my car problems, and prices for repairs are, in general, much lower than in the U.S. or Canada. I suspect that other big-name dealerships give similar satisfactory service. Often they will take your car right away and make repairs in just a few hours, sometimes minutes. Production of Hondas began in Guadalajara in 1993, so Honda parts should now be more widely available throughout Mexico.

If your car breaks down on the road, help might already be on the way. Green, radio-equipped repair trucks manned by uniformed, English-speaking officers patrol the major highways during daylight hours to aid motorists in trouble. The **"Green Angels"** will perform minor repairs and adjustments free, but you pay for parts and materials.

ACCIDENTS When possible, many Mexicans drive away from accidents to avoid hassles with police. If the police arrive while the involved persons are still at the scene, everyone may be locked in jail until blame is assessed. In any case, you have to settle up immediately, which may take days of red tape. Foreigners without fluent Spanish are at a distinct disadvantage when trying to explain their side of the event.

Three steps may help the foreigner who doesn't wish to leave the scene of an accident as the Mexicans do: If you're in your own car, notify your Mexican insurance company, whose job it is to intervene on your behalf. If you're in a rental car, notify the rental company immediately and ask how to contact the nearest adjuster. (You did buy insurance with the rental—right?). Finally, if all else fails, ask to contact the nearest Green Angels, who may be able to explain to officials that you are covered by insurance. See also "Mexican Auto Insurance" in Section 7, "Getting There," "By Car," above.

PARKING   When you park your car on the street, lock up and leave nothing within view inside (day or night). I use guarded parking lots, especially at night, to avoid vandalism and break-ins. This way you also avoid parking violations. When pay lots are not available, dozens of small boys will surround you as you stop, wanting to "watch your car for you." Pick the leader of the group, let him know you want him to guard it, and give him a peso or two when you leave. Kids may be very curious about the car and may look in, crawl underneath, or even climb on top, but they rarely do any damage.

BY RV

Touring Mexico by recreational vehicle is a popular way of seeing the country. Many hotels have hookups. RV parks, while not as plentiful as in the U.S., are available throughout the country.

BY FERRY

In the Yucatán ferries take passengers between Puerto Juárez and Isla Mujeres, Playa Linda and Isla Mujeres, and Playa del Carmen and Cozumel.

HITCHHIKING

You see Mexicans hitching rides, for example, at crossroads after getting off a bus, but as a general rule hitchhiking isn't done. It's especially unwise for foreigners, who may be suspected of carrying large amounts of cash.

SUGGESTED ITINERARIES

IF YOU HAVE 5 DAYS

Since Mérida and Cancún are both popular gateways to the Yucatán, I've included two five-day suggestions for planning your trip. The first is based in Mérida and the second itinerary starts in Cancún.

A TOUR BASED IN MÉRIDA

Day 1: Arrive in Mérida. Settle in, get your bearings, change some money, adjust to the heat, and explore the market. Have dinner in one of the downtown restaurants.

Day 2: Tour the city, stopping at each of the historic buildings near the Plaza Mayor, and along the Paseo de Montejo. Save time for shopping, and don't miss the free nightly entertainment in Mérida's local parks.

Day 3: Leave Mérida, and if you're driving, stop at Mayapán on your way to Uxmal. These two sites, and perhaps a quick stop in Ticul, will fill your day. Return to Mérida for the night, or stay at Uxmal or Ticul.

Day 4: If you stay near Uxmal, spend Day 4 touring Kabah, Sayil, Labná, Xlapak, and the Grutas (Caves) de Loltún. If you're absolutely fascinated by ruins, head for Campeche to spend the night, stopping on the way at Edzná. Otherwise return to Mérida.

Day 5: Ride from Mérida through henequén country to Chichén-Itzá. Find a hotel room, have lunch, perhaps take a nap, then hike out to the ruins and tour until closing time,

A TOUR BASED IN CANCÚN

Day 1: Immediately upon arrival, pick up your rental car at the airport and head down the coastal Highway 307 south of Cancún and spend the night at one of the coastal inns, resorts, or villages—Playa del Carmen, Pamul, Xpuha, Punta Bete, Puerto Aventuras, Akumal, or Tulum. You can also go by bus from Cancún to Playa del Carmen, but other stops are more difficult.

Day 2: The next day explore as you like, then head down the coast to Tulum and see the ruins. After the ruins you have four good choices: You can continue on down the Punta Allen Peninsula to one of the small inns; or take the turnoff just past the ruins inland to the ruins of Cobá and spend the night there; or head back to Cancún, stopping at Xel-Ha Lagoon for snorkeling en route; or return to Playa del Carmen and take the ferry to Cozumel and spend the next day diving or exploring the island.

Day 3: If you continue inland to Cobá, get to the ruins of Cobá early and be ready to leave at 11am before the heat sets in. Continue north on the road to Chemax, Valladolid, and the ruins of Chichén-Itzá. Settle into your hotel. Or instead of Chichén-Itzá, head back to Cancún for two days of relaxation before returning home.

Day 4: If you stay at Chichén-Itzá, spend the morning at the ruins, then head to Cancún in the afternoon and spend the night there.

Day 5: Take it easy.

IF YOU HAVE 10 DAYS

You can touch all the high points of the Yucatán in a week by rental car, but you'll be traveling fast. Ten days is better, two weeks is excellent, and you can easily spend three weeks or more if you travel off the beaten track or by bus. The following itinerary uses Cancún as the launching point of a vacation, winding up the journey relaxing in Cancún before heading home.

Days 1–5: Spend these days as suggested in the Cancún-based tour above.

Day 6: Mérida is easy to reach from any of the suggested places above by bus, or by plane from Cozumel and Cancún. On the day of arrival, plan to settle in, get your bearings, change money, and adjust to the heat.

Day 7: While in Mérida take a self-guided walking tour of this hospitable and colonial city. Save some time for the market.

Day 8: By bus or by car, be sure to see Uxmal. The stone carvings on the temples are the most elaborate and beautiful in the Yucatán. If you're driving be sure to stop at Mayapán, another site. These two sites, and perhaps a quick stop in Ticul will fill your day. The nearby town of Ticul is a convenient alternative lodging base if you're driving. If you are pressed for time, in one long day, by scheduled bus or by car, you can skip Mayapán and Ticul and see Uxmal and the other nearby ruins on the Puuc Route—Kabah, Sayil, Labná, and Xlapak. Have lunch en route (bring it along) or at Oxkutzkab (if you're driving).

Day 9: Return to Cancún, get settled in, and relax. In the evening try one of the many Tulum Avenue restaurants or an outdoor eatery in a shopping center near the Convention Center.

Day 10: Relax in Cancún.

9. WHERE TO STAY

BUDGET ACCOMMODATIONS Mexican hotels, like hotels throughout the world, have an assortment of rooms in a range of prices. Rooms with bath or air conditioning are always more expensive. In addition, rooms with a view of the street may be more expensive (and noisier) than those with windows opening onto an airshaft. Rooms may be furnished with a single bed, a double bed, or two twin beds; the best buy is for two people to take the double bed—twins are almost always more expensive. Ask for *una cama matrimonial*. When the desk clerk asks "How many beds?" don't necessarily answer "Two." Or if the clerk shows you a room with two beds, ask if he has one with a double bed. The price the desk clerk quotes you for a room often won't be the cheapest room he has available. Ask to see a cheaper room (*Quiero ver un cuarto más barato, por favor*)—it can't hurt.

The maximum price a hotel can charge for its rooms is no longer controlled by the Mexican government. Often desk clerks will quote a lower price than their normal one if business is slack or if you suggest a slight reduction. Room rates are required to be posted in plain view near the reception desk, and as a rule they are. Ask the clerk to show you the *tarifa*. Be sure to ask if the quoted rate includes the 10% tax.

In the hotel listings throughout this book, note that all rooms have private bath unless I have noted otherwise at the beginning of a particular hotel's write-up.

Finally, test the beds if you intend to stay any length of time. Price often has nothing to do with the comfort of the beds. Often the cheaper hotels will have beds bought at different times, so one room may have a bad bed while another has a good one.

HOLIDAY RESORTS Travelers heading for resorts like Cancún, Cozumel, Playa del Carmen, and Isla Mujeres should write ahead for hotel reservations on major holidays (Mexican as well as international). Christmas through New Year's and Easter week are the worst for crowding. If you discover it's a holiday when you're en route to the resort, plan to arrive early in the day.

Several readers have written to me about difficulties they encountered in making reservations at moderately priced and budget establishments by mail, and even by toll-free reservation numbers. Some report no answer or no record of their request (or deposit check) when they've arrived. Or they are quoted a higher price than one they might have paid by just arriving without a reservation. I've experienced the same frustrations. Here's a suggestion: At budget hotels, only make reservations during high season if you are going to a beach area. Off-season, just arrive and find out what's available by calling when you arrive. If you truly want a reservation, write or fax well in advance, saying in your letter that you'll forward a deposit upon receipt of a confirmation. Or, instead, call the hotel, make the reservation, get the name of the person who takes the reservation, and then send your deposit by registered mail, return receipt requested—all of which can take a good deal of time. If the clerk asks where you're calling from, pick someplace nearby in Mexico; if you say the United States or some distant Mexican city, the quoted rate could be two to three times the current local price; if they think you're nearby, they know you can easily find out the true rate. If in doubt about the price on arrival, ask the price as though you're just another tourist looking for a room. Don't tell them you've made a reservation and see what price they quote you. If it's a lot lower than the price quoted in the reservation, accept the lower price and register. If you've paid a deposit, make sure it's applied to your bill. You may have to debate the point with them a bit, but it's worth it.

If you choose to stay in a first-class resort, my best advice is to look for a package deal through a travel agent or tour operator. Sometimes packages, which may include airfare, some meals, transfers to and from the airport, or other amenities, work out to be much cheaper than what you'd pay if you booked each component of your trip separately.

VILLAS & CONDOS Renting a private villa or condominium home for a vacation is a popular vacation alternative. The difference between the two, of course, is that villas are usually freestanding and condos may be part of a large or small complex and may seem more like a hotel. Often the villas are true private homes, in exclusive neighborhoods and rented out seasonally by their owners. Either accommodation comes with private kitchen and dining area, maid service, and pool. Often a full-time cook, maid, or gardener/chauffeur is on duty. Prices may be as low as $80 a night, or may be as high as $500. Rates are seasonal, with the best deals between May and October.

Three companies specializing in this type of vacation rental are: **Creative Leisure,** 951 Transport Way, Petaluma, CA 94954-1484 (tel. 707/778-1800, or toll free 800/426-6367; **Mexico Condo Reservations,** 5801 Soledad Mountain Rd., La Jolla, CA 92037 (tel. 619/275-4500, or toll free 800/262-4500, 800/654-5543 in Canada); and **Casa Cozumel,** V.I.P. Services, Apdo. Postal 312, Cozumel, Q. Roo 77600 (tel. 987/2-2259; fax 987/2-2348), which only has listings on the island of Cozumel. All three have brochures with photographs of potential properties.

YOUTH HOSTELS Mexico has some clean, adequate, and low-priced hostels built and maintained by the government. For a list, contact **SETEJ,** Hamburgo 305, in Mexico City (tel. 5/211-0743).

A source of information on inexpensive youth-hostel tours is the **Agencia Nacional de Turismo Juvenil,** Glorieta del Metro Insurgentes, Local C-11, Mexico 6, D.F. (tel. 5/211-6636), at the Insurgentes Metro plaza.

CAMPING It's easy and relatively cheap to camp south of the border if you have a recreational vehicle or trailer. It's more difficult if you have only a tent. Some agencies selling Mexican ar insurance in the U.S. (including Sanborn's) will give you a free list of campsites if you ask. The AAA also has a list of sites.

Campgrounds tend to be slightly below U.S. standards. Remember that campgrounds fill up just like hotels during the winter rush-to-the-sun and at holiday times, so get there early.

10. WHERE TO DINE

You can save more money on meals than on any other expense of your trip, but I rush to add that eating well is one of the most important things you can do to make your trip enjoyable. Avoid "junk" foods, a luxury item in Mexico. Good nutrition is one of the keys to avoiding or mitigating the dread "turista" diarrhea (see Section 3, "Health & Insurance," above).

BREAKFAST Breakfast is the most overpriced meal in the world, and Mexico is no exception. Drop by a panadería or pastelería (bakery or pastry shop) and produce market, and get a few delicious sweet rolls or some pastry and fruit for incredibly low prices. This, plus perhaps a glass of milk, can keep you going until you have your big meal at noon.

If you pack an immersion coil and have a heat-resistant plastic cup, instant coffee or a tea bag, and powdered milk, you'll be able to make your own coffee or tea in the morning at a fraction of the restaurant price. Coffee in Mexico normally costs 75¢ to $1 a cup. Having a coil or hot pot is also very handy if you are ill and can only stomach chamomile tea, instant soup, or bouillon. Coffee (ground and instant), tea bags, powdered milk (*leche en polvo*), and bouillon cubes are all readily available in Mexico, and I've indicated the location of pastry shops in most cities.

LUNCH Your best value by far will be to eat a big meal at noon. Most of Mexico is warm or hot during most of the day, so plan to be up and out to see the local sights early in the morning after a light breakfast. Then relax and collect your thoughts over a large lunch at about 1 o'clock and take it easy during the hottest part of the day. Have a light supper before returning to your hotel. This is what Mexicans do, and so most restaurants offer a **comida corrida,** or lunch special, of several courses at a fixed price between 1 and 4pm. Usually the meal will include soup, pasta, main course, dessert, and coffee, and will cost $3.50 to $9. The comida corrida, however, isn't always the cost-saving tanker-upper it once was. Portions are smaller these days, and often the price doesn't include dessert or a drink. One sign of a good comida is the number of Mexicans the place attracts; look to see what others are having. Sometimes a main course alone is the best bargain.

DINNER For dinner you'll want to eat lightly, having eaten heavily at 1 or 2pm, and if you can make do with a good bowl of soup and a plate of enchiladas you'll need to spend very little. Avoid the long, luxurious dinners so popular in Europe and the U.S., unless you've decided to splurge. Such evening meals are not truly Mexican, and are therefore more expensive.

MARKETS Every town in Mexico has a market, and those found in the cities are often fabulous modern affairs. A full range of local produce, cheese, eggs, bread, and inexpensive fresh fruit is sold. The location of the market is given for most towns; if in doubt, ask for the *mercado*. Avoid milk and cream in open containers. In most places you should be able to find modern factory-packaged milk; if not, the powdered whole milk sold everywhere is almost as good (much better than powdered skim milk sold in the U.S.).

11. SHOPPING

The charm of Mexico is nowhere better expressed than in its arts and crafts. Hardly a tourist will leave this country without having bought at least one handcrafted item. Mexico is famous for textiles, ceramics, baskets, and onyx and silver jewelry, to mention only a few.

Prices for the crafts are really dependent on your bargaining ability. It's very helpful to visit a government fixed-price shop (usually called the Artes Populares or

FONART) before attempting to bargain. This will give you an idea of the cost versus quality of the various crafts.

Note: Though many of the craft regions mentioned below are not in or near the states mentioned in this book, stores throughout Mexico, including those in the Yucatán peninsula, commonly sell these items.

Following, now, are the various crafts, in alphabetical order.

Baskets: Woven of reed or straw—Halacho and Becal in the Yucatán, Oaxaca, Copper Canyon, Toluca, Puebla, Mexico City.

Blankets: Saltillo, Toluca, Santa Ana Chiautempan, north of Puebla, Oaxaca, and Mitla (made of soft wool with some synthetic dyes; they use a lot of bird and geometric motifs). Make sure that the blanket you pick out is in fact the one you take since often the "same" blanket in the wrapper is not the same.

Glass: Hand-blown and molded—Monterrey, Tlaquepaque, and Mexico City.

Guitars: Made in Paracho, 25 miles north of Uruapan on Highway 37.

Hammocks and Mosquito Netting: Mérida, Campeche, Mazatlán. See market section in Mérida (Chapter 5) for details on buying.

Hats: Mérida (Panama), made of sisal from the maguey cactus; finest quality weaving; easy to pack and wash. San Cristóbal de las Casas, Chiapas, is a good place for varied regional hats.

Huaraches: Leather sandals, often with rubber-tire soles—San Blas, Mérida, Mexico City, Guadalajara, Hermosillo, San Cristóbal de las Casas, and in fact most states.

Huipils: Handwoven, embroidered or brocaded overblouses indigenous to almost all Mexican states but especially to Yucatán, Chiapas, Oaxaca, Puebla, Guerrero, and Veracruz. Most of the better huipils are used ones bought from the village women. Huipils can be distinguished by villages; look around before buying— you'll be amazed at the variety.

Lacquer Goods: Olinala, Guerrero, northeast of Acapulco, is known for ornate lacquered chests and other lacquered decorative and furniture items. Pátzcuaro and Uruapan, west of Mexico City, are also known for gold-leafed lacquered trays.

Leather Goods: Monterrey, Saltillo, León, Mexico City, San Cristóbal de las Casas, and Oaxaca.

Masks: Wherever there is locally observed regional dancing you'll find mask makers. The tradition is especially strong in the states of Guerrero, Chiapas, Puebla, Oaxaca, Michoacán.

Onyx: Puebla (where onyx is carved), Querétaro, Matehuala, Mexico City.

Pottery: Ticul (in the Yucatán), Tlaquepaque, Tonalá, Oaxaca, Puebla, Michoacán, Coyotepec, Izúcar de Matamoros, Veracruz, Copper Canyon, Dolores Hidalgo, and Guanajuato.

Rebozos: Women's or men's rectangular woven cloth to be worn around the shoulders, similar to a shawl—Oaxaca, Mitla, San Cristóbal de las Casas, Mexico City, and Pátzcuaro. Rebozos are generally made of wool or a blend of wool and cotton, but synthetic fibers are creeping in, so check the material carefully before buying. Also, compare the weave from different cloths since the fineness of the weave is proportional to the cost.

Serapes: Heavy woolen or cotton blankets with a slit for the head, to be worn as a poncho—Santa Ana Chiautempan (near Tlaxcala), San Luis Potosí, Santa María del Río (south of San Luis Potosí), Chiconcoac (near Texcoco), Saltillo, Toluca, Mexico City.

Silver: Taxco, Mexico City, Zacatecas, Guadalajara. Sterling silver is indicated by "925" on the silver, which certifies that there are 925 grams of pure silver per kilogram, or that the silver is 92.5% pure. A spread-eagle hallmark is also used to indicate sterling. Look for these marks or you may pay a high price for an inferior quality that is mostly nickel, or even silverplate called alpaca.

Stones: Chalcedony, amber, turquoise, lapis lazuli, amethyst—San Cristóbal de las Casas, Querétaro, San Miguel del Allende, Durango, Saltillo, San Luis Potosí. The cost of turquoise is computed by weight, so many pesos per carat. Amber is mined in the state of Chiapas.

Textiles: Oaxaca, Chiapas, Santa Ana near Puebla, Guerrero, and Nayarit are known for their excellent weaving, each culturally distinct and different.

Tortoiseshell: It's illegal to bring it into the U.S.

 MEXICO

Abbreviations Dept.=apartments; Apdo.=post office box; Av.=Avenida; Blv.=Bulevar (boulevard); Calz.=Calzada (boulevard). *C* on faucets stands for *caliente* (hot), and *F* stands for *fría* (cold). In elevators, *PB* (*planta baja*) means ground floor.

American Express Wherever there is an office, I've mentioned it.

Business Hours In general, Mexican businesses in larger cities are open between 9am and 7pm; in smaller towns many close between 2 and 4pm. Most are closed on Sunday. Bank hours are 9 or 9:30am to 1pm Monday through Friday. A few banks in large cities have extended hours.

Camera and Film Take full advantage of your 12-roll film allowance by bringing 36-exposure rolls. Also bring extra batteries: AA batteries are generally available, but AAA and small disk batteries for cameras and watches are rarely found. A few places in resort areas advertise color film developing, but it might be cheaper to wait until you get home. If you're a serious photographer, bring an assortment of films of various speeds as you will be photographing against glaring sand, in gloomy Maya temples, and in dusky jungles. Proper filters are a help. See also "Photography," below.

Cigarettes Cigarettes are much cheaper in Mexico (even U.S. brands) if you buy them at a grocery store or drugstore and not at a hotel tobacco shop.

Climate See Section 2, "When to Go," earlier in this chapter.

Crime See "Legal Aid" and "Safety," below, and "Bribes" and "Scams" in Section 1, "Information, Entry Requirements & Money," earlier in this chapter.

Currency See Section 1, "Information, Entry Requirements & Money," earlier in this chapter.

Customs Mexican Customs inspection has been streamlined. At most ports of entry entering tourists are requested to punch a button: If the resulting light is green, you go through without inspection; if it's red, your luggage or car may be inspected thoroughly or briefly.

Doctors and Dentists Every embassy and consulate is prepared to recommend local doctors and dentists with good training and modern equipment; some of the doctors and dentists even speak English. See the list of embassies and consulates under "Embassies and Consulates," below, and remember that at the larger ones a duty officer is on call at all times. Hotels with a large clientele of foreigners are often prepared to recommend English-speaking doctors. Almost all first-class hotels in Mexico have a doctor on call.

Documents Required   See Section 1, "Information, Entry Requirements & Money," earlier in this chapter.

Driving Rules   See Section 8, "Getting Around," earlier in this chapter.

Drug Laws   Briefly, don't use or possess illegal drugs in Mexico. Mexicans have no tolerance of drug users and jail is the solution, with very little hope of getting out until the sentence (usually a long one) is completed or heavy fines or bribes are paid. (*Important note:* It isn't uncommon to be befriended by a fellow user only to be turned in by that "friend," who then collects a bounty for turning you in. It's no win!) Bring prescription drugs in their original containers. If possible, pack a copy of the original prescription with the generic name of the drug.

I don't need to go into detail about the penalties for illegal drug possession upon return to the U.S. Customs officials are also on the lookout for diet drugs sold in Mexico, possession of which could also land you in jail in the U.S. because they are illegal there. If you buy antibiotics over the counter (which you can do in Mexico), say, for a sinus infection, and still have some left, you probably won't be hassled by U.S. Customs.

Drugstores   Drugstores (*farmacias*) will sell you just about anything you want, with prescription or without. Most are open Monday through Saturday from 8am to 8pm. If you need to buy medicines after normal hours, ask for the *farmacia de turno*—pharmacies take turns staying open during the off-hours. Find any drugstore and in its window may be a card showing the schedule of which farmacia will be open at what time.

Electricity   The electrical system in Mexico is 110 volts, 60 cycles, as in the U.S. and Canada. However, in reality it may cycle more slowly and overheat your appliances. To compensate, select a medium or low speed for hairdryers, though it may still overheat. Older hotels still have electrical outlets for flat two-prong plugs; you'll need an adapter for using any modern electrical apparatus that has an enlarged end on one prong, or which has three prongs to insert. Many first-class and deluxe hotels have the three-holed outlets (*trifacicos* in Spanish). Those that don't *may* loan adapters, but to be sure, it's always better to carry your own.

Embassies and Consulates   They provide valuable lists of doctors, and lawyers, as well as regulations concerning marriages in Mexico. Contrary to popular belief, your embassy cannot get you out of a Mexican jail, provide postal or banking services, or fly you home when you run out of money. Consular officers can provide you with advice on most matters and problems, however. Most countries have a representative embassy in Mexico City and many have consular offices or representatives in the provinces.

The Embassy of **Australia** in Mexico City is at Jaime Balmes 11, Plaza Polanco (tel. 5/395-9988); it's open Monday through Friday from 8am to 1pm.

The Embassy of **Canada** in Mexico City is at Schiller 529, in Polanco (tel. 5/724-7900; it's open Monday through Friday from 9am to 1pm and 2 to 5pm (at other times the name of a duty officer is posted on the embassy door).

The Embassy of **New Zealand** in Mexico City is at Homero 229, 8th Floor (tel. 5/250-5999); it's open Monday through Thursday from 9am to 2pm and 3 to 5pm, and on Friday from 9am to 2pm.

The Embassy of the **United Kingdom** in Mexico City is at Lerma 71, at Rio Sena (tel. 5/7-2569 or 7-2593); it's open Monday through Friday from 8:30am to 3:30pm. There's an honorary consul in Mérida, Calle 58 no. 450 (tel. 99/21-6799).

The Embassy of the **United States** in Mexico City is right next to the Hotel María Isabel Sheraton at Paseo de la Reforma 305, at the corner of Río Danubio (tel. 5/211-0042, or 5/211-4536 for emergencies). There's a U.S. consul in Mérida (tel. 9/925-5011). In addition, a consular agent resides in Cancún (tel. 988/4-2411), open from 9am to 2pm and 3 to 6pm.

Emergencies   The 24-hour **Tourist Help Line** in Mexico City is 5/250-0151.

Etiquette   As a general rule, Mexicans are very polite. Foreigners who ask questions politely, and say "Please" and "Thank you" will be rewarded. On the other hand, Mexicans will brazenly step ahead of you in lines, especially at ticket counters. The corrective words are *"La cola está atrás,"* which means "the end of the line is back there." Mexicans are also very formal; an invitation to a private home, no matter how humble, is an honor. And although many strangers will immediately begin using the familiar form of the pronoun *tú* and its verb form, if you want to be correct, the formal *usted* is still preferred until a friendship is established. When in doubt use the formal form and wait for the Mexican to change to the familiar. Mexicans are normally uncomfortable with our "dutch treat" custom of dining, and will usually insist on paying. It can be touchy and you don't want to be insulting. But you might offer to get the drinks or insist on paying the tip. If you're invited to a home, it's polite to bring a gift, perhaps a bottle of good wine or flowers.

Guides   Most guides in Mexico are men. Many speak English (and occasionally other languages) and are formally trained in history and culture to qualify for a federally approved tourism license. Hiring a guide for a day at the ruins, or to squire you around, may be a worthwhile luxury if you establish boundaries in the beginning. Be specific about what you want to do and how long you want the service. The guide will quote a price. Discussion may reduce the initial quote. If your guide is using his own car, is licensed (something he can prove with a credential), and speaks English, the price will be higher and is generally worth it. If you are together at lunch, it's customary to buy the guide's meal. When bus tours from the U.S. diminished a few years ago, many licensed English-speaking guides became taxi drivers, so it isn't unusual to find incredibly knowledgeable taxi drivers who are experienced guides. These licensed guides/taxi drivers often have a permanent spot outside the better hotels and are available for private duty. If the service has been out of the ordinary, a tip is in order—perhaps 10% of the daily rate. On bus tours, the recommended tip is $1.50 to $2 per day per person.

Hitchhiking   Generally speaking hitchhiking is not a good idea in Mexico. Take a bus instead—they're cheap and go everywhere.

Holidays   See Section 2, "When to Go," earlier in this chapter.

Information   See Section 1, "Information, Entry Requirements & Money," earlier in this chapter, and specific city chapters for local information offices.

Language   The official language is Spanish, but there are at least 50 Indian languages spoken and more than four times that many Indian dialects. English is most widely spoken in resort cities and in better hotels. It's best to learn some basic Spanish phrases.

Legal Aid   International Legal Defense Counsel, 111 S. 15th St., Packard Building, 24th Floor, Philadelphia, PA 19102 (tel. 215/977-9982), is a law firm specializing in legal difficulties of Americans abroad. See also "Embassies and Consulates" and "Emergencies," above.

Mail   Mail service south of the border tends to be slow and erratic. If you're on a two-week vacation, it's not a bad idea to buy and mail your postcards in the Arrivals lounge at the airport to give them maximum time to get home before you do.

For the most reliable and convenient mail service, have your letters sent to you c/o the American Express offices in major cities, which will receive and forward mail for you if you are one of their clients (a travel-club card or an American Express traveler's check is proof). They charge a fee if you wish them to forward your mail.

If you don't use American Express, have your mail sent to you care of *Lista de Correos* (General Delivery), followed by the Mexican city, state, and country. In Mexican post offices there may actually be a "lista" posted near the *Lista de Correos* window bearing the names of all those for whom mail has been received. If there's no list, ask and show them your passport so they can riffle through and look for your letters. If the city has more than one office, you'll have to go to the central post office—not a branch—to get your mail. By the way, in many post offices they return mail to the sender if it has been there for more than 10 days. Make sure people don't send you letters too early.

In major Mexican cities there are also branches of U.S. express-mail companies such as Federal Express and DHL as well as private mail boxes such as Mail Boxes Etc.

Maps   AAA maps to Mexico are quite good and available free to members at any AAA office in the U.S.

Newspapers and Magazines   The English-language newspaper *The News*, published in Mexico City, carries world news and commentaries, and a calendar of the day's events including concerts, art shows, and plays. Newspaper kiosks in larger Mexican cities will carry a selection of English-language magazines.

Passports   See Section 1, "Information, Entry Requirements & Money," earlier in this chapter.

Pets   Taking a pet into Mexico entails a lot of red tape. Consult the Mexican Government Tourism Office nearest you (see Section 1, "Information, Entry Requirements & Money," earlier in this chapter).

Photography   All archeological sites and many museums have restrictions on the use of personal cameras. At archeological sites visitors using their own video cameras are charged $8.50. A similar charge is permitted at all sites for still cameras; some sites charge it while others do not. It's courteous to ask permission before photographing anyone. In San Cristóbal de las Casas and surrounding villages, Indians have religious reasons for not wishing to be photographed. Some villages in that area prohibit photography of any kind.

Police   Police in general in Mexico are to be suspected rather than trusted; however, you'll find many who are quite helpful with directions, even going so far as to lead you where you want to go.

Radio/TV   Many hotels now have antennas capable of bringing in U.S. TV channels. Large cities will have English-language stations and music.

Restrooms   The best bet in Mexico is to use restrooms in restaurants and hotel public areas. Always carry your own toilet paper and hand soap, neither of which is in great supply in Mexican restrooms. Public facilities, usually near the central market, vary in cleanliness and usually have an attendant who charges a few pesos for toilet use and a few squares of toilet paper. Pemex gas stations have improved the maintenance of their restrooms along major highways. No matter where you are, even if the toilet flushes with paper, there'll be a waste basket for paper disposal. Many people come from homes without plumbing and are not accustomed to toilets that will take paper, and will throw paper on the floor rather than put it in the toilet—thus you'll see the basket no matter what quality of place you are in. On the other hand, the water pressure in many establishments is so low that paper won't go down. There's often a sign saying "do," or "don't" flush paper.

Safety   Whenever you're traveling in an unfamiliar city or country, stay alert. Be aware of your immediate surroundings. Wear a moneybelt and don't sling your camera or purse over your shoulder. This will minimize the possibility of your becoming a victim of crime.

Crime is more of a problem in Mexico than it used to be. Although you will feel physically safer in most Mexican cities than in comparable big cities at home, you must take some basic, sensible precautions.

First, remember that you're a tourist, and an obvious target for crime. Beware of pickpockets on crowded buses and in markets. Guard your possessions very carefully at all times; don't let packs or bags out of your sight even for a second (the big first-class bus lines will store your bag in the luggage compartment under the bus, and that's generally all right, but keep your things with you on the less responsible village and some second-class buses on country routes).

Next, if you have a car, park it in an enclosed or guarded lot at night. Vans are a special mark. Don't depend on "major downtown streets" to protect your car—park it in a private lot with a guard, or at least a fence.

Women must be careful in cities when walking alone, night or day. Busy streets are no problem, but empty streets (even if empty just for afternoon siesta) are lonely places.

Important warning: Agreeing to carry a package back to the States for an acquaintance or a stranger could land you in jail for years if it contains drugs or some other contraband. Never do it no matter how friendly, honest, or sincere the request. Perpetrators of this illegal activity prey on innocent-looking single travelers and especially senior citizens.

Allowing anyone into your room whom you don't know could invite an instant robbery. This includes someone announcing him or herself (by phone or at your hotel room door) as room service bringing a "free" meal or drinks as compliments of the house—or anything you didn't order. When you open the door expectantly, robbers burst in. Always use caution before opening your door to anyone. When in doubt, call hotel security or the reception desk.

Taxes   There's a 10% tax on goods and services in Mexico, which may or may not be included in the posted price.

Telephone and Fax   Telephone area codes are gradually being changed all over the country. The change may affect the area code and first digit, or area code only. But some cities are adding exchanges and changing whole numbers. Often a personal or business telephone number is changed without notification to the subscriber! Though a recorded message may come on to tell you a phone is busy (after you've already heard the busy signal), telephone courtesy messages announcing a phone number change are almost nonexistent in Mexico. You can try operator assistance for difficult-to-reach numbers, but often the phone company doesn't provide them with new numbers.

Fax machines are often turned off when offices are closed. And many fax numbers are also regular telephone numbers; for these you have to ask for the fax tone—"*por favor darme el tono por fax.*" Then you wait for the tone and send your fax.

Telephone etiquette in Mexico does not require the answerer to suggest taking a message or having someone return the call; you'll have to suggest it. Although many businesses do, phone etiquette doesn't necessarily require answering with the business name; you have to ask if you have the right place.

Most of the old coin-operated **public pay phones** have been replaced by Ladatel phones, which usually use both coins (the old 100-peso coin), and a special card. Cards are purchased in denominations of 10, 20, and 30 New Pesos at pharmacies, bookstores, and grocery stores near Ladatel phones. The card entitles you to a certain amount of credit; as you talk you can watch the money tick away on the phone's special display. These are expensive, costing about 75¢ a minute for a long distance or local call. Instead of using a Ladatel phone for a local call, if it's a quick call, try to use the phone of a local merchant, or one in a hotel lobby. Also see the Appendix for detailed information about using pay phones and making long-distance calls.

Time   Central standard time prevails throughout most of Mexico. The west-coast states of Sonora, Sinaloa, and parts of Nayarit are on mountain standard time. The state of Baja California Norte is on Pacific standard time, but Baja California Sur is on mountain time.

Beginning in the spring of 1995, Mexico will adopt daylight saving time to save on energy costs.

Tipping   Throw out the ironclad 15% tipping rule in budget restaurants no matter what other travel literature may say. Do as the locals do: For meals costing under $3, leave the loose change; for meals costing $4 to $5, leave 6% to 10%, de-pending on service. Above $5, you're into the 10% to 15% bracket. Some of the more crass high-priced restaurants will actually add a 15% "tip" to your bill—leave nothing extra if they do. Remember also to tip on the actual price—before tax.

Bellboys and porters will expect about 25¢ to 50¢ per bag depending on the quality of hotel. You needn't tip taxi drivers unless they've rendered some special service—carrying bags or trunks.

Tourist Offices   See Section 1, "Information, Entry Requirements & Money," earlier in this chapter, and also specific city chapters.

Visas   See Section 1, "Information, Entry Requirements & Money," earlier in this chapter.

Water   Most hotels have decanters or bottles of purified water in the rooms, and the better hotels have either purified water from regular taps or special taps marked AGUA PURIFICADA. In the resort areas, especially the Yucatán, hoteliers are be-ginning to charge for in-room bottled water. Virtually any hotel, restaurant, or bar will bring you purified water if you specifically request it, but you'll usually be charged for it.

Wire Funds   If you need cash in a hurry, *Dineros en Minutos* (Money in Minutes) is affiliated with Western Union and makes wire cash transactions at Electrika, furniture and electronic stores in Mexico. Your contact on the other end presents cash to Western Union, which is credited by Electrika, and presented (in pe-sos) to you. The service only recently began in Mexico but 500 outlets are planned.

CHAPTER 3

CANCÚN

Today Cancún (pop. 350,000) is the magic word in Mexican vacations. Besides existing as a premier resort destination on its own, it enjoys a prime location in relation to other places on the Yucatán's tourist circuit: Cancún is 125 miles northeast of Chichén-Itzá, 80 miles north of Tulum, 105 miles northeast of Cobá, and 10 miles west of Isla Mujeres.

Less than two decades ago, however, the name Cancún meant little to anyone. Perhaps a resident of Puerto Juárez or Isla Mujeres knew the spot by its configuration—a hook-shaped island of powdery limestone sand, lined with coral reefs, on the Caribbean side of the Yucatecan coast.

The idea for Cancún began in the early 1960s when bank visionaries, wishing to create jobs for Mexico's future, conceived the plan of developing new resort areas. Several years of intense searching highlighted three undeveloped areas at what today are known as the Bays of Huatulco and Ixtapa on Mexico's Pacific coast, and Cancún, facing the Caribbean Ocean on the Yucatán peninsula. Eventually the bankers convinced the government to go along. Huatulco was favored as the first development, but Cancún won out because officials thought it would be the hardest to develop and would take the longest. It was on completely untouched land more than 100 miles from a settlement of any kind. Roads, highways, public transportation, running water, and electricity were nonexistent. Recruited construction help were Maya-speaking Indians who were unskilled in construction and who didn't speak Spanish. Absolutely everything had to be brought in. Incredible as it may seem now that Cancún has more than 18,000 hotel rooms, it opened in 1974 with one hotel and a lot of hype. Meanwhile Cancún City popped up on the mainland to house the working populace that flocked here to support the resort.

Today, luxury hotels line the 14-mile hook-shaped island. In fact, the island boasts an enormous variety of modern architectural styles that get grander and more lavish each year. Cancún City grew up with hotels designed for the budget-minded traveler and a downtown area chock-a-block with restaurants all trying to outdo each other to attract clientele.

Detractors say the resort is homogenized U.S. and not Mexico at all. There's a lot of truth to that. People who know only Cancún don't really know Mexico or its people. But it's the country's most popular destination, and one reason people return

WHAT'S SPECIAL ABOUT CANCÚN

Beaches
All 12 miles of powdery white beaches on Cancún Island are open to the public.

Excursions
Day trips to Sian Ka'an Biosphere Reserve, the ruins of Tulum, and the island and beach resorts to the north and south.

Restaurants
Hundreds of restaurants, from world-class to Formica-class, cater to just about every culinary whim and budget.

Shopping
Downtown markets, small shops, and island shopping centers offer an incredible variety of goods from local crafts to decorator designs and clothing galore.

Nightlife
Flashy discos, restaurants, pier dancing, and lobby bars keep Cancún wide awake until the wee hours.

---

is precisely because it looks a lot like home—Miami being the favorite city of comparison. True, with all its modern glitz, it isn't the charming colonial Mexico that you see inland in the Yucatán and elsewhere in Mexico away from coastal development. But it is the epitome of Mexico's mega-coastal resorts of today. The pace is fast; traffic zooms; and restaurant, condo, and timeshare hawkers vie for customers. Familiar U.S. franchise restaurants seem to be wherever you look, while nonfranchise fine-dining establishments scramble to compete.

In 1994, 20 years after the first hotel opened, Cancún finally seems to have come of age. There are only a few spaces left for giant hotels. Shopping centers that took so long to fill are complete now and extend practically the length of the island, offering more imported goods from around the world than in the past as well as designer fashions and furniture.

It's the ideal site for a resort—the coast is lush Yucatecan jungle, and the long island, with its fine sandy beaches, is perfect for seaside hotels. The Caribbean waters are incredibly blue and limpid, temperatures (both air and water) are just right, and the coral reefs and tropical climate guarantee brilliant underwater life for snorkeling and scuba diving. Maya ruins at Tulum, Chichén-Itzá, and Cobá are a short drive away, as are the snorkeling reserves of Xcaret and Xel-Ha. And for a change of scene the older, less expensive island resorts of Isla Mujeres and Cozumel are close at hand. The coast south of Cancún, which includes the village of Playa del Carmen, is exploding with resorts in all price ranges almost all the way to Tulum.

1. ORIENTATION

ARRIVING

BY PLANE **Mexicana Airlines** flies from Chicago, Dallas/Fort Worth, Guadalajara, Los Angeles, Mexico City, Miami, and New York City. **Aeroméxico** offers service from Mexico City, Houston, Mérida, New York City, and Tijuana.

Regional carriers **Aero Cozumel** and **Aero Caribe** (both affiliated with Mexicana) fly from Havana, Mexico City, Tuxtla Gutiérrez, Villahermosa, Cozumel, Mérida, Oaxaca, Veracruz, and Ciudad del Carmen. **American Airlines** has flights from Dallas/Fort Worth and Raleigh/Durham. **Continental** flies from Houston, New Orleans, and New York. **Northwest** has year-round flights from Tampa and winter flights from Memphis. **United** has numerous connecting flights from the U.S. **Taesa** flies from Mexico City, Ciudad Juárez, Tijuana, Acapulco, Chetumal, and Cozumel.

Special vans run from Cancún's international airport into town for $10 per person. Cab rates from the airport range from around $10 to $15 for a trip to Club Med, to $27 for a ride to the Zona Hotelera (Hotel Zone), to $35 for taking you to the Punta Sam car-ferry to Isla Mujeres. There's no van transportation to the Puerto Juárez people-ferry to Isla Mujeres. The least expensive way to get there is to take the van to the bus station in downtown Cancún and from there bargain for a taxi, which should cost around $7 or $8. Most major rental-car companies have outlets at the airport, so if you are renting a car, consider picking it up and dropping it off at the airport to save on these exorbitant airport transportation prices.

BY BUS The **bus station** is in downtown Cancún City at the intersection of Avenidas Tulum and Uxmal, within walking distance of several of my hotel suggestions. Both first- and second-class buses operate from here, but each has its own ticket window and waiting room. In addition, other ticket offices are around the corner from the station on Tulum. Because the area is now so congested with arriving and departing buses and taxis, I wouldn't be surprised if a new station is built in a less central area during the life of this book.

DEPARTING

BY PLANE There is no collective service from Cancún City or the Hotel Zone to the airport, so you'll have to hire a taxi from Cancún City for around $12 to $18 or from the Hotel Zone for around $15 to $20.

All the airlines have offices in town and/or at the airport: **Aeroméxico** is at Avenida Cobá 80 (tel. 84-3571 or 84-2728). **Aero Cozumel** and **Aero Caribe** are at Avenida Tulum 99 at Uxmal (tel. 84-2000). **American** is represented at the airport (tel. 84-2651 or 84-2947 for reservations), as is **Continental** (tel. 84-2540). **Mexicana Airlines** has an office Avenida Cobá 39 (tel. 87-4444). **United** is at the airport (tel. 84-2528).

BY BUS The bus station, though conveniently located in downtown Cancún, is small and often overcrowded with prospective passengers and the streets surrounding it are clogged with buses.

Autotransportes Playa Express (tel. 84-1984) runs minibuses between Cancún and Playa del Carmen almost every half hour between 6am and 9pm from the corner of Tulum and Pino (at one end of the bus station). Tickets are purchased onboard. **Caribe Inter** (tel. 84-1365) has 10 buses to Mérida, seven to Chetumal, three to Valladolid, four to Playa del Carmen, and two to Felipe Carrillo Puerto. There are at least 24 **Autotransportes del Caribe** buses daily to Mérida, Valladolid, and Chichén-Itzá; five buses to Villahermosa; three to Coatzacoalcos; seven to Mexico City; and six to Playa del Carmen, Chetumal, and stops in between. **Primera Clase** (tel. 84-1378) offers buses to Tizimin, Chichén-Itzá, Valladolid, Playa del Carmen, Tulum, and Chetumal. Despite its name it isn't a deluxe line. **Caribe Express** (tel. 87-4174) offers deluxe service to Mérida ($3^1/_2$ hours), Campeche (7 hours), and Chetumal (5 hours). Caribe Express buses are air-conditioned, and have restrooms, refreshments, and video movies. Buy tickets at least a day in advance from the air-conditioned office at the station. **ADO** (tel. 84-1378) buses go to Mérida and Valladolid almost twice hourly until 11:30pm. **Oriente Premier** (tel. 84-1378) has deluxe service to Mérida, with the first at 6am and the last at midnight. **Expreso de Oriente** (tel. 84-5542), on Tulum around the corner from the bus station, has 11 deluxe departures to Mérida, the first at 7am and the last at 2:45am. Passengers are picked up in front of their ticket office/waiting room.

If you have a long wait at the station, escape across the street to the Hotel Plaza Caribe for air conditioning, sandwiches, and soft drinks.

BY FERRY For ferry service to Cozumel or to Isla Mujeres, see Chapter 4.

TOURIST INFORMATION

The **State Tourism Office** (tel. 98/84-8073) is centrally located downtown on the east side of Avenida Tulum between the Ayuntamiento Benito Juárez building and Comermex Bank, both of which are between Avenidas Cobá and Uxmal. The office is open Monday through Sunday from 9am to 9pm. The addresses and rates of hotels are listed here, as well as ferry schedules.

Many people (the friendliest in town) offer information in exchange for listening to a spiel about the wonders of a Cancún time-sharing or condo purchase. Expect to spend no less than half a day of your vacation if you get suckered in by these sales professionals and don't expect to receive the promised gift for listening.

Pick up a free copy of the monthly publication *Cancún Tips* and a tabloid-size publication, *Cancún Scene*. Both are useful and have fine maps. The publication is owned by the same people who own the Captain's Cove restaurants, a couple of sightseeing boats, and time-share hotels, so the information, while good, is not completely unbiased. Don't be surprised if during your stay, one of their army of employees touts the joys of time-sharing.

CITY LAYOUT

There are two Cancúns: **Cancún City,** on the mainland, has restaurants, shops, and less expensive hotels, as well as all the other establishments that make life function—pharmacies, dentists, automotive shops, banks, travel and airline agencies, and car-rental firms, all within an area about nine blocks square.

The city's main thoroughfare is **Avenida Tulum.** Heading south, Avenida Tulum becomes the highway to the airport and the ruins of Tulum and Chetumal, as well as the turnoff (right) to connect to the toll road to Chichén-Itzá and Mérida. Heading north, it joins the Mérida–Puerto Juárez highway that goes past the Isla Mujeres ferries and on into the Yucatán peninsula to Mérida.

The famed **Zona Hotelera,** or **Zona Turística,** stretches out along **Isla Cancún** (Cancún Island), a sandy strip 14 miles long, shaped like a "7." It's now joined by bridges to the mainland at the north and south ends. **Avenida Cobá** from Cancún City becomes **Paseo Kukulkán,** the island's only main traffic artery. Cancún's international airport is just inland from the base of the "7."

FINDING AN ADDRESS The street-numbering system remains from Cancún's beginning days of city lots. Addresses are still given by the number of the building lot and by the *manzana* (block) or *super-manzana* (group of city blocks). Some streets have signs with names, although the establishments along the street may refer to the street only by its number, as Retorno 3. In short, it is very difficult to find a place in Cancún City just by the numbers. The city is still relatively small and the downtown section can easily be covered on foot. On the island, addresses are given by kilometer number on Kukulkán or by reference to some other well-known location.

2. GETTING AROUND

BY BUS   In town, almost everything is within walking distance. Frequent **Ruta 1** or **2** (marked *Hoteles*) city buses operate from the mainland to the beaches along the Avenida Tulum, the main street, all the way to Punta Nizuc at the far end of the Zona Turística on Cancún Island. **Ruta 8** buses, go to Puerto Juárez/Punta Sam for ferries to Isla Mujeres. Get them in front of the tourism office on Avenida Tulum. Both these city buses operate *only between 8am and 10pm daily*. Buses cost about 85¢ per ride.

BY TAXI   Settle on a price in advance. The trip from Cancún City to the Hotel Camino Real, for example, should cost $6.50; from Cancún City to the airport, fare should be $10 to $12. In Cancún proper, most runs are about $3 to $5.

BY MOPED   Although the racetracklike traffic on Kukulkán has slowed with the imposition of speed zones, mopeds are still a dangerous way to cruise around. Downtown Cancún, like the island thoroughfare, is very congested. If a moped is your choice, however, rentals start at $25 for a day. A credit-card voucher is required as security for the moped. You should receive a crash helmet (it's the law) and instructions on how to lock the wheels when you park, as well as how to maneuver the moped on the road. Do read the fine print on the back of the rental agreement that states your liability for repair or replacement of the moped in case of accident, theft, or vandalism. There's generally no personal accident insurance, so you rent at considerable risk.

BY RENTAL CAR   There's really no need for a car to get around Cancún, since bus service is good, taxis on the mainland are relatively inexpensive, and most things in Cancún City are within walking distance. But if you do rent, the cheapest way is to arrange for the rental before you leave your home country. Otherwise, if you rent on the spot after arrival, the daily cost of a rental VW Beetle will be around $65. If you're arriving by air, you'll save considerably on taxi fare by picking up and dropping off the car at the airport. *Important note:* Speed zones have finally been established and posted on Paseo Kukulkán in the hotel zone, slowing cars to around 60 kilometers (40 miles) per hour in most of the zone. New traffic lights have also been installed to further control traffic on the island, and in town raised cement pedestrian walkways across Tulum Avenue make motorists slow down while people cross. Police ticket speeders frequently, so be careful. For seeing the rest of the Yucatán, or taking a couple of days down the coast toward Tulum, I recommend renting a car, since public transportation is sparse. (See Section 8, "Getting Around," in Chapter 2.)

 CANCÚN

American Express   The local office is located at Avenidas Tulum 208 and Agua (tel. 84-1999, 84-4243, or 87-0831). Hours Monday through Friday are 9am to 2pm and 4 to 6pm, and Saturday from 9am to 1pm.

Area Code   The telephone area code is 98.

Babysitters   Ask at your hotel.

Bookstores   See "Newspapers and Magazines," below.

Car Rentals   See "Getting Around," earlier in this chapter.

Climate   It's hot. The rainy season is May through October. August through October is the hurricane season, which brings erratic weather. October, but especially November, can be cloudy, windy, somewhat rainy, and even cool, so a cotton sweater is handy as is rain protection.

Consulates   The U.S. consular agent is in the Maruelos Building at Av. Nader 40 (tel. 98/84-2411). The agent is available Monday through Friday from 9am to 2pm and 3 to 5pm; the office is open Monday through Friday from 9am to 2pm and 3 to 6pm. In an emergency, call the U.S. Consulate in Mérida (tel. 99/47-2285).

Crime   Car break-ins are just about the only crime to speak of, but they happen frequently, especially around the shopping centers in the Zona Hotelera. VW Beetles and Golfs are frequent targets. Don't leave valuables in plain sight.

Currency   See Section 1, "Information, Entry Requirements & Money," in Chapter 2.

Currency Exchange   Most banks are downtown along the Avenida Tulum, and are usually open Monday through Friday from 9:30am to 1:30pm. There are also a few *casas de cambio* (exchange houses), and downtown merchants are eager to change cash dollars. Island stores don't offer good exchange rates. Avoid changing money at the airport as you arrive, especially the first place you see, where the rates are worse than any you'll be quoted in town and even more unfavorable than those at other facilities farther inside the airport concourse.

Decompression Chamber   The area's only decompression chamber is in the Total Assist Hospital. (See "Emergencies," below.)

Doctors   Ask at your hotel or call one of the hospitals listed under "Emergencies," below.

Drugstores   Next to the Hotel Caribe Internacional, the Pharmacy Escanto, Av. Yaxchilán 36 at Sunyaxchen (tel. 84-4083 or 84-9330) is open 24 hours.

Emergencies   For first aid, **Cruz Roja** (the Red Cross; tel. 84-1616) is open 24 hours and is located on Avenida Yaxchilán between Avenidas Xcaret and Labná, next to the Telemex building. **Total Assist,** a small nine-room emergency hospital with English-speaking doctors, at Claveles 5, SM22 at Tulum, is open 24 hours (tel. 84-1058 or 84-1092). The desk staff may have limited English. **Clínica Quirurgica del Caribe,** at SM63, Mz Q, Calle 3 inte. no. 36, is open 24 hours (tel. 84-2516). *Urgencias* means "Emergencies."

Holidays   See Section 2, "When to Go," in Chapter 2. Because holidays are generally when North American visitors come to Cancún, many hotels and restaurants will prepare turkey and dressing on Thanksgiving and Christmas, play familiar holiday music, and plan other traditions to make the visitor feel at home.

Hospitals   See "Emergencies," above.

Laundry and Dry Cleaning   At Tulum and Crisantemas, Ela Lavandería has self-service washers and driers, or they'll do your laundry for you. It's open Monday through Saturday from 9am to 7pm. Ask about dry cleaning at your hotel.

Lost Property   File a written report with the police (tel. 84-1913). See also "Scams," in Chapter 2.

Luggage Storage and Lockers   Hotels will generally tag and store excess luggage while you travel elsewhere.

Newspapers and Magazines   For English-language newspapers and books, go to Fama on Avenida Tulum between Tulipanes and Claveles (tel. 84-6586), open daily from 8am to 10pm. (Avoid filling out a contest flier here, which results in a call from time-share promoters.)

Photographic Needs For batteries and film, try Omega on Avenida Tulum at Tulipanes (tel. 84-3860).

Police To reach the police (*seguridad pública*) dial 84-1913 or 84-2342.

Post Office The main post office (tel. 84-1418) is at the intersection of Avenidas Sunyaxchen and Xel-Ha. It's open Monday through Friday from 8am to 7pm and Saturday from 9am to 1pm.

Radio and TV The 24-hour Radio Turquesa (dial 105.1) has broadcasts in English, Spanish, and French, and personal messages in English (tel. 87-0498 or 87-0499).

Religious Services Check the local phone book.

Restrooms There are few public restrooms. Use those in restaurants, hotels, and other public establishments.

Safety There is very little crime in Cancún. People in general are safe late at night in touristed areas; just use ordinary common sense. As in any other coastal resort, don't take money or valuables to the beach. See "Crime," above.

Swimming on the Caribbean side presents real dangers from undertow. See "Sports & Recreation," below in this chapter for information on flag warnings.

The island's decompression chamber is at the Total Assist Hospital (see "Decompression Chamber," above).

Seasons Technically, high season is December 15 through Easter, and during this period, accommodation prices are higher. During the low season, May through November, prices are reduced 30% to 60%. Some hotels are starting to charge high-season rates between July and September to take advantage of school-holiday and European visitors.

Shoe Repairs In Spanish it's *reparación del calzado*. Try El Cosario, in the market, stall 28, SM28, where Avenidas Tankah and Xpuhil converge.

Taxes See "Fast Facts: Mexico," in Chapter 2.

Taxis See Section 2, "Getting Around," earlier in this chapter.

Telephones The area code for Cancún that once was 988 is now 98. All local numbers now have six digits instead of five; all numbers begin with 8. If a number is written 988/4-1234, when in Cancún you must dial 84-1234.

Useful Telephone Numbers Contact the police at 84-1913; call for tourist information at 84-8073.

3. ACCOMMODATIONS

Now that there are so many hotels competing for the market in Cancún, hoteliers have not raised prices as dramatically as in the past—a definite boon for vacationers. Cancún City has many good hotels that are moderately priced or in the budget range. During off-season (from April to November), prices go down and it doesn't hurt to bargain for a further price reduction. Hotels also often have discounted prices from February up to Easter week.

The hotel listings in this chapter begin on Cancún Island, the most expensive place to stay, and finish in Cancún City, where bargain lodgings abound.

CANCÚN ISLAND

VERY EXPENSIVE

CAMINO REAL CANCÚN, Paseo Kukulkán, Punta Cancún (Apdo. Postal 14), Cancún, Q. Roo 77500. Tel. 98/83-0100, or toll free 800/722-6466 in the U.S. Fax 98/83-1730. 381 rms and suitoo. A/C MINIBAR TV TEL

$ Rates: High season $220–$1,095 single or double. Low season $170–$770 single or double. Package deals provide the best value. **Parking:** Daily fee for guarded parking adjacent to hotel.

On four acres, right at the tip of Punta Cancún, and designed by Mexican architect Ricardo Legorreta, the Camino Real is among the island's most appealing places to stay. It has a choice location, a lavish country club–style layout, and dramatic architecture that inspired many other buildings in Cancún. The Camino Real is also a member of Leading Hotels of the World.

The rooms are elegantly outfitted with pink breccia-marble floors, tropical high-backed raffia easy chairs, and drapes and spreads in light, soft pastel colors. Some rooms in the new 18-story, 87-room Camino Real Club make truly elegant use of Mexican touches, such as lacquered armoires and chests from Olinalá, Guerrero; couches festooned in purple, pink, and yellow pillows; or a color theme based on deep purple and turquoise. Standard rooms in this section are much like hotel rooms in the rest of the resort. Master suites, with expansive views, have swivel TVs, large dining tables with four chairs, and hot tubs on the balconies. Camino Real Club guests receive a complimentary continental breakfast daily in the Beach Club lobby, as well as complimentary cocktails and snacks there each evening. Lower priced rooms have lagoon views.

Dining/Entertainment: La Brisa, under a giant palapa by the beach, serves all three meals and specializes in seafood; it features a large salad bar. Open 24 hours, Azulejos offers an international menu that emphasizes open-flame grilled meat and a Mexican fiesta on Saturday nights. Children can look forward to their own menus in both La Brisa and Azulejos. The Snack Shack by the pool is open during pool hours. The lobby bar features Mexican music nightly from 5:30 to 7:30pm, and later, the oceanview Azucar Disco swings into action Monday through Saturday at 9:30pm.

Services: Laundry and room service, travel agency, car rental, in-room safety boxes, babysitting (with advance notice).

Facilities: A beautiful freshwater pool and a private saltwater lagoon with sea turtles and tropical fish grace the grounds. There's also a private beach, a sailing pier, and a water-sports center (with sailboard and boat rentals, among other offerings). Three lighted tennis courts, beach volleyball, boutiques, and barber and beauty shops complete the facilities.

CANCÚN SHERATON RESORT, Paseo Kukulkán km 13.5, Cancún, Q. Roo 77500. Tel. 98/83-1988, or toll free 800/325-3535 in the U.S. Fax 98/85-0974. 748 rms and suites. A/C MINIBAR TV TEL

$ Rates: High season $210–$300 single or double. Low season $160–$300 single or double. **Parking:** Free.

These three lavish, pyramid-style buildings on their own vast stretch of beach impress you first with a lobby awash in large expanses of green tiles and a dramatic stainless-steel sculpture of birds in flight. Emerald lawns extend in every direction from the main buildings, hammocks hang in a shady palm grove, and a small reconstructed Maya ruin crowns a craggy limestone hillock.

FROMMER'S SMART TRAVELER: HOTELS

1. The budget hotels are in Cancún City. If you walk into one of them off a Cancún City street you may be quoted one price for a room. However, if you call or write from the U.S. or Canada, the quoted rate for the same room may be considerably higher because they think that if you are writing or calling for reservations, they've got your business—so they might as well jack up the price. Beware.
2. If you call for a reservation, say you are calling from a nearby city in Mexico (they usually ask) or right in town. More than likely you'll get a fair quote.
3. During the low season (except Thanksgiving) there are plenty of budget and moderately priced rooms, so just arrive and see what's available.
4. Because of a February lull in visitors, hotels lower prices that month, making a mini-low season. On the other hand because of European and Mexican vacationers, some hoteliers make July and August a mini-high season by raising prices.
5. On Cancún Island, never pay the "rack rate," the hotel's published rate to the general public. Package rates through hotels, airlines, and tour companies can cut the cost considerably. Even during high season there may be promotional specials.
6. To save money on a package, select the least expensive hotel, then spend time at the restaurants and beaches of those on the higher end of the package scale.
7. Consider travel time to and from Cancún before purchasing a two- or three-day package (you could spend half your time traveling).
8. Cancún has become a mecca for high school and college students during Easter week and the week before and after it. Hotels often cater to them with plenty of high-decibel music by the pool and on the beach.

Rooms and suites are luxurious, with views of the Caribbean (to the east) or of the lagoon (to the west). Guest units are supplied with purified tap water and smoke detectors. In the V-shaped tower section, all units have in-room security boxes, and guests enjoy the services of a personal butler who attends to a variety of tasks from shoe shines to snack service. There's a no-smoking floor, and rooms are available for disabled guests.

Dining/Entertainment: The airy Yan Kin Grill, open from noon to 11pm daily, is perched above the beach. La Duna is the venue for a variety of special feasts, including a daily breakfast buffet from 6:30am until noon and a lavish Sunday brunch. In the Towers you'll find Cardinale, open from 6 to 11pm and offering homemade Italian pastas; and La Fonda, open daily from 7am to 5pm, for a Mexican meal. There are five more bars on the premises. The lobby bar offers live music from noon to midnight.

Services: Laundry and room service, travel agency, car rental, massage, and babysitting.

Facilities: Three swimming pools, six lighted tennis courts with tennis pro on duty, beach, fitness center with sauna, steam bath and whirlpool, mini-golf, aerobics, swimnastics, arts and crafts, Spanish classes, children's playground, basketball court, table games, pharmacy, beauty and barber shop, business center, flower shop, and boutiques.

CONTINENTAL VILLAS PLAZA, Paseo Kukulkán km 11, Cancún, Q. Roo 77500. Tel. 98/83-1022, or toll free 800/882-6684 in the U.S. Fax 98/85-1403. 638 rms. A/C MINIBAR TV TEL

$ Rates: High season $250–$320 single or double. Low season $145–$190 single or double. **Parking:** Free.

From a distance, this hotel appears to be a large complex of pink Spanish colonial villas, which indeed it is. It goes on for blocks along the Paseo Kukulkán, so it may be no surprise to learn that there are hundreds of guest rooms here: 261 in the villas, and 377 in the "Towers." It makes you think you've landed in a brand-new Spanish-colonial country club; the grounds are that well kept. Rooms are decorated with a tropical inspiration, with the appropriate bamboo furniture and tranquil colors. Each room has a separate living area, and either a balcony or terrace. In-room safety boxes and purified tap water are pluses.

Dining/Entertainment: The hotel's restaurants include Le Buffet with international food, open from 6pm to midnight daily; Rancho Grande, off the main lobby, open from 6 to 11pm for Mexican food; La Palapa, open for breakfast only from 7 to 11am; Paradise Cove by the beach, open from 11am to 5pm; and Las Conchas, open from 7am to 5pm, serving a breakfast buffet and light lunches beside the main pool. Las Cupulas, in the villas section, serves Italian cuisine nightly from 7 to 11pm. The lobby bar with live entertainment (and a happy hour each afternoon) is a popular place in the evenings.

Services: Room and laundry service, travel agency, massage, car rental, and babysitting.

Facilities: Three pools, two tennis courts, two racquetball/squash courts, beach, marina, pharmacy, boutiques, liquor store, and beauty and barber shop.

FIESTA AMERICANA CANCÚN, Paseo Kukulkán km 7.5, Cancún, Q. Roo 77500. Tel. 98/83-1400, or toll free 800/223-2332 in the U.S. Fax 98/83-2502. 281 rms. A/C MINIBAR TV TEL

$ Rates: High season $265–$270 single or double. Low season $170–$185 single or double. **Parking:** Free.

Resembling a charming jumble of an old-world city street with colorful stucco walls and randomly placed balconies and windows, the Fiesta Americana Cancún echoes the charm of another time and place. Smaller than most island hotels, it was built originally with honeymooners in mind and so it's Cancún's most intimate hotel. Quiet and relaxing, on a nice beach and calm bay, rooms are beautifully furnished and all have balconies facing the ocean. Units also offer purified tap water, remote-control TVs, and hairdryers. Some have in-room safety-deposit boxes. The location is ideal: right across the street from shopping malls and many restaurants and near the Convention Center.

Dining/Entertainment: For formal dinners, try the Condesa del Mar, with pastel colors, lace tablecloths, a silver candelabra, and international cuisine; it's open evenings from 6 to 11pm. The Chula Vista, open 7 to 10:30am and 7 to 11pm, is the place for a buffet breakfast and dinner. At poolside, the Palapa Chac-Mool provides light meals and fast food. Loco Coco is the pool's swim-up bar. The lobby bar is open most of the day, with piano entertainment in the evenings between 8 and 11 pm. Finally, Caliente Sports/TV Betting Bar fronts the property and is open to the street and boasts numerous big-screen TVs bringing in the lastest sporting events. It's open from 9am to 2am daily.

Services: Laundry and room service, travel agency, and wedding arrangements.

Facilities: One swimming pool, water-sports rental on the beach, boutiques, wheelchairs.

FIESTA AMERICANA CORAL BEACH, Paseo Kukulkán km 9.5, Cancún, Q. Roo 77500. Tel. 98/83-2900, or toll free 800/223-2332 in the U.S. Fax 98/83-3173. 602 suites. A/C MINIBAR TV TEL

$ Rates: High season $340 single or double. Low season $265 single or double.

Call it awesome, spectacular, beautiful, overwhelmingly sophisticated. It's enormous in a Mexican way and grandly European in its lavish public halls and lobby. This hotel, which opened in 1991, is positively majestic. There's elegant dark green granite from France, deep red granite from South Africa, black and green marble from Guatemala, beige marble from Mexico, a canopy of stained glass from Guadalajara, lavish ironwork fashioned by Mexican artisans, furniture from the Yucatán, and hardwood floors from Texas. The elegant choices are, of course, carried into the guest rooms, which are decorated with more marble, area rugs, and tasteful use of Mexican decorative arts. All rooms have balconies facing the ocean, plus remote-control TVs and hairdryers. Master suites have double vanities, dressing room, bathrobes, whirlpool baths, and large terraces. Two concierge floors feature daily continental breakfast and evening cocktails, and a 24-hour reception-cashier. Two junior suites are equipped for handicapped guests.

The hotel's location is a good one, on Punta Cancún, opposite the Convention Center, and within walking distance of shopping centers and restaurants.

Dining/Entertainment: Coral Reef is an elegant gourmet restaurant offering seafood, with an ocean and pool view; it's open daily from 6pm to midnight. La Joya, an elegant Mexican restaurant, serves lunch and dinner. Viña del Mar is a café-style restaurant with international food and an ocean view. Open 7am to noon and 5:30 to 11:30pm, it features many specialty meals and a daily breakfast buffet. Both the Sunset Snack Bar and Contoy Island serve the pool and beach from 11am to 5pm. Five bars should suit just about everyone—especially the elegant lobby bar, where you'll enjoy soft live music in the evenings. It's open from 4pm to midnight.

Services: Laundry and room service, travel agency, car rental, and massage.

Facilities: A 660-foot-long free-form swimming pool; swim-up bar; 1,000 feet of beach; three indoor tennis courts with stadium seating; gymnasium with weights, sauna, and massage; water-sport rentals on the beach; business center; tennis pro shop; fashion and spa boutiques; and beauty and barber shops.

HOTEL MELIA CANCÚN, Paseo Kukulkán km 14, Cancún, Q. Roo 77500. Tel. 98/85-1114, or toll free 800/336-3542 in the U.S., 91-800/2-1779 in Mexico. Fax 98/85-1263. 450 rms and suites. A/C MINIBAR TV TEL

$ Rates: High season $275 single, $285 double. Low season $185 single, $195 double.

You can't miss seeing this hotel with its expansive and palatial exterior. Inside its eight stories are dripping with vines. The circular interior is a jungle of plants set against a fountain. The marble-and-teakwood backdrop is decorated with majolica pottery from Guanajuato and lacquer chests from Olinalá, Guerrero. The spacious rooms, all with sitting areas and balconies, are appropriately stylish and feature hairdryers, remote-control TVs, in-room security boxes, and purified tap water. There are four rooms specially equipped for handicapped guests on the first floor, all with extra-wide bathrooms.

Dining/Entertainment: Ailem (which is Melia spelled backwards) is a formal and elegant spot, serving French cuisine Tuesday through Sunday from 7 to 11pm. Don Pepe, a casual place, serves from 7am to 11pm and on Sunday there's a brunch from noon to 5pm. Quetzal, open 7am to midnight, offers a morning breakfast buffet and an à la carte menu the rest of the day. Caribe, by the pool, specializes in seafood and is open from 10:30am to 5pm. Drinks and snacks can be had

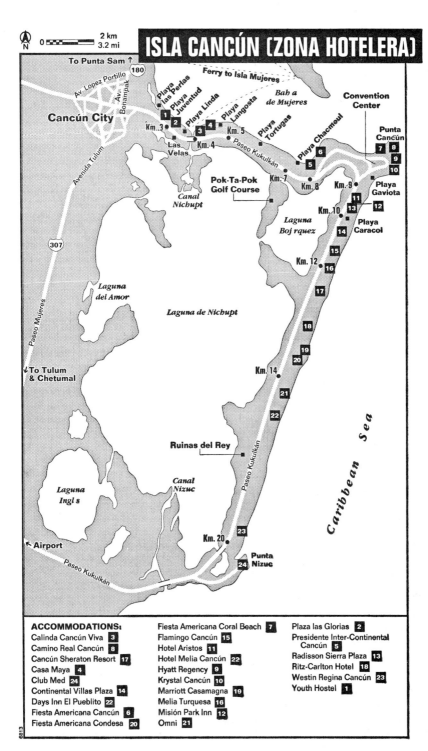

ISLA CANCÚN (ZONA HOTELERA)

0 — 2 km / 3.2 mi

To Punta Sam ↑
180
Av. Lopez Portillo
Ferry to Isla Mujeres
Bahía de Mujeres
Convention Center

Cancún City
Av. Bonampak

Playa las Perlas
Playa Juventud
Playa Linda
Playa Langosta
Playa Tortugas
Playa Chacmool
Punta Cancún

Km. 3
Las Velas
Km. 4
Km. 5
Paseo Kukulkán
Km. 7
Km. 8
Km. 9
Playa Gaviota
Playa Caracol

Avenida Tulum

Canal Nichupt

Pok-Ta-Pok Golf Course

Laguna Bojórquez

Km. 10
Km. 12

307

Laguna del Amor

Laguna de Nichupt

Km. 14

Paseo Mujeres

↓To Tulum & Chetumal

Caribbean Sea

Ruinas del Rey

Canal Nizuc

Paseo Kukulkán

Laguna Inglés

Km. 20

← Airport
Paseo Kukulkán

Punta Nizuc

6813

by the beach at El Patio, from 10am to 7pm daily. Five bars serve all guests all day. The lobby bar, open 10am to midnight, features Latin rhythms from 8pm.

Services: Laundry and room service, travel agency, car rental, and baby cribs and babysitters.

Facilities: Two pools; beach; nine-hole golf course on the property; three lighted tennis courts; Ping-Pong; gymnasium with massage, sauna, whirlpool, facials, aerobics, weights, hydromassage showers, and dressing room; and beauty and barber shop. During high season or times of high hotel occupancy there's a full daily list of activities for children posted in the lobby.

MARRIOTT CASAMAGNA, Paseo Kukulkán km 20, Cancún, Q. Roo 77500. Tel. 98/85-2000, or toll free 800/228-9290 in the U.S. Fax 98/85-1385. 450 rms and suites. A/C MINIBAR TV TEL

$ Rates: High season $260–$316 single or double. Low season $205–$230 single or double.

Enter through a half-circle of Roman columns, then a long dome entry and a wide lavishly marbled 44-foot-high lobby, and you'll know luxury is the hallmark here. The lobby expands in three directions with wide Mexican cantera-stone arches finished off outdoors where columns vanish into shallow pools like Roman baths. All rooms have computer-card entry; most have balconies and contemporary furnishings with tiled floors, ceiling fans (besides air conditioning), and a rose, mauve, and earth-tone color scheme. All suites occupy corners and have enormous terraces, ocean views, and TVs in both the living room and bedroom. Purified tap water, scales, irons and ironing boards, fire detectors, and alarm clocks are other pluses.

Dining/Entertainment: Mikado is an authentic Japanese steakhouse, open for lunch and dinner. La Capilla, outdoors, serves all three meals. The Bahía Club, by the beach, serves fresh seafood and snacks for lunch; La Isla is a poolside bar and grill that's open during pool hours. The lobby bar features nightly mariachi music, while Sixties nightclub features hits from the '50s through the '70s, with space for dancing.

Services: Laundry and room service, travel agency, and car rental.

Facilities: Beach; swimming pool; two lighted tennis courts; health club with saunas, lockers, whirlpool, aerobics, and juice bar; and beauty and barber shop.

RITZ-CARLTON HOTEL, on Retorno del Rey, off Paseo Kukulkán km 13.5, Cancún, Q. Roo 77500. Tel. 98/85-0808, or toll free 800/241-3333 in the U.S. Fax 98/85-1015. 272 rms, 100 suites. A/C MINIBAR TV TEL **Parking:** Free, guarded.

$ Rates: High season $332–$545 standard single or double, $600–$3,000 suite. Low season $285–$445 standard single or double, $445–$3,000 suite.

On 7½ acres, the nine-story Ritz-Carlton in Cancún is easily the island's most elegant hotel in the finest traditional European sense. People who stay here are accustomed to the finest of everything—impeccable gloved service, crystal chandeliers, stained glass, thick molding, elegant marble, luxurious upholstered mahogany furniture, large sprays of fresh flowers, silver and crystal in the dining rooms, and lush carpets throughout in muted reds and blues.

That's just the grandly scaled public areas. The spacious guest rooms are equally sumptuous. Each room has remote-control TVs, safety-deposit boxes, electronic locks, and maid service twice daily. Suites are large, and some have a large dressing area, two TVs, balconies, and one and a half baths. Marble baths throughout have telephones, separate tubs and showers, lighted makeup mirror, weight scales, and hair dryers. Floors 8 and 9 are for Ritz-Carlton Club members, who have special amenities including five mini-meals a day. Prices depend on whether your room is oceanfront, or ocean or garden view. While the hotel will still be expensive no matter what, their packages may offer some cost-saving incentives and are worth exploring.

Dining/Entertainment: On the ground level, The Café, a stylishly casual glass-walled restaurant with evening trio entertainment, is open from 7am to 11pm daily. The Dining Room, with a large expanse of beveled windows, features northern Italian cuisine in total elegance daily from 7pm to midnight. The Grill, a stylish English pub, offers grilled specialities, nightly entertainment, and a dance floor. Considered one of Cancún's finest restaurants, it's open from 7pm to 1am daily. The Caribe Bar and Grill is open for snacks during pool hours. The lobby bar opens at 5pm daily and offers live music between 7:30 and 11pm.

Services: Laundry and dry cleaning, room service, travel agency, concierge.

Facilities: A swiming pool, three tennis courts, fully equipped gym with exercise equipment, massages and lockers, pharmacy/gift shop, boutiques, beauty and barber shops.

EXPENSIVE

HOLIDAY INN CROWNE PLAZA, Paseo Kukulkán, Zona Hotelera, Cancún, Q. Roo 77500. Tel. 98/85-1022, or toll free 800/465-4329 in the U.S. Fax 98/85-0313. 366 rms and suites. A/C MINIBAR TV TEL

$ Rates: High season $207–$402 single or double. Low season $175–$370 single or double. **Parking:** Free.

The circular entry of the Holiday Inn rises from the street level, revealing a dramatic hot-pink sculpture. Inside the architecture is just as futuristic, with soaring buttresses and a glass-covered atrium that requires neck-craning to see completely. Sea breezes sweep through the totally open lobby. Outside, the oceanside pool is filled to the brim and its edge seems to disappear into the sea. The carpeted rooms are furnished in painted pastels and have ocean views and narrow furnished balconies. Rooms come with hairdryers, remote-control TVs, and in-room security boxes. Two floors are no-smoking.

Dining/Entertainment: Bella Vista is open from 7am to midnight. Los Gallos serves Mexican food and Alghero is a Mediterranean eatery. Both are open daily from 6pm to midnight. La Palapa, by the pool, is open from noon to 5pm.

Services: Laundry and room service, travel agency, and massage.

Facilities: Two tennis courts, four swimming pools (one indoor), beach, health club, sauna, whirlpool, beauty shop, and boutiques.

HYATT CANCÚN CARIBE, Paseo Kukulkán km 10.5, Cancún, Q. Roo 77500. Tel. 98/83-0044, or toll free 800/233-1234 in the U.S. Fax 98/83-1514. 198 rms. A/C MINIBAR TV TEL

$ Rates: High season $260 single or double, $335 Regency room. Low season $180 single or double, $230 Regency room. **Parking:** Free.

This sedate Hyatt hotel is south of Punta Cancún. Because of its dramatic crescent shape, all units face the sparkling Caribbean and have terraces on which to enjoy the view. Regency rooms have lighted makeup mirrors, weight scales, hairdryers, robes, and in-room security boxes. Regency guests also receive a complimentary continental breakfast, evening drinks, and crudités—but best of all, they have use of their own pool. Between the hotel and the beach is a pool complex built to resemble a Maya village. A replica of Chaac-Mool gazes out to sea, like any sunbather.

Note that there are two Hyatt hotels in Cancún.

Dining/Entertainment: The Cocay Café serves both a breakfast and lunch buffet daily, dining is accompanied by a Mexican trio in the evenings. La Concha is the poolside snack bar. The Blue Bayou serves Cajun-style food from 6:30 to 11pm daily. Pizza's a restaurant serving just that from 11am to 5pm. There's live music in the Casis Bar nightly starting at 8pm. The Frisco bar by the pool is open from 10am to 5pm daily.

Services: Room and laundry service, travel agency, and car rental.

Facilities: Swimming pool, beach, beauty shop, pharmacy, and boutiques.

KRYSTAL CANCÚN, Paseo Kukulkán km 7.5, Cancún, Q. Roo 77500. Tel. 98/83-1133, or toll free 800/231-9860 in the U.S. Fax 98/83-1790. 316 rms. A/C MINIBAR TV TEL

$ Rates: High season $195–$230 single or double. Low season $150–$190 single or double. **Parking:** Free.

The Krystal Cancún lies on Punta Cancún with the Camino Real and Hyatt Regency, near the Convention Center, many shops, restaurants, and clubs. The Krystal uses lots of luscious, cool marble in its decoration, and displays striking textile "pictures" hanging on the walls of its public spaces. The guest rooms, in two buildings, have luxury appointments, with bamboo furniture, drapes and spreads in earthy tones, two double beds, and water views. The hotel's tap water is purified, and there are ice machines on every floor.

Should you decide to rent one of the presidential suites, you'll get your own private pool. Club Krystal rooms come with hairdryer, makeup mirror, weight scales, in-room safety box and robe, complimentary continental breakfast, and evening canapés and drinks; guests in those rooms also have access to the Club Lounge, a rooftop sun lounge, with a whirlpool and concierge service.

Dining/Entertainment: Bogart's, a chic dining room with a Moroccan "Casablanca" theme, is open daily from 7pm to midnight. The luxurious Hacienda El Mortero, a replica of a colonial hacienda, serves Mexican cuisine nightly from 6pm to midnight. For a casual bite, there's Aquamarina, the hotel coffee shop, open from 7am to 11pm, and the Beach Club down by the beach serves snacks all day. By the pool, the Cascada bar is open from 9am to 5pm, and Rarotonga, which specializes in seafood, is open from 9am to 11pm. In the evening there's live entertainment in the lobby bar from 7pm to 12:30am. Christine's, one of the most popular discos in town, is open nightly from 10pm to 4am. The hotel also features theme nights throughout the week.

Services: Laundry, room service, travel agency, and car and moped rental.

Facilities: A long swimming pool complex comes complete with waterfall and seven Ionic columns, all overlooking the Caribbean and a beach of limestone boulders and creamy sand (where there's fairly safe swimming). The pool complex has a built-in optical illusion: The waterfall cascades toward the sea, and from certain positions it appears that the pool and the ocean are joined. Other facilities include a pharmacy; a barber and beauty shop; boutiques and a silver shop; two tennis courts with an on-duty tennis pro; a racquetball court; a dive shop; and a fitness club with whirlpool, sauna, and massage facilities.

RADISSON SIERRA PLAZA, Paseo Kukulkán, Cancún, Q. Roo 77500. Tel. 98/83-2444 or 83-3655, or toll free 800/333-3333 in the U.S. and Canada. Fax 98/83-3486. 260 rms. A/C MINIBAR TV TEL

$ Rates: High season $160–$245 single or double. Low season $110–$190 single or double. **Parking:** Free.

There's a luxurious South Seas feel here with lots of potted palms dotting the interior, along with rattan furniture, brass, hot-pink and purple area rugs, and wood louvered doors in the guest rooms. The hotel has its own marina and lagoon in front, along with both lagoonview and oceanview pools.

Each standard room has a balcony, sitting area, combination bathtub/shower, hairdryer, and ceiling fan. Master suites have standard amenities and lots of extras like Berber carpets, large living/dining areas, and kitchens with their own private entries (for all those catered parties you'll no doubt be throwing). In the junior suites, the living and sleeping areas are divided by handsome dresser/TV consoles, and there are separate bathtubs and showers. The lowest-priced rooms have lagoon views; more expensive ones are either oceanfront or oceanview. The hotel's tap water is purified, and there are ice machines on each floor.

Dining/Entertainment: Aquarellas is open from 7am to 11pm daily. El Sol, the snack bar by the pool, is open during pool hours. The lobby bar has trio music nightly from 7 to 10pm. La Luna serves snacks from 10am to 5pm daily.

Services: Room and laundry service, travel agency, and car rental.

Facilities: Swimming pools, two lighted tennis courts, health club, beach, marina, and water-sports rental.

WESTIN REGINA CANCÚN, Paseo Kukulkán km 20, Cancún, Q. Roo 77500. Tel. 98/85-0086, or toll free 800/228-3000 in the U.S. Fax 98/85-0074. 385 rms. A/C MINIBAR TV TEL

$ Rates: High season $202–$230 single or double. Low season $165–$190 single or double. **Parking:** Free, adjacent.

The strikingly austere but grand and beautiful architecture, immediately impressive with its elegant use of stone and marble, is the stamp of architect Ricardo Legorreta. It's divided into two sections, the main hotel and the more exclusive six-story hot-pink tower section. Standard rooms are unusually large and beautifully furnished in cool, contemporary furniture. Those on the sixth floor have balconies and first-floor rooms have terraces. Rooms in the six-story tower section rooms all have ocean or lagoon views, oodles of marble, furniture with Olinalá lacquer accents, cool bedspreads with a Mediterranean flair along with Berber carpet area rugs, oak tables and chairs, and marble terraces with lounge chairs. Rooms feature electronic locks, safety boxes, and sprinkler/smoke alarm systems and ceiling fans in addition to air conditioning.

Dining/Entertainment: Arecife, a three-tiered restaurant, is open 6:30 to 11:30pm. El Palmar is the popularly priced restaurant, open daily from 7am to 11pm. The Sunrise Bar and Grill by the beach and pool is open from 10am to 5pm. The smaller Sunset Bar is open the same hours and offers light snacks. The lobby lounge is open for light snacks and drinks between 4pm and midnight.

Services: Laundry and room service, babysitting, concierge, travel agency, car rental, boutiques, pharmacy/gifts, beauty and barber shop, purified tap water, and ice machine on each floor.

Facilities: Five swimming pools; four whirlpools; beach; two lighted tennis courts; gymnasium with Stairmaster, bicycle, weights, aerobics, sauna, steam massage, and steam room.

MODERATE

CALINDA CANCÚN VIVA, Paseo Kukulkán km 8.5, Cancún, Q. Roo 77500. Tel. 98/83-0800, or toll free 800/228-5151 in the U.S. Fax 98/83-2087. 210 rms. A/C TV TEL

$ Rates: $143–$500 single or double. **Parking:** Free.

It has a blockhouse look from the street side, but on the ocean side of the Calinda Cancún Viva you'll find a small but pretty patio garden and a beach that is safe for swimming. You have a choice of rooms with either lagoon or ocean view (the latter are on the high end of the price scale). At least 162 rooms have refrigerators and 64 have kitchenettes.

Dining/Entertainment: The main restaurant, La Fuente, serves all three meals. La Palapa and La Parilla are both beside the pool for drinks and light meals; Bar La Terraza is in the lobby.

Services: Laundry and room service, travel agency.

Facilities: Swimming pool for adults and one for children, one lighted tennis court, water-sports equipment rental, marina, pharmacy, and gift shop.

CLUB MED, Punta Nizuc, Paseo Kukulkán km 22, Cancún, Q. Roo 77500. Tel. 98/85-2409, or toll free 800/258-2633 in the U.S. and Canada. Fax 98/85-2290. 410 rms. A/C

$ Rates: (including all meals and activities): High season $184 per person double per day, $1,100 per person double per week. Low season $143 per person double per day. $825 per person double per week. Single occupancy available at an extra charge. Land-and-air packages available from selected cities and zones. Children 12 and over are welcome.

Club Meds are the standard setters among all-inclusive resorts and this one is no exception. Set on a secluded, exquisitely manicured peninsula, it's more like a country club than a hotel resort. Activities, all of which are included in the price, as are the meals, are spread out all over the grounds so that there's no feeling of bumping into crowds. There are more room varieties here than at most other Club Meds. Rooms are in two- and three-story buildings (no elevator); all have two full beds that can be moved. Some units have views of the gardens and others of the ocean. The clientele includes a mixture of people from the U.S. and Canada, and many guests from France and other countries where there is a big interest in the Yucatán. Staff members speak languages from around the world. Club Med lies at the far end of Paseo Kukulkán, nearer the airport than town.

Dining/Entertainment: The main dining room serves family-style buffet meals. La Palapa is an open-air seafood bistro by the water's edge for lunch and dinner, and El Rancho is a steakhouse on the beach, which converts to a disco in the evenings. Every evening the staff performs anything from comedy or magic routines in the bar to a full-scale song-and-dance show in the auditorium.

Services: Travel agency.

Facilities: Sports include waterskiing from a special beach, windsurfing, snorkeling in a protected reserve at the village, eight composition tennis courts with four lit for night play, fitness center, aerobics/calisthenics, volleyball and basketball, Ping-Pong and bocce ball, and sailing. There's an extra charge for scuba diving and excursions to Isla Mujeres, horseback riding, and deep-sea fishing. There's also a pharmacy and boutiques.

FLAMINGO CANCÚN, Paseo Kukulkán km 11.5, Cancún, Q. Roo 77500. Tel 98/83-1544. Fax 98/83-1029. 162 rms. A/C MINIBAR TV TEL

$ Rates: High season $167 single or double. Low season $105 single or double. **Parking:** Free; unguarded across the street in the Plaza Flamingo.

The Flamingo seems to have been inspired by the dramatic slope-sided architecture of the Camino Real. But the Flamingo is considerably smaller, with guest rooms forming a quadrangle or courtyard in which you'll find the swimming pool. It's in the heart of the island hotels, opposite the Flamingo Shopping Center and close to other hotels, shopping centers, and restaurants.

Dining/Entertainment: La Joya Restaurant and Don Francisco Restaurant are both open daily from 7am to 11pm. El Coral is the lobby bar.

Services: Laundry and room service, travel agency, and car rental.

Facilities: Swimming pool and beach.

MISIÓN PARK INN, Paseo Kukulkán km 9.5, Cancún, Q. Roo 77500. Tel. 98/83-1755, or toll free 800/448-8355 in the U.S. Fax 98/83-1136. 189 rms. A/C MINIBAR TV TEL

$ Rates: High season $175–$190 single or double. Low season $115–$150 single or double.

With the inn's ingenious design, each room has views of both the lagoon and ocean. Public spaces throughout the hotel have lots of dark wood, cream-beige stucco, red tile, and pastel accents. A big swimming pool is next to the beach. Rooms are smallish but comfortable, with bamboo furniture offset by pastel-colored cushions and bedspreads; bathrooms have polished limestone vanities.

Dining/Entertainment: Khan-Nab is the Mexican speciality restaurant open from 7am to 11pm. There's live music nightly in the lobby bar and the bar by the pool serves guests during pool hours. Batacha also has live music for dancing from 9pm to 4am Tuesday through Sunday.

Services: Laundry and room service, travel agency, and car rental.

Facilities: Pool, beach, pharmacy, and gift shop.

PRESIDENTE INTER-CONTINENTAL CANCÚN, Paseo Kukulkán km 7, Cancún, Q. Roo 77500. Tel. 98/83-0200, or toll free 800/327-0200 in the U.S. Fax 98/83-0200. 292 rms. A/C MINIBAR TV TEL

$ Rates: High season $120–$285 single or double. Low season $120–$184 single or double. **Parking:** Free.

Elegant and spacious without being spread out, the Presidente sports a modern design using lavish expanses of marble and wicker accents. Rooms, with king-size beds and private balconies, have tastefully simple unfinished pine furniture, in-room safes, and remote-control TVs. Sixteen rooms on the first floor have patios with outdoor whirlpool tubs. There are two Club Floors: The President Club Floor has 14 junior suites and one presidential suite. The Caribbean Club Floor has 35 deluxe rooms without balconies but with full-length mirrors, weight scale, and hairdryers. Both offer robes, magnified makeup mirrors, complimentary continental breakfast, evening drinks and canapés, and use of a private key-activated elevator. Two rooms are available for the handicapped and two floors are reserved for nonsmokers.

Coming from Cancún City, you'll reach the Presidente on the left before you get to Punta Cancún—it's behind the golf course and next to million-dollar homes.

Dining/Entertainment: Open for dinner only, the Mediterráneo offers fine dining, spotlighting dishes from France, Greece, Italy, Spain, and Morocco. El Caribeño is a large breezy palapa, three-level restaurant by the beach and pool, serving all meals. Waiters will leave a pot of coffee on the table at breakfast.

Services: Room and laundry service, travel agency, car rental, and irons supplied on request.

Facilities: Two landscaped swimming pools with a waterfall, whirlpools, fitness center, a private and safe beach, lighted tennis courts, water-sports equipment rental, and marina.

BUDGET

DAYS INN EL PUEBLITO, Paseo Kukulkán km 17.5, Cancún, Q. Roo 77500. Tel. 98/85-0422, or toll free 800/325-2525 in the U.S. Fax 98/85-0422.

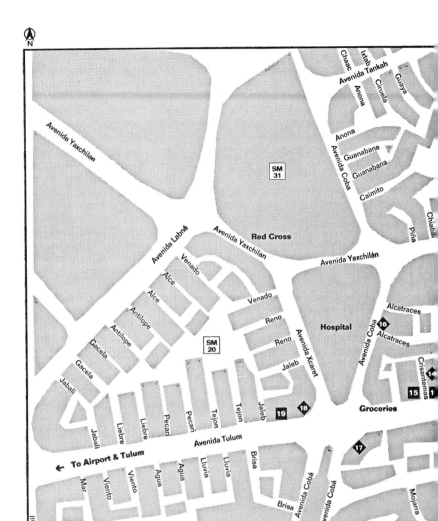

N

Avenida Tankah
Chaac
Ixtab
Ciruela
Guaya
Anona

Avenida Yaxchilan

Anona
Avenida Cobá
Guanabana
Guanabana
Caimito

SM 31

Chiaba
Piña

Avenida Labná
Red Cross
Avenida Yaxchilan

Avenida Yaxchilán

Venado
Alce
Alce
Antilope
Antilope
Gacela
Gacela
Jabali

Venado
Reno
Reno
Jaleb

Avenida Xcaret

Hospital

Alcatraces
Avenida Cobá
16
Alcatraces

Crisantemas

SM 20

15
1

Jabali
Liebre
Liebre
Pecari
Pecari
Tejon
Tejon
Jaleb
Jaleb

19
18

Groceries

Avenida Tulum

← To Airport & Tulum

Brisa
Lluvia
Lluvia
Agua
Agua
Viento
Viento
Mar

17

Avenida Cobá

Brisa

Mojarra

SM 4

Nube

Avenida Cobá

Avenida Sayil

Mar
Fuego
23

Fuego
Tierra
Tierra
Cielo
Cielo
Nube

22

To Hotel Zone →

Sierra
Sierra

20
21

Robalo
Juriel
Robalo

Avenida Bonampak

6814

MEXICO CITY
Cancun ★

ACCOMMODATIONS:

Hotel Antillano **13**
Hotel Cancún Handall **19**
Hotel Cotty **7**
Hotel Hacienda Cancún **2**
Hotel Parador **8**
Hotel Plaza Carrillo's **12**
Hotel Plaza del Sol **4**

Hotel Rivemar **15**
Hotel Tankah **1**
Posada Lucy **5**

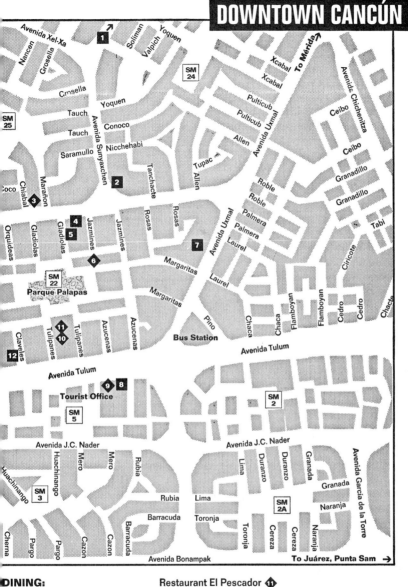

DOWNTOWN CANCÚN

DINING:

Ciao Pastelería **21**
La Dolce Vita **20**
Gory Tacos **10**
La Fondue **22**
La Habichuela **6**
Périco's **3**
Pizza Rolandi **17**

Restaurant El Pescador **11**
Restaurant Los Almendros **23**
Restaurant Pop **9**
Restaurant Rosa
  Mexicano **14**
Super Deli **18**
El Tacolote **16**

239 rms (all with bath). A/C TV TEL

$ Rates: High season $95–$115. Low season $109–$115.

This is one hotel where the low-season rates are strangely higher than high-season rates. Dwarfed by its ostentatious neighbors, El Pueblito has several three-story buildings (no elevators) terraced in a V shape down a gentle hillside toward the sea. A meandering swimming pool with waterfalls runs between the two series of buildings. Rooms have modern furnishings with rattan furniture, bedspreads too short for the beds, travertine marble floors, and large bathrooms. Many have balconies facing the pool or sea. The hotel does not post swimmer warning flags even during extremely dangerous swimming conditions, so use caution in ocean swimming here. There are two restaurants and a bar. Try to get a ground floor room, since a two- or three-story flight of stairs could get old. The prices are a bit high, so be sure to ask about special discount packages. It's on the south end of the Hotel Zone, near Punta Nizuc.

HOTEL ARISTOS, Paseo Kukulkán km 12 (Apdo. Postal 450), Cancún, Q. Roo 77500. Tel. 98/83-0011, or toll free 800/527-4786 in the U.S. Fax 98/83-0079. 244 rms. A/C MINIBAR TV TEL

$ Rates: High season $105–$115 single or double. Low season $80–$105 single or double.

One of the island's first hotels, the Aristos has an adobe-style facade that's more in keeping with the times than its former 1970s look. Rooms are neat and cool, with red-tile floors, small balconies, and yellow Formica furniture. All rooms face either the Caribbean or the paseo and lagoon; rooms with the best views (and no noise from the paseo) are on the Caribbean side. This is one hotel that caters to students on spring break with daily bands by the pool.

There's one restaurant and several bars. Room service, laundry service, a travel agency, and babysitting make life easier. If you'd rather not swim in the central pool, there's a wide stretch of beach one level below the pool and lobby. Watersports equipment is available at the marina, and there are two lighted tennis courts.

CANCÚN CITY

EXPENSIVE

HOTEL PLAZA DEL SOL, Av. Yaxchilán 31, Cancún, Q. Roo 77500. Tel. 98/84-3888. Fax 98/84-1934. 87 rms. A/C TV TEL

$ Rates: High season $100 single or double. Low season $57–$83 single or double.

Don't be put off when I say that this is part of a shopping and office complex. It's a charming oasis in the midst of a busy resort city. There are at least a dozen restaurants within a few minutes' walk. The rooms are furnished in Mexican textiles and pale earth tones; they have two double beds, wall-to-wall carpeting, and piped-in music. Some units have color TVs. Take a dip in the hotel's small swimming pool or else the hotel's four-times-a-day (except Monday) shuttle can whisk you out to the hotel's beach club at the Hotel Maya Caribe. Other facilities include a restaurant, coffee shop, lobby bar, pool bar, travel agency, and shopping arcade. You'll find it near the intersection of Sunyaxchen, catercorner from Perico's Restaurant.

MODERATE

ANTILLANO HOTEL, Calle Claveles 37, Cancún, Q. Roo 77500. Tel. 98/84-1532. Fax 98/84-1878. 46 rms. 2 suites. A/C TV TEL

$ Rates: High season $50 single, $58 double. Low season $43 single, $50 double.

This modern wood-and-stucco hotel is one of the nicer downtown establishments. There's a small bar to one side of the reception area. Rooms overlook Tulum, the side streets, and the interior pool. Each has one or two double beds, a sink area separate from the bathroom, red-tile floors, and a small TV. To find it, head half a block west of Tulum, opposite the restaurant Rosa Mexicana.

HOTEL CANCÚN HANDALL, Av. Tulum 49 at Cobá, Cancún, Q. Roo 77500. Tel. 98/84-1122. Fax 98/84-6352. 50 rms. A/C TV TEL
$ Rates: High season $65 single or double. Low season $48 single or double.
Popular with tour groups, this well-managed two-story hotel has rooms with tile floors, sinks outside the bath areas, and colorful bedspreads. TVs are small but bring in U.S. channels. All rooms have windows but there's not much of a view. Rooms on the front facing Tulum will be noisier, but the air conditioning drowns out most of the din. On the second floor there's a pleasant outdoor lounge area and on the ground floor in back, a small lap pool and lounge area. Free coffee and rolls are offered mornings in the lobby. The hotel is one block west of Cobá, opposite the Hotel America.

HOTEL HACIENDA CANCÚN, Av. Sunyaxchen 39–40, Cancún, Q. Roo 77500. Tel. 98/84-3672. Fax 98/84-1208. 40 rms. A/C TV
$ Rates: High season $43 single or double. Low season $31 single or double. **Parking:** Free.
Rooms at the Hacienda Cancún, some of which hold up to six people, are clean, and plainly furnished but very comfortable. All have windows but no views. There's a nice small pool in the back and a restaurant in front. The hotel is a member of Las Perlas beach club in the hotel zone. It's at Avenida Yaxchilán next to the Hotel Caribe Internacional and opposite 100% Natural.

HOTEL PLAZA CARRILLO'S, Calle Claveles 5, Cancún, Q. Roo 77500. Tel. 98/84-1227. Fax 98/84-2371. 43 rms (all with bath). A/C TV TEL
$ Rates: $51 single or double.
Though it was one of the first hotels in downtown Cancún, Carrillo's is in great shape. Rooms are very comfortable and well-kept, with fresh paint and tile floors. Beds are on concrete platforms and a little low to the floor. The pool is in the center behind the streetside restaurant. Guests here have privileges at the Club de Playa by the Verano Beat Hotel on the island. And the hotel provides free transportation to it at 10am, noon, and 2pm. The location is excellent, just half a block off Tulum near the Parque Palapas. Parking spaces are available around the park.

PARADOR HOTEL, Av. Tulum 26, Cancún, Q. Roo 77500. Tel. 98/84-1922. Fax 98/84-9712. 66 rms. A/C TV TEL
$ Rates: High season $50 single; $54 double. Low season $39 single; $46 double.
One of the most popular downtown hotels, the three-story Parado is conveniently located. Guest rooms are arranged around two long, narrow garden courtyards leading back to a swimming pool (with separate children's pool) and grassy sunning area. The rooms are modern, with two double beds, showers, and cable TV. Help yourself to bottled drinking water in the hall. There is a restaurant and bar. It's at Avenida Tulum and the traffic circle next to Pop's restaurant.

BUDGET

HOTEL CANTO, Av. Yaxchilán at Retorno 5, Cancún, Q. Roo 77500. Tel. 98/84-1207. Fax 98/84-9262. 23 rms. A/C TV TEL
$ Rates: $35 single or double.

With three stories, the Hotel Canto is tall enough to stand out, modern enough to satisfy, and cheap enough to please. Though maintenance could be better, rooms are tidy and freshly painted. Each room has a window but no views, and a small TV with U.S. channels. It's behind the Hotel Caribe Internacional; the entrance is on Tanchacte.

HOTEL RIVEMAR, Av. Tulum 49–51, (Apdo. Postal 334), Cancún, Q. Roo 77500. Tel. 98/84-1199. Fax 98/84-1996. 36 rms. A/C TV TEL
$ Rates: $32 single or double.

It's hard to be better located than the Rivemar, right in the heart of down town Cancún. Rooms are clean, with tile floors, two double beds, and small bathrooms. All units have windows, some with street views and others with hall view. The hotel faces Tulum at Crisantemas.

HOTEL TANKAH, Av. Tankah 69, SM24, Cancún, Q. Roo 77500. Tel. 98/84-4446. 42 rms. A/C (29 rms) FAN (13 rms) TEL
$ Rates: $32 single or double with fan; $36 single or double with A/C.

This modest little hotel has a tiled lobby and heavily stuccoed walls. Some rooms have windows only onto the corridor and all come with the bathroom sink conveniently outside the bathroom area. Ten rooms have TVs. It's at the corner of Avenida Xel-Ha, near Plaza Bonita and opposite Restaurant Linus.

POSADA LUCY, Gladiolas 25, SM22, Cancún, Q. Roo 77500. Tel. and fax 98/84-4165. 26 rms. 9 suites. A/C
$ Rates: $30–$35 single; $46–$58 double. Discounts for longer stays.

One of Cancún's budget standbys, the Posada Lucy is good for a long-term stay. Six units have small living rooms. Two of the units have refrigerators and small kitchen areas. Rooms overall are small and come with one or two double beds. It's away from the hubbub of Tulum, but within quick proximity of all the action. It's one block east of Yaxchilán at Alcatraces, and one block west of Jardín Palapa.

4. DINING

Restaurants change names with amazing rapidity in Cancún, so the restaurants I've chosen are a mix of those with dependable quality and staying power, and those that were new or newly thriving when I checked them for this edition. Whether they will be there when you travel is anyone's guess. Restaurants that survive tend to be more expensive, but good values still exist. And many of the survivors have menus and ambience aimed at the package-tour traveler who comes into Cancún City for "an authentic Mexican dining experience."

On the other hand, Cancún has been invaded by U.S. franchise restaurants, which you will see in more than one location—almost everywhere you look. Among them are Wendy's, Subway, McDonalds, Pizza Hut, Tony Roma's, Ruth's Chris Steak House, KFC, Burger King, etc. Among the most economical chains are Vips and Denny's, which are also in several locations.

ON CANCÚN ISLAND
VERY EXPENSIVE
CAPTAIN'S COVE, Paseo Kukulkán km 15. Tel. 85-0016.

Cuisine: INTERNATIONAL.

$ Prices: Breakfast buffet $7; appetizers $5.50–$9; seafood dishes $17–$38; meat dishes $13–$21; children's menu $3.50–$5.

Open: Daily 7:30am–11pm.

Though far from everything, sitting almost at the end of Paseo Kukulkán, the Captain's Cove continues to pack them in on several dining levels. Diners face big open windows overlooking the lagoon and Royal Yacht Club Marina. At breakfast there's an all-you-can-eat buffet. Lunch and dinner main courses of steak and seafood are the norm and there's a menu catering especially to children. For dessert there are flaming coffees, crêpes, and key lime pie. From the dock here you can also sign up for a lobster dinner cruise from 4:30 to 7:30pm for around $70. To save the cost of an expensive taxi from downtown Cancún, take the local bus and get off at the Omni Hotel, which is across the street.

GRIMOND'S MANSION, Pez Volador no. 8. Tel. 83-0704 or 83-0438.

Cuisine: FRENCH/INTERNATIONAL. **Reservations:** Recommended in high season.

$ Prices: Appetizers $5.50–$11.25; main courses $14–$36.

Open: Dinner daily 6pm–midnight.

An evening here is like an evening in a manor home in the Provence region of France instead of tropical Cancún. Warmly sophisticated, with antique sideboards, fabric-covered walls, lacy window coverings, fresh cut flowers at each table, and soft piano music in the background, the setting is casually refined without being stuffy. Outside is a terrace facing the ocean where you can dine as well—weather permitting. Alain Grimond, a native of Lyon, France, is the owner and chef and you'll probably see his gracious, tall, lanky figure supervising the service and kitchen when you dine. The menu is rich with choices from France, often gently mixed with specialties from Mexico. Among the entrées are fish stuffed with huitlacoche (a native Mexican delicacy) with coriander sabayon, lamb filet in a crust with a parsley sauce, and duck breast with honey vinegar sauce. Among the very tempting desserts you'll find hot apple pie with Yucatán honey and flaming crêpes. It's in a house beside the Casa Maya Hotel near km 4, on the island.

EXPENSIVE

CARLOS 'n' CHARLIE'S, Paseo Kukulkán km 4.5. Tel. 83-0846.

Cuisine: MEXICAN.

$ Prices: Main courses $10–$20.

Open: Lunch daily 11:45am–5pm; dinner daily 6pm–midnight; dancing daily 10pm–3am.

Another of the popular Carlos Anderson restaurants, Carlos 'n' Charlie's features an eclectic decor—fish, hats, pigs, and carrots dangling from the T-shirt-draped ceiling, under a casual palapa facing the lagoon. The menu is written on a sack and includes some delicious specialties such as black bean soup, seafood crêpes, fajitas, barbecue, and even spaghetti for a "sad tummy." The lunch menu is less expensive and is a shortened version of the dinner menu. There's open-air pier dancing nightly after 10pm, for which there's a cover charge if you don't order food. The restaurant is on the lagoon side opposite the Hotel Casa Maya.

EL CARIBEÑO, in the Presidente Hotel, Paseo Kukulkán km 7.5. Tel. 83-0200.

Cuisine: INTERNATIONAL.

$ Prices: Breakfast buffet $12–$14; appetizers $6–$12; main courses $10–$20.

Open: Daily 7am–11pm.

FROMMER'S SMART TRAVELER: RESTAURANTS

1. Count on high prices in Cancún City along Avenida Tulum and in the shopping centers on Paseo Kukulkán on the island.
2. Breakfast and lunch prices are somewhat lower than what you'd pay in the evening along Avenida Tulum, which hosts Cancún City's evening promenade. Restaurateurs compete by placing enticing display plates of their specialties at their restaurant entrances, along with friendly hawkers who implore you to try their place. A packed restaurant therefore may have more to do with the personality and persuasive powers of the hawkers than the food itself.
3. Since main courses at dinner begin around $15 in most restaurants on Tulum, especially those on the south side, it pays to get a recommendation from current diners before venturing in. Most of these restaurants have a few tables overlooking the street, so ask any streetside-table occupant "How's the food?"
4. If you walk just a block or two off Tulum or other avenidas, prices will be much lower for any meal.

If you're looking for that perfect place for leisurely dining by the beach, El Caribeño is it. Good food and service are the norm. It's under a huge thatched palapa, with open sides so you can daydream between courses by day, and at night hear the water lapping on shore and see lights sparkling from as far away as Isla Mujeres. At breakfast there's a sumptuous buffet with made-to-order omelets, Mexican specialties, and a gorgeous array of tropical fruits. The lunch menu is extensive, portions are large, and there's lots to choose, from sandwiches to seafood. The dinner menu is shorter and more expensive, but lunch selections are available—just ask to see the lunch menu.

PLANET HOLLYWOOD, Flamingo Shopping Center, Paseo Kukulkán km 11. Tel. 85-3022 or 85-0366.
Cuisine: INTERNATIONAL.
$ Prices: Appetizers $7.50–$14; main courses $10–$20.
Open: Daily 11am–2am.
The brainchild of Sylvester Stallone, Bruce Willis, and Arnold Schwarzenegger is making a splash in Cancún. It's glittery and trendy inside with a star-studded ceiling and several levels of dining surrounded by Hollywood memorabilia, all centered on a dance floor. Even when there's no live band, the music is mega loud, so you come here to be seen, drink, or eat, but not to casually chat. The menu includes buffalo wings, Texas nachos, pizza, pasta, and grilled platters of steak, chicken, or seafood.

MODERATE

CAPTAIN'S COVE II, in the Langosta Shopping Center, Paseo Kukulkán km 5. Tel. 83-0669.
Cuisine: INTERNATIONAL.
$ Prices: Breakfast buffet $6.25; main lunch courses $8–$30; main dinner courses $6–$35; kids' menu $3–$5.
Open: Daily 8am –11pm.
Though it's open for all three meals, Captain's Cove II is especially noteworthy for its breakfast, with a splendid tranquil ocean view and cool breezes through giant

open windows while joggers huff past and seagulls bathe in a small tidal pool. Ask about the La Bamba breakfast/Isla Mujeres cruise special, which takes off from the dock by the restaurant. There's live music some nights. It's between the Hotel Casa Maya and Playa Linda Beach.

SEÑOR FROG, Paseo Kukulkán km 4.5. Tel. 83-2931.
  Cuisine: INTERNATIONAL.
$ **Prices:** Appetizers $6–$9; main courses $9–$12.
  Open: Daily noon–2am.
    While lively music entertains, a stuffed bear holds the menu as you enter and a life-size papier-mâché frog stands in the corner. Paper streamers will soon dangle from you as they do from the bear, the frog, the rafters, and the other patrons. Take notice of certain "House Rules"—"no smelling, grinning, chewing with mouth open." Walk across the sawdust-covered floor for a seat near the bandstand, the oyster bar, or the lagoon. The menu offers hamburgers and fries, pastas, oysters, tacos, and quesadillas. There's a cover charge after 7:30pm for those who don't order dinner, and reggae music is played from 7:30pm until 2am. Señor Frog is next to Carlos 'n' Charlie's and opposite the Hotel Casa Maya.

CANCÚN CITY

VERY EXPENSIVE

LA DOLCE VITA, Av. Cobá 87, near Av. Nader. Tel. 84-1384.
  Cuisine: ITALIAN. **Reservations:** Required.
$ **Prices:** Appetizers $7–$20; main courses $13–$25.
  Open: Daily noon–11pm.
    La Dolce Vita is among the most pleasant, popular, and elegant small downtown restaurants. A small sunken sidewalk terrace dining area is supplemented with larger interior rooms, all done in soft, pleasing colors. The Italian menu is fine, full, and very tempting. Appetizers include pâté of quail liver and sautéed shrimp in garlic and herbs. There's always seafood soup. You can order pastas such as green ragliolini with lobster médaillons, or rigatoni Mexican style (with chorizo, mushrooms, and chives) as an appetizer or as a main course. Other main courses include tournedos of beef, veal with morel mushrooms, scampi, and various fish. Desserts are all the traditional Italian favorites.

LA FONDUE, Av. Cobá at Calle Agua. Tel. 84-1697.
  Cuisine: FRENCH.
$ **Prices:** Appetizers $5–$21; main courses $10.50–$32; fixed-price menu $25.
  Open: Dinner daily 4:30–11:30pm.
    French-owned and very authentic, La Fondue guarantees that you'll enjoy every minute of a meal here from the attentive service straight through to dessert. There's à la carte dining, as well as a set menu that allows you to have a five-course meal, such as hearts of palm or avocado stuffed with shrimp; onion soup; salad; a fondue of beef, cheese, chicken, steak, or fish; and a dessert such as chocolate fondue or chocolate mousse. The attractive restaurant is dimly lighted and pleasant, and elegant without being overly formal. La Fondue is two blocks south of the Hotel America facing the street at street level in the Plaza America shopping complex.

LA HABICHUELA, Margaritas 25. Tel. 84-3158.
  Cuisine: GOURMET SEAFOOD/BEEF/MEXICAN. **Reservations:** Recommended in high season.

$ Prices: Appetizers $6.50–$13.50; seafood and steaks $12–$33; Mexican dishes $6.50–$23.
Open: Daily 1–11:30 pm

Opened in 1977, La Habichuela is one restaurant with staying power and consistently good food. In a garden setting with tables covered in pink-and-white linens, and soft music in the background, it's an ideal setting for romance and gourmet dining. For an all-out culinary adventure try the Habichuela (string bean) soup; the huitlacoche crêpes; shrimp with tomatoes, yellow peppers, olives, and capers; and the Maya coffee with Xtabentun. Grilled seafood and steaks are excellent as well. The restaurant is a few steps from the northwest end of the Parque Palapas on Margaritas.

RESTAURANT ROSA MEXICANO, Claveles 4. Tel. 84-6313.
Cuisine: MEXICAN HAUTE. **Reservations:** Recommended for parties of six or more.
$ Prices: Appetizers $6–$14; main courses $14–$18; lobster $30.
Open: Dinner daily 5–11pm.

For a nice evening out, try this beautiful little place that has candlelit tables and a plant-filled patio in back. Colorful paper banners and piñatas hang from the ceiling, efficient waiters wear bow ties and cumberbunds color-themed to the Mexican flag, and a trio plays romantic Mexican music nightly. The menu features "refined" Mexican specialties. Try the pollo almendro, which is chicken covered in a cream sauce and sprinkled with ground almonds, served with rice and vegetables. The steak tampiqueño is a huge platter that comes with guacamole salad, quesadillas, beans, salad, and rice. The restaurant is a half a block west of Tulum.

EXPENSIVE

RESTAURANT EL PESCADOR, Tulipanes 28, off Av. Tulum. Tel. 84-2673.
Cuisine: SEAFOOD.
$ Prices: Seafood $19–$29; Mexican plates $8.50–$10.
Open: Daily 11am–10:30pm.

There's often a line at this restaurant, which serves well-prepared and moderate- to high-priced fresh seafood. You can sit on the streetside patio, in an interior dining room, or upstairs. Feast on cocktails of shrimp, conch, fish, or octopus; Créole-style shrimp (*camarones a la criolla*); charcoal-broiled lobster; and stone crab. There's a Mexican specialty meal as well. It's one block west of Tulum.

MODERATE

MI RANCHITO, Av. Tulum 15–16, 1-B. Tel. 84-7814.
Cuisine: MEXICAN.
$ Prices: Breakfast $3–$4; appetizers $4–$6; main courses $8–$28.
Open: Daily 8am–midnight.

A lot of Mexican-style fun awaits you at Mi Ranchito. There's sidewalk and interior (but open-air) dining in the restaurant, which is festooned with piñatas, balloons, and serapes hanging from the ceiling. At night three bands battle one another, or a group of mariachis goes into full song. An open grill laden with shish kebabs, shrimp kebabs, T-bone steaks, filets of fish, chickens, and fajitas, lures you in. It's a lively and popular spot, located in front of the Banco del Atlántico near the intersection with Avenida Cobá.

100% NATURAL, Av. Sunyaxchen 6. Tel. 84-1617.
Cuisine: NATURAL FOODS.

$ Prices: Breakfast $4.50–$6; spaghetti $7–$12; shakes $3.50–$5; sandwiches and Mexican plates $7–$12.
Open: Daily 8am–midnight.

For great mixed-fruit and vegetable shakes and salads, the ever-popular 100% Natural is *the* place. Quench your thirst with delicious fruit-combination shakes of orange, pineapple, strawberry, and banana, with fruit only or with milk added. Full meals include large portions of chicken or fish, spaghetti, or soup and sandwiches. 100% Natural is located between Yaxchilán and Saramuelo, opposite the Hotel Caribe Internacional.

PIZZA ROLANDI, Cobá 12. Tel. 84-4047.
Cuisine: ITALIAN.
$ Prices: Pasta $7–$8; pizza $7–$13.
Open: Daily 1pm–11pm.

The outdoor patio of this restaurant is usually very crowded, so elbow your way in. They serve a hearty, wood-oven, cheese-and-tomato pizza and a full selection of Italian specialities and desserts as well as beer and mixed drinks. It's on the left on Cobá, half a block east of Tulum going toward the island.

RESTAURANT LOS ALMENDROS, Av. Bonampak and Sayil. Tel. 84-0807.
Cuisine: YUCATECAN.
$ Prices: Appetizers $2–$4; main courses $7–$12.
Open: Daily 10am–10:30pm.

The illustrated menu here shows color pictures of the typical Yucatecan dishes served. Some of the regional specialties include lime soup, poc-chuc, chicken or pork pibil, and appetizers such as panuchos yucatecos. The combinado yucateco is a sampler of typical Yucatecan main courses—pollo poc-chuc, sausage, and escabeche. Wine and beer are served. Los Almendros is six blocks south of Cobá, almost at Sayil and opposite the bullring.

RESTAURANT POP, Av. Tulum 26. Tel. 84-1991.
Cuisine: MEXICAN.
$ Prices: Breakfast $4–$7; fixed-price meals $7–$12.
Open: Mon–Fri 7am–11pm, Sat–Sun 8am–11pm; fixed-price meals served noon–10:30pm.

Look for the green awnings of the popular air-conditioned Restaurant Pop. Like the branch in Mérida, the fare tends to the light, simple, and delicious with such staples as hamburgers, and specialties such as Cuban sandwiches on a long baguette, or chicken breast Louisiana style. There are 11 set meals to choose from and all come with soup, rice, main course, and choice of beer, wine, sangría, or soft drink. It's on the east side of Tulum at Uxmal.

BUDGET

GORY TACOS, Tulipanes 6. No phone.
Cuisine: MEXICAN.
$ Prices: Breakfast $3.25–$4; sandwiches $2.50–$4; tacos $4.25–$4.75; grilled specialties $9–$10.
Open: Mon–Sat 9am–11pm, Sun 2–11pm.

Once you find this good and inexpensive restaurant, you may return often. It's clean, small, and casual, with 10 pine benches and pink-tile tables. The hamburgers are close to Stateside fixings and the french fries are thick and fresh—a full order is huge. Sandwiches come in big fresh rolls; the quesadillas are thick with cheese and enveloped in fresh flour tortillas. Besides fast food you can order grilled fish, beef, and chicken, all of which come with french fries, beans, salad, and tortillas. It's next to El Pescador restaurant.

EL TACOLOTE, Cobá 19. Tel. 87-3045.
Cuisine: MEXICAN.
$ Prices: Steaks $11–$14; tacos 80¢–$5; beer $1.25–$2.
Open: Daily 5pm–1:30am.

The ranch theme of red brick, wagon wheels, dark wood tables and chairs, and an open grill is fitting for a place specializing in grilled meats. Steaks are the specialty and northern Mexico–style charro beans are a staple. Tacos come eight ways, plain and really loaded with choices of chile, cheese, bacon, mushrooms, and al pastor. A few tourists are beginning to find the place, but it's usually busy with Mexican families—always a tip-off to good, decently priced food. It's at the corner of Alcatraces opposite the IMSS Hospital.

SPECIALTY DINING
FUN & ENTERTAINMENT

PERICO'S, Yaxchilán 71. Tel. 84-3152.
Cuisine: MEXICAN/SEAFOOD.
$ Prices: Appetizers $6–$7; main courses $7–$19.
Open: Daily noon–2am.

Made of sticks to resemble a large Maya house, Perico's has a Guadalupe Posada and Emiliano Zapata theme, a ceiling full of baskets, and walls hung with a collection of old musical instruments, photos, and dance masks. It's always booming. The extensive menu offers well-prepared steaks, seafood, and traditional Mexican dishes for moderate rates (except lobster). Witty waiters are part of the fun, and don't be surprised if everybody dons huge Mexican sombreros to bob and snake around the restaurant in a conga dance. It's fun whether you join in or not. There's marimba music from 7 to 11:30pm. To find it, go west of Tulum on Cobá, and it's between Sunyaxchen and Cobá.

PASTRIES

CIAO PASTELERÍA, Cobá 30. Tel. 84-1216.
Cuisine: PASTRIES/COFFEE.
$ Prices: Pastries $1.25–$2; special coffees $4.75–$7.75.
Open: Mon–Sat 10am–10pm.

Like a little French café, with half-curtain windows, a few wood tables and chairs, and a display case of delightful pastries served by the slice (or by the whole cake if you like) Ciao Pastelería looks more like it belongs in Georgetown or Greenwich Village. Try a croissant plain, with butter, or filled with chocolate or jam. There's a full menu of mixed drinks, plus hot and cold coffees and many innovative mixtures. This is a good place to escape from the beach scene for early-morning goodies or after-dinner dessert.

As you're going toward the Hotel Zone, it's on the left (north) side of Cobá, almost next to La Dolce Vita.

A DELICATESSEN

SUPER DELI, Tulum at Xcaret/Cobá. Tel. 84-1412.
Cuisine: DELICATESSEN.
$ Prices: Appetizers $2.75–$8; sandwiches $7–$10; pizzas $6.75–$9.25.
Open: Daily 24 hours.

You can't miss the trendy awning and outdoor restaurant at Super Deli. It's very popular for light meals anytime, and inside is a medium-size grocery store with an excellent delicatessen. This is the place to stock up on make-in-your-room sandwiches, snacks for the road, beer, wine, and cheese, and there are canned goods and coffee too.

Look for it on the west side of Tulum, a half a block south of Xcaret/Cobá next to the Hotel Handall.

There's another (smaller) branch on the island in the Plaza Nautilus.

5. ATTRACTIONS

Although most people come to Cancún to kick back and relax on the beach, options for exploring beyond your selected beach chair are numerous.

SUGGESTED ITINERARIES

IF YOU HAVE TWO DAYS Settle in and hit the beach on your first day. In the evening head for Tulum Avenue and select an inviting place from the many restaurants there. Or stroll the shopping areas near the Convention Center and try one of the outdoor restaurants—great for people-watching.

Spend Day 2 at the beach as well. In the evening try one of the "fun" restaurants like Perico's, then rev up at a late-night disco and work off the evening meal. Or, instead of the beach, take one of the all-day yacht trips to Isla Mujeres, the casual island 10 miles offshore (you can also go there on your own by ferry from Puerto Juárez). If you've never seen Maya ruins, take a day trip by bus to Tulum, or take a charter flight to Chichén-Itzá and return in the late afternoon.

IF YOU HAVE THREE DAYS Spend the first two days as suggested above. On Day 3, catch an early bus to the laid-back coastal village of Playa del Carmen, or take a day trip to the new lagoon park of Xcaret.

IF YOU HAVE FIVE DAYS OR MORE Since air service to Cancún is so good, it's a good place to start your exploration of the Yucatán, winding up at Cancún again to relax before returning home. Or it's a good place from which to take day trips in between taking it easy. See Chapter 2, "Planning a Trip to Mexico & the Yucatán," for more extensive itineraries.

THE TOP ATTRACTIONS

CITY TOUR The first thing to do is explore the sandy, once-deserted island that is this billion-dollar resort's reason for being just to see the fabulous resort and get your bearings. The frequent Ruta 1 or Ruta 2 bus, marked *Hoteles*, and those marked *Turismo* run from the mainland city along the full 12 miles to the end of the island and cost 85¢ per ride. You can get on and off anywhere to visit hotels, shopping centers, and beaches. The best stretches of beach are dominated by the big hotels.

PLEASURE BOAT & FERRY EXCURSIONS The island of Isla Mujeres, just 10 miles offshore, is one of the most pleasant day trips from Cancún. At one end is the **El Garrafon National Underwater Park,** which is excellent for snorkeling. And at the other end is a delightful village with small shops, restaurants and hotels, and Norte beach, the island's best stretch of sand. See Section 8, "Easy Excursions," for more on Isla Mujeres. There are two ways to get there: by public ferry from Puerto Juárez, which takes around 45 minutes; and by one of the day-long pleasure boats.

It's easy to go on your own. The Puerto Juárez **public ferries** are just a few miles from downtown Cancún. From Cancún City, take the Ruta 8 bus from in front of the tourism office; the ferry docks in downtown Isla Mujeres. Then take a taxi from the ferry to Garrafon Park. You can stay as long as you like and return by ferry, but be sure to ask about the time of the last returning ferry—don't depend on the posted hours. Taxi fare from downtown Cancún to the pier will cost around $6 to $8. The ferry costs $1.75 to $4 one-way. (For more details and ferry schedule see the section on Isla Mujeres in Chapter 4.)

Pleasure boat excursions to Isla Mujeres are a favorite pastime here. Modern motor yachts, trimarans, even old-time sloops take swimmers, sunners, and snorkelers out into the limpid waters, usually dropping anchor at **Isla Mujeres' Garrafon Beach** for snorkeling around the coral reef, then stopping for lunch and going on to downtown Isla Mujeres for shopping. Most Isla Mujeres trips last five hours, and include continental breakfast, lunch, and usually an open bar. The cost is $40 per person. The day-long trips can be booked through a travel agent. Or you can arrive 30 minutes before departure and buy a ticket—but confirm the sailing time first.

Tour companies are also beginning to offer travelers cruises that emphasize Cancún's natural attributes. The lagoons along the Hotel Zone are ideal spots for spotting herons, egrets, and crabs in the mangroves. These are often billed as **jungle cruises,** and they often include time for lagoon snorkeling. Other excursions go to the **reefs** in glass-bottom boats so that you can have a near scuba-diving experience seeing many colorful fish. But the reefs are a distance from shore and impossible to reach on windy days with choppy seas. Still other boat excursions visit **Isla Contoy,** a national bird sanctuary island. However, if you are planning to spend time in Isla Mujeres, the Contoy trip is easier and more pleasurable to take from there.

The operators and names of boats offering excursions change often. To find out what's available when you are there, check with a local travel agent or hotel tour desk which should have a wide range of options. You can also go to the Playa Linda Pier either a day before or the day of your intended outing and buy your own ticket. If you go on the day of, arrive at the pier around 8:45am since most boats leave around 9 or 9:30am.

RUINAS EL REY Cancún has its own Maya ruins. They're less impressive than Tulum, Cobá, or Chichén-Itzá, but still of interest. The ruins are about 13 miles from town, at the southern reaches of the Zona Hotelera, almost to Punta Nizuc. Look for the Royal Maya Beach Club on the left (east), and then the ruins on the right (west). Admission is $3.50 daily from 8am to 5pm.

The Maya fishermen built this small ceremonial center and settlement very early in the history of Maya culture. It was then abandoned, and later resettled near the end of the Postclassic Period, not long before the arrival of the conquistadores. The platforms of numerous small temples are visible amid the banana plants, papayas, and wildflowers.

BULLFIGHTS Cancún has a small bullring near the northern (town) end of Paseo Kukulkán opposite the Restaurant Los Almendros. Bullfights are held every Wednesday at 3:30pm during the winter tourist season. There are usually four bulls. Travel agencies in Cancún sell tickets for $45 for adults, $25 for children.

A THEME PARK Cancún's version of an entertainment theme park may be **Mexico Mágico,** an outrageously colorful multi-acre operation on Bulevar Kukulkán. Inside are variety shows from folkloric, flamingo, and pre-Hispanic dancing to mariachis and comedy Mexican style. Printed nightly schedules, with a map, tell you what's showing when and where, and you can pick any event that interests you. Three or four dinner shows vary nightly and cost extra—around $30 each per person. There are usually two or three dinner shows each evening with seatings at 6:30 and 8pm or at 7, 9, and 11pm. Outside the entertainment pavilions are shops selling imported crafts from Asia and Europe, objects seldom seen in Mexico—Chinese porcelain, Moroccan rugs, clothing from Indian and Japan, etc. Several eateries sell fast food such as tacos, hot dogs, nachos, hamburgers, beer, and soft drinks. General admission is $20 per person. However, when I was there, many hotel tour and concierge desks had free coupons to cover the admission, so look around before paying full fare. *One caveat:* Few of the entertainment pavilions are covered, so during the rainy season shows may be rained out, or you may spend lots of time waiting for the rain to clear so the shows can start again. There's no drainage, so the streets inside Mexico Mágico become rivers.

SHOPPING Although shops in Cancún are more expensive than their equivalents in any other Mexican city, most visitors spend a portion of their time browsing.

There are several open-air **crafts markets** easily visible on Avenida Tulum in Cancún City.

Malls on Cancún Island are air-conditioned, sleek, and sophisticated. Most of these come one after another between km 7 and km 12 along Paseo Kukulkán—**Costa Brava/La Mansion, Plaza Lagunas, Mayfair, Plaza Terramar, El Parian, Plaza la Fiesta, Plaza Caracol,** and **Plaza Flamingo.** More are farther out on the island. These malls offer fine shops selling anything from fine crystal and silver to designer clothing and decorative objects. Numerous restaurants are interspersed among the shops and centers, many with prices higher than their branches on the mainland. Store hours generally are daily from 10am to 8 or 10pm. Stores in malls near the Convention Center generally stay open all day, but some, and especially in malls farther out, close between 2 and 5 pm.

Cancún's "people" **market,** selling food, spices, housewares, piñatas, party supplies, etc., is behind the post office at Sunyaxchen and Xelha. It's open Monday through Saturday from 9am to 1pm and 4 to 9pm and Sunday from 9am to 2pm. There you can also find Disco Tinhorot II (tel. 84-3728), with a large selection of Mexican tapes and CDs. It's open market hours.

6. SPORTS & RECREATION

THE BEACHES All of Mexico's beaches are public property. Be especially careful on beaches fronting the open Caribbean—the spine of the island's "7"—as the undertow can be deadly. Swim where there's a lifeguard. By contrast, the waters of Mujeres Bay (Bahía Mujeres) at the top of the "7" are usually calm. Get to know Cancún's water-safety pennant system, and make sure to check the flag at any beach or hotel before entering the water. Here's how it goes:

White=Excellent
Green=Normal conditions (safe)
Yellow=Changeable, uncertain (use caution)
Black or Red=Unsafe! Use the swimming pool instead

FROMMER'S FAVORITE
CANCÚN EXPERIENCES

Beach Lazing Spend at least two days with nothing more on your agenda than relaxing poolside or beachside, ordering refreshing drinks, reading a book, and watching the cerulean Caribbean.

An Excursion to Isla Mujeres Plan at least a day trip to this colorful village. Spend several hours snorkeling at Garrafon National Park and another couple of hours lingering over lunch. Stay overnight or longer if you can spare the time. For a local experience take the public ferry there from Puerto Juárez, rather than the more commercialized yacht cruise.

Touring Sian Ka'an Biosphere Reserve Spend a long day in the wilds of Quintana Roo's jungle coast exploring lagoons and spotting tropical birds.

Dining Around Though restaurants are expensive here, part of a Cancún vacation is looking forward to finding the next fabulous restaurant, of which there are many.

Taking a Self-styled City Tour From Cancún City board a city bus marked "Zona Hotelera" and ride it to the end of the line and back admiring the incredible differences in modern architecture on Cancún Island.

Shopping Cancún's modern shopping centers come complete with snazzy boutiques and numerous indoor and outdoor restaurants. They're interesting to explore even if you're not in the shopping mood.

Lagoon Snorkeling Tote the snorkeling gear and plan at least one day in the clear lagoons among the colorful fish at either Xel-Hal or Xcaret.

Here in the Caribbean, a storm can come up and conditions change from safe to unsafe in a matter of minutes, so be alert: If you see dark clouds heading your way, make your way to shore and wait until the storm passes and the green flag is displayed again.

Playa Tortuga (Turtle Beach) is the public beach, where, besides swimming, you can also rent a sailboard and take lessons.

WATER SPORTS Many beachside hotels have water-sports concessions, which include rental of rubber rafts, kayaks, and snorkeling equipment. On the calm Nichupté Lagoon and Laguna Bojórquez side are outlets for renting sailboats, water jets, and water skis. Prices vary and are often negotiable, so check around.

Besides **snorkeling** at **Garrafon National Park** (see Isla Mujeres in Chapter 4), travel agencies offer an all-day excursion to the natural wildlife habitat of **Isla Contoy,** which usually includes time for snorkeling. It costs more than if you do it on your own from Isla Mujeres.

You can go to one of the numerous piers or travel agencies to arrange a day of **deep-sea fishing** for around $80 an hour for up to four people.

Scuba trips run around $60 and include two tanks. **Scuba Cancún,** Paseo Kukulkán, km 5 on the lagoon side (tel. 83-1011; 9am to 2pm only fax 84-2336), offers a four-hour resort course for $100. Full certification takes four to five days and costs around $350. Scuba Cancún also offers diving trips to 12 nearby reefs including Cuevones at 30 feet and out to the open ocean at 54 to 56 feet. The latter is offered in good weather only. The average dive is around 35 feet. One-tank dives cost $45 and two-tank dives cost $66.

For windsurfing, go to the Playa Tortuga public beach where there's a **Windsurfing School** (tel. 84-2023) with equipment for rent.

SPORTS WAGERING This form of entertainment seems to be sweeping Mexico's resort destinations. Mounted TV screens around the room at **LF Caliente** (tel. 83-3704), at the Fiesta Americana Hotel, show all the action in racetrack, jai-alai, football, soccer, etc., in a bar/lounge setting. Besides watching you can place bets. **Espectáculos Deportivos de Cancún** (tel. 83-3900 or 83-3901) is a huge building on Bulevar Kukulkán km 4.5 next to the Playa Linda Pier. Inside are two separate operations. Straight ahead as you enter are live **jai-alai** games (13 each day), which begin at 7pm and run until the wee hours. You can watch the games from the arena in cushioned chairs upstairs in the restaurant. Admission is $8. Bets begin at $3. To the left as you enter is **Super Book,** with 12 satellite dishes poised to capture major U.S. sporting events, as well as horse and dog races. Action begins here daily at 1pm and runs until midnight. There's a restaurant and bar as well. There's no admission. Bets begin at $2.

7. EVENING ENTERTAINMENT

One of Cancún's attractions is its active nightlife. Sometimes there's entertainment enough just strolling along thriving Tulum Avenue, where hawkers of food show off enticing sample plates to lure in passersby. But there are also dark depths of snazzy discos and a variety of lobby entertainment at island hotels.

Several of my recommended restaurants (see "Dining," above), such as Carlos 'n' Charlie's and Señor Frog on the island and Périco's in Cancún City, offer dancing, music, and fun at a fraction of the price of discos.

CONVENTION CENTER The long awaited Convention Center is open with slick (and I mean slick) marble floors, arcades of fashionable shops and restaurants, entertainment, meeting rooms, an auditorium, and a 600-foot tower with a restaurant on top. The center's **Mexican Fiesta** had not yet resumed when I checked, but should be offering a dinner and show when you travel.

THE PERFORMING ARTS Several hotels host Mexican fiesta nights including a buffet dinner and a folkloric dance show; admission including dinner ranges for $30 to $50. The **Ballet Folklórico de Mexico** appears Monday through Saturday nights in a two-hour show at the Continental Villas Plaza (tel. 85-1444, ext. 5690). The **Hyatt Regency Cancún** (tel. 83-1234) has a dinner, folkloric, and mariachi fiesta Tuesday through Friday nights, as does the **Camino Real** (tel. 83-1200). **El Mexicano** restaurant (tel. 84-4873) in the Costa Blanca shopping center has two nightly dinner shows—one Mexican and one tropical, as well as live music for dancing. The Mexican Fiesta at the new Convention Center had not reopened when I checked, but it may be offering shows when you travel.

THE CLUB & MUSIC SCENE Many of the big hotels have nightclubs, usually a disco or at least live music and a lobby bar. Expect to pay a cover charge of between $14 and $20 per person in the discos or show bars. Add drinks ($5 to $9 each) and tips to these prices, and you'll see that a night in fabulous Cancún is not all that cheap.

Flashy **Christine's** (tel. 83-1133), at the Hotel Krystal on the island, is one of the most popular discos. Observe the dress code of no shorts and no jeans. Open from 9:30pm nightly.

Dady'O, km 9.5, is one of the newest discos on the island. It opens at 9:30pm nightly.

La Boom, Bulevar Kukulkán km 3.5 (tel. 83-1152), is two things: On one side there's a video bar and on the other it's a two-level disco with the required thump-thump of cranium-cracking loud music. There's blessed air conditioning in both places. Each night there may be a special client-getting attraction like no cover, free bar, ladies night, bikini night, etc. It's open nightly from 10pm until 4am. A light show at 11:30pm begins in the disco.

Azúcar Bar Caribeño, adjacent to the Hotel Camino Real (tel. 83-0100), offers spicy tropical dance music of the salsa, merengue, and bolero kind with bands from Cuba, Jamaica, and the Dominican Republic. It's open nightly from 9pm to 4am.

Tequila Sunrise Grill Bar & Fiesta, in the Mayfair Shopping Center, may be a restaurant, but it was the liveliest place for dancing on my last visit and there's no cover. It's open daily from 7pm to 4am.

There's always something going on in the spacious lobby bar of the **Continental Plaza and Villas** (tel. 83-1400). In the evenings, for the price of drinks, you can enjoy an assortment of entertainment ranging from light rock and roll to popular Mexican ballads.

8. EASY EXCURSIONS

See Section 5, "Attractions," earlier in this chapter, for details on yacht and ferry excursions to Isla Mujeres.

SIAN KA'AN BIOSPHERE RESERVE Eighty miles south of Cancún begins the Sian Ka'an Biosphere Reserve, a 1.3 million–acre area set aside in 1986 to preserve tropical forests, savannas, mangroves, canals, lagoons, bays, cenotes, and coral reefs—all of which are home to hundreds of birds and land and marine animals (see Chapter 4 for details). The Friends of Sian Ka'an, a nonprofit group based in Cancún offers **biologist-escorted day trips** from Cancún daily (weather permitting) for $115 per person. The price includes lunch, round-trip van transportation to the reserve, guided boat/birding trip through one of the reserve's lagoons, and use of binoculars. For reservations contact them at Amigos de Sian Ka'an, Plaza America, Av. Cobá 5, 3rd Floor, Suites 48–50 (tel. 84-9583), or make reservations through a Cancún travel agent.

COASTAL EXPLORATION—RUINS TO RESORTS Day-long excursions, or perhaps even an overnight stay, are easy using Cancún as a base. Day trips to the **Maya ruins** to the south at **Tulum** are operated daily by Cancún agencies and this should be your first goal, then perhaps the *caleta* (cove) of **Xel-Ha** or the new lagoon day trip to **Xcaret** (see Chapter 4), all of which are easily arranged by travel agencies. As long as you are going south, consider venturing inland to the ruins of

Cobá or a night or two on the island of **Cozumel**, or one of the budget resorts on the **Tulum coast** or **Punta Allen** south of the Tulum ruins. **Isla Mujeres** is an easy day trip off mainland Cancún (see Chapter 4). Although I don't recommend it, by driving fast or catching the buses right or by charter plane, one can go inland to **Chichén-Itzá**, explore the ruins, and return in a day, but it's much better to spend several days seeing Chichén-Itzá, Mérida, and Uxmal. See the following chapters for transportation details and further information on all of these destinations.

ISLA MUJERES, COZUMEL & THE CARIBBEAN COAST

The jungle and beach-dotted coast from Cancún south to Chetumal has been dubbed the **Costa Turquesa** (Turquoise Coast), and from Cancún to Tulum it's known as the **Tulum Corridor.** White powdery beaches stretch from Cancún to Chetumal for 230 miles, and in underwater parks snorkelers and divers can swim past coral swarming with many colorful fish.

All along Highway 307 you'll see signs pointing to new developments, some of which are under construction and others consisting of nothing more than a big sign and a pipe dream that may never materialize. Though these expensive resort developments are rising up in a frenzy, numerous small, inexpensive hideaways dot the coastline a short distance from the highway. And almost 100 miles of this coast, from Tulum to halfway between Felipe Carrillo Puerto and Chetumal, have been saved from developers and set aside as the Sian Ka'an Biosphere Reserve.

SEEING THE CARIBBEAN COAST

This coastline, all in the state of Quintana Roo, is best experienced in a car. It's not impossible to get about by bus, but it requires careful planning, more time, and oodles of patience. Hitching a ride with other travelers is another possibility, but I don't recommend hitchhiking on the highway.

The present two-lane Highway 307 south of Cancún is flanked by jungle on both sides, except where there are beaches and beach settlements. Traffic, which was once scarce, is dangerously dense now. See the "Traveler's Advisory," below.

Puerto Morelos, the car-ferry port to Cozumel, is a 45-minute drive from Cancún; the drive to the laid-back beachside village of Playa del Carmen takes an hour; Xcaret Lagoon and Pamul are a little over an hour away. The drive to Akumal takes an hour and forty-five minutes; to Xel-Ha and Tulum, around two hours; and to Chetumal, about five hours.

WHAT'S SPECIAL ABOUT THE CARIBBEAN COAST

Archeology
Pre-Hispanic remains at Cobá and Tulum.

Newly discovered ruins and reexcavation of sites between Bacalar and Escarcega.

Beaches
250 miles of white powdery beaches stretching south from Cancún to Chetumal.

National Parks
Isla Contoy National Wildlife Reserve, on an uninhabited island off Isla Mujeres, with hundreds of birds, and sea turtle nests. Chancanab Lagoon in Cozumel, Garrafon on Isla Mujeres, Xel-Ha south of Cancún, and 20 miles of reefs off Cozumel Island—four famed underwater parks.

Sian Ka'an Biosphere Reserve, with hundreds of species of birds and animals.

Nature
Turtle nesting and hatching on Cozumel, Punta Allen, and Isla Contoy between June and September.

Birding, especially on Cozumel Island, Punta Allen Peninsula, Bacalar, Chunyaxche, and Boca Paila Lagoon; near the ruins of Cobá, Ascención, and Espíritu Santo bays; and around Felipe Carrillo Puerto.

Water Sports
Cozumel, Mexico's premier diving playground.

Akumal, Pamul, and Isla Mujeres, secondary dive sites.

Chinchorro Reef, relatively undiscovered by divers.

The most popular agency-led tour is to the ruins of Tulum, followed by a stop at Xel-Ha for a swim and snorkeling in the beautiful clear lagoon. The once-placid and little-known Xcaret Lagoon opened in 1991 as a full-blown tourist attraction for people who plan to spend the day. There are frequent buses between Cancún and Chetumal which stop at the most inhabited places—Playa del Carmen, Tulum, and Felipe Carrillo Puerto. These buses will also let you off on the highway if you want to go to Xel-Ha, Xcaret, or Pamul, for example, but you'll have to walk the mile or so from the highway to your destination. On the return you'll have to walk back and wait to flag a passing bus, and be willing to be passed by if it is full.

Passenger ferries go to Isla Mujeres from Puerto Juárez near Cancún, and car-ferries leave from Punta Sam, also near Cancún. A car/passenger ferry runs between Puerto Morelos (south of Cancún) and Cozumel. Passenger ferries also run between Playa del Carmen and Cozumel—the preferred way to go.

Though Chetumal is the capital of Quintana Roo state, it has little to recommend it. Staying in or near Bacalar is preferable to Chetumal. Both are jumping-off points for entering Guatemala and for visiting the newly expanded "Rio Bec" ruin route between Bacalar and Escarcega.

TRAVELER'S ADVISORY Highway 307 is a four-lane road from Cancún almost to Puerto Morelos. Possibly a four-lane highway will be constructed to parallel it all the way to Chetumal. Until that happens, you'll have to be very careful after the road narrows to two lanes at Puerto Morelos. Traffic is quite heavy from Cancún to Tulum and drivers go too fast. A stalled or stopped car is hard to detect and there are no shoulders for pulling off the roadway. **Follow these precautions for a**

safe journey: Never turn left while on the highway (it's against Mexican law anyway). In other places in Mexico, where there are shoulders, you pull off to the right shoulder, then make your left turn. On this road and elsewhere on the peninsula, always go to the next road and turn around and come back to the turnoff you want. Occasionally a specially constructed right-hand turnoff, such as that at Xcaret, allows motorists to pull off to the right in order to cross the road when traffic has passed. Don't speed and don't follow the next car too closely. There have been many accidents and fatalities on this road lately and these precautions could save your life. After Tulum, traffic is much lighter, but use these precautions anyway.

Gas is available at Tulum, Felipe Carrillo Puerto, and Chetumal. If you are going beyond Tulum, tank up there since the next gas station is 60 miles ahead at Felipe Carrillo Puerto. There's no gas at Cobá, so Tulum is also the place to fill up before heading inland. Stations stay open only from around 8am to around 7pm; most stations have regular (Nova) and unleaded gas (Magna Sin).

Except in Cancún, Isla Mujeres, Playa del Carmen, and Cozumel, **exchanging money** is difficult along this coast. And with the exception of Cancún, Isla Mujeres, and Cozumel, **mosquitoes** are numerous and fierce on this coast so bring plenty of mosquito repellent that has "deet" as the main ingredient. (Avon's Skin So Soft, a bath oil with a popular-but-unofficial use as a good-smelling and effective mosquito repellent in the States, is almost useless here.)

1. ISLA MUJERES

10 miles N of Cancún

GETTING THERE From Mérida Air service was discontinued a few years ago but appears to have started again on **Aerolineas Bonanza,** Calle 56 no. 579, between Calles 67 and 69 (tel. 99/28-0496 or 24-6228). From Mérida there's one flight Monday through Friday at 12:55pm, returning at 2:10pm. On Saturday there's an additional flight that leaves Mérida at 7:30am and returns from Isla Mujeres at 8:45am. In Isla Mujeres the office is in the Hotel Perla del Caribe (tel. 987/7-0120 or 7-0306). You can also fly from Mérida to Cancún, and proceed from there by bus and ferry (see below).

First- and second-class buses leave from the Mérida bus station several times a day. Your destination is **Puerto Juárez near Cancún,** from which you take a ferryboat to the island (see ferry schedule, below).

From Cozumel There are daily flights between Cozumel and Cancún; from the Cancún airport proceed to the Puerto Juárez ferry terminal east of downtown Cancún. Or you can take a ferry from Cozumel to Playa del Carmen, then a bus to Puerto Juárez, then another ferry to Isla Mujeres (see below for ferry and bus information from Cozumel).

From Cancún Passenger ferryboats from mainland Cancún go to Isla Mujeres from **Puerto Juárez;** the **passenger/car-ferry** leaves from **Punta Sam** a short distance from Puerto Juárez on the same road. To get to the latter two ports, take any Ruta 8 city bus from Avenida Tulum.

From Puerto Juárez Puerto Juárez is the dock for the passenger boats to Isla Mujeres. Passenger boats run the 45-minute trip many times daily to and from Cancún and Isla Mujeres at a cost of $1.75 to $4. There is no ticket office; pay as you board. The helpful **tourism office** at the dock provides information about hotels; the price of taxis to downtown Cancún (around $6), the Cancún airport ($17), or Hotel Zone ($6–$15); and about ferry schedules in Cancún, Isla Mujeres, Playa del Carmen, and Cozumel. It's open sporadically. Taxi fares are posted in the parking lot fronting the pier.

From Punta Sam If you are taking a vehicle to Isla Mujeres, you'll use the Punta Sam port a little farther past Puerto Juárez. The ferry runs the 40-minute trip daily all year except in bad weather. Cars should arrive an hour in advance of the ferry departure to register for a place in line and pay the posted fee. Passengers without a car pay $2 each. However, Isla Mujeres is so small that a vehicle isn't necessary.

For total, laid-back, inexpensive Caribbean relaxation, it's hard to beat Isla Mujeres, once called the "poor man's Cancún." Isla's prices have gone up considerably in the last several years but have slowed down a bit recently. It's a bargain compared to Cancún, and I much prefer it over Cancún and Playa del Carmen. Sandy brick streets front low-rise buildings in town, where there's little vehicular traffic. There's no formal nightlife. Rested and suntanned visitors hang out in open-air cafés, talk, and trade paperback novels until about 10pm when restaurateurs and shop owners start to yawn and the whole island beds down.

There are two versions of how Isla Mujeres got its name. The more popular one claims that pirates parked their women here for safekeeping while they were marauding the Spanish Main. The other account attributes the name to conquistador Francisco Hernandez de Córdoba, who was reportedly impressed by the large number of female terra-cotta figurines he found in temples on the island.

ORIENTATION

ARRIVING Ferries arrive at the dock in the center of town. Taxis are always lined up in front and ask around $2 to $4 to take you to almost any hotel—a rip-off. The price gets cheaper if you wait until all passengers have left the area. Unless you're loaded with luggage you don't need transportation since most hotels are close by.

PUERTO JUÁREZ PASSENGER FERRY SCHEDULE

Cancún to Isla Mujeres	Isla Mujeres to Cancún
6:15am	7:30am
9:00	8:30
9:30	9:30
10:00	10:30
11:00	11:30
Noon	12:30pm
1:00pm	1:30
2:00	2:30
3:00	3:30
4:00	4:30
5:00	5:00
6:00	5:30
7:00	6:30
8:00	7:30

PUNTA SAM CAR-FERRY

Cancún to Isla Mujeres	Isla Mujeres to Cancún
7:15am	6:00am
9:45	8:30
Noon	11:00
2:30pm	1:15pm
5:15	4:00
10:00	7:15

ISLAND LAYOUT Isla Mujeres is about 5 miles long and 2¹/₂ miles wide. The **ferry docks** are right at the center of town, within walking distance of most hotels. The street running along the waterfront is **Rueda Medina,** commonly called the *Malecón.* The **market** (Mercado Municipal) is by the post office on **Calle Guerrero,** an inland street at the north edge of town, which, like most streets in the town, is unmarked. Norte Beach (formerly Coco Beach) is the best beach.

GETTING AROUND The newest form of transportation on Isla Mujeres is the electric **golf cart,** available for rent at many hotels for $10 per hour. They're a convenient mode of transportation, if you don't want to fiddle with a moto and if you understand that they don't go more than 20 miles per hour.

Another way to see the island is to rent a **"moto,"** the local sobriquet for motorized bikes and scooters. If you don't want to fool with gears and shifts, rent a fully automatic one for around $25 per day or $6 per hour. They come with seats for one person, but some are large enough for two. Take time to get familiar with how the scooters work and be careful on the road as you approach blind corners and hills where visibility is poor. There's only one main road, with a couple of offshoots so you won't get lost. Do be aware that the rental price does not include insurance and any injury to yourself or the scooter will come out of your pocket.

FAST FACTS

Area Code The area code for Isla Mujeres is 987. The first digit for all telephone numbers on the island has been changed from 2 to 7.

Hospital The Hospital de la Armada (tel. 7-0001), on Medina at Ojon P. Blanco, has the island's only decompression chamber. It's a half mile south of the town center.

Post Office/Telegraph Office The correo is on Calle Guerrero, by the market.

Supermarket The Super Mercado Betina faces the main plaza, and is open daily from 7am to 10pm.

Telephone There's a long-distance telephone office in the lobby of the Hotel María José, Avenida Madero at Medina. Open Monday through Saturday from 9am to 1pm and 4 to 8pm.

Tourist Information The **City Tourist Office** is on Hidalgo in a pink wooden building facing the Plaza Principal and next to the Palacio Municipal. It's open Monday through Friday from 9am to 2pm and 6 to 8pm (tel. 987/7-0316).

Tourist Seasons Isla Mujeres' tourist season (when hotel rates are higher) is a bit different than other places in Mexico. High season runs December through May—a month longer than in Cancún; some hotels raise their rates in August and some hotels raise their rates beginning in mid-November. Low season is June through mid-November.

WHAT TO SEE & DO

THE BEACHES

There are three beaches, one in town, **Playa Norte** (formerly Playa Cocoteros), extending around the northern tip of the island to your left as you get off the boat; another at **Garrafon National Park,** about three miles south; and **Playa Langosta,** along the Caribbean edge of the Laguna Makax.

Playa Norte, the best beach, is beautiful and easily reached on foot from the village. Playa Langosta is a public beach with several rather high-priced palapa-style restaurants. Consider bringing your own refreshments. Local buses go to Playa Langosta as far as the El Paraíso restaurant on the beach.

WATER SPORTS

SWIMMING Wide Playa Norte is the best swimming beach, with Playa Langosta second. There are no lifeguards on duty in Isla Mujeres, and the system of water-safety flags used in Cancún and Cozumel isn't used here. Be very careful.

SNORKELING By far the most popular place to snorkel is **Garrafon National Park** at the southern end of the island where you'll see numerous schools of colorful fish. The well-equipped park has beach chairs, changing rooms, lockers, showers, and a snack bar. Taxis from the central village cost around $4 one-way. Admission costs $2 and lockers rent for $1.75.

Another excellent location is around the lighthouse in the **Bahía de Mujeres** (bay) opposite downtown, where the water is about six feet deep. Boatmen will take you for around $10 per person if you have your own snorkeling equipment, or $15 more if you use theirs.

Note: No matter where you snorkel, remember that coral cuts like a knife and causes painful infection.

DIVING Several dive shops have opened on the island, most offering the same trips. The traditional dive center is **Buzos de México,** on Rueda Medina at Morelos (tel. 7-0274), next to the boat cooperative. **Bahia Dive Shop,** on Rueda Medina 166 across the street from the car-ferry dock (tel. and fax 987/7-0340), is a full-service shop with dive equipment for sale and rent. The most complete shop on the island, Bahia offers a wide variety of diving options, including resort and certification classes and knowledgeable, certified divemasters. **Carnavalito Dive Shop,** Rueda Medina 7 at Madero (tel. and fax 987/7-0118), also sells equipment. The most popular reefs are Manchones, Banderas, and Cuevones, all 30- to 40-foot dives costing $50 to $65 for a two-tank trip. Cuevas de los Tiburones (Caves of the Sleeping Sharks) is Isla's most famous dive site and costs $60 to $80 for a two-tank dive. Your chance of actually seeing sharks, by the way, is less than 50%. The best season for diving is from June through August, when the water is calm.

FISHING To arrange a day of fishing ask at the **Sociedad Cooperativa Turística** (boatmen's cooperative; tel. 7-0274) or the travel agency mentioned under Isla Contoy below. The cost can be shared with four to six others and includes lunch and drinks. All year you'll find bonito, mackerel, kingfish, and amberjack. Sailfish and sharks (hammerhead, bull, nurse, lemon, and tiger sharks) are in good supply in April and May. In winter, large grouper and jewelfish are prevalent. Four hours of fishing cost around $120 or eight hours for $250. The cooperative is open Monday through Saturday 8am to 1pm and 5 to 8pm. Sunday hours are 7:30 to 10am and 6 to 8pm.

OTHER ATTRACTIONS

MAYA RUINS   Just beyond the lighthouse, at the southern end of the island, is a pile of stones that once formed a small Maya pyramid before Hurricane Gilbert. Believed to have been an observatory built to the moon goddess Ixchel, now it's reduced to a rocky heap. The location on a lofty bluff overlooking the sea is still worth seeing. If you are at Garrafon National Park and want to walk, it's not too far. Turn right from Garrafon. When you see the lighthouse, turn toward it down the rocky path.

A PIRATE'S FORTRESS   The Fortress of Mundaca is about 2¹/₂ miles in the same direction as Garrafon, about half a mile to the left. The fortress was built by the pirate Mundaca Marecheaga who in the early 19th century arrived at Isla Mujeres and proceeded to set up a blissful paradise in a pretty, shady spot while making money from selling slaves to Cuba and Belize.

SHOPPING

Shopping is a casual activity here—few glittery, sleek shops and none of the hard-sell you find in Acapulco. Prices are also cheaper. You'll find silver, Saltillo serapes, Oaxaca rugs, masks, Guatemalan clothing, pottery, blown glassware, and T-shirts in abundance. One store stands out from the rest.

LA LOMA, Guerrero 6. Tel. 7-0446.
   At this store you'll find a great variety of good folk art, including Huichol yarn "paintings," masks, silver, chains and coins, a good selection of textiles, Oaxaca wood carvings, Olinalá lacquer objects, and colorful clay candelabras from Izúcar de Matamoros. You'll see it opposite the left side of the church and almost next to the Hotel Rocamar. It's open Monday through Saturday from 10am to 3pm and 5 to 8pm.

WHERE TO STAY

There are plenty of hotels in all price ranges in Isla Mujeres. Rates are at their peak during high season, December through May, which is the most expensive and most crowded time to go.

EXPENSIVE

HOTEL CABAÑAS MARÍA DEL MAR, Av. Carelos Lazo 1, Isla Mujeres, Q. Roo 77400. Tel. 987/7-0179. Fax 987/7-0213. 52 rms. A/C
$ Rates (including continental breakfast): High season $85 single or double; $75 bungalow; new "castle" section $85–$90 single or double. Low season $45–$66 single or double; "castle" $45–$75 single or double.
A good choice, the Cabañas María del Mar is located on Playa Norte, a half block from the Hotel Nabalam. There are three completely different sections to this hotel. The two-story section behind the reception area and beyond the garden offers nicely outfitted rooms facing the beach, all with two single or double beds, refrigerators, and balconies with ocean views. Eleven single-story cabañas closer to the reception and pool are rather dark. The newest addition, El Castillo, is across the street and built over and beside Buho's restaurant. It contains all "deluxe" rooms, but some are larger than others; the five rooms on the ground floor all have large patios. Upstairs rooms have small balconies. Most have one double bed, but two come with two single beds. All have ocean views, blue-and-white tile floors, and tile lavatories,

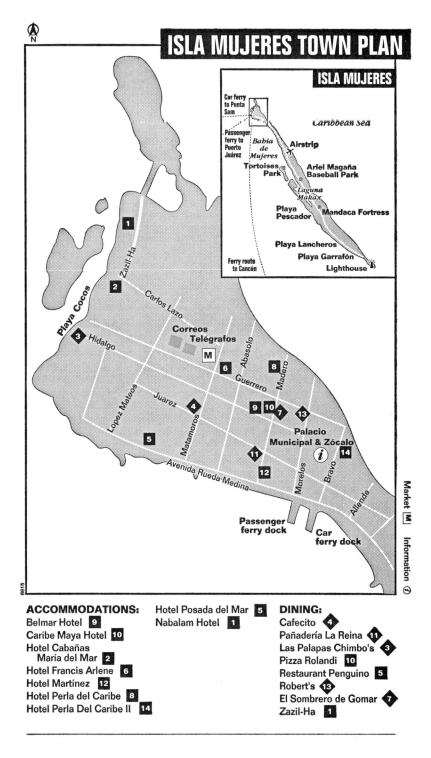

ISLA MUJERES TOWN PLAN

ISLA MUJERES

Car ferry to Punta Sam

Passenger ferry to Puerto Juárez

Bahía de Mujeres

Airstrip

Caribbean Sea

Tortoises Park

Ariel Magaña Baseball Park

Laguna Makax

Playa Pescador

Mandaca Fortress

Ferry route to Cancún

Playa Lancheros

Playa Garrafón

Lighthouse

Zazil-Ha

Playa Cocos

Hidalgo

Carlos Lazo

Correos
Telégrafos

M

Abasolo

Madero

Guerrero

Lopez Mateos

Juarez

Matamoros

Palacio
Municipal & Zócalo

Avenida Rueda Medina

Morelos

Bravo

Allende

Passenger
ferry dock

Car
ferry dock

Market M   Information ⓘ

ACCOMMODATIONS:
Belmar Hotel **9**
Caribe Maya Hotel **10**
Hotel Cabañas
   María del Mar **2**
Hotel Francis Arlene **6**
Hotel Martínez **12**
Hotel Perla del Caribe **8**
Hotel Perla Del Caribe II **14**

Hotel Posada del Mar **5**
Nabalam Hotel **1**

DINING:
Cafecito **4**
Pañadería La Reina **11**
Las Palapas Chimbo's **3**
Pizza Rolandi **10**
Restaurant Penguino **5**
Robert's **13**
El Sombrero de Gomar **7**
Zazil-Ha **1**

6815

and are outfitted in cool cotton bedspreads and natural-toned neocolonial furniture. There's a small, unkempt pool in the garden. The owners also have a bus for tours and a boat for rental, as well as car and moto rental.

To get here from the pier walk left one block, then turn right on Matamoros. After four blocks, turn left on Lazo, the last street. The hotel is at the end of the block.

HOTEL NABALAM, Zazil Ha 118, Isla Mujeres, Q. Roo 77400. Tel. 987/7-0279. Fax 987/7-0446. 19 suites. A/C FAN

$ Rates: High season $95 single or double. Low season $80 single or double.

This two-story hotel near the end of Norte Beach is a fine addition to the island's lodgings with its comfortable rooms on a quiet, ideally located portion of the shore. Each spacious room includes two double beds, ceiling fan, table and chairs, and either a balcony or patio. The hotel's restaurant, Zazil-Ha, is one of the best on the island. (See "Where to Dine," below.)

From the pier, walk left one block, then right on Matamoros for four blocks, and left on Lazo, the last inland street; walk straight to the next street, then turn right; the hotel is a half a block down on the left.

HOTEL PERLA DEL CARIBE, Av. Madero 2 (at Guerrero), Isla Mujeres, Q. Roo 77400. Tel. 987/7-0444. Fax 987/7-0011. 86 rms. A/C (44 rms) FAN (42 rms)

$ Rates: High season $80–$95 single or double. Low season $50–$76 single or double. Ask about discounts and packages.

This establishment is located on the eastern shore where a heavy surf crashes rhythmically against a newly built seawall. Rooms have ordinary motellike furnishings and little balconies with sea views. A nice-size swimming pool and sunning patio face the ocean. The restaurant serves all three meals and there's a TV lounge off the lobby. A hotel representative often meets the ferries to transport guests and their luggage to the hotel. The hotel also rents golf carts to buzz around town for around $10 an hour. Inquire about off-season discounts and package rates—otherwise, the hotel is somewhat overpriced.

From the pier, walk left one block, turn right at Hotel María José, and walk four blocks straight ahead; the hotel office is on the right.

HOTEL PERLA DEL CARIBE II, Av. Norte Bravo 1, Isla Mujeres, Q. Roo 77400. Tel. 987/7-0586. Fax 987/7-0101. 30 rms (all with bath). FAN

$ Rates: High season $76 single or double. Low season $52–$65 single or double.

This hotel (formerly the Hotel Rocamar) is perched on the high ground at the opposite end of town from the ferry dock, with a commanding view of the sea. Prices go up or down depending on the season and whether you want an ocean view or park and street view. Everything's done in nautical style here, with what seems like every conch shell ever opened in the restaurant going to line the garden walkways. Rope and hawsers are employed as trim, and even the bathroom sinks are mounted in Lucite tops chock-full of seashells. Sea breezes and ceiling fans keep the spacious rooms cool. A restaurant and bar are on the lower level and a pleasant, small pool faces the ocean.

From the pier walk right three blocks on Medina, then turn left on Bravo and go three blocks to the end.

HOTEL POSADA DEL MAR, Av. Rueda Medina 15, Isla Mujeres, Q. Roo 77400. Tel. 987/7-0300. Fax 987/7-0266. 40 rms. A/C TEL

$ Rates: High season $70 single, $80 double. Low season $45 single, $55 double.

Attractively furnished, this long-established hotel faces the water and a wide beach three blocks north of the ferry pier. The rooms are in a large garden palm grove in either a three-story hotel building or in one-story bungalow units. For the spacious quality of the rooms and the location, this is among the best buys on the island. A seldom-used but wide and appealing stretch of Playa Norte is across the street. A casual palapa-style restaurant and a pool are set back on the front lawn and the popular Pinguino's Restaurant fronts the street. See "Where to Dine" below. Ask about cost-saving packages.

From the pier go left three blocks; the hotel is on the right.

MODERATE

HOTEL BELMAR, Av. Hidalgo, Isla Mujeres, Q. Roo 77400. Tel. 987/7-0430. Fax 987/7-0492. 10 rms. A/C TV TEL
$ Rates: High season $42 single, $47 double. Low season $31 single, $37 double.
Situated above Pizza Rolandi, this hotel is run by the same people who serve up those wood-oven pizzas. The simple but stylish rooms come with two twin or two double beds and handsome tile accents. Prices are high considering the lack of views, but the rooms are very pleasant and a strong TV antenna brings in U.S. channels.

From the pier walk left half a block, then turn right on Abasolo. Go straight two blocks and turn left on Hidalgo; the hotel is half a block on the right.

HOTEL FRANCIS ARLENE, Guerrero 7, Isla Mujeres, Q. Roo 77400. Tel. and fax 987/7-0310. 12 rms. A/C or FAN
$ Rates: High season $30 single, $35 double. Low season $25–$29 single, $30–$35 double.
The Magaña family operates this neat little two-story inn behind their family home, which is built around a small shady courtyard. You'll notice the tidy cream-and-white facade of the building from the street. Rooms are clean and comfortable, with tile floors and all-tile baths, and soap and towels laid out on the bed. Downstairs rooms have refrigerators and stoves and each upstairs room comes with refrigerator and toaster. All have balconies or patios.

From the ferry dock turn right, then left on Abasolo for two longish blocks. Turn left again on Guerrero. It's on the right.

BUDGET

HOTEL CARIBE MAYA, Av. Madero 9, Isla Mujeres, Q. Roo 77400. Tel. 987/7-0190. 26 rms. A/C or FAN
$ Rates: High season $20 single, $36 double. Low season $14 single, $20 double.
The rooms in this basic three-story hotel contain furniture that may have seen service in some older and long-gone establishment, green-tile floors, nylon ruffled bedspreads, over-the-bed reading lights, and showers. Upstairs rooms are brighter.

To get here from the main pier, turn left and go one block, then right 1½ blocks onto Avenida Madero. It's between Guerrero and Hidalgo.

HOTEL MARTÍNEZ, Av. Madero 14, Isla Mujeres, Q. Roo 77400. Tel. 987/7-0154. 14 rms. FAN
$ Rates: $18 single or double.
Don't judge the hotel by the cluttered patio as you enter. Guests have been returning to this three-story hotel (no elevator) for years because the basics are dependable. The rooms are freshly painted, the sheets and towels are white (although well used), and each painted bedside table has a seashell lamp. An outdoor sitting area on the second floor catches great cross breezes, as do the rooms.

To get here from the ferry pier, turn left, then walk two blocks and turn right. The hotel is on the right.

WHERE TO DINE

The **Municipal Market**, next door to the telegraph office and post office on Avenida Guerrero, has several little cookshops operated by obliging and hardworking señoras and enjoyed by numbers of tourists. They set out their steel tables and chairs emblazoned with soft-drink logos early in the morning, and serve up cheap, tasty, filling food all day. Drop by to see what's cooking.

MODERATE

LAS PALAPAS CHIMBO'S, Coco Beach. No phone.
Cuisine: SEAFOOD.
$ Prices: Breakfast $3–$5; sandwiches and fruit $3–$6; seafood $7–$11.
Open: Daily 8am–6pm.

If you're looking for the best beachside palapa-covered restaurant where you can wiggle your toes in the sand while scarfing down fresh seafood, this is the place. Locals recommend it as their favorite on Norte Beach. Try the delicious fried fish (a whole one), which comes with rice, beans, and tortillas.

PINGUINO, in the Hotel Posada del Mar, Av. Rueda Medina 15. Tel. 7-0300.
Cuisine: MEXICAN/SEAFOOD.
$ Prices: Breakfast $3–$6; main dishes $7–$12; lobster $27.
Open: Daily 7am–9pm; bar open to midnight.

The best seats on the waterfront are on the deck of this new restaurant/bar, especially in late evening when islanders and tourists arrive to eat, drink, and dance. This is the place to splurge on lobster—though you'll pay dearly, you'll get a large, sublimely fresh lobster tail with a choice of butter, garlic, or secret sauces. Breakfasts include fresh fruit, yogurt, and granola, or healthy platters of eggs, served with homemade wheat bread. The manager, Miguel, whips up some potent concoctions at the bar. The band, playing nightly from 9pm to midnight, will make you want to dance until they quit. Pinguino is in front of the hotel, three blocks north of the ferry pier.

PIZZA ROLANDI, Av. Hidalgo s/n. Tel. 7-0429.
Cuisine: ITALIAN.
$ Prices: Appetizers $3.50–$12; main courses $6.50–$18; pizza $6–18; cuisine menu $3.75–$31.
Open: Daily 1pm–midnight.

Pizza Rolandi, the chain that saves the day with dependably good, reasonably priced food in otherwise expensive resorts, comes through in Isla Mujeres as well. The casual dining room, in an open courtyard of the Hotel Berny, is the scene for consumption of plate-size pizza, pasta, and calzones cooked in a wood oven. There's also a more expensive cuisine menu with fish, beef, and chicken dishes. Guitarists often perform in the evenings. You'll find Rolandi's between Madero and Abasolo.

RESTAURANT EL SOMBRERO DE GOMAR, Av. Hidalgo 35. Tel. 7-0142.
Cuisine: GRILLED SEAFOOD/STEAK.
$ Prices: Main courses $5.75–$12; margarita $4; beer $1.75.
Open: Daily 7am–11pm.

Among Isla Mujeres's most dependable old standbys, the Gomar has an ice-cream parlor on the ground floor and an upstairs restaurant overlooking the street that's festooned with colorful sombreros and Saltillo serapes. The prices are a little high, but the service and food are good. And you can order such favorites as grilled lobster, T-bone steaks, and baked potatoes while overlooking all the action on this busy crossroads at the corner of Madero.

ZAZIL-HA, at the Hotel Nabalam, Norte Beach. Tel. 7-0279.
   Cuisine: INTERNATIONAL.
$ Prices: Breakfast $4.75–$6.75; main courses $5.75–$14; platter meals $12.
   Open: Daily 7:30am–9:30pm.
At this restaurant you can enjoy some of the island's best food while sitting among the palms and gardens at tables on the sand. The serene environment is enhanced by the food—terrific pasta with garlic, shrimp in tequila sauce, fajitas, delicious mole enchiladas, and more, plus great nachos. It's likely you'll return for several more meals before you leave. It's almost at the end of Calle Zazil-Ha.

BUDGET

CAFECITO, Calle Juárez. No phone.
   Cuisine: CREPES/ICE CREAM/COFFEES.
$ Prices: Coffee drinks $1–$3; crêpes $3–$5; breakfast $3–$5; main courses $5.50–$9.75.
   Open: Fri–Wed 8am–noon and 6–10pm.

 Begin the day with a croissant and cream cheese, or end it with a hot-fudge sundae. Or stop by for the most flavorful cup of coffee on the island. Crêpes are served with yogurt, ice cream, fresh fruit, or chocolate sauces as well as with ham and cheese; eggs are served with fresh croissants. Dinners include fish and curried shrimp. The café is one block east of Medina at the corner of Matamoros.

PANADERÍA LA REINA, Av. Madero. Tel. 7-0419.
   Cuisine: BAKERY.
$ Prices: Cookies 35¢ each; pan dulce 50¢.
   Open: Mon–Sat 7am–9pm.
This bakery near Hotel Osorio is perhaps your best bet for an inexpensive breakfast. Go early morning or mid-afternoon—in the evening the selection is a bit picked over. There's a refrigerator of juices and yogurt too. It's one block from Medina at the corner of Avenida Juárez.

ROBERT'S, on Morelos between Hidalgo and Guerrero. No phone.
   Cuisine: MEXICAN.
$ Prices: Breakfast $2.50–$4; main courses $7–$14; tacos and tortas $1.25–$4.
   Open: Daily 8am–midnight.
Look for the house with a hot-pink facade and white plastic tables and chairs. Popular with locals and undiscovered by tourists, Robert's has some of the island's most economical meals. The menu includes a variety of dishes including pork, chicken, and seafood, plus hamburgers and tacos. Robert's faces the church on the central plaza.

AN EXCURSION TO ISLA CONTOY

 If at all possible, plan to visit this pristine uninhabited island 19 miles by boat from Isla Mujeres, set aside as a national wildlife reserve in 1981. The oddly shaped, 3.8-mile-long island is covered in lush vegetation and harbors

FROMMER'S NATURE NOTES
THE MAGNIFICENT FRIGATE BIRD

Among Yucatán's shore birds the "magnificent frigate bird" is one of the most abundant and visible. It's deserving of its honorable name, for its wing-span of up to eight feet makes it the longest in the world among birds with comparable body weight. Once you learn to distinguish the frigate birds' al-most bat-shaped wings silhouetted against a clear blue sky, you'll notice them often. But if the bird is frightened on its nest, those same graceful wings that cruise effortlessly on thermals can also become hopelessly entangled in tree limbs.

Both males and females have shiny black feathers and the female sports a patch of white at her throat. During mating season the males inflate their bal-loon-like, bright-red throat pouches, soaring in front of prospective mates or puffing up handsomely among the mangrove branches beside a group of indif-ferent female

Though they live and nest in mangroves at the water's edge, the frigate birds don't have water-repellent feathers and will drown if they fall in. A pair of frigate birds raise one offspring per season that reaches its own maturity in about six years. They mate and nest from March through June and Septem-ber through December in large colonies; they're easy to see on Isla Contoy, in the Sian Ka'an, and Punta Allen.

70 species of birds as well as a host of marine and animal life. Bird species that nest on the island include pelicans, brown boobies, frigates, egrets, terns, and cormorants. Flocks of flamingos arrive in April. June, July, and August are good months to plan an overnight trip to witness turtles nesting. Most excursions troll for fish, which will be your lunch, anchor en route for a snorkeling expedition, and leisurely skirt the is-land for close viewing of the birds without disturbing the habitat. After arrival, there's time to snorkel, laze on the gorgeous beach, or walk in search of birds. A modern visitor's center has excellent displays in Spanish, English, and French ex-plaining the climate, wildlife, and geology of the island.

The trip from Isla Mujeres takes a minimum of an hour and a half one-way, more if the waves are choppy. Due to the tight-knit boatmen's cooperative, prices for this excursion are the same everywhere, $40. You can buy a ticket at the coop-erative, **Sociedad Cooperativa Turística** (tel. 7-0274) on Avenida Rueda Medina, next to Mexico Divers and Las Brisas restaurant, or at one of several travel agencies, such as **La Isleña,** on Morelos between Medina and Juárez (tel. 7-0036). La Isleña is open daily from 6am to 9pm.

Three types of boats go to Contoy. Small boats have one motor and seat eight or nine people. Medium-size boats have two motors and hold 10 passengers. Large boats have a toilet and hold 16 people. Some boats have a sun cover, others do not. Boat captains should respect the cooperative's regulations regarding capacity and should have enough life jackets to go around. I highly recommend the services of boat-owner **Ricardo Gaitan,** who, besides the day trip, offers the only overnight excursion. Ask for him at the cooperative or write to him directly: P.O. Box 42, Isla Mujeres, Q. Roo 77400. He speaks English, and his large boat, the **Estrella del Norte,** comfortably holds 16 passengers. If you spend the night on the island, be sure to take along mosquito repellent. An inflatable mattress wouldn't be a bad idea, although bedding is provided.

EN ROUTE SOUTH ALONG THE COAST

To enjoy fully the wealth of attractions that the Yucatán has to offer, you must wander farther from your Cancún/Isla Mujeres base. Chapter 5 has full information on points west of Cancún such as Chichén-Itzá and Mérida. Let's look now at what lies south of Cancún, on the way to the island of Cozumel and beyond.

If you don't have your own car, transport along the Caribbean coast presents problems although public transportation has improved. Though there are dozens of buses a day down the coast (see Chapter 3), you may end up waiting along the sweltering highway for an hour or more only to have a jam-packed bus roar right by you.

After Cancún, Playa del Carmen has the next-best selection of bus services. If you're driving be sure to read the "Traveler's Advisory," earlier in this chapter.

Despite the comical name, one of the most educational attractions in the area is **Croco Cun,** a zoological park where crocodiles are raised. Though far from grand, the park has exhibits of crocodiles at all stages of development, as well as animals of many species that once roamed the Yucatán peninsula. Guides give a very informative tour. The snake exhibit is fascinating, though it may make you think twice about roaming in the jungle. The rattlesnakes and boa constrictors are particularly intimidating, and the tarantulas are downright enormous. Children enjoy the guides' enthusiastic tours, and are entranced by the spider monkeys and wild pigs. Wear plenty of bug repellent, and allow an hour or two for the tour, followed by a cool drink in the restaurant. Croco Cun is open daily from 8am to dark. Admission is $5; free for children under 6. The park is at km 33 on Highway 307.

About a half a mile before you reach Puerto Morelos is the 150-acre **Jardín Botánico** opened in 1990 and named after Dr. Alfredo Barrera, a biologist who studied the jungle. It's a natural, protected showcase for native plants and animals and open Tuesday through Sunday from 9am to 4pm. Admission is $2.75 and it's worth the money and every minute of the hour or more it will take to see it. Slather on the mosquito repellent, though. The park is divided into six parts: the epiphyte area (plants that grow on others), Maya ruins, ethnographic area with a furnished hut and typical garden, mangroves, the chiclero camp about the once-thriving chicle (chewing gum) industry, and the nature park where wild vegetation is preserved. Wandering through the marked paths you'll see the dense jungle of plants and trees named and labeled in English and Spanish. Each label has the plant's scientific and common names, use of the plant, and the geographic areas where it is found in the wild. It's rich in bird and animal life too, but to catch a glimpse of something you'll have to move quietly and listen carefully.

2. PUERTO MORELOS

21 miles S of Cancún

GETTING THERE   By Bus   Buses from Cancún's bus station going to Tulum and Playa del Carmen usually stop here, but be sure to ask in Cancún if your bus makes the Puerto Morelos stop.

By Car   Drive south from Cancún along Highway 307.

ESSENTIALS   The local area code is 987. There's one public telephone in Puerto Morelos at the *caseta de larga distancia* (tel. 987/4-5086) next to the Zenaida Restaurant a block south of the main entry street leading to the highway. You can make calls there and supposedly they'll take messages and pass along hotel-reserva-tion requests. It's open Monday through Saturday from 8am to 1pm and 4 to 7pm. On the highway, near the Puerto Morelos junction, you'll see a gas station on the left.

━━━━━━━━━━━

Most people come here to take the car-ferry to Cozumel, several hours away. Puerto Morelos has begun to resume the building boom that was beginning when Hurricane Gilbert came through.

WHERE TO STAY

CABAÑAS PUERTO MORELOS, Apdo. Postal 1524, Cancún, Q. Roo 77501. Tel. 987/1-0004. 4 cabañas.
$ Rates: High season $450–$750 per week, $70 per night. Low season $275–$450 per week, $50 per night.

If you're looking for something comfortable and reasonable, away from the crowds and near the beach, this is a good place to consider, especially for a long stay. Connie and Bill Butcher created this shady hideaway with lots of extra touches. It consists of three one-bedroom cabañas and a two-bedroom house. (Higher prices are for the two-bedroom house.) Rooms, all with tile floors, have kitchens equipped with coffee makers and juicers, plus bottled water, several beers, and soft drinks to get you started. You'll also find paperback books and colorful furniture with folk art accents. There's a shady place outside for dining or lounging. The Butchers are known for their willingness to help guests enjoy the area. Most rooms are booked in advance from the U.S., but you can take a chance on a vacancy if you're in the area. This spot is 12 miles from the Cancún airport. To find it from the Puerto Morelos zócalo: turn left at the edge of the zócalo as you come from the highway. Go three blocks and it's on the left behind a white wall and gate. Ring the bell.

Reservations: Contact Niki Seach, 7914 NE. Ochoa, Elk River, MN 55330 (tel. 619/441-7630).

CARIBBEAN REEF CLUB, Villa Marina, Puerto Morelos, Q. Roo 77500. Tel. 987/1-0191, or toll free 800/322-6286. Fax 987/1-0190. 18 apts. A/C and FAN TV
$ Rates: High season $90–$200. Low season $65–$150.

Opened in 1991, these new units of a developing condominium complex on the beach come with marble floors, neutral-toned furniture, and windows on the garden all facing the ocean. All come with one bedroom (most with two double beds), com-bination kitchenette with living room (and sleeper sofa), remote-control TV, and two bathrooms with showers (some have a combo tub/shower). Besides air conditioning, each also has a fan. In high season the units are rented as a whole (kitchenette in-cluded), but in low season they can be separated. There's a nice-size pool next to the beach. There's also complimentary use of snorkeling gear, Sunfish sailboats, and windsurf boards. A comfortable and breezy beachfront restaurant on the property serves all three meals daily between 8am and 9pm.

To find it follow directions through Puerto Morelos to the ferry pier and the complex is just beyond it.

OJO DE AGUA, Calle Ejer Mexicano, Puerto Morelos, Q. Roo 77500. Tel. 99/25-0292 in Mérida. Fax 99/28-3405. 16 rms. FAN
$ Rates: High season $55–$60 single or double. Low season $50–$60 single or double.

This family-style two-story hotel on the beach is ideal for a long weekend or extended stay especially in the 12 rooms with kitchens. All rooms have white-tile floors, natural-toned furniture, and table and chairs. Most rooms have one double and one twin bed, but two come with king-size beds. There's a free-form pool by the ocean. The restaurant operates seasonally, more or less depending on hotel occupancy, so don't count on it.

To find it, from the zócalo turn left on the last street which parallels the ocean. The hotel is at the far end on the left.

Reservations: In Mérida, contact the hotel at Calle 12 no. 96, Mérida, Yuc. 97050. The office is between Calles 21 and 23.

POSADA AMOR, Apdo. Postal 806, Cancún, Q. Roo 77500. Tel. and fax 987/1-0033. 20 rms (10 with bath).
$ Rates: $21–$25 single or double without bath, $30–$35 single or double with bath.
The simple, cheery little rooms with screens and mosquito netting are quite plain but adequate and clustered around a patio in back of the restaurant. The posada's restaurant is rustic and quaint like an English cottage with whitewashed walls, small shuttered windows, and open rafters, and decorated with primitive paintings and flowers on each table. Prices are reasonable, with main courses costing $7 to $12 or so. It's open daily from 7:30am to 10pm.

To get here, when you enter town, turn right; with the town square on the left, follow the main street leading to the ferry and the hotel is on the right.

WHERE TO DINE

LOS PELICANOS, on the oceanside behind and right on the zócalo. Tel. 1-0014.
Cuisine: SEAFOOD.
$ Prices: Main courses $4–$20; lobster $25.
Open: Daily 10am–10pm.
In this village of few restaurants, Los Pelicanos has an almost captive audience for beachside dining. You'll notice the inviting restaurant down a block or two right of the zócalo on the street paralleling the ocean. Select a table inside under the palapa or outside on the terrace (but wear mosquito repellent in the evenings). From the terrace you have an easy view of pelicans swooping around the dock. The seafood menu has all the usual offerings from ceviche to conch three ways to shrimp, lobster, and fish. There's grilled chicken and steak for nonseafood eaters.

THE CAR-FERRY TO COZUMEL

The dock (tel. 987/1-0008) is the largest establishment in town and very easy to find. The car-ferry schedule is a complicated one and may change, so double-check it before arriving. On Monday and Tuesday the ferry leaves at 1pm; on Wednesday at 10am; on Thursday, Saturday, and Sunday at 6am; and on Friday at 5am.

Cargo takes precedence over cars. Some 25 to 30 cars can fit on each ferry but there's space for only two to four camper vehicles. Officials suggest camper drivers stay overnight in the parking lot to be first in line for tickets. In any case, always arrive at least two hours in advance of the ferry departure to purchase a ticket and to get in line. The trip to Cozumel takes three to four hours.

Since passenger-boat service between Playa del Carmen and Cozumel is quite frequent now, I don't recommend that foot passengers trying to reach Cozumel bother with this boat.

Check return schedules upon arrival in Cozumel. The return voyage from Cozumel leaves the car-ferry dock, south of town near the Hotel Sol Caribe. Get there early to buy your ticket and get in line. During long bouts of bad weather, the boat has been kept docked for as long as a week.

EN ROUTE TO PLAYA DEL CARMEN

Heading south on Highway 307 from Puerto Morelos, the village of **Muchi** is the next landmark. It's only 20 miles from Puerto Morelos to **Playa del Carmen,** so you'll be there in a half hour or less. However, you'll pass several small beach resorts en route. Less than three miles before Playa del Carmen, you'll see a sign pointing left to **Punta Bete,** which is the place-name for a fine beach—not a town. For an out-of-the-way place on a private beach, turn left here to the Cabañas Xcalacoco, for which you'll see a faded sign on the highway.

Continuing on the highway toward Playa del Carmen and less than a mile past the Punta Bete turnoff is another sign pointing left to two more beachfront resorts, Las Palapas and the Shangri-La Caribe. In both places, if you come between July and October, you can walk the beach at night to watch for **turtles** lumbering ashore to lay their eggs, or watch the eggs hatch and the tiny vulnerable turtles scurry to the ocean in the last two months. However, turtles will not lay eggs where there is too much light, so as development continues (and more lights are installed) we'll see fewer turtles nesting.

WHERE TO STAY

The hotels that follow are listed in the order that travelers will pass them.

CABAÑAS XCALACOCO, Carretera Cancún-Tulum km 52 (Apdo. Postal 176), Playa del Carmen, Q. Roo 77710. No phone. 7 cabañas.

$ Rates: $35 one bed; $40 two beds; RV and campers $4 per person. Discounts in low season. **Parking:** Free.

The narrow, overgrown road isn't much and you may even wonder if it's the right one. Have faith and keep bearing right. Soon you'll reach the beach and the compound with cabañas facing the ocean. Though close to Playa del Carmen, you might as well be a thousand miles from civilization for the secluded feeling you get. It's a real hideaway. The cabañas are tidy, whitewashed concrete buildings with small porches all right on the beach. All have bathrooms; five have king-size beds, and the others have two double beds each. Since there's no electricity, kerosene lamps light rooms in the evenings. Camping facilities are available for those in recreational vehicles and others wishing to hang a hammock under a thatched-roof covering. For these folks there's a shower and bathroom but no electricity. An excellent small restaurant on the premises serves guests, but it's always a good idea to bring along packaged and canned snacks, water, and soft drinks. Owners Ricardo and Rosa Novelo can arrange snorkeling and fishing trips for up to four people.

LA POSADA DEL CAPITÁN LAFITTE, Carretera Cancún-Tulum km 62, Playa del Carmen, Q. Roo. Tel. 987/3-0214. Fax 987/3-0213. 40 bungalows. A/C FAN

$ Rates (including breakfast and dinner): Low season $80–$90 single; $90–$340 double. Christmas, New Year's, Thanksgiving, and part of Feb are higher. Minimum three-night stay. No credit cards. **Parking:** Free.

You'll see the sign on the highway pointing left toward Capitán Lafitte, and then you'll drive a mile down a rough dirt road that heads east from the highway. The single-story, white stucco bungalows are smallish but very comfortable, stylishly furnished, and equipped with tile floors, small tiled bathrooms, and either two double

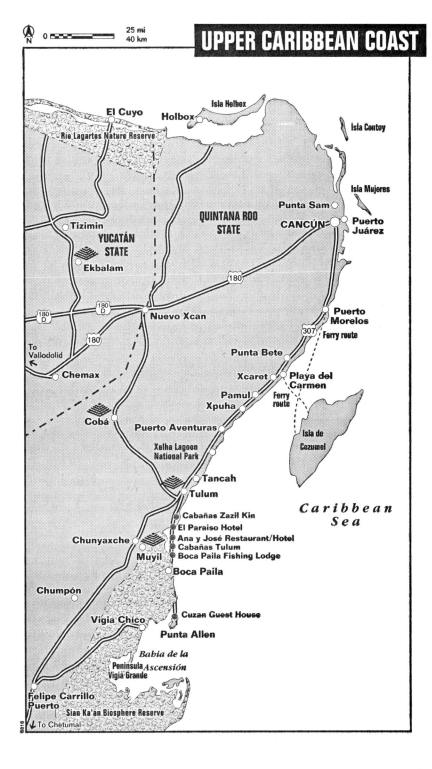

beds or one king-size bed and an oceanfront porch. There's 24-hour electricity (a plus you learn to value on this coast). Guests can receive coffee in the room as early as 6:30am. You'll find a large raised swimming pool and sunning deck, dining room, clubhouse, restaurant, and dive shop. There's a turtle patrol during summer on nearby beaches known as nesting grounds for green and loggerhead turtles. Divers from North America make up virtually the entire clientele here.

Information and reservations: Contact Turquoise Reef Group, Box 2664, Evergreen, CO 80439 (tel. 303/674-9615, or toll free 800/538-6802 in the U.S.). Reservations can also be made in Mérida (tel. 99/23-0485 or 24-1585; fax 99/23-7142). During high season rooms are usually booked well in advance.

SHANGRI-LA CARIBE, Carretera Cancún-Tulum km 69.5 (Apdo. Postal 116), Playa del Carmen, Q. Roo 77710. Tel. 987/2-2888. Fax 987/3-0500. 70 rms. FAN

$ Rates (including breakfast and dinner): High season $75 single; $100–$470 double. Christmas, New Year's, and part of Feb higher; low-season discounts. **Parking:** Free.

Only a mile or so before the Playa del Carmen turnoff, you can't miss signs for Shangri-La Caribe on the highway which point left a mile down a semipaved road. The two-story, high-domed, palapa-topped bungalows meander to the ocean linked by sidewalks and edged by tropical vegetation. All come with two double beds, nice tile baths, and a hammock strung on the patio or balcony. Prices get higher the closer you get to the beach and for two-bedroom casas.

Dining/Entertainment: One restaurant serves all three meals and the bar is open long hours.

Services: Car rental and taxi tours to nearby lagoons and ruins.

Facilities: The large inviting pool is surrounded by a sun deck and there are horses to rent at $40 an hour. The Cyan-Ha Diving Center on the premises offers diving, snorkeling, and fishing trips, and equipment rental for these sports. May and June are best for fishing with abundant marlin, sailfish, and dorado.

Information and Reservations: Contact Turquoise Reef Group, Box 2664, Evergreen, CO 80439 (tel. 303/674-9615, or toll free 800/538-6802 in the U.S.). Reservations can also be made in Mérida (tel. 99/23-0485 or 24-1585; fax 99/23-7142).

---

3. PLAYA DEL CARMEN

20 miles S of Puerto Morelos, 44 miles S of Cancún

GETTING THERE By Bus There are five bus stations in Playa del Carmen, all on Avenida Principal (the main street). **Transportes de Oriente** is one and a half blocks north of the ferry and main square. **Autotransportes del Caribe** is across the street, near the corner of Avenida Principal and Avenida 5. **Expresso de Oriente** is in the same area on Avenida Principal. The **ADO** station is four blocks north of the ferry dock and two north of the zócalo. **Autotransportes Playa Express** is opposite Transportes del Caribe a half a block from Avenida 5. It has minibus service from Cancún every half hour from 6am to 8pm. From Cancún, Transportes de Orients runs one confirmed-seat bus. Seven de paso ADO buses pass through Playa del Carmen on the way to Cancún. The first is at 6:30am. Seven ADO buses go to Valladolid, Chichén-Itzá, and Mérida; and one to Tulum at 10:45am; several second-class buses run the same routes.

By Car The turnoff to Playa del Carmen from Highway 307 is plainly marked and you'll arrive on the town's widest street, Avenida Principal/Avenida Juárez (not that there's a street sign to that effect).

By Ferry Of the three ferries from Cozumel mentioned below, the water jet **WJ México** is the fastest by 10 to 15 minutes. If the water is choppy, take precautions against seasickness. See the schedule in the accompanying table.

DEPARTING By Bus **Autotransportes Playa Express** buses depart every half hour for Cancún. **Autotransportes del Caribe** buses are all de paso to Cancún, Xel-Ha, Tulum, and Felipe Carrillo Puerto. **Transportes de Oriente** runs five buses to Cancún, the first at 5am and the last at 6:30pm, as well as buses to Tulum, Valladolid, and Cobá at 5 and 10am and 5pm. **ADO** also goes to Villahermosa and Mexico City from here.

By Ferry See the schedule in the accompanying table.

This little Caribbean village came into being because of the passenger-boat service to Cozumel. But it's developed quite a tourist trade of its own. With the opening of the luxurious Hotel Continental Plaza Playacar near the ferry dock in 1991, and the nearby all-inclusive Diamond Resort in 1992, "progress" is more rapid than ever and developers have plans for untouched and beautiful beaches both north and south of the village. Travelers have discovered that Playa del Carmen's long stretches of white beach are far better than those on Cozumel.

Playa del Carmen is finally getting government attention as it moves towards becoming a major coastal city. The town doubled in size in 1993 and authorities set aside more land for the town across Highway 307. By the turn of the century, Playa del Carmen is projected to have a population of more than 50,000. In 1992, new sewage and water lines were laid throughout town and the town finally received telephone service. By early 1993, many of the dirt streets had been covered with concrete. Avenida 5 became a pedestrians-only walkway for five blocks. The town cut its political apron strings from Cozumel and became independent, complete with its first elected mayor, within its own separate *municipio*. Avenida Principal/Avenida Juárez leads into town and has always been considered "main street." Now four-lane Avenida 30, five blocks away from the beach, has been paved and is positioned as another "main street." Builders are busy sectioning off housing developments for local use (as opposed to touristic use). Time-share hawkers ply their fake-friendly ways in Playa now, but not in the numbers present in Cancún. Topless sun bathing, though against the law in Mexico, seems condoned here including leisurely topless beach strolling anywhere there's a beach. It's so casually topless, in fact, that there's a sign in the post office to the effect of "No topless in here." Nightlife consists of pleasant strolls and sitting at streetside cafés, listening to music until 10 or 11pm.

Playa's loss of innocence in 1993 was inevitable given the tremendous growth on this coastline and Playa's position in the center of it. Still, Playa is a relatively peaceful place where you can hang out on the beach for hours without feeling the need to explore. But get there quick—it's changing fast.

ORIENTATION

ARRIVING The ferry dock in Playa del Carmen is a block and a half from the main square, and within walking distance of hotels. The fare one-way is between $7 and $10.

FERRY SCHEDULE FROM COZUMEL TO PLAYA DEL CARMEN

WJ México	*Xelha* and *Cozumeleño*
4am	4am
6:30	6:30
8	7:45
9	8:30
11	9
1:30pm	10:45
3:15	1:15pm
4	3:45
5:30	5:30
6:30	7:45
8	

FERRY SCHEDULE FROM PLAYA DEL CARMEN TO COZUMEL

WJ México	*Xelha* and *Cozumeleño*
5:30am	5:30am
7:30	7:30
9:30	9:30
10:15	10:20
Noon	Noon
2:15pm	2:15pm
4	4
5:30	5:15
6:30	6:30
7:30	8:45
8:45	

CITY LAYOUT   Street signs are fairly visible throughout the village. The main street, **Avenida Principal/Avenida Juárez,** leads into town from Highway 307, crossing Avenida 5 one block before it ends at the beach next to the main plaza or zócalo. **Avenida 5** leads to the ferry dock, two blocks from the zócalo, but it's closed to vehicular traffic. Most restaurants and hotels are either on Avenida 5, or a block or two off of it. The village's beautiful beach parallels Avenida 5 and is only a block from it.

GETTING AROUND   Taxis are available but unless you are going to the highway, just about everything is a short walk from hotels, restaurants, the ferry, and zócalo.

FAST FACTS

Area Code   The telephone area code is 987.

Laundry   There's a launderette, Lavandería Yee, on Avenida 5 on the left. It's open Monday through Saturday from 8am to 8pm and on Sunday and holidays from 7am to noon.

Long-distance Telephone   Most hotels have telephone service now. The Hotel Playa del Carmen on Avenida Principal is open for long-distance service Monday through Saturday from 7am to 2pm and 3 to 9pm.

Parking   Because of the pedestrians-only blocks and increasing population and popularity of Playa, parking close to hotels has become more difficult. There was talk of prohibiting vehicular traffic inside the village by corraling all vehicles into a pay lot that would be served by special taxis.

Post Office   The post office is on Avenida Principal, three blocks north of the zócalo on the right past the Hotel Playa del Carmen.

Seasons   High season is December through Easter, plus August. November is becoming quite popular with Europeans and some innkeepers are raising prices then as well. Low season is all other months.

Spanish Lessons   The Centro Bilingue de Playa del Carmen (tel. and fax 987/3-0550) offers informal classes in conversational Spanish as well as Spanish geared toward government and business. Classes in Maya were in the planning stages—check on the status. For a reasonable fee they'll arrange transport to the Cancún airport and confirm airline tickets. The school is in the village proper, but ask for the exact address when you make enrollment plans.

WHAT TO SEE & DO

Playa's main attraction is its fine, wide beach; most people come just to relax and enjoy it. Other attractions include offshore scuba diving and snorkeling and day trips to beaches at nearby Xcalacoco, Punta Bete, Xcaret, Pamul, or Xpuha.

The island of Cozumel is a 45-minute ferry ride away. A bit farther afield are the ruins of Tulum and Cobá.

At the Maya-Bric Hotel, the **Tank-Ha Dive Shop** (tel. 3-0302) rents diving and snorkeling gear and arranges trips to the reefs. Snorkeling trips cost $25 and include soft drinks and equipment. Two-tank dive trips are $60; resort courses are available. You can make arrangements for most of these on your own with local taxi drivers, but get the price established in advance.

Jaguar Tours, Calle 12 Norte (tel. 987/3-0456), has a variety of local trips, many of which are focused on nature such as cave diving and snorkeling in lagoons and cenotes. For more information write Apdo. Postal 126, Playa del Carmen, Q. Roo 77710.

WHERE TO STAY

There are motel-style hotels on Avenida Principal, but the more interesting hostelries are the cabaña-style inns along the beach and on Avenida 5.

VERY EXPENSIVE

CONTINENTAL PLAZA PLAYACAR, Frac. Playacar km 62.5, Playa del Carmen, Q. Roo 77710. Tel. 987/3-0100, or toll free 800/882-6684 in the U.S. Fax 987/3-0105. 204 rms. A/C TEL

$ Rates: High season $200 single or double. Low season $140 single or double.

Playa del Carmen's most lavish and comfortable hotel opened in 1991 on 308 acres spreading out along the beach beyond the ferry pier. Almost 200 Maya ruins were found during development of the resort. The entry leads through a sunny, wide marble lobby beyond which you see the pool and beach. The large, beautifully furnished rooms all have in-room safety boxes, purified tap water, tile floors, large baths, wet bars with refrigerators, and balconies with ocean views. To find it from the ferry pier, turn left when you get off the ferry and follow the road a short distance until you see the Playacar sign.

Dining/Entertainment: La Pergola, with pool, beach, and ocean view, serves international food daily from 7 to 11am and 6 to 11pm. La Sirena, the poolside restaurant, is open from 7am to 6pm daily. The stylish and welcoming lobby bar is open between 11am and 1am daily with live music in the evenings.

Services: Room and laundry service, babysitting, gift shop and boutiques, travel agency, and tours to nearby archeological zones and lagoons.

Facilities: Oceanside pool, water-sports equipment, one lighted tennis court.

EXPENSIVE

HOTEL MOLCAS, 1 Sur y Av. 5, Playa del Carmen, Q. Roo 77710. Tel. 987/3-0070 or 3-0135. Fax 987/3-0071. 35 rms. A/C

$ Rates: High season $75 single, $86 double. Low season $58 single, $75 double.

Built in the 1970s this is Playa's first hotel, built to accommodate ferry passengers when the service first started. It's a graceful, two-story, colonial-style hotel with tile floors and comfortable rooms. The restaurant faces the ferry and is a comfortable place to sip a cool drink and watch the comings and goings of tourists and the ferry.

MODERATE

ALBATROS ROYALE, Apdo. Postal 31, Playa del Carmen, Q. Roo 77710. Tel. 987/3-0001, or toll free 800/527-0022 for reservations in the U.S. 31 rms. FAN

$ Rates: High season $50–$65 single or double. Low season $35–$45 single or double.

Almost next door to the Cabañas Albatros, the new "deluxe" sister hotel rises up two stories on a narrow bit of land facing the beach. The white-stucco and thatch-roofed architecture is typical of the style seen often on this coast, and there's a meandering garden-lined path leading to the rooms. The large rooms are modern and comfortable, with tile floors, large tile bathrooms with marble vanities and showers, over-bed reading lights, balconies or porches, and ocean views. Hammocks swing outside each door. Most have two double beds but seven have queen-size beds. Parking is on the street.

From Avenida Principal walk four blocks north on Avenida 5, then right half a block; the hotel is on the left.

BUNGALOWS YAX HA, Apdo. Postal 84, Playa del Carmen, Q. Roo 77710. No phone. 4 rms. FAN

$ Rates: $40–$80 single or double large bungalow; $30–$60 single or double small bungalow.

This little grouping of rustically comfortable bungalows is set back in an idyllic setting of shady sand pathways edged by tropical plants and conch shells. No two are alike inside although each one has a covered porch and kitchen. For example, the thatch-roofed Casa Alta has a single bed downstairs with the living room and kitchen. A ladder goes to the loft sleeping area with a double bed. Casa Rodonda sleeps four people in two separate rooms. The other two cottages have concrete roofs—a plus considering mosquitoes—and a single cot and double bed in one bedroom.

It's right on the beach at the corner of Calle 10 between Calles 8 and 10.

CABAÑAS ALBATROS, Apdo. Postal 31, Playa del Carmen, Q. Roo 77710. Tel. 987/3-0001, or toll free 800/527-0022 in the U.S. 18 bungalows. FAN

$ Rates: High season $40–$50 cabaña for one or two. Low season $30–$40 cabaña for one or two.

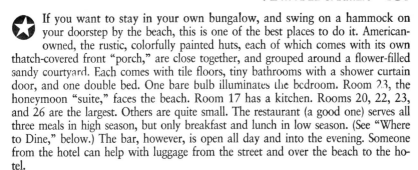 If you want to stay in your own bungalow, and swing on a hammock on your doorstep by the beach, this is one of the best places to do it. American-owned, the rustic, colorfully painted huts, each of which comes with its own thatch-covered front "porch," are close together, and grouped around a flower-filled sandy courtyard. Each comes with tile floors, tiny bathrooms with a shower curtain door, and one double bed. One bare bulb illuminates the bedroom. Room 23, the honeymoon "suite," faces the beach. Room 17 has a kitchen. Rooms 20, 22, 23, and 26 are the largest. Others are quite small. The restaurant (a good one) serves all three meals in high season, but only breakfast and lunch in low season. (See "Where to Dine," below.) The bar, however, is open all day and into the evening. Someone from the hotel can help with luggage from the street and over the beach to the hotel.

From Avenida Principal walk three blocks north on Avenida 5, then right one block to the beach; the hotel is half a block down on the beach.

CABAÑAS NUEVO AMANECER, Calle 4 Norte no. 3 (Apdo. Postal 59), Playa del Carmen, Q. Roo 77710. No phone. 14 rms. FAN
$ Rates: $25–$35 single or double.

American-owned and well kept, the rooms are connected by a thatched-roof walkway. Each tidy cabaña also has a thatched roof, well-screened windows, mosquito netting over the bed, tile floors and baths, one double bed, and a hammock. A spare bed can be added. Laundry service is available.

It's on the landward side off Avenida 5, 1½ blocks from the beach, 4½ blocks from the ferry, and 2½ blocks from the bus station.

CUEVO PARGO, Calle 8 s/n, Playa del Carmen, Q. Roo 77710. Tel. and fax 987/3-0351. 13 rms (11 with bath). FAN
$ Rates: High season $30–$65 single or double. Low season $25–$45 single or double.

New owners Sandy and Bill Dillon gave the Cuevo Pargo a splendid cleaning and revamp and are adding new rooms. Set in a small patch of undisturbed jungle, and linked by stone pathways, it's cooler than any place in town and comes complete with its own cenote. Rooms are rustic but comfortable and come with small charms like rock walls and unusual architecture—no two are alike. Two of the bungalows share two baths, which are separate for men and women. Three bungalows have kitchens. One room has a loft bed with a living area below. The hotel's tiny restaurant serves a limited menu of charcoal-broiled hot dogs and hamburgers (with U.S. beef), homemade potato salad, and Texmex chili; plans were in the works to expand the menu. The Safari bar, to the left after you enter, is a good place to come for an evening drink and meet fellow travelers. The bar is open daily from 3pm to midnight. Happy hour is between 5 and 6pm and from 7 to 8pm. There's a TV with U.S. channels in the lobby.

From Avenida Principal walk four blocks north on Avenida 5, then right half a block; the hotel is on the left half a block from the beach.

HOTEL ALEJARI, Calle 6 (Apdo. Postal 166), Playa del Carmen, Q. Roo 77710. Tel. 987/3-2754. Fax 987/3-2155. A/C (5 rms) FAN (10 rms)
$ Rates: High season $40 single or double; $66 single or double with kitchenette; $60 single or double two-story unit with kitchen. Low season $35 single or double; $58–$65 single or double two-story unit with kitchen. **Parking:** Free; guarded.

Built around a fastidiously kept, flower-filled inner yard, this small hotel lies on the beach side just off Avenida 5 and half a block from the beach. Rooms are clean, with white walls, ruffled bedspreads, and a small vanity with mirror in the bedrooms.

Ground-level rooms have two double beds. Rooms with kitchens have a kitchen and living room downstairs, and the bedroom, with a king-size bed, is up a narrow stairway.

LA RANA CANSADA, Calle 10, Playa del Carmen 77710. Tel. 987/3-0389. 7 rms (all with bath).

$ Rates: High season $45 single or double. Low season $25 single or double.

The "Tired Frog" is one of the most simply pleasant inns in the village. Open again after several years, it's had a complete facelift. Rooms face an inner courtyard with a small snack bar under a large thatched palapa where guests can lounge and read. Paperbacks are available at the front desk. Hammocks are strung on the covered porch outside the row of rooms. The rooms are simple, but very neat, with fresh paint, new tile floors, and bathroom fixtures. Some have concrete ceilings and some have thatched roofs. Doors and windows are well screened, but each room comes with a box of mosquito-repellent coils to light. Guests receive a key to the outside gate. It's a block and a half inland from the beach.

To find it, from the main plaza walk five blocks north on Avenida 5 and turn left on Calle 10; the hotel is on the left.

MAYA-BRIC HOTEL, Av. 5 Norte, Playa del Carmen, Q. Roo 77710. Tel. and fax 987/3-0011, 24 rms. A/C or FAN

$ Rates: High season $45 single or double. Low season $25 single; $30 double.

The colorful exterior and flowers of this two-story, beachfront inn will catch your eye. The well-kept rooms have two double beds and stucco walls. There's a small, clean swimming pool. A restaurant by the office serves breakfast and dinner during high season. The Tank-Ha Dive Shop located here (see "What to See & Do," above) arranges daily diving and snorkeling trips. It never hurts to ask for an additional discount on rooms here.

It's between Calles 8 and 10, 4½ blocks (north) past the zócalo, on the right.

BUDGET

BANANAS CABAÑAS, Av. 5 at Calle 6, Playa del Carmen, Q. Roo 77710 Tel. 987/3-0036. 15 rms (9 with bath). FAN

$ Rates: High season $25–$35 single; $27–$41 double. Low season $18–$25 single; $22–$27 double.

The formerly run-down Bananas Cabañas experienced a total revamp in 1993. Rooms were gutted, painted, and refurnished. Though not finished when I checked, they looked better than the last worn-out incarnation and should be a much better choice at bargain prices when they're finished. The higher prices are for rooms with a private bath. The hotel is behind Limones Restaurant.

MOM'S HOTEL, Av. 30 at Calle 4. Tel. 987/3-0315. 12 rms (all with bath). FAN

$ Rates: High season $25 single; $30 double. Low season (May–June and Sept–Nov) $15 single; $20 double. Discounts for lengthy stays.

Though away from the beach, this is a good choice if all the beachside inns are full, or for a long stay. Rooms, all facing the interior courtyard, are fairly large and sunny, and come with tile floors, one or two double beds, and bedside reading lights. There's a small pool in the courtyard and Mom's restaurant, as you enter, is a good one for all meals. Six more rooms are being added.

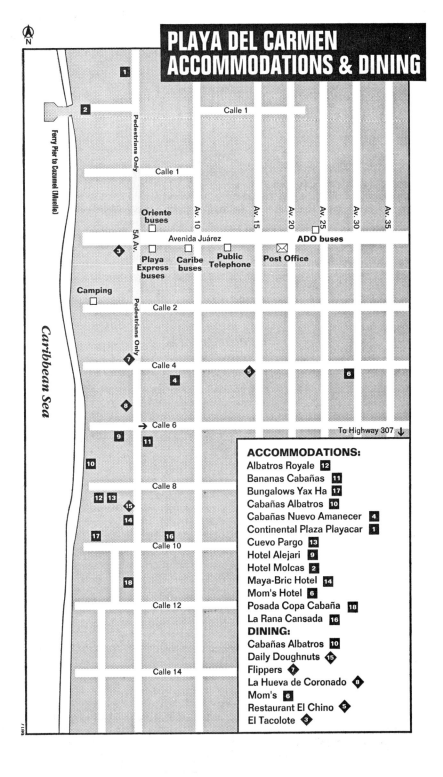

PLAYA DEL CARMEN
ACCOMMODATIONS & DINING

N

Ferry Pier to Cozumel (Muelle)

Caribbean Sea

Calle 1

Pedestrians Only

Calle 1

Oriente buses

Av. 10

Av. 15

Av. 20

Av. 25

Av. 30

Av. 35

5A Av.

Avenida Juárez

ADO buses

Playa Express buses

Caribe buses

Public Telephone

Post Office

Camping

Pedestrians Only

Calle 2

Calle 4

Calle 6

To Highway 307

Calle 8

Calle 10

Calle 12

Calle 14

ACCOMMODATIONS:
Albatros Royale **12**
Bananas Cabañas **11**
Bungalows Yax Ha **17**
Cabañas Albatros **10**
Cabañas Nuevo Amanecer **4**
Continental Plaza Playacar **1**
Cuevo Pargo **13**
Hotel Alejari **9**
Hotel Molcas **2**
Maya-Bric Hotel **14**
Mom's Hotel **6**
Posada Copa Cabaña **18**
La Rana Cansada **16**
DINING:
Cabañas Albatros **10**
Daily Doughnuts **15**
Flippers **7**
La Hueva de Coronado **8**
Mom's **6**
Restaurant El Chino **5**
El Tacolote **3**

POSADA COPA CABAÑA, Apdo. Postal 103, Playa del Carmen, Q. Roo
77710. Tel. 987/3-0218. 4 rms. 2 cabañas. FAN
$ Rates: High season $30 single; $40 double. Low season $25 single, $30 double.

Hammocks are stretched in front of each room and on the porch of each cabaña at this pleasant inn that occupies a shady yard set back on Avenida 5 between Calles 6 and 8. The clean, simply furnished rooms have one or two double beds on cement platforms, and pink-and-gray tile floors. Vanity and sinks are conveniently placed outside the bathrooms in each one. There's good cross ventilation through well-screened windows.

CAMPING

Playa del Carmen has many little camping sites down along the water. Turn to the left at the beach and head for the **Camping Cabañas Las Ruinas** (no phone), right on the beach and across the street from a tiny Maya ruin. Everyone pays a refundable entry deposit of $8.50 and cabin renters deposit $20. Hammocks rent for $2, and sheets, towels, and blankets (no pillows) rent for 75¢. Lockers cost $1; security boxes cost $5. Hammock space in a covered palapa comes with a locker and costs $5. Small cabins cost $10 to $15; tent, trailer, camper, or auto space costs $5. A shady palapa serves as a restaurant and general gathering area. Coming in from the highway, turn left (north) on the town's main street, go one block, and turn right.

A YOUTH HOSTEL

From the bus station, walk toward the highway and follow the signs to the local youth hostel. A bed in an 18-bunk room with cold water costs $5. This includes sheets, pillowcase, and a locker. You can also rent a cabaña for $17 with shared bath. It's a 10- to 15-minute walk from the bus station.

WHERE TO DINE

MODERATE

CABAÑAS ALBATROS, on the beach at the corner of Calle 6. Tel. 3-0001.
Cuisine: MEXICAN/ITALIAN.
$ Prices: Breakfast $3.50–$8; appetizers $2–$6; main courses $5–10.
Open: Breakfast daily 7–11am; lunch daily 12:30–3pm; dinner daily in high season 6–10pm. Happy hour noon–1pm and 4–6pm.

On the beach, this is a good place to meet Americans who live here and while away some hours munching and people-watching. The food is dependably good. The lunch menu has nachos (loaded or plain), fruit, submarine sandwiches, hamburgers, ceviche, soup, seafood, fajitas, salads, and tacos. The evening menu in season features seafood and a few offerings from the lunch menu. From Avenida Principal walk three blocks north on Avenida 5 then turn right one block on Calle 6 to the beach and turn left; the hotel/restaurant is half a block down the beach.

FLIPPERS, Av. 5 at Calle 4. No phone.
Cuisine: MEXICAN/GRILLED MEAT.
$ Prices: Grilled specialties $7–$20; seafood platter $29.
Open: Daily 3–10:30pm.

There's almost always a crowd at Flippers, which is noticeable from the street for its nautical theme, created by fishnets and ropes under a thatched palapa. There's an extensive bar list as well as a varied menu that includes hamburgers, poc-chuc, beef tampiqueña, and grilled seafood.

LA HUEVA DE CORONADO, Av. 5. No phone.
Cuisine: MEXICAN.
$ Prices: Breakfast $4–$7; main courses $5–$16.
Open: Daily 9am–midnight.

Another of Playa's popular restaurants with a breezy nautical decor, this one is especially popular at breakfast. The menu also offers beef, chicken, and fish as main courses. Try the filling and well-prepared plate-lunch special.

BUDGET

DAILY DOUGHNUTS, Av. 5 between Calles 8 and 10. Tel. 3-0396.
Cuisine: DOUGHNUTS/CROISSANT SANDWICHES.
$ Prices: Doughnuts 70¢; centers 20¢; sandwiches $1.90; molletes 50¢; coffee 75¢.
Open: Daily 7am–9pm.

Paulino and Federico Suárez, a pair of enterprising Mexico City youths, opened this delicious doughnut shop in 1993. The variety is mouthwatering—50 kinds in all, with terrific toppings, all glazy or chocolatey or nutty or combined, and flavored with coffee, almonds, cream, blueberries, strawberries, peanut butter, and more. The Chiapan blend they use makes the best cup of coffee in town. To be sure their doughnuts get around, youths take variety batches on large tricycles around town, and you can buy from them too. Load up the night before for breakfast in your room or on your patio, or get it fresh that morning.

EL TACOLOTE, Av. Juárez. Tel. 3-0066.
Cuisine: GRILLED MEATS & SEAFOOD.
$ Prices: Main courses $3.50–$12.25.
Open: Daily 9am–9pm. Shortened hours in low season.

You may have enjoyed the branch of this restaurant in Cancún. And you'll likely enjoy this one, too, with its cool patio in back. There's a good selection of tacos, hamburgers, and mixed brochettes. The vegetarian plate is grilled shrimp with peppers. The "gringas" plate comes with flour tortillas, grilled pork, and cheese. Charro beans are among the side orders. The restaurant faces the main plaza.

MOM'S, Av. 30 at Calle 4. Tel. 3-0315.
Cuisine: HOME COOKING.
$ Prices: Breakfast $2–$5.75; lunch and dinner $3.85–$7.
Open: Daily 7am–9pm.

Where else but at home do you think of having sandwiches of fried eggs or peanut butter and jelly, or perhaps meatloaf, apple cobbler, and homemade vanilla ice cream? Mom's has it. At Christmas and Thanksgiving you can depend on turkey with all the traditional fixings. Other standard menu offerings include soup and salad, chicken salad, and daily lunch and dinner specials such as fish in a basket. A TV with U.S. channels is tuned to the news, or sports if there's an important game. This is a good place to meet resident foreigners. To find it, walk five blocks west on Calle 4 and it's on the right, inside Mom's Hotel, and facing the open interior courtyard.

RESTAURANT EL CHINO, Calle 4 at Av. 15, No phone.
Cuisine: YUCATÁN/MEXICAN.
$ Prices: Breakfast $1.25–$3.85; main courses $5–$7.75.
Open: Daily 8am–11pm.

Locals highly recommend this place and so do I. Though slightly off the popular Avenida 5 row of restaurants, it has its own cool ambience with tile floors and plastic-covered tables set below a huge palapa roof with whirring ceiling fans.

Among the offerings to enjoy at breakfast are cornflakes, pancakes, and blended fruit drinks. Main courses include some regional favorites such as poc-chuc, chicken pibil, and Ticul-style fish. Other selections include lobster and shrimp crêpes, brochettes of beef, chicken or shrimp, fajitas, ceviche, and sandwiches.

EN ROUTE TO COZUMEL
& THE LOWER CARIBBEAN COAST

From Playa del Carmen you can go by ferry to Cozumel (see the ferry schedule earlier in this section for details) or continue south to Akumal, Tulum, Punta Allen, and Chetumal on Highway 307. Or it's an easy trip inland to Cobá from the turnoff at Tulum.

4. COZUMEL

12 miles E of Playa del Carmen, 44 miles S of Cancún

GETTING THERE By Plane Aero Cozumel (tel. 2-0928, 2-0503, or 2-0877; fax 987/2-0500 in Cozumel; tel. 4-2862 in Cancún)—a Mexicana affiliate—has numerous flights to and from Cancún. **Continental** (tel. 2-0847 or 2-0487) has flights from Houston. **Mexicana,** Melgar Sur 17 at Calle Salas (tel. 2-0157, 2-0263, or at the airport 2-0405; fax 2-2945), flies from Dallas/Fort Worth, Miami, and Mérida. **Taesa** (tel. 2-4220) flies from Cancún.

By Bus Buses from Cancún go to Playa del Carmen where there are frequent passenger ferries to Cozumel (see Section 3, above).

By Car See Section 2, "Puerto Morelos," above, for car-ferry information. Or you could drive to Playa del Carmen, find a reliable place to leave your car, and take the passenger ferry from Playa del Carmen.

By Ferry There are several passenger ferries running between Cozumel and Playa del Carmen. **WJ México,** the modern water jet, makes the trip in 40 to 45 minutes compared to 50 to 60 on the **Xelha** and **Cozumeleño.** The *WJ México* costs $10 one-way and is enclosed, usually air-conditioned, with cushioned seats and video entertainment. *Cozumeleño* and *Xelha* run open-air vessels with canopies for $6.75. Both companies have ticket booths at the main pier. Be prepared for seasickness on windy days. For the ferry schedules, see Section 3, "Playa del Carmen," above, or go to the pier. The passenger ferry lets off passengers at the central village plaza. Cruise passengers and the car-ferry dock south of town.

DEPARTING Taxis, no collective vans, go to the airport for $6 to $8. For the schedule of ferry departures, see the section on Playa del Carmen, earlier in this chapter. For the car-ferry, check in Cozumel at the car-ferry dock.

SPECIAL EVENTS Carnaval/Mardi Gras is Cozumel's most colorful fiesta. It begins the Thursday before Ash Wednesday with daytime street dancing and nighttime parades on Thursday, Saturday, and Monday, with the last being the best.

C ozumel's name comes from the Maya word *Cuzamil,* meaning "land of the swallows." It's Mexico's largest Caribbean island, 28 miles long and 11 miles wide, but only 3% developed, leaving vast stretches of jungle and uninhabited shoreline. The only town is San Miguel de Cozumel, usually just called San Miguel.

During pre-Hispanic times the island was one of three important ceremonial centers (Izamal and Chichén-Itzá were the other two). Salt and honey, trade products produced on the island, further linked Cuzamil with the mainland where they put ashore at the mainland ruins we know today as Tulum. The site was occupied when Hernán Cortés landed here in 1519. Before his own boat docked, Cortés's men sacked the town and took the chief's wife and children captive. According to Bernal Díaz del Castillo's account, everything was returned. Diego de Landa's account says that Cortés converted the Indians and replaced their sacred Maya figures with a cross and a statue of Mary in the main temple at Cozumel.

After the Spanish conquest the island was an important port, but diseases brought by the foreigners decimated the population and by 1570 it was almost uninhabited. Later inhabitants returned, but the War of the Castes in the 1800s severely curtailed Cozumel trade. Cozumel continued on its economic roller coaster and after the caste war Cozumel again took its place as a commercial seaport. Merchants exported henequén, coconuts, sugarcane, bananas, chicle, pineapple, honey, and wood products. In 1955 Hurricane Janet all but demolished the coconut palm plantations. In the mid-1950s Cozumel's fame as a diving destination began to grow. Real development of the island as a resort vacation evolved along with Cancún's beginning in the mid-1970s.

Today Cozumel is one of the Yucatán's top resort destinations, and the country's diving capital. If Cancún is the jet-set's port of call and Isla Mujeres is the poor man's Cancún, Cozumel is a little bit of both. More remote than the other two, this island (pop. 50,000) is a place where people come to get away from the day-tripping atmosphere of Isla Mujeres or the mega-development of Cancún.

All the necessaries for a good vacation are here: excellent snorkeling and scuba places, sailing and water sports, expensive resorts and modest hotels, elegant restaurants and taco shops, even a Maya ruin or two. If, after a while, you do get restless, the ancient Maya city of Tulum, the lagoons of Xel-Ha and Xcaret, or the nearby village of Playa del Carmen provide convenient and interesting excursions.

ORIENTATION

INFORMATION   The **Tourism Office** (tel. 987/2-0972) is on the second floor of the Plaza del Sol commercial building facing the central plaza. It's open Monday through Friday from 9am to 3pm.

CITY LAYOUT   San Miguel's main waterfront street is called **Avenida Rafael Melgar,** running along the western shore of the island. Passenger ferries dock right in the center, opposite the main plaza and Melgar. Car-ferries dock south of town near the hotels Sol Caribe, La Ceiba, and Fiesta Inn.

The town is laid out on a grid, with avenidas running north and south, calles running east and west. The exception is **Avenida Juárez,** which runs right from the passenger-ferry dock through the main square and inland. Juárez divides the town into northern and southern halves.

Heading inland from the dock along Juárez, you'll find that the avenidas you cross are numbered by fives: "5a Av.," "10a Av.," "15a Av." If you turn left and head north, calles are numbered evenly: 2a Norte, 4a Norte, 6a Norte. Turning right from Juárez heads you south, where the streets are numbered oddly: la Sur (also called Adolfo Salas), 3a Sur, 5a Sur. The scheme is more systematic than it is practical.

ISLAND LAYOUT   The island is cut in half by one road which runs past the airport and ruins of San Gervasio to the almost uninhabited southern coast of the island. The northern part of the island has no paved roads. It's scattered with small badly ruined Maya sites, from the age when "Cuzamil" was a land sacred to the moon goddess Ixchel. San Gervasio is accessible by motor scooter and car.

Most inexpensive hotels are in the town of San Miguel. Moderate to expensive accommodations are north and south of town. Many cater to divers. Beyond the hotels to the south is **Chancanab National Park,** centered on the beautiful lagoon of the same name. Beyond Chancanab is **Playa Palancar,** and, offshore, the **Palancar Reef** (arrecife). At the southern tip of the island is **Punta Celarain** and the lighthouse.

The eastern, seaward shore of the island is mostly surf beach, beautiful for walking but dangerous for swimming.

GETTING AROUND

You can walk to most destinations within town. The trip from town to the Chancanab Lagoon by taxi costs from around $8. For a day at the beach, finding some like-minded fellow travelers and sharing the cost of a cab is the most economical way to go. Taxis should charge no more than $8 from the town center to the farthest hotels.

Car rentals are as expensive here as in other parts of Mexico. Open-top jeeps are popular for rental, but be aware that they are easy to roll, and many tourists have been injured or killed using them. See Chapter 2, Section 8 for specifics.

Moped rentals are all over the village and cost about $25 a day, but terms and prices vary. Carefully inspect the actual moped you'll be renting to see that all the gizmos are in good shape: horn, light, starter, seat, mirror. And be sure to note all damage to the moto on the rental agreement. Most importantly, read the fine print on the back of the moped-rental agreement, which states if you are not insured, you are responsible for paying for any damage to the bike (or for all of it if it is stolen or demolished), and you must stay on paved roads. It's illegal to ride a moto without a helmet. Be careful of sunburn; there's a tendency to forget that riding in the sun all day is the same as lying on the beach all day.

Important note: North-south streets have the right of way.

FAST FACTS

American Express   The local representative is Fiesta Cozumel, Av. Melgar 27 (tel. 2-0831; fax 2-0433).

Area Code   The area code is 987.

Bookstore   The Agencia de Publicaciones Gracia, next to the Farmacia Juaquin, is a small store facing the zócalo at Avenida 5 (tel. 2-0031). It has a good selection of English-language novels and magazines. Open Monday through Saturday from 8am to 10pm and Sunday from 10am to 2pm and 6 to 10pm.

Climate   October through December there can be strong winds all over the Yucatán as well as some rain. May through September is the rainy season.

Decompression Chamber   The new decompression chamber (*cámara de decompreción)* is at Discover Cozumel Diving (tel. 2-2387) on Calle 5 Sur one block off Melgar between Melgar and Avenida 5 Sur (tel. 2-2387 or 2-0280). Normal store hours are 8am to 1pm and 4 to 8pm.

Diving   If you intend to dive, remember to bring proof of your diver's certification. Underwater currents can be very strong here, so be cautious.

Doctors   Cozumel has several English-speaking American and Mexican doctors in residence. Your hotel can help you contact one.

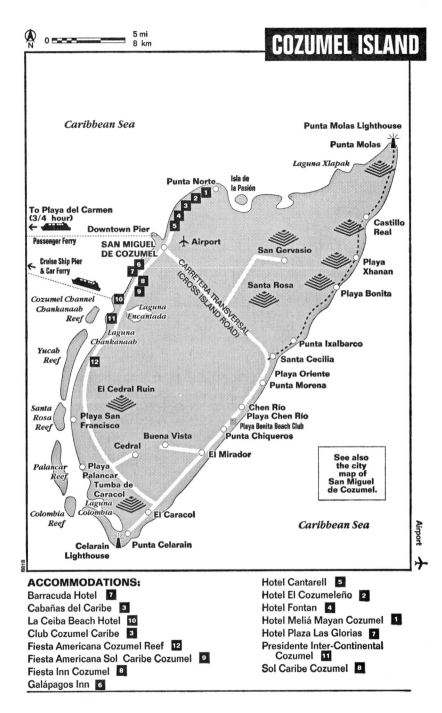

COZUMEL ISLAND

0 | 5 mi
0 | 8 km

N

Caribbean Sea

Punta Molas Lighthouse

Punta Molas

Laguna Xlapak

Punta Norte
Isla de
la Pasión

1

2

3

4

5

To Playa del Carmen
(3/4 hour)

Downtown Pier

Passenger Ferry

Castillo
Real

SAN MIGUEL
DE COZUMEL

Airport

San Gervasio

Playa
Xhanan

Cruise Ship Pier
& Car Ferry

6

7

Santa Rosa

Playa Bonita

8

9

Cozumel Channel

Chankanaab
Reef

10

Laguna
Encantada

Laguna
Chankanaab

11

Punta Ixalbarco

Yucab
Reef

12

Santa Cecilia

Playa Oriente

Punta Morena

El Cedral Ruin

Chen Río
Playa Chen Río
Playa Benita Beach Club
Punta Chiqueros

Santa
Rosa
Reef

Playa San
Francisco

Buena Vista

Cedral

El Mirador

Palancar
Reef

Playa
Palancar
Tumba de
Caracol

Laguna
Colombia

Colombia
Reef

El Caracol

Caribbean Sea

Airport

Celarain
Lighthouse

Punta Celarain

CARRETERA TRANSVERSAL
(CROSS ISLAND ROAD)

See also
the city
map of
San Miguel
de Cozumel.

8818

ACCOMMODATIONS:
Barracuda Hotel **7**
Cabañas del Caribe **3**
La Ceiba Beach Hotel **10**
Club Cozumel Caribe **3**
Fiesta Americana Cozumel Reef **12**
Fiesta Americana Sol Caribe Cozumel **9**
Fiesta Inn Cozumel **8**
Galápagos Inn **6**

Hotel Cantarell **5**
Hotel El Cozumeleño **2**
Hotel Fontan **4**
Hotel Meliá Mayan Cozumel **1**
Hotel Plaza Las Glorias **7**
Presidente Inter-Continental
Cozumel **11**
Sol Caribe Cozumel **8**

IMPRESSIONS

At this writing there were no telephones on Cozumel, and only about one crackly radio connection which usually made an unsuccessful effort at taking down reservations for those arriving. Practically no food is grown on Cozumel, aside from the plentiful lobster and fish, so that everything must be brought in by plane or ship. This goes for fuses for the power system, nails for the buildings, tissue for the bathroom and every can of food on the island.
—JOHN WILHELM, *GUIDE TO MEXICO,* 1966

Laundry   The Express Laundry on Salas, between Calles 5 Sur and 10 Sur, has do-it-yourself washers and driers, and will do dry cleaning. Open Monday through Saturday from 8am to 9pm, Sunday from 8:30am to 3pm.

Post Office   The post office (correos) is on Avenida Rafael Melgar at Calle 7 Sur, at the southern edge of town. It's open Monday through Friday from 9am to 6pm, Saturday from 9am to 6pm.

Seasons   High season is Christmas through Easter. November and December can be very windy, and too dangerous to dive.

Telephone   Long-distance telephones are on Salas between 5 Avenida Sur and 10 Avenida Sur on the exterior of the telephone building. Use a credit card to get an American operator, or push the star button twice then 09 for the U.S. and Hawaii, wait for an operator, give your area code and number and credit-card number; make it collect; or have a pile of 100-peso coins ready to feed the phone.

WHAT TO SEE & DO

TOURING THE ISLAND

Travel agencies can book you on a group tour of the island for around $30, depending on whether your tour includes lunch and a stop for snorkeling. A taxi driver charges $50 for a three-hour tour. You can easily rent a motorbike or car for half a day to take you around the southern part of the island (42 miles). *Important note:* If you drive yourself in the downtown area, be aware that north-south traffic has the right of way. Be careful, they don't slow down.

North of town, along Melgar (which becomes Carretera Pilar), you'll pass a yacht marina and a string of Cozumel's first hotels as well as some new condominiums. A few of the hotels have nice beaches, which you are welcome to use. On Cozumel this public ownership is more important than ever, since beaches are relatively few as most of the island is surrounded by coral reefs. This road ends just past the hotels; you can backtrack to the transversal road that cuts across the island from west (the town side) to east and link up with the eastern highway which brings you back to town.

The more interesting route begins by going **south** of town on Melgar (which becomes Costera Sur or Carretera a Chankanaab) past the Hotel Barracuda and Sol Caribe. About five miles south of town you'll come to the big Sol Caribe and La Ceiba Hotels, and also the car-ferry dock, for ferries to Puerto Morelos. Go snorkeling out in the water by the Hotel La Ceiba and you might spot a **sunken airplane,** put there for an underwater movie. Offshore, from here to the tip of the island at Punta Celarain, 20 miles away, is **Underwater National Park,** so designated to protect visitors from damaging the reefs. Dive masters warn not to touch or destroy the underwater growth.

FROMMER'S NATURE NOTES

THE SACRED CEIBA

Sacred to the Maya, the beautiful deciduous ceiba (*say*-bah) tree, with leaves spreading into a tall, thick canopy, is better known elsewhere as the kapok tree. Its seeds burst with a puffy cotton that's used for insulation and for stuffing mattresses and life jackets. For the Maya it represented creation and figured heavily in planting rituals to assure good crops. In Maya hieroglyphics and painting, the ceiba is represented by a breast. While a tree ripe with seeds signaled a good harvest, young Maya girls were warned to avoid touching the ripe seeds for fear of developing large, pendulous breasts—evidently an undesirable thing.

Certainly the tree is hard to ignore. At maturity a ceiba can stand more than 100 feet tall and 10 feet wide. Sharp, wide spines cover its smooth surface when it's young, but appear only on the upper parts of older trees. In its depths the Maya believed the turkey-footed Xtabay lived. A fearsome creature, she dragged her victims to nearby caves and choked the life from them, then returned to her residence inside a bent ceiba tree. How this squares with the tree as a symbol of creation isn't quite clear. This handsome tree is found all along Mexico's coasts, but it was most revered in the Yucatán.

CHANCANAB NATIONAL PARK This **lagoon** and **botanical garden** is a mile past the big hotels and 5½ miles south of town. It has long been famous for the color and variety of its sea life. The intrusion of sightseers began to ruin the marine habitat so now visitors must swim and snorkel in the open sea, not in the lagoon. The **beach** is wide and beautiful, with plenty of shady thatched umbrellas to sit under and the snorkeling is good—lots of colorful fish. Arrive early to stake out a chair and palapa before the cruise-ship visitors arrive. There are restrooms, lockers, a gift shop, several snack huts, a restaurant, and a snorkeling gear–rental palapa.

Surrounding the lagoon, a botanical garden linked by shady paths has 352 species of tropical and subtropical plants from 22 countries and 451 species from Cozumel. Several Maya structures have been re-created within the gardens to give visitors an idea of Maya life in a jungle setting. There's a small natural history museum as well. Admission to the park costs $5.50. Open daily from 8am to 4:30pm.

GOOD BEACHES After another 10 miles, you'll come to **Playa San Francisco,** and south of it, **Playa Palancar**—on Cozumel (besides the beach at Chancanab Lagoon) they're the best. Food (usually overpriced) and equipment rentals are available.

PUNTA CELARAIN After Playa San Francisco, you plow through the jungle on a straight road until you're 17½ miles from town. Finally, you emerge near the southern reaches of the island on the east coast. The **lighthouse** you see in the distance is at **Punta Celarain,** the island's southernmost tip. The sand track is unsuitable for motorbikes, but you can drive to the lighthouse in about 25 minutes.

THE EASTERN SHORE The road along the east coast of the island is wonderful. There are views of the sea, the rocky shore, and the pounding surf. On the land side are little farms and scrubby forests. Exotic birds take flight as you approach, and monstrous (but harmless) iguanas skitter off into the undergrowth.

Most of the east coast is unsafe for swimming because the surf can create a deadly undertow, which will pull you far out to sea in a matter of minutes. There are always cars pulled off along the road here, with the occupants spending the day on the beach but not in the churning waters. Three **restaurants** catering to tourists are along this part of the coast, complete with sombrero-clad iguanas for a picture companion.

Halfway up the east coast, the paved eastern road meets the paved transversal road (which passes the ruins of San Gervasio) back to town, 9¹/₂ miles away. The east-coast road ends when it turns into the transversal, petering out to a narrow track of sandy road by a nice restaurant in front of the **Chen Río beach;** vehicles, even motorbikes, will get stuck on the sand road. If you are a birdwatcher, leave your vehicle on the highway here and walk straight down the sandy road. A lagoon paralleling it on the left is full of waterfowl. Go slowly and quietly and at the least you'll spot many herons and egrets. Farther on are Maya ruins.

HORSEBACK RIDING South of town, on the way to the Chancanab Lagoon about 3¹/₂ miles you'll see a sign pointing left down an unpaved road a short distance to the Rancho San Manuel where you can rent horses. There are only seven horses, though, and a guide and soft drink are included in the price. Rides cost $20 an hour. It's open daily from 8am to 4pm.

MAYA RUINS One of the most popular trips is to **San Gervasio** (100 B.C.–A.D. 1600). A road leads there from the airport or you can continue on the eastern part of the island following the paved transversal road. The worn sign to the ruins is easy to miss, but the turnoff (left) is about halfway between town and the eastern coast. Stop at the entry gate and pay the 75¢ per vehicle road-use fee. Go straight ahead over the potholed road to the ruins about two miles farther and pay $5.50 per person to enter. Personal cameras cost $8.50 each to use.

When it comes to Cozumel's Maya remains, getting there is most of the fun, and you should do it for the trip, not for the ruins. The buildings are conserved, but crudely made and would not be much of a tourist attraction if they were not the island's only cleared and accessible ruins. More significant than beautiful, the site was once an important Maya ceremonial center where they gathered, coming even from the mainland. The important deity here was Ixchel, known as the goddess of weaving, women, childbirth, pilgrims, the moon, and medicine. Although you won't see any representations of her at San Gervasio today, Bruce Hunter (*A Guide to Ancient Maya Ruins*) writes that priests hid behind a large pottery statue of her and became the voice of the goddess speaking to pilgrims and answering their petitions. She was the wife of Itzamná, about whom there is more to learn in Izamal. Tour guides charge $12 for a tour for one to six people, but it's not worth it. Find a copy of the green booklet *San Gervasio,* sold at local checkout counters or bookstores and tour the site on your own. Seeing it takes 30 minutes.

A HISTORY MUSEUM The **Museo de la Isla de Cozumel,** on Melgar between Calles 4 and 6 Norte, is more than just a nice place to spend a rainy hour. On the first floor an excellent exhibit showcases endangered species, the origin of the island, and its present-day topography and plant and animal life including an explanation of coral formation. Upstairs showrooms feature the history of the town, artifacts from the island's pre-Hispanic sites, and colonial-era cannon, swords, and ship paraphernalia. It's open daily from 10am to 6pm. Admission is $3.50; guided tours in English are free. There's a very expensive rooftop restaurant open long hours.

BOAT EXCURSIONS

Boat trips are another popular pastime at Cozumel. Some excursions include snorkeling and scuba diving or a stop at a beach with lunch. Various types of tours are offered, including a glass-bottom-boat tour lasting 1½ hours for $15.

AN EXCURSION TO SIAN KA'AN BIOSPHERE RESERVE

On the mainland south of Cozumel is the Sian Ka'an Biosphere Reserve, 1.3 million acres set aside to protect hundreds of species of birds, animals, and plants (see Section 6, below, for details). **Viajes Internacionales Palancar,** 10a Av. Sur no. 124, Cozumel, Q. Roo 77600 (tel. 987/2-2259; fax 987/2-2348), offers day-long excursions to the reserve from Cozumel for $115 per person. A minimum of four persons is required for the trip which leaves at 8am and returns at 7pm and includes a guided boat tour of the reserve with an English-speaking guide, box lunch, and drinks.

AN EXCURSION TO PLAYA DEL CARMEN & XCARET

One of the easiest do-it-yourself excursions from Cozumel is to Playa del Carmen, a laid-back mainland resort village just a 25- to 45-minute ferry ride away (see Section 3, above). From there it's a short taxi ride to the newly opened Xcaret underwater park (see Section 5, below). Both offer fine beaches and are ideal for a day of lazing.

WATER SPORTS

SNORKELING Anyone who can swim can go snorkeling. Rental of the snorkel (breathing pipe), goggles, and flippers should only cost about $5 for a half day; a snorkeling trip costs $30 to $40. The brilliantly colored tropical fish provide a free dazzling show. Chancanab Park is one of the best places to go on your own for an abundant show of colorful fish.

SCUBA DIVING This is Mexico's dive capital. Various establishments other island rent scuba gear—tanks, regulator with pressure gauge, buoyancy compensator, mask, snorkel, and flippers. Many will also arrange a half-day expedition in a boat complete with lunch for a set price. Sign up the day before, if you're interested. A day of diving costs around $45 to $55 and includes two tanks. However, if you are a dedicated diver, you'll save many dollars by buying a diving package that includes air, hotel, and usually two dives a day. There's a decompression chamber on the island (see "Fast Facts," above).

The underwater wonders of the famous **Palancar Reef** are offshore from the beach of the same name. From the car-ferry south to Punta Celarain are more than 20 miles of offshore reefs. In the famous blue depths divers find caves and canyons small and large, colorful fish, and an enormous variety of sea coral. The **Santa Rosa Reef** is famous for its depth, sea life, coral, and sponges. **San Francisco Reef,** off the beach by the same name south of town, has a drop-off wall, but it's still fairly shallow and the sea life is fascinating. The **Chankanab Reef,** where divers are joined by game fish, is close to the shore by the national park of the same name. It's shallow and good for novice divers, as is **La Ceiba Reef. Yucab Reef,** next going south on the eastern road after Chancanab has beautiful coral. Numerous vessels on the island operate daily diving and snorkeling tours so the best plan, if you aren't traveling on a prearranged dive package, is to shop around and sign up for one of those. Of Cozumel's many dive shops two are among the top:

Agua Safari, next to the Vista del Mar Hotel, Melgar at Avenida 5 and the Hotel Plaza Las Glorias (tel. 2-2588, ext. 746); and **Deportes Aquáticos** at Melgar and Calle 8 Norte (tel. and fax 2-0640).

You can save money by renting your gear at a beach shop and diving from shore. The shops at the Plaza Las Glorias and La Ceiba hotels are good places for shore diving—you'll find plenty to see as soon as you enter the water. It costs between $5 and $7 to rent one tank and weights. One-tank afternoon boat dives are also a good deal at $25 to $30.

WINDSURFING   Sailboards are for rent at several hotels south of town.

One of Mexico's top windsurfing champions, Raúl De Lille, offers windsurfing classes and equipment rentals at the beach in front of Sol Cabañas del Caribe, on the north side, and at Playa Bonita on the windward side. For information call 2-0017; fax 987/2-1942.

FISHING   The best months for fishing are April through September, when the catch will be blue and white marlin, sailfish, tarpon, swordfish, dolphinfish, wahoo, tuna, and red snapper. A half day of fishing costs $250. Viajes Internacionales Palancar, 10a Av. Sur no. 124 (tel. 2-2259), can arrange fishing trips. The Cozumel Angler's Fleet at the marina north of town offers a variety of fishing options including half-day, full-day, and two- and four-day fishing packages, either fishing and nothing else or a package with hotel. For advance reservations contact them at P.O. Box 341, Cozumel, Q. Roo 77600 (tel. toll free 800/253-2701 in the U.S.; fax 987/2-1135).

SHOPPING

Shopping has improved beyond the ubiquitous T-shirt shops into expensive resortwear, silver, and better decorative and folk art. Most of the stores are on Melgar.

If you want to pick up some Mexican tapes and CDs head to **Discoteca Hollywood,** at Juárez 421 (tel. 2-4090). It's open Monday through Saturday from 9am to 10pm and bills itself as the "Paradise of the Cassette." The selection and quantity are large.

EVENING ENTERTAINMENT

Cozumel is a town frequented by sports-minded visitors who play hard all day and wind down early at night. People sit in outdoor cafés around the zócalo enjoying the cool night breezes until the restaurants close. **Carlos 'n' Charlie's** (see "Where to Dine," below) is always one of the liveliest places in town.

Scaramouche, on Avenida Melgar, two blocks south of the zócalo, is by far the most visible and popular disco. It's open 9:30pm until 3am. There's usually a cover charge, but it varies.

WHERE TO STAY

Cozumel's hotels are in three separate locations: The oldest resorts, most of which are expensive, line beaches and coral and limestone outcroppings north of town, while the more budget-oriented inns are in the central village; other expensive hotels lie south of town. Since tourism to Cozumel has been down the last couple of years, many hoteliers have not raised their prices as dramatically as in the past. Generally speaking, they've been so cautious and fickle that prices may even be less expensive than the ones quoted here by the time you travel.

Note: There's one **central reservations number** for many (not all) of the island's hotels—toll free 800/327-2254 in the U.S. and Canada, or 305/670-9439 in Miami.

NORTH OF TOWN

I'll start with the northernmost hotels going through town, and move onward to the end of the southern hotel zone. Like beaches south of town, those along the northern shore appear sporadically and some hotels have enclosed them with retaining walls. **Carretera Santa Pilar** is the name of Melgar's northern extension, so just take Melgar north and all the hotels are lined up in close proximity to each other on the beach a short distance from town and the airport.

Very Expensive

HOTEL EL COZUMELEÑO, Carretera Santa Pilar km 2 (Apdo. Postal 53), Cozumel, Q. Roo 77600. Tel. 987/2-0050, or 2-0149, or toll free 800/437-3923 in the U.S. Fax 987/2-0381. 100 rms. A/C TEL
$ Rates: High season $162 single, $175 double. Low season $130–$140 single or double. **Parking:** Free.
The five-story Hotel El Cozumeleño is located on Santa Pilar beach, with one of the largest stretches of coral-free sand in the area. The expansive marble-floored lobby scattered with pastel groupings of chairs and couches is a popular gathering place. The glassed-in dining room looks out onto the Caribbean, as do all of the spacious and nicely furnished guest rooms. There's a very nice palm-shaded swimming pool.
Note: The toll-free reservation number listed above answers in Mexico and there's no one to make reservations or give prices between 1 and 5pm.
Dining/Entertainment: La Veranda restaurant is outside on the terrace just off the lobby and is open daily for breakfast from 7:30 to 10:30am and dinner from 6:30 to 10:30pm. El Cocal, by the beach and pool, is open daily between 11:30am and 4:30pm.
Services: Laundry and room service, travel agency, auto and moped rental.
Facilities: Two swimming pools, one tennis court, water-sports equipment rental.

HOTEL MELIA MAYAN PLAZA, Carretera Santa Pilar km 3.5 (Apdo. Postal 9), Cozumel, Q. Roo 77600. Tel. 987/2-0411, or toll free 800/336-3542 in the U.S. Fax 987/2-1599. 220 rms. A/C MINIBAR TV
$ Rates: High season $170–$195 single or double. Low season $150–$175 single or double. **Parking:** Free.
The plush renovation of this establishment creates the impression of a completely new top-quality hotel. The low-key, elegant lobby, with pale gray marble floors and rose and pale green accents, is a welcome respite on arrival. Since it's such a comfortable lobby, and there's a small bar at one end, guests frequently congregate among the inviting couch groupings. The spacious and beautifully furnished rooms all have ocean views from either a balcony or patio. Some of the standard rooms are right on the beach. If you want a nice, quiet, and secluded getaway removed from traffic (what little there is in Cozumel) and town, this is the place. It's at the end of the paved northern shore road.
Dining/Entertainment: La Isla Restaurant with beach and ocean views is open daily from 7:30am to 10:30pm. La Palapa by the pool is open daily between 11am and 6pm. La Iguana snack bar is open daily from 10am to 5pm. Ask about special once-or-twice-a-week fiestas featuring regional dancing and buffet dining.

Services: Travel agency; room and laundry service; motorcycle, car, and bicycle rental.

Facilities: Two swimming pools, one of the longest stretches of beach on the island, two tennis courts, water-sports equipment for rent on the beach.

Expensive

CABAÑAS DEL CARIBE, Carretera Santa Pilar km 4.5 (Apdo. Postal 9), Cozumel, Q. Roo 77600. Tel. 987/2-0017, or 2-0072, or toll free 800/336-3542 in the U.S. Fax 987/2-1599. 48 rms. A/C

$ Rates: High season $135 single, $140 double. Low season $115 single, $125 double. **Parking:** Free.

Built in two sections, the hotel gives you two choices of room styles. Standard rooms in the two-story section adjacent to the lobby are smallish (but very nice) and decorated in southwest colors of apricot and blue. All have small sitting areas and either a porch or balcony facing the beach and pool. The one-story bungalow/cabaña section has a similar decor but rooms are larger and have patios on the beach.

Dining/Entertainment: The main restaurant is in a glassed-in terrace on the beach, plus there's a poolside spot for snacks.

Services: Travel agency.

Facilities: Swimming pool; water-sports equipment for rent including sailboats, jet skis, and diving, snorkeling, and windsurfing equipment; pharmacy; gift shop.

Moderate

CLUB COZUMEL CARIBE, Carretera Santa Pilar km 4.5 (Apdo. Postal 43), Cozumel, Q. Roo 77600. Tel. 987/2-0100, or toll free 800/327-2254 in the U.S. Fax 987/2-0288. 260 rms. A/C

$ Rates (including meals, airport transfers in Cozumel, and water sports): High season $125–$150 per person. Low season $115 per person. Overnight accommodations aboard the MV *Oceanus* $75 per person double occupancy for members, $100 per person double occupancy for nonmembers.

In this, the largest hotel in the northern zone, many rooms are in the older nine-floor "tower" section. Others, in the three-story section adjacent to the lobby, have ocean-view balconies and are closer to the action and the beach. There's a small stretch of beach between coral outcroppings which adjoins another beach held by a rock wall. The hotel operates on an all-inclusive plan; you pay one price and receive almost everything the hotel has to offer: drinks, meals, tennis, water sports, and lodging. The grounds are spacious and relaxing with tall palms and tropical plants and lots of lounge chairs. Call for details of current offerings and reservations; often the last night is free in a seven-night stay.

Dining/Entertainment: Two restaurants serve all meals at scheduled hours. The Barefoot Disco is open nightly and movies are often shown there before the disco opens.

Services: Car rental, massages, daily organized recreation.

Facilities: Two pools, two lighted tennis courts, pharmacy, boutique, and aerobics. Included in the all-inclusive cost—sailing, kayaking, windsurfing, snorkeling, daily dives, and cruises; dive shop with all equipment; resort course for beginning divers as well as PADI-certification classes. The MV *Oceanus* is the hotel's liveaboard 100-foot diving ship specializing in overnight diving and shark-photo trips. Diver's logbook and certification required.

SAN MIGUEL DE COZUMEL

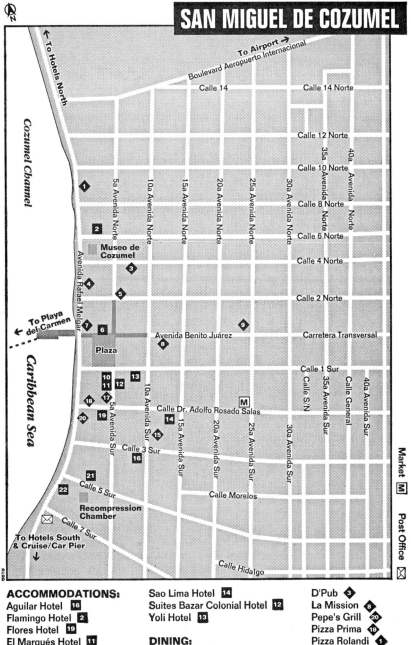

ACCOMMODATIONS:
Aguilar Hotel **16**
Flamingo Hotel **2**
Flores Hotel **19**
El Marqués Hotel **11**
Mary Carmen Hotel **10**
Maya Cozumel Hotel **21**
Mesón San Miguel **6**
Safari Inn Hotel **22**

Sao Lima Hotel **14**
Suites Bazar Colonial Hotel **12**
Yoli Hotel **13**

DINING:
Café Caribe **15**
Café del Puerto **7**
Carlos 'n' Charlie's Restaurant **4**
Coco's Restaurant **17**

D'Pub **3**
La Mission **8**
Pepe's Grill **20**
Pizza Prima **18**
Pizza Rolandi **1**
Sports Page
   Restaurant **5**
Waffle House **9**

HOTEL FONTAN, Carretera Santa Pilar km 2.5, Cozumel, Q. Roo 77600. Tel. 987/2-0300. Fax 987/2-0105, 48 rms. A/C TV TEL

$ Rates: High season $90 single, $110 double. Low season $70 single, $75 double. **Parking:** Free.

Ⓢ Rooms on all four floors have been freshly painted and updated and each has a private balcony; most have ocean views. Bathrooms all have showers. There's a nice swimming pool by the beach (held up by a retaining wall) and surrounded by lounge chairs. There's a restaurant and a bar, plus a dock for water sports. The Fontan provides excellent value for your money.

HOTELS IN TOWN

Very Expensive

HOTEL PLAZA LAS GLORIAS, Av. R. Melgar km 1.5, Cozumel, Q. Roo 77600. Tel. 987/2-2000, or toll free 800/342-2644 in the U.S. Fax 987/2-1937. 163 suites. A/C TV TEL

$ Rates: High season $185. Low season $145. Low-season discounts available. **Parking:** Free.

This new all-suite hotel has the best of both of Cozumel's worlds: It's the equivalent of five blocks from town center, so it's within walking distance of town, and it has most of the top-notch amenities of its resort neighbors farther out on the island. Beyond the expansive, comfortable lobby is the pool, a multilevel deck, a shored-up beach, and the ocean. The large, nicely furnished rooms all have separate sunken living rooms and balconies with ocean views. You have a choice of two double beds or a king-size bed.

Dining/Entertainment: During high season there's usually a buffet at breakfast and lunch. The main restaurant features different specialties nightly. There's palapa dining outside for all meals (weather permitting). The popular lobby bar features a large-screen TV which brings in major sports events. In high season there's often live entertainment (soft music) there as well.

Services: Laundry and room service, travel agency, concierge.

Facilities: Swimming pool by the beach, diving pier, dive shop, organized pool games, and recreational director.

Moderate

HOTEL AGUILAR, Calle 3 Sur no. 95, Cozumel, Q. Roo 77600. Tel. 987/ 2-0307. Fax 987/2-0769. 32 rms. A/C FAN

$ Rates: High season $30 single, $35 double. Low season $20 single, $25 double.

Behind the Aguilar's clean white stucco walls you'll find a quiet little retreat around a plant-filled courtyard that's still within walking distance of downtown action. The spotless rooms come with stenciled walls, over-bed lights, tile floors, two (firm) double beds covered in chenille spreads, and glass louvered windows with good screens. Besides air conditioning, each room also has a fan. A nice pool is in the center and you can rent a car (though the rates are expensive), a boat, or a motorscooter in the lobby.

HOTEL BARRACUDA, Av. Rafael Melgar (Apdo. Postal 163), Cozumel, Q. Roo 77600. Tel. 987/2-0002 or 2-1243. Fax 987/2-0884 or 2-3633. 50 rms. A/C FAN

$ Rates: High season $70 single, $85 double. Low season $55 single, $60 double.

You might not think much of this plain pink building a short walk south of town, but the view from within is outstanding. Rustic carved wood furnishings decorate

FROMMER'S SMART TRAVELER:
HOTELS

1. Cozumel has a good selection of hotels in all price ranges. You'll have no trouble finding a room from May through November, but during high season, mid-December through April (and especially Christmas and Easter), I recommend calling or writing ahead for reservations.
2. Hotels in the downtown area are the least expensive and only a short walk from restaurants and dive shops.
3. Because hotel prices are so high, never book a room without first checking on package possibilities, especially those with air transportation included.
4. Because occupancy has been low the last several years, even in high season, many of the costlier hotels offer attractive high-season discounts during certain weeks. There's a lull in travel and therefore possibly lower hotel rates in early January, late February, and late March.
5. Dive packages are among the best packages and often include options for a nondiving companion.
6. Booking a budget hotel and then arranging diving separately (either in advance or on arrival) is becoming a popular economic option especially during low season.
7. Remember when choosing an outlying hotel that taxis charge $5 to $8 for a one-way ride to town—a consideration if you plan to dine around or do much shopping.

the cozy rooms, all with balconies looking out to sea. There's a refrigerator in each room as well. An inner hallway leading to the rooms blocks out the noise from the road. There's no pool, but lounge chairs are lined up on an elevated strip of sand, and stairs lead down to a good snorkeling area. There's a good dive shop and a small oceanfront café serving breakfast and snacks. The hotel is on Costa Sur, a five-minute walk from town.

HOTEL MARY-CARMEN, 5a Av. Sur no. 4, Cozumel, Q. Roo 77600. Tel. 987/2-0581, 27 rms. A/C FAN
$ Rates: High season $50 single or double. Low season $45 single or double.
Watched over by eagle-eyed señoras, the two stories of rooms here surround an inner courtyard shaded by a large mamey tree. Rooms are clean and carpeted, with well-screened windows facing the courtyard. Most have two double beds. The Hotel Mary-Carmen is half a block south of the zócalo on the right.

HOTEL MAYA COZUMEL, Calle 5a Sur no. 4, Cozumel, Q. Roo 77600. Tel. 987/2-0011. Fax 987/2-0781. 38 rms. A/C TEL
$ Rates: High season $48 single, $55 double. Low season $42 single, $48 double. Diving packages available.
This bright apricot-and-white hotel, three blocks down Melgar from the town center, has upbeat rooms, with light tile floors and comfortable leather chairs. Through a glass wall in the lobby you can see the grassy rear courtyard surrounding the swimming pool. The desk clerk can arrange tours, diving packages, and car rentals. From the zócalo, walk three blocks south on Melgar, and turn left on 5a Sur; the hotel is on the left.

HOTEL SAFARI INN, Melgar at Calle 5 Sur (Apdo. Postal 41), Cozumel, Q. Roo 77600. Tel. 987/2-0101. Fax 987/2-0661. 12 rms. A/C
$ Rates: $40 single or double.

⭐ The nicest budget hotel in town is above and behind the Aqua Dive Shop. Natural colors and stucco pervade the interior of this three-story establishment. The huge rooms come with firm beds, a built-in sofa, and tiled floors. The hotel caters to divers and offers some good dive packages.

To find it, walk south on Melgar 3½ blocks; the hotel faces the Caribbean at the corner of Calle 5 Sur.

HOTEL SUITES BAZAR COLONIAL, Av. 5 Sur no. 9 (Apdo. Postal 286),
  Cozumel, Q. Roo 77600. Tel. 987/2-0506. Fax 987/2-1387. 28 rms. A/C
$ Rates: High season $50 single, $55 double. Low season $45 single, $50 double.

⭐ Across the street from El Marqués is a collection of shops, and this nice four-story hotel—with elevator. It's a good deal for the money. The lobby is far back past the shops. You get a quiet, spacious, furnished studio or a one-bedroom apartment with red-tile floors on the first floor. Second- and third-floor rooms have a kitchenette. From the zócalo, walk half a block on Av. 5a Sur; the hotel is on the left.

MESÓN SAN MIGUEL, Av. Juárez 2. Cozumel, Q. Roo 77600. Tel. 987/
  2-0233 or 2-0323. Fax 987-2-1820. 97 rms. A/C TEL
$ Rates: High season $70 single or double. Low season $40 single or double.
You couldn't ask for a better location, facing the main plaza in San Miguel, and that's what you are paying for. There's a nice large swimming pool on the property, but no beachfront, and few rooms with any view of the sea. Rooms are comfortable but dated, with worn carpets. Virtually any restaurant in town is just a few minutes' walk from the hotel's front door.

Budget

HOTEL FLAMINGO, Calle 6 Norte no. 81, Cozumel, Q. Roo 77600. Tel.
  987/2-1264. 22 rms. FAN
$ Rates: High season $25 single, $30 double. Low season $18 single, $25 double.
Built in 1986, the Flamingo offers three floors of quiet rooms, a grassy inner courtyard, and very helpful management. Second- and third-story rooms are spacious. All have white-tile floors, and rooms on the front have balconies overlooking the street. Some doubles have one bed; others have two. Soft drinks and bottled water are available from the refrigerator in the lobby. You get a lot for your money here. To find the Flamingo, walk north on Melgar from the zócalo three blocks and turn right on Calle 6; the hotel is on the left.

HOTEL FLORES, Calle Adolfo Rosado Salas 25, Cozumel, Q. Roo 77600.
  Tel. 987/2-1429. Fax 987/2-2475 33 rms. A/C FAN
$ Rates: $20–$25 single, $23–$27 double.
The three-story Flores (no elevator) is a good downtown choice. Some rooms have windows facing interior halls and stairs. Corner rooms have two windows to the outside and are bright and cheerful. The Flores is a block west of Melgar a few doors from the Hotel Suites Elizabeth.

HOTEL EL MARQUÉS, 5a Av. Sur no. 12, Cozumel, Q. Roo 77600. Tel.
  987/2-0677. Fax 987/2-0537. 40 rms. A/C
$ Rates: High season $35 single or double. Low season $30 single or double.
The three stories of sunny rooms have gold trim and Formica-marble countertops, French provincial overtones, gray-and-white tile floors, and two double beds. Third-floor rooms have good views. The staff is friendly and attentive. To find it from the zócalo, walk south on Melgar one block to Rosado Salas and turn left; the hotel is on the left.

HOTEL SÁO LIMA, Rosado Salas 260, Cozumel, Q. Roo 77600. No phone. 20 rms. FAN

$ Rates: $16 single; $18 double.

This small, two-story whitewashed hotel has basic rooms with two double beds or a double and a twin. Rooms on both floors face each other, separated by a narrow garden running down the middle. It's 2½ blocks west of Melgar between Avenidas 10 and 15 Sur.

HOTEL YOLI, Calle 1 Sur no. 164, Cozumel, Q. Roo 77600. Tel. 987/2-0024. 10 rms. FAN

$ Rates: $15 single; $18 double.

Clean and very simple, the Yoli (or Yoly) is also one of the most colorful and cheerful hotels in town. Yellow door trim contrasts with aqua doors and aqua-tile walls in the hallways. Your room may have a freshly painted fuchsia or pink wall—or maybe both. Furnishings are old-fashioned but comfortable, and lighted with a circular fluorescent fixture on the wall. Towels and soap are laid out on each bed. You'll find it between the main plaza and 10a Avenida Sur, 1½ blocks west of Melgar and half a block west of Avenida 5 Sur.

HOTELS SOUTH OF TOWN

The best beaches are south of town, but not all the best ones have hotels on them. Each hotel has either a swimming pool, a tiny cove, a dock, or all three. You'll be able to swim, sun, and relax at any of these hotels and most are diver-oriented. **Costera Sur,** also called **Carretera a Chankanab,** is the southern extension of Melgar, so just follow Melgar south through town to reach these hotels, which are, generally speaking, farther apart than those north of town.

Very Expensive

FIESTA AMERICANA COZUMEL REEF, Costera Sur km 7.5, Cozumel, Q. Roo 77600. Tel. 987/2-2622, or toll free 800/465-4329 in the U.S. Fax 987/2-2666. 160 rms. A/C TEL

$ Rates: High season $190–$225 single or double. Low season $165–$200 single or double.

Cozumel's newest and southernmost hotel opened in 1992. Entry to the large, luxurious, marble-filled lobby is via a circular drive to the back. Rooms are beautifully furnished with pastel tile floors and natural-toned furniture, and all have balconies and ocean views. Each unit is equipped with a hairdryer, and the hotel's tap water is purified. Three rooms are specially designed for the handicapped, and the second floor is all no-smoking. It's located beyond the Presidente Hotel.

Dining/Entertainment: Miramar Caribbean Grill is the hotel's elegant restaurant, open daily from 6 to 11pm The casual Reef Restaurant is open from 6am to 6pm. La Palapa, across the road by the beach, is open daily from 10am to 5pm.

Services: Room and laundry service; travel agency; car; motorbike, and bicycle rental; babysitting.

Facilities: Large pool in front, two lighted tennis courts, workout room with equipment, dive shop with dive-boat pier, water sports and equipment rental, walled-in beach across the street, roped-off snorkeling area, jogging trail through the jungle in back of the hotel, gift shop, pharmacy.

PRESIDENTE INTER-CONTINENTAL COZUMEL, Costera Sur km 6.0, Cozumel, Q. Roo 77600. Tel. 987/2-0322, or toll free 800/327-0020 in the U.S. Fax 987/2-1360. 253 rms. A/C MINIBAR TV TEL

$ Rates: High season $235–$330 single or double. Low season $170–$265 single or double. Discounts and packages available. **Parking:** Free.

The first thing you'll notice here is the palatial scale of the place and the masterful, stylishly grand combination of marble with hot-pink stucco and stone as you enter. Near the Chancanab Lagoon, the hotel, surrounded by shady palms, spreads out on a beautiful beach with no close neighbors.

There are four categories of rooms. The spacious superior rooms are on the first and second floors of the tower and all have balconies and garden views. Large deluxe rooms on the third to fifth floors have balconies and ocean views. Deluxe beachfront rooms have comfortable patios and direct access to the beach on the ground floor and on the second-floor balconies with ocean views. The no-smoking rooms are all on the fourth level, and two rooms are set aside for handicapped guests. Naturally each category of room has a different price. Absolutely ask about discounts and packages here.

Dining/Entertainment: The Arrecife restaurant serves international specialties and is open daily from 6pm to midnight. Caribeño, by the pool and beach, is open from 7am to 7pm.

Services: Room and laundry service, travel agency, car and motorbike rental.

Facilities: Swimming pool, two tennis courts, water-sports equipment rental, dive shop and dive-boat pier, pharmacy, boutiques.

SOL CARIBE COZUMEL, Costera Sur km 3.5 (Apdo. Postal 259), Cozumel, Q. Roo 77600. Tel. 987/2-0700, or toll free 800/223-2332 in the U.S. Fax 987/2-1301. 321 rms. A/C MINIBAR TV TEL

$ Rates: High season $200 tower-section room, $150 garden room, $184 ocean-view room. Low season $156 tower-section room, $135 garden room, $145 ocean-view room. **Parking:** Free.

On the landward side of the road, just north of the car-ferry dock, is the island's largest hotel, which has rooms on 9 and 10 floors in two separate sections. The entrance is dramatic, beneath a vast wooden canopy, surrounded by tropical greenery and splashing fountains, with rocks and replicas of Maya statuary here and there. Lush big-leafed plants and trees are spread throughout the hotel grounds and provide deep shade by the huge swimming pool (which has its own swim-up bar). Rooms have ocean or garden views, and the hotel's tap water is purified. Those units in the new tower section all have balconies, as do suites in the older, original section. The hotel's own beach cove is just across the road.

Dining/Entertainment: La Gaviota (The Seagull), for fine dining, is open daily from 7 to 11pm. The coffee shop, La Casa del Pescador, is open daily from 7 to 11am and again from 1 to 5pm. The lobby bar offers live music nightly and happy hour between 5 and 7pm. There's also a swim-up bar in the pool, and a snack bar, the Marlin Azul, at the beach across the street. Ask about the Mexican fiesta night.

Services: Room and laundry service, travel agency, car and motorbike rental.

Facilities: Swimming pool, three lighted tennis courts, dive shop and dive pier, water-sports equipment rental, rock-walled beach across the street, pharmacy, gift shop, beauty shop.

Expensive

LA CEIBA BEACH HOTEL, Costera Sur km 4.5 (Apdo. Postal 284), Cozumel, Q. Roo 77600. Tel. 987/2-0815, or toll free 800/437-9609. Fax 800/235-5892. 113 rms. A/C MINIBAR TV TEL

$ Rates: High season $110 single, $135 double. Low season $105 single, $110 double. Diving packages available. **Parking:** Free.

Across from the Sol Caribe, on the beach side of the road, La Ceiba is named for the lofty and majestic tree, sacred to the Maya, which grows in the tropics. It's a popular hotel and the large lobby seems to always be abustle with guests. Rooms all have ocean views and balconies, and bathrooms have combination tubs and showers. The swimming pool is only steps from the beach.

The emphasis here is on water sports, particularly scuba diving, and if this is your passion, be sure to ask about the special dive packages when you call for reservations.

Dining/Entertainment: The Galleon Bar/Restaurant, off the lobby, has walls shaped like an old ship. It's open daily from 7am to 11pm. Chopaloca by the beach is open daily from 9am to 11pm.

Services: Laundry and room service, travel agency.

Facilities: Large, free-form swimming pool by the beach, tennis court, water sports, dive shop and dive-boat pier, roped-off area for snorkeling.

FIESTA INN, Costera Sur km 1.7, Cozumel, Q. Roo 77600. Tel. 987/2-2899, or toll free 800/223-2332 in the U.S. Fax 987/2-2154. 178 rms. A/C TV TEL
$ Rates: High season $120 single or double. Low season $80 single or double. **Parking:** Free.

New in 1989, the Fiesta Inn is built around a grassy inner yard with an enormous swimming pool decked out with lounge chairs. Most of the nicely furnished rooms face the inner grounds and all have furnished balconies. Some no-smoking units are available. The hotel's tap water is purified, and there is an ice machine on each floor. The beach, reached by an underground tunnel, is across the road.

Dining/Entertainment: One restaurant serves all meals.

Services: Laundry and room service, travel agency.

Facilities: Enormous pool, one tennis court, beach across the road with dive shop and dive-boat pier, boutique, pharmacy.

Moderate

GALÁPAGOS INN, Costera Sur km 1.5 (Apdo. Postal 289), Cozumel, Q. Roo 77600. Tel. 987/2-0663 or 2-1933, or call Aqua-Sub Tours toll free 800/847-5708 in the U.S. or 713/783-3305 in Texas. 54 rms. A/C
$ Rates (including all meals and two days diving): High season three-night package $440 per person. Low season three-night package $300 per person. Longer diving packages available and lower rates for nondivers.

Homey, shady, and done in colonial style with white stucco and red-brick accents, this older inn is usually peopled by divers who have signed up for one of the several money-saving three-, five-, and seven-night package deals. The inn, located a mile south of the main square, has its own small swimming pool and a bit of walled-in beach. A row of hammocks swings under a long thatched roof by the ocean where there's nothing but the sound of surf and breezes. Some rooms have balconies or terraces on the beach. All have ocean views. One restaurant serves all meals with specific meal times. The bar, with drinks only, is open daily from 7 to 11pm. There's a fully equipped dive shop and dives take off from the hotel's pier.

WHERE TO DINE

There are cheap ways to eat well in Cozumel. On Calle 2 Norte, half a block in from the waterfront, is the **Panificadora Cozumel,** excellent for a do-it-yourself breakfast, or for picnic supplies. It's open from 6am to 9pm daily. Cookshops in the **market** always have something brewing; just look for what's hot and freshly cooked.

VERY EXPENSIVE

CAFÉ DEL PUERTO, Melgar 3. Tel. 2-0316.
   Cuisine: INTERNATIONAL. **Reservations:** Recommended.
   $ Prices: Appetizers $3.50–$12; main courses $14–$45.
   Open: Dinner daily 5–11pm.

For a romantic dinner with a sunset view, try this restaurant. After being greeted at the door, climb the spiral staircase to the main dining area or continue to a higher loft overlooking the rest of the dining room. Soft piano music entertains in the background. The service is polished and polite and the menu sophisticated, with main courses like mustard steak flambé, shrimp brochette with bacon and pineapple, and prime rib. You'll find the Café del Puerto opposite the zócalo and the passenger-ferry pier.

PEPE'S GRILL, Av. Rafael Melgar at Salas. Tel. 2-0213.
   Cuisine: GRILLED SPECIALTIES. **Reservations:** Recommended.
   $ Prices: Appetizers $4–$12; main courses $14–$35; children's menu $12.
   Open: Dinner daily 5–11:30pm.

Pepe's started the grilled-food tradition in Cozumel and continues as a popular trendsetter with low lights, soft music, solicitous waiters, and excellent food—witness the perpetual crowd. Tables are open to sea breezes, and failing that, ceiling fans move the air. The menu is extensive, with flame-broiled specialties such as beef filet Singapore and shrimp Bahamas. The children's menu offers breaded shrimp and fried chicken. For dessert try the cajeta crêpes.

EXPENSIVE

CARLOS 'n' CHARLIE'S, Melgar 1. Tel. 2-0191.
   Cuisine: MEXICAN.
   $ Prices: Appetizers $3.50–$12; main courses $8–$18.
   Open: Mon–Sat 9am–midnight, Sun 5pm–midnight.

As always with this popular chain of restaurants, the emphasis is on good clean fun *and* consistently good but expensive food. In Cozumel the beat is loud and lively; you hear it before you see it on the second floor. There's a moose head over the stairs and the ceiling is full of T-shirts and auto tags. Menu offerings include spaghetti, barbecue ribs, Yucatecan specialties, crêpes, tacos, steak, and fish. The restaurant faces Avenida Melgar 1½ blocks north of the zócalo, between Calles 2 and 4 Norte.

D' PUB, Calle 4 Norte 140. Tel. 2-4132.
   Cuisine: INTERNATIONAL.
   $ Prices: Main courses $7–$20.
   Open: Dinner Mon–Sat 5pm–midnight.

Though new, this Caribbean-style island house, with its front porch and cut-out wood trim, looks like the few remaining wooden houses from Cozumel's past. Inside it's a handsome combination English pub and gracious garden dining establishment. In the main room as you enter, casual couches and conversational areas are conducive to leisurely drinking and chatting. Farther on there's dining inside or outside on the patio fronting the manicured inner courtyard. The eclectic menu includes fish and chips, barbecue chicken, dip roast-beef sandwiches, fajitas, stir-fried vegetables with meat or shrimp, rack of lamb, seafood, and steaks. Whatever you have, top it off with apple pie à la mode. The restaurant is in the middle of the block between 5a Avenida Norte and 10a Avenida Norte.

FROMMER'S SMART TRAVELER:
RESTAURANTS

1. Restaurants along Melgar and around the zócalo will be more expensive and not necessarily better than those a block or more away.
2. For inexpensive do-it-yourself meals you can pick up fruit, vegetables, and picnic fixings at the municipal market or at one of the delicatessens I've recommended.
3. Have your main meal at lunch, when restaurant prices are generally lower.
4. For inexpensive drinks, take advantage of hotel bar happy hours, which usually offer two drinks for one price during the late afternoon.

MODERATE

LA MISSION, Av. Juárez 23. Tel. 2-1641.
Cuisine: GRILLED MEAT/MEXICAN.
$ Prices: Seafood dishes $9.50–$16; meat dishes $7.50–$13; Mexican specialties $8–$11.
Open: Daily 3pm–midnight.

You can tell by the crowds that this is a popular restaurant; foreign patrons often leave saying, "We'll see you next year." The first thing you notice is the open, colorfully tiled kitchen on the right where cooks prepare the dependably good food for which La Mission is known. The tender fajita platter comes with guacamole, beans, rice, and fresh flour tortillas. The owner says, "If you don't like it, don't pay." La Mission is a short walk from the zócalo between 10a and 15a Avenidas Sur.

PIZZA PRIMA, Calle Salas 109. Tel. 2-4242.
Cuisine: ITALIAN.
$ Prices: Small pizzas $6.90–$10; large pizzas $9.25–$13.75; pastas $5.75–$15.50; subs $3.45–$4.75.
Open: Thurs–Tues 1–11pm.

This is one of the few good Italian restaurants in Mexico. Everything is fresh—the pastas, calzones, and pizza sourdough. Owner Albert Domínguez grows most of the vegetables on his hydroponic on the island. The menu changes daily and might include shrimp scampi, fettuccine with pesto, crab ravioli with cream sauce, etc. The fettuccine Alfredo is wonderful, as is the puff-pastry garlic bread and crispy house salad. The sub sandwiches are big and varied, and among them is a "Philly" cheese steak, a "mama mía" meatball, and chicken parmesan. The large pizza easily feeds three adults. Dining is upstairs on the breezy terrace. Domínguez also owns Western Fried Chicken around the corner (right) from Pizza Prima. Pizza Prima's bright orange building is visible just off Melgar between Calles 5 and 10 Sur.

PIZZA ROLANDI, Melgar between Calles 6 and 8 Norte. Tel. 2-0946.
Cuisine: ITALIAN.
$ Prices: Appetizers $4.50–$8; main courses $9.25–$15; pizza $8.50–$11.
Open: Mon–Sat 11:30am–11:30pm.

Deck chairs and glossy wood tables make the inviting interior garden at Pizza Rolandi a restful place in daytime; it's a romantic, candlelit spot at night. The specialty here (as in their branches in Isla Mujeres and Cancún) is wood oven–baked pizzas. But for a change look for pasta prepared five ways and the weekly specials, which may be a special pizza, pasta, or fish with an Italian twist. The Rolandi is four blocks north of the zócalo on the landward side of Melgar.

THE SPORTS PAGE, 5a Av. Norte at Calle 2 Norte. Tel. 2-1199.

Cuisine: AMERICAN.

$ Prices: Breakfast $4.50–$6; appetizers $5.50–$17; main courses $7.50–$20; hamburgers $5–$7.

Open: Daily 9am–11pm.

Though Mexican-owned, the Sports Page is very American, right down to the authentic hamburgers and fries, the satellite-TV antenna to catch U.S. sports action, and U.S. team pennants and T-shirts on the walls. The menu, too, caters to Americans, with luxury nachos, burgers, fajitas, tacos, lobster, steak, and sandwiches. A block north of the zócalo, it's air-conditioned, and prices are given in dollars.

THE WAFFLE HOUSE, Av. Juárez 499. No phone.

Cuisine: BREAKFAST/DESSERTS.

$ Prices: Waffles $3.50–$6; breakfast $5–$7.

Open: Daily 8am–1pm and 6–9pm.

Jeanie De Lille, the island's premier pastry chef, bakes crisp, light waffles and serves them in many ways, including the waffle ranchero with eggs and salsa. Hash browns, homemade breads, and great coffee are other reasons to go a bit out of your way to find this place. Stop by for coffee and caramel or a chocolate torte in the evening. Hours may vary in low season. The Waffle House is five blocks inland from the malecón, at the corner of Avenida 25 Norte.

BUDGET

CAFÉ CARIBE, 10a Av. Sur. Tel. 2-3621.

Cuisine: PASTRIES/COFFEE.

$ Prices: Coffee $1–$3.50; pastries $1.50–$4.50.

Open: Mon–Sat 8am–noon and 5–9pm.

This cute little eatery behind a fuchsia and dark green facade shows promise. The menu is a great one to start or finish the day, or for something in between. You'll find ice cream, milk shakes, freshly made cheesecake and carrot cake, and croissants filled with cheese and cream or ham and cheese. Nine different coffees are served, including Cuban, espresso, and Irish. It's between Salas and 3 Sur opposite Delikatessen & Deli's Café.

CASA DE DENIS, 1 Sur 16. Tel. 2-0067.

Cuisine: MEXICAN.

$ Prices: Appetizers $1.50–$2.50; main courses $2–$6.

Open: Mon–Sat 7am–11pm.

Behind a yellow-frame facade and with only five tables, decked out in checkered cloths, Casa de Denis is nearly always full. The small kitchen turns out decent Mexican fast food—tacos, enchiladas, pork and fries, chicken mole, and more. It's popular with locals and tourists alike and the service is swift. It's half a block off the zócalo.

COCO'S, Av. 5 Sur no. 180. Tel. 2-0241.

Cuisine: MEXICAN/AMERICAN.

$ Prices: Breakfast $2.50–$5; plate lunch $3–$7; hamburger $4.75–$6.

Open: Mon–Fri 7am–3pm, Sat–Sun 7am–noon.

Once discovered, Coco's becomes a favorite. Tended by owners Terri and Daniel Ocejo, it's clean and welcoming to the tourist, right down to the free coffee refills and the ready ice water. Here you can indulge in Stateside favorites like hash browns, cornflakes and bananas, barbecue sandwiches, hamburgers, baked potatoes prepared three ways, and more. It's hard to top the breakfast special, which comes with two eggs, two pancakes, toast, coffee, and your choice of ham, bacon, or sausage. A plate lunch might include a choice of breaded fish or barbecued chicken served with a choice of baked or fried potato, vegetable, and salad. A gift section at the front includes gourmet coffee, local honey, and bottles of hot pepper, chocolate, rompope, and vanilla; plus there's a paperback-book exchange. It's at the corner of Salas. It's closed the last two weeks of September and the first week in October.

5. FROM AKUMAL TO TULUM

Of the fledgling resorts south of Playa del Carmen, **Akumal** is one of the most developed, with pricey resort hotels and bungalows scattered among the graceful palms that line the beautiful beach and bay. **Puerto Aventuras** is a privately developed, growing resort city aimed at the well-heeled traveler. **Pamul** has always been an idyllic hideaway on a gorgeous beach, and now a few other places have opened, including a family-owned area called **Xpuha,** 2½ miles beyond Pamul on a wide gorgeous beach.

Those seeking little-known and inexpensive getaways flock down the **Punta Allen Peninsula** south of Tulum, where the beaches are great and the generator shuts down at 10pm (if there is one). A few beach cabañas now have reliable power, telephones, and hot showers. If the offbeat beach life is what you're after, grab it now before it disappears. You'll also enjoy a swim in the nearby lagoon of **Xel-Ha,** one of the coast's prettiest spots. And the new parklike development of **Xcaret** will appeal to many for an all-day excursion.

The impressive Maya ruins at **Cobá,** deep in the jungle are a worthy detour from your route south. You don't need to stay overnight to see the ruins, but there are a few hotels.

EN ROUTE SOUTH FROM PLAYA DEL CARMEN   Bus transportation from Playa del Carmen south is no longer as chancy as it used to be, but it's still not great. Buses leave fairly frequently between Playa and Chetumal, stopping at every point of interest along the way. There's even bus service to and from Cobá three times a day. There are four bus companies in Playa. Though buses originate here, you may be told you can't buy tickets ahead of time. Ask the price anyway and make sure the bus driver doesn't overcharge you. (Get into the habit of asking for receipts.) If you choose to leave the driving to someone else, be sure to find a driver you like; remember you'll be with him all day.

XCARET

Three miles south of Playa del Carmen is the turnoff to Xcaret, a 150-acre specially built tourist destination that promotes itself as an ecological park. It's meant to be a place to spend the day. It's open daily from 9am to 5:30pm.

To build it, however, they rearranged quite a bit of nature. If you're looking for a place to escape the commercialism of Cancún, this may not be it; it's expensive and somewhat contrived, and may even be very crowded. All this may diminish the advertised "natural" experience. Children, however, seem to love it and the setting is beautiful. Once you're past the entry booths (built to resemble small Maya temples), walking paths meander around a natural bathing cove and the snorkeling lagoon. You'll see remains of a group of Maya temples, and have access to swimming beaches with canoes and pedalboats, limestone tunnels to snorkel through, marked palm-lined pathways, and a visitors center with lockers, first aid, and gifts. There's a museum, a "farm," and a botanical garden. Visitors aren't allowed to bring in food or drinks so you're at the mercy of the high-priced restaurants. Personal radios are a no-no, as is the use of suntan lotion in the lagoon (the chemicals in lotion will poison the lagoon habitat).

The price of $17 per person entitles you to all the facilities—boats, life jackets, and snorkeling equipment for the underwater tunnel and lagoon, and lounge chairs and other facilities. However, there are often more visitors than equipment (such as chairs and snorkels) so bring a beach towel and your own snorkeling gear. Travel agencies in Cancún offer Xcaret as a day trip at a much higher price, which includes transportation and admission, than what you'd pay to come on your own. You'll also see Xcaret's colorfully painted buses hauling people from Cancún.

PAMUL

Sixty miles south of Cancún, 10 miles south of Xcaret, and a half mile east of the highway is Pamul, which in Maya means "a destroyed ruin." Here you can enjoy a beautiful beach and a safe cove for swimming—it's a delightful place to leave the world behind.

A PADI- and SSI-certified dive instructor moved to Pamul a few years ago from the U.S. and opened **Scuba Max** (tel. and fax 987/4-1729), a fully equipped dive shop next to the cabañas. Using three 38-foot boats, he takes guests on dives five miles in either direction. Or if it's too choppy, the reefs in front of the hotel are also excellent. The cost per dive is $45 if you have your own equipment or $65 if you rent. They also have a branch in the Costa del Mar Hotel in Playa del Carmen.

The **snorkeling** is excellent in this protected bay and the one next to it.

WHERE TO STAY & DINE

CABAÑAS PAMUL, Carretera Cancún-Tulum km 85. (Apdo. Postal 83), Playa del Carmen, Q. Roo 77710. Tel 987/4-3240. 7 bungalows; 82 trailer spaces (all with full hookups). FAN
$ Rates: High season $45 single, $50 double. Low season $25 single, $30 double. July–Aug $30 single, $40 double.

When you reach this isolated, relaxing hotel you'll see coral and white beachfront bungalows with covered porches steps away from the Caribbean. Each cabaña has two double beds, tile floors, rattan furniture, ceiling fans, hot water, and 24-hour electricity. A small, reasonably priced restaurant by the office serves excellent but simple meals and reasonably priced beer and soft drinks, but bring some nonperishable snacks and bottled drinks—you're miles from stores and other restaurants. For stays longer than a week ask for a discount, which can sometimes be as much as 10% to 20%. Trailer guests have six showers and bathrooms separate for men and women. Laundry service is available. Turtles nest here June through September.

The Pamul turnoff is clearly marked on the highway. Bus drivers will let you off on the highway; then it's almost a mile on a straight, narrow, paved-but-rutted road to the cabañas.

XPUHA

Almost three miles beyond Pamul on the left is an area known as Xpuha (Ish-poo-*hah*). When I was there it was marked by three separate crude signs pointing to narrow rough roads cutting through the jungle. Any of the roads will lead to all three

FROMMER'S NATURE NOTES
SEA TURTLES OF THE YUCATÁN

At least four of Mexico's nine marine turtles nest on the beaches of Quintana Roo—the loggerhead, green, hawksbill, and leatherback varieties. Of these, the leatherback is almost nonexistent, and the loggerhead is the most abundant— but all are endangered.

Most turtles lay eggs on the same beach year after year, and as often as three times in a season (usually between 10pm and 3am). Lights of any kind repel them, including flashlights and camera flash. The female turtle's strenuous trancelike digging with back flippers for more than an hour leaves its head and legs flushed. Depositing the 100 or more eggs takes only minutes, then she makes the nest invisible by laboriously covering it with sand, and disappears into the sea. Each soft-shelled egg looks like a ping-pong ball.

Hatchlings scurry to the sea 45 days later, but successful incubation depends on the temperature and depth of the nest. When conditions are right, the hatch rates of fertile eggs are high; however, because of predators only 5% of those that finally make it to the sea live to return.

Despite recent efforts to protect Mexico's turtles, the eggs are still considered an aphrodisiac and there's a market for them; turtles are killed for their shells and meat as well. Since turtle life expectancy is more than 50 years, killing one turtle kills thousands more. Costly protection programs include tagging the female and catching the eggs as they are deposited and removing them to a protected area and nest of identical size and temperature.

places. All are nicely spaced apart in a row, and all face an incredibly beautiful beach once owned by *cocoteros* (coconut growers). Two of their descendents have opened budget inns here in this gorgeous setting. The other offers a for-pay day beach, where guests are charged a price to spend the day. Though they call these inns "villas," the name implies much more than the reality of simply furnished, white concrete buildings. The **restaurant** of the Villas Xpuha, offers excellent, home-style cooking (great fresh fish platters), and it's open daily from 7am to 8pm. It's ideal for day-trippers who want to spend the day on the beach and have restaurant facilities too; the owners request that visitors not bring food. As long as you use the restaurant, there's no charge for the two public bathrooms and showers. Within walking distance there's a huge lagoon and the reef is not far offshore.

WHERE TO STAY & DINE

VILLAS DEL CARIBE XPUHA, Carreterra Cancún-Tulum km 88, Playa del Carmen, Q. Roo. No phone. 8 rms.
$ Rates: High season $50 single or double. Low season $30 single, $35 double.
Not quite as nice as its neighbor Villas Xpuha, this inn is still a good choice. The two stories of rooms face the beach, with communal porches for lounging. Rooms have blue-tile floors and matching blue walls and come with one or two double beds, all-tile bathrooms, and windows facing the beach. One room has a kitchen. There's 24-hour electricity and hot water here, too. They have radio communication with the Hotel Flores in Cozumel (tel. 987/2-1429), so if you're there, you can reserve a room ahead (or vice versa).

VILLAS XPUHA AND RESTAURANT, Carreterra Cancún-Tulum km 88 (Apdo. Postal 115), Playa del Carmen, Q. Roo 77710. No phone. 5 rms. FAN

$ Rates: High season $50 single or double. Low season $35 single or double.

The five rooms line up in a row, and four have a porch area on the beach and ocean. One is an island-style wooden structure. Inside the rooms are plain but clean, with nice tile floors and bathrooms, two single beds, two plastic chairs, hammock hooks, and a place for a suitcase, but no closet. A single bare bulb in the center of the ceiling provides light and two windows open to the porch. Count on 24-hour electricity and hot water.

PUERTO AVENTURAS

Sixty-five miles south of Cancún and five miles south of Pamul, you'll come to the new, city-size development of Puerto Aventuras on Chakalal Bay. Though it's on 900 oceanfront acres, you don't see the ocean unless you walk through one of the two hotels. A complete resort, it includes a state-of-the-art marina, two hotels, multitudes of fashionable condominiums winding about the grounds and around the marina, and a nine-hole golf course, which should have 18 holes by December 1996.

WHAT TO SEE & DO

A MUSEUM Even if you don't stay here, the **Museo CEDAM** is worth a stop. CEDAM is the Spanish acronym for Center for the Study of Aquatic Sports of Mexico, and the museum houses the **history of diving** on this coast from pre-Hispanic times to the present. Besides dive-related memorabilia there are displays of pre-Hispanic pottery, figures and copper bells found in the cenote of Chichén-Itzá, shell fossils, and sunken ship contents. It's open Wednesday through Monday (closed Tuesday) from 11am to 1pm and 2 to 7pm.

A DOLPHIN SHOW Three times a day there's a dolphin show in a roped-off area of the marina. The first 30 minutes of the hour-long show is educational; the next 30 minutes is for spectators to swim with the dolphins. Life jackets are provided as well as showers and changing rooms. The cost is $65 per person.

SPORTS & RECREATION

BOATING Kayaks and pedalboat rentals are available at the Hotel Club de Playa.

DIVING/SNORKELING Diving and snorkeling arrangements can be made at the Hotel Club de Playa.

GOLF Until the full 18-hole golf course is ready in 1996, golfers can use the practice green and the nine-hole course, which is completed. Rental of clubs is $16 a day, carts are $25 an hour, and the greens fee is $30.

HORSEBACK RIDING Riding arrangements are made at the Hotel Club de Playa.

TENNIS Both the Oasis and Hotel Club de Playa have two courts each, available at a cost of $10 per hour.

WHERE TO STAY & DINE

HOTEL OASIS PUERTO AVENTURAS, Carretera Puerto Juárez–Chetumal km 295, Puerto Aventuras, Q. Roo 77710. Tel. 987/2-3000, or toll free 800/446-2747. Fax 987/3-5051. 309 rms and suites. A/C TV TEL

$ Rates: High season $350–$800 one- to three-bedroom unit, low season $225–$550 one- to three-bedroom unit.

Built on a grand scale, the Hotel Oasis makes lavish use of space and travertine marble both in the open and flowing public areas and in the guest rooms. The seven stories are built in a U-shape, facing Chakalal Bay. Suites come with one bedroom, two double beds, and a Murphy bed. Junior suites have a large sitting area and two bedrooms; and master suites have three bedrooms, large separate living and dining areas, and two balconies. Some master suites have a jet tub on the balcony. Rooms have either an ocean view or overlook the marina.

Dining/Entertainment: There are two restaurants, a disco, and lobby bar.

Services: Room and laundry service, travel agency, mini-cart transportation within the development. Package prices may include transportation from Cancún.

Facilities: Two pools, beach, one tennis court, super deli/market, gift shop, pharmacy, use of sports facilities and rental equipment at Hotel Club de Playa.

AKUMAL

Continuing on the highway a short distance, you come to **Akumal,** a resort development built around and named after a beautiful lagoon. Signs point the way in from the highway, and the white-arched Akumal gateway is less than a half mile toward the sea. The resort complex here consists of five distinct establishments which share the same wonderful, smooth palm-lined beach, and the adjacent **Half Moon Bay** and **Yalku Lagoon.** The hotel's signs and white entry arches are clearly visible from Highway 307.

WHAT TO SEE & DO

You don't have to be a guest here to enjoy the beach, **swim** in the beautiful clear bay, and eat at the restaurants. It's an excellent place to spend a day while on a trip down the coast. Ask at the reception desk about **horseback rides** to Chemuyil ($30) and tours of the **Sian Ka'an Biosphere Reserve** ($115). For **scuba diving,** two completely equipped dive shops with PADI-certified instructors serve the hotels and bungalows in this area. Both are located between the two hotels. There are almost 30 dive sites in the region (from 30 to 80 feet) and dives cost around $50 to $65 each. Both shops offer resort courses as well as complete certification. **Fishing** trips can also be arranged through the dive shops. You're only 15 minutes from good fishing. Two hours minimum costs $150 to $175 and each additional hour is $25 for up to four people with two fishing lines.

WHERE TO STAY & DINE

HOTEL-CLUB AKUMAL CARIBE VILLAS MAYA, Carretera Cancún-Tulum (Hwy. 307) km 63. Tel. 987/2-2532. 73 rms. A/C TEL

$ Rates: High season $90 single or double bungalows, $110 single or double hotel room. Low season $65 single or double bungalow, $90 single or double hotel room.

The white arches you drive under and the entry are not impressive, but the lodging varieties here are. The 48 spacious **Villas Maya Bungalows** have beautiful tile floors and comfortable, nice furniture, all with fully equipped kitchens. The 21 rooms in the new three-story **beachfront hotel** are similarly furnished but with small kitchens (no stove), a king-size or two queen-size beds, pale tile floors, and stylish Mexican accents. The **Villas Flamingo** are four exquisitely designed and luxuriously (but comfortably) furnished two-story homes facing Half Moon Bay.

Each has one, two, or three bedrooms; large living, dining, and kitchen areas; and a lovely furnished patio just steps from the beach. The hotel has its own pool separate from other facilities on the grounds. Akumal's setting is truly relaxing and there's a restaurant facing the beach and lagoon.

Reservations: Arrangements can be made by writing to P.O. Box 13326, El Paso, TX 79950 (tel. 915/584-3552, or toll free 800/351-1622 in the U.S. outside Texas, 800/343-1440 in Canada).

CHEMUYIL & XCACEL

Next down the highway (70 miles south of Cancún and 3 miles south of Akumal) is the beach and trailer part at **Chemuyil,** developed by the government as "the most beautiful beach in the world"—or so says the sign on the highway. The once-beautiful beach of deep drifting sand is ugly and packed. Yellow blight disease has felled the towering palms. There's a snack bar and medical clinic. There's a fee for each adult to enter and to camp overnight, but it's really not worth even a stop.

More idyllic, **Xcacel** is 1½ miles south of Chemuyil, and ¼ mile east of the highway. It's a gorgeous palm-shaded place where you can stay for the day for $1.75 or pitch your tent or park your van for $3 per person per night, including use of changing rooms, toilets, and showers. There's a nice restaurant here as well, but you can cookout in a portable grill (yours) as long as you bring your own charcoal and don't cook on the beach.

When I was last there, a state-supervised volunteer group had established a **"save the turtle" program** on the beach left of the restaurant. It's unfunded, so visitor donations are critical and there's a contribution box at the entrance to the turtle area. For as long as it lasts, visitors can see the turtles in shaded water flats before they are released. Loggerheads are so rare that this may be your only chance to ever see one. At least half of the remaining loggerhead turtles nest between here and Cancún—or will until driven away by development. In 1991 the volunteers protected 550 loggerhead and green turtle nests and more than 2,500 of these endangered species have been hatched, tagged, and released. Four biologists patrol the beach nightly between May and September, but they don't want help from visitors. Use of flashlights on the beach at night is prohibited because it confuses the turtles when they are about to nest or when the hatchlings are ready to go to sea.

Author's note: Chemuyil and Xcacel were popular when there were no other accessible places on the coast. There are other, lesser known options available now, so if you're looking for a place to spend the day with no admission cost, but even more beautiful beaches with a restaurant and shower and bathroom facilities, then Xcalacoco, Pamul, and the Villas Xpuha at Xpuha are better choices—all of which you pass before reaching Chemuyil and Xcacel. Each has a few plain, but comfortable cabaña units for overnight stays as well. At these places it's courteous to buy food and drinks from the restaurants in exchange for entering their property (your only access) to use the otherwise public beach. See the descriptions for each one above.

XEL-HA

The Caribbean cost of the Yucatán is carved by the sea into hundreds of small *caletas* (coves) that form the perfect habitat for tropical marine life, both flora and fauna. Many caletas remain undiscovered and pristine along the coast, but **Xel-Ha,** eight miles south of Akumal and a mile and a half from Xcacel, is enjoyed daily by snorkelers and scuba divers who come to luxuriate in its warm waters, palm-lined shore, and brilliant fish. Xel-Ha (pronounced *Shell*-hah) is a bit of paradise for swimming, with no threat of undertow or pollution. Proximity to the ruins at Tulum makes Xel-Ha a good place for a dip when you've finished clambering around the Maya castles.

The short eight-mile hop north from Tulum to Xel-Ha can be done by bus. When you get off at the junction for Tulum, ask the local restaurant owner when the next buses come by. Otherwise you may have to wait as much as two hours on the highway. Most tour companies from Cancún or Cozumel include a trip to Tulum and a swim at Xel-Ha in the same journey.

The entrance to Xel-Ha is a half mile in from the highway. You'll be asked to pay a $5 per person "contribution" to the upkeep and preservation of the site. Children under 12 are admitted free. It's open daily from 8am to 4:30pm.

Once in the park, you can rent snorkeling equipment and an underwater cameras—but it's much cheaper to bring your own. You can also buy an outrageously priced drink or a meal, change clothes, and take showers. When you swim, be careful to observe SWIM HERE and NO SWIMMING signs. The greatest variety of fish can be seen right near the ropes marking off the "no swimming" areas, and near any groups of rocks. Xel-Ha is an exceptionally beautiful place!

Just south of the Xel-Ha turnoff on the west side of the highway, don't miss the **Maya ruins** of ancient Xel-Ha. You'll likely be the only one there as you walk over limestone rocks and through the tangle of trees, vines, and palms. There's a huge, deep, dark, and daring cenote to one side and a temple palace with tumbled-down columns, a jaguar group, and a conserved temple group. A covered palapa on one pyramid guards a partially preserved mural.

6. TULUM, PUNTA ALLEN & SIAN KA'AN

To get your bearings, think of Tulum as three distinct areas. First, there's the **junction** of Highway 307 and the Tulum access road where you'll find two small hotels, two restaurants, and a Pemex gas station. Second, on Highway 307, about 1½ miles past the Tulum junction is the Mexican **village** of Tulum. Third, a turn at the Tulum junction (before the Tulum village) and by the restaurants (mentioned above) will take you a half mile to the **ruins of Tulum** and a collection of small restaurants, snack shops, and souvenir stands. Enter the ruins here. The road past the Tulum ruins parking lot heads south along the narrow Punta Allen Peninsula to Boca de Paila, a portion of the Sian Ka'an Biosphere Reserve, and Punta Allen, the lobster-fishing village at the tip end. Though most of this 30-mile-long peninsular stretch of sandy potholed road is uninhabited, there are several modest but comfortable inns along this fabulous beach, south of the ruins.

TULUM ARCHEOLOGICAL SITE

At the end of the Classic period in A.D. 900 the Maya civilization began to de cline and most of the large ceremonial centers were deserted. During the Postclassic period (A.D. 900 to the Spanish conquest), small rival states developed with a few imported traditions from the Mexicans. Tulum is one such walled city-state, eight miles south of Xel-Ha. The Maya seaport was built in the 10th century as a fortress overlooking the Caribbean. Aside from its spectacular setting, Tulum is not an impressive city when compared to Chichén-Itzá or Uxmal. There are no magnificent pyramidal structures as are found in the classic Maya ruins. The stone carving is crude and the site looks as though it was put together in a hurry or by novice apprentices rather than skilled masters. The primary god here was the diving god, depicted on several buildings as an upside-down figure above doorways. Seen at the Palace at Sayil and Cobá, this curious, almost comical figure is also known as the bee god.

The most imposing building in Tulum is the large stone structure on the cliff called the **Castillo (castle)**, actually a temple as well as a fortress, once covered with stucco and painted. In front of the Castillo are several unrestored palacelike buildings partially covered with stucco. And on the beach below, where the Maya once came ashore, tourists frolic, combining a visit to the ruins with a dip in the Caribbean.

The **Temple of the Frescoes**, directly in front of the Castillo, contains interesting 13th-century wall paintings inside the temple, but entrance is no longer permitted. Distinctly Maya, they represent the rain god Chaac and Ixchel, the goddess of weaving, women, the moon, and medicine. On the cornice of this temple is a relief of the head of the rain god. If you get a slight distance from the building you will see the eyes, nose, mouth, and chin. Notice the remains of the red-painted stucco on this building—at one time all the buildings at Tulum were painted a bright red.

Much of what we know of Tulum at the time of the Spanish conquest comes from the writings of Diego de Landa, third bishop of the Yucatán. He wrote that Tulum was a small city inhabited by about 600 people, who lived in dwellings situated on platforms along a street and supervised the trade traffic from Honduras to the Yucatán. Though the city was walled, most of the inhabitants probably lived

FROMMER'S NATURE NOTES

STONE CRABS

Since the late 1940s fishermen from Campeche have been harvesting the deep reddish-brown and cream-colored stone crab, prized for the delicate sweet meat of its enormous claw. *Menipe mercenaria,* or "cangrejo moro" as it's called in Mexico, is found all along the Gulf coast, including Florida as well as the Mexican state of Campeche, both of which harvest the crab commercially (as does Cuba).

In the Caribbean fishing village of Punta Allen, in Mexico's Quintana Roo state, fishermen are attempting to develop a stone crab industry to supplement the erratic lobster fishing there. Using traps woven from a local vine, fishermen capture the slow-moving crabs and remove the largest claw—very carefully, as the forceful pinch of a stone crab claw is enough to sever a human finger. The live crab is returned to the water where it regenerates the large claw within a year; meanwhile, the crab uses the smaller claw to feed and defend itself.

The female crab lays eggs (500,000 with each spawning) several times a season from March through October. Called *manitas de cangrejo* (little crab hands) on menus in Mexico, the fleshy legs are usually steamed or boiled and served with fresh lime.

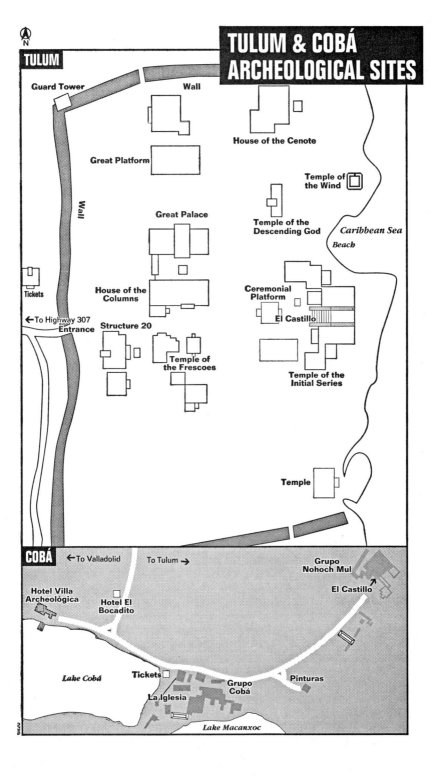

TULUM & COBÁ ARCHEOLOGICAL SITES

TULUM

N

Guard Tower

Wall

House of the Cenote

Great Platform

Wall

Temple of the Wind

Great Palace

Temple of the Descending God

Caribbean Sea

Beach

Tickets

House of the Columns

Ceremonial Platform

El Castillo

← To Highway 307
Entrance

Structure 20

Temple of the Frescoes

Temple of the Initial Series

Temple

COBÁ

← To Valladolid

To Tulum →

Grupo Nohoch Mul

Hotel Villa Arqueológica

Hotel El Bocadito

El Castillo

Lake Cobá

Tickets

Pinturas

Grupo Cobá

La Iglesia

Lake Macanxoc

outside the walls leaving the interior for the priestly hierarchy and religious ceremonies. Tulum survived about 70 years after the conquest, when it was finally abandoned.

Because of the excessive number of visitors this site receives, it is no longer possible to climb the ruins. Visitors are asked to remain behind roped-off areas to view them. Admission is $5. There's an additional charge of $8.50 for a permit to use a video camera at the site. Licensed guides solicit at the entrance and charge $15 for a 90-minute tour in English, French, or Spanish. They will point out many architectural details that you may otherwise miss, but their historic information may not be up-to-date. Pay bathrooms are behind the ticket booth.

WHERE TO STAY & DINE NEAR TULUM JUNCTION

HOTEL ACUARIO AND RESTAURANT EL FAISAN, Carretera Cancún-Tulum (Hwy. 307) km 127 (Apdo. Postal 80), Tulum, Q. Roo. Tel. 988/4-4856 in Cancún. 12 rms. A/C TV
$ Rates: $55 single or double.
The Hotel Acuario and Restaurant El Faisan y Venado are found here, along with a small grocery store where you can pick up snacks and bottled water. The grocery store is on the front and the restaurant and rooms are in the back around a small pool. The rooms and pool always seem to be undergoing changes and repairs. Rooms are modern and comfortable, although housekeeping and maintenance are often lacking. The price and menu at the restaurant are similar to those at Crucero's (across the street).

MOTEL EL CRUCERO, Carretera Cancún-Tulum (Hwy. 307), Apdo. Postal 4, Tulum, Q. Roo Tel. 987/3-0230 or 3-0232. 16 rms. FAN
$ Rates: High season $14 single, $19 double.
This motel has a very good and festive restaurant, where main courses cost $6. The pollo pibil is excellent. The guest rooms, however, are quite basic and may have hot water. There's also a tiny "convenience store."

SOUTH OF THE RUINS/PUNTA ALLEN PENINSULA

About three miles south of the ruins, the pavement ends and becomes a narrow sandy road, with many potholes during the rainy season. Beyond this point is a 30-mile-long peninsula called **Punta Allen,** split in two at a cut called **Boca Paila,** where a bridge connects the two parts of the peninsula and the Caribbean enters a large lagoon on the right. It is included in the far-eastern edge of the 1.3-million-acre **Sian Ka'an Biosphere Reserve** (see below). Along this road you'll find several cabaña-type inns, all on beautiful beaches facing the Caribbean. Taxis from the ruins can take you to most of these, then you can find a ride back to the junction at the end of your stay.

WHAT TO SEE & DO

Besides lazing around or going on and **birding expeditions** between June and August (July is best) sea **turtles** nest on the beaches along here. Alfonso Herrera and wife María Guadalupe Breseño, local residents who live at Rancho Kan Zuul next to the Cabanas Tulum, are state employees hired to protect the nests (*nido* in Spanish) and see that the hatchlings, born 45 days later, have a safe journey to the sea. They protect around 1,500 nests of three different types of turtles a season with an average of 90 to 170 eggs each. It takes the turtles about 90 exhausting minutes to dig the nests with back flippers, and tourists can watch. But please, no flash pictures or flashlights. Light disorients the turtles, making them switch directions and upset the laborious nesting process. The turtles lumber ashore at night, usually between 10pm and 3am. If you participate, a tip to the family would be courteous.

SIAN KA'AN BIOSPHERE RESERVE Down the peninsula, a few miles south of the Tulum ruins, you'll pass the guardhouse of the Sian Ka'an Bio sphere Reserve, which in 1986 set aside 1.3 million acres to preserve tropical forests, savannas and mangroves, coastal and marine habitats, and 70 miles of coastal reefs. The area is home to jaguar, puma, ocelot, margay, jaguarundi, spider and howler monkeys, tapir, white-lipped and collared peccary, manatee, brocket and white-tailed deer, crocodiles, and green, loggerhead, hawksbill, and leatherback sea turtles. It also protects 366 species of birds, including ocellated turkey, great curassow, parrots, toucans and trogons, white ibis, roseate spoonbill, jabiru stork, wood stork, flamingo, and 15 species of herons, egrets, and bitterns. It's separated into three parts: a Core Zone, restricted to research; a Buffer Zone, where visitors and families already living there have restricted use; and a Cooperation Zone, outside the reserve but vital to its preservation. If you drive on Highway 307 from Tulum to an imaginary line just below the Bahía (bay) of Espíritu Santo, all you see on the Caribbean side is the reserve; but except at the **ruins of Muyil/Chunyaxche** (see "En Route to Felipe Carrillo Puerto," below), there's no access. At least 22 archeological sites have been charted within Sian Ka'an. The best place to sample the reserve is the Punta Allen peninsula, part of the Buffer Zone. The inns were already in place

---

FROMMER'S ARCHEOLOGY NOTES
SIAN KA'AN BIOSPHERE RESERVE

At least 22 pre-Hispanic sites have been discovered within the Sian Ka'an Biosphere Reserve. Early this century the Carnegie Institute and Tulane University found Cacakal (known as Platanal), Nohkú (or Punta Pájaros), Chacmool (called locally Santa Rosa), and Canché Balan in the region around Asunción Bay and Espíritu Santo Bay. Thomas Gann found Tantamán (called Tampalám) near Punta Herrero and in 1926 discovered the Maya-made canal connection of Vigia del Lago to the inland ruins of Chunyaxche (Muyil) plus the ruins of Chenchomac. Eleven years later Alberto Escalona Ramos of the Mexican Scientific Expedition came upon the ruins of Las Milpas near Vigía Chico.

Probably the most thrilling written account of all comes in *The Lost World of Quintana Roo*, written by Frenchman Michel Peissel, a young untrained archeologist who explored the area on foot on two trips between 1958 and 1963. He discovered at least 17 new sites when the area was still sparsely settled, inhabited by chicle and coconut plantation caretakers. Most sites date from the last Postclassic era between A.D. 1200 and 1500, when the Maya civilization was in decline.

But there is evidence of occupation for at least 2,000 years. The people were fishermen, who hunted manatee and turtle, and engaged in conch trading with Honduras and Belize, as well as important centers such as Cozumel. The goods went inland via Maya-made canals through the jungle, which included not only the Muyil connection but canals connecting Asunción and Espíritu Santo bays. (*Author's note:* I am indebted to the Friends of Sian Ka'an for this background information.)

when the reserve was created. Of these only the Caphe Ha Guest House and the Cuzan Guest House (see below) offer trips for birding. But anywhere here, bring your own binoculars and birding books and have at it—the bird life is rich.

At the Boca Paila bridge you can often find fishermen who'll take you into the lagoon on the landward side, where you can fish and see plenty of bird life; but it's unlikely the boatman will know bird names in English or Spanish. Birding is best just after dawn, especially during the April-through-July nesting season.

Day trips to the Sian Ka'an are led from Cozumel (see Section 4, above) and by a biologist from the **Friends of Sian Ka'an in Cancún.** For more information about membership, the reserve, or trip reservations write them at: Plaza America, Av. Cobá no. 5, 3a Piso, Suite 48–50, Cancún, Q. Roo 77500 (tel. 988/4-9583; fax 988/7-3080). From Cozumel **Viajes Internacionales Palancar,** 10a Av. Sur no. 124, Cozumel, Q. Roo 77600 (tel. 987/2-2259; fax 987/2-2348), offers day-long excursions to the reserve.

WHERE TO STAY & DINE

Lodgings here vary in quality: some are quite comfortable, but simple, while others are a lot like camping out. One or two have electricity for a few hours in the evening; many don't have hot water. The first one is a half mile south of the ruins and the farthest one is 30 miles south. Bring plenty of mosquito repellent and mosquito netting, and a flashlight. From October through December winds may be accompanied by nippy nights, so come prepared; hotels don't have blankets.

EL PARAÍSO, Punta Allen Peninsula km 1 (Apdo. Postal 61), Tulum, Q. Roo. Tel. 987/2-3636 or 987/2-2001 in Cozumel. Fax 987/2-1717. 10 rms (all with bath). FANS
$ Rates: High season $42 single, $56 double. Low season $28 single, $34 double.
The eye-appealing row of apricot-colored cement-walled rooms looks like a motel lined up near the island road. The splendid, palm-studded beach and water are part of the property 100 yards or so farther on after you turn in the entrance. This was formerly a plain but clean little inn, but on my last visit rooms were dingy and the bathrooms dirty and smelly although supposedly ready for the next guest—me. The two thin towels were dingy, too, and as rough as sandpaper. The management also instituted high-season prices in the middle of November—a month early. Each room comes with tile floors, two double beds and no bedspreads, hot water, bottled drinking water, and electricity from 6 to 10pm. The rooms are linked by a breezy covered common porch set with comfy chairs. The hotel's large restaurant is near the water and open daily from 7am to 9pm. It's a half mile south of the Tulum ruins immediately beyond Cabañas Don Armando.

RESTAURANT Y CABAÑAS ANA Y JOSÉ, Carretera Tulum km 7 (Apdo. Postal 80), Tulum, Q. Roo. Tel. 98/80-6021. Fax 98/80-6022. 16 rms.
$ Rates: High season $58 single or double. Low season $46 single or double.
This place started as a restaurant and blossomed into a comfortable inn on the beach. All cabañas have tiled floors, one or two double beds, bathrooms with cold-water showers in eight rooms, little patios, and electricity between 5 and 10pm. The rock-walled cabañas in front are a little larger, with some facing the beautiful wide beach just a few yards off. The only drawback is the lack of cross-ventilation in some of the rooms, which can be uncomfortable at night without electricity and fans. The inn also offers massage, yoga, and bicycle rentals.

The excellent, screened-in restaurant, with sand floors under a palapa, is open daily from 8am to 9pm. It's four miles south of the Tulum ruins.

CABAÑAS TULUM, Punta Allen Peninsula km 7. Tel. 98/25-8295 in Mérida. 18 rms (all with bath). FAN

$ Rates: High season $37 single or double. Low season $28 single or double.

Next door to Ana and José's (see above) is a row of bungalows facing a heavenly stretch of ocean and beach. Each bungalow includes a cold-water shower, two double beds, screens on the windows, a table, one electric light, a nice-size tile bathroom, and a veranda where you can hang a hammock. The electricity is on from 6:30 to 10:30pm only, so bring candles or a flashlight. A small restaurant serves beer, soft drinks, and all three meals for reasonable prices. The cabañas are often full between December 15 and Easter, and July and August, so make reservations. It's four miles south of the ruins.

BOCA PAILA FISHING LODGE, Apdo. Postal 59, Cozumel, Q. Roo 77600. Tel. and fax 987/872-0053 or 872-1176. 8 cabañas. FAN

$ Rates (for six days and seven nights, including all meals and a private boat and fishing guide for each cabaña): High season (Dec 15–May 31) $2,350 single, $1,825 per person double. Low season $1,880 single, $1,460 per person double. Ask about prices for nonangler sharing a double with an angler. Nonfishing drop-in prices July–Sept, $75 per person with three meals; $50 per person without meals.

Easily a top contender for the most hospitable spot along this road, the white stucco cabañas offer a friendly beachside comfort that makes it an ideal choice. Spread out on the beach and linked by a nice walkway, each individual unit has a mosquito-proof palapa roof, large tiled rooms comfortably furnished with two double beds, rattan furniture, hot water in the bathrooms, wall fans, 24-hour electricity, and comfortable screened porch. The Boca Paila attracts a clientele that comes to bone fish in the saltwater flats. Prime fishing months are March through June. But when occupancy is low, nonfishing guests can be accommodated with advance notice. The lodge is about midway down the Punta Allen Peninsula, just before the Boca Paila bridge.

Reservations: Contact Frontiers, P.O. Box 959, 100 Logan Rd., Wexford, PA 15090 (tel. 412/935-1577, or toll free 800/245-1950; fax 412/935-5388).

CAPHE HA GUEST HOUSE, Carretera Tulum–Punta Allen. No phone. 2 rms (1 with bath).

$ Rates (including breakfast and dinner): $100 single; $175–$200 double.

This secluded guesthouse, owned by Sue Brown Baker, is set in a dense coconut palm grove on a long, fabulous palm-lined beach. There are no restaurants, other inns, or telephones nearby. Lodging is in two mosquito-proof, solar-powered, one-bedroom cottages and a main house; one cottage has a private bath and one shares a bath with the main house. Rates include as many guided fishing, diving, and birding excursions as guests want. Guests have the run of the main house, and everyone usually pitches in to help with the family-style meals. During the rainy season the potholes are full of water, so allow ample time to arrive before 3pm "mosquito time," as Baker suggests. Ask for directions when you make reservations.

Reservations: For information/reservations in the U.S., contact Jeff Frankel in New York (tel. 212/219-2198). Reservations are required.

CUZAN GUEST HOUSE, Punta Allen. 9 rms (4 with bath).

$ Rates: $20–$50 single or double; seven-day fly-fishing package available.

About 30 miles from the Tulum ruins, you reach the end of the peninsula and Punta Allen, Yucatán's best-known lobster-fishing village. Isolated and rustic, it's part Indiana Jones, part Robinson Crusoe, and certainly the most laid-back end-of-the-line spot you'll find for a while. There's 24-hour solar-powered electricity. And there's a palm-studded beach, town center, lobster cooperative, a few streets with modest homes, and a lighthouse at the end of a narrow sand road, dense with coconut palms and jungle on both sides. It's a welcome sight to see the beachside Cuzan Guest House and its sign in English that reads STOP HERE FOR TOURIST INFORMATION. As one guest wrote, "The end of the world never looked so good." A stay here could well be the highlight of your trip, provided you're a flexible traveler.

Two rooms are Maya-style oval-shaped stucco buildings with concrete floors and a shared bathroom with a shower between them. Two huts with magnificent water views have private baths. The remainder of the accommodations are very comfortable teepee-shaped thatched palapa huts with concrete floors and double beds, all with shared bath. The real charmer here is the sand-floor restaurant run by co-owner Sonja Lillvik, a Californian who makes you feel right at home. If it's lobster season you may have lobster at every meal and always a deliciously different recipe. But you may also enjoy a pile of scrumptious stone crabs. She arranges **fly-fishing** trips for bone, permit, snook, and tarpon to the nearby saltwater flats and lagoons of Ascension Bay. The $25 per person boat tour of the coastline that she offers is a fascinating half day of **snorkeling,** slipping in and out of mangrove-filled canals for **birdwatching,** and skirting the edge of an island rookery loaded with frigate birds. November through March is frigate mating season and the male frigate shows off his big billowy red breast pouch to impress potential mates. The overnight **Robinson Crusoe Tour** costs $100 per person and includes boat travel to remote islands, beaches, reefs, ruins (Muyil/Chunyaxche), jungles, and lagoons, and birdwatching. Or you can go kayaking along the coast or simply relax in a hammock on the beach or in your room.

Reservations: Contact Apdo. Postal 24, Felipe Carrillo Puerto, Q. Roo 77200 (tel. and fax 983/4-0385 in Felipe Carrillo Puerto).

EN ROUTE TO COBÁ

About a mile south of the turnoff to Tulum, on Highway 307, is the road to Cobá, another fascinating Maya city 40 miles inland. If you're driving, turn right when you see the signs to Cobá, and continue on that road for 40 miles. (There's no gas at Cobá, so fill up in Tulum.) When you reach the village, proceed straight until you see the lake and the road curves right; go left. The entrance to the ruins is at the end of that road past some small restaurants.

7. COBÁ

105 miles S of Cancún

GETTING THERE & DEPARTING   By Bus   From Playa del Carmen there are three buses to Cobá. Two buses leave Valladolid for Cobá at 4:30am and 1:15pm, but they may fill early, so buy tickets as soon as possible. Several buses a day leave Cobá: At 6:30am and 3pm a bus goes to Tulum and Playa del Carmen, and at noon and 6:30 and 7pm there's a bus to Valladolid. Buses arrive and depart from in front of the Hotel El Bocadito.

The highway into Cobá becomes one main paved street through town, which passes El Bocadito restaurant and hotel on the right (see "Where to Stay & Dine," below) and goes a block to the lake. If you turn right at the lake you reach the Villas Arqueológicas a block farther. Turning left will lead past a couple of informal/primitive restaurants on the left facing the lake, and to the ruins, straight ahead, the equivalent of a block. The village is small and poor, gaining little from visitors passing through to see the ruins. Used clothing (especially for children) would be a welcome gift.

SEEING THE RUINS

The Maya built many breathtaking cities in the Yucatán, but few were grander in scope than Cobá—however, much of the 42-square-mile site on the shores of two lakes is unexcavated. A 60-mile-long *sacbe* (pre-Hispanic raised road) through the jungle linked Cobá to Yaxuná, once an important and large Maya center 30 miles south of Chichén-Itzá. It's the Maya's longest-known sacbe and at least 50 more shorter ones spoke off here to distant ruins in the jungle. An important city-state, Cobá, which means "water stirred by the wind," flourished between A.D. 632 (the oldest carved date) until after the founding of Chichén-Itzá around A.D. 800, when it slowly faded in importance and population until it was finally abandoned. Current scholarly thinking places Cobá as an important link in the trade route between the Yucatán Caribbean coast and inland cities. Architecturally its two towering temples more resemble those south of it at Tikal in Guatemala and the Río Bec ruins near Chetumal than others in Mexico's Maya land. And there is evidence that the royalty of Cobá was linked to that of the Maya of Guatemala as well.

Once in the site, keep your bearings, as it's very easy to get lost on the maze of dirt roads in the jungle. Bring your bird and butterfly books; this is one of the best places to see both. Branching off from every labeled path you'll notice unofficial narrow paths into the jungle, used by locals as shortcuts through the ruins. These are good for scouting for birds, since stillness quickly envelops you as you leave tourist chatter on the path—the better to see and hear the birds, but be careful to remember the way back. Wildflowers—lantana and daisies among them—add color to the vine-twisted jungle floor. There's the constant hum of bees, and numerous butterflies flitter about.

The **Grupo Cobá** boasts a large, impressive pyramid, **the Temple of the Church** (La Iglesia), which you'll find if you take the path bearing right after the entry gate. Walking to it, notice unexcavated mounds on the left. Though the urge to climb the temple is great, the view is better from El Castillo in the Nohoch Mul group farther back at the site.

From here return back to the main path and turn right. You'll pass a sign pointing right to the ruined **juego de pelota (ballcourt),** but the path is obscure.

Continuing straight ahead on this path for 10 or 15 minutes you'll come to a fork in the road. Left and right you'll notice jungle-covered, unexcavated pyramids and at one point you'll cross a raised portion crossing the pathway—this is the visible remains of the sacbe to Yaxuná. Throughout the area, intricately carved stelae stand by pathways, or lie forlornly in the jungle underbrush. Though protected by crude thatched roofs, most are so weatherworn as to be indiscernible.

The left fork leads to the **Nohoch Mul** group, which contains **El Castillo,** the highest pyramid in the Yucatán (higher than the great El Castillo at Chichén-Itzá and the Pyramid of the Magician at Uxmal). When I was last there visitors were still permitted to climb to the top. From that magnificent lofty position you can see unexcavated, jungle-covered pyramidal structures poking up through the forest all around—ah, if only there was money for further excavation. The right fork (more or less straight on) goes to the **Conjunto Las Pinturas.** Here, the main attraction is the **Pyramid of the Painted Lintel,** a small structure with traces of the original bright colors above the door. You can climb up to get a close look. Though maps of Cobá show ruins around two lakes, there are really only two excavated buildings to see after you enter the site. *Note:* Because of the heat, visit Cobá in the morning, or after the heat of the day has passed. Mosquito repellent and comfortable shoes are imperative.

Admission is $4.50; children under 12 are admitted free daily. Sunday and holidays it's free to everyone. A camera permit costs $8.50. The site is open daily from 8am to 5pm.

WHERE TO STAY & DINE IN COBÁ

EL BOCADITO, Calle Principal, Cobá, Q. Roo. No phone. 8 rms. FAN
$ Rates: $12 single or double.
El Bocadito, on the right as you enter town, could take advantage of being the only game in town besides the much more expensive Villas Arqueológicas—but it doesn't. Next to the hotel's restaurant of the same name, the rooms are arranged in two rows facing an open patio. They're simple, with tile floors, two double beds, no bedspreads, ceiling fan, and washbasins separate from the toilet and cold-water shower cubicle. It's agreeable enough and always full by nightfall; to secure a room, arrive no later than 3pm. The clean, open-air **restaurant** has good meals at reasonable prices, served by a friendly, efficient staff. Busloads of tour groups stop here at lunch (always a sign of approval). I enjoy Bocadito's casual atmosphere. There's a bookstore, with English-language books, and a gift shop adjacent to the restaurant.

Reservations: Apdo. Postal 56, Valladolid, Yuc. 97780.

VILLA ARQUEOLÓGICA COBÁ, Cobá, Q. Roo. Tel. 5/203-3086 in Mexico City, or toll free 800/258-2633 in the U.S. 44 rms. A/C
$ Rates: $72 single, $84 double.
Operated by Club Med, but nothing like a large Club Med village, this lovely lakeside hotel is a five-minute walk from the ruins. The hotel has a French polish and the restaurant is usually top-notch, though expensive. Breakfast costs $15; lunch and dinner, $25. The rooms, built around a plant-filled courtyard and beautiful swimming pool, are stylish and soothingly comfortable. The hotel also has a library of books on Mesoamerican archeology (with books in French, English, and Spanish). Make reservations; this hotel fills with tour groups. To find it, drive through town and turn right at the lake; the hotel is straight ahead on the right.

EN ROUTE TO FELIPE CARRILLO PUERTO

From the Cobá turnoff, the main road, Highway 307, heads southwest through Tulum village. About 14 miles south of the village are the ruins of **Muyil** (ca. A.D. 1–1540) at the settlement of **Chunyaxche,** on the left-hand side. Tulane University, in conjunction with the Institución Nacional de Antropología de México, has done extensive mapping and studies; but of the more than 100 or so buildings, caves, and subterranean temples, only a couple of buildings have been excavated. Postsherds discovered in 1989 by archeologists show that Muyil was probably inhabited from A.D. 1 until the conquest of Mexico in 1519. A recently discovered sacbe runs almost a mile from the center of the site to the Muyil Lagoon. Excavations revealed mortarless rock walls, tombs with the remains of two people, and 2,500-year-old pottery pieces. One of the objects of this research is to find evidence of an inland port, since **canals** link the site to the Caribbean nine miles east at Boca Paila.

The Friends of Sian Ka'an in Cancún (see Section 6, above) organizes trips through the canals from Boca Paila. The Cuzan Guest House in Punta Allen also

FROMMER'S ARCHEOLOGY NOTES
SACBEOB—ANCIENT MAYA ROADS

The Maya built raised roads called sacbeob (that's plural—the singular is sacbe), meaning "white roads." Filled with stone rubble and smoothed with white limestone plaster, the roadbeds were elevated as much as three feet over the existing landscape. Widths of sacbeob varied from nine to at least 60 feet, and support of the roads, with retaining walls and culverts for drainage and access, varied depending on the terrain. These lofty paths are generally believed to have been constructed for ceremonial rather than commercial purposes. Many, such as the 60-mile-long sacbe linking Cobá and Yaxuná, may well have been originally constructed to consolidate power and as a show of strength over rival cities. At Chichén-Itzá visitors follow a broad tree-lined sacbe to the famous cenote, where remains of animals, humans, and their possessions were discovered.

guides visitors here through the lagoons and canals. *Note:* The mosquito and dive-bombing fly population is fierce, but this is one of the best places along the coast for birding—go early in the morning. For a truly exciting account of this site and the Quintana Roo coast when it was unexplored territory as recently as the early 1960s, try to find a copy of *The Lost World of Quintana Roo,* by Frenchman Michel Peissel, published in 1963. He explored the coast from Tulum to Belize on foot and was particularly captivated by the ruins he found at Chunyaxche.

Admission is $2.50; free for children under 12 and free for everyone on Sunday and festival days. It's open daily from 8am to 5pm.

After Muyil and Chunyaxche, the highway passes 45 miles of jungle-bordered road.

Important note: If you're driving farther, fill up the tank at Tulum. The next chance is at Felipe Carrillo Puerto, 60 miles farther. There's no gas at Cobá.

8. FELIPE CARRILLO PUERTO

134 miles S of Cancún

GETTING THERE   By Bus   There's frequent bus service from Cancún and Playa del Carmen. The bus station is right on the zócalo. From there it is a 10-minute walk east down Calle 67, past the cathedral and banks, to Avenida Juárez. Turn left onto Juárez and you'll find the recommended hotels and restaurants, and the traffic circle I use as a reference point.

By Car   Coastal Highway 307 from Cancún leads directly here. The highway goes right through town, becoming Avenida Benito Juárez. Driving from the north, you will pass a traffic circle with a bust of the great Juárez. The town market is here.

ESSENTIALS   The telephone area code is 983. Banks here don't exchange foreign currency.

F elipe Carrillo Puerto (pop. 47,000) is a busy crossroads in the jungle along the road to Ciudad Chetumal. It has gas stations, a market, a small ice plant, a bus terminal, and a few modest hotels and restaurants.

Since the main road intersects the road back to Mérida, Carrillo Puerto is the turning point for those making a "short circuit" of the Yucatán peninsula. Highway 184 heads west from here to Ticul, Uxmal, Campeche, and Mérida. Highway 295 goes north to Valladolid.

As you pass through, consider its strange history: This was where the rebels in the War of the Castes took their stand, guided by the "Talking Crosses." Some remnants of that town (named Chan Santa Cruz) are still extant. Look for signs in town pointing the way. For the full story, refer to Chapter 1, where there's a section on Yucatán's fascinating history.

WHERE TO STAY

HOTEL SAN IGNACIO, Av. Juárez s/n, Felipe Carrillo Puerto, Q. Roo. Tel. 983/4-0122. 12 rms. FAN
$ Rates: $14 single; $20–$23 double.
This small, simple hotel surrounds a parking lot. The rooms are bright and clean but spare in furnishings. In case the office is closed, the dueña lives next door across the back parking lot and she's thrilled to have guests. Get to bed early—this town wakes up at dawn.

The Restaurant 24 Horas is practically next door. The hotel is on the left, one block south of the Hotel/Restaurant Faisán y Venado.

HOTEL/RESTAURANT EL FAISAN Y VENADO, Av. Juárez s/n, Felipe Carrillo Puerto, Q. Roo. Tel. 983/4-0043. 21 rms. A/C (8 rms) or FAN (13 rms).
$ Rates: $16 single; $28 double.
This hotel is adjacent to the popular restaurant of the same name. The tidy rooms, with hot water, are plain, functional, and comfortable. Realistic photographs of the rooms are on display in the restaurant. Thirteen have TV. The restaurant is one of the townfolks' favorites. Modern with an airy dining room looking onto the street, it's a good place for a stop if you're just passing through. Main courses run $4 to $5 and it's open daily from 6am to 10pm.

To find it, go one block south from the traffic circle and it's easy to see on the left.

WHERE TO DINE

Besides the popular Faisán y Venado, mentioned above, there's **Danesa Ice Cream Parlor** next door to the Restaurant 24 Horas (below).

RESTAURANT 24 HORAS, Av. Juárez s/n. Tel. 4-0020.
  Cuisine: MEXICAN.
$ Prices: Breakfast $2.50–$4.75; main courses $3.50–$8.50.
  Open: Daily 24 hours.
Comfortable and open to breezes, this restaurant displays a Maya glyph picture stone on one wall. Come for breakfast; it's the only place in town open early. A full breakfast includes scrambled eggs, ham, instant coffee, and fruit. You'll see it on the left opposite the Pemex gas station.

9. MAJAHUAL, XCALAK & THE CHINCHORRO REEF

Continuing south from Felipe Carrillo Puerto, you'll come to the turnoff (left) onto Highway 10, 1½ miles after Limones, to the coastal settlements of Majahual and Xcalak, the latter named after the tiny village at the tip end of the peninsula. If you're sampling this coast's offbeat offerings, if you're a diver looking for new underwater conquests, and if you're a roll-with-the-punches kind of traveler, you won't want to miss this remote and relatively undeveloped (for the moment) area. Bird lovers will find an abundance of colorful birdlife.

Yellow blight disease has made raising coconut palms here no longer possible, except, so far, at plantations beyond Xcalak. And the fishing village of Xcalak, once with a population as large as 1,200 before the 1958 hurricane, now has only 200 inhabitants. The route is littered with closed, or half-open, rustic inns and erratically operating hut-restaurants, and many For Sale signs. One sign trumpets "Big development coming, lots for sale." A plethora of shady deals await the greedy and unwary, so before you get Xcalak buying fever, beware of fast talkers who may not have clear title to the land they are selling.

Just to orient yourself, the turnoff from Highway 307 is 163 miles southeast of Cancún, 88 miles southeast of Tulum, and 70 miles southeast of the small village of Limones. *Important notes:* Absolutely don't make this sojourn without a large quantity of strong mosquito repellent with deet as a main ingredient. Your last chance for gas is at Felipe Carrillo Puerto, although if you're desperate, the tire repairman's family in Limones might sell you a liter or two. Look for the big tire leaning against the fence. Except for the makeshift arrangement at Limones, there's no gas between Felipe Carrillo Puerto and Chetumal. From the turnoff at Highway 307 to Xcalak takes around two hours. Slow down at settlements. Residents aren't expecting much traffic and dogs and children play on the road.

After the turnoff from Highway 307 follow this paved road straight 30 miles to the end. (On the way you'll pass another turnoff on the left to El Placer, which is a stretch of private beachfront homes.) When you get to the end and see the Caribbean and the beach, turn right onto the narrow sand road. This barely inhabited place is Majahual, significant for the military guard station where you'll be stopped. Tell them you're a tourist: *"Estoy turista."* They have the right to search your car for drugs and weapons, but they probably won't. Because of its remote location but easy access to Belize at the end of the peninsula, this isolated area is at times a clandestine link for drug trafficking between the two countries.

From Majahual it's 35 miles to the end of the road at Xcalak. The narrow sand road follows the beach with clear views of the Caribbean and it has plenty of potholes, similar to the road running to Punta Allen. This one, however, is maintained more regularly.

Getting here without a car is possible via minivan from Chetumal, where one minivan leaves Chetumal daily at 7am and arrives at Xcalak around 10am. It returns to Chetumal at 1pm. More people than the van should hold will be squeezed in, and perhaps a goat or pig will be strapped on top. There's a 2,800-foot **paved runway** at Xcalak. To summon a taxi before landing, pilots fly over Xcalak and tip the wings twice.

Offshore 22 miles is **Chinchorro Reef Underwater National Park,** a 24-mile-long, 8-mile-wide oval-shaped reef with a depth from 3 feet on the reef's interior to 3,000 feet on the exterior. Locals claim it's the last virgin reef system in the Caribbean. Until recently it was almost impossible to dive here due to the reef's distance from shore and the remote land accessibility to it. It's invisible from the ocean side, so one of its diving attractions is the number of shipwrecks—at least 30 of them—along the reef's eastern side. One is on top of the reef. Divers have counted 40 cannon at one wreck site. On the west side are walls and coral gardens, but it's too rough to dive there. Even though there's boat access now, wave heights of four to six feet mean getting to the reef can be a thrilling, upsetting, or even white-knuckle ride. And because of bad weather or high waves it's often impossible to make the trip at all. However, diving five minutes offshore from the Costa de Cocos Resort is highly rewarding when weather prohibits Chinchorro diving, so a good diving experience is still available.

WHERE TO STAY & DINE FROM MAJAHUAL TO XCALAK

En route along the peninsula you'll pass small settlements, some of which offer rooms, camping, or a place to hang your hammock; many look deserted. Of those who are open, not all are reputable. Travelers anywhere along here should expect inconveniences. When things break down or food items run out, replacements are a long way off. This could mean the dive boat is broken indefinitely, the beer or vegetable truck doesn't show up, or the generator that powers the water, toilets, and kitchen is off for hours or days. Bring your own purified drinking water. Generator electricity is the norm (perhaps only a few hours in the evening), so a flashlight is handy for stumbling around when lights are out. In addition to mosquito repellent, you might want to stow a package or two of mosquito coils as well. Campers should bring mosquito netting. A couple of restaurants in Xcalak offer good seafood and Mexican specialties. Ask at Costa de Cocos about which one is currently offering the best food and service.

COSTA DE COCOS DIVE RESORT, Carretera Majahual-Xcalak km 52. Q.
Roo. 8 cabañas. FANS
$ Rates (including breakfast and dinner): $50 single; $35 double with one bed, $40 double with two beds; $30 triple. Dive package (daily rate including dives, breakfast, and dinner) $125 single, $105 double with one bed, $95 triple. Three-night minimum stay with dive package.
Far and away the most sophisticated hostelry along this route, it's a welcome respite in a palm grove just before the fishing village of Xcalak, which is a half mile farther at the end of the peninsula. The beautifully constructed thatch-roofed cabañas are fashioned after Maya huts but with sophisticated details like limestone walls halfway up, followed by handsomely crafted mahogany-louvered and screened windows, beautiful wood plank floors in the bedroom, large tile bathrooms, comfortable furnishings, and shelves of paperback books. Hot water and mosquito netting were being added to each room when I was there. Nice as it is, it still won't hurt to inspect your shoes daily for hidden critters—this is the jungle, after all. All dive equipment is available and included in dive packages or rented separately for day guests. The resort operates a 40-foot dive boat for diving Chinchorro. Water-sports equipment for rent includes an ocean kayak and windsurf board. PADI open-water certification can be arranged also at an additional cost. Beer and soft drinks are sold at the resort, but bring your own liquor and snacks. Besides the rates quoted above there are separate diving rates for individuals without package arrangements.

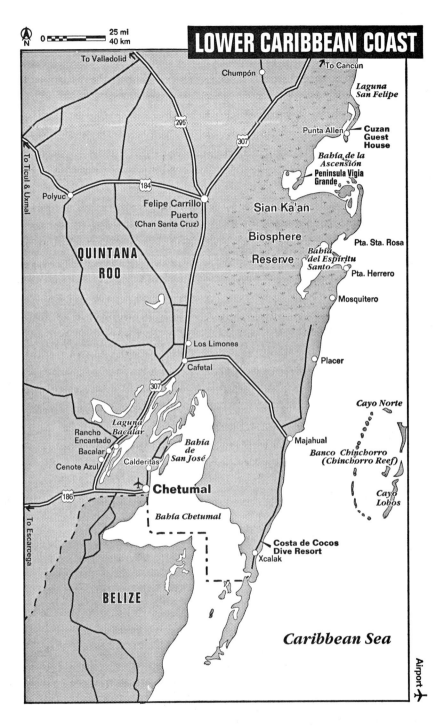

Reservations in the U.S.: Tel. 708/529-4473, or toll free 800/443-1123; fax 813/488-4505.

10. LAGO BACALAR

65 miles S of Felipe Carrillo Puerto, 23 miles N of Chetumal

GETTING THERE By Bus Buses going south from Cancún and Playa del Carmen stop here.

By Car Signs into Bacalar are plainly visible from Highway 307.

If you can arrange it, a stop in Bacalar sure beats staying in Chetumal or Carrillo Puerto. The crystal-clear, spring-fed waters of Lake Bacalar, which is slightly over 65 miles long, empty into the Caribbean. Spaniards fleeing coastal pirates used Maya pyramid stones to build a fort in Bacalar, which is now a small **museum.** The area is very quiet—the perfect place to swim and relax. At least 130 species of **birds** have been counted in the area. If you're in your own car, take a detour through the village of Bacalar and down along the **lakeshore drive.** To find the lakeshore drive go all the way past town on Highway 307 and you'll see a sign pointing left to the lake. When you turn left, that road is the lakeshore drive. You can double back along the drive from there to return to the highway. The Hotel Laguna is on the lakeshore drive. From here it's a 30-minute drive to Chetumal and to the Corozol Airport in Belize.

WHERE TO STAY

HOTEL LAGUNA, Costera de Bacalar no. 143, Bacalar, Q. Roo. Tel. 983/ 2-3517 in Chetumal. 22 rms, 4 bungalows. FAN

$ Rates: $45 single or double.

The Laguna is off the beaten path, so there are almost always rooms available, except in winter when it's full of Canadians. Rooms overlook the pool and have a lovely view of the lake. The water along the shore is very shallow, but you can dive from the hotel's dock into 30-foot water. The hotel's restaurant is fine, with main courses costing about $5 to $12. It's open daily from 8am to 8pm.

To find it go through town toward Chetumal. Just at the edge of town you'll see a sign pointing left to the hotel and the lakeshore drive.

RANCHO ENCANTADO, Carretera Felipe Carrillo Puerto–Chetumal, (Apdo. Postal 233), Chetumal, Q. Roo 77000. Tel. and fax 983/8-0427. 10 casitas (8 with bath). FAN

$ Rates (including continental breakfast and dinner): Nov–Apr $86–$120 single or double. May–Oct $70–$96 single or double. ($17.50 per person less without food.)

Rancho Encantado's immaculate stucco-walled, tile-roofed casitas are spread out on a shady manicured lawn beside the shores of Lago Bacalar. Each spacious and beautifully kept room has mahogany-louvered windows, cedar ceilings, shiny red-tile floors, handsome blue-tile kitchenette, table and chairs, living room, porch with chairs, and hammocks strung between trees. Casita 8 sleeps five people and Casita 1 sleeps four. Two Maya-style cabañas share a bath. The large palapa-topped restaurant, beside the lake, serves all three meals; the food is excellent. You can swim from the hotel's dock. A massage therapist on staff charges $40 per session. Managers here keep abreast of developments at the nearby archeological sites and are the only source of current information before you reach the ruins. Special packages and excursions can be arranged in advance from the hotel's U.S. office. Among them are day trips to the nearby ruins, an extended visit to Calakmul, a Yucatecan-style cookout, outings along the coast and lake, and trips to Belize. Groups interested in birding, yoga, archeology, etc., are invited to bring a leader and use Rancho Encantado as a base. To find it, look for the hotel's sign on the left about 1½ miles before Bacalar.

Reservations: P.O. Box 1644, Taos, NM 87571; tel. toll free 800/748-1756 in the U.S. during weekday office hours, fax 505/751-0972.

WHERE TO DINE

Besides the excellent lakeside restaurant of **Rancho Encantado** (see "Where to Stay," above), you may also enjoy the **Restaurant Cenote Azul,** a comfortable open-air thatch-roofed restaurant on the edge of the beautiful Cenote Azul. In both places entrées cost from $5 to $13. To get there, follow the highway to the south edge of town and turn left at the restaurant's sign and follow that road around to the restaurant. At Rancho Encantado you can swim in Lago Bacalar, or at the Restaurant Cenote in the placid Cenote Azul—but without skin lotion of any kind, since it poisons the cenote.

EXCURSIONS FROM BACALAR

A few miles west of Bacalar begins the Yucatán's southern ruin route, generally called the Río Bec region (named after a group of ruins in the area), which, until recently, enjoyed little attention. All that is about to change. Within the last several years, the Mexican government has spent millions of pesos to conserve previously excavated sites and uncover heretofore unexcavated ruins. It's an especially ruin-rich, but little explored, part of the peninsula. With the opening in late 1994 of **Dzibanche,** an extensive "new" site, together with other new discoveries at existing ruins, the region is poised to become the peninsula's "newest" tourist destination. With responsible guides, other jungle-surrounded, but difficult-to-reach sites *may* also be available soon—Payan, Hormiguero, Río Bec, Manos Rojas—but most of these are currently reached only by four-wheel-drive vehicles. Touristic services (restaurants, hotels, guides, visitor centers, etc.), will trail ruin development for a while, but this area is definitely worth watching and visiting now.

Just nine miles from the edge of Bacalar is the turnoff from Highway 307 to Highway 186, leading to the Río Bec ruin route as well as to Escarcega, Villahermosa, and Palenque. Get an early start and all of the ruins mentioned below, except Calakmul, can be easily visited in a day from Bacalar. These sites will be changing, however, since swarms of laborers are still busy with further exploration. Evidence shows that these ruins, especially Becán, were part of the trade route that linked the Caribbean coast at Cobá to Edzná and the Gulf coast.

There are no visitor facilities or refreshments at these sites, so bring your own water and food. However, in the village of Xpujil (just before the ruins of Xpujil), the **Restaurant Concha Caribe** has very good food and is becoming a hangout for ruins enthusiasts—note the wall of photos and descriptions of little-known sites.

Entry to each site is $3.50 to $4.50 and all are free on Sunday. Wear loads of mosquito repellent.

DZIBANCHÉ Dzibanché (or Tzibanché) means "place where they write on wood." Excavation began in 1993, and the site should be open to the public in late 1994. Scattered over 25 square miles, it's both a Pre- and Postclassic site occupied for around 700 years. When I was there, two enormous and adjoining acropoli had been cleared. The site shows influence from Río Bec, Petén, and the Teotihuacán site near Mexico City. The Temple of Lintels in Acropolis 2 has Teotihuacán-style *tablud tablero* (slant and straight facade) architecture, a rarity in the Yucatán. Despite centuries of an unforgiving wet climate, a wood lintel, in good condition and with a date carving, still supports a partially preserved corbeled arch on top of this building. A formal road to these ruins was nonexistent when I was there and there are no signs. However, it's off to the right, approximately 30 miles from the Highway 307 turnoff. Ask at Rancho Encantado near Bacalar (see "Where to Stay," above) about guides and access.

KOHUNLICH   Kohunlich, 26 miles from the intersection of Highways 186 and 307, dates from around A.D. 100 to 900. Turn left off the road and the entrance is less than a mile ahead. From the parking area you enter the grand parklike site, crossing a large and shady ceremonial area flanked by four large pyramidal edifices.

Continue walking and just beyond this grouping you'll come to Kohunlich's famous **Pyramid of the Masks** under a thatched covering. The masks, actually large three-foot-high plaster faces, are on the facade of the building. Besides characteristic Olmec undulating lips, the masks show vestiges of blue and red paint. It's speculated that masks covered much of the facade of this building.

During recent excavations two intact pre-Hispanic-age skeletons and five decapitated heads were uncovered that were once probably used in a ceremonial rite. Rambling in the woods beyond this structure and the main ceremonial area you can see the remains of other jungle-covered buildings.

XPUJIL   Xpujil (also spelled Xpuhil) means either "cat tail" or "forest of kapok trees," and the site flourished between A.D. 400 and 900. It was discovered in 1936 by Karl Ruppert and John H. Denison during investigations sponsored by the Carnegie Institute. Ahead on the left after you enter, a rectangular-shaped ceremonial platform 6½ feet high and 173 feet long holds three once-ornate buildings. These almost conical edifices, with false stairs, resemble the towering ruins of Tikal in Guatemala and rest on a lower building with 12 rooms. Unfortunately, they are so ruined that one can only ponder how it might have been. A rendering by Maya scholar Tatiana Proskouriakoff shows masks of the rain god on the center of the tower buildings and lining the upper portion of the lower building connecting the towers. Portions of the latter are still visible. To the right after you enter are two newly uncovered structures, one of which is a large acropolis. From the highway, a small sign on the right points to the site, which is just a few yards off the highway and 49 miles from Kohunlich.

BECÁN   Becán, once surrounded by a moat, means "canyon formed by water" and dates from the early to the late Classic period—600 B.C. to A.D. 850. Discovered in 1936 at the same time Xpujil was found, the site is about 4½ miles beyond Xpujil. Extensive excavations began in 1991 and will continue through 1997. Following jungle paths beyond the first visible group of ruins, you'll see at least two recently excavated acropoli. Though Becán was abandoned by 850, ceramic remains indicate there may have been a resurgence of population at the site between A.D. 900 and 1000, and it was still used as a ceremonial site as late as A.D. 1200 by a few remaining agricultural groups. So far it is believed that Becán was a major player in a trade route that linked Cozumel, Cobá, the Petén area of today's Guatemala, the site of Edzná, and the Gulf coast of Mexico.

The 6,201-foot moat encircling the 47-acre site is 33 feet wide and 16½ feet deep. The moat was, of course, a defensive measure although it's believed that it wasn't filled with water, but instead spiny plants were planted in and around it to repel unwanted visitors. Archeologists calculate that it took 350 men 350 days to construct such a moat. Prior to the recent excavations, only one of Becán's four sections was partially cleared. It's visible on the right side of the highway, about a half mile to the right down a rutted road.

CHICANNÁ   Slightly over a mile beyond Becán, on the left side of the highway, is Chicanná, which means "house of the mouth of snakes." It's a small site with trees loaded with bromeliads and a central square surrounded with five buildings. The most outstanding edifice features a monster-mouth doorway and an ornate stone facade with more superimposed masks. It's similar to one at Copán in Honduras.

CALAKMUL   When excavations at Calakmul are finally finished, this site could be one of the most exciting on the peninsula and will likely find recognition equal to Chichén-Itzá, Uxmal, and Palenque as must-see ruins during a Yucatán visit. But right now you have to be a rugged pioneer to see it. The turnoff on the left for Calakmul is located 145 miles from the intersection of Highways 186 and 307 just after the village of Conhuas. From Escarcega to the turnoff to the right is approximately 63 miles. From there it's almost 40 miles on a rugged road that's impassable during the rainy season from May through October, and requires a four-wheel-drive vehicle other times. This area is both a **massive Maya archeological zone** with at least 60 archeological sites, and a 178,699-acre rain forest designated in 1989 as the **Calakmul Biosphere Reserve,** which includes territory in both Mexico and Guatemala. It's the largest tropical reserve in Mexico and occupies almost 13% of Campeche state.

The Archeological Zone   Every dry season since 1982 archeologists have been excavating the ruins of Calakmul, which dates from 100 B.C. to A.D. 900 and is the largest of the area's 60 known sites. At its zenith at least 60,000 people may have lived around the site, but by the time of the Spanish conquest of Mexico in 1519, fewer than 1,000 people were here. Nearly 7,000 buildings have been discovered and mapped. Discoveries include more stelae than at any other Maya site, and tombs with jade jewelry and masks and other important burial memorabilia, and at least one building that exceeds the size of any other known in the Maya world. Portions of Calakmul's tomb contents, including a jade mask and jewelry, are on display in the Regional Museum of Campeche in Campeche. In *A Forest of Kings,* Linda Schele and David Freidel tell of wars between Calakmul, Tikal, and Naranjo (the latter two in Guatemala) and how Ah-Cacaw, king of Tikal (75 miles south of Calakmul) captured King Jaguar-Paw in A.D. 695 and later Lord Ox-Ha-Te Ixil Ahau, both of Calakmul. *National Geographic* featured Calakmul in its October 1989 issue about La Ruta Maya. From January to May the site is open Tuesday through Sunday from 7am to 7pm. Admission is $4.50.

Calakmul Biosphere Reserve   Set aside in 1989, this is the peninsula's only high-forest selva, a rain forest that annually records as much as 16 feet of rain.

IMPRESSIONS

As one walks among the ruins one realizes that the archeologist not only must be well grounded in the rudiments of his calling but must be a detective, a construction engineer, an executive, and a jigsaw-puzzle expert as well. As one walks among the unrestored ruins one sees laid out on the ground broken stones which are for all the world like pieces of a jigsaw puzzle.
—LEONIDAS W. RAMSEY, *TIME OUT FOR ADVENTURE,* 1934

Among the plants are cactus, epiphytes, and orchids. Endangered animals found here include the white-lipped peccary, jaguar, and puma. So far more than 250 species of birds have been recorded. At the moment there are no guided tours in the reserve and no overnight stays or camping is permitted. But a hint of the region can be seen around the ruins.

EN ROUTE TO CHETUMAL

As you approach the end of the lake, Highway 307 intersects Highway 186. Turn right, and you're headed west to the ruins of Kohunlich, Xpujil, Becán, and Calakmul (see "Excursions from Bacalar," above), and the town of Escarcega, the village and ruins of Palenque, and Villahermosa; turn left, and you'll be going toward Chetumal.

11. CHETUMAL

85 miles S of Felipe Carrillo Puerto, 23 miles S of Lago Bacalar

GETTING THERE & DEPARTING   By Plane   Aero Caribe (Mexicana) has daily flights to and from Cancún and three times weekly between Chetumal and the ruins of Tikal in Guatemala. **Taesa** flies from Cancún.

By Bus   The bus station, **Autotransportes del Caribe** (tel. 2-0740), is 20 blocks from town center on Insurgentes at Niños Héroes.

Eight direct first-class buses a day go to Cancún via Tulum, Playa del Carmen, and Puerto Morelos; eight go to Mérida. With changes en route, four first-class buses a day go to Mexico City, and one a day goes to Villahermosa (a seven- to eight-hour trip). **Caribe Express** (tel. 2-7889 or 2-8001) has deluxe buses to Mérida at 5pm and midnight and to Cancún at 6pm and 12:30am. This service features a 28-seat bus with video movies, steward service, and refreshments.

Second-class bus service includes routes daily to Tulum and the coast (two buses), Mérida (four buses), Campeche (two buses), Villahermosa (four buses), San Andrés Tuxtla, Veracruz, and Mexico City (one bus). Sixteen second-class buses run to and from Bacalar daily.

To Belize: Two companies make the run from Chetumal, through Corozal and Orange Walk, to Belize City. **Batty's Bus Service** runs 10 buses per day and **Venus Bus Lines** (in Corozal; tel. 04/2-2132) has seven daily buses, the first at 11am. The 2pm bus is express with fewer stops. A ticket to Corozal costs $1.25. Seven buses go to Belize City (tel. 02/7-3354 in Belize); it costs $6. The first leaves at 4am and the last at 10am. Though it's a short distance from Chetumal to Corozal, it may take as much as an hour and a half, depending on how long it takes the bus to pass through Customs and Immigration.

By Car   It's a 2¹/₂-hour ride from Carrillo Puerto. If you're heading to Belize you'll need a passport and special auto insurance, which you can buy at the border. You can't take a rental car over the border, however. To get to the ruins of Tikal in Guatemala you must first go through Belize to the border crossing at Ciudad Melchor de Mencos. For more details on crossing into Guatemala and Belize see *Frommer's Costa Rica, Guatemala & Belize on $35 a Day*. You'll arrive following Obregón into town. Niños Héroes is the other main cross street. When you reach it, turn left to find the hotels mentioned below.

ESSENTIALS   The telephone area code is 983. Chetumal has many "no left turn" streets, with hawk-eyed traffic policemen at each one. Be alert; they love to nail visitors and may even motion you into making a traffic or pedestrian violation, then issue a ticket.

Quintana Roo became a state in 1974, and Chetumal (pop. 170,000) is the capital of the new state. While Quintana Roo was still a territory, it was a free-trade zone to encourage trade and immigration between neighboring Guatemala and Belize. The old part of town, down by the river (Río Hondo), has a Caribbean atmosphere and wooden buildings, but the newer parts are modern Mexican. There is lots of noise and heat, so your best plan would be not to stay—it's not a particularly interesting or friendly town.

WHERE TO STAY & DINE

HOTEL CONTINENTAL CARIBE, Av. Héroes 171, Chetumal, Q. Roo 77000. Tel. 983/2-1100. Fax 983/2-1676. 75 rms. A/C TV TEL
$ Rates: $70 single, $75 double. **Parking:** Free.
This modern hotel, across from the central market, has nice rooms and a swimming pool. The moderately priced restaurant is large, well staffed, and open from 7:30am to 11pm daily. You'll find it on the right side of Héroes.

HOTEL JACARANDA, Obregón 201, Chetumal, Q. Roo 77000. Tel. 983/2-1455. 46 rms. A/C (21 rms) FAN (25 rms) TEL
$ Rates: $20 single; $25 double.
This semimodern, two-story hotel is undistinguished except for its low prices. It's located down the hill from the market, at Avenida Héroes. The restaurant, a brightly lit, Formica-furnished place, has efficient service and good food at low prices. It's closed Sunday and holidays but otherwise open from 7am to 11pm.

HOTEL PRÍNCIPE, Av. Héroes 326, Chetumal, Q. Roo 77000. Tel. 983/2-4799 or 2-5167. Fax 983/2-5191. 51 rms. A/C
$ Rates: $35 single, $56 double.
Located between the bus station and the center of town, my favorite hotel offers nice rooms arranged around a central courtyard. The inexpensive restaurant serves all three meals. It's located six blocks south of the bus station.

MOVING ON FROM BACALAR & CHETUMAL

From Bacalar and Chetumal you have several choices. You can go south to Belize and Guatemala (though not in a rental car) and after Bacalar, you can cut diagonally across the peninsula to Mérida or retrace your steps to Cancún.

You can take Highway 186 west to Escarcega, Villahermosa, and Palenque, but I don't recommend it. It's a long, hot, and lonely trip on a highway that is often riddled with potholes after you cross into Campeche state. Permanent *Zona de deslave* signs warn motorists that parts of the roadbed are missing entirely or so badly dipped as to cause an accident. The road improves from time to time, but annual rains cause constant problems.

At the Campeche state line there's a military guard post with drug-sniffing dogs; every vehicle is searched. A military guard post at the Reforma intersection just before Bacalar requires motorists to present the identification they used to enter Mexico (birth certificate or passport), plus their Tourist Permit. Other photo identification may be required, as well as information on where you are staying or where you are headed. The whole procedure should take only minutes.

CHAPTER 5

MÉRIDA & THE MAYA CITIES

1. MÉRIDA
• **WHAT'S SPECIAL ABOUT MÉRIDA & THE MAYA CITIES**
2. MAYAPÁN & TICUL
3. UXMAL
4. CAMPECHE
5. CHICHÉN-ITZÁ
6. VALLADOLID

Beautiful Mérida, the Yucatán's cultural center, is the natural launching point for seeing the Yucatán's major archeological sites, with good roads to the ruins branching out like spokes on a wheel. Easy trips to the Gulf coast and the Yucatán's upper coast can be made from Mérida as well. It's only 75 miles west of Chichén-Itzá, 60 miles east of Celestún, and 50 miles north of Uxmal. It's especially good for a driving trip because there are no mountains, roads are fairly well maintained, traffic is light, and stopping in the many rock-walled villages is a delight. In Mérida and throughout Yucatán's central portion, in and around the ruins, there are numerous choices for economical lodging.

1. MÉRIDA

900 miles E of Mexico City, 200 miles SW of Cancún

GETTING THERE   By Plane   Mexicana flies to Mérida from Mexico City and Miami. **Aeroméxico** flights arrive from Cancún, Miami, and Mexico City. **Aerocaribe** (a Mexicana affiliate) provides service from Cozumel, Chetumal, Cancún, Oaxaca, Villahermosa, and Guadalajara. **Taesa** flies from Cozumel. **Continental** provides service from Houston. **Aviateca** flies from Guatemala City and Houston. **Aviacsa** provides service from Cancún, Monterrey, Villahermosa, Tuxtla Gutiérrez, Oaxaca, and Mexico City.

By Train   From Valladolid the train arrives at 8am; from Tizimín at 5pm; and from Campeche at 9:30pm. From Palenque (using a train that originates in Mexico City) the arrival time varies anywhere between 1am and 8pm. This is a second-class train without sleeping or dining cars.

By Bus   Service is provided by the ADO Line, Expresso de Oriente, Autotransportes del Sur, Caribe Express, Autotransportes Peninsulares, Autotransportes del Caribe, and Autotransportes del Sureste.

By Car   Highway 180 from Cancún, Chichén-Itzá, or Valladolid leads into Calle 65, past the market, and within one block of the Plaza Mayor. Highway 281 from Uxmal (via Muna and Umán) becomes Avenida Itzáes. If you arrive by that route, turn right on Calle 63 to reach the Plaza Mayor. From Uxmal (via Ticul and the ruins of Mayapán) the road passes through Kanasin before joining Highway 180 from Valladolid into Mérida.

WHAT'S SPECIAL ABOUT MÉRIDA & THE MAYA CITIES

Architecture
Mérida, with its colonial architecture and the beautiful Museum of Anthropology.

Archeology
Uxmal, the most beautiful of the Yucatán's pre-Hispanic Maya cities. Chichén-Itzá, grand Maya site famed for its architecture and the appearance of the shadow-and-light serpent each September.

Maya Villages
Tinum, a whitewashed, rock-walled village, where visitors can stay with the locals.
Ticul, village of tricycle taxis and seamstresses noted for their elaborate embroidered shifts.

Nature
Flamingo sanctuaries, near Celestún, where thousands of flamingos winter, and near Río Lagartos, where they nest in the spring and summer.

A Fortified City
Campeche's unique walled fortifications surround the city; many of the baluartes are museums.

Crafts
Beautiful multicolored baskets woven in damp caves in Halacho.
Panama-hat weavers in Becal.
Hammock weavers in every village.
Silver- and gold-filigree work created throughout the Yucatán.

A traffic loop encircles Mérida, making it possible to skirt the city and head for a nearby city or site. Directional signs are generally good into the city, but going around it on the loop requires constant vigilance.

The eight-lane toll highway (*autopista*) between Mérida and Cancún was completed in 1993 and cuts the driving time between the two cities from five hours to about four hours. The highway begins about 35 miles east of Mérida at Kantuníl, intersecting with Highway 180. It ends at Nuevo Xcan, which is about 50 miles before Cancún. Tolls one way cost about $50.

DEPARTING By Plane **Mexicana** is at Calle 58 no. 500 at Calle 61 (tel. 24-6623), and at Calle 56-A no. 493, at Paseo de Montejo (tel. 24-7421 or 23-0508). Mexicana's airport phone number is 46-1332. **Aeroméxico** is at Montejo 460 between Calles 37 and 35 (tel. 27-9000) and at the airport (46-1305). **Aerocaribe** is at Paseo Montejo 500 (tel. 28-6786) and at the airport (tel. 28-6790). **Continental** is at the airport (tel. 46-1390). **Aviateca** has an office on Calle 58 between Calles 45 and 43 (tel. 24-4354). **Taesa** is at the airport (tel. 46-1826), as is **Aviacsa** (tel. 46-1344). You'll have to take a taxi from the city to the airport; the fare is nearly $8.

By Train The train station is about six blocks northeast of the Plaza Mayor at Calle 55 between Calles 46 and 48. I don't recommend long train trips in this part of Mexico. The cars are uncomfortable (no sleeping or dining cars) and slow, and tourists aboard are easy marks for thieves.

The train to Mexico City starts out on time at 9pm from Mérida and arrives in Palenque around 9am, but could take twice the scheduled 36 hours to reach the capital. Trains depart daily for Valladolid at 1pm (a four-hour trip) and for Progreso (a three-hour trip) at 2pm. On short runs the train is generally on time.

Tickets go on sale one hour before departure; the **train information booth** (tel. 27-7701) is open Monday through Saturday from 7am to 10pm and on Sunday from 8am to 3pm. From downtown buses to the train station line up on Calles 59 and 61, directly behind the Cepeda Peraza Park.

By Bus   The Central Camionera is seven blocks southwest of the Plaza Mayor at Calle 68, between Calles 69 and 71.

To Uxmal: Autotransportes del Sur (24-9055) buses depart at 6 and 9am, and 12 and 3pm; return trips are at 11:30am and 3:30 and 7:30pm. The same company also offers one bus daily on the Mérida-Uxmal-Kabah-Sayil-Labná-Xlapak route. The trips cost $18, departing Mérida at 8am, returning at 2pm. The driver allows passengers to spend around 90 minutes at Uxmal and 30 minutes at each of the other archeological sites before returning. There is no evening departure for the sound and light show at Uxmal.

To Chichén-Itzá: There are first-class ADO (tel. 24-7868) buses at 7:30am and 3:30pm. If you're planning a day trip (something I don't recommend if you enjoy seeing the impressive ruins) take the 7:30am bus and reserve a seat on the 3:30pm return bus.

There is one second-class bus to Pisté at 2:30pm on Autotransportes del Sur.

To Valladolid and Cancún: Expresso de Oriente (tel. 26-0031) offers luxury service—video, bathroom, and refreshments—to Cancún (a five-hour trip) 22 times daily between 3am and midnight. The line also has five deluxe buses daily to Valladolid between 6:30am and 11:15pm. Caribe Express has nine deluxe buses daily to Cancún between 7:15am and 10pm. Autotransportes del Sur has service to Valladolid at 6:15am, and 12:15 and 6:15pm. Autotransportes del Caribe goes to Cancún at 6:30am and 5:30 and 11:45pm. ADO has 10 buses to Valladolid and on to Playa del Carmen between 5am and midnight.

To Playa del Carmen, Tulum, and Chetumal: Ten ADO buses go to Valladolid and on to Playa del Carmen between 5am and midnight. ADO also has deluxe buses to Chetumal via Ticul at 10:10am and 5:30pm. Caribe Express (tel. 24-4275) buses to Playa del Carmen and Tulum depart at 6:15am and 11pm. Caribe Express buses to Chetumal depart at 7:30 and 10:30am and 1, 10, and 11pm. Autotransportes Peninsulares (tel. 24-1844) offers Servicio Plus deluxe service to Chetumal at 8:30am and 6pm.

To Campeche: Autotransportes Peninsulares has deluxe service to Campeche at 8am and 3pm. ADO has first-class service to Campeche at 8am and 4:30 and 7:15pm. Autotransportes del Sur (tel. 24-9374) buses leave every 30 minutes from 6am to 11:30pm.

To Palenque and San Cristóbal de las Casas: ADO has first-class service to Palenque at 8am and 10pm. Autotransportes del Sureste has second-class service to Palenque and San Cristóbal de las Casas at 6pm.

By Car   See "En Route to . . ." at the end of this section for suggested routes from Mérida to other destinations in the region.

Mérida (pop. 558,000), capital of the state of Yucatán, has been the major city in the area ever since the Spanish founded it in the mid-1500s on the site of the defeated Maya city of Tihó. Although the modern city is a major touristic crossroads to the archeological ruins of the peninsula and its glitzy coasts, the city is easygoing and the friendliness of its people remains a trademark.

Downtown Mérida is full of fine examples of colonial-era architecture. Vestiges of the opulent 19th-century era of Yucatán's henequén boom remain in the ornate

IMPRESSIONS

*As a cure for jumpy nerves, business worries, and all that, I prescribe a trip to Mérida.
Instead of jumping from an apartment window I suggest as a better way out—at least a
week on a bench in the shaded plazas of Mérida. This seat should be just across from an
open cantina and within sound of rustling Mayan skirts. I shall be surprised if this
prescription does not prove a cure.*
—LEONIDAS W. RAMSEY, TIME OUT FOR ADVENTURE, 1934

---

mansions sprinkled throughout the city. In the market and elsewhere, you'll notice
items woven of a sisal fiber from the henequén plant; it's used to make hammocks,
baskets, purses, shoes, table mats, twine, rope, and packing material.

ORIENTATION

ARRIVING By Plane Mérida's airport is eight miles from the city center, on
the southwestern outskirts of town, where Highway 180 enters the city. The airport
has desks for car rentals, hotel reservations, and tourist information. **Taxi tickets** to
town are sold outside the airport doors under the covered walkway. A colectivo
ticket for up to five people costs $8 each, but you have to wait for the five to as-
semble. Private taxis cost $12 and can be shared by up to four persons.

City bus no. 79 ("Aviación") operates between the town center and the airport. This is the cheapest way to go, with a one-way ticket costing only 50¢, but
the buses are not all that frequent. Other city buses run along the Avenida Itzáes,
just out of the airport precincts, heading for downtown.

By Train For city buses from the train station, go left out the front door of the
train station to the corner where city buses ("Estación") pick up passengers and follow a route along Calle 55. You are also within walking distance of several hotels
and the town center.

By Bus From Mérida's main bus station you are only six blocks from Plaza
Mayor and within walking distance of several hotels. Local buses into town stop on
the corner to the left of the bus station front door.

INFORMATION The most convenient source of information is the downtown
branch of the **State of Yucatán Tourist Information Office,** in the hulking edifice known as the Teatro Peón Contreras, on Calle 60 between Calles 57 and 59
(tel. 24-9290 or 24-9389). It's open daily from 8am to 8pm. Other information
booths are staffed at the airport and bus station and on Calle 62 next to the Palacio
Municipal at roughly the same hours.

CITY LAYOUT As with most colonial Mexican cities, Mérida's streets were laid
out in a grid. **Even-numbered streets** run north-south; **odd-numbered streets**
run east-west. In the last few decades, the city has expanded well beyond the grid,
and several grand boulevards have been added on the outskirts to ease traffic flow.

When looking for an address, you'll notice that street numbers progress very
slowly due to the many unnumbered dwellings and -A, -B, and -C additions. Example: Getting from 504 to 615-D on Calle 59 takes 12 blocks.

The center of town is the very pretty **Plaza Mayor** (sometimes called the Plaza
Principal), with its shady trees, benches, vendors, and a social life all its own.
Around the plaza are the massive cathedral, the Palacio de Gobierno (state government headquarters), the Palacio Municipal, and the Casa de Montejo. Within a few
blocks are several smaller plazas, the University of Yucatán, and the sprawling
market district.

Mérida's most fashionable address is the broad, tree-lined boulevard called **Paseo de Montejo** and the surrounding neighborhood. The Paseo de Montejo begins seven blocks northwest of the Plaza Mayor and is home to Yucatán's anthropological museum, several upscale hotels, and the American consulate. New highrise deluxe hotels are opening just off the Paseo on **Avenida Colón,** another shaded boulevard that also contains some of the city's finest old mansions. Within the next few years this neighborhood will become Mérida's more exclusive tourism zone, with fine restaurants and boutiques for the travelers drawn to the new hotels.

GETTING AROUND

BY BUS   City buses are the cheapest way to go, charging only 50¢ for a ride. You can take one to the large, shady Parque Centenario on the western outskirts of town. Look for the bus of the same name ("Centenario") on Calle 64. Most buses on Calle 59 go to the zoo or Museum of Natural History. Those marked "Estación" go to the train station. "Central" buses stop at the bus station and any bus marked "Mercado" or "Correo" (post office) will take you to the market district.

BY TAXI   Taxi drivers are beginning to overcharge tourists in Mérida the way they do in Mexico City. Taxi meters start at $3.50.

BY CAR   Rental cars are handy for your explorations of Mayapán, Uxmal, and Kabah, but you don't need one to get around Mérida, or to reach Chichén-Itzá or Cancún. Rental cars are very expensive these days in Mexico, averaging $45 to $65 per day for a VW Beetle.

Keep these tips in mind as you scour the city for a rental-car deal: Don't be impressed by a very low daily charge, unless it includes unlimited mileage. Keep in mind that you can often get lower rates if you arrange the rental before you leave the U.S. and for more than a day or two.

Important note: Deductibles range between $250 and $1,000, so don't fail to get that information before you sign up. For more information, see "Car Rentals," in Chapter 2.

BY HORSE-DRAWN CARRIAGE   Look for a line of carriages near the cathedral, and in front of the Hotel Casa del Balam, then haggle for a good price. An hour's tour of the city costs around $12.

ON FOOT   Most tourist attractions are within easy walking distance form the Plaza Mayor.

FAST FACTS

Area Code   The telephone area code is 99.

Bookstore   The Librería Dante, Calle 60 at Calle 57 (tel. 24-9522), has a selection of English-language cultural history books on Mexico. It's open Monday through Friday from 8am to 9:30pm, Saturday from 8am to 2pm and 4 to 9:30pm, and Sunday from 10am to 2pm and 4 to 8pm.

Climate   November through February the weather can be chilly, windy, and rainy. You'll need a light jacket or sweater for winter, and thin, cool clothes for summer days. Light rain gear is suggested for the brief showers of late May, June, and July, but there's a chance of rain all year in the Yucatán.

Consulates   The **U.S. consulate** is at Paseo de Montejo 453, at the corner of Avenida Colón (tel. 99/25-5011 or 25-5554), near the Holiday Inn. It's open Monday through Friday from 7:30am to 4pm. There is a specific schedule for visas and traveler's problems: Visa matters are dealt with only on Monday, Wednesday, and Friday from 7:30 to 11am; other kinds of problems are considered the same days from noon to 3:30pm and on Thursday until 4pm. The telephone number of a duty officer is posted at the entrance. The **British vice-consulate** is at Calle 53 no. 489, at the corner of Calle 58 (tel. 99/28-6152). Though in principle it's open Monday through Friday from 9:30am to 1pm, you may find no one there. The vice-consul fields questions about travel to Belize as well as British matters.

Currency Exchange Banamex, in the Palacio Montejo on the Plaza Mayor, has a currency exchange that usually provides a better rate of exchange than other banks, but the lines are often maddeningly long. Hours are Monday through Friday from 9:30am to 1:30pm. As an option, there's a money-exchange office just as you enter the bank gates, and more banks are located on and off Calle 65 between Calles 62 and 60.

Doctors If you're suffering from "Montezuma's revenge," see "Health & Insurance," in Chapter 2 for tips. If it gets serious, ask your hotel to call a doctor after you've got an estimate of his fee.

Hospitals The city's Hospital O'Horan is on Avenida Itzáes at Calle 59-A (tel. 99/24-4111), north of the Parque Centenario.

Post Office Mérida's main post office (correo) is in the midst of the market at the corner of Calles 65 and 56. It's open Monday through Friday from 8am to 5pm, and Saturday from 8am to 2pm.

Seasons There are two high seasons: one in July and August, when the weather is very hot and humid and when Mexicans most commonly take their vacations; and one between December 15 and Easter Sunday, when northerners flock to the Yucatán to escape winter weather and when weather in the Yucatán is cooler.

Telephones Long-distance casetas are at the airport and the bus station. Look also for the blue-and-silver Ladatel phones that are appearing in public places all over Mexico. Remember that international calls, while getting cheaper, are still extremely expensive; but at least from a caseta you won't pay the hotel "service charge." Also see "Telephones & Mail," in the Appendix. *Important note:* Telephone numbers are being changed throughout the city so if you have difficulty reaching a number, ask the telephone operator for assistance.

WHAT TO SEE & DO

Mérida is pretty and congenial, but summers are also very hot—up to 108°F (42°C) prior to the muggy rainy months (June through September). I recommend you snatch a quick breakfast and begin touring early. When the midday heat is at its worst, have lunch and a siesta, and issue forth in the evening, refreshed and ready for the next round.

If you're lucky enough to be visiting November through January or February, you'll be able to spend most of the day outdoors without discomfort.

IMPRESSIONS

Nothing I had read had prepared me for Mérida. Here was a city with a personality all its own, immaculately clean with its blue, buff, and pink buildings. There are no large buildings in Mérida to dwarf the others, for the whole city is in scale. It has up-to-date buses, electric lighting fixtures, and the most interesting little black horse-drawn carriages, which keep running to and fro or stand beneath the shadows at the curbs.
—LEONIDAS W. RAMSEY, *TIME OUT FOR ADVENTURE,* 1934

SUGGESTED ITINERARIES

Since Mérida is an interesting as well as economical city from which to tour the Yucatán, here are a few suggestions on planning your visit. If you have a little more time for branching out and exploring the surrounding regions, see Chapter 2, "Planning a Trip to Mexico & the Yucatán," for more extensive itineraries.

IF YOU HAVE TWO DAYS Settle in and get your bearings on your first day: Change some money, adjust to the heat, and explore the market or tour the city using the walking tour in this chapter. Have dinner in one of the downtown restaurants.

On your second day, tour the city, stopping at each of the historic buildings near the Plaza Mayor, and along the Paseo de Montejo. Save time for shopping, and don't miss the free nightly entertainment in the local parks. Or if you'll be leaving without seeing the nearby ruins, get an early start and take either an agency-led bus tour to Uxmal, or the public-bus tour that takes you to Uxmal and the circuit of ruins close to it all in one day.

IF YOU HAVE THREE DAYS Spend your first two days as outlined above; then on Day 3, get an early start and head for the flamingo sanctuary at Celestún. Take a boat tour of the sanctuary, have lunch there, and return to Mérida in time for one of the city's entertainment events in the parks.

SPECIAL EVENTS

Many Mexican cities offer weekend concerts in the park, but Mérida is unique in Mexico for its almost daily, high-quality public events, most of which are free.

Sunday Each Sunday from 9am to 5pm there's a fair, called **Domingo en Mérida** (Sunday in Mérida), the heart of which is held in the Plaza Mayor. The downtown area is blocked from traffic for the day and comes alive with children's art classes, antiques vendors, and food stands, as well as concerts of all kinds. At 11am in front of the Palacio del Gobierno, musicians play anything from jazz to semiclassical and folkloric music. Also at 11am the police orchestra performs Yucatecan tunes at the Santa Lucía park. At 11:30am marimba music brightens the Parque Cepeda Peraza (Parque Hidalgo) on Calle 60 at Calle 59. At 1pm, in front of the Palacio Municipal on the Plaza Mayor, folk-ballet dancers reenact a typical Yucatecan wedding. All events are free.

Monday The **City Hall Folkloric Ballet** and the **Police Jaranera Band** perform at 8pm in front of the Palacio Municipal. The music and dancing celebrate the feast after the branding of cattle on Yucatecan haciendas. Among the featured performers are dancers who perform with trays of bottles or filled glasses on their heads—quite something to see. Free admission.

Tuesday The theme for Tuesday entertainment (held in Santiago Park at 9pm) is **Musical Memories.** The park is on Calle 59 at Calle 72. Tunes range from South American and Mexican to North American. Free admission. Also at 9pm in the Teatro Peón Contreras on Calle 60 at Calle 57, the **University of Yucatán Folkloric Ballet** presents *Yucatán and its Roots.* Admission is $5.

Wednesday The **University of Yucatán Folkloric Ballet,** along with guitarists and poets, performs at 8pm at the Mayab Culture House on Calle 63 between Calle 64 and 66. Free admission.

Thursday Typical Yucatecan music and dance is presented at the **Serenade** in Santa Lucía park at 9pm. Free admission.

Friday   at 9pm in the patio of the University of Yucatán, Calle 60 at 57, the **University of Yucatán Folkloric Ballet** performs typical regional dances from the Yucatán. Free admission.

WALKING TOUR — MÉRIDA

Start: Plaza Mayor.
Finish: Palacio Canton.
Time: Allow approximately two hours, not counting browsing or time out for refreshment.

Downtown Mérida is a visitor's visual delight, with several tree-shaded parks and fine examples of both colonial and late 19th-century architecture. It's all within an easy stroll of the:

1. Plaza Mayor, flanked east and west by Calles 61 and 63 and north and south by Calles 60 and 62. It began its history as the Plaza de Armas, a training field for Montejo's troops. Later called the Plaza Mayor, it was renamed the Plaza de la Constitución in 1812, then the Plaza de la Independencia in 1821. Other common names for it include Plaza Grande, Plaza Principal, and zócalo. Today this beautiful town square, now shaded by topiary laurel trees, is dressed out in manicured shrubs and lawns with plenty of pleasant iron benches. Numerous public entertainment events take place there throughout the year.

On the east side of the plaza stands the:

2. Cathedral, built between 1561 and 1598. It looks like a fortress, as do many other early churches in the Yucatán. (That was actually their function in part for several centuries, as the Maya did not take kindly to European domination.) Much of the stone in the cathedral's walls came from the ruined buildings of Maya Tihó. Inside, decoration is sparse, with altars draped in fabric gaily embroidered like a Maya woman's shift. The most notable feature is a picture over the right side door of Ah Kukum Tutul Xiú visiting the Montejo camp.

To the left of the main altar is a smaller shrine with a curious burnt cross, recovered from the church in the town of Ichmul, which burned down. The figure was carved by a local artist in the 1500s from a miraculous tree that burned but did not char. The figure, along with the church, broke out in blisters as the flames enveloped it. The local people named it **Cristo de las Ampollas** (Christ of the Blisters). Also take a look in the side chapel (open from 8 to 11am and 4:30 to 7pm), which has a life-size diorama of the Last Supper. The Mexican Jesus is covered with prayer crosses that were brought by supplicants asking for intercession.

To the right (south) of the cathedral is a:

3. Seminary and the former site of the archbishop's palace. The palace was torn down during the Mexican Revolution (1915); part of the seminary remains, but is now used for shops.

On the south side of the square is the:

4. Palacio Montejo, also called the Casa de Montejo. Started in 1549 by Francisco Montejo, "El Mozo," it was occupied by Montejo descendants until the 1970s. It now houses a bank branch (Banamex), which means you can get a look at parts of the palace just by wandering in during banking hours Monday through Friday from 9:30am to 1:30pm. Note the arms of the Spanish kings and of the Montejo family on the plateresque facade, along with figures of the conquistadores standing on the heads of "barbarians" overcome by their exploits. Look closely and you'll find the bust of Francisco Montejo the Elder, his wife, and his daughter.

Facing the cathedral, across the plaza from the west side is the:

5. **Palacio Municipal** (City Hall), with its familiar clock tower. It started out as the *cabildo,* the colonial town hall and lockup, in 1542. It had to be rebuilt in the 1730s, and rebuilt again in the 1850s, when it took on its present romantic aspect.

On the north side of the plaza is the:

6. **Palacio de Gobierno,** dating from 1892. Large murals painted between 1971 and 1973 decorate its interior walls. Scenes from Maya and Mexican history abound, and the painting over the stairway combines the Maya spirit with ears of sacred corn, the "sunbeams of the gods." Nearby is a painting of the mustached, benevolent dictator Lázaro Cárdenas, who in 1938 expropriated 17 foreign oil companies and was hailed as a new Mexican liberator. The palace is open Monday through Saturday from 8am to 8pm and on Sunday from 9am to 5pm.

REFUELING STOP Should you decide to take a break before continuing up Calle 60 from the Plaza Mayor you won't be disappointed at the **Dulcería y Sorbetería Colón,** on the north side of the Plaza Mayor. It's a delightful, inexpensive restaurant spilling onto the covered *portales* facing the plaza. The fare is simple—delicious pastries, soft drinks, and milk shakes.

EXPLORING CALLE 60 Continuing north from the Plaza Mayor up Calle 60 you'll see several of Mérida's old churches and little parks. Several stores along Calle 60 cater to tourists, selling gold-filigree jewelry, pottery, and folk art. A stroll along this street leads to the Parque Santa Ana and continues on to the fashionable boulevard Paseo de Montejo and its Museo Regional de Antropología.

On your left as you leave the Plaza Mayor, the:

7. **Teatro Daniel de Ayala** offers a continuous schedule of performing artists from around the world. Opposite the theater, the:

8. **Museo de la Ciudad de Mérida** is housed in the Seminario de Ildefonso, which began as one of the city's first hospitals. In the 1920s the state's collection of archeological treasures was kept here; now the museum's photographs, drawings, and dioramas illustrate the city's history.

Three-fourths of a block farther is the:

9. **Parque Cepeda Peraza** (also called the Parque Hidalgo), named for the 19th-century Gen. Manuel Cepeda Peraza and part of Montejo's original city plan. Small outdoor restaurants front hotels on the park, making it a popular stopping-off place anytime of the day.

REFUELING STOP Any one of the several outdoor restaurants on the Parque Cepeda Peraza makes an inviting respite. My favorite is **Giorgio,** where you can claim a table and write postcards while bartering for hammocks, amber jewelry, and baskets displayed by wandering artisans. It's in front of the Gran Hotel.

Bordering Parque Cepeda Peraza is the:

10. **Iglesia de Jésus,** or El Tercer Orden (The Third Order), built by the Jesuit order in 1618. The entire city block in which the church stands was part of the Jesuit establishment, and the early schools developed into the Universidad de Yucatán.

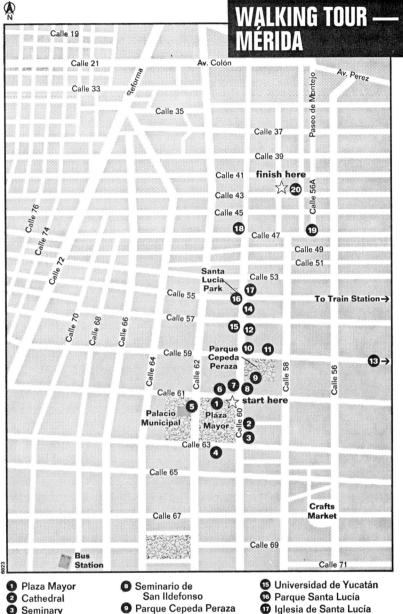

WALKING TOUR — MÉRIDA

Calle 19
Calle 21
Av. Colón
Reforma
Calle 33
Calle 35
Paseo de Montejo
Av. Perez
Calle 37
Calle 39
Calle 41
finish here
☆ ⓴
Calle 56A
Calle 43
Calle 45
⓲
Calle 47
⓳
Calle 49
Calle 51
Santa Lucía Park
Calle 53
⓱
Calle 55
⓰
⓮
To Train Station →
Calle 57
⓯ ⓬
Calle 59
Parque Cepeda Peraza
⓾ ⑪
⓭ →
Calle 61
⑥ ⑦ ⑧
⑨
Calle 58
Calle 56
⑤
① ☆ start here
Palacio Municipal
Plaza Mayor
②
Calle 60
③
Calle 63
④
Calle 65
Calle 67
Crafts Market
Calle 69
Bus Station
Calle 71

Calle 76, Calle 74, Calle 72, Calle 70, Calle 68, Calle 66, Calle 64, Calle 62

0823

1. Plaza Mayor
2. Cathedral
3. Seminary
4. Palacio Montejo
5. Palacio Municipal
6. Palacio de Gobierno
7. Teatro Daniel de Ayala
8. Seminario de San Ildefonso
9. Parque Cepeda Peraza
10. Iglesia de Jesús
11. Biblioteca Cepeda Peraza
12. Teatro Peón Contreras
13. Convento de la Mejorada
14. Parque de la Madre
15. Universidad de Yucatán
16. Parque Santa Lucía
17. Iglesia de Santa Lucía
18. Parque Santa Ana
19. Paseo de Montejo
20. Palacio Canton/Museo Regional de Antropología

Beside the church is the:

11. The Biblioteca (library) Cepeda Peraza, founded by the general in 1867.

Next on your right is the:

12. Teatro Peón Contreras, an enormous beige edifice, designed by Italian architect Enrico Deserti in the early years of this century. In one corner you'll see a branch of the State Tourist Information Office facing the park. The main theater entrance, with its Carrara marble staircase and frescoed dome, is a few steps farther. Domestic and international performers appear here frequently.

East on Calle 59 five blocks past the park and the church is the:

13. Former Convento de la Mejorada, a late-1600s work of the Franciscans.

Backtracking to Calle 60, you'll next see the:

14. Parque de la Madre (also called the Parque Morelos), which contains a modern statue of the Madonna and Child. The statue is a copy of the work by Lenoir which stands in the Luxembourg Gardens in Paris.

On the west side of Calle 60, at the corner of Calle 57, is the:

15. Universidad de Yucatán, founded in the 19th century by Felipe Carrillo Puerto with the help of General Cepeda Peraza. The founding is illustrated by the fresco (1961) by Manuel Lizama.

A block farther on your left, past the Hotel Misión Park Inn is the:

16. Parque Santa Lucía. Surrounded by an arcade on the north and west sides, the park once was the place where visitors first alighted in Mérida from their stagecoaches. On Sundays Santa Lucía park is the center of a popular downtown street fair and several evenings a week hosts popular entertainment. And on Thursday nights performers present Yucatecan songs and poems.

Facing the park is the ancient:

17. Iglesia de Santa Lucía (1575).

To reach the Paseo de Montejo, continue walking north on Calle 60 to the:

18. Parque Santa Ana, five blocks up Calle 60 from the Parque Santa Lucía.

Turn right here on Calle 47 for a block and a half, then turn left onto the broad, busy boulevard known as the:

19. Paseo de Montejo, a broad, tree-lined thoroughfare lined with imposing banks, hotels, and several old 19th-century mansions erected by henequén barons, generals, and other Yucatecan potentates. It's Mexico's humble version of the Champs-Elysées.

REFUELING STOP Before or after tackling the Palacio Canton (below), a good place for a break and for watching life on the paseo is the lobby restaurant of the **Hotel Paseo Montejo,** which has excellent regional specialties. It's on Paseo Montejo, a block and a half north of the Palacio Canton.

At the corner of Calle 43 is the:

20. Palacio Canton, which houses the **Museo Regional de Antropología** (anthropology museum; tel. 23-0055). Designed and built by Enrico Deserti, the architect who designed the Teatro Peón Contreras, it's the most impressive mansion on Paseo Montejo. It was constructed between 1909 and 1911, during the last years of the Porfiriato, as the home of Gen. Francisco Canton Rosado. The general enjoyed his palace for only six years before he died in 1917. The house was converted into a school and later became the official residence of Yucatán's governor.

Admire the building itself as you walk around. It's the only paseo mansion that you'll get to visit. Be sure to examine the little art deco elevator—a great luxury at one time.

This is an interregional museum, not only of the state but also of the rest of the peninsula and Mexico, including displays on cosmology, pre-Hispanic time computation and comparative timeline, musical instruments, weaving examples, and designs and stone carving from all over the country.

On the right as you enter is a room used for changing exhibits, usually featuring "the piece of the month." After that are the permanent exhibits, with captions mostly in Spanish only. Starting with fossil mastodon teeth, the exhibits take you down through the ages of the Yucatán's history, giving special attention to the daily life of its inhabitants. You'll see how the Maya tied boards to babies' skulls in order to reshape the heads (giving them the slanting forehead that was then a mark of great beauty) and how they filed teeth to sharpen them, or drilled teeth to implant jewels. Enlarged photos show the archeological sites and drawings show the various styles of Maya houses and how they were constructed. The one of Mayapán, for instance, clearly shows the city's ancient walls. Even if you know only a little Spanish, the museum provides a good background for Maya explorations. The museum is open Tuesday through Saturday from 8am to 8pm, and Sunday from 8am to 2pm. Admission is $4.50; free on Sunday. There's a museum bookstore on the left as you enter.

MORE ATTRACTIONS

West of the Plaza Mayor, along Avenida Itzáes between Calle 59 and Calle 85, lies the large **Parque Centenario,** a fine place for an afternoon stroll, especially with children. There's a small train that runs around the park, and a small but interesting zoo with Yucatecan animals. The cages are close to shady walkways, so it's easy to get a good look at the hairless dogs, numerous monkey and pigeon varieties, alligators, flamingos, parrots, jaguars, pumas, leopards, and lions. Throughout the park, sandy play areas and swings act as magnets for children. There's no admission and it's open daily from 8am to 7pm.

The small **Museo de Historia Natural** is just down the block from the Parque Centenario on Calle 59 at Calle 84, housed in an old mansion that was once a military hospital. Among the interesting displays is the skull of a hippopotamus, and a large dried insect display including a sizable variety of butterflies and the maquech beetle of Maya lore (see "Shopping," below, for more about the maquech). Admission is free; it's open Tuesday through Sunday from 8am to 6pm.

Four blocks east of the Plaza Mayor, the **Museo Regional de Arte Popular** (no phone) on Calle 59 between Calles 50 and 48, displays regional costumes, pottery, and folk art of the Yucatán. There's a small bookstore and large salesroom with quality crafts from throughout Mexico. Hours are Tuesday through Saturday from 8am to 8pm.

SHOPPING

Mérida is known for hammocks, guayaberas (typical men's shirts), and Panama hats. But there are also good buys in Yucatán-made baskets and pottery, as well as crafts from all over Mexico, especially at the central market. Mérida is also the place to pick up prepared *achiote*, a mixture of ground achiote, oregano, garlic, masa, and other spices used in Yucatecan cuisine, especially on grilled meat and fish—I don't leave Yucatán without it.

Mérida's bustling **market district,** bounded by Calles 63 to 69 and Calles 62 to 54, is a few blocks southeast of the Plaza Mayor. The streets surrounding the market can be as interesting and crowded as the market itself. Heaps of prepared achiote are sold in the food section or it's sometimes found bottled and already mixed with the juice of the sour orange. Buy the prepared achiote if you are heading home from Mérida since it needs refrigeration.

CRAFTS

LA CASA DE ARTESANÍAS, Calle 63 no. 513, between Calles 64 and 66. Tel. 23-5392.

This beautiful restored monastery doubles as a regional crafts showplace and saleshop and bookstore. There's a bulletin board listing cultural events, and an inexpensive cafeteria. It's open Monday through Saturday from 8am to 8pm.

CRAFTS MARKET, in a separate building of the main market, Calle 67 at Calle 56.

Look for a large pale green building behind the post office. Climb the steps and wade into the clamor and activity, browsing for leather goods, hammocks, Panama hats, Maya embroidered dresses, men's formal guayabera shirts, and craft items of all kinds.

MUSEO REGIONAL DE ARTESANÍAS, Calle 59 no. 441, between Calles 50 and 48.

This is a branch of the Museo Nacional de Artes e Industrias Populares from Mexico City. Displays of regional costumes and crafts occupy front rooms. In the back is a large room full of crafts from all over Mexico, including filigree jewelry from Mérida, and folk pottery, baskets, and wood carving from the Yucatán. It's open Tuesday through Saturday from 8am to 8pm, and Sunday from 9am to 2pm. Admission is free.

HAMMOCKS

The supremely comfortable Yucatecan fine-mesh hammocks (*hamacas*) are made of string from several materials. Silk is wonderful, but extremely expensive, and only for truly serious hammock-sleepers. Nylon is long-lasting. Cotton is attractive, fairly strong, and inexpensive, but it wears out sooner than nylon. There are several grades of cotton string used in hammocks. Here's how to proceed: Look at the string itself. Is it fine and tightly spun? Are the end loops well made and tight? Open the hammock and look at the weave. Are the strings soiled? Are there many mistakes in the pattern of the weave?

To see if the hammock is large enough, grasp the hammock at the point where the wide part and the end strings meet, and hold your hand level with the top of your head. The body should touch the floor; if not, the hammock is too short for you. Keep in mind that any of these hammocks is going to look big when you stretch it open, but many will seem small when you actually lie in them.

Hammocks are sold as *sencillo* (single, 50 pairs of end strings, about $15), *doble* (double, 100 pairs of end strings, $20), *matrimonial* (larger than double, 150 pairs of end strings, about $25). The biggest hammock of all is called *una hamaca de quatro cajas*, or sometimes *matrimonial especial*, and it is simply enormous, with 175 pairs of end strings; if you can find one, it'll cost you about $30. Buy the biggest hammock you can afford. You'll be glad you did. The bigger ones take up no more room, and are so much more comfortable, even for just one person. (To get long life from your hammock, always remember to remove your shoes and avoid contact between buttons or zippers and the weave.)

Where should you buy your hammock? Street vendors will approach you at every turn, "*¿Hamacas, señor, señorita?*" Their prices will be low, but so is their

IMPRESSIONS

For me hammocks had always been associated with the danger of falling out of them, their discomfort, and the Navy. I was soon to revise this opinion when I tried out a Mayan hammock, and had agreed with the local legend that the hammock was a present from the gods to mankind. The Yucatán hammock is an honest hammock and does not play dirty tricks in the middle of the night like the other hammocks of the world ... and to be on the safe side I bought what is known as a "matrimonial hammock," one so large that it could sleep two people lengthwise or even abreast.
—MICHEL PEISSEL, THE LOST WORLD OF QUINTANA ROO, 1963

quality. If you buy from these vendors, be sure to examine the hammock carefully. Booths in the market will have a larger selection at only slightly higher prices.

I've been recommending **La Poblana, S.A.**, Calle 65 no. 492, between Calles 60 and 58, for years with no complaints. Sr. William Razu, the owner, is usually on the job and ready to whip out dozens of hammocks for your inspection. Prices are marked, so don't try to bargain. If you've spent some time in the market for hammocks, and you seem to know what you're talking about, Sr. Razu may usher you upstairs to a room wall-to-wall with hammocks, where you can give your prospective purchase a test run. La Poblana sells ropes and mosquito nets for hammocks as well, and also Maya women's dresses and men's guayaberas. Hours are Monday through Saturday from 8am to 7pm.

MAQUECH—THE LEGENDARY MAYA BEETLE

One of the most unusual items for sale in the Yucatán is the live maquech beetle. Storekeepers display bowls of the large dusty brown insects that have long black legs and backs sprinkled with multicolored glass "jewels," with each insect attached to a small gold chain. The chain hooks to a small safety pin and behold, you have a living brooch to wear. One version of the maquech legend goes that a Maya princess became the forbidden love object of a Maya prince. Without her knowledge, he crept into her garden one night, and just as they met he was captured by the princess's guards. To save the prince, a sorceress turned him into a beetle and put him on a decaying tree near where he was captured. When the princess recovered from her faint, she looked for the prince where she had last seen him and found the bejeweled beetle instead. In an instant she knew it was the prince. Using a few strands of her long hair, she harnessed the beetle and kept it over her heart forever. Another version has it that the prince asked a sorceress to put him close to the heart of his beloved princess. So, because he was very rich, she turned him into a jeweled beetle pin. Either way, putting one close to your heart costs between $7 to $10 and comes with a piece of its favorite wood, a nice little box with air holes to carry it in, the chain, and a safety pin. U.S. Customs, however, doesn't permit the beetle to cross the border, so plan to find it a home before you leave Mexico.

PANAMA HATS

Another very popular item are these soft, pliable hats made from the palm fibers of the jipijapa in several towns along Highway 180, especially Becal, in the neighboring state of Campeche. There's no need to journey all the way to Campeche, however, as Mérida has the hats in abundance. Just the thing to shade you from the fierce Yucatecan sun, the hats can be rolled up and carried in a suitcase for the trip home. They retain their shape quite well.

Jipi hats come in three grades, judged by the quality (pliability and fineness) of the fibers and closeness of the weave. The coarser, more open weave of fairly large fibers will be sold for a few dollars (or by street vendors in Cancún and Cozumel for up to $10!). The middle grade, a fairly fine, close weave of good fibers, should cost about $15 in a responsible shop. The finest weave, truly a beautiful hat, can cost more than $50.

In **La Casa de los Jipis,** Calle 56 no. 526, near Calle 65, a tried-and-true *sombrerería,* a phlegmatic señora will show you the three grades of hats, grumbling all the while. Find your size, more or less, and the señora will tie a ribbon around the hat for final adjustment. If you'd like to see how the hats are blocked, wander into the depths of the rear of the store.

WHERE TO STAY

Mérida is a budget traveler's paradise. Most hotels offer at least a few air-conditioned rooms, and a few of the places also have swimming pools. You may find absolutely every room taken in July and August.

VERY EXPENSIVE

CASA DEL BALAM, Calle 60 no. 48, Mérida, Yuc. 97000. Tel. 99/24-8844, or toll free 800/624-8451 in the U.S. Fax 99/24-5011. 54 rms, 2 suites. A/C MINIBAR TV TEL

$ Rates: $125 single or double; $165 suite. **Parking:** Free.

One of Mérida's most popular and centrally located hotels is built around a lush interior courtyard. In two sections of three and six stories respectively, the colonial-style rooms are accented with Mexican textiles, folk art, dark furniture, iron headboards, and tile floors with area rugs. It's hard to top this place for location and comfort. There's a travel agency and a rental-car agency in the lobby, as well as a popular restaurant and bar with trio entertainment in the evenings. The tables scattered around the courtyard have become a favorite romantic spot for evening cocktails and appetizers.

The owners also run the Hacienda Chichén-Itzá hotel, at the entrance of the ruins of Chichén-Itzá, so you can make arrangements here to stay there.

To find the hotel, walk three blocks north of the Plaza Mayor.

HOTEL EL CONQUISTADOR, Paseo Montejo 458, Mérida, Yuc. 97000. Tel. 99/26-2155. Fax 99/26-8829. 161 rms, 9 suites. A/C TV TEL

$ Rates: $110 single; $118 double. **Parking:** Free.

Its well-maintained rooms, excellent restaurants, and solarium pool make this the nicest hotel on Paseo Montejo, much in demand with small tour groups and business travelers. The view from the 10th-floor rooftop solarium and the rooms on the upper floors is spectacular; try to get a room facing downtown. The rooms are decorated in blue and white, each with two double or one king-size bed and a large tiled bathroom.

The hotel's main dining room attracts a crowd of locals for its lavish breakfast buffet, which is served daily. There's also room service, a laundry, a travel agency, car rentals, and meeting rooms. It's one block from the museum on the east side of the street.

HYATT REGENCY MÉRIDA, Calle 60 no. 344, Mérida, Yuc. 97000. Tel. 99/25-6722, or toll free 800/228-9000 in the U.S. Fax 99/25-7002. 300 rms and suites. A/C MINIBAR TV TEL

$ Rates: $165–$200 single or double.

When it opened in 1994, the Hyatt Regency was the tallest building in Mérida, at 17 stories high. It's also the most luxurious hotel in town, far surpassing the services and style Mérida is accustomed to. The large, modern rooms have in-room movie channels on satellite TV, 24-hour room service, direct-dial long-distance phone service, and personal safes. Regency Club rooms take up two floors of the hotel; guests here receive complimentary continental breakfast and evening cocktails and hors d'oeuvres, special concierge service, and private lounges and board rooms.

The elegant hotel offers guests several restaurants and bars (including a swim-up bar), a complete business center, travel agency, and shops. It's at the intersection of Calle 60 and Avenida Colón.

EXPENSIVE

HOTEL MISIÓN PARK INN, Calle 60 no. 491, Mérida, Yuc. 97000. Tel. 99/23-9500, or toll free 800/448-8355. Fax 99/23-9500. 147 rms. A/C TV TEL

$ Rates: $66 single or double; $85–$150 suite.

The Misión Park Inn is actually a large modern addition grafted onto a gracious older hotel. The location, right across the street from the university and the Teatro Peón Contreras, at the corner of Calle 57, and only two short blocks from the Plaza Mayor, is excellent. Enter the hotel's cool lobby from the noisy street, and you'll find yourself in an oasis complete with bubbling fountain, high ceilings, and a nice little swimming pool. Though the public rooms are colonial in style, the guest units are Spartan in a modern way with blond furniture, tile floors, drapes and shutters, and two double beds in most rooms. Some of the suites have small kitchens and separate living-room areas.

One restaurant serves all meals. La Trova Bar has live piano entertainment Monday through Saturday evenings. There's also laundry and room service, and a travel agency.

MODERATE

CASA MEXILIO GUEST HOUSE, Calle 68 no. 495, Mérida, Yuc. 97000. Tel. and fax 99/28-2505, or toll free 800/532-6802 in the U.S. 7 rms, 1 suite. FAN

$ Rates (including breakfast): High season $60–$70 single or double. Low season $50–$60 single or double.

Those preferring the atmosphere of a private home rather than a hotel may find this 19th-century town house a perfect alternative. Guests have the run of the three-story home, which is built around indoor and outdoor patios. Each room is different and throughout the house pleasant decorative use is made of Mexican crafts. On the back patio there's a small swimming pool and whirlpool. In the upstairs living room guests have use of the stereo and TV and books on archeology. Breakfast is taken in the pleasant dining room beside the kitchen. The hotel is connected with the Turquoise Reef Group, which has inns on Mexico's Caribbean coast between Cancún and Playa del Carmen. You can make reservations here for those inns, as well as sign on for a variety of trips in the Yucatán.

GRAN HOTEL, Calle 60 no. 496, Mérida, Yuc. 97000. Tel. 24-7730. Fax 99/24-7622. 30 rms. A/C (10 rms) FAN (20 rms) TEL

$ Rates: $60 single; $65 double; $72 junior suite. **Parking:** Free, three blocks away.

Perhaps the finest example of old-time hotel architecture in the city, the Gran Hotel offers an ambience that's 19th-century rather than colonial, and it's all the more enjoyable for that. Marble stairs lead to the three stories of rooms surrounding a plant-filled central court. Corinthian columns and fancy ironwork vie for your attention with lofty portals and heavy worked wood trim. The freshly painted high-ceilinged rooms have ornate wood door frames, and old-timey tile floors. Heavy windows and drapes cut down on the noise from the plaza; turning on the air conditioner helps as well. A few exercise machines are kept in a locked workout room; fee for their use is $5. El Patio Español, the hotel restaurant, is off the lobby. You're paying for history, ambience, and location more than state-of-the-art hotel comfort.

It's ideally located on the Parque Cepeda Peraza, next to the Hotel Caribe, half a block north of the Plaza Mayor between Calles 59 and 61.

HOTEL CARIBE, Calle 59 no. 500, Mérida, Yuc. 97000. Tel. 99/24-9022, or toll free 800/826-6842 in the U.S. Fax 99/24-8733. 18 rms, 38 suites. A/C (37 rms) FAN (19 rms) TV TEL

$ **Rates:** $36 single with fan, $40–$45 single with A/C; $42 double with fan, $45–$50 double with A/C; $65–$75 suite for two with fan or A/C. **Parking:** Free; guarded.

Step inside the entry of this small, two-story central city hotel and discover a colonial-style jewel. Nicely coordinated furnishings accent new pastel-colored tile floors. Comfortable sitting areas along the three stories of covered but open-air walkways become like an extended living room, offering a cozy respite any time of day. On the top floor there's a small swimming pool, sun deck, and great views of the cathedral and town. The interior restaurant is arranged around a quiet central courtyard, while the hotel's sidewalk café, El Mesón, is set out in front in the shady Parque Cepeda Peraza. Entry is on the Parque Cepeda Peraza, a half block north of Plaza Mayor.

HOTEL COLONIAL, Calle 62 no. 476, Mérida, Yuc. 97000. Tel. 99/23-6444, or toll free 800/428-3088 in the U.S. Fax 99/28-3961. 73 rms. A/C TV TEL

$ **Rates:** $63 single or double.

For price and location, it's hard to beat this bright, modern, multistoried hotel with two elevators. A small swimming pool is on the ground floor behind the lobby, while the top story holds a partially covered plant-filled deck with tables and chairs and great city views. Coordinated pastel furnishings in each of the newly refurbished rooms lend a touch of class usually found in more expensive hotels. It's north of the Plaza Mayor at the intersection of Calles 62 and 57 near the University of Yucatán.

HOTEL DEL GOBERNADOR, Calle 59 no. 535, Mérida, Yuc. 97000. Tel. 99/23-7133, or toll free 800/227-0212 in the U.S. Fax 99/28-1590. 61 rms, 16 junior suites. A/C TV TEL

$ **Rates:** $60 single or double. Additional person $5 extra. Parking: Free.

Modern and comfortable, this hotel is one of Mérida's most popular. Built on three levels around an interior swimming pool, all rooms have tile floors and bathrooms with showers. To the left of the lobby is a cozy restaurant, and the hotel offers laundry service. It's three blocks west of the Parque Cepeda Peraza, at the intersection of Calles 59 and 66.

HOTEL POSADA TOLEDO, Calle 58 no. 487, Mérida, Yuc. 97000. Tel. 99-23/4355. 19 rms, 1 suite. A/C (16 rms) FAN (3 rms)

$ **Rates:** $43 single with fan, $48 single with A/C; $48 double with fan, $54 double with A/C; $66 suite with A/C. **Parking:** Free; next door.

I'm fond of this colonial inn, which was once a private mansion. It's a cross between a garden dripping with vines and a fading museum with beautifully kept antique furnishings. Most rooms have no windows, but high ceilings and appropriately creaky hardwood floors are standard. The rooftop lounge area is excellent for

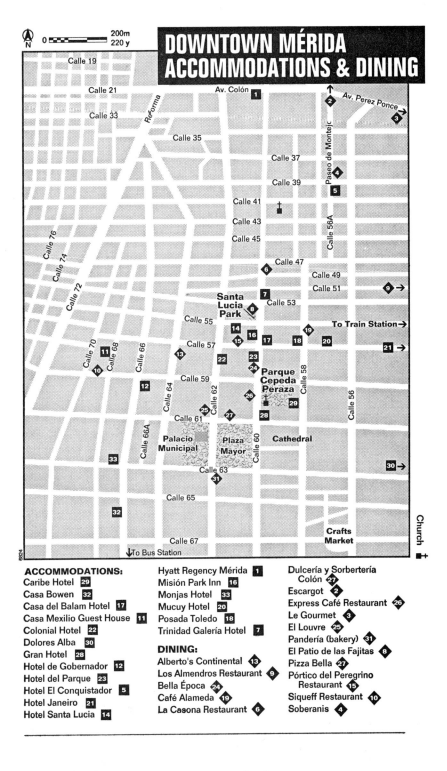

DOWNTOWN MÉRIDA
ACCOMMODATIONS & DINING

0 | 200m
    | 220 y

Calle 19
Calle 21
Av. Colón **1**
Calle 33
Reforma
Av. Perez Ponce **2** **3**
Calle 35
Paseo de Montejo
Calle 37
Calle 39 **4**
5
Calle 41
Calle 43
Calle 45
Calle 56A
Calle 76
Calle 74
Calle 72
Calle 47 **6**
Calle 49
Calle 51 **9** →
7
Santa Lucia Park **8** Calle 53
Calle 55
14
16 **19** **To Train Station** →
Calle 57 **15** **17** **18** **20**
Calle 70
Calle 68
Calle 66
11 **13** **21** →
10 **22** **23**
12 **24**
Calle 59 **26** **Parque Cepeda Peraza**
Calle 64
Calle 62
Calle 58
25 **29**
Calle 61 **27** **28**
Calle 56
Calle 66A
Palacio Municipal **Plaza Mayor** Calle 60 **Cathedral**
33
Calle 63 **30** →
31
Calle 65
32
Crafts Market
Calle 67
↓To Bus Station
Church

ACCOMMODATIONS:
Caribe Hotel **29**
Casa Bowen **32**
Casa del Balam Hotel **17**
Casa Mexilio Guest House **11**
Colonial Hotel **22**
Dolores Alba **30**
Gran Hotel **28**
Hotel de Gobernador **12**
Hotel del Parque **23**
Hotel El Conquistador **5**
Hotel Janeiro **21**
Hotel Santa Lucia **14**

Hyatt Regency Mérida **1**
Misión Park Inn **16**
Monjas Hotel **33**
Mucuy Hotel **20**
Posada Toledo **18**
Trinidad Galería Hotel **7**

DINING:
Alberto's Continental **13**
Los Almendros Restaurant **9**
Bella Época **24**
Café Alameda **19**
La Casona Restaurant **6**

Dulcería y Sorbertería Colón **27**
Escargot **2**
Express Café Restaurant **26**
Le Gourmet **3**
El Louvre **25**
Pandería (bakery) **31**
El Patio de las Fajitas **8**
Pizza Bella **27**
Pórtico del Peregrino Restaurant **15**
Siqueff Restaurant **10**
Soberanis **4**

viewing the city in the cool of the evening. Ten rooms have TVs and some have phones. Two of the grandest rooms have been remodeled into a spectacular suite with lavender and blue walls decorated with ornate cornices and woodwork. The enormous bedroom and separate living room are furnished with the hotel's best antiques; the bathroom and closet are larger than the rooms in some budget hotels. Two air conditioners struggle to keep the cavernous space cool.

The Posada Toledo is on Calle 58 at the corner of Calle 57, 7 blocks west of the train station, and 2½ blocks northeast of the Plaza Mayor.

BUDGET

CASA BOWEN, Calle 66 no. 521-B, Mérida, Yuc. 97000. Tel. 99/21-6809.
25 rms. A/C (5 rms) FAN (20 rms)

$ Rates: $18 single or double with one bed and fan; $20 double with two beds and fan; $30 double with A/C; $26 double with two beds, kitchen, and fan. **Parking:** Free; limited.

Formed from a lovely old mansion plus a modern addition next door, this hospitable, family-run inn is one of the best budget hotels in Mexico. The lobby and courtyard are filled with plants, rattan rockers, and comfortable sitting areas. Among the extras is a paperback-book lending library, a rooftop clothesline, well-screened windows, an English-speaking management, and several comfortable sitting areas in both sections. Rooms vary in size, with decoration generally created around a colonial theme. All are clean, with tile floors and nice-sized windows.

It's on Calle 66 at the corner of Calle 65. From the bus station walk out the front door, turn right, and walk one block. At Calle 66 turn left and walk two blocks. It's on the left. It's three blocks southwest of the Plaza Mayor.

HOTEL DOLORES ALBA, Calle 63 no. 464, Mérida, Yuc. 97000. Tel. 99/ 28-5650, or 21-3745. Fax 99/28-3163. 40 rms. A/C (4 rms) FAN (36 rms)

$ Rates: $28 single with fan, $32 single with A/C; $32 double with fan; $38 double with A/C; $42 triple with fan; $48 triple with A/C. **Parking:** Free; guarded, limited.

The Sanchez family converted their family home into a comfortable hotel with a large open court, and a smaller courtyard with a nice clean swimming pool. The rooms, decorated with local crafts, all have showers. A small dining room opens for breakfast. The Sanchez family also operates the Hotel Janeiro in Mérida, and the Hotel Dolores Alba outside Chichén-Itzá, so you can make reservations here for the other hotels.

It's between Calles 52 and 54, four blocks west of the Plaza Mayor, and a block north of the market.

HOTEL JANEIRO, Calle 57 no. 435, Mérida, Yuc. 97000. Tel. 99/23-3602.
22 rms. A/C (12 rms) FAN (10 rms)

$ Rates: $28 single with fan; $36 single or double with A/C. **Parking:** Free; limited.

Owned by the same family that runs the Dolores Alba, the Janeiro sports the results of a refurbishing that has improved the rooms. In a quiet courtyard in back there's a little swimming pool and patio tables. You can make reservations here for the owners' hotel near Chichén-Itzá.

The Janeiro lies between Calles 48 and 50. From the train station walk out the front door, turn right to the next block, then left one block and right on Calle 57. It's half a block on the right.

HOTEL MONJAS, Calles 66 no. 509 at 63, Mérida, Yuc. 97000. Tel. 99/ 28-6632. 26 rms. FAN

$ Rates: $16 single with one bed; $18 double with one bed, $22 double with two beds. With its inviting modern appearance, the lobby outperforms the guest units at this two-story hotel. But the basically furnished rooms are clean, and each includes a ceiling fan, and either one or two double beds or a double and a twin. The location is excellent, slightly away from traffic and city hubbub. A small snack bar in the lobby functions on weekends selling sandwiches; breakfast pastries and soft drinks are sold anytime.

From the Plaza Mayor walk two blocks west on Calle 63. The hotel is on the right corner. From the bus station, turn right out the front door and walk one block. Turn left on Calle 66 and walk four blocks. It's on the left.

HOTEL MUCUY, Calle 57 no. 481, Mérida, Yuc. 97000. Tel. and fax 99/ 23-7801. 22 rms. FAN
$ Rates: $20 single; $25 double; $30 triple.

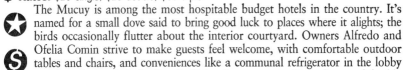

The Mucuy is among the most hospitable budget hotels in the country. It's named for a small dove said to bring good luck to places where it alights; the birds occasionally flutter about the interior courtyard. Owners Alfredo and Ofelia Comin strive to make guests feel welcome, with comfortable outdoor tables and chairs, and conveniences like a communal refrigerator in the lobby and laundry and clothesline facilities for guest use. Two floors of freshly painted rooms, with window screens, showers, and ceiling fans, are lined up on one side of the flower-filled garden. The owners live on the premises, and Señora Comin speaks English.

The hotel is 3½ blocks northeast of the Plaza Mayor, and five blocks west of the train station between Calles 56 and 58.

HOTEL SANTA LUCÍA, Calle 55 no. 508, Mérida, Yuc. 97000. Tel. and fax 99/28-2672. 51 rms. A/C or FAN TV TEL
$ Rates: $26 single with fan, $30 single with A/C; $30 double with fan, $36 double with A/C. **Parking:** Free; guarded.
Though this small hotel opened in 1990, it still looks brand new. The rooms are in a three-story building with windows facing the inner hallways or the courtyard, with its long, inviting swimming pool. The management is very attentive and helpful, providing information on tours, restaurants, and sights. They also run the Hotel San Clemente in Valladolid. The hotel is just west of Santa Lucía park between Calles 60 and 62.

TRINIDAD GALERÍA, Calles 60 no. 456 at 51, Mérida, Yuc. 97000. Tel. 99/23-2463. 31 rms, 1 suite, A/C (2 rms) FAN (29 rms)
$ Rates: $26 single with fan, $33 single with A/C; $33 double with fan, $39 double with A/C; $50 suite with A/C and TV. Ask about seasonal discounts. **Parking:** Free; limited.
Once an enormous home, this rambling structure has been transformed into a hotel that includes a small shaded swimming pool, a communal refrigerator and shared dining room, oodles of original art and antiques, and lots of relaxing nooks with comfortable furniture. A lush garden enhances the inner courtyard. Upstairs a covered porch, decorated with antiques and plants, runs the length of the hotel, providing yet another place to read or converse. Rooms are darkish and simply furnished, and most don't have windows, but the overall ambience of the hotel is comparable to that of more expensive inns.

It's on Calle 60 at the corner of Calle 51, three blocks north of Santa Lucía park and six blocks north of the Plaza Mayor.

WHERE TO DINE

EXPENSIVE

ALBERTO'S CONTINENTAL, Calle 64 no. 482. Tel. 28-5367.

Cuisine: LEBANESE/YUCATECAN/ITALIAN. **Reservations:** Recommended.

$ Prices: Main courses $12–$24.

Open: Daily 11am–11pm.

Created from a fine old town house, with large rooms built around a plant- and tree-filled patio that's framed in Moorish arches, this is one of Mérida's most elegant settings for dining. Cuban floor tiles from a bygone era and antique furniture and sideboards create an Old World mood. The tables are covered with white cloths and flickering candles at night. The eclectic menu includes tahini, tabbouleh, carne en brochette, and steaks al carbón. There's a sampler plate of four Lebanese favorites, plus traditional Yucatecan specialities such as pollo pibil and fish Celéstun (bass stuffed with shrimp). Or go Italian with spaghetti and veal parmesan. Polish off your selections with Turkish coffee. Alberto's is at the corner of Calle 57.

LA BELLA ÉPOCA, in the Hotel del Parque, Calle 60. Tel. 28-1928.

Cuisine: YUCATECAN/MEXICAN/MIDDLE EASTERN. **Reservations:** Recommended.

$ Prices: Appetizers $4–$10; soups and salads $4–$8; main courses $8–$16.

Open: Daily noon–midnight.

The ideal time to dine at this elegant yet casual restaurant is just before 8pm on a Sunday evening, when you can claim one of the tables for two set on small balconies overlooking the strollers and calesas that pass by the Parque Madre. The menu is beyond extensive—so don't promise your taste buds any special treats until you've checked on their availability. It's easy to linger for hours over course after course, starting with the multiethnic appetizers, including *sikil-pak*, a dip made with ground pumpkin seeds. The Mexican and Yucatecan main courses are the best, and there are plenty of choices for vegetarians. Save room for flaming *crepas cajetas* (caramel crêpes) and café de olla. Valet parking is available.

LA CASONA, Calle 60 no. 434. Tel. 23-8348.

Cuisine: CONTINENTAL/ITALIAN. **Reservations:** Recommended.

$ Prices: Appetizers $2.50–$7.75; pasta courses $6–$10; meat courses $9.75–$15.

Open: Daily 1pm–midnight.

A gracious old Mérida house and its lush interior garden make for a charming and romantic restaurant. The cuisine is continental, especially Italian, so you can choose among such dishes as filet mignon with brandy and cream, linguine with mushrooms, or lasagne. It's also a fine place to wind up the day sipping espresso or cappuccino. It's nine blocks north of the Plaza Mayor, at the corner of Calle 47.

ESCARGOT, Paseo Montejo Norte 250. Tel. 44-2477.

Cuisine: CONTINENTAL/FRENCH. **Reservations:** Recommended.

$ Prices: Appetizers $4–$10; main courses $8–$20.

Open: Tues–Sun 1pm–1am.

Chef Yannig, who gained local fame at his now-defunct Yannig's restaurant, has moved to this elegant spot beside the Amarantus nightclub, the hottest nightspot for young, wealthy Méridianos. Yannig continues to please diners with his sea bass Pompadour covered in mushrooms and a white wine sauce, and the green peppercorn beef. The peach Melba is a favorite dessert, though the crêpes are also worth saving room for.

The restaurant is near the country club; catch the 52 bus at Calle 59 between Calles 56 and 58.

LE GOURMET, Perez Ponce 109. Tel. 27-1970.

Cuisine: FRENCH/SEAFOOD.

$ Prices: Breakfast $1.75–$7.50; appetizers $2.75–$19; main courses $8–$30.

Open: Mon–Thurs 1–11:30pm, Fri–Sat 1pm–midnight, Sun noon–5pm.

Behind stained-glass windows, and sporting marble floors and art on the walls, Le Gourmet is especially favored by Mérida upper crust. While the specialty here is seafood (try the pompano in puff pastry), there are almost as many beef selections to choose from, but only a few chicken dishes. Ask for the chef's suggestions, which change daily. Take the Villas Hacienda 52 bus and the restaurant is just after Calle 50. Return to town on the 52 Norte bus.

RESTAURANTE PÓRTICO DEL PEREGRINO, Calle 57 no. 501. Tel. 28-6163.

Cuisine: MEXICAN/INTERNATIONAL. **Reservations:** Recommended.

$ Prices: Appetizers $3–$6; main courses $7–$15.

Open: Daily noon–11pm.

This romantic restaurant captures the spirit of 19th-century Mexico with its shady little garden court and a cross-topped gateway. If the weather is too warm for outdoor dining, escape to the air-conditioned dining rooms decorated with antique mirrors and elegant sideboards; there's also a modern streetside salon. The extensive menu offers soup, fish filet, grilled gulf shrimp, spaghetti, pollo pibil, and coconut ice cream topped with Kahlúa. You'll find the Pórtico del Peregrino 2½ blocks north of the main square, between Calles 60 and 62, next door to Pop and across from the university.

MODERATE

LOS ALMENDROS, Calle 50-A no. 493. Tel. 28-5459.

Cuisine: YUCATECAN.

$ Prices: Appetizers $4.50–$5.50; main courses $6–$10; daily specials $7.50.

Open: Daily 9am–11pm

The original Los Almendros is at Ticul, deep in the Maya hinterland, but the branch in Mérida has become a favorite spot for sampling local delicacies. Colorful chairs and tables get you into a festive mood. Ask to see the menu, with color photographs of the offerings and descriptions in English. Poc-chuc, a marinated and grilled pork, was created in Mérida at this restaurant. It faces the Plaza de Mejorada between Calles 57 and 59, six blocks east of Parque Cepeda Peraza.

EL PATIO DE LAS FAJITAS, Calle 60 no. 467. Tel. 28-3782.

Cuisine: MEXICAN

$ Prices: Appetizers $5–$6.50; main courses $8–$10; comida corrida $6–$7.50; beer $2.

Open: Mon–Sat 1–11pm.

Fajitas are the specialty at this mansion-turned-restaurant where you dine around a central courtyard decorated with plants and colorful tablecloths. The fajitas, grilled before you on the patio, are made of small strips of marinated pork, chicken, or beef, or whole shrimp, all sizzled on an iron griddle with a dash of garlic and lime juice. Each order comes with guacamole, tortillas, and fresh Mexican salsa cruda. The portions are not large, and you may want to order a baked potato on the side. The menu also offers an economical fixed-price meal in the afternoon, which can include soup, poc-chuc, or pollo mole, rice, beans, and tortillas (but not your drink). The restaurant is four blocks north of the Plaza Mayor, at the corner of Calle 53.

SIQUEFF RESTAURANT, Calle 59 no. 553. Tel. 24-7465.

Cuisine: LEBANESE/INTERNATIONAL.

$ Prices: Lebanese specialties $3–$7.50; main courses $3–$12.
   Open: Daily 11am–7pm.
In a former mansion that's lost its polish, you can still admire the grand mahogany-framed doors around the Moorish arched central patio with halls and rooms that lead to who knows where. Siqueff is popular with Mérida's middle class, so there are almost always several large families enjoying a meal. Lebanese specialties are listed under "varios"; the menu Arabe is a little bit of everything. You can also have stone crab legs from Mexico's Gulf coast, and paella Valenciana.

SOBERANIS, Calle Montejo 468. Tel. 27-7186.
   Cuisine: SEAFOOD.
$ Prices: Appetizers $3.50–$9; main courses $7–$18.
   Open: Daily 8am–11pm.
Part of a popular chain that's also represented in Cancún, Progreso, and Cozumel, Soberanis has dependably good meals. At this branch you can sit outside on the patio or inside. Besides full seafood meals, there are also sandwiches and a few selections of beef or chicken.

BUDGET

Calle 62 between the main plaza and Calle 57 has a short string of small super-cheap food shops. Budgeteers are sure to find things to fit the appetite and the wallet if they begin at the plaza and go for a couple of blocks. To make your own breakfast, try the **Panificadora Montejo,** at the corner of Calles 62 and 63, the southwest corner of the main plaza, and choose from a dozen or more delectable breakfast treats. For those (like me) who can't start a day without fresh orange juice, juice bars have sprouted up all over Mérida. Several of these thirst-quenching establishments are on or near the main plaza.

CAFE ALAMEDA, Calle 58 no. 474. Tel. 28-3635.
   Cuisine: YUCATECAN/MIDDLE EASTERN.
$ Prices: Appetizers $2–$4.50; breakfast $2.50–$4; main courses $4–$9.
   Open: Mon–Sat 8am–10pm.
At about 10am on weekdays the Alameda is filled with businessmen all eating the same late breakfast—a shish kebab of marinated beef, a basket of warm pita bread, and coffee. If eggs are more your style, order them with beans; otherwise you'll get a small plate with a little pile of eggs. Vegetarians are in luck here, with choices of tabbouleh, hummus, cauliflower or spinach casseroles, and veggie tamales. The umbrella-shaded tables on the back patio are nice.

CAFE-RESTAURANT EXPRESS, Calle 60 no. 509. Tel. 28-1691.
   Cuisine: MEXICAN.
$ Prices: Breakfast $1.75–$4; main courses $5.50–$7.50; fixed price meal $6.50; sandwiches $2–$4.
   Open: Daily 7am–11pm.
One of the most popular meeting places in town faces the Parque Cepeda Peraza. Waiters snap to attention and hordes of local residents—mainly men—sit and idle the hours away, totally oblivious to the surroundings, with all attention focused on the sidewalk or at least a newspaper. The vast menu includes Spanish-style pork, pollo pibil, and huachinango milanesa (red snapper). You can also while away some time here with good, strong coffee. It's opposite the Parque Cepeda Peraza, near the corner of Calle 59.

DULCERÍA Y SORBETERÍA COLÓN, Calle 61 no. 500. Tel. 28-1497.
   Cuisine: PASTRIES.

$ Prices: Pastries 65¢–$1.50; ice cream $1.50; soft drinks 40¢; milk shakes $1.65.
Open: Daily 8am–11:30pm.

Bent-wire café tables and chairs are set out here on the portico facing the Plaza Mayor at the corner of Calle 62. For after-dinner ice cream or delicious Mexican pastries and cakes, this is the best vantage point for people-watching in the late afternoon or evening. Try their exotic tropical-fruit ice creams such as coconut or papaya, but pick a time of day when auto traffic (with its noise and smelly fumes) is not so heavy around the square.

EL LOUVRE, Calle 62 no. 499. Tel. 24-5073.
Cuisine: MEXICAN.
$ Prices: Main courses $2.50–$5.25; fixed-price lunch $5–$7.50.
Open: Daily 24 hours.

This big open restaurant feeds everybody who comes to Mérida at one time or another—including farm workers and townspeople. But they know tourists are looking for value, so there's an English menu. The comida corrida might include beans with pork on Monday, pork stew on Tuesday, etc., plus there are sandwiches, soup, and other full meals. It's half a block north of the Plaza Mayor.

PIZZA BELLA, Calle 61 and Plaza Mayor. Tel. 23-6401.
Cuisine: ITALIAN.
$ Prices: Breakfast $2.50–$3.50; pizza $6–$11.50; spaghetti $3.50–$5.50.
Open: Daily 8am–midnight.

A popular little eatery, Pizza Bella is festooned in red-checked tablecloths; its waiters are decked out in red caps. Elbow your way in or grab one of the outside tables and enjoy pizza prepared 10 ways, or spaghetti plain, bolognese, or with garlic. If you're not hungry, they serve mixed drinks, espresso, and cappuccino. Pizza Bella faces the Plaza Mayor, next to the Dulcería y Sorbetería Colón at the corner of Calle 62.

EVENING ENTERTAINMENT

For a full range of free or low-cost evening entertainment and Mérida Sunday activities, see "Special Events," earlier in this section.

Teatro Peón Contreras, at Calles 60 and 57, and the **Teatro Ayala,** on Calle 60 at Calle 61, host a wide range of performing artists from around the world. Stop in and see what's showing.

Action at the hotel bars, lounges, and discos depends on the crowd of customers presently staying at each hotel. Most of Mérida's downtown hotels, however, are filled with tour groups whose members prefer to rest after an exhausting day.

EASY EXCURSIONS FROM MÉRIDA
CELESTÚN NATIONAL WILDLIFE REFUGE

This flamingo sanctuary and offbeat fishing village on the Gulf coast is a 1½-hour drive from Mérida. To get here, take Highway 281 (a single-lane road) past numerous old henequén haciendas. There are also frequent buses from Mérida.

One telephone at the Hotel Gutiérrez (99/28-0419) serves as the public phone for the entire village. There's a bank, gas station, and grocery store. Bus tickets are purchased at the end of the row of market stalls on the left side of the church. When I checked, buses to Mérida left at 7am and 2, 4, and 6:30pm. Celestún hotels don't furnish drinking water, so bring your own or buy it in town.

What to See and Do

THE WILDLIFE REFUGE   The town is on a narrow strip of land separated from the mainland by a lagoon. Crossing over the lagoon bridge, the 14,611-acre wildlife refuge spreads out on both sides without visible boundaries. You'll notice the small boats moored on both sides. They are waiting to take visitors to see the flamingos. Besides flamingos, anytime of year you may see frigate birds, pelicans, cranes, egrets, sandpipers, and other waterfowl feeding on shallow sandbars. Of the 175 bird species that come here, at least 99 are permanent residents. At least 15 duck species have been counted. Flamingos are found here all year; some nonbreeding flamingos remain year-round even though the larger group takes off around April to nest on the upper Yucatán peninsula east of Río Lagartos. A 1½- to two-hour flamingo-sighting trip costs around $30 for four persons, or twice that if you stay a half day. The best time to go is around 7am and the worst is midafternoon when sudden storms tend to come up. Be sure not to allow the boatmen to get close enough to frighten the birds; they've been known to do it for photographers, but it will eventually cause the birds to permanently abandon the habitat. Your tour will take you a short distance into the massive mangroves, which line the lagoon, to a sulfur pool where the boatman kills the motor and poles in so you can feel the sultry air, the density of the jungle, and see other birds.

SPECIAL EVENTS   December 8 is the **feast day of the Virgen de la Concepción,** the patron saint of the village. On the Sunday nearest July 15, a colorful procession takes Celestún's venerated figure of the Virgin of Concepción to meet the sacred figure of the Virgin of Asunción on the highway leading to Celestún. Returning to Celestún, they float away on decorated boats and later return to be ensconced at the church during a mass and celebration.

Where to Stay

To find local restaurants and hotels, follow the bridge road a few blocks to the end. On the last street, Calle 12, paralleling the oceanfront, you'll find a few hotels with decent rooms but marginal housekeeping standards. Always try to bargain for better rates, which could be 30% less in the off-season.

HOTEL AGUILAR, Calle 12, Celestún, Yuc. 97367. 12 rms.
$ Rates: $15 single; $20 double.
Across Calle 12 from the beach, the single-story Aguilar is set back from the street and built around a sandy courtyard. The spacious rooms have hot and cold water, good cross-ventilation, screened windows, tile floors, hammock hooks, one or two double beds, and bathrooms with showers. A small grocery store is in front.
   To get here, turn right on Calle 12 and go four blocks. It's on the right (landward side) between Calles 5 and 7.

HOTEL GUTIÉRREZ, Calle 14 at Calle 13, Celestún, Yuc. 97367. Tel. 99/ 28-0419. 18 rms.
$ Rates: $15 single; $20 double.
Although this hotel appears to be the nicest in town, with its three stories of rooms all on the beach, its housekeeping standards are noticeably lax and promised hot water may never appear. Buy drinking water in the lobby. The hotel also serves as the town's long-distance telephone office. To find it turn left on Calle 12; it's on the right about two blocks.

HOTEL MARÍA DEL CARMEN, Calle 12 no. 111, Celestún, Yuc. 97367. Tel. 99/28-0152. 9 rms (all with bath). FAN
$ Rates: $15 single; $20 double.

New in 1992, this clean two-story hotel on the beach is a welcome addition to Celestún's modest lineup of hotels. Spare, but clean and large, the rooms all have marble-tile floors, two double beds with sheets but no bedspread, screened windows (check the screens for holes), and small balconies or patios facing the ocean. Best of all, there's hot water in the bathrooms (not necessarily a hallmark of other Celestún hotels). Some bathrooms lack toilet seats, however. Lorenzo Saul Rodríguez and María del Carmen Gutiérrez own the hotel and are actively involved in local conservation efforts, particularly in protecting the sea turtles that nest on the beach in early summer. Look for the sign for Vista del Mar, the hotel's restaurant; the rooms are behind it past a large parking lot.

Where to Dine

RESTAURANT CELESTÚN, Calle 12, on the waterfront.
 Cuisine: SEAFOOD/MEXICAN.
$ Prices: Main courses $3–$10; soft drinks $1; beer $1.50.
 Open: Daily 10am–6pm.
I highly recommend this ocean-view restaurant, owned by Elda Cauich and Wenseslao Ojeda, where the service is friendly and swift. Tables and chairs fill a long room that stretches from Calle 12 to the beach. The house specialty is a super-delicious shrimp, crab, and squid omelet (called a "torta"). But if you are a fan of stone crabs (*manitas de cangrejo* on the menu), this is definitely the place to chow down. Trapped fresh in the Gulf by Celestún fishermen, they come freshly cooked and seasoned with fresh lime juice. Other local specialties include mullet (*liza*) and caviar de Celestún (mullet eggs). To find the restaurant, follow the bridge road to the waterfront and the restaurant is immediately left, on Calle 12.

DZIBILCHALTÚN

This Maya site and **national park,** nine miles north of Mérida along the Progreso road and 4½ miles east off the highway, is worth a stop. Though it was founded about 500 B.C. and flourished around A.D. 750, Dzibilchaltún was in decline long before the conquistadores' arrival. But the remains of a 16th-century church suggest it had a large enough population to require a church and may have been occupied until A.D. 1600, almost a hundred years after the arrival of the Spaniards. Discovered in 1941, this site has been studied many times over the years, and more than 8,000 buildings have been mapped. The site covers an area of almost 10 square miles with a central core of almost 65 acres. At its peak as many as 40,000 people centralized their commerce and religion here. At least 12 sacbeob, the longest of which is 4,200 feet, have been unearthed; they link the areas within the confines of the site and, unlike at other Yucatán sites, none links Dzibilchaltún to other cities. Dzibilchaltún means "place of the stone writing" and at least 25 stelae have been unearthed, many of them reused in buildings built after original ones were covered or destroyed.

Today the most interesting buildings are grouped around the **Cenote Xlacah,** the sacred well, and include a complex of buildings around Structure 38, the **Central Group** of temples, the raised **causeways** (or sacbeob), and the **Seven Dolls Group,** centered on the **Temple of the Seven Dolls.** It was beneath the floor of the temple that those seven weird little dolls (now in the museum) were discovered. The site is so huge (and the sun so fierce) it seems daunting to wander through the vegetation-filled site searching out the remains of the groupings here. But it's more pleasurable now that the Yucatán State Department of Ecology has added nature trails here and published a booklet (in Spanish) of birds and plants seen at various points along the mapped trail. En route you'll see pyramidal remains too. The booklet tells where in the park you are likely to see specific plants and birds, such as the splendid turquoise-browed motmot or the Aztec parakeet.

There's a small museum at the site with exhibits of stelae, figurines, pottery, and a group of seven strange clay dolls that show a variety of diseases and birth defects.

A Museum of the Maya is scheduled to open in 1995, on the grounds of Dzibilchaltún. It will be a replica of a Maya village of houses, called *nas*, staffed by Maya demonstrating traditional cooking, gardening, and folk art techniques.

To get there by bus from Mérida, go to the Progreso bus station at Calle 62 no. 524, between Calles 65 and 67. There are five buses per day Monday through Saturday at 7:10 and 9am, and 1, 2, and 3:20pm to the pueblo of Chanculob; it's a one-kilometer walk to the ruins from there. On Sunday there are only three buses to Chanculob, at 5:40 and 9am and 2pm. The return bus schedule is posted at the ticket window by the ruins. The last bus is at 4:15pm.

The site and nature trails are open daily from 9am to 5pm. Admission is $6, and free on Sunday.

PROGRESO

For another beach escape go to Progreso, a modern city facing the Gulf less than an hour from Mérida. Here the Malecón, a beautiful oceanfront drive, fronts a vast beach lined with coconut palms that's popular on weekends. A long pier or *muelle* (pronounced mu-wey-yeh) shoots out into the bay to reach water deep enough for oceangoing ships, and a few seafood restaurants face the Malecón.

From Mérida, buses to Progreso leave the special bus station (on Calle 62 at no. 524, between Calles 65 and 67) every 15 minutes during the day, starting at 5am. The trip takes 45 minutes.

In Progreso, the bus station is about four blocks south of Calle 19, which runs along the beach.

EN ROUTE TO MAYAPÁN, TICUL & UXMAL

There are two routes to the splendid archeological zone of Uxmal (Oosh-*mahl*) about 50 miles south of Mérida. The most direct one is on Highway 261 via Umán, the Hacienda Yaxcopoíl, and the ruins of Oxkintoc and Muna; the other route follows Highway 18 through Kanasin, the ruins of Mayapán, Ticul, and Santa Elena, on a scenic but meandering trip through numerous interesting villages. Both routes are described below.

It's possible to see Uxmal on a day trip by bus from Mérida. Sunday is a good day to go, since admission is free and means a savings of $24 per person, if you go to Uxmal and nearby ruins, or $30 if Loltún is included. **Autotransportes del Sur** in Mérida has a special day trip to Uxmal and nearby ruins (see "Departing," at the beginning of this section).

The best way to visit the sites is to rent a car, stay two nights in Uxmal or Ticul, and allow two full days of sightseeing.

VIA YAXCOPOÍL & MUNA From Mérida via Umán, it's 20 miles to the Hacienda Yaxcopoíl and 40 miles to Muna on Highway 261. Uxmal is 10 miles from Muna.

Ten miles beyond Umán is **Yaxcopoíl**. This tongue-twisting Maya name belongs to a fascinating old hacienda on the right side of the road between Mérida and Uxmal. It's difficult to reach by bus.

Take a half hour to tour the house, factory, outbuildings, and museum. You'll see that such haciendas were the administrative, commercial, and social centers of vast private domains—almost little principalities—carved out of the Yucatecan jungle. It's open Monday through Saturday from 8am to dusk and Sunday from 9am to 1pm.

A Stop En Route at Oxkintok   When you leave Yaxcopoíl, you still have almost 30 miles to drive to reach Uxmal. On the way you'll pass Oxkintok, a Maya archeological site that's newly opened to the public. To get there continue on Highway 180 south through Umán, past the hacienda of Yaxcopoíl and the village of Maxcanú. Just as you would to reach Uxmal, turn left at the crossroads of Highways 180 and 184. At the village of Calcehtok you'll see a sign pointing right to the ruins of Oxkintok, which are down a dirt road about ¾ of a mile. This is also an easy trip either from Tikul or Uxmal. Only 35 miles south of Mérida and 28 miles northeast of Uxmal, it dates from Preclassic times—perhaps as early as 300 B.C. Excavations by the Spanish government between 1985 to 1991, under the auspices of Mexico's Instituto Nacional de Antropología e Historia (INAH), have cleared the site and made it available to tourists.

Although it is not a newly discovered site, and before recent excavations it suffered extensive looting, new discoveries still thrilled archeologists. It covers almost three square miles. Although the architecture is predominantly Puuc, as in other sites nearby, scholars believe it was an important crossroads because there is great evidence of influence from as far away as the Usumacinta River (which borders Guatemala), Campeche, and the Petén area of southern Yucatán and northern Guatemala. The greatest construction phase took place from A.D. 300 to 550, but building and habitation continued until at least the late Classic period around A.D. 1000. Archeologists mapped more than 200 buildings during their six seasons of work. At least 12 are pyramids, and numerous tombs were uncovered yielding heretofore undiscovered tombs deep inside the pyramids and many jade masks. Other remarkable discoveries include a crocodile carved from a conch shell, a human figure carved possibly from the rib bone of a manatee, numerous hieroglyphs, carved lintels, and stelae.

Visible today are three groups of structures—the Santunsat, Ch'ich Palace, and the Devil's Palace. Of these the most interesting is probably the Santunsat, which was isolated and for some unknown reason not included in the grand urban plan of the city. Its depths hid a labyrinth of tunnels, passageways, stairs, and rooms, one of which was a tomb. Scholarly interpretation of this building concludes that the three levels may represent the underworld, the earth, and the universe. Because of the placement of windows it was probably also an observatory. Villagers from the surrounding area believe it was a place of religious learning and initiation. In Maxcanú one legend says it was from this group of buildings that the first men to populate the area came. And still others believe it still harbors *aluxes* and *duendes* (miniature mythical characters). The 10-room Ch'ich Palace still has two of the four anthropomorphic columns that once decorated the portico. The Devil's Palace is so named because of an anthropomorphic column with holes in its head that supports the northern portico. Archeologists did not pursue the regional legend that says Oxkintok is linked to Mérida (once the ancient Maya city of Tihó) by an underground tunnel.

Visually the site doesn't begin to rival Uxmal or Chichén-Itzá, but it's interesting if you are following a ruins itinerary. The site is open daily from 8am to 5pm. Admission is $6, and free on Sunday; use of a video camera costs an additional $8.50.

VIA KANASIN, MAYAPÁN & TICUL Taking Calle 67 east, head out of Mérida toward Kanasin and Acanceh (Ah-*kahn*-keh), about 12 miles. When Calle 67 ends, bear right, then left at the next big intersection. Follow the wide, divided highway complete with speed bumps. At Mérida's *circunvalación* (road that circles the city), you'll see signs to Cancún. You can either cross the circunvalación and go straight into Kanasin or turn and follow the Cancún signs for a short distance then follow the signs into Kanasin.

In Kanasin, watch for signs that say CIRCULACIÓN. As in many Yucatán towns, you're being redirected to follow a one-way street through the urban area. Go past the market, the church, and the main square on your left, and continue straight out of town. The next village you come to, at km 10, is San Antonio Tehuit, an old henequén hacienda. At km 13 is Tepich, another hacienda-centered village, with those funny little henequén-cart tracks crisscrossing the main road. After Tepich comes Petectunich, and finally Acanceh.

A Stop En Route at Acanceh Overlooking Acanceh's main square, there's a partially restored pyramid to the left of the church, and the large **Stucco Palace** a couple of blocks from there. There's little stucco left on the palace, but to find it, follow the street to the right of the market, turn right at the first corner, left at the next one, and right again. The grass-covered pyramid is about halfway down the block. A few animal figures in stucco relief are preserved under a makeshift cover on top. You'll have to find the custodian, Anatolio Narvaez, to unlock the gate to either pyramid; his house is on the street to the right of the main square and about halfway down opposite the market. Even if you just see the pyramid from the street without tracking down Sr. Narvaez for the key, it's a good excuse to detour through the village with its whitewashed rock walls and tidy oval-shaped thatched huts.

From Acanceh's main square, turn right (around the statue of a smiling deer) and head for **Tecoh,** with its huge crumbling church (5½ miles away) and **Telchaquillo** (seven miles farther). This route takes you past several old Yucatecan haciendas, each complete with its big house, chapel, factory with smokestack, and workers' houses.

Shortly after the village of Telchaquillo, a sign on the right side of the road will point to the entrance of the ruins of Mayapán.

2. MAYAPÁN & TICUL

MAYAPÁN

Founded by the man-god Quetzalcoatl (Kukulkán in Maya) in about A.D. 1007, Mayapán ranked in importance with Chichén-Itzá and Uxmal and covered at least 2½ square miles. For more than two centuries it was the capital of a Maya confederation of city-states that included Chichén and Uxmal. But before the year 1200 the rulers of Mayapán ended the confederation by attacking and conquering Chichén, and by forcing the rulers of Uxmal to live as vassals in Mayapán. Eventually a successful revolt by the captive Maya rulers brought down Mayapán, which was abandoned during the mid-1400s.

Though ruined, the main pyramid is still impressive. Next to it is a large cenote (natural limestone cavern, used as a well), now full of trees, bushes, and banana plants. Beside it is a small temple with columns and a fine high-relief mask of Chaac, the hook-nosed rain god. Jungle paths lead to other small temples, including

El Caracol, with its circular tower. These piles of stones give no idea of how the walled city of Mayapán appeared in its heyday. Supplied with water from 20 cenotes, it had more than 3,000 buildings in its enclosed boundaries of several square miles. Today, all is covered in dense jungle.

Admission is $6, and free on Sunday. Use of a video camera costs an additional $8.50. The site is open from 8am to 5pm daily.

FROM MAYAPÁN TO TICUL The road is a good one but directional signs through the villages are nonexistent. Stop and ask for directions frequently. From Mayapán continue along Highway 18 to Tekit (five miles), turn right, and go to Mama on a road as thrilling as a roller-coaster ride (4⅓ miles), then turn right again for Chapab (eight miles).

If you're ready for a break, take time out to visit the **tortilla factory** in Chapab. Turn left when you see a building named Centro Educativo Comunitario Chapab and the factory is a couple of blocks farther on the left. As you came into town you probably noticed young Maya girls with masa dough up to their elbows carrying large pans and buckets of it atop their heads. They're returning from the daily ritual of corn grinding and they'll use the masa to make their own tortillas at home. Other youngsters are carrying out large stacks of finished tortillas hot off the press. The Matos Sabino family owns the factory and they don't mind if you stop in and watch the action, which goes on daily from 8am to around 3pm. Better yet, buy some tortillas, fill them with avocados, tomatoes, and cheese and have a picnic on the lawn across the street.

After Chapab you reach Ticul (6¼ miles), the largest town in the region.

TICUL

GETTING THERE There are frequent buses from Mérida. The Ticul bus station is near the town center on Calle 24 between Calles 25 and 25A. For car information see the routes above.

Driving has become very difficult in Ticul, since cars, buses, trucks, and bicycles all compete for space on the narrow, potholed streets. Consider parking several blocks from the center of town and walking from there. Directional signs that allow drivers to bypass the most congested part of town are beginning to appear.

DEPARTING There are first-class buses to Mérida daily at 7 and 10am and 5:30 and 7pm. Also check with the drivers of the minivans that line up across from the bus station.

Buses run twice hourly to Muna, where you can change buses to Uxmal.

ESSENTIALS The telephone area code is 997.

SPECIAL EVENTS Ticul's annual festival, complete with bullfights, dancing, and carnival games, is held during the first few days of April.

Many of the 27,000 inhabitants of this sprawling town make their living embroidering *huipiles* (the Maya women's shiftlike dress), weaving straw hats, making shoes and gold-filigree jewelry, and shaping pottery. Workshops and stores featuring most of these items are easy to find, especially in the market area.

The market, most hotels, and Los Almendros, Ticul's best-known restaurant, are on the main street, **Calle 23,** also called the Calle Principal.

SHOPPING

Ticul is best known for the cottage industry of huipil embroidery and the manufacture of ladies' dress shoes, and it's a center for large-size, commercially produced pottery. Most of the widely sold sienna-colored pottery painted with Maya designs comes from Ticul. If it's a cloudy, humid day the potters may not be working, since part of the process requires sun-drying. But they still welcome visitors to make purchases of finished pieces.

ARTESANÍAS POPULARES, Calle 21 no. 239, between Calles 32 and 34.
The Chan family, owners of the Hotel Bougambillias Familiar, also own a pottery factory that produces much of the Maya motif pottery you see for sale in the Yucatán, as well as more traditional pottery for gardeners. Drop in between 8am and 5pm Tuesday through Friday and Saturday until noon.

WHERE TO STAY

Only 12 miles northeast of Uxmal, Ticul is an ideal spot from which to launch regional sightseeing and avoid the high cost of hotels at Uxmal.

HOTEL BOUGAMBILLIAS FAMILIAR, Calle 23 no. 291A, Ticul, Yuc.
97860 Tel. 997/2-0139. 20 rms. FAN
$ Rates: $20 single; $28 double with one or two beds.
Ticul's nicest inn is more like a motel, with parking outside the room section. The half-circle drive into the arched entrance is lined with plants and pottery from the owner's local factory. Ceiling-height windows don't let in much light, but the spotlessly clean rooms have saggy beds, cool tile floors, and ready hot water. In back is the hotel's pretty restaurant, Xux-Cab (see "Where to Dine," below).
To find it, follow Calle 23 through Ticul on the road to Muna. It's on the right before you leave town and past the Santa Elena turnoff.

HOTEL SAN MIGUEL, Calle 28 no. 195, Ticul, Yuc. 97860. No phone. 20
rms. FAN
$ Rates: $9 single; $15 double with one bed; $18 double with two beds.
Some people might call the simply furnished rooms in the Hotel San Miguel Mexican cell-block style. Though it's not the Ritz, the price is right and each room has a private bath and a window on a narrow exterior corridor facing a sunny wall. It's mere steps from the market. From the market, walk half a block north, then turn left on Calle 28; the narrow doorway to the hotel is on the left.

WHERE TO DINE

Good restaurants are few in Ticul, but besides those listed here, don't overlook the busy **market** on Calle 23, where you can pick up fresh fruit and grab a bite at one of the little eateries.

LOS ALMENDROS, Calle 23 no. 207. Tel. 2-0021.
Cuisine: YUCATECAN.
$ Prices: Appetizers $3.75–$4.25; main courses $6–$8.
Open: Daily 9am–7pm.
Set in a big old Andalusian-style house, this is the original of a chain with branches now in Mérida and Cancún. The Maya specialties include *papadzules* (sauce-covered, egg-filled tortillas), poc-chuc, and the spicy pollo ticuleño. As in the Mérida branch, the qualify of food varies. Ask for the illustrated menu in English that explains the dishes in detail. To find Los Almendros, walk two blocks south of the market and it's on the left.

RESTAURANT LOS DELFINES, Calle 27, no. 216. No phone.
Cuisine: MEXICAN.
$ Prices: Appetizers $3.75–$7.50; main courses $4–$7.
Open: Daily 8am–6pm.

The new owners of my favorite, Restaurant Delfine, bought the name and reopened in a beautiful garden setting near the center of town. The menu is similar to the old Delfine's with chiles rellenos stuffed with shrimp, carne raja asado with achiote, pork, garlic-flavored fish, and other seafood. If the restaurant appears to be closed, just bang on the large metal doors and someone will open.

From Calle 23 (main street) go past the market and turn left on Calle 23. Go two blocks and turn right on Calle 27; it's on the left half a block farther.

XUX-CAB, Calle 21, behind the Hotel Bougambillias Familiar. Tel. 2-0139.
Cuisine: REGIONAL.
$ Prices: Main courses $5–$7.
Open: Daily 8am–8pm.

This partly open-air and partly sheltered restaurant showed promise at first, but is often disappointing because although the menu lists 16 *platillos* (plate meals), only a few may actually be offered. Ask what they have, then decide what to order. Then who knows—a delicious appetizer may appear gratis with your alcoholic drink. Roving musicians often play in the afternoon and evening, making it a pleasant place to relax and eat. To find it, pass through central Ticul on Calle 23, towards Muna several blocks past the market; turn into the Hotel Bougambillias and park in back.

AN EXCURSION TO YAXNIC CAVES

Just outside the village of Yotolín (also spelled Yohtolín), which is between Ticul and Oxkutcab, are some impressive caves called **Yaxnic** (Yash-*neek*), on the grounds of the old, private Hacienda Yotolín. Virtually undeveloped and full of colored stalactites and stalagmites, the caves are visited by means of a perilous descent in a basket let down on a rope.

Arranging this spelunking challenge takes time, but since the thrill may be worth it, here's the procedure. Several days (or even weeks or months) before your intended cave descent, go to Yotolín and ask for the house of the *comisario*. He will make the proper introductions to the hacienda owners, who in turn will tell you how to prepare for the experience.

EN ROUTE TO UXMAL

From Ticul to Uxmal follow the main street through town. At the edge of town turn left at the sign to Santa Elena. It's 10 miles to Santa Elena; then, at the highway, cut back right for about two miles to Uxmal.

Or drive straight through Ticul, and it's 14 miles to Muna. At Muna, turn left and head south on Highway 261 to Uxmal, 10 miles away.

3. UXMAL

50 miles S of Mérida, 12 miles SW of Ticul

GETTING THERE By Bus Autotransportes del Sur buses (tel. 24-9055 in Mérida) to Uxmal depart from Mérida at 6 and 9am, noon, and 3pm; return trips are at 11:30am and 3:30 and 7:30pm—wait at the highway by the turnoff to the ruins, across from the Hacienda Uxmal hotel. The same company offers one bus daily on the Mérida-Uxmal-Kabah-Sayil-Labná-Xlapak route, departing at 9am. The trip costs $18, departing Mérida at 8am, returning at 2pm. The driver allows passengers to spend around 90 minutes at Uxmal and 30 minutes at each of the other archeological sites before returning. There is no evening departure for the sound-and-light show at Uxmal.

By Car   Two routes are described above, either on Highway 261 from Mérida returning through Muna, or via Highway 18 from Mérida via Kanasin and Mayapán. *Note:* There's no gasoline at Uxmal, so top off the tank in Mérida, Muna, or Ticul before continuing

ESSENTIALS   Admission   Admission to the archeological site of Uxmal is $6; to Kabah, Sayil, Labná, Xlapak, or Loltún, it's $6 each. A Sunday visit to the ruins will save money since admission is free to Uxmal and other recommended sites nearby, except Loltún, where admission is $2.50 on Sunday.

Information   The visitor's center at the ruins is open daily from 8am to 10pm, and has a restaurant, toilets, a first aid station, and shops selling soft drinks, ice cream, film, batteries, and books.

Restaurants   Restaurants at hotels near Uxmal and at the visitor's center are expensive, so if you're coming for the day, the smartest thing to do is bring a lunch.

Uxmal consists of the archeological site and its visitor's center, four hotels, and a highway restaurant. There are no phones except those at the hotels. Most public buses pick up and let off passengers on the highway at the entrance to the ruins. Close to Uxmal are other sites—Sayil, Kabah, Xlapak, Labná, and Loltún—worth visiting; see "Easy Excursions from Uxmal," below.

SEEING THE RUINS

After passing through the admission area and visitor's center, prepare yourself for one of the highlights of your Yucatán vacation, for the ruins of Uxmal, noted for their rich geometric stone facades, are the most beautiful in the Yucatán. Remains of an agricultural society indicate that the area was occupied possibly as early as 800 B.C. However, the great building period took place a thousand years later between A.D. 700 and 1000, during which time the population probably reached 25,000. Then Uxmal fell under the sway of the Xiú princes (who may have come from the Valley of Mexico) after the year 1000. Four and a half centuries later the Xiú conquered Mayapán (1440s), and not long after, the glories of Maya ended when the Spanish conquistadores arrived.

The site is open daily from 8am to 5pm. Admission is $6 (free on Sunday), and there's an $8.50 charge to bring in a video camera. Parking is $1.

Guided Tours   Guides at the entrance of Uxmal give tours in a variety of languages and charge $25 for one person or a group. The guides frown on this (they'd rather you pay as a single), but you can hang around the entrance and ask other English-speakers if they would like to join you in a tour and split the cost. As at other sites, their information is not up-to-date, but you'll see areas and architectural details you might otherwise miss.

The Pyramid of the Magician   As you enter the ruins, note the *chultún* (cistern) inside the entrance to the right. Besides the natural underground cisterns

FROMMER'S ARCHEOLOGY NOTES
THE SERPENT MOTIF

Throughout Mesoamerica the serpent motif appears embellished in stone and gold, on murals, ceramics, and shells. Through its connection to water and land, the serpent represented fertility to the native cultures. Life depended on the land's production, so it is no wonder that this visually striking motif was so frequently represented.

It's memorable as much for its frequent renditions throughout Mesoamerica as it is for the fabulous artistry required to produce it. A stone rattlesnake undulates across the facade of the Nunnery complex at Uxmal. The Governor's Palace there projects 103 masks of Chaac (the rain god) rising and falling across its facade like a slithering serpent.

Light and shadow during the summer and winter solstices at Chichén-Itzá's El Castillo create the body of a serpent on the stairway, connecting to the multi-ton head and open mouth of a serpent. At Chichén-Itzá's Temple of the Warriors, and other places, a human head often appears from the wide-open mouth of a serpent.

This motif appeared in the Yucatán before Toltec influence. Quetzalcoatl, the legendary god/king of the Toltecs, was characterized as a serpent wearing the feathers of the queztal bird, as was Kukulkán (the Maya representation of Quetzalcoatl). Vision serpents, yet another form of the plumed serpent, appear in Maya carvings, often in association with bloodletting (induced to produce hallucinations).

(such as cenotes) formed in the porous limestone, chultunes were the principal source of water for the Maya.

Just beyond the chultún, Uxmal's dominant building, the Pyramid of the Magician (also called the Soothsayer's Temple), with its unique rounded sides, looms majestically on the right as you enter. The name comes from a legend about a mystical dwarf who reached adulthood rapidly after being hatched from an egg, and who built this pyramid in one night. Beneath it are five temples, since it was common practice for the Maya to build new structures atop old ones, even before the old structures were ruined.

The pyramid is unique because of its oval shape, height and steepness, and its odd doorway on the opposite (west) side near the top. The doorway''s heavy ornamentation, a characteristic of the Chenes style, features 12 stylized masks of the rain god Chaac and the doorway itself is a huge open-mouthed Chaac mask.

The View from the Top   The tiring and even dangerous climb is worth it for the view. From on top you can see Uxmal's entire layout. Next to the Pyramid of the Magician, to the west, is the Nunnery Quadrangle and left of it a conserved ballcourt, south of which are several large complexes. The biggest building among them is the Governor's Palace, and behind it lies the partially restored Great Pyramid. In the distance is the Dovecote, a palace with a lacy roofcomb (false front) that looks perfect for an apartment complex for pigeons. From this vantage point note how Uxmal is special among Maya sites for the use of broad terraces or platforms constructed to support the buildings; look closely and you'll see that the Governor's Palace is not on a natural hill or rise, but on a huge square terrace, as is the Nunnery Quadrangle.

The Nunnery The 16th-century Spanish historian Fray Diego López de Cogullado gave the building its name because it resembled Spanish monasteries. Possibly it was a military academy or a training school for princes, who may have lived in the 70-odd rooms. The buildings were constructed at different times: The northern one was first, then the southern one, then east, then west, with the western building having the most richly decorated facade composed of intertwined stone snakes and numerous masks of the hook-nosed rain god Chaac.

The corbelled archway on the south was once the main entrance to the Nunnery complex; as you head toward it out of the quadrangle to the south, look above each doorway in that section for the motif of a Maya cottage, or *na*, looking just as they do throughout the Yucatán today. All of this wonderful decoration has been restored, of course—it didn't look this good when the archeologists discovered it.

The Ballcourt The unimpressive ballcourt is preserved to prevent further decay. Keep it in mind to compare with the magnificent restored court at Chichén-Itzá.

The Turtle House Up on the terrace south of the ballcourt is a little temple decorated with colonnade motif on the facade, and a border of turtles. Though small and simple it's one of the gems of Uxmal.

The Governor's Palace In size and intricate stonework, this is Uxmal's masterwork, an imposing three-level edifice with a 320-foot-long mosaic facade done in the Puuc style. Puuc means "hilly country," the name given to the hills nearby and thus to the predominant style of pre-Hispanic architecture found here. Uxmal has many examples of Puuc decoration, characterized by elaborate stonework from door tops to the roofline. Fray Cogullado, who named the Nunnery, also gave this building its name, and the Governor's Palace may have been just that: the administrative center of the Xiú principality, which included the region around Uxmal. It probably had astrological significance as well. For years scholars pondered why this building was constructed slightly turned from adjacent buildings. Originally they thought the strange alignment was because of the sacbe, which starts at this building and ends 11 miles distant at the ancient city of Kabah. But recently scholars of archeoastrology (a relatively new science) discovered that the central doorway, which is larger than the others, is in perfect alignment with Venus. Before you leave the Governor's Palace, note the elaborate stylized headdress patterned in stone over the central doorway. Standing back from the building on the east side, note how the 103 stone masks of Chaac undulate across the facade like a serpent and end at the corners where there are columns of masks.

The Great Pyramid A massive, nine-level, partially restored structure, it has interesting motifs of birds, probably macaws, on its facade, as well as a huge mask. The view from the top is wonderful.

The Dovecote It wasn't built to house doves, but it could well do the job in its lacy roofcomb, a kind of false front on a rooftop. The building is remarkable in that roofcombs weren't a common feature of temples in the Puuc hills, although you will see one (of a very different style) on El Mirador at Sayil.

Light-and-Sound Show A 45-minute sound-and-light show is staged each evening, in Spanish for $3 at 7pm, and in English for $4 at 9pm. The special sound-and-light bus from Mérida only stays for the Spanish show. If you stay for the English, you'll have to take a taxi back to Mérida. After the impressive show, the chant "Chaaac, Chaaac" will echo in your mind for weeks.

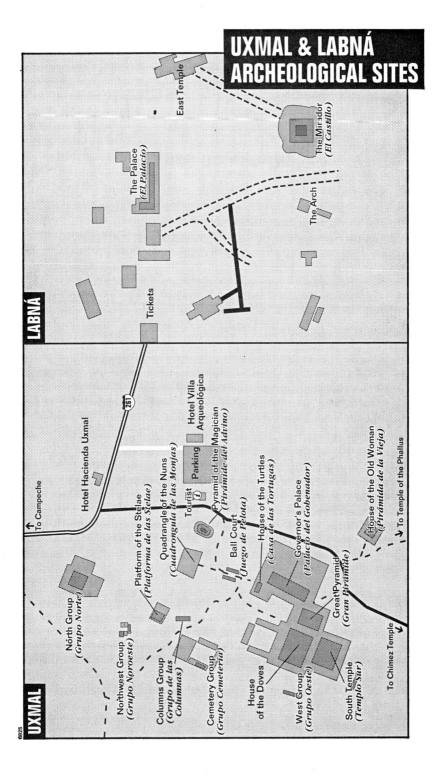

UXMAL & LABNÁ ARCHEOLOGICAL SITES

LABNÁ

East Temple

The Palace
(El Palacio)

The Mirador
(El Castillo)

The Arch

Tickets

UXMAL

← To Campeche

Hotel Hacienda Uxmal

261

North Group
(Grupo Norte)

Northwest Group
(Grupo Noroeste)

Platform of the Stelae
(Plataforma de las Stelae)

Quadrangle of the Nuns
(Cuadrángula de las Monjas)

Columns Group
(Grupo de las Columnas)

Cemetery Group
(Grupo Cemetería)

Tourist
ℹ

Parking

Hotel Villa Arqueológica

Pyramid of the Magician
(Pirámide del Adivino)

Ball Court
(Juego de Pelota)

House of the Turtles
(Casa de las Tortugas)

Governor's Palace
(Palacio del Gobenador)

House of the Doves

West Group
(Grupo Oeste)

Great Pyramid
(Gran Pirámide)

South Temple
(Templo Sur)

House of the Old Woman
(Pirámide de la Vieja)

↘ To Temple of the Phallus

To Chimez Temple ↘

6825

IMPRESSIONS

At Uxmal the buildings have a truly artistic grandeur which makes them among the most glorious structures of the world. Versailles, medieval cathedrals, the tombs of the Moguls in India, the Parthenon itself, have little or no edge on the architectural beauty and majesty of Uxmal.
—MICHEL PEISSEL, *THE LOST WORLD OF QUINTANA ROO*, 1963

WHERE TO STAY

Unlike Chichén-Itzá, which has several classes of hotels from which to choose, Uxmal has (with one exception) only one type: comfortable but expensive. This might just be the place to blow your budget. If you've already done that by renting a car, more affordable rooms can be found at nearby Ticul.

HOTEL HACIENDA UXMAL, Carretera Mérida-Uxmal km 80, Uxmal, Yuc. 97844. Tel. 99/25-2122, or toll free 800/235-4079 in the U.S. 75 rms. A/C (10 rms) FAN (65 rms) TV

$ Rates: High season $125 single or double; low season $95 single or double.
One of my favorites, this is also the oldest hotel in Uxmal. Located on the highway across from the ruins, it was built as the headquarters for the archeological staff years ago. Rooms are large and airy, exuding a whisper of well-kept yesteryear, with patterned tile floors, heavy furniture, and well-screened windows. All rooms have ceiling fans, and air conditioning and TV are being added to all the rooms.

Guest rooms surround a handsome central garden courtyard with towering royal palms, a bar, and a swimming pool. Other facilities include a dining room and gift shop. Meals are expensive here: breakfast costs $6 to $10; lunch $8 to $16; dinner $18 to $22. A guitar trio usually plays on the patio in the evenings. Checkout time is 1pm, so you can spend the morning at the ruins and take a swim before you head out on the road again. It's on the highway opposite the road entrance to the ruins.

Mayaland Resorts, owners of the hotel, offers tour packages that include free car rentals for the nights you spend at their hotels, with no minimum stay. Mayaland also has a transfer service between the hotel and Mérida for about $30 each way.

Reservations: Contact Mayaland Resorts, Av. Colón 502, Mérida, Yuc. 97000 (tel. 99/25-2122, or toll free 800/235-4079 in the U.S.; fax 99/25-2397).

HOTEL MISIÓN PARK INN UXMAL, Carretera Mérida-Uxmal km 78, Uxmal, Yuc. 97844. Tel. and fax 99/24-7308, or toll free 800/437-7275 in the U.S. 49 rms. A/C FAN

$ Rates: $75 single; $80 double.
Though it's a distance from the archeological site, the open U form of this hotel, centered around a lovely pool, gives every room a view of the ruins. Each of the large, comfortable rooms has a balcony or terrace, but nary a stick of patio furniture for relaxing while enjoying the view of the distant rippling Puuc hills and nearby ruins protruding above the jungle. The public areas, however, are comfortably furnished. The hotel restaurant, like the others in Uxmal, is quite expensive: Breakfast runs $6; lunch or dinner, $12 to $15. The hotel is 1¼ miles north of the ruins on Highway 261.

RANCHO UXMAL, Carretera Mérida-Uxmal km 70, Calle 26 no. 166, Ticul, Yuc. 97860. No phone. 20 rms. A/C or FAN

$ Rates: $30 single or double; $5 per person campsite. **Parking:** Free; guarded.
This modest little hotel is an exception to the high-priced places near Uxmal, and it

gets better every year. Air conditioning has been added to six of the rooms, which have good screens, hot water showers, and 24-hour electricity. The restaurant has improved as well, and a full meal of poc-chuc, rice, beans, and tortillas costs about $6. It's a long hike to the ruins from here, but the manager will help you flag down a passing bus or combi, or even drive you himself if he has time. A primitive campground out back has electrical hookups and use of a shower. The hotel is 2¼ miles north of the ruins on Highway 261.

VILLA ARQUEOLÓGICA, Ruinas Uxmal, Uxmal, Yuc. 97844. Tel. 99/24-7053, or toll free 800/258-2633 in the U.S. 40 rms. A/C
$ Rates: $72 single; $84 double. **Parking:** Free; guarded.

This Club Med operation sports a beautiful layout around a plant-filled patio and a pool. It also offers a tennis court, library, and an audiovisual show on the ruins in English, French, and Spanish. The hotel driveway starts at the ruins parking lot. The serene rooms have two oversized single beds. French-inspired meals are à la carte only and cost $15 for breakfast and $25 for lunch or dinner. It's easy to find; just follow signs to the ruins, then turn left to the hotel just before the parking lot at Uxmal.

WHERE TO DINE

CAFÉ-BAR NICTE-HA, in the Hotel Hacienda Uxmal, across the highway from the turnoff to the ruins. Tel. 24-7142.
Cuisine: MEXICAN.
$ Prices: Soups and salads $2–$4; pizzas and enchiladas $8; main courses $8–$13; fixed-price lunch $12.50.
Open: Daily 1–8pm.

This small restaurant attached to the Hotel Hacienda Uxmal is visible from the crossroads entrance to the ruins. The food has improved greatly, but the prices are unreasonably high. If you eat here, take full advantage of the experience and spend a few hours by the swimming pool near the café—use is free to customers. This is a favorite spot for bus tours, so come early.

LAS PALAPAS, Hwy. 261. No phone
Cuisine: MEXICAN.
$ Prices: Breakfast $3; comida corrida $7–$8.50; soft drinks $1.
Open: Daily 9am–5pm.

Three miles north of the ruins on the road to Mérida you'll find this pleasant restaurant with open-air walls and a large thatched palapa roof. The personable owner, María Cristina Choy, has the most reasonable dining prices around. Individual diners can sometimes become lost in the crowd if a busload of tourists arrives, but otherwise the service is fine and the food is quite good. The comida corrida comes with meat, salad, rice, and beans.

There's also a small gift shop there with regional crafts and a few books. The owner's brother-in-law was opening a trailer park nearby.

EASY EXCURSIONS FROM UXMAL
THE OTHER MAYA CITIES

South and west of Uxmal are several other Maya cities worth exploring. Though smaller in scale than either Uxmal or Chichén-Itzá, each has its gems of Maya architecture. The facade of masks on the Palace of Masks at Kabah, the enormous palace at Sayil, and the fantastic caverns of Loltún may be among the high points of your trip. These sites are best photographed in the afternoon light.

All of these sites are currently undergoing excavation and reconstruction, and some buildings may be roped off when you visit.

Getting There   Kabah is 17 miles southeast of Uxmal. From there it's only a few miles to Sayil. Xlapak (Shla-*pahk*) is almost within walking distance (through the jungle) from Sayil, and Labná just a bit farther east. A short drive east from Labná brings you to the caves of Loltún.

If you aren't driving, a daily bus from Mérida goes to all these sites, with the exception of Loltún. (See "By Bus" under "Departing," at the beginning of Section 1, earlier in this chapter for more details.)

To reach Loltún by public transportation, take a bus running every half hour from Mérida to the town of Oxkutzcab, a 1¾-hour trip. From there, a truck (or more expensive, a taxi) will take you the additional 20 minutes to the caves. But there's no reliable return transportation unless your taxi waits.

KABAH   If you're off to Kabah, head southwest on Highway 261 to Santa Elena (8½ miles), then south to Kabah (8 miles).

The ancient city of Kabah is on both sides along the highway. From Uxmal, turn right into the parking lot.

The most outstanding building at Kabah is the huge **Palace of Masks,** or Codz Poop ("rolled-up mat"), named from a motif in its decoration. You'll notice it first on the right up on a terrace. Its outstanding feature is the Chenes facade, completely covered in a repeated pattern of 250 masks of the rain god Chaac, each one with curling remnants of Chaac's elephant trunk–like nose. There's nothing like this facade in all of Maya architecture. For years stone-carved parts of this building lay lined up in the weeds like pieces of a puzzle awaiting the master puzzlemaker to put them in place. Now workers are positioning the parts in place, including the broken roofcomb. Sculptures from this building are in the museums of anthropology in Mérida and Mexico City.

Once you've seen the Palace of Masks, you've seen the best of Kabah. But you should take a look at the other buildings. Just behind and to the left of the Codz Poop is the **Palace Group** (also called the East Group), with a fine Puuc-style colonnaded facade. Originally it had 32 rooms. On the front you see seven doors, two of them divided by columns, which is a common feature of Puuc architecture. Recent restoration has added a beautiful L-shaped colonnaded extension to the left front. Further restoration is underway at Kabah, so there may be more to see when you arrive.

Across the highway, a large, conical dirt-and-rubble mound (on your right) was once the **Great Temple,** or **Teocalli.** Past it is a **great arch** that was much wider at one time, and may have been a monumental gate into the city. A sacbe linked this arch to a point at Uxmal. Compare this corbelled arch to the one at Labná (below), which is in much better shape.

The site is open daily from 8am to 5pm. Admission is $6, but free on Sunday; use of a video camera anytime costs $8.50.

SAYIL   Just about three miles south of Kabah is the turnoff (left/east) to Sayil, Xlapak, Labná, Loltún, and Oxkutzcab. And 2½ miles along this road are the ruins of Sayil (which means "place of the ants").

Sayil is famous for **El Palacio,** the tremendous, more-than-100-room palace that is a masterpiece of Maya architecture. Impressive for its simple grandeur, the building's facade, on three terraced levels, is breathtaking with its rows of columns and colonettes, which give it a Minoan appearance. On the second level, notice the upside-down stone figure of the diving god over the doorway; it's a motif used at

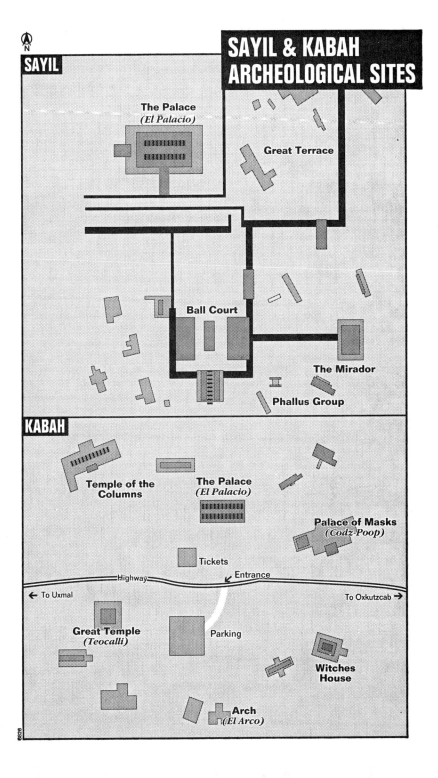

Tulum several centuries later and signifies the god of bees and honey. From the top of El Palacio there's a great view of the Puuc hills. Sometimes it's difficult to tell which are hills and which are unrestored pyramids, as little temples peep out at unlikely places from the jungle. The large circular basin on the ground below the palace is an artificial catch basin for a chultún (cistern), since this region has no natural cenotes (wells) to catch rainwater.

Off in the jungle past El Palacio is **El Mirador,** a small temple with an oddly slotted roofcomb. Beyond El Mirador, a crude **stele** has a phallic idol carved on it, with greatly exaggerated proportions.

It's open daily from 8am to 5pm. Admission is $6 Monday through Saturday, free on Sunday.

XLAPAK   Xlapak (pronounced Shla-*pahk*) is a small site with one building; it's 3½ miles down the road from Sayil. The **Palace at Xlapak** bears the masks of the rain god Chaac. It's open from 8am to 5pm daily and the admission is $6 (free on Sunday); to use your video camera costs an additional $8.50.

LABNÁ   Labná, which dates between A.D. 600 and 900, is 18 miles from Uxmal, and only 1¼ miles past Xlapak. Like other sites in the Yucatán, it's also undergoing significant restoration and conservation. Description placards fronting the main buildings are in Spanish, English, and German.

The first thing you see on the left as you enter is **El Palacio,** a magnificent Puuc-style building, much like the one at Sayil but in poorer condition. There is an enormous mask of Chaac over a doorway with big banded eyes, a huge snout nose, and jagged teeth around a small mouth that seems on the verge of speaking. Jutting out on one corner is a highly stylized serpent's mouth, out of which pops a human head with a completely calm expression. From the front here you can gaze out to the enormous grassy interior grounds flanked by vestiges of unrestored buildings and jungle. And from El Palacio you can walk across the interior grounds on a newly re-constructed sacbe leading to **Labná's corbelled arch,** famed for its ornamental beauty and for its representation of what many such arches must have looked like at other sites. This one has been extensively restored, although only remnants of the roofcomb can be seen, and it was part of a more elaborate structure that is completely gone. Chaac's face is on the corners of one facade, and stylized Maya huts are fashioned in stone above the doorways. You pass through the arch to **El Mirador,** or **El Castillo,** as the rubble-formed, pyramid-shaped structure is called. Towering on the top is a singular room crowned with a roofcomb etched against the sky. There's a refreshment and gift stand with bathrooms at the entrance. It's open daily from 8am to 5pm. Admission is $6 (free on Sunday). There's an extra $8.50 fee to use your video camera.

LOLTÚN   The caverns of Loltún are 18½ miles past Labná on the way to Oxkutzcab, on the left side of the road. The fascinating caves, home of ancient Maya, were also used as a refuge and fortress during the War of the Castes (1847–1901). Inside, you can examine statuary, wall carvings and paintings, chultunes (cisterns), and other signs of Maya habitation, but the grandeur and beauty of the caverns alone is impressive.

In front of the entrance is an enormous stone phallus. The cult of the phallic symbol originated in the south of Veracruz and appeared in the Yucatán between A.D. 200 and 500. The entrance fee is $6, $2.50 on Sunday, and 1½-hour-long tours in Spanish are given at 9:30 and 11am, and 1:30, 2, and 3pm every day. Before going, confirm these times at the information desk at Uxmal.

To return to Mérida from Loltún, drive the 4½ miles to Oxkutzcab, and from there head north on Highway 184 to Ticul (12 miles), Muna, and Mérida (65 miles).

OXKUTZCAB

Oxkutzcab (Ohsh-*kootz*-kahb, pop. 21,000), seven miles from Loltún, is the heartland of Yucatán's fruit-growing region, particularly known for oranges. The tidy village, centered by a beautiful 16th-century church and the market, is worth a stop if for no other reason than to eat at La Cabaña Suiza before heading back to Mérida, Uxmal, or Ticul. During the last week in October and first week in November is the **Orange Festival** and the village goes all out with a carnival and orange displays in and around the central plaza.

Where to Stay

LOS TUCAÑES, Calle 64 no. 999, Oxkutzcab, Yuc. 97860. Tel. 99/75-0348. 20 rms. A/C FAN

$ Rates: $20 single or double with fan; $26 single or double with A/C. **Parking:** Free; guarded.

If you have a car, Oxkutzcab is an ideal place to stay while you're touring the Puuc region. The town is far quieter than Ticul, and accommodations and meals far less expensive than those at Uxmal. Archeologists and anthropologists working in the area use Los Tucanes as their base. All rooms have hammock hooks and saggy mattresses; red, gold, and black is the predominate color scheme. The hot water is unpredictable. The hotel boasts the only disco between Mérida and Campeche, the Centro Nocturna El Huerto. The restaurant (with pool table) is open daily from 9am to 9pm. The potential for nighttime noise is high; bring earplugs. Los Tucanes is by the hospital on the outskirts of town. Entering from Mérida, turn left one block after the Pemex station.

Where to Dine

LA CABAÑA SUIZA, Calle 54 no. 101. Tel. 99/75-0057.
  Cuisine: CHARCOAL-GRILLED MEAT/MEXICAN.
$ Prices: Meat dishes $5.50; soft drinks and orange juice $1.
  Open: Daily 7:30am–6:30pm.

It's worth a trip from Loltún, Ticul, or Uxmal just to eat the delicious charcoal-grilled meat at this unpretentious eatery, dripping with colorful plants, that lies in a quiet neighborhood. Park in the gravel courtyard, then take a seat at one of the metal tables either under the palapa roof or outdoors where caged birds sing. Señora María Antonia Puerto de Pacho runs the spotless place with an iron hand, and either she or one of her daughters provides swift, friendly service. The primary menu items include filling portions of charcoal-grilled beef, pork, or chicken, all of which are served with salad, rice, tortillas, and a bowl of delicious bean soup. But you can also find a few Yucatecan specialties such as costillos entomatados, escabeche, queso relleno, and pollo pibil. The restaurant is between Calle 49 and Calle 51, three blocks south of the main square.

EN ROUTE TO CAMPECHE

From Oxkutzcab, head back 27 miles to Sayil, then south on Highway 261 to Campeche (78 miles). Along the way are several ruins and caves worth visiting.

XTACUMBILXUNA CAVES Highway 261 heads south for several miles, passing through a lofty arch marking the boundary between the states of Yucatán and Campeche. Continue on through Bolonchén de Rejón (Bolonchén means "nine wells").

About 1¾ miles south of Bolonchén a sign points west to the **Grutas de Xtacumbilxuna** (though the sign spells it XTACUMBINXUNAN). Another sign reads IT's WORTH IT TO MAKE A TRIP FROM NEW YORK TO BOLONCHÉN JUST TO SEE XTACUMBILXUNA CAVES (JOHN STEPHENS—EXPLORER). The caves are open whenever the guide is around, which is most of the time. Follow him down for the 30- or 45-minute tour in Spanish, after which a 50¢ to 75¢ tip is customary.

Legend has it that a Maya girl escaped an unhappy love affair by hiding in these vast limestone caverns, which wouldn't be hard to do, as you'll see. If she hid there, she left no trace. Unlike the fascinating caves at Loltún, filled with traces of Maya occupation, these have only the standard bestiary of limestone shapes: a dog, an eagle, a penguin, madonna and child, snake, and so on—figments of the guide's imagination.

CHENES RUINS On your route south, you can also take a detour to see several unexcavated, unspoiled ruined cities in the Chenes style. You have to be adventurous for these; pack some food and water. When you get to Hopelchén, take the turnoff for Dzibalchén. When you get to Dzibalchén (25½ miles from Hopelchén), ask for directions to Hochob, San Pedro, Dzehkabtún, El Tabasqueño, and Dzibilnocac.

EDZNÁ From Hopelchén, Highway 261 heads west, and after 26 miles you'll find yourself at the turnoff for the ruined city of Edzná, 12½ miles farther along to the south.

Once a network of Maya canals crisscrossed this entire area, making intensive cultivation possible and no doubt contributing to Edzná's wealth as a ceremonial center. But today it is more historically important than impressive to see and perhaps not worth the $6 entrance fee and the few minutes it takes to walk it all. What you'll see at this "House of Wry Faces" (that's what Edzná means) is a unique pyramid of five levels with a fine temple, complete with roofcomb on top. Several other buildings surround an open central yard. Farther back new excavations have revealed a structure with several fine stucco masks on the facade similar to those of Kohunlich in the Río Bec region near Chetumal.

The buildings at Edzná were mostly in the heavily baroque Chenes style; however, no vestiges of the distinctive decorative facades remain at Edzná. *Note:* The afternoon light is better for photographing the temple.

Back on Highway 261, it's 8½ miles to the intersection with Highway 180, and then another 19 miles to the very center of Campeche.

4. CAMPECHE

157 miles SE of Mérida, 235 miles NE of Villahermosa

GETTING THERE By Plane Aeroméxico flies once daily to and from Mexico City.

By Train Trains arrive from Palenque, Mérida, and Mexico City.

By Bus Campeche is well connected with Mérida and Villahermosa, and there are four daily buses from Uxmal.

By Car Highway 180 goes south from Mérida, passing near the basket-making village of Halacho, and Becal, the town of Panama-hat weavers. At Tenabo take the shortcut (right) to Campeche rather than going farther to the crossroads near Chencoyí. From Uxmal, Highway 261 passes near some interesting ruins and the Xtacumbilxuna caves.

DEPARTING   By Plane   The airport is several miles northeast of town. There's no collective transportation from town and taxis charge around $6 for the trip. **Aeroméxico** (tel. 6-6659) has offices at the airport. Local travel agencies can also make arrangements.

By Train   The train station is two miles northeast of the downtown waterfront, on Avenida Héroes de Nacozari, which intersects Avenida de los Gobernadores. Trains from Campeche depart for Palenque at 8am and 11pm for the nine-hour trip; and for Mérida at 5:30pm, arriving at 10:30pm. Be careful fo thievery on the train between Campeche and Palenque.

By Bus   The **Camioneros de Campeche** line (tel. 6-2332) runs second-class buses to Mérida every half hour, a two- to three-hour trip. There are direct buses to Mérida at 7am and 1:30 and 5:30pm, three daily buses to Uxmal at 7 and 11am and 5pm, and two buses to Edzná at 8am and 2:30pm (this bus drops you off and picks you up one kilometer away from the ruins). These tickets are sold on the Calle Chile side of the bus station at the Camioneros de Campeche ticket booth. **ADO** (tel. 6-0002), in the front of the station, has one first-class *de paso* bus to Palenque at 11pm and to Mérida every half hour from 5am to midnight. **Omnibus Caribe Express** has direct, deluxe service to Mérida and Cancún. Tickets are available at the main bus station, but the buses depart from the Plaza Super Diez on Avenida Ruíz Cortínez. The line may have its own terminal by the time you travel; check with the tourist office for the latest information.

By Car   For the "vía corta" (short way) to Celestún or Mérida, go north on Avenida Ruíz Cortínez, bearing left to follow the water (this becomes Avenida Pedro Saliz de Barando, but there's no sign). Follow the road as it turns inland to Highway 180, where you turn left and you're on your way (there's a gas station at the intersection). The route takes you through Becal, a village of Panama-hat makers, and Halacho, a village known for beautiful basket-making. Stores in both villages close between 2 and 4pm.

To Edaná and Uxmal, go north on either Cortínez or Gobernador and turn right on Madero, which becomes Highway 281. To Villahermosa, take Cortínez south; it becomes Highway 180.

Campeche (pop. 172,000), capital of the state bearing the same name, is a pleasant, beautifully kept coastal town with a leisurely pace.

Founded by Francisco de Córdoba in 1517 and claimed for the Spanish crown by the soldier Francisco de Montejo the Elder in 1531, it was later abandoned and refounded by Montejo the Younger in 1540. To protect against pirates who pillaged the Gulf coastal towns, the townspeople built a wall around the city in the late 1600s. Remnants of these walls, called *baluartes* (bulwarks), are among the city's proudest links with the past.

You'll be able to enjoy this charming city without the crowds, because tourists bypass Campeche on their way to Mérida in favor of the road via Kabah and Uxmal.

ORIENTATION

ARRIVING   If you arrive by plane, you'll have to take a taxi into town (for about $6) from the airport, which is several miles northeast of town.'

Campeche's **train station** is far from town, near the airport. Taxis await trains, but don't be too slow in getting to them, as they are the only means of transportation and you are very far from town. You'll have to pay whatever they charge, since there's no other means of transportation and they aren't regulated.

The **bus station** is seven long blocks from the Plaza Principal. Turn left out the front door, walk one block, and turn right at Calle 49. Go straight for five blocks, and turn left onto Calle 8; the plaza is three blocks ahead. Taxis cost around $3.

INFORMATION The **State of Campeche Office of Tourism** (tel. 981/6-5593 or 6-7364) is in the Baluarte Santa Rosa on the south side of town on Circuito Baluartes between Calles 12 and 14. It's open Monday through Friday from 9am to 9pm, Saturday from 9am to 7pm, and Sunday from 9am to 1pm.

CITY LAYOUT Most of your time in Campeche will be spent within the confines of the old city walls. The administrative center of town is the modernistic **Plaza Moch-Couoh** on the waterfront, next to which rises the modern office tower called the Edificio Poderes or Palacio de Gobierno, headquarters for the State of Campeche. Beside it is the futuristic Cámara de Diputados, or Casa de Congreso (state legislature's chamber), which looks like an enormous square clam. Just behind it, the **Parque Principal** (central park) will most likely be your reference point for touring.

Campeche boasts a systematic street-naming plan: Streets running roughly north to south have even numbers, and those running east to west have odd numbers. In addition, the streets are numbered so that numbers ascend toward the south and west. After walking around for five minutes you'll have the system down pat.

GETTING AROUND

Most of the recommended sites, restaurants, and hotels are within walking distance of the Parque Principal. Campeche isn't easy to negotiate by bus so I recommend taxis for the more distant areas.

FAST FACTS

American Express Local offices are at Calle 59 no. 4–5 (tel. 1-1010), in the Edificio Belmar on the side street opposite the Hotel Baluartes. Hours are 9am to 2pm and 5 to 7pm Monday through Friday and Saturday until noon. They don't cash traveler's checks, however.

Area Code The telephone area code is 981.

Mail The post office (correo) is in the Edificio Federal at the corner of Avenida 16 de Septiembre and Calle 53 (tel. 981/6-2134), near the Baluarte de Santiago. The telegraph office is here as well.

WHAT TO SEE & DO

With its city walls, clean brick-paved streets, friendly people, easy pace, and orderly traffic, Campeche is a lovely city, worthy of at least a day in your itinerary. Besides exploring the museums built within the city walls, stroll the streets (especially Calles 55, 57, and 59), and enjoy the typical Mexican colonial-style architecture while looking through large doorways to glimpse the colonial past: high-beamed ceilings, Moorish stone arches, and interior courtyards.

INSIDE THE CITY WALLS

As the busiest port in the region during the 1600s and 1700s, Campeche was a choice target for pirates. The Campechaños began building impressive defenses in

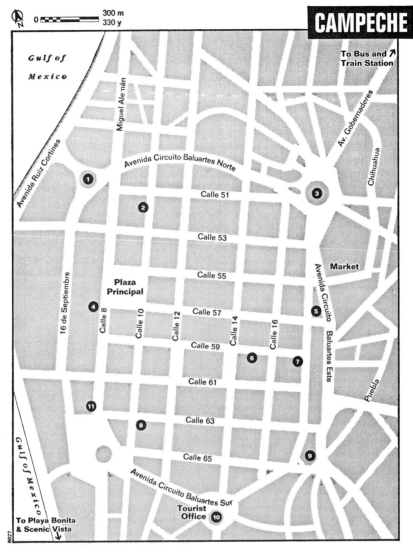

CAMPECHE

Gulf of Mexico

0 |====| 300 m
        330 y

To Bus and ↗
Train Station

Miguel Alemán

Av. Gobernadores

Chihuahua

Avenida Circuito Baluartes Norte

Calle 51

Calle 53

Calle 55

Market

Avenida Circuito Baluartes Este

Plaza
Principal

16 de Septiembre

Calle 8

Calle 10

Calle 12

Calle 14

Calle 16

Calle 57

Calle 59

Calle 61

Calle 63

Calle 65

Puebla

Gulf of Mexico

To Playa Bonita
& Scenic Vista

Avenida Circuito Baluartes Sur

Tourist
Office

Campeche

MEXICO CITY

Baluarte de la Soledad ❹
Baluarte de San Pedro ❸
Baluarte de Santiago ❶
Baluarte San Francisco ❺
Baluarte San Juan ❾
Baluarte Santa Rosa ❿
Mansión Carvajal ❷
Museo de Arte de Campeche ❽
Museo de la Ciudad ⓫
Museo Regional de Campeche ❻
Puerta de Tierra ❼

1668 and by 1704 the walls, gates, and bulwarks were in place. Today five of the seven remaining bulwarks are worthy of a visit.

A good place to begin is the pretty little zócalo, or **Plaza Principal,** bounded by Calles 55 and 57 running east and west and Calles 8 and 10 running north and south. Construction of the church on the north side of the square began in 1650, and was finally completed a century and a half later.

For a good introduction to the city, turn south from the park on Calle 8 and walk five blocks to the Museo de la Ciudad (city museum).

BALUARTE DE SAN CARLOS/MUSEO DE LA CIUDAD, Circuito Baluartes and Av. Justo Sierra. No phone.

A permanent exhibition of photographs and plans shows the city and its history. A model of the city shows how Campeche looked in its glory days and gives a good overview for touring within the city walls.

Admission: 50¢.

Open: Tues–Sun 9am–2pm and 4–8pm.

MUSEO DE ARTE DE CAMPECHE, Calles 10 and 63. Tel. 6-1424.

For colonial glitter with a touch of modern art, visit this museum, which is actually the restored Templo de San José (1640), where traveling exhibits of Mexican art are displayed. It's just three blocks inland from the Baluarte de San Carlos/Museo de la Ciudad.

Admission: Free.

Open: Tues–Fri 9am–1pm and 4–8pm.

MUSEO REGIONAL DE CAMPECHE, Calle 59 no. 36, between Calle 14 and Calle 16. Tel. 6-9111.

Two and a half blocks farther inland from the Museo de Arte de Campeche is the city's best museum, which is worthy of a prolonged visit. Housed in the former mansion of the Teniente de Rey (Royal Governor), it features original Maya artifacts, pictures, drawings, and models of Campeche's history.

The exhibit on the skull-flattening deformation of babies practiced by the Maya includes actual deformed skulls. Another highlight is the Late Classic (A.D. 600–900) Maya stele carved in a metamorphic rock that does not exist in Yucatán, but was brought hundreds of miles from a quarry.

Many clay figures show scarified faces and tools used for cutting the face, such as manta ray bones, obsidian, and jade. Other unusual pre-Hispanic artifacts include clay figures with movable arms and legs, and jade masks and jewelry from the tomb of Calakmul, a site in southern Campeche that is undergoing study and excavation.

Among the other Calakmul artifacts found in Structure VII are the remains of a human between 30 and 40 years old—you can see demonstrated the burial custom of partially burning the body, then wrapping it in a woven straw mat and cloth. In pottery vessels they discovered beans, copal, and feathers, all items deemed necessary to take the person through the underworld after death.

A model of the archeological site at Becán shows Maya society in daily life. Other displays demonstrate Maya architecture, techniques of water conservation, aspects of their religion, commerce, art, and their considerable scientific knowledge.

If you speak Spanish, ask for Kantun Puch Leocadio, a museum custodian who will walk with you through the museum pointing out things you might miss and joyfully imparting his considerable knowledge. There's a bookstore on the left as you enter.

Admission: $4.50.

Open: Tues–Sat 8am–8pm, Sun 8am–1pm.

PUERTA DE TIERRA [LAND GATE], Calle 59 at Circuito Baluartes/Av. Gobernadores.

Portraits of pirates and city founders are the attraction at this small museum. The five-ton, 1732 French cannon in the entryway was found in 1990. On Friday at 8pm there's a light-and-sound show.

Admission: Free; $3.35 for light-and-sound show.
Open: Tues–Sat 8am–2pm and 4–8pm, Sun 8am–2pm.

BALUARTE DE SAN PEDRO, Circuito Baluartes/Av. Gobernadores, at Calle 51.

Traffic skirts this prominent baluarte, which houses the **Exposición Permanente de Artesanías**. There's a small selection of crafts including intricately carved bull-horn jewelry (don't mistake it for the prohibited tortoiseshell), baskets, pottery, embroidered dresses, hats, and packaged food products, all from the state.

Admission: Free.
Open: Mon–Fri 8am–2pm and 4–8pm, Sat 9am–noon.

MANSIÓN CARVAJAL, Calle 10 no. 584. No phone.

Restoration was completed in 1992 on this early 20th-century mansion, originally the home of the Carvajal family, owners of a henequén plantation. In its latest transformation, the blue-and-white Moorish home is used for government agencies. Join the crowd purposefully striding along the gleaming black-and-white tile and up the curving marble staircase. No signs mark the entrance to the building—look for fresh blue-and-white paint inside the entrance on the west side of Calle 10 between Calles 53 and 51.

Admission: Free.
Open: Mon–Sat 9am–2pm and 4–8pm.

BALUARTE DE SANTIAGO, intersection of Av. 16 de Septiembre and Calle 49.

This is the northernmost of the seaside bulwarks, now Campeche's **Jardín Botánico** (Botanical Gardens), a shady place with both common and exotic plants. More than 250 species of plants and trees share what seems like a terribly small courtyard. Some are identified, and a film explaining the garden is shown when the projector is working.

Admission: Free.
Open: Tues–Fri 9am–3pm and 5–9pm, Sat–Sun 9am–1pm.

BALUARTE DE LA SOLEDAD, intersection of Calles 57 and 8, opposite the Plaza Principal.

This bastion houses the Sala de Estelas, or Chamber of Steles, a display of Maya votive stones brought from various sites in this ruin-rich state. Many are badly worn, but the excellent line drawings beside the stones allow you to admire their former beauty.

Admission: Free.
Open: Tues–Sat 8am–8pm, Sun 8am–1pm.

MORE ATTRACTIONS

A SCENIC VISTA For the best view of the city and sea, go south from the tourism office on Avenida Ruíz Cortínez and turn left on Ruta Escénica, which winds up to the **Fuerte San Miguel**. Built in 1771, this fort is the most important of the city's defenses. Santa Anna used this fort when he attacked the city in 1842. Though it was formerly a museum, its use was undetermined on my last visit. The view is dramatic, whether the building is open or not.

BEACHES The Playa Bonita is four miles west out of town, but it's often dirty.

WHERE TO STAY

Though Campeche's tourist trade is small, there are some good places to stay. If business is slow, the rates given below may be discounted.

EXPENSIVE

RAMADA INN, Av. Ruíz Cortínez 51 (Apdo. Postal 251), Campeche, Camp. 24000. Tel. 981/6-2233 or 6-4611, or toll free 800/272-6234 in the U.S. Fax 981/6-1618. 120 rms. A/C TV TEL
$ Rates: $90 single; $100 double; $115 junior suite. **Parking:** Free.
Extensively remodeled in 1990, the handsomely furnished rooms at the Ramada Inn all have tile floors and balconies facing the ocean. The restaurant, bar, and coffee shop are popular with local citizens—always a good recommendation. There's a large swimming pool, a discotheque, and a fenced parking lot behind the hotel. It's on the main oceanfront boulevard, two blocks west of the Plaza Principal and next to the Hotel Baluartes.

MODERATE

HOTEL BALUARTES, Av. Ruíz Cortínez 61, Campeche, Camp. 24000. Tel. 981/6-3911. Fax 981/6-2410. 100 rms. A/C TV TEL
$ Rates: $72 single; $78 double. **Parking:** Free.
Right on the ocean, this was the city's original luxury hotel. It's still a nice place, but not refurbished and modern like the Ramada next door. Many of the rooms have a sea view, and there is a swimming pool, and a restaurant and bar. You're close to all the major sights. The Baluartes is at the corner of Calle 61, two blocks west of the Plaza Principal.

BUDGET

HOTEL AMERICA, Calle 10 no. 252, Centro, Campeche, Camp. 24000. Tel. 981/6-4588. 52 rms. FAN
$ Rates: $30 single; $36 double; $40 triple. **Parking:** Free; unguarded.
Old but clean and well kept, this is a good, centrally located lodging choice. The rooms, housed in two stories (no elevator), have one, two, or three double beds and come with tile floors. Corner rooms will be quieter than those with windows on the street. The Hotel America is between Calles 59 and 61.

HOTEL LÓPEZ, Calle 12 no. 189, Campeche, Camp. 24000. Tel. 981/6-3021. 39 rms A/C (25 rms) FAN (14 rms) TEL
$ Rates: $36 single or double with A/C; $29 single or double with fan.
Near restaurants and most major sights, this old three-story hotel is a good budget choice. The rooms, tiled from floor to ceiling, are semiclean and well lit. The hotel's second-floor restaurant is open daily from 7am to 6pm. The hotel is between Calles 61 and 65, 3½ blocks southeast of the Plaza Principal.

LA POSADA DEL ÁNGEL, Calle 10 no. 307, Campeche, Camp. 24000. Tel. 981/6-7718. 15 rms. A/C
$ Rates: $24 single; $28 double.
Opposite the cathedral and half a block north of the Plaza Principal, you'll find the three-story La Posada del Ángel. Rooms are a little dark, with glass louvered windows opening onto a narrow hall. All are clean and freshly painted and come

with either two double beds or a single and a double. Carpeted halls in the upper two stories should cut down on noise.

WHERE TO DINE

To sample authentic regional food try colados, which are delicious regional tamales; tacos de salchicha (an unusual pastry); cazón de Campeche (a tasty shark stew); and pan de cazón, another shark dish for those with more adventurous palates.

MODERATE

LA PIGUA, Av. Miguel Alemán no. 197A. Tel. 1-3365.
  Cuisine: SEAFOOD/MEXICAN.
  $ Prices: Appetizers $3–$10; main courses $7–$15.
  Open: Daily noon–6pm.
You can easily pass the entire afternoon in this junglelike dining room, with glass walls between the diners and the trees. Couples and business acquaintances practice the art of doing lunch, Mexican style, spending hours over a multicourse meal. The most filling meal on the menu is the plateful of rice with octopus and shrimp; the most unusual are chiles rellenos stuffed with shark. This is where you should splurge on shrimp, seafood cocktails, and a dessert of local fruits in syrup and liqueurs. To reach La Pigua walk north on Calle 8, cross the Avenida Circuito by the botanical garden, where Calle 8 becomes Miguel Alemán. The restaurant is 1½ blocks north, on the east side of the street.

RESTAURANT BAR MARANGANZO, Calle 8 no. 268. Tel. 1-3898 or 1-3899.
  Cuisine: STEAKS/REGIONAL.
  $ Prices: Main courses $6–$17.
  Open: Daily noon–midnight.
Stylish and popular, the place is filled at lunchtime with Campeche's office workers and on Sunday's with the city's upper crust. Its owners are the same folks who run La Parroquía, and the menu is similar (but higher priced and without sandwiches) and the decor is completely different. You'll be greeted by hostesses wearing regional costumes who'll seat you at one of the cloth-covered tables. Besides regional specialties, there's filet mignon and mixed brochette. Trios entertain in the afternoon and a pianist takes over in the evenings.

RESTAURANT MIRAMAR, Calle 8 no. 293. Tel. 6-2883.
  Cuisine: SEAFOOD/MEXICAN.
  $ Prices: Appetizers $2–$3.50; main courses $7.50–$15; sandwiches $2.50–$4.
  Open: Mon–Fri 8am–midnight, Sat 8am–1pm, Sun 11am–7pm.
One of the best choices in Campeche is very near the town hall building at the corner of Calle 61. The decor is airy and pleasant, with light-colored stone arches, dark wood, and ironwork. The menu offers typical Campeche seafood dishes: lightly fried, breaded shrimp (ask for "camarones empanizados"); arroz con mariscos (shellfish and rice); and pargo poc-chuc. For dessert there's queso napolitana, a very rich, thick flan. Ask about the changing daily specials.

BUDGET

PANADERÍA NUEVA ESPAÑA, Calle 10 no. 256. Tel. 6-2887.
  Cuisine: BAKERY.
  $ Prices: Most items 35¢–$2.50.
  Open: Daily 6:30am–9:30pm.

Just off the Plaza Principal, this is Campeche's best downtown bakery. Besides the usual shelves of assorted breads and pastries, you can also stock up on food for the road—mayonnaise, catsup, cheese, butter, yogurt, and fruit drinks. This is the place to try the unusual tacos de salchicha, also called *feite*.

LA PARROQUÍA, Calle 55 no. 9. Tel. 6-8086.
  Cuisine: MEXICAN.
$ Prices: Breakfast $2–$4.50; main courses $3.35–$10; comida corrida $5.
  Open: Daily 24 hours.

After several years of announcing it, La Parroquía, the popular local hangout, finally moved—across the street. (Another, very similar looking restaurant occupies their old space, so don't get them confused.) The same friendly waiters are on hand, offering the same inexpensive fare, which includes great breakfasts and colados, the delicious regional tamal. Selections on the comida corrida might include pot roast, pork, or fish, served with rice or squash, beans, tortillas, and fresh fruit-flavored water.

5. CHICHÉN-ITZÁ

112 miles E of Cancún, 75 miles W of Mérida

GETTING THERE   By Plane   Day trips on charter flights from Cancún can be arranged by travel agents in the U.S. or Cancún.

By Bus   From Mérida, first-class **ADO** buses leave at 7:30am and 3:30pm. If you go round-trip in a day (a 2½-hour trip one-way) take the 7:30am bus and reserve a seat on the return bus.

You'll arrive in the village of Pisté, at the bus station next to the Pirámide Inn. From Pisté there's a sidewalk to the archeological zone, which is a mile or so west of town. Taxi drivers don't haggle here, so try to find as many people as possible to pile in and split the minimum one-way fare of $5.

By Car   Chichén-Itzá is on the main highway (no. 180) between Mérida and Cancún.

DEPARTING   There are direct buses to Cancún at 1:15 and 5:15pm and to Mérida at 3pm. De paso buses to Mérida also leave hourly from 7:15am to 5:15pm. The bus station office is open daily from 6am to 6pm.

ESSENTIALS   The telephone area code is 985. Pisté is 1½ miles from the ruins.

VILLAGE LAYOUT   The small town of Pisté, where most hotels and restaurants are located, is about 1½ miles from the ruins of Chichén-Itzá. Public buses from Mérida, Cancún, Valladolid, and elsewhere discharge passengers here. A few hotels are at the edge of the ruins, and one, the Hotel Dolores Alba, is about 1½ miles from the ruins on the road to Valladolid.

The fabled pyramids and temples of Chichén-Itzá are the Yucatán's best-known ancient monuments. You must go, since you can't really say you've seen the Yucatán until you've gazed at the towering El Castillo, seen the sun from the Maya observatory called El Caracol, or shivered on the brink of the gaping cenote that may have served as the sacrificial well.

This Maya city was established by Itzáes, perhaps sometime during the A.D. 800s. Linda Schele and David Friedel, writing in *A Forest of Kings* (William Morrow,

1990), cast doubt on the legend that Kukulkán (also called Quetzalcoatl by the Toltecs—a name also associated with a legendary god) came here from the Toltec capital of Tula and, along with Putún Maya coastal traders, built a magnificent metropolis combining the Maya Puuc style with Toltec motifs (the feathered serpent, warriors, eagles, and jaguars). Reading of Chichén's bas-reliefs and hieroglyphs fails to support that legend, but instead shows that Chichén Itzá was a continuous Maya site influenced by association with Toltecs, but not by an invasion. The truth about Kukulkán's role in the Yucatán is once again in question. (See also Chapter 1, "Introducing Mexico & the Yucatán.")

Spend at least the night at Chichén-Itzá (actually in Pisté) and two nights if you can, and take your time seeing the ruins in the cool of the morning and afternoon after 3pm; take a siesta during the midday heat. The next morning get to the ruins early; when the heat of the day approaches, catch a bus to your next destination. This may involve paying the admission fee more than once (unless you're there on a Sunday when it's free), but the experience is worth it. Day trips generally arrive when it's beginning to get hot, rushing through this marvelous ancient city in order to catch another bus or have lunch. They leave just as the once-fierce sun burnishes the temples a benevolent gold.

THE MAYA CALENDAR

To understand Chichén-Itzá fully, you need to know something about the unique way in which the Maya kept time on several simultaneous calendars.

Although not more accurate than our own calendar, the intricate Maya calendar systems begin (according to many scholars) with 3114 B.C., before Maya culture existed. From that date, the Maya could measure time—and their life cycle—to a point 90,000,000 years in the future! For now, just note that they conceived of world history as a series of cycles moving within cycles.

The Solar Year The Maya solar year consisted of 365.24 days. Within that solar year there were 18 "months" of 20 days each, for a total of 360 days plus a special five-day period.

The Ceremonial Year A ceremonial calendar, completely different from the solar calendar, ran its "annual" cycle at the same time. But this was not a crude system like our Gregorian calendar, which has saints' days, some fixed feast days, and some movable feasts. It was so intricate that the ordinary Maya depended on the priests to keep track of it. Complex and ingenious, the ceremonial calendar system consisted of 13 "months" of 20 days—but within that cycle of 260 days were another 20 "weeks" of 13 days. The Maya ceremonial calendar "interlaced" exactly with the solar calendar. Each date of the solar calendar had a name, as did each date of the ceremonial calendar; so every day in Maya history had two names, which were always quoted together.

IMPRESSIONS

Into this well (Chichén-Itzá) they were and still are accustomed to throw men alive as a sacrifice to the gods in times of drought; they held that they did not die, even though they were not seen again. They also threw in many other offerings of precious stones and things they valued greatly; so if there were gold in this country, this well would have received most of it, so devout were the Indians in this.
—Friar Diego de Landa, Yucatán Before and After the Conquest, 1566

The Double Cycle After 52 solar years and 73 ceremonial "years," during which each day had its unique, unduplicated double name, these calendars ended their respective cycles simultaneously on the very same day, and a brand-new, identical double cycle began. Thus, in the longer scheme of things, a day would be identified by the name of the 52-year-cycle, the name of the solar day, and the name of the ceremonial day.

Mystic Numbers As you can see, several numbers were of great significance to the system. The number 20 was perhaps most important, as calendar calculations were done with a number system with base 20. There were 20 "suns" (days) to a "month," 20 years to a *katun*; and 20 *katuns* (20 times 20, or 400 years) to a *baktun*.

The number 52 was of tremendous importance, for it signified, literally, the "end of time"—the end of the double cycle of solar and ceremonial calendars. At the beginning of a new cycle, temples were rebuilt for the "new age," which is why so

---

 FROMMER'S ARCHEOLOGY NOTES

MAYA CONSTRUCTION STYLES

Chenes Style The baroque examples of Maya architecture, Chenes buildings are elaborately embellished from top to bottom with separately cut stone pieces, often with many representations of Chaac, the Maya rain god. As with the Río Bec style, doorways are often open mouths of a fierce-looking Chaac with pointed teeth. Though the Chenes heartland is in the states of Campeche and Quintana Roo, Yucatán's ruins also have excellent Chenes-style buildings. Good examples are the Nunnery Annex at Chichén-Itzá, and the high up doorway on the Temple of the Magician at Uxmal, and at Kabah where 250 Chaac masks cover the stunning facade of the Codz Poop.

Puuc Style The name Puuc refers to a region, a culture, and an architectural style. The Yucatán's only hilly area, south of Mérida, is known as the Puuc (Maya for hills or mountains), and gives the region's architecture its name. Architecturally elaborate stonework, often mosaic-like, generally begins from the top of the doorline to the roofline and includes many masks of Chaac, appearing with an elephant trunk-like hook nose. In other places, these masks appear on the facade as well as ornamental corner ends of buildings. Puuc buildings are also embellished with a series of short stone columns, giving the buildings a beautiful, almost Greek appearance.

Río Bec Style Found particularly in the states of Campeche and Quintana Roo, and south in Guatemala, the style takes its name from the ruins of Río Bec, located south of Xpuhil off Highway 186 between Chetumal and Escarcega. Río Bec architecture is characterized by roofcombs, which adorn rooftops like latticework false fronts. Frequently, doorways are elaborate stonework mouths of Chaac, but also called "monster mouths." Steep pyramids are frequently almost cone-shaped, with narrow stairs leading to the top that they are impossible to climb. Examples of Río Bec style are at Xpuhil, Becán, Chicaná, and Calakmul. Away from the traditional Río Bec area, roofcombs also appear in several places such as Palenque, Uxmal, and Kabah.

many Maya temples and pyramids hold within them the structures of earlier, smaller temples and pyramids.

Their Concept of Time   The Maya did not consider time "progress." They thought of it as the wheel of fate, spinning endlessly, determining one's destiny by the combinations of attributes given to days in the solar and ceremonial calendars. The rains came on schedule, the corn was planted on schedule, and the celestial bodies moved in their great dance under the watchful eye of Maya astronomers and astrologers. *The Blood of Kings* (see "Recommended Books," Chapter 1) has an especially good chapter on the Maya calendar.

As evidence of the Maya obsession with time, Chichén's most impressive structure, El Castillo, is an enormous "time piece."

SEEING THE RUINS

The main entrance and huge visitor's center, where you pay admission, is beside the parking lot and consists of a museum, auditorium, restaurant, bookstore, and restrooms. You can see the site on your own or with a licensed guide. These guides are usually waiting at the entrance and charge around $30 for one to six people. Although the guides frown on it, there's nothing wrong with your approaching a group of people who speak the same language and asking if they would like to share a guide with you. The guide, of course, would like to get $30 from you alone and $30 each from other individuals who don't know each other and still form a group. Don't believe all the history the guides spout—some of it is just plain out of date, but the architectural details they point out will be enlightening.

There are actually two parts of Chichén-Itzá, which dates from around A.D. 600 to 900: the northern (new) zone, which shows distinct Toltec influence; and the southern (old) zone, which is mostly Puuc architecture. The site occupies four square miles and it takes a strenuous full day (from 8am to noon and 2 to 5pm) to see all the ruins, which are open daily from 8am to 5pm. Admission is $6, free for children under 12, and free for all on Sunday and holidays. A permit to use your own video camera costs an additional $8.50. Parking costs $1. You can use one ticket to reenter in the same day, but you'll have to pay again to reenter on another day.

Chichén-Itzá's sound-and-light show was completely revamped in 1993, with new computerized light and sound systems. The show now rivals that at Uxmal (long considered the best) and is well worth seeing. The Spanish version is shown nightly at 7pm and costs $3; the English version is at 9pm and costs $4. The show may be offered in French and German as well. Ask at your hotel.

EL CASTILLO   As you enter from the tourist center, the beautiful 75-foot El Castillo pyramid is straight ahead. It was built with the calendar in mind: There are a total of 364 stairs plus platform to equal 365 (days of the year); 52 panels on each side represent the 52-year cycle of the Maya calendars; and nine terraces on each side of the stairways total 18 terraces, to represent the 18-month Maya solar calendar. If this isn't proof enough of the mathematical precision of this temple, come for the spring or fall equinox (March 21 and September 21 between 3 and 5pm). On those days, the seven stairs of the northern stairway plus the serpent-head carving at the base are touched with sunlight; they become a "serpent" formed by play of light and shadow. It appears to descend into the earth as the sun hits each stair from the top, ending with the serpent head. To the Maya this was a fertility symbol: The golden sun has entered the earth—time to plant the corn.

El Castillo, also called the Pyramid of Kukulkán, was built over an earlier structure. A narrow stairway entered at the western edge of the north staircase leads into the structure, where there is a sacrificial altar-throne of a red jaguar encrusted with jade. The stairway is open at 11am and 3pm, and is claustrophobic, usually crowded, humid, and uncomfortable. A visit early in the day is best. No photos of the figure are allowed.

MAIN BALLCOURT (JUEGO DE PELOTA)   Northwest of El Castillo is Chichén's main ballcourt, the largest and best preserved anywhere and only one of nine ballcourts built in this city. Carved on both walls of the ballcourt are scenes showing Maya figures dressed as ball players, decked out in heavy protective padding. The carved scene also shows a kneeling headless player with blood shooting from the neck, looked upon by another player holding the head.

Players on two teams tried to knock a hard rubber ball through one or the other of the two stone rings placed high on either wall, using only their elbows, knees, and hips (no hands). According to legend, the losing players paid for defeat with their lives. However, some experts say that the victors were the only appropriate sacrifices for the gods. Either way, the game must have been exciting, heightened by the marvelous acoustics of the ballcourt.

THE NORTH TEMPLE   Temples are at both ends of the ballcourt. The North Temple has sculptured pillars and more sculptures inside, as well as badly ruined murals. The acoustics of the ballcourt are so good that from the North Temple a person speaking can be heard clearly at the opposite end, about 450 feet away.

TEMPLE OF JAGUARS   Near the southeastern corner of the main ballcourt is a small temple with serpent-columns and carved panels showing warriors and jaguars (tigers). Up the flight of steps and inside the temple, a mural was found that chronicles a battle in a Maya village.

TZOMPANTLI (TEMPLE OF THE SKULLS)   To the right of the ballcourt is the Temple of the Skulls, with rows of skulls carved into the stone platform. When a sacrificial victim's head was cut off, it was stuck on a pole and displayed in a tidy row with others. Just in case skulls became scarce, the architects provided these rows of skulls. Also carved into the stone are pictures of eagles tearing hearts from human victims. The word Tzompantli is not Maya, but came from central Mexico with the Toltecs. Reconstruction using scattered fragments may add a level to this platform and change the look of this structure by the time you travel.

PLATFORM OF THE EAGLES   Next to the Tzompantli, this small platform has reliefs showing eagles and jaguars clutching human hearts in their talons and claws; there's also a head coming out of the mouth of a serpent.

PLATFORM OF VENUS   East of the Tzompantli and north of El Castillo, near the road to the Sacred Cenote, is the Platform of Venus. In Maya-Toltec lore, Venus was represented by a feathered monster, or a feathered serpent with a human head in its mouth. It's also called the Tomb of Chac-Mool because a Chac-Mool figure was discovered "buried" within the structure.

SACRED CENOTE   Follow the dirt road, actually an ancient sacbe, that heads north from the Platform of Venus and after five minutes you'll come to the great natural well that may have given Chichén-Itzá (The Well of the Itzáes) its name. This was a well used for ceremonial purposes, not for drinking water, and according to legend, sacrificial victims were drowned in this pool to honor the rain god Chaac. Anatomical research done early this century by Ernest A. Hooten showed that bones of both children and adults were found in the well. Judging from Hooten's evidence, they may have been outcasts, diseased, or feeble-minded.

Edward Thompson, American consul in Mérida and a Harvard professor, bought the hacienda of Chichén early this century, explored the cenote with dredges and divers, and exposed a fortune in gold and jade. Most of the riches wound up in Harvard's Peabody Museum of Archeology and Ethnology. Later excavations, in the 1960s, brought up more treasure; studies of the recovered objects show offerings brought from throughout the Yucatán, and even farther away.

TEMPLE OF THE WARRIORS/GROUP OF THE THOUSAND COLUMNS

Due east of El Castillo is one of the most impressive structures at Chichén, the Temple of the Warriors (Templo de los Guerreros), named for the carvings of warriors marching along its walls. It's also called the Group of the Thousand Columns, after the many columns flanking it. Since recent restoration, hundreds more columns have been rescued from the rubble and put in place, setting off the temple more magnificently than ever. Climb up the steep stairs at the front to reach a figure of Chac-Mool, and several impressive columns carved in relief to look like enormous feathered serpents. South of the temple was a square building called the market *(mercado)* by archeologists. Its central court is surrounded by a colonnade. Beyond the temple and the market, in the jungle, are mounds of rubble, parts of which are being reconstructed.

The main Mérida-Cancún highway used to cut straight through the ruins of Chichén, and though it has now been diverted, you can still see the great swath it cut. South and west of the old highway's path are more impressive ruined buildings. On the way to these buildings is a shady stand selling cold drinks.

TOMB OF THE HIGH PRIEST (TUMBA DEL GRAN SACERDOTE)

Past the refreshment stand, to the right of the path, is the Tomb of the High Priest, which stood atop a natural limestone cave in which skeletons and offerings were found, giving the temple its name.

This building was being reconstructed when I was there, and workers were unearthing other smaller temples in the area. As the work progresses some buildings may be roped off, and others will open to the public for the first time. It's fascinating to watch the archeologists at work, meticulously numbering each stone as they take apart what appears to be a mound of rocks, then reassemble them into a recognizable structure.

Next building along, on your right, is the **House of Metates (Casa de los Metates),** named after the concave corn-grinding stones used by the Maya. Past it is the **Temple of the Stag (Templo del Venado),** fairly tall though ruined. The relief of a stag that gave the temple its name is long gone.

The next temple, **Chichan-chob (Little Holes),** has a roofcomb with little holes, three masks of the rain god Chaac, three rooms, and a good view of the surrounding structures. It's one of the older buildings at Chichén, built in the Puuc style during the Late Classic period.

OBSERVATORY (EL CARACOL)

Construction of the Observatory, a complex building with a circular tower, was carried out over a long time. No doubt the additions and modifications reflected the Maya's increasing knowledge of celestial movements, and their need for ever more exact measurements. Through slits in the tower's walls, Maya astronomers could observe the cardinal directions and the approach of the all-important spring and autumn equinoxes, and the summer solstice. The temple's name, which means "snail," comes from a spiral staircase within the structure which is now closed off.

On the east side of El Caracol, a path leads north into the bush to the **Cenote Xtoloc,** a natural limestone well that provided the city's daily water supply. If you see any lizards sunning there, they may well be xtoloc, the lizard for which the cenote is named.

TEMPLE OF PANELS Just to the south of El Caracol are the ruins of a steambath (Temazcalli), and the **Templo de los Tableros,** named for the carved panels on top. This was once covered by a much larger structure, only traces of which remain.

EDIFICE OF THE NUNS (EDIFICIO DE LAS MONJAS) If you've visited the Puuc sites of Kabah, Sayil, Labná, and Xlapak, the enormous Nunnery here will remind you at once of the "palaces" at the other sites. Built in the Late Classic period, a new edifice was built over an older one. Suspecting that this was so, Le Plongeon, an archeologist working earlier in this century, put dynamite in between the two and blew part of the newer building to smithereens, thereby revealing part of the old. You can still see the results of Le Plongeon's indelicate exploratory methods.

On the eastern side of the Nunnery is an **annex (Anexo Este)** in highly ornate Chenes style, with Chaac masks and serpents.

THE CHURCH (LA IGLESIA) Next to the annex is one of the oldest buildings at Chichén, ridiculously named The Church (La Iglesia). Masks of Chaac decorate two upper stories. Look closely and you'll see among the crowd of Chaacs an armadillo, crab, snail, and tortoise. These represent the Maya gods called *bacah,* whose job it was to hold up the sky.

TEMPLE OF OBSCURE WRITING (AKAB DZIB) The temple is along a path east of the Edifice of the Nuns. Above a door in one of the rooms are some Maya glyphs, which gave the temple its name, since the writings have yet to be deciphered. In other rooms, traces of red handprints are still visible. Reconstructed and expanded over the centuries, at least part of this building is very old, and may well be the oldest at Chichén.

OLD CHICHÉN (CHICHÉN VIEJO) For a look at more of Chichén's oldest buildings, constructed well before the Toltecs arrived, follow signs from the Nunnery southwest into the bush to Old Chichén (Chichén Viejo), about half a mile away. Be prepared for this trek with long trousers, insect repellent, and a local guide. The attractions here are the **Temple of the First Inscriptions (Templo de los Inscripciones Iniciales),** with the oldest inscriptions discovered at Chichén, and the restored **Temple of the Lintels (Templo de los Dinteles),** a fine Puuc building.

WHERE TO STAY AT PISTÉ/CHICHÉN-ITZÁ

If you want to make a reservation, be advised that it is difficult to reach Chichén by phone; however, many hotels have reservation services in Mérida or Mexico City.

EXPENSIVE

HACIENDA CHICHÉN-ITZÁ, Zona Arqueológica, Chichén-Itzá, Yuc. 97751. Tel. 985/6-2513 or 6-2462. 18 rms (all with bath). FAN
$ Rates: $88 single or double. **Closed:** Off-season.
A romantic hotel a short walk from the back entrance to the ruins, the Hacienda Chichén-Itzá consists of bungalows built years ago for those who were excavating the ruins. Each cottage is named for an early archeologist working at Chichén. There's a pool, which is open to those who drop in for lunch. The dining room is outside under the hacienda portals overlooking the grounds. But any meal is expensive: Breakfast is $7, lunch around $14, and dinner $20.

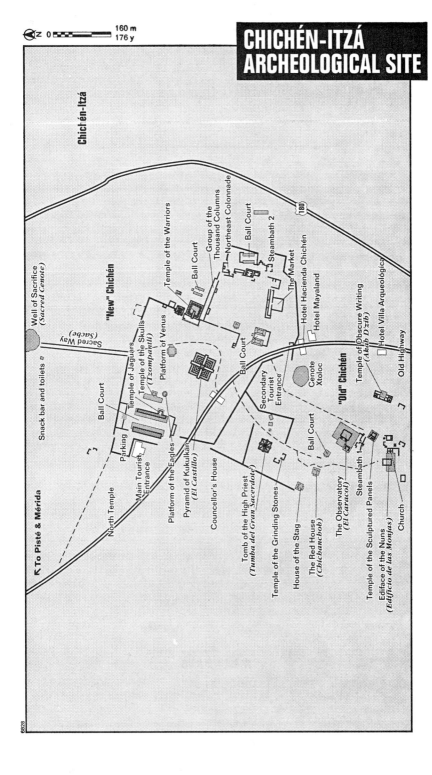

CHICHÉN-ITZÁ ARCHEOLOGICAL SITE

0   160 m
     176 y

Chichén-Itzá

To Pisté & Mérida

Well of Sacrifice
(Sacred Cenote)

Sacred Way
(Sacbe)

"New" Chichén

Snack bar and toilets

Ball Court

Parking

Main Tourist Entrance

North Temple

Platform of the Eagles

Pyramid of Kukulkán
(El Castillo)

Councellor's House

Temple of Jaguars

Temple of the Skulls
(Tzompantli)

Platform of Venus

Temple of the Warriors

Ball Court

Group of the Thousand Columns

Northeast Colonnade

Ball Court

Steambath 2

The Market

Hotel Hacienda Chichén

Hotel Mayaland

Ball Court

Secondary Tourist Entrance

Cenote Xtoloc

"Old" Chichén

Temple of Obscure Writing
(Akab D'zib)

Hotel Villa Arqueológica

Old Highway

Tomb of the High Priest
(Tumba del Gran Sacerdote)

Temple of the Grinding Stones

House of the Stag

The Red House
(Chichanchob)

The Observatory
(El Caracol)

Ball Court

Steambath 1

Temple of the Sculptured Panels

Ediface of the Nuns
(Edificio de las Monjas)

Church

180

6828

IMPRESSIONS

The architects of pre-Colombian America were more fortunate than most of those of Europe. Their masterpieces were never condemned to invisibility, but stood magnificently isolated, displaying thier three dimensions to all beholders. European cathedrals were built within the walls of cities; the temples of the aboriginal American seem, in most cases, to have stood outside.
—ALDOUS HUXLEY, *BEYOND THE MEXIQUE BAY,* 1934

The hacienda is closed from May through October, though the owners were re-considering this policy and it may be open year-round. It's often booked solid in the high season; advance reservations are strongly recommended.

Reservations: Contact Casa del Balam, Calle 60 no. 48, Mérida, Yuc. 97000 (tel. 99/24-8844, or toll free 800/223-4084 in the U.S.; fax 99/24-5011).

HOTEL MAYALAND, Zona Arqueológica, Chichén-Itzá, Yuc. 97751. Tel. 985/6-2777. 164 rms (all with bath). A/C or FAN TV

$ Rates: High season $125 single or double. Low season $95 single or double. **Parking:** Free; guarded.

In operation since the 1930s, this is a long-time favorite by the ruins. No other hotel quite captures the feel of a ruins experience with the front doorway framing El Caracol (the observatory) as you walk outside from the lobby. Rooms in the main building, connected by a wide, tiled veranda, have air conditioning and TV, tiled baths (with tubs), and colonial-style furnishings. Romantic oval-shaped Maya huts with beautifully carved furniture, palapa roofs, and mosquito netting, are tucked around the wooded grounds. The grounds are gorgeous, with huge trees and blossoming ginger plants. There's a long pool and lounge area, and a restaurant that serves only fair meals at fixed prices, about $20 for a full lunch or dinner. You're better off ordering light meals and snacks by the pool or in the bar. Mayaland has a shuttle service between the hotel and Mérida for about $35 each way.

The Hotel Mayaland is a great bargain if you take advantage of their rental-car deal. If you rent a car through their office in Mérida or Cancún your accommodations are free, with no minimum stay.

Reservations: Contact Mayaland Resorts, Av. Colón 502, Mérida, Yuc. 97000 (tel. 99/25-2122, or toll free 800/235-4079 in the U.S.; fax 99/25-7022).

HOTEL VILLA ARQUEOLÓGICA, Zona Arqueológica, Chichén-Itzá, Yuc. 97751. Tel. 985/6-2830, or toll free 800/258-2633 in the U.S. 32 rms. A/C

$ Rates: $90 single, $100 double.

Operated by Club Med, the Villa Arqueológica is almost next to the ruins and built around a swimming pool. The very comfortable rooms are like those at Uxmal and Cobá, each with two oversized single beds. There are tennis courts, and the hotel's rather expensive restaurant features French and Yucatecan food (breakfast is $15, lunch and dinner are $25).

Reservations: Reserve through Av. Presidente Masaryk 183, Mexico City, D.F. 11570 Mexico (tel. 5/254-7077).

MODERATE

HOTEL MISIÓN PARK INN CHICHÉN-ITZÁ, Carretera Mérida-Valladolid km 119, Pisté, Yuc. 97751. Tel. Caseta Pisté 985/6-2462, ext. 104, or toll free 800/437-7275 in the U.S. 42 rms. A/C

$ Rates: $75 single, $80 double. **Parking:** Free.

This two-story hotel, with comfortable rooms, is built around a pretty pool and a grassy inner lawn. The expensive restaurant-bar is popular with tour groups. You can drop in for breakfast ($6), lunch, or dinner ($10). Driving through Pisté, you'll see the hotel on the right if you're coming from Valladolid or on the left if you're arriving from Mérida.

PIRÁMIDE INN, Carretera Mérida-Valladolid km 117, Pisté, Yuo. 97751.
Tel. Caseta Pisté 985/6-2462 (leave a message). Fax 985/6-2671. 44 rms. A/C
$ Rates: $50 single or double.

Less than a mile from the ruins at the edge of Pisté, this hospitable inn has large motellike rooms equipped with two double beds or one king-size bed; but do check your mattress for its sag factor before accepting the room. Hot water comes on between 5 and 9am and 5 and 9pm. Water is purified in the tap for drinking. There is a pool in the midst of landscaped gardens, which include the remains of a pyramid wall. Try to get a room in the back if street noise bothers you. If you're coming from Valladolid it's on the left, and from Mérida look for it on the right.

BUDGET

HOTEL DOLORES ALBA, Carretera Valladolid–Chichén-Itzá km 122, Yuc.
97751. No phone. 18 rms. A/C (3 rms) FAN (15 rms)
$ Rates: $24 single; $28 double; $32 triple; $38 cottage for four. A/C $6 extra.

You're a mile from the back entrance to the ruins if you stay at the Dolores Alba. The nice rooms are clean, with matching furniture, tile floors and showers, and well-screened windows. There's a swimming pool on the front lawn.

The hotel restaurant serves good meals at moderate prices. Breakfast costs between $2.80 and $5, and main courses at other meals run around $6.50. But you should realize that when it comes to dining you have little choice—the nearest alternative restaurant, or tienda where you can pick up your own supplies, is several miles away.

Free transportation is provided to the ruins anytime, but you'll have to get back on your own (about a 30-minute walk). The Dolores Alba in Mérida, also recommended, is owned by the same family, so either hotel will help you make reservations.

If you go to Chichén-Itzá by bus from Mérida, ask for a ticket on a bus that is going past the ruins—to Valladolid or Puerto Juárez—and then ask the bus driver to stop at the Dolores Alba. Or take a taxi from the ruins to the hotel. It's 1½ miles past the ruins on the road going east to Cancún and Valladolid.

Reservations: Contact the Hotel Dolores Alba, Calle 63 no. 464, Mérida, Yuc. 97000 (tel. 99/28-5650; fax 99/28-3163).

POSADA CHAC MOOL, Carretera Mérida-Valladolid, Pisté, Yuc. 97751.
No phone. 5 rms. FAN
$ Rates: $16 single; $20 double; $23 triple. **Parking:** Free.

Clean, plain, and relatively new, this no-frills single-story motel opened in 1990. The basically furnished rooms have new mattresses, red-tile floors, and well-screened windows. Little tables and chairs outside each room on the covered walkway make an inviting place to enjoy a self-made meal. The posada is at Calle 15, next to the Central Handcraft Market, and almost opposite Hotel Misión.

WHERE TO DINE

Food is available near the ruins in the expensive hotels. In Pisté there's little difference between the prices or fare at any of the restaurants. Most of the better spots cater to large groups, which converge on them for lunch after 1pm. Competition is moving in, however, and there may be more restaurants open by the time you travel.

LA FIESTA, Pisté, Carretera Mérida-Valladolid. No phone.
   Cuisine: REGIONAL/MEXICAN.
$ Prices: Main courses $8–$12; comida corrida $10.
   Open: Daily 7am–9pm (comida corrida served 12:30–4pm).

Lively in decor, with Maya motifs on the wall and colorful decorations, this is one of Pisté's long-established restaurants, catering especially to tour groups. Though expensive, the food is very good. You'll be quite satisfied, unless you arrive when a tour group is being served, in which case service to individual diners usually suffers.

PUEBLA MAYA, Pisté, Carretera Mérida-Valladolid. No phone.
   Cuisine: MEXICAN.
$ Prices: Fixed-price lunch buffet $12.
   Open: Daily 1–5pm.

Opposite the Pirámide Inn, the Puebla Maya looks just like what its name implies, a Maya town with small white huts flanking a large open-walled palapa-topped center. Inside however, you'll cross an artificial lagoon, planters drip with greenery, and live musicians play to the hundreds of tourists filling the roomful of tables. Service through the huge buffet is quick, so if you've been huffing around the ruins all morning, you have time to eat and relax before boarding the bus to wherever you are going.

AN EXCURSION TO GRUTAS (CAVES) DE BALANKANCHE

The Grutas de Balankanche are 3½ miles from Chichén-Itzá on the road to Cancún and Puerto Juárez. Expect the taxi to cost about $8. Taxis are usually on hand when the tours let out. The entire excursion takes about 1½ hours and the three-mile walk inside is hot and humid. The natural caves became wartime hideaways. You can still see traces of carving and incense-burning, as well as an underground stream which served as the sanctuary's water supply. Outside take time to meander through the botanical gardens where most of the plants and trees are labeled with their common and scientific names. Admission is $4. Use of your video camera will cost an additional $8.50. Children under 6 years of age aren't admitted. Guided tours are given daily in English at 11am, 1 and 3pm; in French at 10am; and Spanish at 9am, noon, 2 and 4pm. The site itself is open from 11am to 5pm. Tours go only if there are a minimum of six people and take up to 30 people at a time. Double check these hours at the main entrance to the Chichén ruins.

6. VALLADOLID

25 miles W of Chichén-Itzá, 41 miles E of Mérida, 75 miles W of Cancún

GETTING THERE   By Train   From Mérida the train departs at 4pm and arrives in Valladolid at 8pm.

By Bus   Almost hourly buses leave from Mérida, passing through Pisté and Chichén-Itzá on the way to Valladolid and Cancún. There are also regular buses from Cancún and at least six daily buses from Playa del Carmen.
   The bus station in Valladolid is at the corner of Calle 37 and Calle 57, 10 very

long blocks from the main plaza, and too far to haul heavy luggage. Taxis are usually in front of the station.

By Car   Highway 180 and the toll road, Highway 180D, link Valladolid with both Cancún and Mérida. From the toll road, the access road leads to Valladolid's main plaza.

DEPARTING   By Train   The train station is at the end of Calle 42 eight blocks from the central plaza. Tickets are on sale between 3 and 5am and 7am to noon. The train to Mérida departs at 3:50am and arrives in Mérida at 8am.

By Bus   Because of the frequency of buses to Mérida and Cancún, advance purchase of tickets isn't usually necessary. To Pisté (the town nearest the Chichén-Itzá ruins), **Autotransportes Oriente** (tel. 6-3449), has de paso buses every hour from 4am to 9:30pm. These same buses go to Mérida. De paso buses on this same line go to Cobá at 4:30am and 1pm. Buses to Tizimin go every hour from 5am to 10pm. **Expresso de Oriente** buses (tel. 6-3630) go to Mérida six times daily, to Playa de Carmen twice, and to Cancún five times. **Autobuses del Centro del Estado** offers five daily buses to Tinum and several other small towns on the way to Mérida.

By Car   There are signs all over town leading motorists to the toll road (cuota) to Mérida, Chichén-Itzá, or Cancún, but I didn't see one indicating how to take the free (libre) road. Calle 39, a one-way street that forms one side of the zócalo, leads to the free highway going to Pisté/Chichén-Itzá, and Mérida. Calle 41, a one-way street on the opposite side of the zócalo, leads to the free highway to Cancún. When you reach the area of Cancún, signs were nonexistent leading into town. Keep following the road as straight as you can and it will let you out on the highway leading to Cancún's airport—turn left to reach Cancún and right to go to the airport.

ESSENTIALS   The telephone area code is 985. The bus and train stations and all hotels and restaurants are within walking distance of Valladolid's pretty main square, the Parque Francisco Canton Rosado. The central plaza is eight long blocks straight ahead from the train station. The bus station is a short two blocks from the central plaza (going left out the front door of the station). From either Chichén or Cancún, the highway goes right past the main square in town. Hotels and restaurants here are less crowded than the competition in Chichén.

Peaceful, slow-paced Valladolid (pronounced "Bay-ah-doh-*leet*"; pop. 45,000) was built upon the site of the original sacred Maya town of Zací. Its sleepy pace today belies a tumultuous past. Montejo the Younger conquered it in 1543, after a long battle with the inhabitants, and renamed it Valladolid in honor of a town in Spain. A few years after Montejo's victory, the Maya revolted again, only to be squashed by the Spaniards, who were saved by reinforcements from Mérida. After the Spanish came the wealthy henequén hacienda owners, who guarded their sovereign right to the town and excluded the Maya. Centuries of Spanish supremacy and festering Maya resentment finally exploded in 1847, when the Maya revolted again in Valladolid, beginning what is known as the War of the Castes, which lasted almost 20 years. (See Chapter 1 for more background on this war.) This time they were armed with weapons purchased from the British in Belize. Though they soon returned, the terrorized Spanish populace fled their homes in Valladolid, and the Maya carried their war to the entire peninsula. Later, just before Mexico's revolution, brought on by President Porfirio Díaz's 30-year hold on the country, citizens of

Valladolid were among the first to speak out publicly against his dictatorship.

Today Valladolid is a regional agricultural center and growing overnight stop for tourists due to its proximity to the ruins of Chichén-Itzá, just 30 miles west.

WHAT TO SEE & DO

The town is centered around a grand central plaza. The fountain in the middle features a statue of a graceful Maya woman wearing an embroidered huipil and pouring water from a clay pot. Fronting the park, the 18th-century **cathedral** on Valladolid's main square, though large and fortresslike, is otherwise bereft of interesting detail. But a few blocks away, the Franciscans built the impressive **Convento de San Bernardino de Sisal** in 1552, under the architectural leadership of Fr. Juan de Mérida, who was also responsible for missions at Izamal and Mani. It's noted for its distinctive Gothic ceiling, retablos, and realistic black Christ in the church, and for the large convent attached to it. Though it's a functioning church today, visitors are welcome. It's on a diagonal street called Calle 41A at Calle 51. To find it follow Calle 41, which runs in front of the cathedral on the square toward Chichén-Itzá. Just after Calle 48, Calle 41 intersects on the left with a diagonal street called Calle 41A, or Calzada de Los Frailes; the Convento is two long blocks straight ahead.

Embroidered Maya dresses can be found at the **Mercado de Artesanías de Valladolid** at the corner of Calles 39 and 44, and from women around the main square. The latter also sell—of all things—Barbie doll–size Maya dresses! Just ask "¿*Vestidos para Barbies?*" and out they come.

The **food market** is on Calle 32 between Calles 35 and 37. Though it's open other days, Sunday morning is when the market is most active and colorful.

WHERE TO STAY

Hotels (and restaurants) here are less crowded and less expensive than the competition in Chichén.

HOTEL MARÍA DE LA LUZ, Calle 42 no. 194, Valladolid, Yuc. 97780. **Tel. 985/6-2071.** Fax 985/6-2098. 30 rms. A/C (17 rms) FAN (13 rms) TV
$ Rates: $29 single; $37 double. **Parking:** Free.
The two stories of rooms here are built around an inner pool that isn't kept very clean. Rooms have been refurbished, with new paint, new tile floors and baths, and new mattresses. A couple of rooms have balconies overlooking the square. The wide, interior covered walkway to the rooms is a nice place to relax in comfortable chairs. It's on the west side of the main square, between Calle 39 and Calle 41.

HOTEL EL MESÓN DEL MARQUÉS, Calle 39 no. 203, Valladolid, Yuc. **97780. Tel. 985/6-2073.** Fax 985/6-2280. 34 rms. A/C
$ Rates: $50 single or double; $58 suite. **Parking:** Free.
This comfortable old colonial-era mansion-turned-hotel, on the north side of the square, offers rooms in both the original 200-year-old mansion and a new addition built around a pool in back. There are several price categories, depending on a room's location and amenities, so be sure to ask what rate you are quoted. Several rooms have TVs. Though otherwise comfortable, the cheaper rooms (with windows on the side street) will contend with an all-night disco. Hot water may not materialize when you want it, so the best advice is clean up when the water's hot and don't depend on it at other times. It's on the main square opposite the church.

HOTEL SAN CLEMENTE, Calle 42 no. 206, Valladolid, Yuc. 97780. Tel. 985/6-2208 or 6-3161. Fax 985/6-3614. 60 rms. FAN
$ Rates: $24 single; $33 double.
This modern white stucco building is at the southwest corner of the square. The view of the church from the second floor is slightly obstructed. The plain but functional rooms are arranged on two floors around a central garden with a swimming pool (which may or may not have water in it). The hotel's restaurant is just off the lobby.

The San Clemente is on the main square at the corner of Calle 21, to the right of the cathedral.

WHERE TO DINE

The lowest restaurant prices are found in the **Bazar Municipal,** a little arcade of shops beside the Hotel El Mesón del Marqués right on the main square. The cookshops open at mealtimes, with tables and chairs set in the courtyard. You won't find many printed menus, let alone one in English. But a quick look around at nearby tables will tell you what's cooking, and a discreet point of a finger will order it. Ask the price though, so you won't be charged something exorbitant when the bill appears.

CASA DE LOS ARCOS RESTAURANT, Calle 39 no. 200-A. Tel. 6-2467.
  Cuisine: MEXICAN/YUCATECAN.
$ Prices: Breakfast $4.50–$5; main courses $6.25–$7.50.
  Open: Daily 7am–10pm.
A lovely, breezy courtyard with a black-and-white tiled floor makes this restaurant especially appealing. Waiters are efficient, and the menu is in English and Spanish. The hearty comida corrida might feature a choice of meat and include red beans, tortillas, and coffee. There's also a full menu of beef, chicken, seafood, and a few Mexican specialties.

From the main square, with Hotel Marqués on your left, take Calle 39 two blocks; the restaurant is on the right, across from the Hotel Don Luis.

HOSTERÍA DEL MARQUÉS, Calle 39 no. 203. Tel. 6-2073.
  Cuisine: MEXICAN/YUCATECAN.
$ Prices: Breakfast $1.75–$4; Mexican plates $2.25–$4.50; main courses $4.50–$7.75; sandwiches $2.25–$4.
  Open: Daily 7am–11pm.
Adjacent to the Hotel del Marqués, facing the main square, this restaurant often spills out onto the hotel's open portals on the interior courtyard where tables are gaily decorated in hot pink and turquoise, with fresh flowers. It's definitely a popular place on the square and often crowded at lunch.

HOTEL MARÍA DE LA LUZ, Calle 42 no. 195. Tel. 6-2070.
  Cuisine: MEXICAN/YUCATECAN.
$ Prices: Breakfast buffet $4.75; main courses $6.50; tamales and sandwiches $2–$3.
  Open: Daily 7am–10pm; breakfast buffet served 7–11am.
There's a touch of class here, with rattan chairs drawn up to cloth-covered tables. Open to the street, on the west side of the main square, this hotel-lobby restaurant is well known for its breezy and inexpensive meals with large portions. Between this and the Mesón del Marqués you'll have the central village "in" gathering spots covered.

FROMMER'S NATURE NOTES

TURQUOISE-BROWED MOTMOT

If you ever see a turquoise-browed motmot swoop across your path, you won't soon forget it—from end to end a mature bird is about a foot long. And if you see one, its mate isn't far behind. The top of the flattish head, the wing tips, and the tail are rimmed in bright blue, something sure to catch the eye. But the most dramatic distinguishing feature is the double tail that extends nakedly from the upper tail feathers and resembles the feather end of an Indian arrow. The motmots nest in limestone, so look for them around caves and cenotes and among stony crags at archeological sites.

EASY EXCURSIONS

TINUM

Adventurous people should consider staying in Tinum, a 30-minute drive from Valladolid, to experience authentic Maya lifestyle. Some years ago, Ms. Bettina McMakin Erdman left Miami to settle in the tiny village of Tinum. She learned the Maya language, became acquainted with the villagers, and soon hosted visitors interested in discovering exactly what it's like to live as the Maya do.

The 17-year tradition of hospitality continues, carried on by Jacinto Pool Tuz, whom everyone knows as Don Chivo. He will arrange for you to board with a Maya family in their *na* (house of sticks with a thatched roof), and to eat with them and share their daily life. The cost, paid directly to the family, is about $12 per day. You'll need to bring a hammock to sleep on. Or, since nearly everyone here makes their own hammocks, you can write ahead to have one made and waiting for you in Tinum. A double-size hammock is best, even for one person, and would cost around $30. Be sure you realize that this is the real thing: You sleep in your hammock, in a *na* with a dirt floor, cook on a fire, and use one of the two bathrooms in Dona Bettina's house. You're welcome for two or three nights.

To get to Tinum, take one of the five daily buses from Valladolid. The trip takes 40 minutes and costs 95¢. By car from Valladolid, head out of town toward Chichén-Itzá; just at the edge of Valladolid you'll see a worn directional sign on your right to Tinum; follow that road straight ahead. The daily train leaves Mérida for Valladolid at 4:30am and stops in Tinum at 7:30am. The bus from Mérida leaves from the Progreso bus station. When you arrive in town ask for directions to the home of Don Chivo; everyone knows him. Advance reservations are necessary, so to make them, write to Sr. Jacinto Pool "Don Chivo," Calle 24 no. 102A, Tinum, Yuc. 97750.

CENOTE DZITNUP

The Cenote Dzitnup, 2½ miles west of Valladolid off Highway 180, is worth a visit, especially if you have time for a dip. Descend a short flight of rather perilous stone steps, and at the bottom, inside a beautiful cavern, is a natural pool of water so clear and blue it's like something from a dream. If you decide to take a swim, be sure you do not have creams or other chemicals on your skin—they damage the habitat for the small fish and other organisms living there. Also, no alcohol, food, or smoking is allowed after you enter the cavern.

Admission is $1. It's open daily from 7am to 5pm.

EKBALAM

Twenty-one miles northeast of Valladolid is Ekbalam, a newly opened archeological site; its Maya name means "black jaguar" or "star jaguar." Excavations are ongoing, and the ruins date from 100 B.C. to A.D. 1200.

To get there from Valladolid, go north on Highway 295 for 11 miles. Watch for the sign pointing right to the village of Hunuku and turn there, following the road for 8½ miles. When you reach Hunuku, a small village, ask someone to point to the dirt road that leads about 1½ miles to the ruins. Willing young boys will probably offer to lead you there. If caretaker Felipe Tuz Cohuo, the site custodian, isn't around, the children can point out the highlights, having absorbed a lot of information during the years the ruins have been excavated by Mexico's Instituto Nacional de Antropología e Historia (INAH) and by archeologists from Tulane University.

To really get a lot out of this site you should be prepared to climb up mountainlike pyramids, with sides made of loose dirt and even looser rocks. Wear good sturdy walking shoes or hiking boots if you have them. As long as this site is relatively unvisited, custodian Tuz may, as he did with me, give a guided rope tour of the site. By means of a long heavy rope, which he adeptly ties to various trees as you go, visitors pull themselves up the slopes or steady themselves on the way down—very clever. Otherwise you must go carefully but unaided if you intend to climb. Some of the important parts can also be seen from the pathway, but climbing is much more rewarding. A tip to him is greatly appreciated. Pencils or ballpoint pens are good gifts for the children.

You can park at the entry sign and walk from there. On 2,500 wooded acres over an area of four square miles, the buildings, which are close together, are grouped around a large central area; along 350 feet of the perimeter are remains of two low walls which the boys can point out on the road leading to the ruins. The largest building, called Structure 1 or "The Tower," is impressive for its 100-foot height as well as its length of 517 feet and width of 200 feet. As you climb to the top, the guide will point out collapsed corbelled arches, filled in with earth and rubble, covering passages to some yet unexplored interior chamber. From the top you can see the highest building of Cobá (30 miles southeast as the crow flies).

Scholars believe Ekbalam was the center of a vast agricultural region. From this lofty vantage point you can see fertile land all around, which still produces corn, cotton, and honey.

Structure 3, also called "The Palace of the Nuns," has a row of corbelled-arch rooms. Though greatly destroyed, this architecture resembles the Puuc style of other Yucatecan sites. The structure got its name from Désirée Charnay, one of the late 19th-century explorers whose writings brought attention to Yucatecan ruins.

Many badly weathered stelae fragments have been found and some are on display under flimsy thatched coverings. Workmen were busy restoring a temple atop one of the enormous mounds during my visit. Other structures show partial walls, some made of irregular rocks and others of carefully fitted and cut rock. Chultunes, or natural limestone water reservoirs, are scattered all over the site; it isn't known yet if any were used for ceremonial purposes. Sacbeob fan out in several directions, but so far none is thought to go farther than a mile or so. Further excavations are planned for "The Tower."

If you do any climbing at all, seeing the area will take a minimum of two hours. The site is open daily from 8am to 5pm. Admission is $3.25.

RÍO LAGARTOS WILDLIFE REFUGE

Fifty miles north of Valladolid (and 25 miles north of Tizimín) on Highway 295 is Río Lagartos, a 118,000-acre refuge established in 1979 to protect the largest nesting population of flamingos in North America. Other protected plant and bird life are included within the park, which includes dunes, mangrove swamps, and tropical forests. There are jaguars, ocelots, sea turtles, and at least 212 bird species, 141 of which are permanent residents. Three fishing villages—Río Lagartos, El Cuyo, and Las Coloradas—are within the range of the park; these three small villages bring 11% of the state's fish to market.

You can make the trip in one long day from Valladolid, but you'll have to leave by at least 5am to get there by 7am, in time to arrange a trip to see the flamingos with one of the local boatmen. There's one poor-quality hotel in Río Lagartos, which I don't recommend. I prefer to overnight in Tizimín (pop. 50,000), 35 miles north of Valladolid. It's a pleasant city, and the agricultural hub of the area. From Tizimín to Río Lagartos it's about a 30-minute drive.

What to See and Do

Río Largartos is a small fishing village of around 3,000 people who make their living from the sea and the occasional tourist who shows up to see the flamingos. Colorfully painted homes face the malecón (the oceanfront street), and brightly painted boats dock along the same half-moon-shaped port.

Plan to arrive in Río Lagartos around 7am and go straight to the dock area. There boatmen will offer to take you on an hour-long trip to the flamingo lagoons, for around $40 for up to six people in a motor-powered wood boat. Ask around for Filiberto Pat Zem, a reliable boatman who takes time to give a good tour; he's a little overeager to frighten the birds, though, so just say no to that.

Although thousands of flamingos nest near here from April to August, it is prohibited by law to visit their nesting grounds. A flamingo nest is a strange thing, actually a conical mound of mud built in shallow water and big enough to hold one egg. Flamingos need mud with particular ingredients including a high salt content in order to multiply. This area has both. On your boat tour you'll probably see flamingos wading in the waters next to Mexico's second-largest salt producing plant—the muddy bottom is plenty salty here. They use their special bills to suck up the mud and have the ability to screen the special contents they need from it. What you see on the boat trip is a mixture of flamingos, frigate birds, pelicans, herons in several colors, and ducks. Don't allow the boatman to frighten the birds into flight for your photographs; it causes the birds to eventually leave the habitat permanently. While Río Lagartos is interesting, if you have time for only one flamingo foray, make it Celestún (west of Mérida). Comparing the two, I've seen more flamingos and more of other kinds of birds at Celestún.

Where to Stay

HOTEL SAN JORJE, Calle 53 no. 411. Tizimín, Yuc. Tel. 986/3-2037. 34 rms. A/C (7 rms) FAN (27 rms)
$ Rates: $29 single; $33 double.
Right on Tizimín's main square, you'll have a bird's-eye view of village life and you'll be within walking distance of restaurants. The three stories of rooms (no elevator) are

plain but comfortable, with tile floors, good beds, and well-screened windows. House-keeping is a bit lax; if your sheets don't seem fresh ask for a replacement.

Occupants of rooms on the north side next to the strip of shops will discover the town's music teacher has a shop in the next building where fledgling musicians prac-tice (each on a different tune at the same time) from 6pm until 8pm; every tentative, squawky, repetitive note will sound as though it originates in your room. The music lesson is followed by regional dance lessons until around 10pm. The prices are too high for the quality of rooms. Ask for a discount.

Where to Dine

PIZZA CAESAR, Calle 53 no. 400. Tel. 3-2152.
  Cuisine: ITALIAN.
$ Prices: Pizzas $4–$12; spaghetti $4–$6; sandwiches $2.50–$4.50.
  Open: Dinner Tues–Sun 5:30–11:30pm.

You'll find this Italian restaurant appropriately decked out in red and white with wood-plank tables and benches and dim lighting. The pizzas are decent and come eight ways. Among the sandwiches you'll find hot ones with salami, ham, cheese, to-mato, and onion, submarines to go, and hamburgers. From the Hotel San Jorje, turn right out the front door and the restaurant is ahead a block or so on the right.

RESTAURANT TRES REYES, on the central plaza. Tel. 3-2106.
  Cuisine: REGIONAL.
$ Prices: Breakfast $3–$6; main courses $6–$11.
  Open: Daily 7:30am–11:30pm.

You can't miss this all-orange restaurant on the main square. Except for the brilliant orange decor, it's a basically plain restaurant serving Yucatecan mainstays of pork, beef, chicken, fish, shrimp, and soup. Sandwiches aren't on the menu, but they have them.

EN ROUTE TO CANCÚN, ISLA MUJERES & MÉRIDA

If you're ready to head onward to Cancún and Isla Mujeres, see "By Car" under "Departing," above, for specific directions on how to find either the toll or free road in Valladolid heading to Cancún, Puerto Juárez (for Isla Mujeres), and Mérida. The 100-mile ride to Cancún on the free road takes about 2 hours, or on the toll road about 1½ hours. If you use the free road, once you reach the city limits of Cancún, you'll have to ask directions into the city since directional signs seem to be nonexist-ent. The toll road stops 50 miles from Cancún, though you continue on paved roads into the city. It stops about 35 miles before Mérida, but directional signs into the city are fairly good.

CHAPTER 6

TABASCO & CHIAPAS

1. VILLAHERMOSA
• **WHAT'S SPECIAL ABOUT TABASCO & CHIAPAS**
2. PALENQUE
3. SAN CRISTÓBAL DE LAS CASAS
4. TUXTLA GUTIÉRREZ

Though technically not part of the Yucatán peninsula, Tabasco and Chiapas are often included in a Yucatán tour because of their Maya connections, so I include them here. These neighbor states span the distance from the Gulf of Mexico to the Pacific Ocean. Tabasco, because of the oil trade along its coast, is more affected by the modern world than Chiapas, which is hemmed in by majestic mountains and an undeveloped coast. Besides oil, Tabasco is noted for its production of tobacco and cacao (chocolate). Chiapas produces cacao, too, and some of the best coffee in Mexico. Both states boast important indigenous influences. The famous Olmec site of La Venta is in Tabasco state (museums in Villahermosa hold its sculptural remains), while numerous Indian groups in the state will speak Maya-related languages. Villahermosa, Tabasco, is considered a main route to the ruins of Palenque and an important gateway to San Cristóbal de las Casas in the state of Chiapas. San Cristóbal is surrounded by indigenous villages, each with language, culture, and craft traditions that are unique in Mexico.

SEEING TABASCO & CHIAPAS

There are several ways to access the Tabasco-Chiapas region. Some people arrive at Villahermosa and go inland by bus to Palenque and San Cristóbal, then leaving the region at Tuxtla Gutiérrez. This works well if you are coming or going to Oaxaca, since commuter planes now connect Tuxtla and Oaxaca and buses frequently make the long trip. Others arrive from the opposite direction via Tuxtla Gutiérrez, then move on to San Cristóbal, Palenque, and Villahermosa. This plan works well if your ultimate destination is the Yucatán peninsula. Presently the airport at San Cristóbal is closed and Palenque's has limited access; but there are airports nearby.

It's easy to discover that Palenque and San Cristóbal de las Casas are the two stellar attractions here. For apportioning time, spend one day in Villahermosa, no less than one day (two nights) at Palenque, and no less than three days (four nights) in San Cristóbal.

---

1. VILLAHERMOSA

89 miles E of Palenque, 100 miles S of Campeche

GETTING THERE   By Plane   Mexicana flies to Villahermosa from Mexico

WHAT'S SPECIAL ABOUT TABASCO & CHIAPAS

Outstanding Museums

La Venta Museum of Archeology and Carlos Pellicer Regional Museum of Anthropology in Villahermosa, two of the country's top museums.

An Outstanding Zoo

Miguel Alvarez del Toro Zoo, in Tuxtla Gutiérrez, one of the best zoos in Mexico.

Shopping

San Cristóbal de las Casas, one of the best villages in Mexico for shopping, with its weavers, potters, and leather workers.

Chocolate, grown and sold around Villahermosa and Comalcalco.

Events and Festivals

Carnaval in Chamula, near San Cristóbal, featuring the ceremonial custom of running on hot embers.

Archeological Sites

Palenque, in a lush tropical setting, with the only pyramid in Mexico built specifically as a tomb.

Bonampak, with magnificent murals that are the greatest battle paintings of pre-Hispanic Mexico.

Comalcalco, near Villahermosa, the only pre-Hispanic center constructed with kilned brick.

Yaxchilán, an important Maya ceremonial jungle site on the Usumacinta River, reached by boat.

Culture

Eight Indian groups in Chiapas, each with distinctive traditions and two different but related Maya languages.

Variations of the rich Maya culture surrounding San Cristóbal de las Casas, Chiapas.

City, Tuxtla Gutiérrez, and Guadalajara. **Aeroméxico** flies from Mexico City, Guadalajara, Mérida, Acapulco, and U.S. gateways. **Aviacsa** flies from Mérida, Mexico City, Tuxtla Gutiérrez, and Oaxaca. **AeroLitoral,** another regional airline, flies from Tampico, Minatitlán, Ciudad Carmen, and Monterrey. **Aerocaribe** flies from Cancún, Cozumel, Tuxtla Gutiérrez, Oaxaca, and Mérida.

By Train The train does connect Mexico City with Villahermosa—or rather, with Teapa, an hour by bus from Villahermosa—but everyone says it's a terrible way to travel. It's dirty, uncomfortable, and dangerous, with only second-class accommodations.

By Bus The first-class bus lines, **Autotransportes Cristóbal Colón** and **ADO**, arrive from Campeche, Mérida, Tuxtla Gutiérrez, San Cristóbal de las Casas, Tapachula, Oaxaca, and Mexico City. The second-class buses on **Sureste** arrive from Tuxtla, Campeche, and Mérida.

By Car At the outset let me warn you about the drive from Chetumal to Villahermosa. Besides the fact that it's an isolated route, the potholes are returning and you're in for hundreds of kilometers of rutted road, washed-away pavement, and dangerous dips. I'll never drive it again.

DEPARTING By Plane For reservations, confirmation, and information contact: **Mexicana** (tel. 16-3785, 16-3132, or 12-1164 at the airport). **Aeroméxico** (tel. 12-6991, 12-1528, or 14-1675 at the airport). **Aviación de Chiapas** (Aviacsa; tel. 14-5770, 14-5780, or 14-4755 at the airport). Aviacsa flies direct to Mérida, Mexico City, and Tuxtla Gutiérrez. **Aerocaribe** (tel. 14-3202) is the regional carrier, with flights to Cancún, Cozumel, Mérida, Oaxaca, and Tuxtla Gutiérrez. Aerocaribe tickets are also available at Mexicana ticket counters. **AeroLitoral,** a subsidiary of Aeroméxico, is at the airport (tel. 13-3614) and has flights to Monterrey.

By Train   Ferrocariles Unidos del Sureste (tel. 93/12-0165) has a station in Teapa, an hour by bus from Villahermosa. The one train daily to Mexico City at 7:35am is not recommended. (See "Getting There," above.)

By Bus   The two bus stations in Villahermosa are about three blocks apart. The first-class **ADO** station (tel. 12-4446), is at Mina and Merino, three blocks off Highway 180. This is one of the nicest bus stations in Mexico, with a clean waiting area, luggage storage at 50¢ per bag, and a decent restaurant. Tickets for most destinations leave from here, and the station houses many lines, including ADO buses. Most ticket booths have computerized ticketing, and you can look at the computer screen and select your seat. Regular **ADO** buses to Palenque leave at 5, 6, 7:10, 9, and 11am, and at 4:30 and 6:05pm. Deluxe service to Palenque leaves at 8am and 1:30pm. **Autotransportes Cristóbal Colón** (tel. 12-2937; fax 93/14-3645) goes to Tuxtla Gutiérrez (where you can make connections to San Cristóbal de las Casas), Tapachula, Oaxaca, and Mexico City. **UNO** (tel. 14-5818) runs luxury buses with 25 seats, smoking and no-smoking sections, self-service refreshments, video movies, and air conditioning. They go to Mexico City, Veracruz, Puebla, and Mérida. You can reserve seats up to two days in advance.

The **Central Camionera de Segunda Clase** (second-class bus station) is on Highway 180/186, near the traffic circle bearing a statue of a fisherman. It's one of the sleaziest stations in Mexico. From the second-class bus station you can ride **Sureste del Caribe** to Tuxtla and Campeche at 6 and 11am, 3 and 7pm; and to Mérida four times daily. **Servicio Somellera** (tel. 12-3973) goes to Comalcalco every 30 minutes. **Autobuses Unidos de Tabasco** travels to Veracruz. Be forewarned that the bus station is horrid, and the buses even worse.

By Car   Paved Highway 195 connects the Tabascan capital of Villahermosa with Tuxtla Gutiérrez, the capital of the state of Chiapas. Between Villahermosa and San Cristóbal de las Casas the road, although paved, may be severely potholed in places. Sometimes a portion of the roadway caves in and traffic slows to one lane to avoid it. These conditions occur more frequently during the rainy season between May and October. The trip to San Cristóbal takes a minimum of five hours from Villahermosa. The paved, mountainous (and very curvy) road between San Cristóbal to Tuxtla is in good condition and the trip takes about 1½ hours.

The road to Palenque is a good one and the drive should take about two hours (three hours by bus).

ESSENTIALS   The telephone area code is 93. American Express is represented locally by Turismo Nieves, Bulevar Simon Sarlat 202 (tel. 93/12-0604 or 12-4390; fax 93/12-5130).

Villahermosa (pop. 265,000), the capital of the state of Tabasco, is right at the center of Mexico's oil boom. But it's on the fringes of just about everything else. Were it not for oil and the city's proximity to the ruins of Palenque, visitors would have little reason to come here since it's 100 miles south of Campeche, and 293 miles south of San Cristóbal de las Casas, both places of greater touristic interest. Nevertheless, oil wealth has helped transform this dowdy provincial town into a more attractive and obviously prosperous modern city, making it a comfortable crossroads in your Mexican journeys.

Prosperity brought a beautiful park surrounding the Parque Museo La Venta; a high-class business, residence, and hotel development called Tabasco 2000, with its gleaming office buildings, convention center, golf course, and exclusive residences; the CICOM development with its theaters and the Museo Regional de Antropología Carlos Pellicer Cámara; and the pedestrians-only shopping area along Avenida Benito Juárez. You really shouldn't miss the fabulous Parque La Venta, which contains the Olmec remains found at La Venta, west of Villahermosa.

The most popular side trip from Villahermosa is to the archeological site of Palenque, covered later in this chapter.

ORIENTATION

ARRIVING Coming in from Villahermosa's airport, which is 6½ miles east of town, you'll cross a bridge over the Río Grijalva and turn left to reach downtown. The airport minibuses charge $8; taxis range from $16. Don't linger in the terminal and expect a minibus to still be at the curb when you're ready. The ticket seller is in cahoots with the taxi drivers and would rather that you take a taxi than a van.

Buses marked "Mercado-C. Camionera," or simply "Centro," leave frequently from the bus station for the center of town. A taxi from either bus station to downtown limits will cost about $2.50 to $5.

If you're arriving by car, know that daytime parking in downtown Villahermosa can be difficult, but there are several parking lots near the hotels recommended here. I suggest using one that's guarded round the clock.

INFORMATION The best source of information is at the **State Tourism Office** in the Tabasco 2000 complex, Paseo Tabasco 1504, SEFICOT building, Centro Administrativo del Gobierno (tel. 15-0693 or 15-0694). It's inconveniently located, opposite the Liverpool department store and enclosed shopping center. It's on the second floor and open Monday through Friday from 8am to 4pm. There are two other branches: the airport office is staffed when flights are due; and La Venta Park has an office open Tuesday through Sunday from 8am to 4pm. The staff can supply rates and telephone numbers for the hotels as well as useful telephone numbers for bus companies and airlines.

CITY LAYOUT The hotels and restaurants I recommend are located off the four main streets: Madero, Piño Suárez, the Malecón, and Grijalva/Ruíz Cortínez. Highway 180 skirts the city, so a turn onto Madero or Piño Suárez will take you into the center of town.

Your point of focus in town can be the **Plaza Juárez,** or main square, bounded by the streets named Zaragoza, Madero, Sanchez, and Carranza. The plaza is the center of the downtown district, with the Río Grijalva to its east and Highway 186 to its north. Within this area is the **pedestrian zona,** with roads closed to traffic for five blocks. This zone is often called **Centro,** or **Zona Luz.** Villahermosa's main thoroughfare is Avenida Madero, running south from Highway 186 past the Plaza Juárez to the river, where it intersects with the riverside avenue, the Malecón.

GETTING AROUND

All the **city buses** converge on Avenida Piño Suárez at the market, and are clearly labeled for Tabasco 2000, Parque La Venta, and Centro; most rides cost about 35¢.

A **taxi** from the center of town to the Parque La Venta is about $6.

If you're getting around **by car,** Villahermosa's streets are well marked with arrows clearly designating the direction of traffic.

WHAT TO SEE & DO

You can hit the high points in a day. If you need to shop for any necessities or luxuries, head to the indoor shopping mall at Tabasco 2000, or the shops lining Avenida Madero.

PARQUE MUSEO LA VENTA, Av. Ruíz Cortínez s/n. Tel. 15-2228.

La Venta was one of three major Olmec cities during the Preclassic period (2000 B.C. to A.D. 300). The mammoth heads you see in the park were found in the tall grass when the ruins of La Venta were discovered in 1938. Today all that remains of the once-impressive city are some grass-covered mounds—once earthen pyramids—84 miles west of Villahermosa. All the gigantic heads and other important sculptures have been moved from the site to this lovely museum/park. Allow at least an hour to wander through the junglelike sanctuary, looking at the 3,000-year-old sculpture and listening to the birds that inhabit the grounds.

On a walk through the park you'll see Olmec relics, sculptures, mosaics, a mockup of the original La Venta, and of course three of the colossal Olmec heads. Carved around 1000 B.C., these heads are 6½ feet high and weigh around 40 tons. The faces seem to be half-adult, half-infantile, with that fleshy "jaguar mouth" that is characteristic of Olmecan art. The basalt rock was transported from the nearest source, over 70 miles from La Venta, which is all the more impressive when you realize they had no wheels to move it. The multiton rock was brought by raft from the quarry to the site. At least 16 heads have been found: four at La Venta, nine at San Lorenzo, and three at Tres Zapotes—all cities of the Olmecs.

On your stroll through the park, notice the other fine stone sculptures and artistic achievements of the Olmecs, who set forth the first art style in Mesoamerica, chiseling their monumental works without using metal. Their exquisite figures in jade and serpentine, which can be seen in the Regional Museum of Anthropology, far excelled any other craft of this period.

Admission: $2; $8.50 per camera for photography permits.

Open: Tues–Sun 8am–4pm. Sound-and-light show Fri–Sat at 7pm and 8:15pm; Tues, Thurs, and Sun at 7pm. **Directions:** Take Paseo Tabasco northeast to Highway 180, turn right, and it's less than a mile on your right, next to the Exposition Park.

MUSEO REGIONAL DE ANTROPOLOGÍA CARLOS PELLICER CÁMARA, Av. Carlos Pellicer 511. Tel. 12-1803.

This museum, on the west riverbank a mile south of the center of town, is architecturally bold and attractive, and very well organized inside. The pre-Hispanic artifacts on display include not only the Tabascan finds (Totonac, Zapotec, and Olmec), but artifacts pertaining to the rest of the Mexican and Central American cultures as well.

The first floor has the auditorium, bookstore, and gift shop, so most of what interests visitors is on the upper floors, reached by an elevator or stairs. The second floor is devoted to the Olmecs, and the third floor to central Mexico, including the Tlatilco and Teotihuacán cultures; the Huasteca culture of Veracruz, San Luis Potosí, and Tampico states; and the west coast cultures of Nayarit state. Photographs and diagrams provide vivid images, but the explanatory signs are mostly in Spanish. Look especially for the figurines that were found in this area, for the illuminated alabaster mask, and for the colorful Codex (an early book of pictographs).

Admission: $2.50.

Open: Daily 9am–7:30pm; gift shop Mon–Sat 9am–8pm.

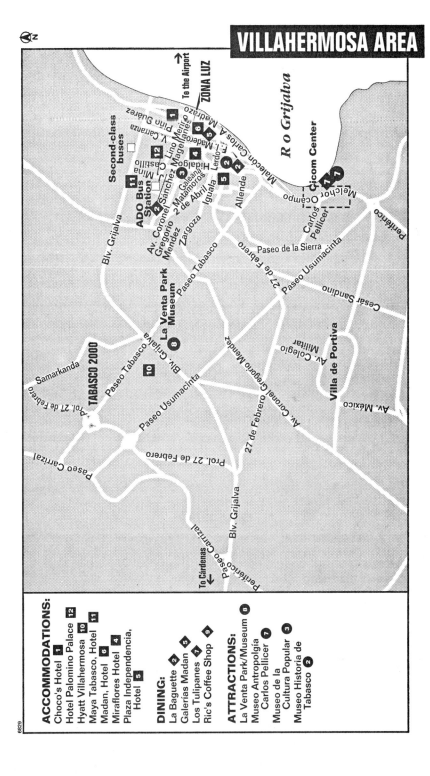

VILLAHERMOSA AREA

ZONA LUZ

To the Airport →

R o Grijalva

Cicom Center

Second-class buses

ADO Bus Station

Mina Castillo

TABASCO 2000

La Venta Park Museum

Samarkanda

Villa de Portiva

To Cardenas ↓

ACCOMMODATIONS:

Choco's Hotel **1**
Hotel Palomino Palace **12**
Hyatt Villahermosa **10**
Maya Tabasco, Hotel **11**
Madan, Hotel **6**
Miraflores Hotel **4**
Plaza Independencia, Hotel **5**

DINING:

La Baguette **2**
Galerías Madan **5**
Los Tulipanes **7**
Ric's Coffee Shop **9**

ATTRACTIONS:

La Venta Park/Museum **8**
Museo Antropolgía Carlos Pellicer **7**
Museo de la Cultura Popular **3**
Museo Historia de Tabasco **2**

6829

MUSEO DE LA HISTORIA DE TABASCO [Casa de los Azulejos], 27 de Febrero and Juárez. Tel. 12-4996.

Take a half hour and see this museum, which presents the history of Tabasco from pre-Columbian times to the present through documents, artifacts, and pictures. Every room is decorated with tiles in the Spanish and Italian baroque style, and the building's blue-and-white-tiled exterior, with wrought-iron balconies, is worth a snapshot. Only some explanations are in English. There's a nice gift shop off the lobby featuring products of the state of Tabasco, and books are for sale in the lobby. The museum is at the corner of 27 de Febrero and Avenida Juárez in the pedestrians-only zone.

Admission: $1.
Open: Daily 9am–8pm.

MUSEO DE CULTURA POPULAR, Calle Zaragoza 810. Tel. 12-1117.

This museum is near the post office, a short three-block walk from the Museo de la Historia. As you enter, on the right there's a small gift shop with baskets, carved gourds, embroidered regional clothing, and chocolate from Tabasco. Displays in the next room show the state's regional clothing and dance costumes. In the back is a Chontal hut, complete with typical furnishings and a recorded conversion of two female villagers talking about the high cost of living. Student guides are often on hand for a free explanation. One of them explained that he grew up in a hut like the one on display, but today there are only two huts like it remaining in his village of Tecoluta. Another room shows ceremonial pottery and household utensils. Located at the intersection of Juárez and Zaragoza, the museum is three blocks north of the Museo de la Historia.

Admission: Free.
Open: Daily 9am–8pm; shop 9am–2pm and 5–8pm.

WHERE TO STAY

The area around the intersection of Avenidas Juárez and Lerdo, the area sometimes referred to as Zona Luz, is now one of the best places to stay; the streets are pedestrian malls closed to traffic. One drawback to this plan is parking, though there are guarded lots on the outskirts of the mall. Room rates in Villahermosa are distressingly high, especially considering what you get.

EXPENSIVE

HYATT VILLAHERMOSA, Av. Juárez 106, Villahermosa, Tab. 86000. Tel. 93/13-4444, or toll free 800/233-1234 in the U.S. Fax 93/15-1235. 209 rms. A/C MINIBAR TV TEL

$ Rates: $140 single or double; $165 Regency Club room.

The Hyatt Villahermosa lives up to the high standards set by this worldwide chain. The beautifully furnished rooms are quiet and comfortable, with two double beds or one king-size bed—state your preference. Floors 6 through 9 hold the Regency Club, where guests receive special amenities, such as separate check-in, daily newspaper, continental breakfast, and evening cocktails. There's also a business center with access to a copy machine and fax; guests can also rent cellular phones. The Hyatt is at Tabasco and Bulevar Grijalva.

Dining/Entertainment: The Bougainvillea restaurant serves international specialties. La Ceiba is a café-style eatery open for all three meals. Two bars are open afternoons and evenings. The video bar La Plataforma is in the concert hall on the back of the grounds and is open Wednesday through Sunday from 8pm to 2am (there's a cover charge).

Services: Room and laundry service, travel agency, car rental.

Facilities: Pool, two tennis courts, boutiques, beauty shop, pharmacy, business center.

MODERATE

HOTEL MAYA TABASCO, Av. Ruíz Cortínez 907 (Apdo. Postal 131), Villahermosa, Tab. 86000. Tel. 93/12-1111 or 12-1825, or toll free 800/528-1234 in the U.S. Fax 93/12-1097. 156 rms. A/C TV TEL

$ Rates: $90 single or double. **Parking:** Free.

You can't go wrong in this comfortable and busy hotel with six floors of carpeted rooms. It's located on the main highway, convenient to the bus station, museums, and downtown. The large rooms have either two single beds, two double beds, or a king-size, with natural-toned colonial-style furniture, which includes a rocker. Some units have individually controlled air conditioning and some are controlled centrally.

Dining/Entertainment: The specialty restaurant El Jardín is open Monday through Saturday from 1pm to 1am. Kukulcán, the more informal restaurant off the lobby, is open daily from 7am to 10:30pm. There's an off-lobby bar open daily. Studio 8, the disco, opens at 9pm Thursday through Saturday (there's a cover charge).

Services: Room and laundry service, travel agency, and car rental.

Facilities: Pool, pharmacy.

BUDGET

HOTEL MADAN, Piño Suárez 105, Villahermosa, Tab. 86000. Tel. 93/12-1650. 20 rms. A/C TV TEL

$ Rates: $40 single; $48 double.

The two-story Hotel Madan is another convenient downtown lodging choice, within walking distance of the pedestrians-only zone and central city museums. The pleasant rooms are clean and carpeted. There's a comfortable sitting room and a cold-water dispenser on the second floor. The Madan is between Reforma and Lerdo, behind the popular Restaurant Galerias Madan.

HOTEL MIRAFLORES, Reforma 304, Villahermosa, Tab. 86000. Tel. 93/12-0022. Fax 93/14-0486. 54 rms. TV TEL

$ Rates: $40 single; $45 double; $50 triple.

Right in the heart of the pedestrian zone, the modern Hotel Miraflores couldn't be better situated. The comfortably furnished rooms have red-tile floors, Santa Fe–motif bedspreads, and nice-sized bathrooms. There's a nice restaurant off the lobby and a coffee shop on the street—great for watching downtown daily life. The Miraflores is at the south end of the pedestrian mall, near Madero.

HOTEL PALOMINO PALACE, Av. Mina 222, Villahermosa, Tab. 86000. Tel. 93/12-8431. 45 rms. A/C

$ Rates: $25 single or double. **Parking:** Free.

Directly across the street from the first-class bus station, the Palomino is surprisingly clean and quiet. The rooms are small, each with a couple of shelves for clothes (no closet) and blue-tiled bathrooms with hot-water showers. Those overlooking Avenida Mina are the noisiest; there are a few rooms away from the street that should be your first choice. There's a restaurant off the lobby open daily from 6am to midnight. The Palomino is a great choice for those just passing through town, and fills up quickly.

HOTEL PLAZA INDEPENDENCIA, Independencia 123, Villahermosa, Tab.
86000. Tel. 93/12-7541 or 12-1120, or toll free 800/528-1234 in the U.S. Fax
93/14-4724. 90 rms. A/C TV TEL

$ Rates: $46 single; $50 double; $55 triple. **Parking:** Free.

Of the many hotels in this price range the Plaza Independencia is by far the
best. The rooms on six floors (with elevator) have avocado drapes and rugs,
and nice bamboo furnishings, including a small desk. Some rooms have
balconies and river views; from the fifth (top) floor you can see the river. It's
the only budget hotel with a pool—a blessing in muggy Villahermosa—
and enclosed parking. There's an off-lobby restaurant open for all meals and
a bar open Monday through Saturday. Try to reserve your room in advance. The
hotel is two blocks south of the pedestrian area by the Plaza de Armas.

WHERE TO DINE

MODERATE

GALERIAS MADAN, Madero 408. Tel. 12-1650.
   Cuisine: MEXICAN.
$ Prices: Breakfast $3–$4.75; comida corrida $8; hamburgers $5–$7.
   Open: Daily 8am–11pm.

Situated in a lobby of shops, this calm, soft pink, air-conditioned restaurant serves a
comida of soup, rice, main course, vegetables, coffee, and dessert. Large windows
look out to the street, and the room has the feel of a hotel coffee shop where
downtown shoppers and business types gather. It's between Lerdo and Reforma.

LOS TULIPANES, CICOM Center, Periférico Carlos Pellicer Cámara 511.
   Tel. 12-9217 or 12-9209.
   Cuisine: SEAFOOD/STEAKS.
$ Prices: Appetizers $4.75–$8; seafood $8.50–$15; beef $13.35–$15.
   Open: Tues–Sun 1pm–1am.

Supremely popular with the local upper class, Los Tulipanes boasts moderately priced food and excellent service. They seem to serve a full house with
ease and on busy days a trio strolls and serenades. Since it's by the Río
Grijalva and the Pellicer Museum of Anthropology, you can combine a visit to the
museum with lunch here. Besides seafood and steaks there are Mexican specialties
such as chiles rellenos, tacos, and shrimp empanadas.

RIC'S COFFEE SHOP, Las Galas, Av. Mina. Tel. 14-0717.
   Cuisine: MEXICAN.
$ Prices: Breakfast $3.50–$8; soup $2–3.50; main courses $4.50–$12.
   Open: Daily 8am–10pm.

A clean, brightly lit coffee shop like something you'd find in the States. Ric's is a
blessing to those stranded at the nearby bus station. Breakfasts are the best deal,
with a pot of coffee included in the price of the meal; special meals served throughout the day include drinks. The air conditioning is powerful, the waiters and wait-
resses are friendly, and the restrooms are large and clean. Ric's is in the Las Galas
shopping center; turn left on Avenida Mina as you exit the bus station and walk
about half a block to the entrance. The center also has several bakeries and juice
stands.

BUDGET

LA BAGUETTE, Juárez 301. No phone.
   Cuisine: BAKERY.

$ Prices: Loaf of bread $1; sweet rolls, pastries, and cookies 25¢–$1.75.
Open: Mon–Sat 9am–9pm.

French bread is, of course, the specialty here, and on the back wall you'll see fresh loaves lined up like two-foot-long sentries. The Danish pastries, lavish French tortes, and chocolate-filled croissants should keep your sweet tooth satisfied. They've added prepared sandwiches and fruit drinks as well. It's in the pedestrian zone, opposite the Museo de la Historia. There are other branches in the Tabasco 2000 shopping center and the Las Galas shopping center by the bus station.

AN EXCURSION TO CHOCOLATE PLANTATIONS & THE RUINS OF COMALCALCO

Fifty miles from Villahermosa is Comalcalco, the only pyramid site in Mexico made of kilned stone. Your route will take you through Tabasco's cacao (chocolate)–growing country where you can visit plantations and factories to see the cacao from the pod on the tree to the finished chocolate bar.

You'll need a car to enjoy the cacao touring, but Comalcalco itself can be reached by bus from Villahermosa. Somellera line buses leave for the town of Comalcalco from the second-class bus station every 30 minutes; ADO has first-class buses at 12:30pm and 8:30pm. From the town of Comalcalco take a taxi or a VW minivan to ruins which are two miles farther. Travel agencies in Villahermosa offer a Comalcalco day-trip for $65. Generally it leaves at 8am and returns around 5pm. The price includes transportation, guide, and entry to the ruins, but not lunch.

By car, the fastest route from Villahermosa is on Highway 180 west to Cárdenas then north on Highway 187. Along the road to Cárdenas are numerous banana plantations and roadside stands loaded with the yellow fruit, one of the primary cash crops of the region. As you come into Cárdenas look for the **Alteza chocolate factory** of the cooperative Industriador de Cacao de Tabasco (INCATAB; tel. 12-0723). There's a sales shop in front where you can buy boxes of chocolate in all its variations—white, milk, and instant, and with varieties of ingredients, including peanuts and sesame seeds. The big boxes of chocolate they sell are actually filled with small wrapped, two-bite bars—great for stocking stuffers or gifts. Tours of the factory can be arranged Monday through Friday between 10am and noon for up to 25 people.

Cárdenas is the center of cacao processing but the fruit itself is grown in plantations in a wide area west of Villahermosa as far south as Teapa and north to the coast. After you turn right at Cárdenas onto Highway 187, you'll begin passing cacao beans.

Twelve miles before Comalcalco, in the village of **Cunduacan,** stop and ask for directions to the **Asociación Agricola de Productores de Cacao.** It's on the main street but the sign isn't visible. Mornings are best for a tour during November through April when there's an abundance of cacao. Here the cacao beans are received from the growers and processing begins. First the beans are fermented in huge tubs for a little over a week and you see the beans in various stages of bubbling. Then they are mechanically dried for 16 hours. A fresh white cacao bean is slightly larger and fatter than a lima bean, but after roasting it's brown and bitter and smaller than a black-eyed pea. The roasted beans are sacked and sent to the INCATAB chocolate cooperative in Cárdenas.

Along this route are many mom-and-pop cacao plantations where families grow and process their own cacao and sell it at local markets and roadside stands rather than to the cooperative. One of these is **Rancho La Pasadita,** 4½ miles before Comalcalco on the right. Look carefully for the sign (it's a bit obscured) but the sign

FROMMER'S NATURE NOTES
CHOCOLATE

Christopher Columbus first sampled chocolate (cacao) in Nicaragua in 1502, but passed up his chance to introduce it to the rest of the world. It was left to Hernán Cortés, Spanish conqueror of Mexico, to popularize it after sampling it with the Aztec emperor Moctezuma (who drank large quantities of the honey-and-pepper-flavored beverage). Thought to be an aphrodisiac introduced to the world by the god Quetzalcoatl, cacao beans were also used as money by the Aztecs. Cortés introduced cacao cultivation to several Caribbean islands and to Africa, and from there it spread to the rest of the world. Today Mexico ranks tenth in the world in production of cacao, with the states of Tabasco and Chiapas leading the way.

Cacao trees produce for 50 years and require a proper blend of humidity and shade. Trees are planted every 1½ feet under the shade of one of three different and much taller trees. The football-shaped, canteloupe-sized fruit begins as a flower on the tree's trunk and branches and matures four months and 20 days later. Men dragging large mesh bags and wielding machetes carefully harvest the pods, carrying them to a central location in the grove. There others whack open the tough outer shell and spill the contents of about 20 beans per pod into large woven baskets. The beans are fermented, dried, and processed into commercial products. The Industriador de Cacao de Tabasco in Cárdenas, Tabasco, on Mexico's Gulf coast, is the biggest processor of cacao in Latin America, averaging 15 million tons a year. Tabasco state, the chocolate capital of Mexico, produces 45 million tons annually, of which 30,000 are sold on the national and international markets, with the U.S. being the largest international buyer. Some of Tabasco's output is grown, processed, and sold by small vendors who make a homemade (*casera*) log-shaped bar mixed with sugar and different flavors suitable for hot chocolate. Besides traditional chocolate, the beans produce butter, moonshine wine, liquor, and a variety of refreshing and hearty drinks.

on the pink-and-blue house says **Chocolate Casero La Pasadita.** Here Aura Arellano has 19 acres of cacao trees that she planted in the 1950s. She will gladly take you out back where the trees grow, and if it's bean season (November through April) you'll more than likely see workers hacking open the football-shaped, canteloupe-size pods and dumping the contents in big wicker baskets. She ferments her beans the traditional way, in a hollowed-out canoe-size container. She dries and toasts the bean on a small *comal* (clay pan) over an open fire until they are hard like a nut, after which she grinds them to a powder, mixes it with sugar to cook and make into logs for hot chocolate that's *casera*, or homemade. These she sells in her living-room storefront for $4. You see this type of chocolate for sale in shops in Villahermosa.

Comalcalco, 25 miles from Cárdenas, is a busy agricultural center with an interesting market where you can buy wicker baskets like those used to ferment cacao, and *pichanchas* (gourd with holes in it) used to mash flavor from fresh cacao beans for a refreshing drink.

The ruins of Comalcalco are about two miles on the same highway past the town; watch for signs to the turnoff on the right. Park in the lot and pay the admission at the visitor's center by the museum. The museum, with many pre-Hispanic artifacts, is small but interesting and worth the 15 minutes or so it takes to see it. Unfortunately all the descriptions are in Spanish, but there's a history of the people who lived here, the Putún/Chontal Maya, a rough people who were traders, spoke a fractured Maya, and were believed to be those who founded or greatly influenced Chichén-Itzá.

The neat, grass-covered site spreads out grandly as you enter, with pyramidal mounds left, right, and straight ahead. Comalcalco means "house of the comals" in Nahuatl. A comal is a round clay pan used for roasting and making tortillas. All about the grounds you see shards of kilned brick that are also evident on the sides of pyramidal structures. These bricks were made with clay mixed with sand and ground oyster shell. Owing to the fragile nature of these ruins there are many NO SUBIR signs warning visitors not to climb certain structures. Others have paths and arrows pointing to the top. From the palace there's a fabulous view of the whole site. On the Acropolis, under a protective covering, are remains of stucco and plaster masks in surprisingly good condition, although there are few of them. Seeing the ruins takes an hour or so. Admission is $5 and the site is open daily from 8am to 5pm. The afternoon light is great for photographs.

2. PALENQUE

89 miles W of Villahermosa, 144 miles S of San Cristóbal

GETTING THERE By Plane The nearby airport at Comitán serves all Palenque charter flights, though the airport was closed when I was there. Check with travel agencies in Villahermosa, Tuxtla Gutiérrez, and San Cristóbal de las Casas for information.

By Train Plans to add a Mexico City–Mérida first-class train that would pass through Palenque never seem to materialize, but *this* could be the year. At this writing, the second-class train does stop at Ladrón, six miles from Palenque, en route from Mexico City to Mérida, but no one favors traveling on it. Horror stories of thefts, breakdowns, and general misery abound.

By Bus From Villahermosa's first-class ADO station there are seven buses to Palenque daily, with the trip taking from 1½ to 3 hours. From San Cristóbal there's one bus that leaves at 10am and arrives in Palenque near midnight. From Tuxtla Gutiérrez there's deluxe service on the Transportes Rudolfo Figueroa line three times daily.

From Mérida the trip to Palenque takes around nine hours. Deluxe Cristóbal Colón buses make the trip comfortable with several movies, snacks, and drinks en route.

By Car Highway 186 from Villahermosa is in good condition and the trip from there and on the Palenque turnoff should take about an hour and a half. From San Cristóbal the paved road is potholed in places, and in some spots the road has washed out, causing traffic to slow to one lane. This is especially true in the rainy season between May and October.

DEPARTING By Plane Charter flights fly in and out of nearby Comitán.

By Bus Three bus stations in Palenque will serve most of your needs for getting in and out of the village. **Auto Transportes Tuxtla** (tel. 5-0369) is on Juárez, on your right about a block from the Pemex station as you enter town. From here there are five buses daily to Tuxtla Gutiérrez, and five to San Cristóbal beginning at 8am. San Cristóbal de las Casas is a six-hour (minimum) trip. The line also has a bus to Agua Azul at 8 and 11:30am; tickets can only be purchased 30 minutes in advance.

Autotransportes Cristóbal Colón (tel. 5-0140) offers deluxe service between Palenque, San Cristóbal, Tuxtla Gutiérrez, Villahermosa, Mérida, and Ocosingo. **Transportes Rudolfo Figueroa** (tel. 5-0369) has deluxe service between Palenque and Tuxtla Gutiérrez with a stop in San Cristóbal at the highway near the main bus station. Passengers are only dropped off here, and cannot board to ride to Palenque or Tuxtla. These are the most deluxe buses traveling this route, with movies shown en route, curtained windows, air conditioning, and heat. If you tend toward claustrophobia or nausea, however, be forewarned that the windows do not open. **Mundo Maya,** another deluxe line, travels between Palenque and San Cristóbal three times daily.

ADO (tel. 5-0000) has one first-class bus daily to Mexico City at 6pm, one to Mérida at 9pm, seven to Villahermosa, one to Chetumal at 10pm, and two to Escárcega at 8am and 9pm.

The **Terminal de Transportes Dag Dug** (no phone) is also known as the **Mérida station,** although only one bus daily goes to Mérida at 5pm, making the eight-hour trip. The bus originates in Palenque, so chances of getting a seat are good if you buy a ticket a day in advance. Two *de paso* buses per day go to Villahermosa, San Cristóbal de las Casas, and Tuxtla Gutiérrez; and one goes to Ocosingo.

ESSENTIALS The telephone area code is 934. Palenque's constant humidity is downright oppressive in the summer months, especially after rain showers. During winter months the damp air can be chilly, especially in the evenings, so bring a jacket. Rain gear is important equipment any time of year.

The town of Palenque (pop. 16,000) would hardly exist were it not for the ruins.

The ruins and town are 31 miles south of Agua Azul, and 10 miles south of Misol Ha. It's a slow-paced, somnolent village accustomed to visitors passing through; it pays them little heed. The customary promenade of young people circling the plaza on weekends waiting for attention from the opposite sex is alive and well, but with modern overtones—few hawk-eyed dueñas oversee their charges from park benches, pairing up goes on in the shadows, there's lively music, and a fair share of youths circle in autos and trucks.

The ruins of Palenque, on the other hand, are one of the most spectacular Maya archeological sites, with roofcombed temples ensconced in lush vegetation high above the savannas. The ruins, located on the edge of the jungle in the state of Chiapas, are part of a reserve known as the **Parque Nacional Palenque.** The surrounding countryside seems to threaten the ruins with extinction once again, and it takes a team of machete wielders to hold the jungle back.

ORIENTATION

ARRIVING Most travelers reach Palenque by bus, arriving near the center of town. Taxis from the station to most hotels cost less than $4. Only those hotels surrounding the zócalo are within walking distance if you're carrying heavy luggage.

INFORMATION The **State Tourism Office** (tel. 5-0760 or 5-0828) is located near the zócalo, behind the Casa de la Cultura on Calle Jiménez. The office is open Monday through Saturday from 9am to 2pm and 4 to 8pm.

TOWN LAYOUT   The **ruins** are about five miles southeast of town. The road from Villahermosa forks just east of town at the impossible-to-miss Maya statue; the ruins are southwest of the statue, and town lies to the east. Palenque has three separate areas where tourists tend to congregate. The most central area is around the **zócalo,** bordered by Avenidas Hidalgo, 20 de Noviembre, Independencia, and Jiménez. **La Cañada** is a more pleasant area located five blocks east of the zócalo, on Merle Green, a partially paved road which runs through a tropical forest neighborhood. Here you'll find a few small hotels and restaurants and stands of artists who carve and paint. Besides the zócalo area, this is the best location for travelers without cars, since town is within a few blocks and the buses that run to the ruins pass by La Cañada. The third tourist zone is along the **road to the ruins,** where small hotels, RV parks, and campgrounds are tucked into the surrounding jungle. This is an ideal location for those with cars.

GETTING AROUND

The cheapest way to get back and forth from the ruins is on the **Chan Balu colectivo buses,** which depart from the terminal at Avenidas Juárez and Allende every 10 minutes from 7am to 7pm; the fare is 50¢. Chan Balu also has buses five times daily to Misol Ha and Agua Azul; the fare is $7. The buses pass La Cañada and hotels along the road to the ruins, but they may not stop if they are full.

   Taxis from town to the ruins cost $7; drivers may charge more from the ruins back to town.

WHAT TO SEE & DO

The real reason for being here is the ruins, which can be toured in a morning; but many people like to savor Palenque, going both in the morning and afternoon with time out for a siesta during the heat of the day. Although there is much new hotel construction on the road into town, the town of Palenque remains small and uncommercialized despite the fame of the ruins. But at the current rate of hotel building, that small-town ambience may not last long; more shops and restaurants continue to open downtown. There are no sights in the town, so if you have time to spare, sit on the main plaza and observe the goings-on. The La Cañada area east of town is a pleasant spot for a leisurely lunch and browsing through Maya reproductions made by local artists.

PARQUE NACIONAL PALENQUE

The ancient Maya city of Palenque was a ceremonial center for the high priests during the Classic period (A.D. 300–900), with the peak of its civilization around A.D. 600–700. Pottery found during the excavations shows that people lived here as early as 300 B.C.

   The archeological site of Palenque underwent several changes in 1994, culminating in the opening of a new museum and visitor's center on the highway to the ruins. The main entrance is still at the top of a hill at the end of the paved highway, where there is a large parking lot, a refreshment stand, and a ticket booth. A second entrance may be established on the highway near the museum, at the foot of a steep pathway leading up the hill beside the Cascada Motiepa waterfall.

   As you enter the ruins from the traditional entrance, the building on your right is the **Temple of the Inscriptions,** named for the great stone hieroglyphic panels found inside and containing the dynastic family tree of King Pacal (most of which is in the Anthropological Museum in Mexico City). The structure is famous for the tomb, or crypt, of Pacal that archeologist Alberto Ruíz Lhuller discovered in its depths in 1952. Pacal began building the temple less than a decade before he died at age 80 in A.D. 683. It took Lhuller and his crew four seasons of digging to clear out the rubble that was put there to conceal the crypt containing the remains of King Pacal. He reigned for 67 years, since he ascended to the throne at age 12. Lhuller's gravesite is opposite the Temple of the Inscriptions on the right as you enter the park. The crypt of Pacal itself is some 80 feet below the floor of the temple and was covered by a monolithic sepulchral slab 10 feet long and 7 feet wide. A plaster tube runs the length of the stairs to the crypt, and was meant to bring air to the five natives (four men and a woman) who were killed and left at the entrance to the crypt when it was sealed; they were to accompany Pacal on his journey through the underworld. Unless you're claustrophobic, you should definitely visit the tomb. The way down is lighted, but the steps can be slippery due to condensed humidity. This is the only pyramid built specifically as a tomb in Mexico. Carved inscriptions on the sides of the crypt, which visitors can't see, show the ritual of the funerary rites carried out at the time of Pacal's death, and portray the lineage of Pacal's ancestors complete with family portraits.

Back on the main pathway, the building directly in front of you is the **Palace,** with its unique watchtower. A new pathway between the Palace and the Temple of the Inscriptions leads to the **Temple of the Sun,** the **Temple of the Foliated Cross,** the **Temple of the Cross,** and **Temple XIV.** This group of temples, now cleared and in various stages of reconstruction, were built by Pacal's son, Chan-Bahlum, who is usually shown on inscriptions as having six toes. Chan-Bahlum's plaster mask was found in Temple XIV next to the Temple of the Sun. It's the one that's often shown nose to nose with a similar one of his father, Pacal, found in Pacal's tomb. Archeologists have recently begun probing the depths of the Temple of the Sun in search of Chan-Bahlum's tomb. Little remains of this temple's exterior carving. Inside, however, behind a fence, a carving of Chan-Bahlum shows him ascending to the throne in A.D. 690. The panels still in place show Chan-Bahlum's version of his historic link to the throne.

The Northern Group, to the left of the Palace, is also undergoing restoration. Included in this area are the **ballcourt** and the **Temple of the Count,** so named because Count Waldeck camped there in the 19th century. Explorer John Stephens camped in the **Palace** when it was completely tree and vine covered, and there he and Catherwood spent sleepless nights fighting off mosquitoes. At least three tombs complete with offerings for the underworld journey were found there. (For a summary of pre-Columbian history, see Chapter 1; for a thrilling insight into the dynasty here, read the Palenque chapter in *A Forest of Kings* by Linda Schele and David Friedel; Morrow, 1990.) The lineage of at least 12 kings has been deciphered from inscriptions left at this marvelous site.

The old museum building just past the Northern Group is now used for artifact storage, and is closed to the public. To the right of the building, a stone bridge crosses the river, leading to a pathway down the hillside to the new museum. The path is lined with rocks and has steps in the steepest area, leading past the **Cascada Motiepa,** a cool, beautiful waterfall that creates a series of pools perfect for cooling weary feet. Benches are placed along the way as rest areas, and some small temples have been reconstructed near the base of the trail. In early morning

FROMMER'S ARCHEOLOGY NOTES
THE CORBELLED ARCH

The corbelled or "false" arch is one of the hallmarks of Maya architecture. The center stone, rather than holding the two sides together, merely caps two sides of a V-shaped arch. This distinctive arch is made by first constructing one side, with each stone jutting out a bit farther than the last and weighting the stones on the back, then building the other side the same way, and finally joining the two with a center stone. These arches can be seen all over the Maya region, but the experience of walking in immense vaulted corbelled-arch rooms is special at Palenque; the famed arch at Labná is one of the most photographed.

and evening you may hear monkeys crashing through the thick foliage by the path; try to keep noise to a minimum and you may spot wild parrots as well. Walking downhill (by far the best way to go), it takes about 20 minutes to reach the main highway. The path ends on the right side of the highway (facing town). The colectivos will stop here if you wave them down. Currently there is not a ticket booth at the foot of the path. If you enter the ruins by making the steep climb up the path, be sure to stop at the main entrance and pay the fee.

Palenque's elaborate new **visitor's center** and **museum** were inaugurated in May 1993, and are located a few steps across the highway from the foot of the path. The complex includes a large parking lot; a refreshment stand serving sandwiches, snacks, and drinks; and two shops with an impressive display of folk art from throughout Chiapas. Vendors sell typical souvenirs along the parking lot by the main entrance to the ruins as well; among them are Lacandón Indians selling bows and arrows. The museum contains reproductions of artifacts from the ruins, including copies of the hieroglyphic panels from the Temple of the Inscriptions.

Admission to the ruins is $6.50; free on Sunday. There's an $8.50 charge for each camera used, and a $1 charge for parking at the main entrance (parking at the visitor's center is free). The site and visitor's center shops and café are open daily from 8am to 5pm; the museum is open Tuesday through Sunday from 10am to 5pm; the crypt is open daily from 10am to 4pm.

WHERE TO STAY

The three main hotel zones are near the fork in the road at La Cañada, in the village, or on the road to the ruins.

IMPRESSIONS

Such a sight in such a barren and god-forsaken spot left a deep impression on me. And if ruins usually have a grand and romantic charm, those of Palenque are unique and stupefying in their unexpected presence in a sea of hostile forest. There before me stood the mystery of the centuries, of a civilization dead and gone yet still strangely present and reflected in the grandiose buildings that proclaim a pride and glory that is no more.
—MICHEL PEISSEL, THE LOST WORLD OF QUINTANA ROO, 1963

IN LA CAÑADA

HOTEL LA CAÑADA, Calle Merle Green, Palenque, Chi. 29960. Tel. 934/ 5-0102. Fax 934/5-0392. 17 rms. A/C (4 rms) FAN (13 rms)

$ Rates: $37 single or double with fan; $42 single or double with A/C; $47 single or double with A/C and TV. **Parking:** Free.

This secluded group of cottages is surrounded by dense woods. The rooms are a bit musty, which comes with the jungle terrain. Señor Carlos Morales Marquez built the hotel in the 1960s, and his sons, who inherited the hotel, now run the place. Some of the rooms are now part of the Hotel Xibalba, run by another of the Morales brothers. La Cañada's palapa restaurant is one of the best in this area. The hotel is on the dirt and gravel road in La Cañada, about half a mile east of the Maya statue.

The noise from the nightclub just down the road can be significant on weekend nights; choose a room as far away from it as possible.

HOTEL MAYA TULIPANES, Calle Merle Green, Palenque, Chi. 29960. Tel. 934/5-0201. Fax 934/5-1004. 33 rms. A/C (12 rms) FAN (21 rms)

$ Rates: $46 single; $57 double; $67 triple. **Parking:** Free.

Maya statues, carvings, and paintings fill the hallways and public areas in this rambling, overgrown comfortable two-story hotel. Some of the windows are even shaped like the Maya corbelled arch. You definitely feel like you're in the jungle here, and the dark shade is a cool respite from the sun's glare.

Adventure-travel groups sometimes fill the hotel. It's one long block east of the Maya statue in La Cañada.

HOTEL XIBALBA, Calle Merle Green, Palenque, Chi. 29960. Tel. 934/5-0411. Fax 934/5-0392. 8 rms. A/C (4 rms) FAN (4 rms)

$ Rates: $30 single or double with fan; $35 single or double with A/C. **Parking:** Free.

Marco Morales Fimbres, one of the sons of the original owner of the Hotel La Cañada, has taken over some of that hotel's best rooms and created his own small inn. Four of the rooms in a modern building are the nicest in the area, with air conditioning and ceiling fans, lots of space, and bathtubs (a rarity in these parts). Four more rooms are located over the owner's Shivalva travel agency, and have showers and fans. The hotel also has the prettiest new restaurant in the area, called Mero Lec.

LA POSADA, Calle Inominada, La Cañada, Palenque, Chi. 29960. Tel. 934/5-0437. Fax 934/5-0193. 16 rms. FAN

$ Rates: $19 single; $25 double. **Parking:** Free.

If the rave reviews scribbled all over the lobby walls are any indication, La Posada is the most popular place in town. Owner Lourdes Chaves de Grajales took over the hotel in 1993 and continued the tradition of providing budget-priced rooms in pleasant surroundings. The original rooms are basic, each with one cement-platform double bed, a portable fan, and a large tiled bath with hot showers; room numbers are painted in Maya symbols. A second story has been added to the building with eight new rooms, all with two beds, fans, and tiled baths. The rooms face a wide lawn where tables and chairs are set out for guests, and the owner reports she has spotted spider monkeys in the nearby trees. Cold sodas, water, beer, and snacks are sold from a refrigerator in the lobby, near the Ping-Pong table.

La Posada is in La Cañada, left off Merle Green on a dirt road just past the Hotel Maya Tulipanes.

IN TOWN
Expensive

HOTEL MISIÓN PARK INN PALENQUE, Domicilio Conocido, Rancho San Martín de Porres, Palenque, Chi. 29960. Tel. 934/5-0241, or toll free 800/448-8355 in the U.S. Fax 934/5 0300. 160 rms. A/C TEL
$ Rates: $96 single or double; $110 triple.

Palenque's most luxurious hotel is a 20-minute walk from the first-class bus station, or a $2 taxi ride. The views of the surrounding, peaceful countryside—from the mountains to the jungle—are beautiful, and the caged parrots nearby add tropical background noises. The spacious rooms, with high-beamed ceilings and cobalt-blue and white walls, are in long, two-story buildings overlooking the gardens; those near the restaurant must bear the music until 10pm. The beds are enormous, the sheets and pillows soft and fragrant, the bathrooms sparkling clean—but the air conditioners are the noisiest I've ever heard. The pool is a blessing after a morning of pyramid climbing or playing tennis on the hotel's courts; there's a hot springs nearby for soaking your weary feet. The restaurant is remarkably good for one that serves busload after busload of European tour groups; it's especially nice on the patio, with candlelight. The hotel's free shuttle goes to and from the ruins six times a day. It's at the far eastern edge of town, left at the end of Cinco de Mayo.

Budget

CHAN-KAH CENTRO, Av. Independencia, Palenque, Chi. 29960. Tel. 934/ 5-0318. Fax 934/5-0489. 17 rms. FAN
$ Rates: $40 single; $46 double; $58 triple.

The only elevator in town is in this impressive five-story, wood-and-stone building overlooking the main plaza and the jungle beyond. Nine rooms have balconies, and the rooms have freshly painted white-brick walls, red-tile floors, large sinks and showers, over-bed reading lights, matching curtains and bedspreads, and soft sheets. There's a separate space for luggage in the bathroom area. Unfortunately, not all rooms are up to par, and some are pathetically small and basic. If you're not satisfied with what's offered, ask to see another room. There have also been some complaints about desk clerks asking higher rates than those agreed upon when reserving rooms. Try to get your reservation rate in writing by fax or mail. When a band is playing in the second-story bar it can be pretty noisy for the rooms in the front of the hotel, but that's not a nightly occurrence. Six rooms have TVs. It's on the plaza, four blocks from the bus stations.

HOTEL CASA DE PAKAL, Av. Juárez 18, Palenque, Chi. 29960. No phone. 15 rms. A/C
$ Rates: $37 single; $47 double; $56 triple.

This bright, relatively new three-story hotel far surpasses most others on Juárez. Air conditioning is a big plus here. Though the rooms are small, they're far brighter and cleaner than those at nearby establishments, and come with either one double or one single bed covered with chenille spreads. It's one block south of the zócalo.

HOTEL MISOL-HA, Av. Juárez 13, Palenque, Chi. 29960. Tel. 934/5-0092. 28 rms. FAN
$ Rates: $28 single; $32.25 double; $37 triple.

Once one of the most popular hotels in town, this place has deteriorated badly. Walk up a flight of stairs to reach the rooms' level. The walls in the rooms show wear, the shower heads are rusty and corroded, even toilet seats are missing in some rooms. Absolutely see your room before agreeing to a price; you may be able to negotiate a discount. The hotel is between the bus stations, and the zócalo on the north side of Juárez. Hotel parking is three block away.

KASHLAN HOTEL, 5 de Mayo 105, Palenque, Chi. 29960. Tel. 934/5-0297. Fax. 934/5-0399. 30 rms. FAN
$ Rates: $25 single; $30 double.
A half block from the bus station and a block from the zócalo, you're well located here. The spiffy clean rooms have interior windows opening to the hall, marble-square floors, nice bedspreads, tile bathrooms, small vanity, and luggage rack. A string of leather signs in a dozen languages says LEAVE YOUR KEY AT THE DESK in the lobby.

ON THE ROAD TO THE RUINS

CHAN-KAH RUINAS, Carretera Palenque km 31, Palenque, Chi. 29960. Tel. 934/5-0318. Fax 934/5-0820. 30 rms. FAN
$ Rates: $76 single; $91 double; $101 triple.
These comfortable little wood-and-stone bungalows are spread out in a beautiful jungle setting with sliding glass doors opening to a small patio facing the jungle. More rooms are being added. Facilities include a large swimming pool—a blessing after the long walk back from the ruins. Taxis are hard to come by here, and charge extra for picking you up at the hotel. A better way to get into town is to walk to the main road and flag down a colectivo or taxi on the road. The hotel has its own restaurant, with adequate but not wonderful food. Christmas holiday prices may be higher than those quoted here, so be sure to ask. And you may be quoted a higher price if you reserve a room in advance from the U.S. It's on the road to the ruins on the left side, 2½ miles northwest of the ruins.

CAMPING NEAR THE RUINS

There are two camping areas near the ruins, on the left-hand side of the road as you head out from town. The first one is very plain, cheap, and unappealing. You'd do better to continue to the next one, **Camp Mayabell,** within the grounds of the national park. Here you're only 1½ miles from the ruins, which are accessible by colectivo or on foot (about 30 minutes). Mayabell has hookups, showers, and palapas in which to hang your hammock. The price is $3 per person, and you can rent a hammock for $1 a night. Mayabell has full hookups for 24 campers for $10 to $15 a day. Bring your own hammock and hang it under a thatched palapa for $3, which includes use of the showers and bathrooms.

The **Restaurant and Trailer Park María del Mar** is at Carretera Palenque Ruinas km 2.7, Palenque, Chi. 29300 (tel. 934/5-0297). This trailer park has 86 trailer hookups, costing $20 a day. Facilities include showers, toilets, sinks, and a pool. The restaurant is open daily from 7am to 10pm.

WHERE TO DINE

Avenida Juárez is lined with many small eateries, none of which is exceptional. A good option are the many markets and panaderías (bakeries) along Juárez. **Panificadora La Tehuanito** has fresh cookies firm enough to withstand hours in the bottom of a purse, and **La Bodeguita** has a beautiful display of fresh fruit—just stick with those you can peel.

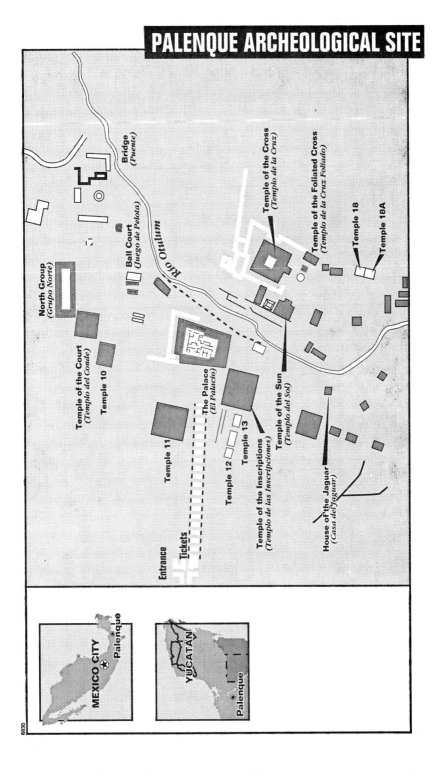

PALENQUE ARCHEOLOGICAL SITE

North Group
(Grupo Norte)

Bridge
(Puente)

Ball Court
(Juego de Pelota)

Río Otulum

Temple of the Cross
(Templo de la Cruz)

Temple of the Foliated Cross
(Templo de la Cruz Foliado)

Temple 18

Temple 18A

Temple of the Court
(Templo del Conde)

Temple 10

Temple 11

The Palace
(El Palacio)

Temple 12

Temple 13

Temple of the Sun
(Templo del Sol)

Temple of the Inscriptions
(Templo de las Inscripciones)

House of the Jaguar
(Casa del Jaguar)

Entrance

Tickets

MEXICO CITY

Palenque

YUCATAN

Palenque

EXPENSIVE

LA SELVA, Carretera Palenque s/n. Tel. 5-0363.
Cuisine: MEXICAN.
$ Prices: Appetizers $5.75–$8; main courses $9.25–$14.
Open: Daily 11am–10pm.

Palenque's traditional "best" restaurant continues to serve top-notch regional cuisine in a pleasant tropical setting. Despite its thatched roof, the dining room is large and refined, adapting well to buses filled with German couples on tour. The Pollo Palenque (chicken with potatoes in a tomato-and-onion sauce) is a soothing choice, and save room for the flan. Mexican wines are served by the bottle. It's a 10-minute walk from the Maya statue toward the ruins.

MODERATE

LA CAÑADA, Calle Merle Green. Tel. 5-0102.
Cuisine: MEXICAN.
$ Prices: Main courses $4.25–$11.50; beer $1.75.
Open: Daily 7am–10pm.

This palapa-topped restaurant tucked into the jungle is said to be one of the best restaurants in town, though it never seems crowded. Though the dining room has a dirt floor, the place is spotless, the service attentive, and the food good, though not exceptional. Breakfast is the best bet, or any of the local specialties—pollo mexicano or bean soup. Near the restaurant, the two-story thatched "club" La Nuit plays disco music and is the most popular dance spot in town. It's in La Cañada, on the left, about midway down the road.

CHAN-KAH CENTRO, Av. Independencia. Tel. 5-0318.
Cuisine: MEXICAN.
$ Prices: Comida corrida $6–$9; quesadillas $3.50.
Open: Daily 7am–11pm.

This attractive restaurant, on the west side of the main plaza, is in the nicest hotel in the center of town, and is the most peaceful place to eat. The menu is in English and Spanish and waiters are extremely attentive, and the food fairly well prepared. The second-story bar overlooks the plaza, and has live music some weekend nights.

RESTAURANT MAYA, Av. Independencia s/n. No phone.
Cuisine: MEXICAN.
$ Prices: Breakfast $5.45; main courses $5.75–$9.25.
Open: Daily 7am–10pm.

The most popular place in town among tourists and locals is on the main plaza near the post office. It's breezy and open, and managed by a solicitous family. A plus at breakfast are the free coffee refills. Try the tamales. It's across the street from the west side of the zócalo.

BUDGET

GIRASOLES, Juárez 189. Tel. 5-0385.
Cuisine: MEXICAN.
$ Prices: Comida del día $9; main courses $3.25–$4.25.
Open: Daily 7am–11pm.

There's always a smattering of locals and foreigners here taking advantage of the good prices. Decor is simple with cloth-covered tables and wicker lampshades on ceiling lights, and fans stirring up the air. It's a good place for resting your feet and

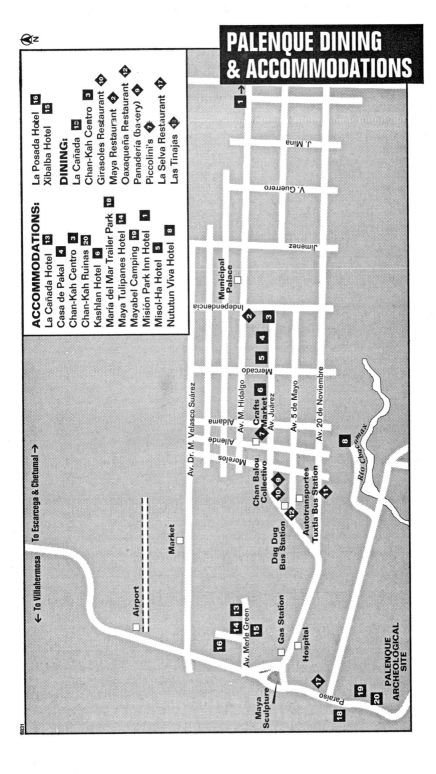

PALENQUE DINING & ACCOMMODATIONS

ACCOMMODATIONS:
La Cañada Hotel **13**
Casa de Pakal **4**
Chan-Kah Centro **3**
Chan-Kah Ruinas **20**
Kashlan Hotel **6**
Maria del Mar Trailer Park **18**
Maya Tulipanes Hotel **14**
Mayabel Camping **19**
Misión Park Inn Hotel **1**
Misol-Ha Hotel **5**
Nututun Viva Hotel **8**

La Posada Hotel **16**
Xibalba Hotel **15**

DINING:
La Cañada **13**
Chan-Kah Centro **3**
Girasoles Restaurant **10**
Maya Restaurant **2**
Oaxaqueña Restaurant **12**
Panadería (bakery) **9**
Piccolini's **7**
La Selva Restaurant **17**
Las Tinajas **11**

← To Villahermosa

To Escarcega & Chetumal →

Airport

Market

Av. Dr. M. Velasco Suárez

Aldama

Morelos

Allende

Av. M. Hidalgo

Av. Juárez

Crafts Market

Chan Balou Collectivo

Dag Dug Bus Station

Autotransportes Tuxtla Bus Station

Av. 5 de Mayo

Av. 20 de Noviembre

Mercado

Independencia

Municipal Palace

Jimenez

V. Guerrero

J. Mina

Río Chacamax

Gas Station

Hospital

Av. Merle Green

Maya Sculpture

Paraíso

PALENQUE ARCHEOLOGICAL SITE

watching the action besides getting a deal on the food. The menu covers the basics with fish, poultry, Mexican specialties, and decent tacos that are more like flautas. Fresh-brewed coffee comes from Chiapas and you can buy it ground by the kilo.

LA OAXAQUEÑA, Av. Juárez at Jorge de la Vega. No phone.
  Cuisine: MEXICAN.
$ **Prices:** Breakfast $3.75; plate lunch "paquete" $5–$8.
  Open: Daily 6am–10pm.

Get a taste of Oaxaca at this bright orange, barnlike restaurant with bamboo walls and windows that look out on the street near the bus stations. There's an enormous list of drinks, the mole is respectable, and the breakfasts basic and filling, but avoid the shrimp omelet. There's a huge list of drinks. It's one block north of the Tuxtla station on the same side of the street.

LAS TINAJAS, Calle 20 de Noviembre s/n. No phone.
  Cuisine: MEXICAN.
$ **Prices:** Breakfast $2.50–$4; main courses $3.50–$7.50.
  Open: Daily 8am–10pm.

Three wooden tables sit on the rickety front porch of this small restaurant, and there are a few more inside. It's a local favorite for the gigantic portions and low prices. One *sope* covered with beans, shredded lettuce, and cheese covers a dinner plate, as does a generous order of *chilaquiles*. The restaurant is one block north of the bus stations, and it's well worth searching out.

PICCOLINI'S, Av. Juárez s/n. No phone.
  Cuisine: PIZZA.
$ **Prices:** Pizza $5–$10; spaghetti $2.50; beer $1.25–$1.75.
  Open: Daily 7am–11pm.

This restaurant near the colectivo station serves Palenque's best pizza at rickety wood tables with red-checked cloths. Travelers from the U.S. are particularly fond of the place, and wolf down the decent-tasting pizza with relish. Don't count on pepperoni—the sausage is spicy Mexican chorizo—but the place does remind you of home. To find it from the zócalo, walk one block west.

EASY EXCURSIONS FROM PALENQUE

AGUA AZUL & CASCADA DE MISOL HA   The most popular excursion from Palenque is the day trip to the Agua Azul cascades. Trips can be arranged through Viajes Shivalva and ATC Tours and Travel, mentioned below, or minivans from the Chan Balu Colectivo Service make the round-trip to Agua Azul and the Cascada de Misol-Ha every day with five round-trips beginning at 9am; the last van departs Agua Azul at 6:30pm. They may wait until six or eight persons want to go, so check a day or two in advance of your proposed trip.

Several new travel agencies have popped up in town, most offering the same tours and services. Prices have become a bit more competitive and it's worth checking out a few of the agencies along Avenida Juárez. Be sure to ask if private or public transportation is used for the tours.

BONAMPAK & YAXCHILÁN   Adventurers might consider the two-day excursion to the Maya ruins of Bonampak and Yaxchilán. The ruins of Bonampak, southeast of Palenque on the Guatemalan border, were discovered in 1946. The mural, discovered on the interior walls of one of the buildings, is the greatest battle painting of pre-Hispanic Mexico. Reproductions of the vivid murals found there are on view in the Regional Archeology Museum in Villahermosa. You can fly or drive to Bonampak. Several tour companies offer a two-day (minimum) tour by four-wheel-drive vehicle to within 4½ miles of Bonampak. You must walk the rest of the way to the ruins, through boot-sucking mud in the rainy season. After camping over-night, you continue by river to the extensive ruins of the great Maya city, Yaxchilán, famous for its highly ornamented buildings. Bring rain gear, boots, a flashlight, and bug repellent. All tours include meals, but vary in price ($80 to $120 per person); some take far too many people for comfort (the seven-hour road trip can be unbear-able). Among the most reputable tour operators is **Viajes Shivalva,** Calle Merle Green 1 (Apdo. Postal 237), Palenque, Chi. 29960 (tel. 934/5-0411; fax 934/5-0392). Office hours are 7am to 3pm. **ATC Tours and Travel,** Avenida Allende at 5 de Mayo in the Hotel Kashlan, Palenque, Chi. 29960 (tel. and fax 934/5-0297), has the most clients and a large number of tours, including a one-day trip to the ru-ins of Tikal, in Guatemala, for five people, and another to Yaxchilán, Bonampak, and Tikal with a minimum of four persons. Besides their office in Palenque, their headquarters are in San Cristóbal opposite the El Fogón Restaurant, so you can make arrangements there as well.

An alternative way to reach Bonampak and Yaxchilán is via tours run by the **Chan Balu Colectivo Service** at Avenidas Juárez and Allende. A minimum of five people is needed to make the trip. The Palenque-Bonampak portion is five to seven hours by road and another 2½-hour hike; an overnight stay in rustic huts with wood-slat beds and no meals or mosquito netting; another two-hour bus ride; a river trip to Yaxchilán; and the long ride back to Palenque. It's a strenuous, no-frills trip that can be absolutely wonderful if you don't expect great service and bring plenty of food and drink, a hammock and net, and plenty of patience. The two-day trip costs about $100 per person.

When negotiating the deal, be sure to ask how many maximum will be in the bus, or you may not have a place to sit for 18 hours of bumpy dirt road.

EN ROUTE TO SAN CRISTÓBAL DE LAS CASAS

After you leave Palenque, you pass the Motel Nututum Viva and then climb into the Chiapan mountains. Six miles out of Palenque, you'll reach a fork in the road; take the right fork to get to **Ocosingo,** your intermediate destination. Most of the road is paved these days, but landslides, potholes, and washouts sometimes slow traffic during the rainy season. After 12½ miles from Palenque (km 47 of the official highway marking system), look for signs to Parque Natural Ejido Misol-Ha (a col-lective farm) on the right. (See "Easy Excursions from Palenque," above, for details.) About 38½ miles from Palenque is the well-marked turnoff, on the right, to **Agua Azul.** From the main road, you must go 2¾ miles on a painfully broken road down the hill into the valley to reach the *ejido* (communal property) and the swimming area. After Agua Azul it's about an hour's ride (40 miles) to Ocosingo, which has a few shops and small restaurants right on the highway. From Ocosingo, you have yet to travel 52 miles to reach the junction with the Pan American Highway 190. From the junction, it's 4½ miles into San Cristóbal. The trip takes around five hours and although the road is in rough condition in spots, the mountain scenery is gorgeous. You'll pass groves of bananas and papayas, then fir and pine forests; as you get closer to San Cristóbal women garbed in colorful regional attire begin to appear on the roadside, gathering sticks for firewood as they go about everyday life in the mountains.

3. SAN CRISTÓBAL DE LAS CASAS

143 miles S of Palenque, 50 miles W of Tuxtla Gutiérrez

GETTING THERE   By Plane   There are no commercial flights to San Cristóbal or nearby Ocosingo at this time, though someday San Cristóbal's airport may once again function. Tour agencies in Palenque and San Cristóbal can arrange flights by charter plane between the two cities for a minimum of four persons, but it's costly and difficult. Plans for an airport near San Cristóbal are in the works, with construction slated for 1995. Check with the tourist office for information.

By Bus   From Palenque: Five **Auto Transportes Tuxtla** buses make the five-hour trip daily. **Transportes Rudolfo Figueroa, Mundo Maya,** and **Cristóbal Colón** have deluxe service several times a day from both Tuxtla Gutiérrez and Palenque. The highway between San Cristóbal and Palenque is paved but portions of it are heavily potholed, washed out, or have dangerous dips. If you are prone to motion sickness, be careful not to eat anything before you get on the bus and carry gum or candy. Buy your ticket the day before your planned departure, if possible.

From Tuxtla Gutiérrez: The best way to get to San Cristóbal from Tuxtla Gutiérrez is to hop on one of the 12 direct buses from the first-class **Cristóbal Colón** bus station for the 1½-hour trip, or one of the deluxe Cristóbal Colón or **Transportes Rudolfo Figueroa** buses. The road between Tuxtla and San Cristóbal is a curvy one and the buses cover it rapidly, so motion sickness is a consideration. The highway climbs to almost 7,000 feet in a matter of 50 miles and the scenery is spectacular.

By Taxi   Taxis from Tuxtla Gutiérrez leave from both the airport or Cristóbal Colón bus station. If you strike a deal with a taxi driver he'll drive four people for around $8 per person to San Cristóbal, but you have to wait for three more passengers to assemble; a solo passenger will pay $30 to $35.

By Car   The road between Palenque and San Cristóbal de las Casas is an adventure in jungle scenery, with some fascinating hideaways to discover on the way. The trip takes about five hours. From Tuxtla it winds through beautiful mountain country and the closer you get to San Cristóbal the more colorfully garbed Indians you'll see along the roadway.

DEPARTING   By Plane   Since San Cristóbal's airport is closed, charter flights use the nearby Ocosingo airport, but they are difficult to arrange. If you need to make flight arrangements on other airlines, contact ATC Tours and Travel across from El Fogón de Jovel Restaurant in San Cristóbal.

By Bus   If you're going to Tuxtla, **Cristóbal Colón** (tel. 8-0291), has hourly first-class buses (called *locales*) from 6:30am to 9:30pm originating in San Cristóbal; nine others pass through (*de paso*) and take on passengers if there's space. Deluxe "Plus" Cristóbal Colón buses depart for Tuxtla at 4 and 5:30pm. Two daily buses go to Villahermosa at noon and 8:15pm and the trip takes seven to eight hours. There's one afternoon bus daily to Oaxaca at 5:15pm; be prepared for a 12-hour trip. Four first-class buses originating in Tuxtla go to Palenque at noon, 5 and 8:15pm, and 1am. Buses for Villahermosa leave at noon and 8:15pm and for Comitán every hour from 6am to 9pm. Deluxe "Plus" buses leave for Mérida at 9:15am and 8pm (a 14-hour trip) and Palenque at 9:15am and 2pm. Or you can sign up for one of the tours to Palenque from San Cristóbal. You have a choice of 17 buses to Tapachula, but they all take at least nine hours.

To ensure a seat on one of the *locales,* purchase your ticket a day or two in advance at the Cristóbal Colón station.

From the second-class bus station, **Transportes Tuxtla** (tel. 8-0504), a total of six buses go to Palenque, two of them with reserved seats at 6am and 12:30pm. There are three distinct bus lines here, and you cannot make reservations on them since the buses originate elsewhere. Be sure you get on the bus whose ticket you hold. Twenty buses throughout the day ply the road to Tuxtla, and five go to Comitán. On **Transportes Fray Bartolomé de las Casas** you can also get buses to a few outlying villages—to Pentalho at 7 and 10am and 1pm, to Chenalho at 1 and 2pm, and San Andrés at 1:45pm. On the latter be sure to check on the availability of return buses *before* starting out.

Autotransportes Lacandonia (tel. 8-1455) also travels from the second-class station to Ocosingo, Agua Azul, and Lagos de Montebello. By the time you visit, the second-class station should have moved to the new government complex under construction on the highway near Insurgentes. Check with the tourist office for information on where the various bus lines are stationed.

To get your bearings in relation to surrounding areas, San Cristóbal (alt. 6,972 ft.; pop. 90,000) is 46 miles southeast of Comitán, only 104 miles southeast of Cuauhtémoc and the Guatemala border, and 282 mountainous miles east of Oaxaca. It's a colonial town set in a lovely valley and it's the major market center for Indians of various tribes from the surrounding mountains. Probably the most visible among them are the Chamulas. The men wear baggy thigh-length trousers and white or black serapes and the women wear blue rebozos, white gathered blouses with embroidered trim, and black wool wraparound skirts. Among the Zinacantecans, the male population dresses in light-pink overshirts with colorful trim and tassels, and sometimes short pants, with hat ribbons (becoming a rare sight) tied on the married men and dangling loose on the bachelors. The women wear beautiful woven shawls of bright pink, blue, black, or beige trimmed in pink, blue, red, or beige with black wool skirts. Tenejapa men wear knee-length black tunics and flat straw hats and the women wear beautiful and heavy wool reddish, rust-color huipils.

San Cristóbal is deep in Mesoamerica where the Maya flourished. In fact, nearly all the Indians in the immediate area speak languages derived from ancient Maya— Tzotzil or Tzeltal. Some don't come into town at all, and one group, the Lacandóns (who number only about 450), live far off in the forests of eastern Chiapas. There are several Indian villages within access of San Cristóbal by road—Chamula, with its weavers and non-Christian church; Zinacantán, whose residents practice a unique religion and wear brilliantly colored clothing; Tenejapa, San Andrés, and Magdalena, known for brocaded textiles; Amatenango del Valle, a town of potters; and Aguacatenango, known for embroidery. Most of these "villages" consist of little more than a church and the municipal government, with homes scattered for miles around and a general gathering only for church and market days (usually Sunday).

Each Maya village elects its own leaders who serve for one year. It's an expensive honor since they must be able to live in the village for a year without an income. Their duties include keeping a home altar for the saints, overseeing the church, preparing religious celebrations, settling disputes, and administering justice for everything (except possibly murder). On market days these leaders sit or walk together and they're most notable because of their colorful ribboned hats and silver studded staffs. A token non-Maya Mexican administrator has a presence in the

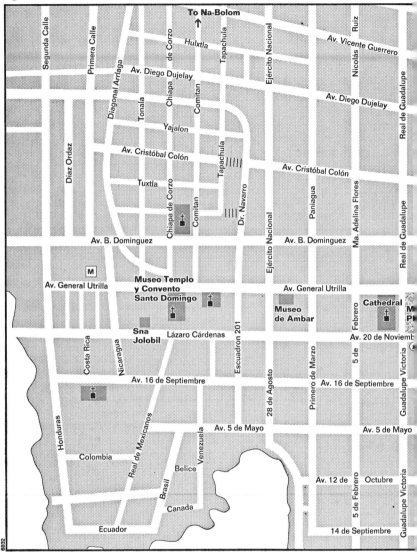

village, but generally doesn't step in unless there's a serious infraction. Until the 1994 uprising in the area, the villagers generally refused to go to the health clinics that were established for them, preferring to rely on trusted outsiders or on folk healers for medicine. However, this attitude may be changing since one of the grievances causing the uprising was lack of health care.

You'll hear the word *Ladino* here and it means non-Indian Mexicans or people who have taken up modern ways, changed their dress, dropped their Indian traditions and language, and live in town. It is both derogatory and descriptive, depending on who is using it and how it's used.

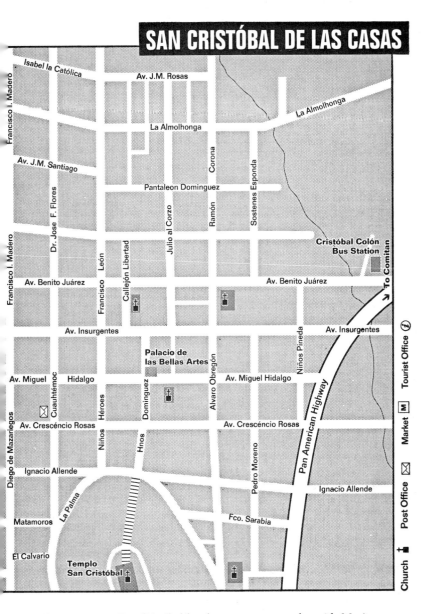

Isabel la Católica

Av. J.M. Rosas

La Almolhonga

La Almolhonga

Francisco I. Madero

Av. J.M. Santiago

La Almolhonga

Dr. José F. Flores

Pantaleon Dominguez

Corona

Sostenes Esponda

Ramón

Julio al Corzo

Francisco I. Madero

León

Francisco

Callejón Libertad

Av. Benito Juárez

Av. Benito Juárez

Cristóbal Colón
Bus Station

To Comitan

Av. Insurgentes

Av. Insurgentes

Niños Pineda

Palacio de
las Bellas Artes

Alvaro Obregón

Av. Miguel Hidalgo

Av. Miguel Hidalgo

Cuauhtémoc

Hidalgo

Héroes

Dominguez

Av. Crescéncio Rosas

Av. Crescéncio Rosas

Diego de Mazariegos

Niños

Hnos

Pedro Moreno

Pan American Highway

Ignacio Allende

Ignacio Allende

La Palma

Matamoros

Fco. Sarabia

El Calvario

Templo
San Cristóbal

Tourist Office ⓘ   Market Ⓜ   Post Office ⊠   Church ✝■

In recent years San Cristóbal has become more popular with Mexicans, not to mention North Americans and Europeans in search of a charming, cool, "unspoiled," traditional town to visit or settle in. As a result, it's no longer quite as quaint as it once was—but it's by no means ruined. Also in recent years Christian missionaries have converted large numbers of indigenous peoples. In some villages they must pay the price by being expelled from their homelands, requiring them to find other homes and work; these people are called *expulsados* (expelled ones). In Chamula, for example, as many as 30,000 have been expelled and many have taken up residence in new villages on the outskirts of San

Cristóbal de las Casas. They still wear their traditional dress although their religious beliefs have changed. Other villages, such as Tenejapa, allow the Christian church to exist and villagers to attend it without prejudice.

Although the influx of tourists is increasing and the influence of outsiders (Mexicans as well) is inevitably chipping away at the culture, the Indians aren't really interested in being like or looking like the foreigners in their midst. They may steal glances at tourists and stare curiously, but mainly they pay little attention to outsiders. Just in case we think they are envious of our clothing, possessions, or culture, I'll repeat an interesting comment made one night during dinner at Na-Bolom with a Maya specialist living in San Cristóbal: "They think we are the remains of a leftover civilization and that we eat our babies."

PHOTOGRAPHY WARNING In and around San Cristóbal taking a photograph can be a risky undertaking because of the native belief that a photograph takes away the soul. Photographers should be very cautious about when, where, and at whom or what they point their cameras. To ensure proper respect by outsiders, villages around San Cristóbal, especially Chamula and Zinacantán, require visitors to go to the municipal building upon arrival and sign an agreement not to take photographs or the punishment will be severe. The penalty for disobeying these regulations is stiff—confiscation of your camera and perhaps a lengthy stay in jail. They mean it! In San Cristóbal the consequences for pointing your camera, even at a chili pepper, are somewhat less—you may be pelted with fruit, vegetables, and stones. Be respectful and ask first. You might even try offering a small amount of money in exchange for taking a picture. Young handcraft vendors will sometimes offer to be photographed for money.

ORIENTATION

ARRIVING The **first-class Cristóbal Colón bus station** is on Highway 190, which runs on the southern outskirts of San Cristóbal. The street that intersects the highway in front of the bus station is Avenida de los Insurgentes, which is straight up from the central plaza. From the station, the main plaza is nine blocks north along Insurgentes (a 10- or 15-minute walk).

The deluxe **Rudolfo Figueroa** buses traveling between Palenque and Tuxtla drop passengers on the side of the highway near the first-class bus station. To catch a cab or minibus, walk over to the station.

The **second-class Transportes Tuxtla station** is on Allende at Calle Moreno, three or four blocks from the Cristóbal Colón station. To get to the central plaza walk east along Moreno to get to Insurgentes, then turn left (north) toward the plaza.

INFORMATION The **Municipal Tourism Office** (tel. 8-0660, ext. 114), on the main square in the town hall next to the cathedral, is well organized with a friendly, helpful staff. The office keeps especially convenient hours: Monday through Saturday

---

IMPRESSIONS

Although many scholarly studies seem to treat Maya civilization as one of history's closed chapters, the Maya did not vanish. Almost one million Maya-speaking people live in Chiapas, the southernmost state of Mexico, and another three million live in Yucatán, Belize, Guatemala, Honduras, and El Salvador.
—Walter F. Morris, Jr., Living Maya, 1987

from 8am to 8pm, and Sunday from 9am to 2pm. Check the bulletin board here for apartments for rent, shared rides to the States, cultural events, and local tours.

CITY LAYOUT The cathedral marks the main plaza, where Avenida de los Insurgentes becomes Utrilla. All streets crossing past the plaza change their names here. The market is nine blocks north along Utrilla, while the bus station is south. From the market, minibuses (colectivos) trundle to outlying villages.

Take note that this town has at least three streets named "Domínguez." There's Hermanos Domínguez, Belisario Domínguez, and Pantaleón Domínguez.

GETTING AROUND

Most of the sites and shopping in San Cristóbal are within walking distance of the plaza.

Colectivo buses to various parts of the city and the outlying villages depart from the public market at Avenida General Utrilla. Buses late in the day are usually very crowded. Always check to see when the last or next bus returns from wherever you are going, then take the one before that—those last buses sometimes don't materialize and you'll be stranded. Experience is speaking!

As traffic increases in the city it often seems quicker to walk to your destination than grab a taxi. Rides from the plaza to most parts of the city are less than $2. There is a taxi stand beside the cathedral at the north side of the plaza.

RENTAL CARS A car comes in handy for trips to the outlying villages, and may be worth the expense when divided among a group. But keep in mind that insurance is invalid on nonpaved roads. There's a Budget rental-car office here at Av. Mazariegos 36 (tel. 8-1871). You'll save money by arranging the rental from your home country. Otherwise a day's rental with insurance will cost $50 in a VW Beetle with manual transmission, the cheapest car to rent.

RENTAL BICYCLES These are a good option for getting around the city; a day's rental is about $10. Bikes are available at **Rent a Bike,** Av. Insurgentes 57 (tel. 8-4157) and at some hotels.

FAST FACTS

Area Code The telephone area code is 967.

Books *Living Maya*, by Walter Morris with photography by Jeffrey Fox (Abrams), is the best book to read for understanding the culture around San Cristóbal de las Casas. *The People of the Bat: Mayan Tales and Dreams from Zinacantán*, by Robert M. Laughlin (Smithsonian), is a priceless collection of beliefs from that village near San Cristóbal.

Bookstore For a good selection of books about local Indians and crafts, go to Librería Soluna, Real de Guadalupe 13B and Insurgentes 27.

Climate San Cristóbal can be very cold day or night all year, but especially during the winter months. Most hotels are not heated although some have fireplaces. Come prepared to bundle up in layers that can be peeled. I always bring heavy socks, gloves, long johns, and a wool jacket, except in June, July, and August when I leave off the latter three. Then I bring a medium-weight jacket or sweater and always some warm footwear. Some sort of rain gear is handy all year as well, but especially in summer when rains can be torrential.

Currency Exchange On the main plaza Banamex is opposite the municipal palace and is open Monday through Friday from 9:30am to 1pm. However, the most convenient place to exchange money is the Money Exchange on Real de Guadalupe 12A, half a block from the plaza and next to the Real del Valle Hotel. It's open Monday through Saturday from 9am to 2pm and 4 to 8pm, and Sunday from 9am to 1pm.

Parking If your hotel does not have parking, use the underground public parking lot (*Estacionamiento*) located in front of the cathedral, just off the main square on 16 de Septiembre. There's a $2 charge per night.

Post Office The post office (correo) is on Avenida Crecencio Rosas and Cuauhtémoc, half a block south of the main square. It's open Monday through Friday from 8am to 7pm for purchasing stamps and mailing letters, 9am to 1pm and 4 to 5pm for mailing packages, and on Saturday and holidays from 9am to 1pm.

Spanish Lessons Centro Bilingue, at the El Puente Café, Real de Guadalupe 55, San Cristóbal de las Casas, Chi. 29250 (tel. 967/4-4157; fax 967/8-3723) offers classes in Spanish.

Telegraph The telegraph office, Calle Diego de Mazariegos 27 (tel. 8-0661), is just past Avenida 5 de Mayo.

SPECIAL EVENTS

In nearby Chamula, **Carnaval,** the big annual festival, occurs three days before Lent. It's a fascinating mingling of the Christian pre-Lenten ceremonies and ancient Maya celebration of the five "lost days" that arise at the end of the 360-day Maya agricultural cycle. Around noon on the Tuesday before Ash Wednesday, groups of village elders run across patches of burning grass as a purification rite, then macho residents run through the streets with a bull. During Carnaval, roads are closed in town and buses drop visitors at the outskirts. *Warning:* No photography of any kind is allowed during the Chamula Carnaval celebrations.

Although perhaps not as dramatic, nearby villages (but not Zinacantán) have celebrations during this time. Visiting them, especially the Sunday before Ash Wednesday, will round out your impression of Carnaval in all its regional varieties. In Tenejapa, the celebrants are still active during the Thursday market after Ash Wednesday.

San Cristóbal explodes with lights, excitement, and hordes of visitors during the week after Easter, when the annual **Feria de Primavera** (Spring Festival) is held. Activities, including carnival rides, foodstalls, handcraft shops, parades, and band concerts, fill an entire week. Hotel rooms are scarce and room prices rise accordingly.

Another spectacle is staged July 22 to 25, the date of the annual **Fiesta of San Cristóbal,** the town's patron saint. The steps up to the San Cristóbal church are lit with torches at night. Pilgrimages to the church begin several days earlier and on the night of the 24th there's an all-night vigil.

WHAT TO SEE & DO

Although San Cristóbal is a mountain town and somewhat hard to get to, it continues to draw more and more visitors. They come to enjoy the scenery, the air, and hikes in the mountains. But most of all they come to bask in the colorful indigenous culture that carries on traditional centuries-old daily life, including such customs as wearing beautifully crafted native garb. The life of the Chiapan Maya swirls around you in San Cristóbal, but most travelers take at least one trip to the outlying villages for a clearer vision of the "living Maya."

NA-BOLOM, Av. Vicente Guerrero 33, San Cristóbal de las Casas, Chi. 29220. Tel. and fax 967/8-1418.

If you're interested in the anthropology of this region, you'll want to visit this house/museum and to stay here if you can. The home, built to house a seminary in 1891, became the headquarters of anthropologists Frans and Trudy Blom in 1951 and the focal point for serious study of the region for outsiders. Frans Blom led many early archeological studies in Mexico, and Trudy was noted for her photographs of the Lacandón Indians and her efforts to save them and their forest homeland. Limited edition sets of her Lacandón photographs are on sale in Na-Bolom and a room showcases a selection of them. A tour of the home includes the displays of pre-Hispanic artifacts collected by Frans Blom, the cozy library with its numerous volumes about the region and the Maya, and the gardens Trudy Blom started for ongoing reforestation of the Lacandón jungle. The tour ends with an excellent 15-minute film on the life of the Bloms, the Lacandóns, and Na-Bolom. Trudy Blom died in 1993, but Na-Bolom will continue as a nonprofit trust.

The 15 guest rooms are named for surrounding villages and are decorated with objects and textiles from them. All except two rooms have fireplaces. Guests are allowed to use the extensive library devoted to Maya literature. Prices for rooms (including breakfast) are $45 single, $50 double, and $55 triple.

Even if you're not a guest here, you can come for a meal, usually a delicious assortment of vegetarian dishes. Just be sure to make a reservation and be on time. The colorful dining room has one large table, and since it's a gathering place for all kinds of visitors, the eclectic mix can make for interesting conversation. After dinner, if there's interest, a host will light a fire in the library, and guests can gather there by the glow of the fire for coffee and conversation amidst more of the Bloms' pre-Hispanic artifacts as well as regional textiles and crafts. Breakfast costs $4, lunch $7.50, and dinner $8.

Admission: Individual tour, $2; group tour and film *La Reina de la Selva,* $3.50.

Open: Individual tours available daily 9am–1:30pm. Group tour and film *La Reina de la Selva* offered Tues–Sun 4:30–7:30pm. **Directions:** Leave the square on Real de Guadalupe, walk four blocks to Avenida Vicente Guerrero, and turn left; Na-Bolom is 5½ blocks up Guerrero, just past the intersection with Comitán.

MUSEO DE ÁMBAR, Plaza Sivan, Utrilla 10. Tel. 8-3507.

From the street it looks like another store selling Guatemalan clothing, but pass through the small shop area and enter the long, narrow museum, a fascinating place to browse. It's the only museum in Mexico devoted to amber, a vegetable fossil resin millions of years old and mined in Chiapas near Simojovel. Owner José Luis Coria Torres has assembled more than 250 sculpted amber pieces as well as a rare collection of amber with insects trapped inside and amber fused with fossils. Amber jewelry and other objects are also for sale.

Admission: Free.

Open: Daily 9am–8pm. **Directions:** From the plaza, walk on Utrillo toward the market and the Museo will be on the left after a couple of blocks.

TEMPLO Y CONVENTO SANTO DOMINGO, Av. 20 de Noviembre.

Women from the various villages around San Cristóbal gather here to sell their weavings and tapestries. Enter through the front door of the carved-stone plateresque facade and inside there's a beautiful gilded wooden altarpiece built in 1560, and walls with saints and gilt-framed paintings. Attached to the church is the ex-Convento Santo Domingo, which now houses a small museum of San Cristóbal and Chiapas. It's five blocks north of the zócalo.

Admission: Church free; museum $2.75 Mon–Sat; free on Sun and holidays.
Open: Museum Tues–Sun 9am–6pm.

THE CATHEDRAL, Av. 20 de Noviembre at Guadalupe Victoria.

San Cristóbal's main cathedral was built in the 1500s and boasts some fine timberwork and a very fancy pulpit.
Admission: Free.
Open: 7am–6pm.

PALACIO BELLAS ARTES, Av. Hidalgo, four blocks south of the plaza.

Be sure to check out this building, four blocks south of the plaza, if you are interested in the arts. It houses sporadic events of dancing, art shows, and other performances, and the schedule of events and shows is usually posted on the door if the Bellas Artes is not open. There's a public library next door.

TEMPLO DE SAN CRISTÓBAL.

For the best overview of San Cristóbal, climb the seemingly endless steps to this church and mirador, or lookout point. Leave the zócalo on Avenida Hidalgo, turn right onto the third street (Hermanos Domínguez); at the end of the street are the steps you've got to climb. A visit here requires stamina. By the way, there are 22 more churches in town, some of which require a strenuous climb up.

HORSEBACK RIDING

The Casa de Huéspedes Margarita and the Hotel Real del Valle (see "Where To Stay," below) can arrange horseback rides for around $20 a day, including a guide. Reserve your steed at least a day before. A horse-riding excursion might go to San Juan Chamula, to nearby caves, or just up into the hills.

SHOPPING

Many Indian villages near San Cristóbal are noted for their weaving, embroidery, brocaded work, leather, and pottery, making the area one of the best in the country for shopping. The craftspeople make and sell beautiful serapes, colorful native shirts, and rebozos in vivid geometric patterns. In leather they are artisans of the highest rating, making the sandals and men's handbags indigenous to this region. There are numerous shops up and down the streets leading to the **market,** all of them willing to sell you anything from string bags and pottery to colorfully patterned ponchos. **Calle Real de Guadalupe** houses more shops than any other street. There's a proliferation of tie-dyed jaspe from Guatemala in bolts and made into clothing, as well as other textiles from that country.

CRAFTS

CENTRAL MARKET, Av. Utrilla.

The market buildings, and the streets surrounding them, offer just about anything you need. Market day in San Cristóbal is every morning except Sunday (when each village has its own local market), and you'll probably enjoy looking at the sellers as much as at the things they sell. Remember, locals generally don't like to be photographed and resent photographs being snapped even of what they are selling. Doing either may make you the object of curses and recipient of flying fruits and vegetables. The mercado is north of the Santo Domingo church, about nine blocks from the zócalo.

EL ENCUENTRO, Real de Guadalupe 63-A. Tel. 8-3698.

Tended by a pair of helpful dueñas, you'll find some of your best bargains here; or at least you'll think the price is fair. The shop carries many regional ritual items such as new and used men's ceremonial hats, false saints, and iron rooftop adornments, plus many huipils and other textiles. It's open Monday through Saturday from 9am to 8pm.

LA GALERÍA, Av. Hidalgo 3. Tel. 8-1547.

This lovely shop beneath a great café has a wonderful selection of paintings and greeting cards by Kiki, a German artist who has found her niche in San Cristóbal. There is also a good selection of Oaxacan rugs and pottery, and unusual silver jewelry. It's open daily from 10am to 9pm.

PLAZA DE LA CALLE REAL, Calle Real de Guadalupe 5.

A number of boutiques are housed in this beautiful old one-story town house. Shop hours vary, but most are open from 10am to 1pm and 4 to 7pm.

TEXTILE SHOPS

CASA DE ARTESANÍAS DIF, Niños Héroes at Hidalgo. Tel. 8-1180.

Crafts made under the sponsorship of DIF (a governmental agency that assists families) are sold in a fine showroom in one of the city's old hacienda-style houses. Here you'll find quality products such as lined wool vests and jackets, bolts of foot-loomed fabrics, Persian-style rugs made at La Albarrada (see below), pillow covers, amber jewelry, and more. In back is a fine little museum showing costumes worn by villagers who live near San Cristóbal. It's open Tuesday through Friday from 9am to 2pm and 4 to 8pm. Saturday, Sunday, and Monday it's open from 10am to 2pm and 5 to 8pm.

LA ALBARRADA, CENTRO DESARROLLO COMUNITARIO DIF, Barrio María Auxiliadora. No phone.

At this government-sponsored school young men and women from surrounding villages come to learn how to hook Persian-style rugs, weave fabric on foot looms, sew, make furniture, construct a house, cook, make leather shoes and bags, forge iron, and grow vegetables and trees for reforestation.

Probably the most interesting for the general tourist is the rug making and weaving. Artisans from Temoaya in the state of Mexico learned rug making from Persians who came to teach them in Mexico in the 1970s. In 1988 the Temoaya artisans traveled to San Cristóbal to teach the craft to area students who in turn have taught others. The beautiful rug designs are taken from brocaded and woven designs used to decorate regional costumes. Visitors should stop at the entrance and ask for an escort. You can visit all the various areas and see students at work, or simply go straight to the weavers. There's a small sales outlet at the entrance selling newly loomed fabric by the meter, leather bags, and rugs and baskets made at another school in the highlands. The rug selection is best here, but there's a Casa de Artesanías DIF in the town center (see above) with these additional crafts and more from around Mexico.

La Albarrada is in a far southern suburb of the city off the highway, right, to Comitán. To get there take the María Auxiliadora *urbano* bus from the corner of 16 de Septiembre and Guadalupe Victoria half a block from the main plaza, or catch it at the market. Ask the driver to let you off at La Albarrada. The same bus returns, passing through town center and ends at the market.

LA SEGOVIANA, Real de Guadalupe 26. Tel. 8-0346.

After a short stint in another location, La Segoviana has moved back to the main shopping street, Real de Guadalupe. For quality and value, this is one of San Cristóbal's premier shops. You'll find beautiful woven sweaters, embroidered native dresses, and other fine crafts tucked in shelves lining the small shop. Ask for help and you'll discover all sorts of treasures tucked away from view. The owner, Don Joaquín Hernánz, disdains the prevalence of Guatemalan goods in San Cristóbal and specializes only in local wares. Hours are daily from 9am to 1:30pm and 4 to 7:30pm.

PLAZA OF SANTO DOMINGO, Av. Utrilla.

The plazas around this church and the nearby Templo de Caridad are filled with women in native garb selling their wares. Here you'll find women from Chamula weaving belts or embroidering, surrounded by piles of loomed woolen textiles from their village. More and more Guatemalan shawls, belts, and bags are included in their inventory. But there are some excellent buys in Chiapan-made wool vests, jackets, rugs, and shawls similar to those at Sna Jolobil, if you take the time to look and bargain. Vendors arrive between 9 and 10am and begin to leave around 3pm.

SNA JOLOBIL, Av. 20 de Noviembre.

The "weaver's house" (in the Maya language) is located in the former convent (monastery) of Santo Domingo, next to the Templo de Santo Domingo, between Navarro and Nicaragua. This cooperative store is operated by groups of Tzotzil and Tzeltal craftspeople, with about 3,000 members who contribute products, help in running the store, and share in the moderate profits. Their works are simply beautiful; prices are set, and high—as is the quality. Be sure to take a look. They're open daily from 9am to 6pm; credit cards are accepted.

TZONTEHUITZ, Calle Guadalupe 74. Tel. 8-2745.

About 3½ blocks from the plaza is one of the best shops on Guadalupe Street near the corner of Diego Dujelay. Owner Janet Giacobone specializes in her own textile designs and weavings. Some of her work is loomed in Guatemala but you can also watch weavers using foot looms in the courtyard. Hours are Monday through Saturday from 9am to 2pm and 4 to 7pm.

UNIÓN REGIONAL DE ARTESANÍAS DE ALTOS DE CHIAPAS, Av. Utrilla 43.

Another cooperative of weavers, this one is smaller than Sna Jolobil, but not necessarily any cheaper, and not as sophisticated in its approach to potential shoppers. It's worth looking around, though, but be prepared to pay cash—no credit cards are accepted. It's open Monday through Saturday from 9am to 2pm and Sunday from 9am to 1pm.

WHERE TO STAY

For really low-cost lodgings, there are basic but acceptable *hospedajes* and *posadas,* which charge around $10 for a single and $13 for a double. Usually these places are unadvertised; if you're interested in a very cheap hospedaje, ask around in a restaurant or café and you're sure to find one. Or go to the tourist office, which often displays notices of new ones on the metal flip rack in the office.

To get you started, I suggest looking on Calle Real de Guadalupe, east out of the main square. Some of the best offerings are here. Other ones, on Insurgentes near the bus station, tend to be noisy. *Important note about hotel prices:* The prices below are the highest the hotels are authorized to charge and are usually only applied during July and August, Easter Week, and Christmas. *At other times rates may be around 20% less.*

EXPENSIVE

CASA MEXICANA, 28 de Agosto 1, San Cristóbal de las Casas, Chi. 29200. Tel. 987/8-0698. Fax 987/8-2627. 29 rms. TV TEL

$ Rates: $70 single; $77 double; $96 triple. **Parking:** Free.

Casa Mexicana opened in 1993 as the most elegant hotel in San Cristóbal, with stunning architecture and amenities unheard of in these parts. The centerpiece of the skylight-covered lobby is a plant-filled rock pond surrounded by ochre pillars and arches reminiscent of the city's historic buildings. As much a gallery as a hostelry, the public spaces are filled with sculptures and art, and several works by Kiki, the artist whose work is featured in La Galería on Hidalgo. Kiki is one of the hotel's owners, and her artistic touch is evident throughout the building. The rooms have peaked wood-beam ceilings, Guatemalan spreads and drapes, and satellite TV; two junior suites have their own hot tubs. Amenities include room service, a sauna, spa, massage service, tennis court, and direct long-distance phones. The restaurant, Los Magueyes, features gourmet European and Mexican cuisine, including mole poblano, beef stroganoff, and goulash. A few tables are set by the pond, a perfect spot for lingering over a drink and plates of sausages and cheeses. Even if you're not staying here, the hotel is well worth a visit. It's at the corner of Utrilla, one block from the Templo de Santo Domingo.

HOTEL FLAMBOYANT ESPAÑOL, 1 de Marzo no. 15, San Cristóbal de las Casas, Chi. 29200. Tel. 967/8-0045 or 8-0762. Fax 967/8-0514. 60 rms. TV TEL

$ Rates: $65 single; $80 double; $85 triple.

The Español reopened in late 1992 after a lengthy renovation, and it set the stage for other luxury hotels. Built around a large tree-shaded courtyard, with a deep sloping red-tile roof, it became a hotel in 1907. Besides the original family home (the part you see upon entry) there are now additional rooms in the back fashioned exactly like those in the original. Each of the large carpeted rooms has beamed ceilings, luxurious multicolored bedspreads, wood-shuttered windows, foot-loomed drapes, and decorative use of regional textiles, plus original watercolors of San Cristóbal streets. Rooms have either a fireplace or portable electric heater—the latter a first in San Cristóbal. Thick blue-and-white tiles cover the large bathrooms. The hotel's warm atrium bar and restaurant look onto the central patio. It's 3½ blocks northwest of the central plaza between Avenida Cárdenas and Avenida 16 de Septiembre.

POSADA DIEGO DE MAZARIEGOS, María Adelina Flores 2 and 5 de Febrero no. 1, San Cristóbal de las Casas, Chi. 29200. Tel. 967/8-0513 or 8-1825. Fax 967/8-0827. 54 rms. TEL

$ Rates: $66 single, $77 double. **Parking:** Free; nearby.

Two separate colonial-style buildings across the street from each other make up this established hotel, one of the best in the city. Both buildings are part of former mansions, each built around a central courtyard. The colonial decor, with little gardens tucked here and there, befits the mountain-town setting. The small rooms in one building have attractive furnishings but little space, yet are warmer than those in the other building, which are larger. Most rooms have TV and fireplaces; wood costs extra. There's a restaurant in one building and a cozy bar in the other, plus a travel agency, gift shop, money exchange, and car-rental agency. A doctor is on call 24 hours and there's laundry service. Local calls made from your room cost 50¢ each. The Posada is at the corner of Utrilla, one block north of the main plaza, where Flores becomes 5 de Febrero.

MODERATE

EL PARAÍSO, Av. 5 de Febrero no. 19, San Cristóbal de las Casas, Chi. 29200. Tel. 987/8-0085. 13 rms. TEL
$ Rates: $33 single; $48 double; $56 triple. **Parking:** Free.
El Paraíso opened in 1993 in a totally new building. The architecture blends modern and traditional touches, with angled tan and blue walls under heavy wood beams and peaked skylights. The rooms have sloping ceilings, wood-framed casement windows facing the courtyard or street, and Guatemalan textiles on the beds (either one king-size or two doubles). Owners Daniel and Teresa Suter-Rodriguez lived in Europe for several years (Daniel is from Switzerland) and between them speak Spanish, English, French, and German. The hotel's pretty, sophisticated restaurant features fondues, salads, and French and Swiss entrées. It's two blocks east of the cathedral at 5 de Mayo.

HOTEL CIUDAD REAL, Plaza 31 de Marzo no. 10, San Cristóbal de las Casas, Chi. 29200. Tel. 967/8-0187. Fax 967/8-0464. 31 rms. TV
$ Rates: $40 single; $48 double.
The location facing the main plaza makes this one of the first hotels tourists see upon arrival. Other hotels have more charm for the same price, so it's location you're paying for more than anything. The first floor holds a large restaurant that sometimes feeds a late-lunch crowd or a few who come for coffee. Unfortunately, noise from the courtyard can be heard in the rooms, which are small but recently remodeled. The rooms on the top floor, with their sloping ceilings, are the most desirable. All have fireplaces, which aren't used. You'll find the hotel on the south side of the main plaza, between Hidalgo and Insurgentes.

HOTEL PALACIO DE MOCTEZUMA, Av. Juárez 16, San Cristóbal de las Casas, Chi. 29200. Tel. 967/8-0352 or 8-1142. Fax 967/8-1536. 42 rms. TEL
$ Rates: $40 single; $50 double. **Parking:** Free; limited.
A good choice near the plaza, this three-story hotel is delightfully overgrown with bougainvillea and geraniums. Fresh-cut flowers tucked around tile fountains are a hallmark here. The rooms have lace curtains on French windows, handsome coordinated drapes and bedspreads, red carpeting, and modern tiled showers. Two suites each have a TV and refrigerator. Overstuffed couches face a large fireplace in the lobby bar, and the cozy restaurant looks out on the interior courtyard. On the third floor there's a solarium with comfortable tables and chairs and great city views. Ask about the owner's new restaurant, Los Esquipules, on the road to Chamula. To find the hotel from the plaza, walk three blocks south on Insurgentes, turn left on León, and the hotel is on the next corner on the left.

HOTEL RINCÓN DEL ARCO, Ejército Nacional 66, San Cristóbal de las Casas, Chi. 29200. Tel. 967/8-1313. Fax 967/8-1568. 36 rms. TEL
$ Rates: $40 single; $50 double. **Parking:** Free.
This is one of my favorite inns in San Cristóbal—partly because of the charming rooms and partly because it's so well managed. The original section of this former colonial-era home is built around a small interior patio, and dates from 1650. Rooms in this part exude a wonderful old charm with tall ceilings and carpet over hardwood floors. Those in the new, adjacent section face a large grassy inner yard and appear architecturally like the original on the outside. Each of the clean, sizable rooms is a bit different. Some are furnished in antiques and others in colonial style, some have small balconies, and all have fireplaces, and drapes and bedspreads foot-loomed to match in the family factory. Owner José Antonio Hernánz is eager to make your stay a good one. (If you

recognize the name, his father owns the Hotel Don Quijote.) There's an excellent restaurant just behind the lobby. The hotel offers special discounted prices to university students, but make arrangements in advance and be able to show university identification. It's removed from the center of town, yet still within walking distance of the major sights. To find it from the plaza, walk three blocks north on Utrilla to Ejército Nacional, turn right and walk five blocks. The hotel is on the corner of Avenida V. Guerrero.

HOTEL SANTA CLARA, Av. Insurgentes 1, San Cristóbal de las Casas, Chi. 29200. Tel. 967/8-1140. 40 rms.
$ Rates: $40 single; $48 double. **Parking:** Free.
There's a certain charm to this old hotel, once called Casa de las Sirenas for the cement mermaids perched on the outer corners of the building. Built hacienda-style it has two two-story wings with red-tile roofs framing a central courtyard; there's even a pair of scarlet macaws squawking from their cages. The rooms have thick carpeting over hardwood, beds with chenille spreads and lots of blankets, but no fireplaces; it can get mighty drafty and cold on winter nights. Check your room first for possible drafts. Twenty rooms have TVs. All in all, despite its exterior charm, you're paying more for location than comfort. The hotel's popular off-lobby restaurant and bar draws crowds in the late afternoon and evening. And there's a swimming pool in the second patio. The hotel faces the plaza on the south side.

POSADA DE LOS ÁNGELES, Calle Francisco Madero 17, San Cristóbal de la Casas, Chi. 29200. Tel. 967/8-1173 or 8-4371. Fax 967/8-2581. 21 rms. TV
$ Rates: $45 single; $50 double.
With beautiful etched-glass doors on the street, you can't help but notice this new inn that opened in 1991. The vaulted ceilings and skylights make the three-story hotel seem much larger and brighter than many others in the city. Rooms have either two single or two double beds and the bathrooms are large, modern, and immaculately clean; windows open to a pretty courtyard with a fountain. The rooftop sun deck is a great siesta spot. To find the posada, walk south on Insurgentes from the plaza one block, turn left on Madero, and walk two blocks; it's between Juárez and Colón.

BUDGET

CASA DE HUÉSPEDES MARGARITA, Calle Real de Guadalupe 34, San Cristóbal de las Casas, Chi. 29200. Tel. and fax 967/8-0957. 26 rms (none with bath).
$ Rates: $7 dorm bed; $15 single; $17 double; $22 triple.
Part hotel, part youth hostel, this establishment has rooms arranged around a courtyard where the young backpackers congregate. The rooms have sagging mattresses and flimsy locks; shared bathrooms are only fair. There's a general lack of organization and security here, but an abundance of information and contacts. The hotel's popular restaurant is filled with youths in the evening, and there is live music at 8pm. Margarita's also has horse rentals, and tours to the nearby ruins of Toniná, Palenque, and the Sumidero Canyon near Tuxtla Gutiérrez. You'll find it 1½ blocks east of the plaza between Avenida B. Domínguez and Colón.

DON QUIJOTE, Colón 7, San Cristóbal de las Casas, Chi. 29230. Tel. and fax 967/8-0346. 22 rms (all with bath). TV
$ Rates: $25 single; $30 double; $35 triple.
This three-story residence built around a small patio has been converted into San Cristóbal's latest budget-priced hostelry. The rooms are small, with tiny closets, but

are carpeted and beautifully coordinated with textiles foot-loomed in the family factory. All have two double beds with over-bed lights, private tiled baths, and plenty of hot water. The lobby is decorated with costumes from area villages and throughout there are old photos of San Cristóbal, and on each floor a mural of Don Quijote and his travels.

HOTEL D'MONICA II, 5 de Febrero no. 18, San Cristóbal de las Casas, Chi. 29200. Tel. 967/8-1363. Fax 967/8-2940. 30 rms (all with bath).
$ Rates: $20 single, $25 double, $30 triple.
Though only two blocks from the main plaza, this small clean hotel is enough off the beaten track to be overlooked in San Cristóbal's central village hubbub. And because it's out of the mainstream, it costs less than it might on a more well-traveled street. Arranged on three floors around a central patio/restaurant, rooms are spacious enough to accommodate both luggage and people. All have firm pine beds, small bathrooms, and tile floors. Don't confuse this hotel with its more expensive sister, the D'Monica I, which is on Insurgentes. The D'Monica II is between Avenida 5 de Mayo and Avenida 16 de Septiembre.

HOTEL FRAY BARTOLOMÉ DE LAS CASAS, Niños Héroes 2, San Cristóbal de las Casas, Chi. 29200. Tel. 967/8-0932. Fax 967/8-3510. 26 rms.
$ Rates: $30 single; $35 double.
This clean, quiet, old colonial inn makes a beautiful impression with a low sloping red-tiled roof supported by dark wood columns around a beautiful red-tile courtyard. The plain rooms are in fair condition. In some the carpets are stained and some showers drip constantly; other rooms are absolutely satisfactory. The courtyard has planters, bentwood furniture, and lots of flowers, and breakfast is served in the small dining room. The hotel is south of the plaza at Insurgents.

HOTEL PLAZA SANTO DOMINGO, Utrilla 35, San Cristóbal de las Casas, Chi. 29200. Tel. and fax 967/8-1927. 29 rms. TV TEL
$ Rates: $25–$30 single; $30–$35 double. **Parking:** Limited.
New in 1992, this hotel is ideally situated across from the Santo Domingo Church, near the bustling market area. Behind the lobby and plant-filled entry courtyard are the rooms, each nicely furnished and carpeted. All come with a small closet and small desk below the TV, set high in the wall. Bathrooms are trimmed in blue-and-white tile and the sink is conveniently placed outside the shower area. A large indoor dining room opened off the lobby in 1993, along with a smaller patio dining area and large bar. All are pleasant, especially the patio tables looking out to the street. This is one of the few places near Santo Domingo and the market where you can get a good meal and use clean restrooms.

POSADA JOVEL, Paniagua 28, San Cristóbal de las Casas, Chi. 29200. Tel. 967/8-1734. 18 rms (5 with bath).
$ Rates: $10 single without bath; $14 double without bath; $16 single or double with bath.
If you're low on funds and want to stay a while in cheery surroundings, then you may find this modest two-story inn to your liking. The bright, freshly painted rooms have tile floors and colorful blanket/bedspreads and basket lamps. Shelves and hooks hold belongings and beds are firm. The posada is between the market and main plaza, 2½ very long blocks east of Utrilla.

POSADA SAN CRISTÓBAL, Insurgentes 3, San Cristóbal de las Casas, Chi. 29200. Tel. 967/8-1900. 10 rms.
$ Rates: $14.50 single; $18 double.

This small quiet hotel, fashioned from a two-story town house and built around a lovely central courtyard, is only one block from the plaza. The small rooms are immaculately clean, with wood floors, simple wood beds and dressers, no heat, and no toilet seats. The showers tend to flood the bathroom floors. While not fancy, it's got charm, convenience, and comfort. The reasonably priced hotel restaurant, Kukulkán, is in back with a view of the courtyard.

REAL DE VALLE, Calle Real de Guadalupe 14, San Cristóbal de las Casas, Chi. 29200. Tel. 967/8-0680. 40 rms.

$ Rates: $28 single; $30 double; $32 triple.

You couldn't ask for friendlier or more helpful staff than the folks at the Real de Valle, two blocks east of the plaza, where the manager is quick to change money, seek medical assistance, arrange tours, and help his guests in any way possible. The 24 new rooms in the back three-story section have new bathrooms, big closets, and a brown-and-cream decor. There's a rooftop solarium with chaise lounges, a small cafeteria, and an upstairs dining room with a big fireplace. The owners recently added fax and photocopy service, a travel agency with personally guided tours, horse rental, laundry service, and Spanish language study. Your money goes a long way here and the location, half a block from the central plaza, is excellent.

WHERE TO DINE

San Cristóbal is one of the country's best dining-out towns. Besides the dining establishments mentioned below, most hotels have their own restaurants and serve good meals. Be sure to look for regional Chiapan food like large tamales, *butifarra* (a delicious sausage), and *posh* (a local firewater similar to aguardiente). But before chowing down or drinking too heavily, remember that you're about a mile and a half high here and food digests more slowly.

Jovel is San Cristóbal's original name and it's used often by businesses. *Coleto* is a term you'll see often in San Cristóbal. It means someone or something from San Cristóbal. Thus you'll see tamales coletos, coleto bread, or coleto breakfast, etc.

MODERATE

EL FOGÓN DE JOVEL, 16 de Septiembre no. 11. Tel. 8-2557.
Cuisine: CHIAPAN.
$ Prices: Corn soup $3.50; Chiapan tamales $5.50; main courses $4–$9.50.
Open: Daily 1–5pm and 7–11pm.

If word of mouth doesn't lead you here, the lively sounds of marimba music will. Chiapan food is served at this handsome old town house, built around a central courtyard. The waiters wear local costumes. Walls are hung with Guatemalan and Chiapan prints and folk art. Dine outside under the portals around the courtyard or in an interior high-ceilinged room. Each dish and regional drink is explained on the menu in Spanish.

To get you started, I highly recommend an order of Chiapan tamales, with three different and filling types. The corn soup is smooth and delicious. The beef-stuffed chile relleno is one of the best buys on the menu. Before your relleno is presented, a basket of steaming warm tortillas arrives along with six condiments of guacamole, refried beans, cheese, salsa Mexicana, green sauce, and hot pickled vegetables for a make-your-own-taco appetizer. It's really enough for two people. Then comes the huge chile relleno together with a pile of rice. Delicious. On a cold afternoon, a cup of warm fruit punch spiked with a shot of posh, a distilled sugar-and-corn drink popular among the locals, really puts bloom on the cheeks. The restaurant is only a block northwest of the plaza.

LA GALERÍA, Av. Hidalgo 3. Tel. 8-1547.
   Cuisine: MEXICAN/AMERICAN.
$ Prices: Yogurt and fruit $3; main courses $3–$9; comida corrida $6.25.
   Open: Daily 8am–11pm.

This is a double treat—a shop of folk art, weaving, pottery, and painting, and a café-restaurant upstairs that serves whole-wheat sandwiches, imaginative meat and soup courses, big fruit salads, and desserts. La Galería is the "in" place for artsy expatriates and tourists; Bonnie Raitt's latest songs play in the background, alternating with the jazzy sounds of Sade. There's a stage on the first floor where salsa and jazz bands appear on occasion, and the best tables in the house are along the upstairs balcony overlooking the stage and courtyard fountain. The bulletin board in the stairwell makes for interesting reading. The shop has a separate street entrance.

LA LANGOSTA, Madero 9. Tel. 8-2238.
   Cuisine: REGIONAL/SEAFOOD.
$ Prices: Breakfast $4; comida corrida $4.75–$9.
   Open: Daily 7am–11pm.

This pretty, upscale restaurant looks more expensive than it really is, and offers an unusual blend of local dishes with a twist. Try the homemade ginger ale, the chalupas (somewhat like tostadas), and the exceptional spicy *mole coleto* (chicken). The glass-top tables, blond wood chairs, and cloth napkins give a sense of class, and there's often soft live music after 9pm. It's a block and a half southeast of the plaza.

LA PARRILLA, Belisario Domínguez 32. Tel. 8-2220.
   Cuisine: GRILLED MEAT.
$ Prices: Tacos $3.50–$4; grilled-meat plates $4.50–$10; side dishes $1.50–$4.
   Open: Mon–Sat 6:30pm–midnight; Sun noon–midnight.

If you're hungering for a rib-sticking, meat-and-potatoes meal, La Parrilla is your place. Guests check off their order on a printed list of selections, available in English and Spanish. Meats are grilled over a wood fire in the main dining room, and include smoked chicken, various types of sausages, pork chops, and beef steaks. Side dishes are ordered separately; don't miss the ranch-style beans and grilled whole onion. Melted cheese (*queso fundido*) comes plain or with mushrooms, smoked sausage, or grilled peppers, and there are several varieties of tacos, quesadillas, and pizzas. The tables by the fireplace in the back dining room are the nicest seats, as long as the TV over the bar is turned low. La Parrilla is in the Cerrillo neighborhood, four blocks east of Real de Guadalupe.

MADRE TIERRA, Insurgentes 19. Tel. 8-4297.
   Cuisine: MEXICAN/VEGETARIAN.
$ Prices: Granola with yogurt $4; comida corrida $8–$10.
   Open: Restaurant daily 8am–9:45pm; bakery Mon–Sat 9am–8pm, Sun 9am–noon.

This restaurant satisfies the hankerings of both meat lovers and vegetarians, and all those seeking a health fix. The bakery specializes in whole-wheat breads, pastries, pizza by the slice, quiche, grains, granola, and dried fruit (and sells a great postcard collection). The restaurant serves the bakery's goods and other fare in an old mansion with wood-plank floors, long windows looking onto the street, and tables covered in colorful Guatemalan jaspe. Classical music plays softly in the background. It's a good place for a cappuccino and pastry or a meal—the comida corrida is very filling. It's opposite the Parque Fray Bartolomé de las Casas, 3½ blocks south of the main plaza.

PARIS-MEXICO RESTAURANT, Madero 20. Tel. 8-0695.

Cuisine: MEXICAN/FRENCH/ITALIAN.

$ Prices: Crêpes $1.75–$5.25; pizza $5.25–$10; comida corrida $5–$5.50.

Open: Daily 7am–11pm.

Decked out with plain, nicely furnished wood tables and chairs, each table topped with a simple red candle, the Paris-Mexico is like a cozy neighborhood café. And it will surely last a while in San Cristóbal—the food is wonderfully prepared from fresh ingredients. The comida corrida might consist of salad, grilled chicken breast, potatoes or rice, fruit salad, and coffee or tea. Or you can choose from three pages of crêpes for breakfast, lunch, dinner, or dessert; pizza made 10 ways; five variations of spaghetti; or from a small selection of beef or chicken dishes. To find it from the plaza, walk a block east on Madero and the restaurant is on the left.

RESTAURANT EL FAISÁN, Madero 2. Tel. 8-2000.

Cuisine: MEXICAN.

$ Prices: Breakfast $2.50–$4.75; main courses $4–$8.50; comida corrida $4.50–$6.50.

Open: Daily 7:30am–11pm; comida corrida served 2–6pm.

Low lighting, clay lanterns, glass-top tables, and native embroidery draw a romantic dinner crowd to this small restaurant. If the tables are full downstairs, don't despair; there's more upstairs. The menu includes delicious pollo a la plancha, cochinita guisado, and quesadillas with sliced red peppers. Wine is served. It's half a block east of the plaza.

RESTAURANT TULUC, Insurgentes 5. Tel. 8-2090.

Cuisine: MEXICAN.

$ Prices: Breakfast $2.75; main courses $3–$9.50; comida corrida $6.

Open: Daily 6am–10pm

This warm and inviting restaurant has lustrous wooden booths and tables all backed with Guatemalan fabric. It's a cozy place for a cup of hot chocolate or espresso coffee, but the comida is an exceptional value here. The three-course meal begins with a generous bowl of soup, then a main dish of your choice, followed by dessert and a fine cup of coffee. The evening menu is equally popular; the specialty is the filete Tuluc, a beef filet wrapped around spinach and cheese, served with fried potatoes and green beans. The Chiapaneco breakfast is a filling quartet of juice, toast, Chiapan tamales, and a choice of tea, coffee, cappuccino, or hot chocolate. The owner speaks seven languages. Restaurant Tuluc is one block south of the plaza.

BUDGET

CAFÉ EL PUENTE, Real de Guadalupe 55. Tel. 8-2250.

Cuisine: MEXICAN.

$ Prices: Breakfast $2–$3; enchiladas $2.50–$4; pastries 50¢–$2.

Open: Daily 8am–9:30pm.

Ex-Californian Bill English has turned a huge old mansion into a café and cultural center where tourists and locals can share information and ideas. The café takes up the main part of the building, with a weaver's shop and travel agency to the side. The Centro Bilingue language school is headquartered here as well, and movies, plays, and lectures are presented nightly in an interior patio and meeting room. It's the kind of place you return to often, for fresh waffles and coffee in the morning, an inexpensive lunch or dinner of brown rice and veggies, or a great salad with Roquefort cheese, and good conversation any time of day. Guests are welcome to post notices, messages, and advertisements on the long bulletin board, well worth checking out if you're looking for a ride, a place to stay, or information on out-of-the-way destinations. El Puente is 2½ blocks north of the plaza.

NORMITA'S COMEDOR FAMILIAR, Av. Juárez at F. Flores. No phone.

Cuisine: MEXICAN.

$ Prices: Breakfast $2.50–$3.50; comida corrida $3.50–$5; pozole $3.45–$4; tacos $1–$3.50.

Open: Daily 8am–10pm.

Normita keeps moving and I keep finding her—eventually—because she serves cheap, dependably good food. Everything is homemade here, from the wood tables and checked tablecloths to the tacos and pozole. It's very humble, with the kitchen taking up one corner of the room (you can watch all the preparations if you like), and tables scattered in front of a large paper mural of a fall forest scene from some faraway place. Normita specializes in short-order mainstays such as tacos, tostadas, sopes, queso fundido, tortas, and Jalisco-style pozole. Enjoy.

SPECIALTY DINING

A Sweetshop

DULCERÍA SAN CRISTÓBAL, Av. Insurgentes 18-A. Tel. 8-1093.

Cuisine: CANDY/COOKIES.

$ Prices: 50¢–$10.

Open: Daily 9:30am–2:30pm and 4–9pm.

San Cristóbal has several sweetshops but this is one of the best, covered wall to wall with delightful confections from hard candy to cookies. There's paraphernalia to make a party, too, from cups, plates, and napkins to confetti.

Coffeehouses

Chiapan-grown coffee is highly regarded and so it's natural to find a proliferation of coffeehouses here, most of which are concealed in the nooks and crannies of San Cristóbal's side streets.

CAFÉ ALTURA, Real de Guadalupe 7. Tel. 8-4038.

Cuisine: COFFEE/HEALTH FOOD.

$ Prices: Soy burgers $2.50; salads $2–$4; coffee 75¢.

Open: Daily 7am–9pm.

A pretty little café in the Pasaje Mazariegos shopping arcade, Café Altura specializes in organic, vegetarian meals. Breakfasts include granola, yogurt, fruit, and whole-wheat breads; vegetable and fruit salads are featured on the lunch and dinner menus. Coffee drinks are priced two for one during the evening happy hour, when soft jazz plays in the background. Grains, granola, teas, and coffee beans are sold in bulk. The pink and purple café sits in the middle of the shopping area.

CAFÉ SAN CRISTÓBAL, Cuauhtémoc 1. No phone.

Cuisine: COFFEE/CAKE.

$ Prices: Coffee 50¢–$1; cake $1.25–$2.

Open: Mon–Sat 9am–10pm, Sun 10am–2pm and 5–10pm.

Not only is this a café, but coffee beans are also sold by the kilogram (2.2 lb.) here for $4. Chess is the game of choice at the few tables and booths; men hunker over their chessboards for hours, drinking coffee and visiting with friends. A cup of coffee here is a calming respite from the rush outside the door. It's two blocks southwest of the plaza.

A Bakery

PANADERÍA MERCANTIL, Mazariego 17. Tel. 8-0307.
   Cuisine: BAKERY.
$ **Prices:** 20¢–$3.
   Open: Mon–Sat 8am 9:30pm.
This bakery offers substantial shelves of freshly baked bread, cookies, and rolls. It's two blocks west of the main plaza between 16 de Septiembre and 5 de Mayo.

EVENING ENTERTAINMENT

Notices around town advertise live music, particularly at the cafés. Another favorite pastime is having friendly conversation at several of my recommended restaurants, particularly the coffeehouses, with their international clientele. Local residents often hang around one of the two movie theaters in town. There's a slim chance that an English-language film will be showing, but there might be one you wouldn't mind watching in Spanish.

EASY EXCURSIONS FROM SAN CRISTÓBAL

TO NEARBY VILLAGES

I highly recommend that you tour the local villages. Several travel agencies in town offer excursions both to nearby villages and the ones listed below, which are farther away. Strangely, except as noted, the cost of the trip includes a driver but does not necessarily include either a bilingual guide or guided information of any kind. For that you pay extra. So if you want to be informed while taking a tour, be sure to ask if the tour is merely transportation or if it includes a knowledgeable guide as well.

One tour is led by a delightful mestiza woman, **Mercedes Hernández Gómez.** Mercedes, a largely self-trained ethnographer, is immensely informed about the history and folkways of the villages. She explains the religious significance of what you will see in the churches, where shamans try to cure Indian patients of various maladies, and she facilitates firsthand contact with Indians. She leads her group to the colectivos at the market where they board a minivan for the village or villages she has selected, and normally return to the plaza about 4pm. She doesn't lead trips on rainy days, but otherwise meet her at the kiosk in the main plaza at 9am. The tour is worth every peso of the $15-per-person charge.

Alex Aranda Pedrero and Raúl García López (tel. 8-3741), a pair of likable and knowledgeable locals, also lead village tours (rain or shine) and meet their groups between 9 and 9:30am in front of the cathedral opposite the tourist office. They call themselves Conozca Chiapas, and have a van to tour in; or if the group is large or has diverse interests, then some will go in the van while the rest use local village buses from the market. The pair are very flexible and will customize a day depending on the desires of the clients. The cost of a regular village tour seeing one or two villages (which depends on if it's a market day or not) costs around $15 per person.

CHAMULA & ZINACANTÁN A side trip to the village of San Juan Chamula really gets one into the spirit of life around San Cristóbal. Sunday, with the market in full swing, is the best day to go for shopping. But other days are good for seeing the village and church more or less unimpeded by anxious children selling their crafts. Colectivos (minibuses) to San Juan Chamula leave the municipal market in San Cristóbal about every half hour, and charge 75¢. Don't expect anyone in these vans to speak English or Spanish. When you arrive, a villager will motion you to a municipal building to pay a small fee and sign a form which in Spanish says you may take pictures of the exterior of the church and nothing else. During Carnaval, no photographs at all are allowed. **Don't dare take pictures inside the church.** Folks, they *really* mean this. During Carnaval in 1990, I met a French photographer who took *one* photograph from a hill above town, after which villagers hiding in the bushes wrestled him to the ground and seized the Nikon he was using; he managed to retain the remainder of his camera gear after a struggle. It was the most expensive photograph he ever took, he lamented.

The village, five miles northeast of San Cristóbal, is the Chamula cultural and ceremonial center. Activity centers on the huge church, the plaza, and the municipal building; each year a new group of citizens is chosen to live in the municipal center as caretakers of the saints, settlers of disputes, and enforcers of village rules. As in other nearby villages on Sunday, the local leaders wear their leadership costumes, with beautifully woven straw hats loaded with colorful ribbon befitting their high position. They solemnly sit together in a long line somewhere around the central square. Chamula is typical of other villages in that men are often away working in the "hot lands" harvesting coffee or cacao, while women stay home to tend the sheep, the children, the corn fields, and the fires. It's almost always women and children's work to gather sticks for fires and you see them along roadsides bent against the weight.

I don't want to spoil your experience of seeing the interior of the Chamula church for the first time by describing it too much. Just don't leave Chamula without seeing it. Stepping from bright sunlight into the candlelit interior, take a few minutes for your eyes to adjust. The tile floor is covered in pine needles amidst a sea of lighted candles stuck to the tile floor. Saints line the walls and before them people are often kneeling and deep in vocalized prayer while passing around bottles of Pepsi. Shamans are often on hand passing eggs over sick people or using a dead chicken in a curing ritual. The saints are similar to those you might see in any Mexican Catholic church, but these take on another meaning to the Chamulas that has no similarity to a Catholic saint other than the name. Visitors can walk carefully through the church to see the saints and their unusual dressing, or stand quietly in the background and observe.

Carnaval takes place just before Lent and is the big annual festival. The Chamulas are not a very wealthy people as their economy is based on agriculture, but the women are the region's best wool weavers, producing finished pieces for themselves and for other villages.

Zinacantán is a wealthier village than Chamula. Before seeing the town's two side-by-side sanctuaries, you must also sign a form, which is more rigid than Chamula's—no photos at all. Once permission is granted and you have paid a small fee, an escort will usually show you the church, but you may also be allowed to see it on your own. Floors may be covered in pine needles here too, the rooms are brightly sunlit, and the experience is an altogether different one than in Chamula.

AMATENANGO DEL VALLE About an hour's ride south of San Cristóbal is Amatenango, a town known mostly for women potters. You'll see their work in San Cristóbal—small animals, jars, and large water jugs—but in the village you can visit the potters in their homes. All you have to do is arrive and walk the dirt streets. Villagers will lean over the walls of family compounds and invite you in to select from their inventory. You may even see them firing the pieces under piles of wood in the open courtyard, or painting them with color derived from rusty iron water. The women wear beautiful red-and-yellow huipils, but if you want to take a photograph, you'll have to pay. To get there, take a colectivo from the market in

San Cristóbal, but before it lets you off, be sure to ask about the return trip schedule.

AGUACATENANGO   Located 10 miles south of Amatenango, this village is known for embroidery. If you've been in San Cristóbal shops before arriving here, you'll recognize the white-on-white or black-on-black floral patterns on dresses and blouses for sale. Their own regional blouse, however, is quite different.

TENEJAPA   The weavers of Tenejapa make some of the most beautiful and expensive work you'll see. The best time to visit is on market days (Sunday and Thursday, but Sunday is best). The weavers of Tenejapa taught the weavers of San Andrés and Magdalena, which accounts for the similarity in their designs and colors. To get to Tenejapa, try to find a colectivo in the very last row of colectivos by the San Cristóbal market, or hire a taxi for around $35. On Tenejapa's main street several stores sell locally woven regional clothing and you can bargain for the price.

OTHER EXCURSIONS

HUITEPEC   Ecological tours to the cloud forest are available through Pronatura, a private nonprofit ecological organization. The forest is a haven for migratory birds, and over 100 species of birds and 600 species of plants have been discovered there. Tours are offered Tuesday, Thursday, and Saturday at 9:30am and cost $7 per person and depart from the Pronatura office at Adelina Flores 21 (tel. 8-0469). To reach the reserve on your own drive on the road to Chamula; the turnoff is at km 3.5. The reserve is open Tuesday through Sunday from 9am to 5pm.

CHINCULTIC RUINS, COMITÁN & MONTEBELLO NATIONAL PARK   Almost a hundred miles southeast of San Cristóbal near the border of Guatemala is the **Chincultic archeological site** and **Montebello National Park,** with 16 multicolored lakes and lush pine forest vegetation.

En route, 46 miles from San Cristóbal is Comitán, a pretty town of 40,000 inhabitants on a hillside, known for its flower cultivation and a sugarcane-based fire water called *comitecho*. It's also the last big town along the Pan American Highway before the Guatemalan border and it's the location of the nearest airport to San Cristóbal.

The recently discovered Chincultic ruins, a late Classic site, have barely been excavated, but the location of the main acropolis, set high up against a cliff, is magnificent to see from below and worth the walk up for the vista. Pay the entry fee at the gate. The trail ahead passes rubble of ruins on both sides. Steep stairs lead up the mountain flanked by more unexcavated tree-covered ruins until you reach the acropolis. From there you can gaze upon the distant Montebello Lakes and miles of cornfields and forest.

The paved road to the lakes passes six of them, all different colors and sizes and ringed by cool pine forests, with car parks and lookouts at most of them. The paved road ends where there's a small restaurant. The lakes are best seen on a sunny day when their famous brilliant colors are best—otherwise the trip is just seeing a series of lakes in a pretty setting.

Most travel agencies in San Cristóbal offer a day-long trip that includes the lakes, the ruins, lunch in Comitán, and a stop in the pottery-making village of Amatenango del Valle. If you're driving, follow Highway 190 south from San Cristóbal through the pretty village of Teopisca, and Comitán, and turn left at La Trintaria where there's a sign to the lakes. After the Trintaria turnoff and before you reach the lakes, there's a sign pointing left down a narrow dirt road to the Chincultic ruins.

RUINS OF TONINÁ   Two hours from San Cristóbal, and eight and a half miles east of Ocosingo, are the Maya ruins of Toniná (which means "house of rocks"), a Classic terraced site covering an area of at least nine square miles. Extensive excavations are underway there during the dry season, although the site has been studied before. As early as A.D. 350 Toniná emerged as a separate dynastic center and has the distinction of having the last recorded date of the long count yet found, that of A.D. 909, on a small stone monument. Another stone discovered there depicted the captured King Kan-Xul of Palenque (younger brother of Chan-Bahlum and son of King Pacal) dated A.D. 711, showing him tied by a rope on his arm but still wearing his royal headdress. An exciting discovery of a huge stucco panel (approximately 15 feet long and 5 feet tall), shows the Lord of Death holding Kan-Xul's head, confirming long-held suspicions that he died at Toniná. At Palenque you see many reliefs carved on stone, but at Toniná, the emphasis was on three-dimensional stone work. Toniná was believed to have been a strong city-state with far-flung ties and influences. Numerous pieces of carved jade have been found there (not a native stone). There are many visible pyramidal platforms and stone carvings. At the moment there are no signs to guide visitors through the site, so you're on your own, or the caretaker can show you around (in Spanish), after which a tip is appreciated. Ask at Casa Margarita in San Cristóbal about guided trips to Toniná for $25 per person with a four-person minimum. The trip includes a bilingual driver, tour of the site, lunch, a river swim, and, during November through February, seeing thousands of swallows swarm near the ruins. You can go on your own by bus to Ocosingo and from there take a taxi to the ruins, but have the taxi wait. The ruins are open daily from 8am to 5pm and admission is $3.50.

PALENQUE, BONAMPAK & YAXCHILÁN   Many visitors want to visit the ruins of Palenque near Villahermosa, and the Bonampak and Yaxchilán ruins on Mexico's border with Guatemala, while they are in San Cristóbal. A trip to Palenque can be accomplished in a long day from San Cristóbal, but I don't recommend a day trip because Palenque should be savored. Bonampak and Yaxchilán are easier to see from Palenque, if you are going there.

   For arranging these trips from San Cristóbal, I highly recommend **ATC Tours and Travel,** by El Fogón restaurant, Calle 5 de Febrero no. 15 at the corner of 16 de Septiembre (tel. 967/8-2550; fax 967/8-3145). They have bilingual guides and good vehicles. They also have a branch in Palenque. See the Palenque section for details on Bonampak and camping overnight at Yaxchilán and see Chapter 2, Section 6, "Adventure & Wilderness Trips," for other ATC regional tours focusing on birds, orchids, textiles, hiking, and camping.

   If you're considering a day trip to the archeological site of Palenque using ATC or a similar travel agency, here's how it works. Starting at 7 or 8am, within three hours you reach the Agua Azul waterfalls where there's a 1½-hour stop to swim. From there it's another 1½-hour drive to Palenque. You'll have about two hours to

---

IMPRESSIONS

In Mexico there is always a brooding sense of the past. Turn off the highway, and the rutted road leads you over humpbacked bridges, past the gates of old haciendas, through the villages where the church stands on the plaza as it always has. The high mesa blossoms pink with cosmos in late August, and far away on the edge of the hills shine the tile domes. Farther up the hills are markets where not everyone speaks Spanish, where women are still wearing garments which they weave for themselves.
—ELIZABETH WILDER WEISMANN, *ART AND TIME IN MEXICO*, HARPER & ROW, 1985

see the site. If your group agrees, you can skip the swim and have more time at Palenque. It'll be a minimum 16-hour day and costs $200 for one or two people, and only slightly more for three or four.

EN ROUTE TO TUXTLA GUTIÉRREZ

Highway 195 winds from Villahermosa and San Cristóbal to Tuxtla, and shouldn't be taken fast. The road also passes through some of the most gorgeous scenery in all Mexico: Emerald-green mountains, thick banana groves, citrus trees growing wild by the roadside, quaint villages, and breathtaking vistas come one after the other as you wind along. These curves, however, may cause motion sickness even to those not normally prone to it. Consider taking a precautionary pill or bring along some hard candy or gum just in case. It's important to get an early start on this road, especially if you're driving from San Cristóbal, for patches of fog often slow traffic until you climb above the clouds. The trip from San Cristóbal to Tuxtla is about 1½ hours; to Villahermosa it's about six to seven hours by car, seven to eight by bus.

4. TUXTLA GUTIÉRREZ

51 miles E of San Cristóbal de las Casas

GETTING THERE   By Plane   Aviación de Chiapas (Aviacsa) flies to Tuxtla from Cancún, Chetumal, Mérida, Mexico City, Guatemala City, Villahermosa, Tapachula, and Oaxaca. **Mexicana** has daily flights from Mexico City, Acapulco, Mérida, Oaxaca, and Villahermosa. **Aerocaribe** flies between Tuxtla and several regional destinations.

By Bus   First-class **Autobuses Cristóbal Colón** runs five daily buses to Tuxtla from Villahermosa, 12 from San Cristóbal, two from Oaxaca, and five from Comitán. Cristóbal Colón and Rudolfo Figueroa deluxe service also runs between Tuxtla, San Cristóbal, and Palenque.

By Car   From Oaxaca or Veracruz, you enter by Highway 190. From Villahermosa or San Cristóbal, you'll enter at the opposite end of town. Eventually, you will end up at the big main square, Plaza Cívica, with its gleaming white church (take a look at the clockwork figures in the tower) and modern buildings.

DEPARTING   By Plane   Mexicana, Av. Central Poniente 206 (tel. 961/2-0020 or 2-5402, and at the airport 3-4921), flies to various destinations around Mexico. Check with the local office of Mexicana about van departures to the airport. They leave from the office or will pick you up at your hotel if you reserve in advance. When the office is closed the van departs from the plaza in front of the Gran Hotel Humberto about two hours before each flight is scheduled to depart. **Aerocaribe,** Bulevar Domínguez 180, a Mexicana affiliate (tel. 961/2-0232; fax 961/2-2053), flies to Oaxaca from Tuxtla's small Aeropuerto Terán and to Cancún and Mexico City from the larger airport 40 minutes from the town center. Aviación de Chiapas, or **Aviacsa,** Av. Central Poniente 1144 (tel. 961/2-6880 or 2-8081; fax 961/3-5029), flies from Aeropuerto Terán to Villahermosa, Tapachula, Oaxaca, Chetumal, Mexico City, Mérida, Cancún, and Guatemala City. Aviacsa seems to have more passengers on its flights from Tuxtla and therefore keeps more to its schedule than does Aerocaribe, which appears to delay flights in order to combine them.

   Important Note: If you're flying on Aerocaribe and Aviacsa, be sure to clarify which airport you'll be departing from. Your ticket may not indicate the right airport, so check with the airline directly or a travel agent in Tuxtla. The smaller Aeropuerto Terán, located a few minutes from Tuxtla's town center, is on the edge of a military base and you may be required to show your ticket to enter. The larger airport is subject to closures and delays because of rain, high winds, and fog. Check ahead if the weather looks bad, and double check which airport you should use. It's possible that the Aeropuerto Terán, closer to town, will be expanded to accommodate larger planes.

By Bus   First-Class **Autotransportes Cristóbal Colón** (tel. 2-2624), runs five daily buses from Tuxtla to Villahermosa; 12 daily buses running on the half hour to San Cristóbal from 5am to 9:15pm; three to Oaxaca; and, to Comitán and Ciudad Cuauhtémoc on the Guatemalan border, every hour from 5:30am until 7pm. The first-class San Cristóbal buses are generally easy to book unless it's a holiday at which time there may be a wait. Deluxe "Plus" buses to Palenque leave at 7am and 6pm.

By Car   From Tuxtla to Villahermosa take Highway 199, then cut north on Highway 195 to Villahermosa. To San Cristóbal, take Highway 199 all the way. Because the road from Tuxtla to San Cristóbal and Villahermosa is mountainous and curvy, don't get in a hurry. It's in good repair to San Cristóbal, but there are many bad spots between San Cristóbal and Palenque. The trip from Tuxtla to Villahermosa takes eight hours by car and the scenery is beautiful.

ESSENTIALS   The area code is 961. The **American Express** representative is Viajes Marabasco, Plaza Bonampak, Loc. 4, Col. Moctezuma (tel. 2-6998; fax 2-4053).

Tuxtla Gutiérrez (alt. 1,838 ft.; pop. 300,000) is the boomtown capital of the state of Chiapas, long Mexico's coffee-growing center, but more recently an oil prospector's meca. To tourists, however, it's a necessary crossroads for getting to San Cristóbal from the Pacific coast, or from the Gulf coast at Villahermosa (173 miles north), Palenque, and San Cristóbal to Oaxaca. The mammoth oil reserves discovered in this wild, mountainous state several years ago have brought people, business, and wealth to Tuxtla. It's not exactly an unpleasant town, but hasn't been able to manage growth with any aesthetic considerations. Tourists are more of a footnote than a necessity. If you have some time to spare, visit the Tuxtla zoo and Sumidero Canyon.

ORIENTATION

ARRIVING   From the **international airport,** it's a 40-minute ride to the center of town. The colectivo into town costs $8, and more if there are only a few passengers. Don't tarry at the airport, though; the vans fill up and leave immediately and taxis charge about five times the price of a colectivo van for the same trip to downtown Tuxtla. Aerocaribe and other commuter flights arrive at Tuxtla's **downtown airport,** a short taxi ride to town center.

The **Cristóbal Colón bus terminal,** 2a Avenida Norte and 2a Calle Poniente, is two blocks west of Calle Central. Taxi drivers solicit riders to San Cristóbal outside the bus station and airport. The going rate of $35 per car can be divided by up to four passengers providing no one has a lot of luggage. You'll have to wait for them to assemble, however, unless fewer than four agree to split the fare.

INFORMATION The **tourist office** (tel. 2-5509 or 2-4535) is in the Secretería de Fomento Económico building (previously called the Plaza de las Instituciones) on Avenida Central/Bulevar Domínguez, near the Hotel Bonampak Tuxtla. It's on the first floor of the plaza and is open Monday through Friday from 8am to 9pm. Most questions can be answered at the information booth in front of the office. There are also information booths at the international airport, staffed when flights are due, and at the zoo, open Tuesday through Sunday from 9:30am to 5pm.

CITY LAYOUT The city is divided by two "Central" streets: Calle Central, running north to south; and Avenida Central (also called Avenida 14 de Septiembre), running east to west. The main highway is Avenida Central (also named Bulevar Domínguez west of downtown). Streets are numbered from these central arteries, with the suffix *norte, sur, oriente, or poniente* designating the direction of progress from the central arteries.

GETTING AROUND

Buses to all parts of the city converge on the Plaza Cívica along Calle Central. **Taxi fares** are more expensive here than in other regions; for example, a taxi across town from the bus station to the tourist office is $5.

WHAT TO SEE & DO

The majority of travelers are simply passing through Tuxtla on their way to San Cristóbal or Oaxaca. The excellent zoo or possibly the Sumidero Canyon is the best place to spend any hours you have to spare.

CALZADA DE LOS HOMBRES ILUSTRES, 1A Oriente Norte at 5A Oriente Norte.

Tuxtla's cultural highlights are clustered in this area, once referred to as the Parque Madero. The park is one part of the area, which also includes the Regional Museum of Anthropology, a botanical garden, a children's area, and the city theater. The museum was closed for renovations when I was there, but will include exhibits on the lifestyles of the people of Chiapas, and some artifacts from the state's archeological sites. In one short stop you can learn about Chiapas's past civilizations, its flora, and its present-day accomplishments

Admission: Park and botanical garden, free; museum $3.50, free on Sun.

Open: Museum Tues–Sun 9am–3pm; botanical garden daily 6am–6pm; children's area Tues–Sun 8am–8pm. **Directions:** The park is 11 blocks northwest of the main plaza. To get there, catch a colectivo along Avenida Central, or walk about 15 minutes west along Calle 5A Oriente Norte.

MIGUEL ÁLVAREZ DEL TORO ZOO [ZOOMAT], Blv. Samuel León Brinois, southeast of downtown.

Located in the forest called El Zapotal, ZOOMAT is one of the best in Mexico, and it's a personal favorite. Its collection of animals and birds indigenous to this area gives the visitor a tangible sense of what Chiapas is like in the wilds. Jaguars, howler monkeys, owls, and many more exotic animals are kept in roomy cages that replicate their home terrain, and the whole zoo is so buried in vegetation that you can almost pretend you're spotting natural habitats. Unlike other zoos I've visited, the animals are almost always on view; many will come to the fence if you make a kissing noise.

Admission: Free; donations solicited.

Open: Tues–Sun 9am–5:30pm. **Directions:** The zoo is about five miles southeast of downtown; buses for the zoo can be found along Avenida Central and at Parque Madero.

SHOPPING

The government-operated **Casa del las Artesanías,** Blv. Domínguez 2035 (tel. 3-3478), moved to this bright pink and purple building in 1993. The shop/gallery features a fine and extensive collection of crafts from throughout the state of Chiapas. Pottery, weaving, jewelry, and wooden articles are grouped by region and type, and fill two stories of showrooms. The displays are informative as well as for sale. It's about 10 blocks from its previous location by the tourist office. It is open Monday through Saturday from 9am to 2pm and 5 to 8pm, and Sunday from 9am to 1pm.

WHERE TO STAY

As Tuxtla booms, the center of the hotel industry has moved out of town, west to Highway 190. As you come in from the airport you'll notice the new motel-style hostelries, all of which are expensive: the Hotel Flamboyant (it's just that, too), the Palace Inn, Hotel Laganja, La Hacienda, and the older Hotel Bonampak Tuxtla. A few less expensive hotels are in the center, but they aren't very good.

GRAN HOTEL HUMBERTO, Av. Central 180, Tuxtla Gutiérrez, Chi. 29000.
 Tel. 961/2-2080 or 2-2504. 112 rms (all with bath). TV TEL
$ Rates: $45 single; $55 double.
This older 10-story inner-city hotel is your best economical bet in booming Tuxtla. It's clean, with tile floors and bathrooms. And it's comfortable enough, with well-kept furnishings (circa 1950) in shades of brown. Purified water comes from open jugs in the hallways. On weekends church bells compete with the nightclub on the ninth floor. But the location is ideal, in the center of town half a block from Plaza Cívica restaurants and the Mexicana Airline office, and a block and half from the Cristóbal Colón bus station.

HOTEL BONAMPAK TUXTLA, Blv. Domínguez 180, Tuxtla Gutiérrez, Chi.
 29030. Tel. 961/3-2050, or toll free 800/528-1234 in the U.S. 70 rms. A/C TV
 TEL
$ Rates: $70 single; $80 double. **Parking:** Free.
This large, sprawling hotel has a swimming pool, tennis court, travel agency, boutique, coffee shop, and elegant restaurant. The rooms facing the street are noisy, even with the air conditioning on, but the interior rooms are blissfully quiet. Many rooms have been remodeled, with new bathroom fixtures, fresh paint, and pastel linens. A shopping plaza is rising next door. The hotel's coffee shop is one of the best in town, often packed with locals and tourists. The extensive menu includes an economical comida corrida, served in the afternoon and early evening. It's on the outskirts of downtown, where Avenida 14 de Septiembre becomes Bulevar Domínguez, opposite the tourist office.

HOTEL ESPONDA, 1 Calle Poniente Norte 142, Tuxtla Gutiérrez, Chi.
 29030. Tel. 961/2-0080 or 2-0731. 52 rms. FAN TEL
$ Rates: $25 single; $28 double; $35 triple. **Parking:** Free.
In a city where inexpensive rooms are hard to come by, the Esponda is an excellent choice. The rooms are in a nondescript five-story building with an elevator; the higher the room, the less street noise disturbs your sleep. The brown, green, and yellow decor is a bit unsightly, but the rooms are perfectly satisfactory, with one, two, or three double beds, showers (without doors or curtains), big closets, and powerful

ceiling fans. It's conveniently located one block from the Plaza Cívica, near the Cristóbal Colón bus station.

WHERE TO DINE

Tuxtla's main plaza, the Plaza Cívica, is actually two plazas separated by Avenida Central. Rimming the edges are numerous restaurants, many of them serving customers outdoors under umbrella-shaded tables. Since they change names with frequency, I won't recommend one restaurant over another. Just stroll the area and pick one that looks interesting, clean, and reasonably priced.

CAFÉ AVENIDA, Av. Central 230 at 1A Calle Paniente.
Cuisine: COFFEE.
$ Prices: Coffee $1 per cup.
Open: Daily 7am–7pm.

There's not much to do in Tuxtla, but for coffee purists I suggest dropping by the Café Avenida (no sign, but it's next to the Hotel Avenida) for a cup or two of the only thing they serve: freshly ground and brewed Chiapan coffee. Huge sacks of beans lean against the counter, the grinder hums away, producing wonderful coffee aromas. The Formica tables have been cleaned so often that the decorative pattern is wearing off. No tea, no sweets, no milk, just coffee, dark roasted (almost burnt), rough flavored, and hearty.

LAS PICHANCHAS, Av. Central Oriente 837. Tel. 2-5351.
Cuisine: MEXICAN.
$ Prices: Tamales $1.50 each; main courses $5–$12.
Open: Daily 12:30pm–midnight; live marimba music 2–4pm and 8–11pm; patio dinner show Tues–Sun 9pm. **Closed:** New Year's Day and two days following Easter.

No trip through Tuxtla Gutiérrez is complete without a meal at this restaurant, which is devoted to the regional food and drink of Chiapas. Colorful cut-paper banners stream from the palm-frond roof and inverted *pichanchas* (pots full of holes used to make nixtamal masa dough) are hung on posts as lanterns. The service is good, but the Spanish-only menu requires an interpreter (or bring your dictionary); next to each item is a description of the meal. Avoid the tired bowl of frijoles Zoques and the uninteresting tasajo (dried, salted beef strips that are reconstituted for a couple of dishes on the menu). For a sample, try the platón de carnes frías (cold meat platter) or the platón de botana regional (a variety of hot tidbits). The former is a tasty sampling of different local sausages plus ham, cheese, and tortillas. I especially like the butifarra. Both feed two or three nicely. You can order with confidence the carne asada a la Chamula, which includes grilled steak, an enchilada, and tostada, along with a small salad and potato chips. Since Chiapan tamales are tastier and larger than any you may have had elsewhere, you must try at least one. Beer and some unusual mixed drinks are offered along with a nice selection of prepared fruit-water drinks. The refreshing *agua de chía* (chia-seed water) is a close cousin to lemonade.

From the Hotel Humberto, in the center of town, walk six to eight blocks south. When you see the black iron gates on the left, enter a patio surrounded by red-brick walls and tables and chairs under an open porch.

EASY EXCURSIONS FROM TUXTLA GUTIÉRREZ

CHIAPA DE CORZO   The small town of Chiapa de Corzo is a 30-minute, eight-mile ride by bus from the main square (buses leave every 15 minutes in the morning, every 30 minutes in the afternoon), or 10 to 15 minutes by taxi. Those going on to San Cristóbal or over the mountains to the Yucatán will pass through this town on their way.

Chiapa has a small museum, on the main square, dedicated to the city's lacquer industry, an interesting church, a colonial fountain, and also a small pyramid, somewhat restored and visible from the road. In the museum you can often see women learning lacquer painting, a regional craft, and sometimes maskmakers give carving demonstrations and lessons.

EL SUMIDERO Another more spectacular trip is to the canyon of El Sumidero, 10 miles northeast of the center of town along a country road. You can hire a taxi for a road tour of the canyon's rim and five lookout points for about $15 an hour. Boat rides through the canyon can be arranged through some travel agencies and hotels in Tuxtla, through the Tuxtla office of **Transportes al Cañon** (tel. 3-3584), or on your own. Take a bus to Chiapa de Corzo and negotiate a ride along the riverbed; the cost should be around $45 for five persons for a two-hour ride. You can also go by bus to Cahuare from the main square and arrange a boat under the Grijalva River Bridge; the rate may be somewhat less here.

APPENDIX

A. TELEPHONES & MAIL
B. BUS TERMS
C. CONVERSION TABLES
D. BASIC VOCABULARY
E. MENU SAVVY

A. TELEPHONES & MAIL

USING THE TELEPHONES

Special Note: Area codes and city exchanges are being changed all over the country. If you have difficulty reaching a number, ask an operator for assistance. Mexico does not have helpful recordings to inform you of changes or new numbers.

Most **public pay phones** in the country have been converted to Ladatel phones, many of which are both coin- and card-operated. Those that accept coins accept the old 100-peso coins, but at some point may begin accepting New Peso coins. Instructions on the phones tell you how to use them. Local calls generally cost the peso equivalent of 75¢ per minute, at which time you'll hear three odd-sounding beeps, and then you'll be cut off unless you deposit more coins. Ladatel cards come in denominations of 10, 20, and 30 New Pesos. If you're planning to make many calls, purchase the 30–New Peso card; it takes no time at all to use up a 10-peso card (about $3.35). They're sold at pharmacies, bookstores, and grocery stores near Ladatel phones. You insert the card, dial your number, and start talking, all the while watching a digital counter tick away your money.

Next is the **caseta de larga distancia** (long-distance telephone office), found all over Mexico. Most bus stations and airports now have specially staffed rooms exclusively for making long-distance calls and sending faxes. Often they are efficient and inexpensive, providing the client with a computer printout of the time and charges. In other places, often pharmacies, the clerk will place the call for you, then you step into a private booth to take the call. Whether it's a special long-distance office or a pharmacy, there's usually a service charge of around $3.50 to make the call, which you pay in addition to any costs if you didn't call collect.

For **long-distance calls,** you can access an English-speaking AT&T operator by dialing the star button twice then 09. If that fails, try dialing 09 for an international operator. To call the U.S. or Canada, tell the operator that you want to make a collect *(una llamada por cobrar)*, station-to-station *(teléfono a teléfono)*, or person-to-person *(persona a persona)* call. Collect calls are the least expensive of all, but sometimes caseta offices won't make them, so you'll have to pay on the spot.

To make a long-distance call from Mexico to another country, first dial 95 for the U.S. and Canada, or 98 for anywhere else in the world. Then, dial the area code and number you are calling.

To call long distance (abbreviated *lada*) within Mexico, dial 91, the area code, then the number. Mexico's area codes *(claves)* may be one, two, or three numbers and are usually listed in the front of telephone directories. In this book the area code is listed under "Fast Facts" for each town. (Area codes, however, are changing throughout the country; see above.)

To place a phone call to Mexico from your home country, dial the international service (011), Mexico's country code (52), then the Mexican area code (for Cancún, for example, that would be 98), then the local number. Keep in mind that calls to Mexico are quite expensive, even if dialed direct from your home phone.

Better hotels, which have more sophisticated tracking equipment, may charge for each local call made from your room. Budget or moderately priced hotels often don't charge, since they can't keep track. To avoid checkout shock, it's best to ask in advance if you'll be charged for local calls. These cost between 50¢ and $1 per call. In addition, if you make a long-distance call from your hotel room, there is usually a hefty service charge added to the cost of the call.

POSTAL GLOSSARY

Airmail **Correo Aéreo**
Customs **Aduana**
General Delivery **Lista de correos**
Insurance (insured mail) **Seguros**
Mailbox **Buzón**
Money order **Giro postale**
Parcel **Paquete**
Post office **Oficina de correos**

Post office box **Apdo. Postal** (abbreviation)
Postal service **Correos**
Registered mail **Registrado**
Rubber stamp **Sello**
Special delivery, express **Entrega inmediata**
Stamp **Estampilla** or **timbre**

B. BUS TERMS

Bus **Autobús**
Truck **Camión**
Lane **Carril**
Nonstop **Directo**
Baggage **Equipajes**
Intercity **Foráneo**
Luggage storage area **Guarda equipaje**
Gates **Llegadas**
Originates at this station **Local**

Originates elsewhere; stops if seats available **De paso**
First (class) **Primera**
Baggage claim area **Recibo de equipajes**
Waiting room **Sala de espera**
Toilets **Sanitarios**
Second (class) **Segunda**
Nonstop **Sin escala**
Ticket window **Taquilla**

C. CONVERSION TABLES

Mexico uses the metric system, as do Canada and Europe. Here are some conversion tables to help you in your shopping and traveling.

METRIC EQUIVALENTS

Here are the metric equivalents for units of length, weight, and liquid measure:

1 inch	=	2.54 centimeters
1 foot	=	30.5 centimeters
1 meter	=	39.37 inches
1 mile	=	1.6 kilometers
1 kilometer	=	0.62 miles
1 pound	=	0.4536 kilograms
1 kilogram	=	2.2 pounds
1 U.S. gallon	=	3.79 liters
1 liter	=	0.26 U.S. gallons

APPROXIMATIONS

Here are a few handy rules of thumb. A pound is slightly less than half a kilogram. A meter is a little more than a yard (3 ft.). A gallon is almost four liters.

An easy way to convert kilometer distances into miles is to multiply the kilometer distance by 0.6; another way of doing the same thing is to think in 3's and 5's, 6's and 10's; 3 miles is about 5 kilometers, 6 miles is about 10 kilometers, so 100 kilometers is about 60 miles.

TEMPERATURE

Use of the metric system includes use of the Celsius (centigrade) thermometer. Here are some reference points:

Fahrenheit	Celsius
0°	-18°
32°	0° (water freezes)
50°	10° (cool weather)
68°	20° (comfortable weather)
88°	30° (hot weather)
98.6°	37° (body temperature)
104°	40° (very hot weather)
212°	100° (water boils)

D. BASIC VOCABULARY

Traveling on or off the beaten track, you will encounter many people in service positions who do not speak English. Many Mexicans who can understand English are embarrassed to speak it. And finally most Mexicans are very patient with foreigners who try to speak their language; it helps a lot to know a few basic phrases.

Berlitz's Latin American Spanish for Travellers, available at most bookstores, cannot be recommended highly enough. But for added convenience, I've include a list of certain simple phrases for expressing basic needs, followed by some menu items presented in the same order in which they'd be found on a Mexican menu.

good day	buenos días	bway-nohss dee-ahss
How are you?	¿Cómo está usted?	koh-moh ess-tah oo-sted
very well	muy bien	mwee byen
thank you	gracias	grah-see-ahss
you're welcome	de nada	day nah-dah
goodbye	adiós	ah-dyohss
please	por favor	pohr fah-bohr
yes	sí	see
no	no	noh
excuse me	perdóneme	pehr-doh-ney-may
give me	déme	day-may
Where is . . . ?	¿Dónde está . . . ?	dohn-day ess-tah
the station	la estación	la ess-tah-see-own
a hotel	un hotel	oon oh-tel
a gas station	una gasolinera	oon-nuh gah-so-lee-nay-rah
a restaurant	un restaurante	oon res-tow-rahn-tay
the toilet	el baño	el bahn-yoh
a good doctor	un buen médico	oon bwayn may-dee-co
the road to . . .	el camino a . . .	el cah-mee-noh ah
to the right	a la derecha	ah lah day-ray-chuh
to the left	a la izquierda	ah lah ees-ky-ehr-dah
straight ahead	derecho	day-ray-cho
I would like	quisiera	keyh-see-air-ah
I want	quiero	kyehr-oh
to eat	comer	ko-mayr

a room	una habitación	*oon*-nuh ha-bee-tah-see-*own*
Do you have . . . ?	¿Tiene usted . . . ?	*tyah*-nay oos-*ted*
a book	un libro	oon *lee*-bro
a dictionary	un diccionario	oon deek-see-own-*ar*-eo
How much is it?	¿Cuánto cuesta?	*kwahn*-to *kwess*-tah
When?	¿Cuándo?	*kwahn*-doh
What	¿Qué?	kay
There is (Is there?)	¿Hay . . .	eye
yesterday	ayer	ah-*yer*
today	hoy	oy
tomorrow	mañana	mahn-*yawn*-ah
good	bueno	*bway*-no
bad	malo	*mah*-lo
better (best)	(lo) mejor	(loh) meh-*hor*
more	más	mahs
less	menos	*may*-noss
no smoking	se prohibe fumar	seh pro-*hee*-beh foo-*mahr*
post card	tarjeta postal	tahr-*hay*-ta pohs-*tahl*
insect repellent	repelante contra insectos	rah-pey-*yahn*-te *cohn*-trah een-*sehk*-tos

1 uno (*ooh*-noh)
2 dos (dohs)
3 tres (trayss)
4 cuatro (*kwah*-troh)
5 cinco (*seen*-koh)
6 seis (sayss)
7 siete (*syeh*-tay)
8 ocho (*oh*-choh)
9 nueve (*nway*-bay)
10 diez (*dee*-ess)
11 once (*ohn*-say)
12 doce (*doh*-say)
13 trece (*tray*-say)
14 catorce (kah-*tor*-say)

15 quince (*keen*-say)
16 dieciseis (de-*ess*-ee-*sayss*)
17 diecisiete (de-*ess*-ee-see-*ay*-tay)
18 dieciocho (dee-*ess*-ee-*oh*-choh)
19 diecinueve (dee-*ess*-ee-*nway*-bay)
20 veinte (*bayn*-tay)
30 treinta (*trayn*-tah)
40 cuarenta (kwah-*ren*-tah)
50 cincuenta (seen-*kwen*-tah)

60 sesenta (say-*sen*-tah)
70 setenta (say-*ten*-tah)
80 ochenta (oh-*chen*-tah)
90 noventa (noh-*ben*-tah)
100 cien (see-*en*)
200 doscientos (dos-se-*en*-tos)
500 quinientos (keen-ee-*ehn*-tos)
1,000 mil (meel)

USEFUL PHRASES

Do you speak English? **¿Habla usted inglés?**
Is there anyone here who speaks English? **¿Hay alguien aquí que hable inglés?**
I speak a little Spanish. **Hablo un poco de español.**
I don't understand Spanish very well. **No entiendo muy bien el español.**
The meal is good. **Me gusta la comida.**
What time is it? **¿Qué hora es?**

May I see your menu? **¿Puedo ver su menú?**
The check, please. **La cuenta, por favor.**
What do I owe you? **¿Cuánto lo debo?**
What did you say? **¿Mande?** (colloquial expression for American "Eh?")
I want (to see) a room **Quiero (ver) un cuarto (una habitación)** for two persons **para dos personas**

with (without) bath. **con (sin) baño.**
We are staying here only one night (one week). **Nos quedaremos aquí solamente una noche (una semana).**
We are leaving tomorrow. **Partimos mañana.**

Do you accept traveler's checks? **¿Acepta usted cheques de viajero?**
Is there a laundry near here? **¿Hay una lavandería cerca de aquí?**
Please send these clothes to the laundry. **Hágame el favor de mandar esta ropa a la lavandería.**

E. MENU SAVVY

GENERAL

almuerzo lunch
cena supper
comida dinner
desayuno breakfast
el menú the menu
la cuenta the check
tampiqueña thinly sliced meat
cocido boiled

empanado breaded
frito fried
poco cocido rare
asado roast
bien cocido well done
milanesa breaded
veracruzana tomato and green olive sauce

BREAKFAST (DESAYUNO)

jugo de naranja orange juice
café con crema coffee with cream
pan tostada toast
mermelada jam
leche milk
té tea
huevos eggs

huevos cocidos hard-boiled eggs
huevos poches poached eggs
huevos fritos fried eggs
huevos pasados al agua soft-boiled eggs
huevos revueltos scrambled eggs
tocino bacon
jamón ham

LUNCH & DINNER

ajo garlic
antojitos Mexican snacks
caldo broth
sopa soup
sopa clara consommé
sopa de lentejas lentil soup
sopa de chícharos pea soup

sopa de arroz dry rice (not soup!)
caldo de pollo chicken broth
menudo tripe soup
salchichas sausages
taco filled tortilla
torta sandwich
tamales rusos cabbage rolls

SEAFOOD (MARISCOS)

almejas clams
anchoas anchovies
arenques herring
atún tuna
calamares squid
camarones shrimp
caracoles snails
corvina bass
huachinango red snapper

jaiba crab
langosta lobster
lenguado sole
lobino black bass
manos de cangrejo stone crab
mojarra perch
ostiones oysters
pescado fish
pez espada swordfish

robalo sea bass/snook
salmón salmon
salmón ahumado smoked salmon

sardinas sardines
solo pike
trucha arco iris rainbow trout

MEATS (CARNES)

ahumado smoked
alambre shish kebab
albóndigas meatballs
aves poultry
bistec steak
cabeza de ternera calf's head
cabrito kid (goat)
callos tripe
carne meat
carne fría cold cuts
cerdo pork
chiles rellenos stuffed peppers
chicharrones pigskin cracklings
chorizo spicy sausage
chuleta chop
chuleta de carnero mutton chop
chuletas de cordero lamb chops
chuletas de puerco pork chops
conejo rabbit
cordero lamb
costillas de cerdo spareribs

falsán phesant
filete de ternera filet of veal
filete milanesa breaded veal chops
ganso goose
hígado liver
jamón ham
lengua tongue
lomo loin
paloma pigeon
pato duck
pavo turkey
pechuga chicken breast
perdiz partridge
pierna leg
pollo chicken
res beef
riñones kidneys
ternera veal
tocino bacon
venado venison

VEGETABLES (LEGUMBRES)

aguacate avocado
aceitunas olives
arroz rice
betabeles beets
cebolla onions
champinones mushrooms
chícharos peas
col cabbage
coliflor cauliflower
ejotes string beans
elote corn (maize)
entremeses hors d'oeuvres
espárragos asparagus

espinaca spinach
frijoles beans
hongos mushroom
jícama potato/turnip–like vegetable
lechuga lettuce
lentejas lentils
papas potatoes
pepino cucumber
rábanos radishes
tomate tomato
verduras greens, vegetables
zanahorias carrots

SALADS (ENSALADAS)

ensalada de apio celery salad
ensalada de frutas fruit salad
ensalada mixta mixed salad

ensalada de pepinos cucumber
  salad
guacamole avocado salad
lechuga lettuce salad

FRUITS (FRUTAS)

chavacano apricot
ciruela prune
coco coconut
durazno peach
frambuesa raspberry

fresas con crema strawberries with
  cream
fruta cocida stewed fruit
granada pomegranate
guanabana green pearlike fruit

guayaba guava
higos figs
lima lime
limón lemon
mamey sweet orange fruit
mango mango
manzana apple
naranja orange

pera pear
piña pineapple
plátano banana
toronja grapefruit
tuna prickly pear fruit
uva grape
zapote sweet brown fruit

DESSERTS [POSTRES]

arroz con leche rice pudding
brunelos de fruta fruit tart
coctel de aguacate avocado
   cocktail
coctel de frutas fruit cocktail
compota stewed fruit
fruta fruit
flan custard

galletas crackers or cookies
helado ice cream
yogurt yogurt
nieve sherbet
pastel cake or pastry
queso cheese
torta cake

BEVERAGES [BEBIDAS]

agua water
brandy brandy
café coffee
café con crema coffee with cream
café de olla coffee with cinnamon
   and sugar
café negro black coffee
cerveza beer
ginebra gin
hielo ice
jerez sherry
jugo de naranja orange juice
jugo de tomate tomato juice

jugo de toronja grapefruit juice
leche milk
licores liqueurs
manzanita apple juice
refrescos soft drinks
ron rum
sidra cider
sifón soda
té tea
vaso de leche glass of milk
vino blanco white wine
vino tinto red wine

CONDIMENTS & CUTLERY

aceite oil
azúcar sugar
copa goblet
cilantro coriander
cuchara spoon
cuchillo knife
mantequilla butter
manteca lard
mostaza mustard
pan bread

bolillo roll
pimienta pepper
sal salt
sopa soup
taza cup
tenedor fork
tostada toast
vinagre vinegar
vaso glass

PREPARATIONS

asado roasted
cocido cooked
bien cocido well done
poco cocido rare
milanesa Italian breaded
empanado breaded
frito fried

a la parrilla grilled
al horno baked
tampiqueño long strip of thinly sliced
   meat
veracruzana tomato, garlic, and onion
   topped

MENU GLOSSARY

Achiote: small red seed of the annatto tree.

Achiote preparada: a prepared paste found in Yucatán markets made of ground achiote, wheat and corn flour, cumin, cinnamon, salt, onion, garlic, oregano. Use mixed with juice of a sour orange or vinegar and put on broiled or charcoaled fish (tikin-chick) and chicken.

Agua fresca: fruit-flavored water, usually watermelon, canteloupe, chia seed with lemon, hibiscus flour, or ground melon-seed mixture

Antojito: a Mexican snack, usually masa-based with a variety of toppings such as sausage, cheese, beans, onions; also refers to tostadas, sopes, and garnachas.

Atole: a thick, lightly sweet, warm drink made with finely ground rice or corn and flavored usually with vanilla; often found mornings and evenings at markets.

Birria: lamb or goat meat cooked in a tomato broth spiced with garlic, chiles, cumin, ginger, oregano, cloves, cinnamon, and thyme, and garnished tableside with onions, cilantro, and fresh lime juice to taste; a specialty of Jalisco state.

Botana: a light snack—an antojito.

Buñelos: round, thin, deep-fried crispy fritters dipped in sugar or dribbled with honey.

Burrito: a large flour tortilla stuffed with beans or sometimes potatoes and onions.

Cabrito: roast kid; a northern Mexico delicacy.

Cajeta: carmelized cow or goat milk often used in dessert crêpes.

Carnitas: pork that's been deep-fried in lard, then steamed, and served with corn tortillas for tacos.

Cazón de Campeche: shark-meat stew, baked in tomato sauce, and traditionally served with pot beans and tortillas.

Ceviche: fresh raw seafood marinated in fresh lime juice and garnished with chopped tomatoes, onions, chiles, and sometimes cilantro, and served with crispy, fried whole corn tortillas.

Churro: tube-shaped, breadlike fritter, dipped in sugar, and sometimes filled with cajeta or chocolate.

Cilantro: an herb grown from the coriander seed chopped and used in salsas and soups.

Chayote: called vegetable pear or mirliton in the U.S., it's a type of green, spiny squash boiled and served as an accompaniment to meat dishes.

Chiles rellenos: poblano peppers usually stuffed with cheese, rolled in a batter, and baked; but other stuffings may include ground beef spiced with raisins.

Chorizo: a spicy red pork sausage, flavored with different chiles and sometimes with achiote, or cumin and other spices.

Cochinita pibil: pig meat wrapped in banana leaves, flavored with pibil sauce, and pit-baked; common in the Yucatán.

Colados: a large rectangular-shaped tamal with strips of chicken, chopped tomato, sliced onion, and epazote steamed in a banana leaf, a specialty in Campeche.

Corunda: a triangular-shaped tamal wrapped in a corn leaf, a Michoacán specialty.

Enchilada: tortilla dipped in a sauce and usually filled with chicken or white cheese and sometimes topped with tomato sauce and sour cream (enchiladas suizas—Swiss enchiladas), or covered in a green sauce (enchiladas verdes), or topped with onions, sour cream, and guacamole (enchiladas potosiños).

Epazote: leaf of the wormseed plant, used in black beans, and with cheese in quesadillas.

Escabeche: a lightly pickled sauce used in Yucatán chicken stew.

Frijoles charros: beans flavored with beer, a northern Mexico specialty.

Frijoles refritos: pinto beans mashed and cooked with lard.

Garnachas: a thickish, small circle of fried masa with pinched sides, topped with pork or chicken, onions, and avocado, or sometimes chopped potatoes, and tomatoes, typical as a botana in Veracruz and the Yucatán.

Gorditas: thickish fried corn tortillas, slit and stuffed with choice of cheese, beans, beef, chicken, with or without lettuce, tomato and onion garnish.

Guacamole: mashed avocado, plain or mixed with onions and other spices.

Gusanos de maguey: maguey worms considered a delicacy and delicious when charbroiled to a crisp and served with corn tortillas for tacos.

Horchata: refreshing drink made of ground rice or melon seeds, ground almonds, and lightly sweetened.

Huevos motuleños: eggs atop a tortilla, garnished with beans, peas, ham, sausage, and grated cheese, a Yucatecan specialty.

Huevos mexicanos: scrambled eggs with onions, hot peppers, and tomatoes.

Huevos rancheros: fried egg on top of a fried corn tortilla covered in a tomato sauce.

Huitlacoche: sometimes spelled "cuitlacoche," mushroom-flavored black fungus that appears on corn in the rainy season; considered a delicacy.

Machaca: shredded dried beef scrambled with eggs or as a salad topping; a specialty of northern Mexico.

Manchamantel: translated means "tablecloth stainer," a stew of chicken or pork with chiles, tomatoes, pineapple, bananas, and jícama.

Masa: ground corn soaked in lime used as basis for tamales, corn tortillas, and soups.

Mixiote: lamb or chicken baked with carrots, potatoes, and sauce in parchment paper from a maguey leaf.

Mole: pronounced "*moh*-lay," a sauce made with 20 ingredients including chocolate, peppers, ground tortillas, sesame seeds, cinnamon, tomatoes, onion, garlic, peanuts, pumpkin seeds, cloves, and tomatillos; developed by colonial nuns in Puebla, usually served over chicken or turkey; especially served in Puebla, state of Mexico, and Oaxaca with sauces varying from red to black and brown.

Molletes: a bolillo cut in half and topped with refried beans and cheese, then broiled; popular at breakfast.

Pan de cazón: three layers of corn tortillas, beans, tomatoes, and cooked shark meat; a specialty of Campeche.

Pan de muerto: sweet or plain bread made around the Days of the Dead (November 1–2), in the form of mummies, dolls, or round with bone designs.

Pan dulce: lightly sweetened bread in many configurations usually served at breakfast or bought at any bakery.

Papadzules: tortillas stuffed with hard-boiled eggs and seeds (cucumber or sunflower) in a tomato sauce.

Pavo relleno negro: stuffed turkey, Yucatán style, filled with chopped pork and beef, cooked in a rich, dark sauce.

Pibil: pit-baked pork or chicken in a sauce of tomato, onion, mild red pepper, cilantro, and vinegar.

Pipián: sauce made with ground pumpkin seeds, nuts, and mild peppers.

Poc-chuc: slices of pork with onion marinated in a tangy sour orange sauce and charcoal-broiled; a Yucatecan specialty.

Pozole: a soup made with hominy and pork or chicken, in a tomato-based broth Jalisco style, a white broth Nayarit style, or green-chile sauce Guerrero style, and topped with a choice of chopped white onion, lettuce or cabbage, radishes, oregano, red pepper, and cilantro.

Pulque: drink made of fermented sap of the maguey plant; best in the state of Hidalgo and around Mexico City.

Quesadilla: flour tortilla stuffed with melted white cheese and lightly fried or warmed.

Rompope: delicious Mexican eggnog, invented in Puebla, made with eggs, vanilla, sugar, and rum.

Salsa mexicana: sauce of fresh chopped tomatoes, white onions, and cilantro with a bit of oil; on tables all over Mexico.

Salsa verde: a cooked sauce using the green tomatillo and puréed with mildly hot peppers, onions, garlic, and cilantro; on tables countrywide.

Sopa de calabaza: soup made of chopped squash or pumpkin blossoms.

Sopa de lima: a tangy soup made with chicken broth and accented with fresh lime; popular in the Yucatán.

Sopa de medula: bone-marrow soup.

Sopa seca: not a soup at all, but a seasoned rice. The name means "dry soup."

Sopa tarascana: a rib-sticking pinto bean–based soup, flavored with onions, garlic, tomatoes, chiles, and chicken broth, and garnished with sour cream, white cheese, avocado chunks, and fried tortilla strips; a specialty of Michoacán state.

Sopa tlalpeña: a hearty soup made with chunks of chicken, chopped carrots, zucchini, corn, onions, garlic, and cilantro.

Sopa tortilla: a traditional chicken broth–based soup, seasoned with chiles, tomatoes, onion, and garlic, bobbing with crisp fried strips of corn tortillas.

Sope: pronounced "*soh*-pay," a botana similar to a garnacha, except spread with refried beans and topped with crumbled cheese and onions.

Tacos al pastor: thin slices of flavored pork roasted on a revolving cylinder dripping with onion slices and the juice of fresh pineapple.

Tacos de salchicha: also alled feite, it's a lightly sweet, flaky crust pastry with a sausage filling; a specialty of Campeche.

Tamal: incorrectly called tamale (*tamal* singular, *tamales* plural); meat or sweet filling rolled with fresh masa then wrapped in a corn husk or a corn or banana leaf, and steamed; many varieties and sizes throughout the country.

Tepache: drink made of fermented pineapple peelings and brown sugar.

Tikin xic: also seen on menus as "tikin chick," charbroiled fish brushed with achiote sauce.

Tinga: a stew made with pork tenderloin, sausage, onions, garlic, tomatoes, chiles, and potatoes; popular on menus in Puebla and Hidalgo states.

Torta: sandwich, usually on bolillo bread, usually with sliced avocado, onions, tomatoes, a choice of meat, and often cheese.

Tostadas: crispy fried corn tortillas topped with meat, onions, lettuce, tomatoes, cheese, avocados, and sometimes sour cream.

Venado: Venison (deer) served perhaps as pipián de venado, steamed in banana leaves and served with a sauce of ground squash seeds.

Queso relleno: "Stuffed cheese" is a mild yellow cheese stuffed with minced meat and spices, a Yucatecan specialty.

Xtabentun: pronounced "shtah-*ben*-toon," a Yucatán liquor made of fermented honey and flavored with anise. It comes *seco* (dry) or *crema* (sweet).

Zacahuil: pork leg tamal, packed in thick masa, wrapped in banana leaves, and pit-baked; sometimes pot-made with tomato and masa; specialty of mid- to upper Veracruz.

INDEX

ACANCEH, 212
Accidents, 59–60
Adventure/wilderness tours, 45–46. See also
    specific destinations
Agua Azul, 274–75
AGUACATENANGO, 297
Ah Kukum Xiú, 10–11
Ailments, common, 38–40
Air travel, 46–47, 53
AKUMAL, 157, 161–62
Alemán, Miguel, 13
Alternative and adventure travel, 45–46
Altitude sickness, 39
AMATENANGO DEL VALLE, 296–97
Amber museum (San Cristóbal), 283
American Express, 76, 138, 228, 300
Amusement parks, 103
Annual events, festivals and fairs, 35–38, 225,
    253, 282. See also specific events
Arch, corbelled, 17, 224, 267
Archeological sites, 17
    Acanceh, 212
    Becán, 180–81
    Bonampak, 274–75
    books about, 26–27
    Calakmul, 181–82
    Cancún, 102
    Chicanná, 181
    Chichén–Itzá, 17, 234–44
    Chincultic, 297
    Cobá, 17, 171–72
    Comalcalco, 262–63
    Cozumel, 142
    Dzibanché, 17, 179–80
    Dzibilchaltún, 209–10
    Edzná, 226
    Ekbalam, 249–50
    El Pital, 5
    Isla Mujeres, 114
    Izapa, 5
    Kabah, 222
    Kohunlich, 180
    La Venta, 256
    Labná, 224
    Loltún, 224
    Mayapán, 212–13
    Muyil, 172
    organized tours of, 45–46, 216, 275,
        298–99
    Oxkintok, 211
    Palenque, 17, 265–67
    photography at, 69
    San Gervasio, 142

Sayil, 222, 224
Sian Ka'an Biosphere Reserve, 167–68
Tonina, 298
Tulum Archeological Site, 163–66
Uxmal, 2, 17, 216–19
Xel-Ha, 163
Xlapak, 224
Xpujil, 180
Yaxchilán, 275
Archeology notes. See also specific topics
    corbelled arch, 267
    Maya construction styles, 236
    sacbeob, 173
    serpent motif, 217
    Sian Ka'an Biosphere Reserve, 167
Architecture, 7, 16–19, 26–27
    Mayan construction styles, 17, 267
        Chenes style, 216–17, 222, 226,
            236, 240
        Puuc style, 7, 211, 217–18, 222,
            224, 235–37
        Río Bec style, 180–82, 218, 222,
            236, 265–67
Art, 16–19, 26–27. See also Folk art and
    crafts
Ash Wednesday, 36
Assumption of the Virgin Mary, 37, 208
Auto insurance, 49, 56. See also Cars and
    driving
Aztecs, 7, 9–10, 16–17, 21, 262

Ballcourts, 17, 23
    Chichén-Itzá, 238
    Cobá, 171
    Palenque, 266
    Uxmal, 218
Baluarte de la Soledad (Campeche), 231
Baluarte de San Carlos/Museo de la Ciudad
    (Campeche), 230
Baluarte de San Pedro (Campeche), 231
Baluarte de Santiago (Campeche), 231
Bananas, 261
Barragán, Luis, 19
Beaches, 2
    Campeche, 232
    Cancún, 103–4
    Chemuyil, 162
    Cozumel, 141–42
    Isla Mujeres, 102, 113
    Playa del Carmen, 124, 129
    Progreso, 210
Becán, 180–81, 230
Beer, 25

Now Save Money on All Your Travels by Joining
FROMMER'S ™ TRAVEL BOOK CLUB
The World's Best Travel Guides at Membership Prices

FROMMER'S TRAVEL BOOK CLUB is your ticket to successful travel! Open up a world of travel information and simplify your travel planning when you join ranks with thousands of value-conscious travelers who are members of the FROMMER'S TRAVEL BOOK CLUB. Join today and you'll be entitled to all the privileges that come from belonging to the club that offers you travel guides for less to more than 100 destinations worldwide. Annual membership is only $25 (U.S.) or $35 (Canada and foreign).

The Advantages of Membership

1. Your choice of *three* free FROMMER'S TRAVEL GUIDES (any *two* FROMMER'S COMPREHENSIVE GUIDES, FROMMER'S $-A-DAY GUIDES, FROMMER'S WALKING TOURS *or* FROMMER'S FAMILY GUIDES—plus *one* FROMMER'S CITY GUIDE, FROMMER'S CITY $-A-DAY GUIDE *or* FROMMER'S TOURING GUIDE).
2. Your own subscription to **TRIPS AND TRAVEL** quarterly newsletter.
3. You're entitled to a **30% discount** on your order of any additional books offered by FROMMER'S TRAVEL BOOK CLUB.
4. You're offered (at a small additional fee) our **Domestic Trip-Routing Kits.**

Our quarterly newsletter **TRIPS AND TRAVEL** offers practical information on the best buys in travel, the "hottest" vacation spots, the latest travel trends, world-class events and much, much more.

Our **Domestic Trip-Routing Kits** are available for any North American destination. We'll send you a detailed map highlighting the best route to take to your destination—you can request direct or scenic routes.

Here's all you have to do to join:

Send in your membership fee of $25 ($35 Canada and foreign) with your name and address on the form below along with your selections as part of your membership package to **FROMMER'S TRAVEL BOOK CLUB, P.O. Box 473, Mt. Morris, IL 61054-0473.** Remember to check off your *three* free books.

If you would like to order additional books, please select the books you would like and send a check for the total amount (please add sales tax in the states noted below), plus $2 per book for shipping and handling ($3 per book for foreign orders) to:

FROMMER'S TRAVEL BOOK CLUB
P.O. Box 473
Mt. Morris, IL 61054-0473
(815) 734-1104

[ ] **YES.** I want to take advantage of this opportunity to join FROMMER'S TRAVEL BOOK CLUB.
[ ] **My check is enclosed.** Dollar amount enclosed_____*
          (all payments in U.S. funds only)

Name_____
Address_____
City_____ State_____ Zip_____
All orders must be prepaid.

To ensure that all orders are processed efficiently, please apply sales tax in the following areas: CA, CT, FL, IL, NJ, NY, TN, WA and CANADA.

*With membership, shipping and handling will be paid by FROMMER'S TRAVEL BOOK CLUB for the three free books you select as part of your membership. Please add $2 per book for shipping and handling for any additional books purchased ($3 per book for foreign orders).

Allow 4–6 weeks for delivery. Prices of books, membership fee, and publication dates are subject to change without notice. Prices are subject to acceptance and availability.

AC1

Please Send Me the Books Checked Below:

FROMMER'S COMPREHENSIVE GUIDES
(Guides listing facilities from budget to deluxe,
with emphasis on the medium-priced)

	Retail Price	Code		Retail Price	Code
☐ Acapulco/Ixtapa/Taxco 1993–94	$15.00	C120	☐ Japan 1994–95 (Avail. 3/94)	$19.00	C144
☐ Alaska 1994–95	$17.00	C131	☐ Morocco 1992–93	$18.00	C021
☐ Arizona 1993–94	$18.00	C101	☐ Nepal 1994–95	$18.00	C126
☐ Australia 1992–93	$18.00	C002	☐ New England 1994 (Avail. 1/94)	$16.00	C137
☐ Austria 1993–94	$19.00	C119	☐ New Mexico 1993–94	$15.00	C117
☐ Bahamas 1994–95	$17.00	C121	☐ New York State 1994–95	$19.00	C133
☐ Belgium/Holland/ Luxembourg 1993–94	$18.00	C106	☐ Northwest 1994–95 (Avail. 2/94)	$17.00	C140
☐ Bermuda 1994–95	$15.00	C122	☐ Portugal 1994–95 (Avail. 2/94)	$17.00	C141
☐ Brazil 1993–94	$20.00	C111	☐ Puerto Rico 1993–94	$15.00	C103
☐ California 1994	$15.00	C134	☐ Puerto Vallarta/Manzanillo/ Guadalajara 1994–95 (Avail. 1/94)	$14.00	C028
☐ Canada 1994–95 (Avail. 4/94)	$19.00	C145	☐ Scandinavia 1993–94	$19.00	C135
☐ Caribbean 1994	$18.00	C123	☐ Scotland 1994–95 (Avail. 4/94)	$17.00	C146
☐ Carolinas/Georgia 1994–95	$17.00	C128	☐ South Pacific 1994–95 (Avail. 1/94)	$20.00	C138
☐ Colorado 1994–95 (Avail. 3/94)	$16.00	C143	☐ Spain 1993–94	$19.00	C115
☐ Cruises 1993–94	$19.00	C107	☐ Switzerland/Liechtenstein 1994–95 (Avail. 1/94)	$19.00	C139
☐ Delaware/Maryland 1994–95 (Avail. 1/94)	$15.00	C136	☐ Thailand 1992–93	$20.00	C033
☐ England 1994	$18.00	C129	☐ U.S.A. 1993–94	$19.00	C116
☐ Florida 1994	$18.00	C124	☐ Virgin Islands 1994–95	$13.00	C127
☐ France 1994–95	$20.00	C132	☐ Virginia 1994–95 (Avail. 2/94)	$14.00	C142
☐ Germany 1994	$19.00	C125	☐ Yucatán 1993–94	$18.00	C110
☐ Italy 1994	$19.00	C130			
☐ Jamaica/Barbados 1993–94	$15.00	C105			

FROMMER'S $-A-DAY GUIDES
(Guides to low-cost tourist accommodations and facilities)

	Retail Price	Code		Retail Price	Code
☐ Australia on $45 1993–94	$18.00	D102	☐ Israel on $45 1993–94	$18.00	D101
☐ Costa Rica/Guatemala/ Belize on $35 1993–94	$17.00	D108	☐ Mexico on $45 1994	$19.00	D116
☐ Eastern Europe on $30 1993–94	$18.00	D110	☐ New York on $70 1994–95 (Avail. 4/94)	$16.00	D120
☐ England on $60 1994	$18.00	D112	☐ New Zealand on $45 1993–94	$18.00	D103
☐ Europe on $50 1994	$19.00	D115	☐ Scotland/Wales on $50 1992–93	$18.00	D019
☐ Greece on $45 1993–94	$19.00	D100	☐ South America on $40 1993–94	$19.00	D109
☐ Hawaii on $75 1994	$19.00	D113	☐ Turkey on $40 1992–93	$22.00	D023
☐ India on $40 1992–93	$20.00	D010	☐ Washington, D.C. on $40 1994–95 (Avail. 2/94)	$17.00	D119
☐ Ireland on $45 1994–95 (Avail. 1/94)	$17.00	D117			

FROMMER'S CITY $-A-DAY GUIDES
(Pocket-size guides to low-cost tourist accommodations
and facilities)

	Retail Price	Code		Retail Price	Code
☐ Berlin on $40 1994–95	$12.00	D111	☐ Madrid on $50 1994–95 (Avail. 1/94)	$13.00	D118
☐ Copenhagen on $50 1992–93	$12.00	D003	☐ Paris on $50 1994–95	$12.00	D117
☐ London on $45 1994–95	$12.00	D114	☐ Stockholm on $50 1992–93	$13.00	D022

FROMMER'S WALKING TOURS
(With routes and detailed maps, these companion guides point out
the places and pleasures that make a city unique)

	Retail Price	Code		Retail Price	Code
☐ Berlin	$12.00	W100	☐ Paris	$12.00	W103
☐ London	$12.00	W101	☐ San Francisco	$12.00	W104
☐ New York	$12.00	W102	☐ Washington, D.C.	$12.00	W105

FROMMER'S TOURING GUIDES
(Color-illustrated guides that include walking tours, cultural and historic
sights, and practical information)

	Retail Price	Code		Retail Price	Code
☐ Amsterdam	$11.00	T001	☐ New York	$11.00	T008
☐ Barcelona	$14.00	T015	☐ Rome	$11.00	T010
☐ Brazil	$11.00	T003	☐ Scotland	$10.00	T011
☐ Florence	$ 9.00	T005	☐ Sicily	$15.00	T017
☐ Hong Kong/Singapore/			☐ Tokyo	$15.00	T016
Macau	$11.00	T006	☐ Turkey	$11.00	T013
☐ Kenya	$14.00	T018	☐ Venice	$ 9.00	T014
☐ London	$13.00	T007			

FROMMER'S FAMILY GUIDES

	Retail Price	Code		Retail Price	Code
☐ California with Kids	$18.00	F100	☐ San Francisco with Kids		
☐ Los Angeles with Kids			(Avail. 4/94)	$17.00	F104
(Avail. 4/94)	$17.00	F103	☐ Washington, D.C. with Kids		
☐ New York City with Kids			(Avail. 2/94)	$17.00	F102
(Avail. 2/94)	$18.00	F101			

FROMMER'S CITY GUIDES
(Pocket-size guides to sightseeing and tourist accommodations and
facilities in all price ranges)

	Retail Price	Code		Retail Price	Code
☐ Amsterdam 1993–94	$13.00	S110	☐ Montréal/Québec		
☐ Athens 1993–94	$13.00	S114	City 1993–94	$13.00	S125
☐ Atlanta 1993–94	$13.00	S112	☐ Nashville/Memphis		
☐ Atlantic City/Cape			1994–95 (Avail. 4/94)	$13.00	S141
May 1993–94	$13.00	S130	☐ New Orleans 1993–94	$13.00	S103
☐ Bangkok 1992–93	$13.00	S005	☐ New York 1994 (Avail.		
☐ Barcelona/Majorca/Minorca/			1/94)	$13.00	S138
Ibiza 1993–94	$13.00	S115	☐ Orlando 1994	$13.00	S135
☐ Berlin 1993–94	$13.00	S116	☐ Paris 1993–94	$13.00	S109
☐ Boston 1993–94	$13.00	S117	☐ Philadelphia 1993–94	$13.00	S113
☐ Budapest 1994–95 (Avail.			☐ San Diego 1993–94	$13.00	S107
2/94)	$13.00	S139	☐ San Francisco 1994	$13.00	S133
☐ Chicago 1993–94	$13.00	S122	☐ Santa Fe/Taos/		
☐ Denver/Boulder/Colorado			Albuquerque 1993–94	$13.00	S108
Springs 1993–94	$13.00	S131	☐ Seattle/Portland 1994–95	$13.00	S137
☐ Dublin 1993–94	$13.00	S128	☐ St. Louis/Kansas		
☐ Hong Kong 1994–95			City 1993–94	$13.00	S127
(Avail. 4/94)	$13.00	S140	☐ Sydney 1993–94	$13.00	S129
☐ Honolulu/Oahu 1994	$13.00	S134	☐ Tampa/St.		
☐ Las Vegas 1993–94	$13.00	S121	Petersburg 1993–94	$13.00	S105
☐ London 1994	$13.00	S132	☐ Tokyo 1992–93	$13.00	S039
☐ Los Angeles 1993–94	$13.00	S123	☐ Toronto 1993–94	$13.00	S126
☐ Madrid/Costa del			☐ Vancouver/Victoria 1994–		
Sol 1993–94	$13.00	S124	95 (Avail. 1/94)	$13.00	S142
☐ Miami 1993–94	$13.00	S118	☐ Washington, D.C. 1994		
☐ Minneapolis/St.			(Avail. 1/94)	$13.00	S136
Paul 1993–94	$13.00	S119			

SPECIAL EDITIONS

	Retail Price	Code		Retail Price	Code
☐ Bed & Breakfast Southwest	$16.00	P100	☐ Caribbean Hideaways	$16.00	P103
☐ Bed & Breakfast Great American Cities (Avail. 1/94)	$16.00	P104	☐ National Park Guide 1994 (avail. 3/94)	$16.00	P105
			☐ Where to Stay U.S.A.	$15.00	P102

Please note: if the availability of a book is several months away, we may have back issues of guides to that particular destination. Call customer service at (815) 734-1104.